THE LATE LORD BYRON

Now it's a d——d hard thing to have to hear and read many things about oneself and not be able to say a word about anything; that's by far the worst of being a Spirit.

A Spiritual Interview with Lord Byron
by 'Quevedo Redivivus'.
(Undated Victorian Pamphlet.)

THE LATE LORD BYRON

POSTHUMOUS DRAMAS BY

Doris Langley Moore

JOHN MURRAY

50 Albemarle Street : London

*To Charles Howard Gordon who housed my books
for three years and read his way through
my little Byron library without
dog-earing a page*

© Doris Langley Moore 1961
Printed by R. and R. Clark, Ltd., Edinburgh

CONTENTS

ILLUSTRATIONS

INTRODUCTION

Many critical enquiries have been devoted to Byron's influence on literature, but no one hitherto has written a book about the aftermath of his
life. There are monographs on individuals whose claim to attention is that
they were, for a period, his companions, and studies of particular problems
and resentments that troubled his survivors; and in 1924 Professor
Samuel Chew gave a spacious bird's-eye view of the poet's whole career as
it looked to the public both while he lived and afterwards. But it has fallen
to my lot to make what seems to be the first fairly detailed survey of the
private arena—in so far as any arena of Byron's was ever private—after
the chief protagonist had departed from it. If I have achieved any success
there should emerge a kind of shadowgraph, the portrait of a man as projected by the conduct of his friends, acquaintances, and enemies after his
death.

Byron's power to conjure up dramas was not extinguished at Missolonghi. Feuds and frauds, comedies and tragedies, continued to gather
about his name throughout the 19th century, and new ones have broken
out in the 20th. I have not found it possible to do more than throw a
fleeting glance towards the later episodes in the posthumous story: they
will make up, if encouragement is not wanting, the contents of a second
volume. The present one begins with the letter that brought the news of
Byron's death to England, and the fantastic act of destruction with which
that news was signalized. It gives a closer view than has yet been attempted
of the struggles of biographers against anti-biographers, the tribulations
of executors, the tensions between widow and sister, and the effect on the
poet's after-fame of the endeavours of all kinds of minor associates to reap
profit from what they could tell or invent about him.

One might suppose that Byron would have become by now a figure as
clearly defined, as convincingly integrated as—say—Samuel Johnson. His
life was perhaps more abundantly documented than that of any Englishman who ever lived—or, at any rate, who ever lived so short a time as
thirty-six years. Besides being exceptionally addicted to the keeping of
records himself, he fulfilled every possible condition for the encouragement of record-keeping by others. He became an object of general
curiosity at twenty-four, and was a noticeable personality at a still earlier
age. His talents were set off by great personal fascination. He was a peer
in an epoch when the nobility held power and privilege that made rank
seem an almost magical dispensation. His fame extended far beyond his
own country and was rendered more piquant by scandals.

It was the sort of fame few poets had enjoyed before and none will ever be able to enjoy again. With the multitude of distractions we take for granted in our own age, it would be perfectly impossible for so concentrated an eagerness to be generated by one young man's occasional books of verse, however splendid or however shocking. All kinds of entertainments, sports, and games have their different stars systematically publicized, and it is difficult even to imagine a time when a poet could go on, year after year, being what we now call front-page news.

But the very magnitude of Byron's renown was a cause of extraordinary distortions of the evidence. To inflate an acquaintanceship into an intimacy, to suggest that three or four meetings were thirty or forty meetings, to tint the picture with the colours the reading public would find congenial—how could these temptations be resisted when there was such a market for 'inside stories' that it seemed the supply could never equal the demand? And there was not only the money; there was the satisfaction of linking oneself in any attitude one chose to assume with a man who, by the mere weight of his fame, could not fail to go down to posterity.

The concern of memoirists to portray themselves in relation to Byron rather than to portray Byron causes a large amount of literature to yield a very small proportion of reliable information. Simply by using verifiable dates as a check upon the expansiveness of the narrators (a surprisingly rare practice to which I have resorted often in these pages), we drastically reduce the significance of some events and prove others to be apocryphal. The brilliant Stendhal, the obtuse John Galt, the socially exuberant Lady Blessington, the socially negligible Medwin, the pious Dallas, the defiant Trelawny—all were alike in this, that their recollections of Byron were contrived to heighten their own stature, and therefore require sifting.

There is one part of the sifting process in which I think I may fairly lay claim to have worked over soil by no means well trodden. I decided to search for the character of the various witnesses as they revealed it in matters not connected with Byron. I read, for example, the lesser known novels of Mary Shelley, Marguerite Blessington, John Galt, and Caroline Lamb; Lady Byron's extensive poetical works and projects for charity and education, Stendhal's correspondence and journals, many whimsical and polemical writings never likely to be reprinted by Leigh Hunt; and miscellaneous letters, speeches, diaries, and publications of John Cam Hobhouse.

A writer's involuntary communications about himself may give us a means of assessing the worth of his disclosures about others. The false refinement and commonplace moralizing of Lady Blessington, the shallow level of her worldly wisdom, the lack of either humour or realism in Mary Shelley's painstaking productions, the perpetual touchy class consciousness

of Galt, are enlightening as to their limitations for dealing with Byron.
The penetrating yet entirely inelastic judgments of Lady Byron on a wide
variety of topics explain why her conception of Byron's character was, in
Professor Marchand's words, 'partially true but tragically inadequate'.
The inveterate literal-mindedness of Hobhouse makes him less entertain-
ing than Stendhal but infinitely more credible.

The good raconteur is often a very poor biographer, and the Age of
Elegance was unfortunately an Age of Anecdote. All kinds of dubious
legends were tolerated with the smiling apology, '*Se non è vero è ben
trovato*'. There was little excuse for such irresponsibility then, there is
none now when the amount of genuine material available is overwhelming. Not only have numberless letters and diaries of the period been
published which were formerly unknown, but the passages hitherto suppressed in printed writings have been restored, in many instances, to the
text. Each epoch gets the kind of biography it can take—that is to say, the
expurgations it needs. It is perhaps something to be said for our own that,
if a man's scale is big enough, we are prepared to accept his complexities
and even his obliquities, realizing that greatness is the product not of
nullity but of resistance, sometimes without victory, to certain stresses;
and that standards of judgment are not immutable. The unpardonable
sins of one generation are the pardonable sins of another, and only
'maladjustments' to the one that follows.

But the asterisks of the Georgians and Victorians were not solely
employed to cover offences against the prevailing moral code. The desire
to avoid wounding the feelings of surviving friends and relatives or their
immediate descendants sets limits to the candour of what is written
within a few decades of a celebrity's death. In this book, however, 'the
evidence of asterisks' will be looked for in vain. I can give the reader a
positive assurance that the object of omissions has been to avoid redundancy and irrelevance, to pass over what is hackneyed, or to obviate as far
as possible the necessity of constantly interrupting the text with explanations; in short, the object any author must have in view who does not want
to produce an interminable work.

Nor have I been much hampered by the omissions of my predecessors.
I had the privilege of an unrestricted and prolonged study of the Lovelace
Papers: the Hobhouse *Journals* still in family possession are freely quoted
in the ensuing chapters: and no facility, great or small, was ever withheld
from me among the Murray archives. The other collections, private and
public, to which I was fortunate enough to be admitted, are named in my
acknowledgments and notes. I have never had occasion to suppress anything at the request of others, nor need to practise evasion for the maintenance of a theory of my own.

That is not to say I have no bias. '*I cannot pretend to be impartial, no, by the Lord, not while I feel.*' So wrote Byron describing his Memoirs, and so I write introducing my shadowgraph. Impartiality in biography seems to me almost an impossibility, and the appearance of it either deception or self-deception. The interest which seduces us into spending years accumulating information upon some notable character must be founded on attraction in the first instance, or at least give rise to attraction (or its opposite) as the work proceeds. But my partiality for my subject has not in the least diminished the intention I started with—to resort to no suppressions.

Byron comes better out of a searching scrutiny than I think most men would. The idea that he was a posturing and untruthful egoist is still expressed from time to time, but never by anyone whose acquaintance with his conduct and his work is more than superficial. Those who have lived longest with him through investigation of his life find him, as his friends did, honest in no common measure. His dangerous 'mobility'— of which he was fully and anxiously aware—makes him an uncertain guide to his own emotions, but, as to facts, he is an excellent one. The more that is published, the more is Byron's veracity attested.

As for his egoism, it never reached the stage of oppressing his companions. Hobhouse, in some touching valedictory verses 'To Lord Byron from his Friends',[1] of small poetic merit but providing a kind of inventory of the reasons why he was loved, speaks of his acts of familiar kindness, generosity, glowing warmth of heart, social charm, his appreciativeness, his ready sympathy, courtesy, playfulness, and steadiness in friendship— none of which eulogies would be applicable to a self-absorbed man. He did not pay lip service to modesty, laying down the law with 'in my humble opinion', neither did he waste much letter paper on polite small talk; but judged by his acts and not his words, he was anything but disregardful of others.

There is scarcely one verdict of the past on Byron, whether it embraces his work, his virtues, or his vices, that has not been reversed, or at any rate revised, in the light of new studies. Even that much-quoted dictum of Goethe's that he was great only while writing poetry—'the moment he reflects he is a child'—now seems what it was, the product of a moment's annoyance. It was naturally seized upon by critics who wanted to dismiss all those reflections of Byron's that were subversive to the established order. The readers of his more mature work will discover that his was a singularly reasonable mind, and that there are few topics on which his thoughts have not worn better than those of most of his contemporaries.

Where he now seems irrational and old-fashioned is precisely that

[1] Murray MSS.

region in which he was once held to be expert—the nature and status of women. No man, whatever degree of independence his thinking may attain, can be completely free from the trammels of his time; and if Byron had unflattering opinions about women, it must be acknowledged that few of those he met were capable of correcting them.

I have not the slightest hope that I will persuade anybody to recognize Byron's merits who is not already disposed to do so. In books as in life we either like people or we do not. If we dislike them, their highest altruism will leave us unmoved; if we like them, we manage to find excuses for their gravest misdemeanours. (A member of that curious little cult, the *aficionados* of Trelawny, has gone so far as to say—in print—that his lies are 'almost endearing', while a Stendhal idolator has described that master's excesses of plagiarism as 'most amusing'.) Reason plays little part in our assessments, but it provides us with pretexts for them.

The pretexts I offer are, at all events, not conjectures. There are few statements I have asked the reader to take on trust. If any appears to be unsupported by reference to a dependable source, it is founded on the cumulative effect of allusions too numerous to be cited. The fact that a very large proportion of the evidence is either new or unhackneyed is due to the response my frequent and sometimes troublesome demands for assistance have met with from many persons and organizations, and in several countries.

It was Byron's great-granddaughter, Lady Wentworth, who first opened to me the family archives referred to herein as the 'Lovelace Papers'. I worked under her roof for some months before her much regretted death in August 1957, and it was an experience that will always be among the high promontories of memory for me, lighted by her own powerful and distinguished personality. Her son, the Earl of Lytton, O.B.E., has acceded to my requests for permission to use the copious extracts I made. His consent is the more generous because he does not necessarily agree with my interpretations of the documents nor approve of my deductions from them.

I am much indebted to Miss C. Draper, M.A., for having aided my researches, and indeed for bringing to Lady Wentworth's notice letters of mine about Byron in the *Sunday Times* that resulted in our association; as well as to the executor, Mr Gladstone Moore, who made it possible for me to continue working with the papers after they left Crabbet Park. The late Mr Walter Beard of Messrs Allen and Unwin, sharing with Miss Draper the duties of literary executor, was unfailingly helpful.

A privilege of the greatest value to this book and to me was the opportunity to read and copy from the numerous manuscript diaries of John Cam Hobhouse, Lord Broughton. This I owe to the kindness and hospitality of Sir Charles Hobhouse, Bt. Lady Hobhouse and Mr and Mrs John Hobhouse have also placed me under obligation. Mr John Hobhouse is the owner of a copy of Dallas's book on Byron with Hobhouse's marginal notes. Mrs Hobhouse, by her wide reading, was able to draw my attention to publications I might otherwise have overlooked.

It is an honour to join the long retinue of authors whose prefaces have expressed gratitude to Sir John Murray, K.C.V.O., D.S.O., for access to his incomparable collection of manuscripts. It will be seen that I have been allowed to make lavish use of documents hitherto unpublished, or only partly published, from this rich source. I have known few pleasures equal to sitting surrounded by Byron's own correspondence in the house that was frequented not only by himself but by many other characters who make an appearance in these pages.

The Roe-Byron Collection at Newstead Abbey and the papers in the Central Public Library, Nottingham, I examined under the expert guidance of the archivist, Miss Violet Walker; and I thank Mr F. C. Tighe, Chief Librarian, and the Nottingham Corporation for allowing quotation. I wrote several times to Miss Walker when I was in doubt about obscure points of Byron family history and received replies that were always of service to me.

The Hon. Sir Harold Nicolson allowed me to have in my keeping for several months the two grand quarto volumes of Moore's *Byron* which had belonged to Hobhouse and were scribbled with his voluminous notes —a treasure Sir Harold subsequently gave to be sold in aid of the London Library.

Other manuscript writings which I consulted in England belong to the British Museum, the Victoria and Albert Museum, the Bodleian Library at Oxford, and the Library of Trinity College, Cambridge. At all these august institutions I was given skilful and courteous assistance.

I much appreciated being allowed entry to the Duke of Devonshire's noble library and manuscript collection at Chatsworth; but I am sorry to confess, after the trouble taken by Mr Thomas Wragg, M.B.E., the Keeper, that the exercise book containing the fruits of my work there were later thrown away by a too tidy housemaid. (In like manner I lost the notes by which I might have established the real authorship of two spurious Byron poems recently ascribed to George Colman the younger, and I have therefore only been able to hint at it.)

Abroad, I had the happiness of going daily for weeks on end to the Keats-Shelley Memorial, Rome, where the manuscripts and library are under the admirable care of Dr Vera Cacciatore, M.B.E. Among their many other good deeds, Dr Cacciatore and her husband, Signore Edoardo Cacciatore, came to my rescue in solving some puzzles of Count Pietro

Gamba's excruciating handwriting. Professor Manara Vaglimigli, Librarian of the Biblioteca Classense, Ravenna, accorded me every possible facility in reading the Gamba Papers, and Signore Lorenzo Minghetti assisted in deciphering further Italian cryptograms. It was perhaps the singularly daunting character of Count Pietro's calligraphy that caused his letters to be neglected for a hundred years. Sir Harold Nicolson was the first, I believe, who was not intimidated.

The multi-lingual librarian in charge of the Gennadius Library in Athens when I was there, Mr Peter Topping, is another of my creditors. His staff too, like that of the Ethnical Library of Greece, and the Ethnological Museum, was most accommodating.

The New York City Public Library and the Morgan Library were delightful haunts to me during my stay in America, which took place at an all too early stage in my researches. I did not have the advantage of working in the libraries of Harvard, Yale, Duke, or Texas, American universities well stocked with Byroniana, but through correspondence with librarians and professors, I have been able to secure photographs or copies of many documents.

To end my list of libraries I must mention with deep respect those where I read only from printed sources—in particular, the London Library, the Reading Rooms of the British Museum in Bloomsbury and at Colindale, the Bibliothèque Nationale in Paris, the Bibliothèque Royale and the Hôtel de Ville in Brussels, the national library in Lisbon and the public library of Bologna.

I owe a large debt to the explorers working in the same field who have so promptly replied to my letters of enquiry. Besides those whose names have already occurred there are Professor Leslie A. Marchand, whose very important three-volume life of Byron was published with so much distinction in 1957, the late Dr E. M. Butler, author of the charming *Byron and Goethe*, the Marchesa Iris Origo and Mr Peter Quennell, both among the most brilliant of contemporary biographers, Professor Mario Praz of Rome, whose knowledge of English literature is remarkable, and Professor Ernest J. Lovell Jr of the University of Texas, a many-sided Byronian and a most obliging one.

In fields adjacent there are Professor Wilfred S. Dowden of the Rice Institute, Texas, an authority on Thomas Moore, Professor William H. Marshall of the University of Pennsylvania, author of the recent *Byron, Shelley, Hunt and the Liberal*, and Professor Willard B. Pope of the University of Vermont, editor—*inter alia*—of Haydon's Journals, quotations from which I have been able, through his kindness, to print correctly. I must also mention Sir Denis Browne, K.C.V.O, F.R.C.S., who has made a study of Byron's lameness, and Lady Anne Hill, whose two

PROLOGUE

Missolonghi
April 20th 1824

Signor Hobhouse,

The misfortune that has befallen us is terrible and irreparable. I scarcely have words to describe it. Lord Byron is dead.

Your friend, my friend and father, the light of this century, the boast of your country, the saviour of Greece is dead.

Although this is the first time that I address myself to you, I feel that I may, through the common tie that binds us, express myself with all the confidence of an old friendship. You will already know that my Lord was struck down by an unforeseen epileptic fit only two months ago. His health however seemed to have improved, and it appeared that the fit had left not the slightest trace. Yet he was always debilitated, both as an effect of that infirmity and because of the severe abstinence which he maintained with the object of preventing a relapse.

On the 10th of this month he was caught in a violent rain while riding on horseback, according to his custom, outside the city. There followed a feverish chill. The symptoms were inflammatory—It looked for a while as if he might have overcome it if he had submitted to the advice of his doctors who ordered him to be bled. He would not have it and the fever increased. Then he submitted, and three or four bleedings were performed, and leeches applied etc., but it was too late. . . .

What an end to his marvellous faculties, which had already borne a strain above human endurance. He died on the 19th of April at half past six in the evening.

. . . I cannot tell you the inconsolable grief of his friends—and of the whole of Greece. In the flower of his prime, and of so many wonderful hopes. . . .

Following the advice of Prince A. Mavrocordato and the leading English people who are to be found here, and because of our long and entire confidence, I have thought myself bound to take on the administration and care of everything connected with him. His papers and his more valuable belongings were sealed immediately after his death— and will be opened in the presence of Prince Mavrocordato and the principal people here. An inventory will be made.

Prologue

I know that he had made a will a long time ago, but I do not know whether he made any later disposition. On the opening of his papers this will be seen and I shall inform you at once.

I will take care of all his things. I have had his body embalmed and will shortly take it to Zante, and from there I will embark with it for England. And you will inform his friends and relatives in what manner you think best. I shall be obliged if you will notify Mr Douglas Kinnaird as his friend and General Agent [Power of Attorney]—and I hope that you will convey to him on my behalf our distress, and the steps that I have taken to bring his remains and his possessions.

Believe me

Your devoted friend
Pietro Gamba.[1]

[1] Murray MSS. in Italian. The writer, Count Gamba, was about twenty-three years old. His letter was carried to Zante by Edward Fowke, one of Byron's suite, and handed to Samuel Barff, his banker there, who was asked to find some means of getting it expeditiously to England. On April 21st, Gamba sent a very similar dispatch to Lord Sidney Osborne at Corfu, who received it on the 25th, and immediately forwarded it by express to London with a covering letter of his own. At the same time, Byron's valet, Fletcher, wrote to the Hon. Augusta Leigh. Thus several communications arrived together on May 14th.

THE LATE LORD BYRON

CHAPTER I

THE BURNING OF THE MEMOIRS[1]

A little after eight in the morning on May 14th, 1824, John Cam Hobhouse was awakened by a loud and unaccustomed rapping at his bedroom door. As he hurriedly rose, already apprehensive, a packet of letters was handed to him labelled 'By Express', and from their postal markings he could see they were of foreign provenance. He was seized with a dreadful foreboding which was not allayed by the sight of a note, delivered at the same time, in the handwriting of Douglas Kinnaird.

It was the seal of this that he broke first. Kinnaird was a convivial person who would not send early-morning messages without reasons of urgency. He was also the man who maintained closer contact than anyone in England with their celebrated friend, Lord Byron, being his banker and trustee and the holder of his Power of Attorney.

The worst, the very worst, anticipations of evil tidings conceivable in Hobhouse's mind were instantly realized. Kinnaird's letter informed him that Byron was dead.

> In an agony of grief, [Hobhouse wrote that night in his diary] such as I have experienced only twice before in my life . . . I opened the despatches from Corfu, and there saw the details of the fatal event.

The first of these two prior agonies was one that Byron had shared—the shock and sorrow of learning, thirteen years before, that a companion they were both devoted to had been drowned, entangled in water weeds, in the Cam. The second was the death of young Captain Benjamin Hobhouse at Quatre Bras. His brother had then set down with moving honesty: 'The whole loss of the British army in that fatal victory is in my mind reduced to one soldier'.

But this third grief was to transcend the others. The gifted young scholar, Charles Skinner Matthews, and the beloved brother, were known only in their own circles, and time, in the natural course of things, could cast his 'kind oblivious shade' over them: whereas Byron was one of the most notable and controversial figures in the Western world, passionately loved, passionately hated, his very name a storm centre: no one who had known him would ever have the remotest possibility of forgetting him, least of all the man who would have to deal with the hundreds of problems he had left behind him—his executor. And he had died at the age of thirty-six in circumstances to draw upon him even more than the usual measure of public attention. A foreign people had gone into mourning for him.

[1] See Appendix 1 for some extended notes on the nature of the Memoirs.

Among the documents which his kinsman, Lord Sidney Osborne, had sent by that portentous express, was the hurriedly printed decree of the Provisional Government of Greece commanding that the Easter festival be suspended, the shops closed for three days, and general mourning observed for twenty days, beginning at sunrise the day after his death with the firing of thirty-seven minute guns.

It was nearly a month since that melancholy tribute had reverberated along the swamps of Missolonghi. The news, though transmitted with all possible speed, could not come faster than sailing ships were able to carry it. Byron had died on the evening of April 19th.

The little printing-press—doubtless the one which the poet had regarded as an absurd and exasperating toy in a country where few could read—must have been working all night to have the official announcement in circulation by the next morning.

> I read this proclamation over and over again [Hobhouse recorded] in order to find some consolation in the glorious conclusion of his life for the loss of such a man, but in vain. All our ancient and most familiar intercourse, the pleasure I had enjoyed in looking back to the days of our amusements at home and our travels abroad, the fond hope with which I had contemplated our again—in our own country—renewing the more than brotherly union which had bound us together, all our tokens of regard, nay, even our trifling differences—all burst upon me and rendered me alive to the deprivation I was now doomed to endure. . . . I shall take some calmer moment for recording some of the particulars of this calamity.

Few that day were the calm moments. First there was a consultation to be held with Kinnaird and Sir Francis Burdett as to the apportionment of the most immediate duties. Sir Francis, another friend who had been concerned in business matters, agreed to break the news to Byron's sister; Kinnaird to distribute the letters from Greece to those most vitally affected, amongst whom was that very featureless Byron cousin, Captain George Anson Byron, R.N., the new lord. Kinnaird also made haste to get an accurate report to the press. Hobhouse wrote some hurried notes to members of Byron's former London circle and, later in the day, followed up Burdett's visit to Mrs Leigh. She was 'in an afflicting condition', causing his own tears to flow afresh and uncontrollably. William Fletcher, who had served Byron as valet since the latter's boyhood, had addressed a letter to her in Hobhouse's care giving her, painfully, in ill-spelt groping phrases, with all the touching eloquence of a complete want of art, a description of her brother's illness and death.

'The reading this letter', said Hobhouse, 'tore my heart to pieces.'

Yet even in the depths of his misery, Hobhouse did not fail to perceive that Fletcher had made a statement which enemies, if they heard of it, would seize upon as an excuse for accusations of either hypocrisy or cowardice: he had spoken of his master's desire in his latter days to have the Bible brought to him. Byron had written works adjudged to be depraved and blasphemous, and when blasphemers turned to the Bible in extremity, their opponents were not slow to make capital of the weakness. Hobhouse knew Byron always had that Bible near him—it was his sister's parting gift when he went into exile—and he was sure that 'unless his mind was shaken by disease', there was not the least likelihood of his having been overcome by religious terrors. Mrs Leigh was adjured to be discreet on this topic, and she acquiesced . . . grudgingly, for she was an orthodox Protestant and would have been glad to think, and let others think, that her brother had been enlightened at the end. But Hobhouse was a very masterful character.

Among the letters entrusted to him by Fletcher, there was also one for Byron's publisher, John Murray, and another for the valet's wife. If these were delivered in person, the first by Hobhouse himself, the second by Kinnaird, due precaution could be taken against rumours of a death-bed conversion. And there was another possibility he was bent upon averting.

> After the first access of grief was over, I determined to lose no time in doing my duty by preserving all that was left to me of my friend, his fame— my thoughts were turned to the Memoirs of his life given to Thomas Moore and deposited by him in Mr Murray's hands for certain considerations. It had so happened that a few days before Thomas Moore had told me that he had made an effort to get the Memoirs out of Mr Murray's hands by coming to some arrangement with Messrs Longmans the booksellers who had promised to advance him 2000 *gs* on his insuring his life—which sum would enable Moore to repay Murray the loan advanced to him—I was not aware whether or not the money had actually been paid to Murray nor consequently in whose hands the Memoirs were.
>
> I called on Kinnaird—it being agreed that Burdett and I should dine with him—Kinnaird very generously wrote a note to Moore offering to give him 2000 £ at once in order to secure the MSS in whose ever hands it was—for the family of Lord Byron—that is to say in order to destroy the said MSS. Burdett came in before the note was written and he also offered to give 2000 £. I said I should be glad to give 1000 £ or what I could for such a purpose, but Kinnaird persisted in sending his note and it was sent.
>
> K. said at the same time that he doubted not the family of Lord Byron or Lady Byron would see the propriety of repaying the money.
>
> We had a melancholy evening, recalling to mind the various excellencies of our dear friend. I shall never forget this dreadful day.[1]

Thus was put in train the measure to secure and destroy the important manuscript which only one of these three distinguished and well-meaning gentlemen had set eyes on, and about the value of which the prime mover

[1] Hobhouse *Journals*, 14 May 1824.

Hobhouse (who had not read it) was by no means equipped to form any judgment. The steps necessary to this drastic and high-handed proceeding occupied a large part of the three following days.

In the meantime, there were expressions of an acute public and private sense of loss on every side. The newspapers, so often hostile, were full of eulogy, the tender-hearted Miss Matilda and Miss Sophia Hobhouse wept tears that seemed unquenchable, and even the lady at Beckenham who had spent eight years meditating on grievances was reported by Captain Byron to be 'in a distressing state'. All these demonstrations gave a sombre satisfaction to Hobhouse who, during nearly half of his thirty-seven years, had coaxed, admonished, quarrelled with, fought for, and loved the object of them; had shared with him experiences so bizarre that they would have seemed far-fetched in a novel; had seen him at his best, noble and generous, and at his worst, capricious and destructive as a fractious child.

And since the verdicts of men of questionable character whose knowledge of Byron was extremely limited have been so often quoted, it may not be irrelevant to consider the private summing-up, of a man of unquestionable character, who had spent as long in his company as all the other commentators put together:

> The *Times* of yesterday announced his death in a manner which is, I think, a fair sample of the general opinion on this event.[1] The writer is, however, mistaken in saying that others may have *been more tenderly beloved* than *Lord Byron*, for no man ever lived who had such devoted friends. His power of attaching those about him to his person was such as no one I ever knew possessed. No human being could approach him without being sensible of this magical influence. There was something commanding, but not overawing in his manner. He was neither grave nor gay out of place, and he seemed always made for that company in which he happened to find himself. There was a mildness and yet a decision in his mode of conversing, and even in his address, which are seldom united in the same person. He appeared exceedingly free, open, and unreserved to everybody, yet he contrived at all times to retain just as much self-restraint as to preserve the respect of even his most intimate friends, so much so that those who lived most with him were seldom, if ever, witnesses to any weakness of character or conduct that could sink him in their esteem.
>
> He was full of sensibility, but he did not suffer his feelings to betray him into absurdities. There never was a person who by his air, deportment, and appearance, altogether more decidedly persuaded you at once that he was well born and well bred. He was, as Kinnaird said of him, 'a gallant gentleman.'[2]

When every allowance has been made for the emotion under which such a passage was written, there is extensive testimony both from

---

[1] An extract from *The Times* announcement is given in Appendix 2.
[2] Hobhouse *Journals*, 16 May 1824.

Hobhouse's own diaries while his friend still lived and a most diverse assortment of other records that Byron did in fact have an extraordinary power of attracting and attaching people: but as is usual with those who enjoy this dangerous privilege, he also had an extraordinary power of attracting and attaching scandals. He not only appeared 'free, open, and unreserved', but he actually was so to an extent which gave a singular vividness to his communications; and, after a fairly complete severance from the fashionable and political circles of London in which Hobhouse himself had never ceased to mix, he had written his reminiscences. As if that were not indiscreet enough, he had annoyed Hobhouse intensely by making a practically unrestricted gift of them to the Irish poet Thomas Moore. Being encumbered with debt, Moore had proceeded with Byron's full approval to assign them to John Murray for two thousand guineas—a transaction Hobhouse chose to describe in these acrimonious words: 'Lord Byron made a present of himself to Mr Moore, and Mr Moore sold his Lordship to the booksellers.'[1]

It was this precious document which Hobhouse with reckless haste had decided to have destroyed. His belief in his own mission to protect his friend's posthumous fame, combined (though this was a motive he could not himself suspect) with his long-standing jealousy of Byron's fondness for Moore, had blinded him utterly to the fact that such a measure would give detractors a first-rate start for any rumours they might care to set afloat, while even admirers would feel that the revelations must have been deplorable.

His moral and material resources were immense. There was the money to buy back the Memoirs. Kinnaird and Burdett and himself were ready to provide it. There was the moral indignation—the more persuasive because he so earnestly felt it—that could make the perfectly open and legitimate bargain between Moore and Murray seem reprehensible. There was the state of tension, in which he could stir up Byron's widow and sister to bring pressure to bear. He wrote to the one and went to see the other.

That sister—or rather, half-sister, the Hon. Augusta Leigh—had never seen the Memoirs, but Hobhouse, who broached the subject to her with urgency, was able to convince her that their destruction must be secured. She was a confused and malleable character, and, moreover, she had been subjected for years to an insidious undermining attack on her affection for her brother—a process giving rise to such anxieties that everything he did or said or wrote seemed fraught with awful possibilities. Like Hobhouse, she had been dismayed at his headstrong folly

[1] *Narrative of Events connected with the Destruction of Lord Byron's Memoirs* compiled by Hobhouse in 1825 from his notes of 1824. Murray MSS.

in persisting in the composition of *Don Juan* despite all sage counsels, and, like Hobhouse again, she deplored his association with Moore; so, though she thought she would 'have sunk at the burden of it',[1] she was prevailed upon to agree to an appointment for the purpose of receiving the manuscript as an object condemned.

Thence arose a vague understanding among the principals that they were meeting to carry out the wishes of Mrs Leigh. That they did not originate with her is shown in a variety of documents, including Hobhouse's diaries, Murray's correspondence, and a Memorandum and letters of her own, all the verifiable details of which can be confirmed from other sources.

Hobhouse had expected difficulties with John Murray, for it would be natural for a publisher who had in hand an asset of such great commercial potentialities to be resolved to guard it. Probably it was with some misgiving that he composed on May 15th, the following note to be delivered by hand at 50 Albemarle Street:

Dear Sir,
   You would confer a favour on me if you would contrive to step here for one moment. I have a letter for you from Fletcher which I wish to put into your hand myself and to know from you whether there is any answer as the Courier that brought me the fatal news yesterday from Lord S. Osborne returns tonight.
                                          Ever yours,
                                          J. C. Hobhouse[2]

He required a good deal from Murray . . . the sight of Fletcher's letter that he might censor it if it ran on about his Lordship's devotion to the Bible, a promise to search out and destroy Byron's indiscreet letters and papers immediately, though their literary and cash value was immense, and a further promise to hand over the Memoirs. All mounting up to a rather tall order, probably the tallest order ever received by a publisher.

But instead of an antagonist, he found an eager ally, one who, for longer than Hobhouse himself, would be glad to take the blame—or, as he certainly supposed, the credit—of having been the chief actor in the drama. John Murray in fact was burning with a belief in his mission not less impassioned than Hobhouse's own. How it had been ignited—whether spontaneously or at the prompting of Lady Byron's friends—remains enigmatical. Certainly those friends flung themselves headlong into the business of getting rid of Byron's testimony.

Not that Lady Byron, any more than her sister-in-law, had read the Memoirs, though a very explicit offer had been made to her to do so by

---

[1] Letter to the Rev. Francis Hodgson, 31 May 1824. Yale University Library MSS.
[2] Murray MSS.

the author of them, who had informed her that they contained a 'long and minute' account of their married life and separation:

> . . . I could wish you to see, read—and mark any part or parts that do not appear to coincide with the truth. The truth I have always stated—but there are two ways of looking at it—and your way may not be mine. I have never revised the papers since they were written. You may read them—and mark what you please. . . . You will find nothing to flatter you—nothing to lead to the most remote supposition that we could ever have been—or be happy together. But I do not choose to give to another generation statements which we cannot arise from the dust to prove or disprove—without letting you see fairly and fully what I look upon you to have been—and what I depict you as being. If seeing this—you can detect what is false—or answer what is charged—do so—*your mark* shall not be erased.[1]

But Lady Byron, whose calculating prudence had been a subject of remark some time before she had committed the one astonishing imprudence of marrying a highly-strung poet, had very deliberately rejected the opportunity. Another woman might have been unable to resist the temptation to learn exactly how a husband whose bitter and eloquent verses disclosed to the world his sense of injury would set forth the mutual disaster of their marriage; but she had realized at once that she would be in a much stronger position if she refused to hear anything resembling a defence. It looked dignified and it baffled the vehement, communicative Byron. She had achieved an exemplary proficiency in this art of baffling.

On receiving that letter nearly four and a half years ago, Lady Byron had at once approached the closest of her numerous confidants, Colonel Francis Hastings Doyle, and asked him to confer with his sister, Miss Selina Doyle, and the lawyer, Stephen Lushington of Doctors' Commons, who had acted for her in the Separation proceedings, and advise what could be done to repress this apparently irrepressible husband.

> If I do not protest against the additional publicity, [she had written] which he intends to give to our domestic concerns, I may seem to sanction the measure—I should not hesitate to add a strong declaration of my resolution to refute misrepresentation, were it not that I fear he might assume this as a pretext for immediate publication—if elated by confidence in his own powers, and desirous of the profit which such a work would produce.[2]

She had followed up this letter with the draft of an answer she might dispatch to Byron, and although it is not the one she sent, it should be quoted as showing her reaction:

[1] LOVELACE, *Astarte*. Letter of 31 Dec. 1819.
[2] 21 Jan. 1820: Lovelace Papers.

. . . I consider the composition of such a Memoir for present or future circulation as wholly unjustifiable, and I would not, even indirectly, appear to sanction it. . . .

In a few days Colonel Doyle wrote conveying Dr Lushington's suggestion that Mrs Leigh should be used as the instrument of suppression:

He conceives that if it were made to appear to Mrs L. that the consequences of this sort of controversy [i.e. Byron's being allowed to give his side of the matrimonial story] . . . would *inevitably* be at last the disclosure of everything which she was most desirous to conceal—that such a letter or communication from her to him wd be sent as wd be likely to operate in deterring him from the commencement of this attack. . . .

If you think that you can make Mrs L. the instrument of conveying that sort of intimidation to Ld B. that may deter him from the course he is about to enter—I think you should not be prevented by any consideration for her *immediate feelings.* . . .[1]

Lady Byron did not need to be told not to consider Augusta Leigh's immediate feelings, because she had long been persuaded that any sufferings she could inflict on her sister-in-law might be the means of saving a soul jeopardized by the ghastly crime of an incestuous love. She had reasons, however, for not using Augusta as her go-between in this instance, and she stated them at great length to her friend.

She wanted, she said, to be able to produce to anyone a copy of her declaration to Lord Byron, and if it were transmitted by Mrs Leigh 'inferences contrary to the truth would be drawn from the fact of my treating her thus confidentially'. Then, she had no reason to think Mrs Leigh could influence her brother. Besides, she might make '*her own comments*'[2] in conveying such a letter, and 'they would combine together against me—he being actuated by revenge—she by fear—whereas, from her never having dared to inform him that she has already admitted his guilt to me with her own, they have hitherto been prevented from acting in concert'.

The objects which it is desirable to accomplish are—1st To prevent the present circulation and future publication of the Memoir.

For this a threat of legal proceedings might be efficacious.

He perhaps knows that the very annunciation of legal proceedings against him might occasion evidence to be offered to me from quarters of which I am at present ignorant. . . . The remotest idea of being summoned to England by any Court of Law would deprive him of that audacity which arises from the security of a foreign residence. . . . 2ndly The second object is—Acting upon right principles, to act as will be most generally approved, in any event. . . .
I have to ask—would not a communication to Lord B. from my father—

---

[1] LOVELACE, *Astarte.* 27 Jan. 1820.
[2] Ibid. 29 Jan. 1820. The italics are Lady Byron's underlining.

authorized by me—answer the desired ends without being liable to the same objection as a letter from myself?—

The chief points in that communication to be—The information of my declining to peruse the MS—A representation of the injurious consequences of its circulation to Ada[1]—and a declaration that I shall consider the existence of such a Memoir (avowedly destined for future publication), especially if it be circulated in MS—at present, as releasing me from even the shadow of an engagement to suppress the facts of my own experience, or the corroborating proofs of Lord B's character and conduct—that reluctant as I have ever been to bring my domestic concerns before the public, and anxious as I have felt to *save from ruin a near connection of his*, I shall feel myself compelled by duties of primary importance, if he perseveres in accumulating injuries upon me, to make a disclosure of the past in the *most authentic* form.[2]

Colonel Doyle had replied to this that, if Mrs Leigh were not to be brought in, Lady Byron had better send 'a letter from yrself short & to the point, without any unnecessary provocation . . . the threat of a third person may make it incumbent upon his pride to revolt. . . .'

He had reiterated the proposal in detail a few days later,[3] explaining that he himself would not care to be the intermediary because, as he stood in no authorized relation to her, there might be 'insinuations'. Dr Lushington was not open to this objection, being her known legal adviser, but his intervention would have to be made through Byron's appointed representative, Kinnaird, 'a very wrong-headed man', of whom it was assumed—quite without foundation—that he might be 'goading Ld B. to the course of publicity'. There was really nothing for it but an answer ostensibly from herself 'affording no handle for any reply'.

It was composed by Dr Lushington, a curt note, which has often been published over Lady Byron's signature, ending with a brief menace about 'consequences' if the book should be published—to which Byron was able to retort that this mysterious threat could be of little avail since, when it was carried out, he would be 'where nothing can touch him further'.

Lady Byron's friends were not a whit less devoted than her husband's and were honoured with even more significant confidences: though unlike Byron, whose lack of reserve was obvious, she had a most discreet and guarded manner and gave the impression each time she offered revelations that they were wrung from her in spite of herself, and so she carried to her listeners the same conviction she always felt herself that she was pursuing a 'Policy of Silence'. By the time of Byron's death, there was a very substantial muster of people who had heard from her own lips the dreadful records of her year of married life, and who thought it grossly

[1] The Hon. Augusta Ada Byron, only child of the marriage.
[2] 29 Jan. Lovelace Papers. The passage between asterisks on p. 19 is omitted from the extensive quotation of the letter in Lovelace's *Astarte*.
[3] 5 Feb. 1820: Lovelace Papers.

unfair for the other party to have left any reminiscences of his own on this topic.

Among these ardent supporters were Vice-Admiral Sir William Hope of the Admiralty Board and his wife, Lady Athlone, who still kept that title by reason of having first been married to the Earl. Sir William lost no time in applying himself to the urgent question—would Lady Byron's representatives agree to repay John Murray the money Moore had been given for the Memoirs if they were handed over for burning? He had every reason to be optimistic because he had been informed by an Admiralty Secretary, John Barrow, who was familiar at Albemarle Street, that Murray was full of readiness to co-operate with any members of Byron's family who might wish to destroy his Memoirs, and it could not be doubted that the money to reimburse him would be raised, for Lady Byron was rich.

Accordingly, two days after Byron's death became known, Sir William called on her solicitor, G. B. Wharton, and not finding him at home, dashed off a letter to him:

> *Admiralty*
> *Sunday Morng*
> *16 May 1824*

My Dear Sir

Having a most sincere esteem for Lady Byron, and considering how much she has already suffered, it would be a most cruel & lamentable circumstance, was She to undergo any further mortifications.

It is to endeavour to prevent this happening, that I now commit to Paper a conversation I had this morning with Mr Barrow one of our Secretarys. . . .

You are aware, I believe, that the late Lord Byron wrote a life of himself, & entrusted the Manuscript to Mr Moore, under the injunction that it was not to be Published in his lifetime. In consequence of Pecuniary difficulties, this manuscript Mr Moore disposed of (I think most fortunately) to Mr Murray the Bookseller under the same injunction as to publication—that period having arrived, Mr Murray naturally looked at it, but he found [it] written in language so horrid & disgusting, that he felt as a man of honour would do, & has *refused* the £2000 guineas [*sic*] he gave fort it, [*sic*] from another in the Trade who at Mr Moore's request wanted to get it back, & yesterday he came to Mr Barrow to state the circumstance, & to know if he could recommend him to any Relation of the Family to whom he might communicate these circumstances. Mr Barrow did not happen to know any person but Mr Wilmot Horton, to whom he recommended him to you. [*sic*] As I have not heard what has passed in that quarter, I am most desirous to give you this early information, and to conjure you not to lose one moment in seeing Mr Murray, for from what Mr Barrow told me, I am sure it would drive to distraction the amiable Lady B. was this [?]unloosed to the Publick in Print—Mr Murray said to Mr Barrow, that he wanted *no Profit*, &

would give back (to be burnt I hope) this abominable manuscript to the
Relations of the family upon being re-imbursed what he had advanced. . . .

I shall either write to, or see Mr Barrow, to ask him to advise Mr Murray
to Keep quiet untill he sees you.

Ever yours truly
Wm Johnstone Hope.[1]

Besides the errors that may be attributed to haste, there are other
curious features here not so easily accounted for. John Murray himself
consistently disclaimed having read the Memoirs. How then can he have
found their language 'horrid and disgusting'? He was well acquainted
with Byron's family and had corresponded with Lady Byron several times
since the Separation. Why should he apply to John Barrow, a stranger to
all concerned, for a recommendation to one of the relatives? Why seek
Barrow's introduction to Wilmot Horton whom he already knew? Yet, if
these were deliberate misrepresentations, Lady Byron's lawyer was hardly
the person to address them to, so we must conclude that the statements
were made in good faith, and that Sir William Hope was a muddle-headed
as well as a meddling person.

John Barrow is nowhere mentioned in the '*Narrative of the circumstances preceding the destruction of the Memoirs of Lord Byron as far as
Mr Wilmot Horton was cognizant of that transaction*', composed within a
fortnight by Wilmot Horton, but that he was very busy behind the scenes
is evident from the lines to John Murray dated the same Sunday:

I enclose you a note from Sir William Hope, who is exceedingly interested
in what concerns Lady Byron; and I have ventured to assure him that you
will take no step hastily, and I have reason to believe you have no other
object than that of being indemnified for the money you gave for the manuscript. It would be well got rid of, if he would take it off your hands and
consign it to the flames.[2]

Before the morning was out he had also sent off a reassurance to the
Admiralty:

My dear Sir William,
I have laid an injunction on Murray who, if I know him at all, will be
ready to do what is right and what I advise him; and I am sure he wishes for
nothing more than sheer indemnification for the Sum which he gave to
Mr Moore, which I believe was 2000 Guineas. I entirely agree with you that
so infamous a document ought never to see the light except that of the fire,
and that 2000 Guineas would be a cheap purchase in comparison to the pain
and anguish the publication of it might inflict on poor Lady Byron & her
friends.

I am, my dear Sir William
very faithfully yours
John Barrow[3]

---

[1] Lovelace Papers. [2] SMILES, Chapter XVII. [3] Lovelace Papers.

Byron in Albanian dress, by Thomas Phillips

These letters make it very hard to see who was taking the initiative in getting Byron's work destroyed. The suggestion of burning certainly seems to have originated with Sir William Hope, if we judge from Barrow's phrase 'I entirely agree with you': but the Horton Narrative shows that, with or without Barrow's influence, Murray was taking steps the day before any of the correspondence last quoted was in existence.

> Mr Murray called on Mr Wilmot Horton on Saturday the 15th Inst. and for the 1st time informed him that he had the memoirs of Lord Byron in his possession. He stated . . . that he had strong reason to believe, although he had never read them himself, that they were entirely unfit for publication— that he well knew the curiosity that would exist in the world on the subject, and that consequently as far as his pecuniary interest was concerned, he should probably gain much more than he had given for them either by publishing or disposing of them,—but that he was perfectly willing to place them in the hands of Lord Byron's family without conditions. Mr Wilmot Horton stated in reply, that he was taken entirely by surprise with respect to this communication,—that he had no authority to act for the family of Lord Byron,—but that he had no hesitation in pledging himself to Mr Murray that he should be indemnified for the Memoirs in question, upon placing them in the hands of the family of Lord Byron, and he requested Mr Murray on no account to suffer these memoirs to leave his possession, until after further communication with him, with which arrangement Mr Murray expressed himself entirely satisfied.[1]

Wilmot Horton could not have believed for an instant that Augusta Leigh, notoriously impecunious, was in a position to pay two thousand guineas to secure the papers. It was not, therefore, of her he was thinking when he pledged himself on behalf of the family, but of Lady Byron. The decision must nevertheless appear to be Augusta's.

She was a cousin of his, and he sometimes acted as her spokesman on those occasions when, according to the code of the day, it was unseemly for a woman to speak for herself. Normally this rôle was filled by a father, brother, or husband, but Augusta's father, Captain Jack Byron, had long been dead, her surviving half-brothers, the Duke of Leeds and Lord Francis Godolphin Osborne, generally kept out of Byron entanglements, and her husband, Colonel Leigh, was an idle and feckless gentleman who lived for horse-racing and no one ever expected him to show the slightest capacity for anything else.

Wilmot and his wife (they had recently added Horton to their name on account of an inheritance) had been close friends of Augusta's and she trusted them still, so far as she dared trust anybody, but unknown to her they had been privy since the break-up of the marriage to all that Lady Byron could tell them of her guilt and depravity, so they were not really

[1] Ibid. and Murray MSS.

well-disposed. Like Augusta's still more intimate friends, the Hon·
Thérèse Villiers and her husband, they were tacitly allies of Lady
Byron's. It was felt that Augusta never could show adequate remorse,
never could abase herself enough to Lady Byron for not having denounced
her publicly, and although she had done penances without number and
abased herself to an extent that now makes profoundly uncomfortable
reading, there was one gesture of submission she had refused to offer.
With something almost like pride, almost like firmness, she had maintained, when several years ago her brother had been expected to visit
England, that she could not bring herself absolutely to shut her doors to
him. This recalcitrance had not been forgiven.

The necessity of preventing any autobiographical writing of Byron's
from reaching the public might well be supposed by Wilmot Horton to be
a matter in which he could serve both ladies equally. Neither could wish
the scandalous chronicle to circulate. Augusta was free from any fear that
her brother would have betrayed her,[1] but it was very plain that if he had
written objectionably about his wife, the repercussions would be painful.
Then there was the fact that Byron, always daring, had been more prone
than ever in recent years to write blasphemies and indecencies. Besides
Don Juan and the deplorable *Cain*, there was a case *pendente lite* at that
very moment against the rash publisher of *A Vision of Judgement*,
indicted as a seditious libel.

Augusta had rooms in St James's Palace and a place at court with
emoluments she could not afford to renounce. She was not a brave or
strong-minded woman, and that she yielded to the various pressures that
were brought to bear on her needs no recondite explanation.

A letter asking for the advice of her firmer, more self-reliant sister-in-
law provides with the sharpness almost of caricature a picture of the
writer—her confusion, weakness, silliness, prejudice, and the dangerous
good nature which showed itself in a too ready desire to please and to
placate. Though it is long and some of its points must be clarified later, it
will bear only the minimum of abridgment:

Sunday Night

My dearest A—I know that you will forgive me for inflicting my perplexities upon you—& I feel most particularly anxious that you sd know
them from myself—on Friday—during my first interview with Mr Hobhouse—he expressed that *now* his first wish was to protect My poor Brother's
fame & then alluded to *the Memoirs* as a subject of anxiety—I asked *who*
had them he replied *Moore*—& told the story of a long squabble between
Moore and Murray about them—which I really could not from nervousness

---

[1] In a letter to the Hon. Mrs Villiers, dated 11 Nov. 1818, Lady Byron wrote: 'I have
had an intimation through Augusta that he was writing his life for publication, and she
did not seem alarmed!' LOVELACE, *Lady Noel Byron*.

comprehend—however it ended in his being *glad Moore* had them, *I* sorry, Murray had them *not*—having of one a good opinion & the other quite the contrary—H—— proceeded to say he did not know what to do—but must. try to work on Moore's feelings abt them, in which he appeared to think his Success doubtful—Yesterday he came—said he had something to tell *I* should be glad to hear—that *it was agreed*—(& he produced a *written paper* with ye agreement stated in it) that Moore Murray Hobhouse & Wilmot Horton sd come *here*—Murray receive 2000 G from Moore & place them the Memoirs in Moores hand who wd resign them into Mine—'*& I advise you Mrs L to burn them* in our presence[']—I started & said, but is Moore to lose £2000! who can make that up to him—upon which H flew into a fit of *vehemence* & never could I understand anything but that I must be a Great fool for *Not* instantly Seizing his Meaning—so I *pretended* I did—& said *very well*—but have you heard from Mr Wilmot that he *will* come—upon which I understood him to know it—he was to attend on your part—this arrangement was repeated in my presence to G[eorge] B[yron] who probably may have told you of it—with ye addition of a suggestion that *he* might also be present—& that D Kinnaird had or wd advance the Money for Moore— when alone with George I exclaimed, "*what can I do?*" for you may imagine my dearest A the horrid task assigned me much as I agree in the expediency of the destruction of this or any thing that may be a disgrace to poor Bs memory—G B comforted me by Saying "*oh never mind you must be only glad they will be burnt*" & so My dear A I thought I must perform this painful duty—with ye sort of feeling I should have if I were doomed to appear in a Court of Justice or something absolutely Necessary—

Today Hobhouse called & said, it is settled—that Moore Murray, *Col Doyle* & myself are to be here at 12 tomorrow for the purpose *above mentioned*—I must tell you tho, that during H s visit yesterday he received a note from Murray, to propose *Col Doyle* instead of *Wilmot*—

. . . Wilmot is just gone—having been *extremely* kind & good natured & all that was amiable—but in ye first place he stated that Col Doyle had never heard *one word* of the arrangement ! ! ! & in the next that he (W) felt that, if it was made I ought to appoint a person to act for me—instead of the thing being transacted here—in which God knows I most perfectly agree—for I wd rather do any thing almost than see any one of the *3* still unseen parties or take any share in the business—W. proposed acting for me—but I told him honestly that I knew there was that sort of feeling still of H[obhouse] &c towards *him*, which wd or might probably revive now so as to occasion a *squabble* which wd be horrible to me—& injurious to the cause—& therefore he said why not leave it to Col Doyle?—I told him I had no objection—but I must tell you that after trying in vain for I do not know how long to discuss what could possibly have induced the Ms [Moore and Murray] to act such a double part—I found that Moore thought if he could but publish the *unexceptionable* parts of the Memoirs—he should make 3000 instead of 2000 ! ! ! upon which I said to Wilmot, then pray let the matter rest *for ye* moment, as to ye destruction of the Memoirs & arrange their safe deposit as you best can—but as you say & I understand Mr Moore says he will only resign them

into *My* hands—if, at a proper time *I* am allowed *any voice* in the affair—
(to which I do not pretend to have any right or claim)—*but* if I have, I am
Most irrevocably determined that not one single line or *word* shall ever be
published, or *not* be burnt—& I only wish I had 3000 Gs to give Moore for
them this moment——

I don't know whether you agree with me dearest A—but there is something to me of *Vanity & Egotism* in writing *one's own life* which I cannot
bear—& there is quite sufficient known by those who may wish to do so, &
can do it well, to answer their purpose without this unfortunate Memoir
having to be read & canvassed & *squabbled* over, for what *one* may think
desirable *another* not so—so here I am—God knows what will happen to-
morrow at 12—for there must be some very mysterious proceedings, which
must be explained by H—— I am *quaking*, for *I am* not *to say Ive seen
W &c*—or allude to him, in short I do dislike having to fabricate or conceal—
Perhaps you can give Me yr opinion by G B— . . . don't plague yr self to
write without he sd be gone—a *line*—just to say My dearest A, what you
think—of course I could not but suppose *Col D* had your *instructions or
consent* to act for you—to this moment I cannot understand it at all. You will
forgive me I know—I am most anxious to know how you are, which I hope
to do from George B tomorrow—*I* am as well as it is possible in my present
circumstances—ye elder children better ye younger fallen sick—God bless
you Dearest A[1]

The mention of a 'double part' acted by Moore and Murray relates
to a proposal by Moore, said to be endorsed in some tentative way by
Murray, that instead of being destroyed the manuscript might be left in
Augusta's keeping. The reference to this in her letter to Lady Byron is
omitted because the matter is dealt with more directly in a protest dispatched by her on the same day, that busy Sunday of notes and messengers,
to Wilmot Horton. (It was he who had conveyed to her in two successive
letters the willingness of Moore and Murray to agree to this expedient.)

Mr Hobhouse has this moment left me, having informed me that it was
decided that Mr Moore, Mr Murray, Col. Doyle and yourself were to be
here at 12 *o'clock to-morrow*—for the purpose of Mr Moore paying Mr
Murray the money for the Memoirs, their being delivered into Mr Moore's
hands and then into mine and from thence into the fire—The *time* has been
settled today—every other part of the intention was *told me* yesterday by
Mr Hobhouse. . . . I have been making up my mind ever since to perform
what *ought* to be done, and was (as I before said) a few minutes ago informed
by Hobhouse of *to-morrow* at 12 being the time—I am more surprised after
this—than I can express to hear of Mr Murray *sending to you* &c &c &c,
still more than ALL—*that I had expressed a wish to have these Memoirs in
my possession!* I declare most solemnly that I never did anything of the
sort— . . . .

I know not what to think or do or to understand in this complicated

[1] Lovelace Papers.

business—it is my *very* decided opinion the Memoirs *ought* to be *burnt*, and I think the sooner the better. . . .[1]

Augusta had become fanatically obstinate in the manner of weak-willed persons when they have been worked upon to take some unwontedly vigorous step.[2] It may not be insignificant that George Byron, who fortified her in her resolution to demolish Byron's records, was another recipient of Lady Byron's confidence, and had, like Colonel Doyle, seen her the day before at Beckenham, and was about to go back there.

Doyle was later to deny that he had any previous knowledge of an intention to burn the manuscript, and to profess that the whole affair had taken him by surprise; and Augusta's long letter confirms that he was not a party to the making of the plan. Yet he must have had more knowledge of what was to happen than he afterwards admitted, else Hobhouse was taking a great deal for granted in writing to Murray on the eve of the pre-arranged ceremony of destruction:

> Mr Moore will be ready with the money at twelve o'clock tomorrow and will meet you at that hour at Mrs Leigh's rooms. Colonel Doyle will, of course, be with you.
>
> You will be good enough to bring all the papers—i.e. the MS and the copy of it made under Mr Moore's eye—the assignment and the bond.[3]

Murray was under the impression that, so far from having stood aloof from the proceedings, Doyle had already offered him whatever he had paid for the Memoirs to hand them over.[4]

Here is Doyle's own declaration to Horton a year later:

> Lady Byron told me at Beckenham, I think the day before, that she had received some communication from Mr Hobhouse on the subject of this manuscript—to the effect, as well as I recollect, that Mr Moore was disposed to deliver it up to Lord Byron's family, and that it was very desirable to obtain it from him—and Lady Byron then requested me to act for her, in the event of its being necessary for her to do anything in the matter. I came to town immediately afterwards but certainly without any *expectation* that I should be called upon to take any steps in the business till I had heard further from her. . . .
>
> My going afterwards to Murray's was quite accidental—you called upon me and requested me to accompany you there, which I did. . . . Lady Byron certainly gave no consent to the *destruction* of the manuscript either directly or indirectly—she never could have known that it was intended to destroy it because I believe that intention was communicated for the first time at the meeting in question.[5]

[1] LOVELACE, *Lady Noel Byron*.

[2] Hobhouse, in his journal entry for 15 May, says that when he told her of the proposed destruction of the Memoirs, 'she did not at first understand it'.

[3] Murray MSS.

[4] Letter to *The Academy*, 29 Sept. 1869.   [5] LOVELACE, *Astarte*.

Doyle's strand in the tangled and knotted skein of responsibility will be seen again less dimly.

During these conferences and letter-writings, Thomas Moore had not been forgotten. He had called on Hobhouse at his Albany chambers while John Murray was in the midst of his first portentous interview, and had been shown into another room to wait, and not invited to emerge till Murray had departed. This was the sort of reception to make him stand on his dignity, and instead of fighting to protect the Memoirs, he fought primarily to assert his own status.

> . . . He complained of Murray [wrote Hobhouse]—he said he had received Kinnaird's note—he would not let any one pay the money—he would pay the money himself—he thought it shameful that Murray had not told me the MSS were his (Moore's)—he had no objection to deliver the MSS to Mrs Leigh but he would do it himself—he would have the grace of this sacrifice himself—he would take the MSS home with him.
>
> All this rather pleased me except the latter part. I did not like his taking the MSS home—considering all that had passed before—especially as he now told me he had suffered several people to see the MSS abroad—and that Lady Burghersh at Florence had actually copied a great part of them—which copy, however, Moore had seen her burn.
>
> I could not help expressing my astonishment that Moore should have even shown the MSS—much less suffered them to be taken out of his sight— he told me Lord Byron had wished him to do so—but he afterwards owned that Lord B's expressions were '*show them to the elect*.'[1]

Moore's object in telling Hobhouse these facts must have been to convince him that burning the Memoirs would be pointless since they had, with Byron's willing assent, been read by 'several' ('many' would have been a more appropriate admission): but the only effect upon Hobhouse was to excite him to quivering resentment. 'Show them to the elect' was almost an insult when they were still unknown to him!

> Now it was impossible B. could mean by these words any person to whom Moore wished to show his intimacy with Lord Byron—which was the true motive for showing about these unjustifiable Memoirs.
>
> Moore also told me that the first part of the Memoirs contained nothing objectionable except one anecdote—namely that Lord B. *had* Lady B. on the sofa before dinner on the day of their marriage—and Moore actually showed this to Lady Burghersh and others— ! ! ! When I told this to Burdett he said 'he ought to have had his brains knocked out for doing so—' that is for showing it.
>
> The second part contained all sorts of erotic adventures and Gifford of the Quarterly who read it at Murray's request said that the whole Memoirs were fit only for a brothel and would damn Lord B. to everlasting infamy if published.

[1] Hobhouse *Journals*, 15 May 1824.

Knowing all this I was anxious to get the MSS destroyed at once—so I proposed that Moore should walk down with me to D. Kinnaird's. We went there and found D. K. at home—Kinnaird entered at once into my views but agreed with Moore that he ought to have the grace of the sacrifice as the property was his.[1]

William Gifford's opinion of the Memoirs would carry more weight if we did not know that he had said the same thing about *Don Juan*; while Hobhouse, for his part, had run the whole gamut of remonstrance against the publication of either that or *Cain*. 'Everlasting infamy' was so freely threatened to Byron in respect of productions which nobody would now wish to do away with, that we need not take the grim words literally.

Moore, though he was one of the 'synod' who had decided *Don Juan* was unpublishable, did not hold that opinion of the Memoirs; but Hobhouse had got him to Kinnaird's house in Pall Mall in order, as he told Augusta, 'to work on his feelings', and this he did so successfully that Moore signed a paper which Kinnaird swiftly drew up for him, copied thus by Hobhouse for his diary:

Mr Moore has the right to demand from Mr Murray the return of the MSS on paying him (Mr M) £2000 for which he holds Mr Moore's Bond at this time, and the MSS as the security for the same. Mr Moore proposes to meet Mr Murray at Mrs Leigh's house and in her presence to pay over to Mr Murray £2000 to receive from Mr Murray the MSS and to hand them over to Mrs Leigh to be entirely at her own absolute disposal.[2]

This was nothing less than outright surrender of Byron's gift to let Augusta do what she would with it—which meant, as Moore was well aware, what Hobhouse had decided she should do.

To understand the reason for Moore's assent to Hobhouse's astounding proposition, we must glance backward to early November 1821, when he learned that two great bulwarks of his social life, Lord Lansdowne and Lord Holland, were united in disliking his transaction with Murray. Lord and Lady Holland had both been allowed to read the book, and had found some comment adverse to Lady Holland in it, and that was what set off the unfortunate train of Moore's misgivings. The disapproval of noblemen, and particularly of these, to whom he was under many obligations, was unendurable to him, and he had soon begun negotiating with Murray for a new contract that would enable him to regain possession of the scripts.

In order to induce John Murray to turn what amounted to an outright purchase into a loan on security, Moore had represented to him that Byron too was having second thoughts about future publication, Murray

[1] Ibid.   [2] Ibid.

being much more likely to do a remarkably obliging thing for Byron than for Moore. What Murray believed may be given in his own words:

. . . In November 1821, a joint assignment of the Memoirs was made to me by Lord Byron and Mr Moore, with all legal technicalities, in consideration of a sum of 2000 guineas. . . . Some months after the execution of this assignment, Mr Moore requested me, as a great personal favour to himself and to Lord Byron, to enter into a second agreement, by which I should resign the absolute property which I had in the Memoirs, and give Mr Moore and Lord Byron, or any of their friends, a power of redemption *during the life of Lord Byron*. As the reason pressed upon me for this change was that their friends thought there were some things in the Memoirs that might be injurious to both, I did not hesitate to make this alteration at Mr Moore's request; and, accordingly, on the 6th day of May, 1822, a second deed was executed, stating that, 'Whereas Lord Byron and Mr Moore are now inclined to wish the said work not to be published, it is agreed that, if either of them shall, *during the life of the said Lord Byron*, repay the 2000 guineas to Mr Murray, the latter shall redeliver the Memoirs' . . .[1]

It is this attestation which had led several biographers to state that, about the time of his mother-in-law's death, Byron began to vacillate and, hoping for reconciliation with his wife, to wish he could reclaim what he had written about her. A number of entries in Moore's journal place it beyond doubt that he was resolved to ask for a new contract many weeks before January 1822, when Lady Noel died, and in fact at a time when Byron himself was vigorously defending—as will presently appear—Moore's right to profit by the Memoirs and his own to have them posthumously published. Nor has anything ever come to light in his correspondence to indicate either that he regretted what he called his anticipated legacy to Moore or that he had hopes in 1822 of a reconciliation with his wife.

The only friends of Byron's who had been actively worrying about the bargain were Holland and Hobhouse, not disinterested parties, and Douglas Kinnaird, who read the Memoirs without turning a hair but took strong exception to the original contract—the one by which 'Mr Moore sold his Lordship to the booksellers'—and who belonged to the anti-Moore faction of Byron's friends. In his capacity of Power of Attorney he had helped to deal with the revision of the terms, and this is another point to be borne in mind when the names of Moore and Byron are found bracketed together in a supposed intention not to publish the manuscripts. Kinnaird, a crony of Hobhouse's, had not liked Byron's renunciation of control. For that reason, he had, from the first, lingered and made difficulties about handing over to Murray the assignment with Byron's signature.

[1] SMILES: Letter to R. Wilmot Horton, 19 May 1824.

Having demonstrated his anxiety to appease his exalted advisers, Moore had not the means to do anything further. The redemption of the pledge needed a large sum even measured by the standards prevailing today when the pound has diminished to about a sixth of the value it then had. He had gone through the motions of doing what the two great lords thought proper, and his inability, after all the fuss he had made, to complete the act of repurchase must have seemed humiliating when he was confronted by Hobhouse and Kinnaird whose disapprobation was patent.

Moore's most persistent foibles were snobbery and the kind of defensive pride that is found chiefly in men who lack security. An Irishman in an epoch when the Irish were still an oppressed people, a grocer's son who had magically won a foothold in the world where birth was usually indispensable to acceptance, his position was rendered still more vulnerable by his being poor—dismally poor compared with Hobhouse, a bachelor free from family cares, whose father was an affluent and indulgent baronet, or Kinnaird, a peer's son with a partnership in a banking business. In consequence, he seemed obliged, the subject of money being raised, to make desperate gestures.

He had exposed all his weakness when, after his futile decision to reclaim the book, he had written in his journal:

> This is, I feel, an over-delicate deference to the opinions of others; but it is better than allowing a shadow of suspicion to approach within a mile of one in any transaction. . . .[1]

'Over-delicate deference' must have been uppermost again when friends of Byron's who were gentlemen by birth informed him what he, as a gentleman himself, ought to do now that Byron was dead. His assent was half-hearted but it was not withheld.

He afterwards announced in the *Morning Chronicle* that he had 'placed the manuscript at the disposal of Lord Byron's sister, Mrs Leigh, with the sole reservation of a protest against its *total* destruction—at least without previous perusal and consultation among the parties'.[2] Hobhouse angrily challenged the existence of the reservation, and since Moore signed the paper it is manifest that he could not have made it with sufficient force; but that he did at least attempt to make it is borne out by another entry in his journal showing he had put forward arguments that to burn 'without any previous perusal or deliberation . . . would be throwing a stigma upon the work, which it did not deserve'.[3] He had also told Wilmot Horton how great an injustice they would do to Byron's memory 'to condemn the work wholly, and without even opening it, as if it were a pest bag'.[4]

---

[1] Moore, *Memoirs*. 22 April 1822.   [2] Letter dated 26 May 1824.
[3] Moore, *Memoirs*. 15 May 1824.   [4] Ibid. 16 May.

Nevertheless, he had somehow been brought to concede the foolish promise. When such words as 'sacrifice' and 'honourable feeling' were the favoured currency, Moore had never let himself be outdone by anyone.

But within hours, or less, he realized that he had gone too far and determined to retract. It is most ironical that he afterwards had to take almost the whole weight of public blame, because in reality his efforts to save the book were strenuous. Besides persuading Longmans, his publisher, to lend him money to buy the property back, and notifying John Murray of his intention, he managed within twenty-four hours to interview severally Samuel Rogers, Henry Brougham, Lord Lansdowne, and Henry Luttrell, all of whom were agreed that total destruction was uncalled for. Luttrell, and perhaps Rogers, had some knowledge of the contents of the alarming manuscript.[1] They were both well acquainted with Byron and might be supposed to have his reputation at heart. Brougham on the other hand had been consulted on Lady Byron's behalf in the Separation, which must have seemed a good reason for hearing his counsels.

Then there were Doyle, acting for Lady Byron, and Horton, vaguely supposed to represent Mrs Leigh. He succeeded in seeing them both, and after a Saturday and Sunday spent in weighty colloquies, he was able to write Hobhouse to the effect that these respectable men had concurred in a 'modification' of the irrevocable course first proposed.

They had reached the conclusion that all parties should together 'peruse and examine' the reminiscences and eliminate what was objectionable, 'rejecting all that could wound the feelings of a single individual, but preserving what was innoxious and creditable to Lord Byron. . . .'[2]

It was not a very satisfactory solution, but seen in perspective it had this merit—it would have given rise to such complicated and lingering disputes that time would have been gained for the outbreak of gentlemanly hysteria to subside. But Hobhouse, on receiving Moore's note on Monday morning, was resolved not to be overborne, and promptly set forth to remonstrate with the most accessible of his opponents, Henry Luttrell, whom he had known for years, and who like himself lived in Albany Court.

On his way to Luttrell's chambers, he happened to meet Moore and, full of righteous anger, told him that 'if the matter were ever publicly discussed, he must say what he thought of the whole transaction'. By playing fast and loose with his promise, Moore had increased the embarrassment of his situation, but he was nerved up now to make a stand.

The hour appointed for the final conference was almost at hand, and

---

[1] See Appendix 3 for conflicting accounts as to whether Rogers actually read the Memoirs or not.   [2] MOORE, *Memoirs*. 16 May 1824.

at Moore's request Luttrell was invited to attend it. The engagement to meet at Augusta's had been altered, and they forgathered in Hobhouse's Albany rooms. Presently John Murray was announced, resolute for doing away with a sensationally interesting unpublished book as, almost certainly, no publisher in history has ever been before or since. So shocked was he when he heard Moore reiterate his suggestion for keeping at least part of the work that, having 'sat down, and in a very determined voice and manner protested that the MSS should be burnt forthwith', he launched into a speech of sheer heroics, which Hobhouse approvingly noted thus:

> I do not care whose the manuscripts are—here am I as a tradesman—I do not care a farthing about having your money or whether I ever get it or not—but such regard have I for Lord Byron's fame and honour that I am willing and am determined to destroy these MSS which have been read by Mr Gifford, who says that they would render Lord Byron's name eternally infamous. It is very hard that I, as a tradesman, should be willing to make a sacrifice which you, as a gentleman, will not consent to.[1]

This from a man who, two days before, had reminded Hobhouse that the sum due to him for redeeming the manuscript was not two thousand pounds, as written in the document Kinnaird had drawn up, but 'two thousand guineas, with interest, and the collateral expenses of stamp, agreement, bond, etc.' was decidedly impressive: but Moore for the moment held out, even when accused by Murray of acting 'anything but like a man of honour'. The tempers of Moore, Murray, and Hobhouse rose, while Luttrell, with a sanity which must have been almost comical where the prevailing tone was altogether quixotic, 'now and then put in a word, saying he could see no harm in reading the manuscript'.

> Mr Hobhouse insisted very strongly on the impropriety of such a proceeding. Mr Moore said that both Mr Wilmot Horton and Colonel Doyle, friends of Lady Byron and of Lord Byron's family, saw no objection to the perusal of the Memoirs. Mr Hobhouse remarked that he could hardly bring himself to believe that; and Mr Murray stated that those two gentlemen themselves were at this moment waiting at his house in order to be present at the destruction of the Memoirs.
> On hearing this, this whole party left Mr Hobhouse's rooms and proceeded to Mr Murray's house in Albemarle Street.[2]

The six people who now met in the famous drawing-room which had witnessed so many pleasanter gatherings fell by a natural division into three pairs—Hobhouse and Murray, hot for destruction; Moore and Luttrell, who alone in that group knew what the book contained, anxious

---

[1] Hobhouse's *Narrative*. Murray MSS.
[2] Ibid. Hobhouse's *Narrative* is written throughout in the third person.

for its total or partial preservation; Horton and Doyle, swayed by Moore's powerful arguments of the day before, yet on the whole favouring the solution that would appeal to Lady Byron.

Kinnaird and Burdett were not present, Kinnaird having been obliged to leave for Scotland, while Burdett's official connection with Byron's affairs had ended after a financial settlement in which he had acted as arbitrator. (It is true that Hobhouse was as yet uncertain that the will by which he had been made executor had not been superseded by a later one, but it would have needed a bold man to dispute his claim to concern himself with a matter touching the after-fame of so very close a friend.)

What took place now was a full-scale altercation, Murray protesting that Moore was not legally entitled to recover the book, the Agreement for which, however, could not be found; Hobhouse pressing the wishes of Mrs Leigh, and Moore so ill-judging as to oppose him with the wishes of Byron. There was nothing better calculated to irritate a man who felt that he owned a proprietary right in Byron—who had conferred with him about his writings since their undergraduate days, interviewed his publisher, corrected his proofs, and brought out a substantial volume of notes to one of his works. To be told of Byron's wishes on a matter both literary and personal by one whom he despised must have been an infusion of wormwood into the cup of his grief—a grief much deeper than the inveterately superficial Moore was capable of feeling.

He was provoked to retort with what he had already said in private to Augusta—that Byron's wishes had changed: at their last meeting, in September 1822, he had expressed uneasiness about his gift, and had only been restrained by delicacy towards Moore from recalling it.[1]

Moore did not believe him, and the conflict reached a degree of bitterness that nearly led to a challenge. Even at the last moment, when the book with the only copy that existed of it had been brought into the room and was about to be torn up and thrown into the flames, he 'still continued his remonstrances, saying: " *Remember I protest against the burning as contradictory to Lord Byron's wishes and unjust to me.*" '[2]

By now a seventh person had joined the company, a boy sixteen years old, John Murray's son, destined to be the third in the unbroken succession of John Murrays whose history as publishers begins in the mid 18th century. He was introduced as the heir to the house, to share in what was recognized as a momentous proceeding. As a man of eighty he could still recall the violence of the quarrel between Moore and Hobhouse.

---

[1] It should be observed that this was several months after the period of his supposed vacillations, which had been used by Moore as a pretext for securing a new contract. In his journal Moore invariably uses the first person singular for recording the negotiations: e.g. 'Determined . . . to throw myself on the mercy of Murray and prevail on him to rescind the deed.' [2] Hobhouse, *Narrative*.

To put down the pretensions of Moore seems by this time to have become Hobhouse's sole—as it was from the first his strongest—motive, for, when his *Narrative* is on the threshold of its culminating point, we find casually dropped into it this most significant passage:

> Some one then asked whether or not the end proposed might not be answered by depositing the manuscripts under seals in the hands of some banker, in order to compare them with any spurious copy of the Memoirs which might afterwards appear. Mr Hobhouse said he could see no objection to this proposal if Mrs Leigh consented, but the proposal was overruled.

'Mr Hobhouse could see no objection.' . . . Then he was not opposed on principle to the preservation of his friend's recollections, but merely, it would appear, determined that they should not be under the jurisdiction of Moore.

The person who ventured by far the soundest idea that had yet been put forward was Wilmot Horton; and as Hobhouse was willing that they should pause and refer the suggestion back to Mrs Leigh, we are left with John Murray and Colonel Doyle as the only possible advocates of instant burning—Luttrell having been from the first on the side of Moore.

If we accept the account contained in his recently quoted letter, Doyle may be ruled out. 'I regarded myself', he informed Horton, 'only as a witness and not as a party to the proceeding.'

Persuaded as he was that his conduct had been meritorious, John Murray would not have been at pains to deny that the last word was with him; but for one who regarded himself only as a witness, Colonel Doyle's behaviour was curious. Hobhouse reports it thus:

> Colonel Doyle then said to Mr Moore "*I understand then that you stand to your original proposal to put the MSS at Mrs Leigh's absolute disposal.*" Mr Moore replied, "*I do but with the former protestation.*" "*Well then,*" said Colonel Doyle, "*on the part of Mrs Leigh, I put them into the fire.*"
> Accordingly Mr Wilmot Horton and Colonel Doyle tore up the Memoirs and the copy of them, and burnt them.[1]

Colonel Doyle's intervention 'on the part of Mrs Leigh' was unwarrantable seeing that he was only, according to his own claim, holding a watching brief for Lady Byron. Though his subsequent denial of being given any definite instructions by her may have been true, it is straining credulity rather far to imagine their having the discussion which sent him hurrying to London, after she had received Hobhouse's urgent letter, without her once uttering an idea as to what the fate of the Memoirs ought to be. She had made her desire to prevent their circulation quite explicit in 1820, and must, one would suppose, have hinted an opinion in

---

[1] Ibid. The italics are Hobhouse's underlining.

1824. The expressions of satisfaction she wrote to at least two correspondents on hearing what had been done prove, at any rate, that Doyle was serving her loyally by putting the most drastic of all ends to the argument.

The pages blazed, pages by the hand that had written *Don Juan*, and also some of the finest prose of his century. Evidently under the impression that the holocaust was some sort of ritual, Wilmot Horton handed a batch of the papers to Hobhouse so that he might take his turn in feeding the fire. He declined, saying that only those empowered by Mrs Leigh should do the work of destruction—a disingenuous excuse from the man who had said to her with so much emphasis: '*You must burn them.*'[1]

He was writer enough to have a glimmering, if there were a lucid interval in his fever, that what was being consumed was something of Byron. As the leaves, torn by the alien hands of Horton and Doyle, blackened and crumbled in the flames, the familiar handwriting must, for a moment at least, have reproached him. If so, his aching conscience served but to make him cruel. He seemed to take a pleasure in every discomfiture that Moore subsequently experienced; and there were many.

The first, over and above the loss of the battle, was the arrival of a solicitor with a draft of the missing Agreement, which fully confirmed Murray's belief that, by neglecting to repay the loan during Byron's lifetime, Moore had totally forfeited his ownership of the Memoirs: after all the high words he was forced to confess lamely that his memory had erred, and that he had never properly read the document.

Then came a crucial dilemma. Murray, as it turned out, had only burned his own property. He had had the satisfaction of making a grandiose speech declaring that he did not care about the money, and now he could do no less than support his words by refusing to have it repaid. Why should Moore, to whom the sum was much greater than it was to Murray, not take him at his word? But pride compelled him to argue that, when he had consented to give up the Memoirs, he had looked upon them as his own.

Hobhouse not only led the chorus of disapprobation for Moore's vagueness in signing contracts without mastering their clauses, but implacably underlined in his *Narrative* Luttrell's reminder, interposed just when it looked as if Moore would consent to let Murray bear the loss: '*Recollect, Moore, you have had the money of Murray.*' Thus urged, there was no other course for one on the defensive but to become more persistent; and Murray, in the customary manner of those who make fine speeches, had it both ways, gaining the credit of his magnanimous words while accepting back in full his two thousand guineas,—with interest and the other little items he had mentioned.

[1] The phrase is as Augusta gives it in a letter to Lady Byron, 6 June 1825.

Still unsated, Hobhouse asked him before they dispersed to own 'that Mr Murray had acted perfectly well and honourably in the business', to which Moore retorted, with a laugh that must have been rather a wry one, that he was like the Irishman who, when a judge enquired if he had anything to say why sentence of death should not be passed upon him, exclaimed: 'Oh nothing, except that by Jasus you've settled it all very nicely amongst you.'

Still Hobhouse would not let it go, but went on telling Moore in a jesting style that must have been unutterably galling, how much he had been in the wrong. That night he unkindly confided to his diary his sympathy with Burdett's remark that 'Moore's conduct might be attributed to *poverty* and *vanity*'. He meant that those disadvantages had actuated Moore in trying to save the Memoirs, but the reverse was really true. Poverty and vanity had deprived him of the courage to stand his ground when the world might suppose that in doing so he had a view to his financial interest.

Not that any degree of courage on his part could have averted the ultimate folly once it was proved that he was legally dispossessed: too many wheels had been set in motion. But the fact remains that he had consented—though protestingly—to what was done while he still believed he had the right to stop it. 'The conclusion cannot be resisted', says his biographer, 'that Moore failed his friend.'[1]

He was determined, however, not to make an admission so damaging either in public or in the privacy of his own meditations, and on the following day, May 18th, restored to something like equanimity by a happy meeting with ladies of the Royal Family, he wrote an afterthought to his account of the scene at Albemarle Street, reminding himself how Hobhouse said Byron had ultimately regretted having given away the Memoirs. 'This if I wanted any justification to myself for what I have done, would abundantly satisfy me as to the propriety of the sacrifice.'[2]

It was a spurious justification introduced as a mere postscript with the words, 'I ought to have mentioned —.' Had Byron's wishes been genuinely in his mind, they would not have been the last consideration he alluded to.

That he was able to convince himself his motives had been such as he would have desired them to be, may be seen from his journal entry for December 15th that year:

> Called upon Hobhouse. . . . Told him (what I feel), that all that has happened since the destruction of the Memoirs convinces me that he was

------

[1] STRONG.   [2] Moore, *Memoirs*.

right in advising their total suppression, as, if the remainder were published, much more mischief would be imagined to have existed in the suppressed part than there is even now. Begged of him to give me some time or other under his hand, for my own satisfaction, *the assurance which had such weight with me in giving up the Memoirs*,[1] that Byron had expressed to him, when they last met, his regret at having put them out of his own power, and that it was only delicacy towards me that prevented him from recalling them; said that I might depend upon it that he would.

Hobhouse's corresponding entry for the same date ends thus:

He [Moore] told me that his conduct had been often attacked even by friends, but that he silenced them by saying that Byron told me his wishes that the Memoirs should not be published. After some more talk on Byron, and his saying several times, 'You were much more his friend than I can pretend to have been,' he went away.

If only Hobhouse had been given that comforting assurance just seven months earlier, if only Moore had not been so assertive of his independence, Byron's autobiography might now have its place on our shelves beside Rousseau's *Confessions*: for what his heart, in the first throes of grief, revolted against (unless all this interpretation is error) was that Moore should be enabled to advertise to the world an intimacy with Byron which might be thought to eclipse his own.

Was he lying when he produced that statement about Byron's regrets for the disposition he had made of the reminiscences? Probably not literally. It is unlikely that, even in the crisis of a struggle in which his profoundest emotions were engaged, that most accurate-minded of men would fling his honesty wholly to the winds: but I believe this to be one of the instances in which he violated the spirit though not the letter of the truth.

He had repeatedly chided Byron for giving away the Memoirs, and Byron had shown an obstinate unrepentance, continuing to present Moore with new portions, and defending both Moore's right to pledge the manuscript to Murray, and his own to do as he pleased with it. On November 23rd, 1821, he was declaring in reply to one of Hobhouse's protests:

With regard to "the Memoirs" I can only say that *Moore* acted entirely with *my approbation* in the whole transaction. . . . Do you really mean to say, that I have not as good a right to leave such an MS after my death as the thousands who have done the same? Is there no *reason* that I should? Will not my life (it is egotism—but you know this is true of all men who have *had* a name even if they survive it) be given in a false and unfair point of

[1] Author's italics.

John Cam Hobhouse at the age of about 45, engraved
from a portrait by A. Wivell

view by others? I mean false as to *praise*, as well as *censure*. If you have any *personal* feelings upon it, I can say, as far as I recollect, that you are mentioned without anything that could annoy you; and if otherwise it shall be cut out.

This is all I can do about them, or indeed am disposed to do.[1]

The assurance that he might cut out anything personally annoying to him could have done little to mollify Hobhouse. Resentment at learning that Byron had put Moore in possession of so important a work without giving a glimpse of it to his closest friend could only be intensified by the announcement that it might possibly contain passages of a questionable kind about himself.

When the new Agreement was made confirming an arrangement with Murray by which Moore was to supply additional anecdotes and information after Byron's death, he was fatuous enough to send off a letter telling his friend that he would be accused of 'purchasing a biographer under pretext of doing a generous action'—to which Byron replied amiably but conclusively that he thought he might have a biographer without purchase 'since most scribblers have two or three gratis'.[2]

That was on July 18th, 1822, nearly three years after Moore had had from him the first seventy-eight folio sheets of the text, those which included the 'long and minute' description of his matrimonial troubles. In all that time he had not retracted, and on August 8th, 1822, he was in fact toying (though Hobhouse was doubtless unaware of this) with the idea of publishing some of the book at once 'to counteract'—and the word should be remembered—the slanders of one John Watkins who had printed his opinion that 'the poet of lust' (Moore) had aptly received as a gift Memoirs by 'the imitator of Juvenal'.

Let me know what you think ,[Byron wrote to Moore] or whether I had better *not*:—at least, not the second part, which touches on the actual confines of still existing matters.[3]

Less than five weeks later, Byron, according to Hobhouse, was voicing those regrets of which he had never given the smallest hint in all the preceding period. It can only be conjectured that if, during Hobhouse's visit to Pisa in September, Byron did lament having put the Memoirs out of his own control, it was because he had not found himself free to act as he pleased when he had had the impulse to publish; and he may well, with that circumstance still in mind, have made some admission—delightful to his friend—that he wished he had not given Moore the book, though he could hardly ask for it back now.

That Hobhouse used his memory disingenuously we may suspect from

---

[1] *Correspondence.*   [2] Ibid.   [3] *L. & J.*

L.L.B.—D

the single clumsy and evasive sentence in which his *Narrative* deals with the important matter of Byron's views:

> Mr Hobhouse said, that his Lordship had, in 1822, expressed himself in connection as to the unfitness of making the use originally intended of the Memoirs.

Such words have not the positive ring of a truth that needs no loophole.

But even the most incontrovertible proof that Byron changed his mind about how and when the Memoirs were to be made public would not have been a justification for what was done with them, seeing that an intention to refrain from publishing a document is in no wise synonymous with an intention to destroy it, and neither Hobhouse, Moore, nor anyone who had known Byron was ever so dishonest as to pretend that he had wished to recall his pages for the purpose of reducing them to ashes. On the contrary, all his references to them in letters and reported conversations are in a style which cannot but lead us to believe that their existence was a source of considerable satisfaction to him.

On this score testimony has come to light by a witness whose romantic and flowery mode of expression should not obscure the extremely valuable mass of first-hand evidence she has provided. This is the much underestimated Countess Guiccioli, author of two books on Byron, one of which has not as yet been published except in the form of extracts. Writing the second work, *La Vie de Lord Byron en Italie*, in her old age and when a most sanctimonious code of morals prevailed, she was obliged to keep up a fiction that her relations with Byron had been platonic, but apart from this almost compulsory hypocrisy, her story, wherever it can be checked, proves trustworthy.

She recalls that when Byron gave Moore the Memoirs—that is, the first batch of them—at his villa on the Brenta in 1819, 'he was beaming. His beautiful face seemed to say that he could resign himself to the injustice of the present in the certainty that these pages would one day do him justice, and that at the same time he was lightening the burden of a friend.' She goes on to comment with bitterness on the treacherous destruction of these writings, which, had they been allowed to survive, would have made materially impossible 'the disgusting fable that has crossed the Atlantic,[1] because they contained down to the tiniest details what had passed between him and Lady Byron'.

At the date in question, Countess Guiccioli had not sufficient command of English to have read the Memoirs, but Byron must have given her some notion of their contents. 'Down to the tiniest details' tallies well

---

[1] Mrs Beecher Stowe's *True Story of Lady Byron*. The Memoirs certainly contained no anticipation of these disclosures. See Appendix 1.

with his own phrase about the description of his married life. She saw him constantly while he proceeded with the work, which he sent off to Moore in successive parcels, and she lived with him till his embarkation for Greece in July 1823. There is one sole point on which all observers are agreed, and that is that he was little disposed to concealment of his feelings: if he had repented of his memoir-writing, his daily companion would not have remained in ignorance of it.

We may securely conclude with her that he would never have sanctioned the irrevocable suppression of the life-story to which he had so long applied himself, any more than he sanctioned the suppression of *Don Juan*, when a conclave of his friends pleaded with him not to print it.

That a group of responsible people should presume to destroy unread a major work by a man whom each of them held to be a genius may seem so strange as almost to defy credence. It is not surprising that the public assumed it was being protected (much against its will) from disclosures of surpassing wickedness; we only marvel that Hobhouse and Murray should completely have failed to see the immense injury they were inflicting on the name they wished to glorify—injury crystallized in the following extract from the *New Monthly Magazine*:

> . . . It *must* be taken for granted that the Memoirs were utterly unfit for publication in any shape; and that Mr Moore and Lord Byron's other friends did not expurgate them only because they were incapable of expurgation.[1]

The public was left unaware that, of the seven who saw Byron's recollections consigned to oblivion, only two had read them, and theirs the voices that were raised in protest. The conclusions drawn by his detractors were inevitable: but if this synthesis of the various first-hand accounts has thrown any light on motives, the fantastic act can now be explained without any such sinister imaginings.

To sum these motives up, Colonel Doyle acted in accordance with what he presumed, having interviewed her, would be the wishes of Lady Byron. Wilmot Horton was also eager to be of service to her, and though he wavered and put forward sensible alternative proposals, he was not disposed to press them. He was ostensibly under directions from Byron's nearest adult relative, and did not understand how completely *she* had been directed by Hobhouse.

Moore suffered the spoliation under duress because he was financially involved and dreaded in his vanity to be thought regardful of self-interest. Had it not been for his fatal snobbery, he might have played a part of real instead of meretricious honour, for he could see the points that Hobhouse and Murray had missed—the slur from which his friend's memory would

[1] May 1827.

never recover. Luttrell was present only as a supporter of Moore. The position of these four participants, the willing and the unwilling, is not ambiguous.

Murray's was more complicated. We must take into consideration his hearty dislike of Byron's later works, and his having had such a deal of trouble over *Don Juan* and *Cain* that he may well have flinched from the prospect of bringing out anything more in, morally speaking, the same line. There was the alarming report of Gifford, his trusted literary adviser, and also the influence of his lawyer, Sharon Turner, who was strongly opposed to his publishing Byron. To these factors must be added his deep distress at Byron's death and sincere desire to avert posthumous scandals, and the urgent representations of Lady Byron's partisans. Nor should we leave out of the account his natural aptitude for a striking gesture. He was taking a stand unique in the trade of bookselling, and the same daring which had inspired him, in 1820, to buy for a huge price a work which could not be published till a man of thirty-two had died, may have been exactly what brought him to the pitch of sacrificing it.

As for Hobhouse, he behaved as if he feared the explosion of grave secrets, but that is very unlikely, for he was well aware, and stated in his *Narrative*, that 'many persons' had already seen the manuscripts. Without any specific revelation in mind, he may well have dreaded indecency and a self-portrait in what Byron had described as 'my finest, ferocious Caravaggio style'—a style that Hobhouse totally failed to appreciate. It might even be hazarded that, having been sharply rebuked for his efforts to demolish *Cain* and *Don Juan*, he was unconsciously resolved to demolish *something*. But no one who had studied Hobhouse's diaries and letters could doubt that, above all, he was impelled by an insensate desire for victory over Moore.

To have entrusted those pages to Moore with *carte blanche* to hand them round as he pleased and no stipulation that they should be shown to Hobhouse was one of the major follies of Byron's life. Hobhouse was unsympathetic at this period to most forms of biographical writing, but he was by no means addicted to the destruction of documents. As Byron's executor, it is actually what he kept when he had the opportunity of expunging it for ever that amazes us. The book his friend had written would have been heavily censored, or its publication delayed for many years, but ultimately, his possessiveness once deferred to, Hobhouse might have proved as vigorous in protecting that ill-fated testament as he was in ensuring its oblivion.

Within twenty-four hours of the burning, Lady Byron received several letters. There was one from her solicitor, Mr Wharton, who had seen Sir William Hope and Lady Athlone, and who reported that their envoy, John Barrow, had been in touch with Murray even before 'Hobhouse & Co', so Murray's promise to give up the property was independent of Hobhouse's advocacy. But he gave full credit to Hobhouse and Kinnaird for their prompt and practical demolition arrangements:

> . . . Its having been so done without your Interference was all that could be wished by you or your friends—In this both her Ladyship and Sir Wm heartily concurred and were most happy to hear the matter was to be so terminated.[1]

Lady Byron replied in a brief note dated May 17th: 'I need only say that your communication has relieved my anxiety.'[2]

Horton's announcement was not written till evening, but it arrived by nightfall because, being at the Colonial Office, he had special facilities.

Downing St
Monday
before 6

Dear Lady Byron
    Do not be alarmed at my sending a *Messenger* over to you (to ease my own pocket at the expense of the Country) but I do so that your mind may be set at rest upon one point *before night*—Doyle & myself were at Mr Murrays by 11, & waited till 12 when I wrote the enclosed letter, which please to return—before I had left the Room however the parties arrived

> Moore
> Luttrell as his friend
> Hobhouse
> Doyle
> W. Horton
> Murray.

& after *an hours* discussion which will not bear abridgements, both copies of the Memoirs *were burnt* in my presence. I will come over & breakfast with you *at 10* on Wednesday, weather & *work* permitting—& would come over this Evening *if I could.* . . .
    Augusta, of course, is very much satisfied at the destruction of the Memoirs. indeed, I am satisfied that it was the only thing to be done, though much remains to be considered respecting it. . . .
    Believe me *always*
                            Your most faithful friend
                                    R. W. Horton[3]

The satisfaction felt by Augusta was, as Lady Byron and her friends apparently believed, because she rejoiced at the suppression of reminiscences which would be incriminating to herself, for they did not move in the fashionable set which had been privileged to read the book and could

[1] Lovelace Papers.   [2] Ibid.   [3] Ibid.

acquit the author of so disgusting a treachery. In the sub-acid correspondence which ensued, Augusta laid stress on having had no motive but the protection of her brother's name, and as to that she took the fullest responsibility—much more than her fair share of it.

> *Whatever* might be said *whoever* might be mentioned in those Memoirs, the disgrace would have been his! He was not there to prevent or to direct—& I feel sure as of My existence that in his life time they wd never have seen light & have every reason to hope from the blessed alteration during the last year, he wd have done his best, had he been spared to have prevented it after his death.[1]

Lady Byron's most explicit utterance to Augusta was slightly at odds with her swift expression of relief to her solicitor. It is contained in a letter of June 1st, 1825:

> . . . I do concur *now* in the expediency and propriety of the destruction, but had the question been *then* submitted to me, they [the Memoirs] certainly would not have been consumed by *my* decision. It is therefore perhaps as well it was not.[2]

The reason why several pens were still preoccupied with the subject more than a year later was that the question was for ever being debated—who, if anyone, should repay Moore for his loss?

Lady Byron, who was liberal in money matters, offered £1000 towards his reimbursement, and Augusta was genuinely eager to provide the remainder, supposing herself to be lifted from financial embarrassment by inheriting as much of Byron's fortune as he was free to leave her. (The bulk of it was tied up in his marriage settlement.) But there were all kinds of hair-splittings as to how the sum should be received, whether directly from the family, or through Murray, or in some other manner. Moore, though longing for the cash, soon grew haughty again. Not knowing that Hobhouse was opposed to any form of restitution, he was rash enough to ask his opinion, and Hobhouse took the chance of making one more thrust —though not by any means his last. His *Narrative* gives the conversation thus:

> . . . Mr Moore said to Mr Hobhouse, "Now tell me, if I had been a rich instead of a poor man, what would you have said?" After hesitating a little, Mr Hobhouse replied, "do you wish me to speak exactly what I think?" "Certainly," said Mr Moore. "Then," replied Mr Hobhouse, "although, if I were your enemy, I should be silent, yet as I am not, I will say that it is my opinion you should *not* take the money."
> Mr Moore took Mr Hobhouse by the hand, and said, "There you spoke as a man of honour, and as a friend; thank you a thousand times. I felt all along I could not take this money; I am now sure I was right."

[1] 6 June 1825: Lovelace Papers.   [2] LOVELACE, *Lady Noel Byron*.

As it is always interesting to compare the descriptions of two good witnesses relating the same incident, and good witnesses are extremely rare among the chroniclers of Byron, Moore's version of the same dialogue, which took place on May 21st, is also given:

> . . . After a little more conversation [Hobhouse] looked earnestly at me and said, "Shall I tell you, Moore, fairly what I would do if I were in your situation?" "Out with it," I answered eagerly, well knowing what was coming, "I would *not* take the money," he replied; and then added, "The fact is, if I wished to injure your character, my advice would be to accept it." This was an honest and manly triumph of good nature. . . .

But many years were to pass before Hobhouse was to cease sniping in a peculiarly ill-natured manner at Moore. The next few days, during which the newspapers persisted in talking of the episode, were fraught with several occasions for disparagement. Though Moore had parted with a sum insanely beyond his means to pay for a measure which he had angrily opposed, and which had turned out after all to involve property not his own, Hobhouse could not bear him to be represented as having made any sacrifice. He viewed Moore's situation with a ruthlessness none the less deadly because it was entirely cloaked from his own eyes in considerations of propriety and gentlemanliness.

Had he realized that Lady Byron would now be able to transmit to future generations her records of her matrimonial life in the certainty that she would be the sole authority, he might not have congratulated himself so warmly on having stifled for ever the only voice that could make an answer—a voice too which he always, publicly and privately, maintained was 'true-spoken'. But there was none of Byron's friends who guessed how busy his widow's pen and tongue had been and would remain over the thirty-six years that lay before her.

The nature of the Memoirs

The Memoirs written by Byron between 1818 and 1821 formed a substantial though uncompleted book. They were produced in three batches, and consisted of over four hundred pages (a hundred sheets) of folio paper —some of it, according to his own description, very long and large. If it was the same as he used for certain compositions at this time, each page would probably have contained not less than three hundred words.

The theory that Byron's friends and family were bent on the concealment of some evil secret, which they supposed he had given away, will not hold water for a moment when confronted with the facts. No one knew better than Hobhouse and Augusta Leigh that, so far from being secret, the bulk of the Memoirs had, with Byron's full sanction, been circulated freely. Augusta wrote to Lady Byron in shocked terms to say that Hobhouse had told her so,[1] and Hobhouse himself recorded:

> Lord Byron gave to Mr Moore the permission to show the manuscript to the 'Elect'. Whom his Lordship meant to designate by that epithet it is not very easy to divine; but on the strength of his permission, Mr Moore showed the Memoirs to many persons. . . .[2]

He showed them indeed to so many persons that, on May 7th, 1820, he noted in his journal:

> Williams . . . has begun copying out Lord B's 'Memoirs' for me, as I fear the original papers may become worn out by passing through so many hands.

These numerous readers, who took no vow of silence, included Lady Burghersh, Lady Davy, Lord and Lady Holland, Richard Hoppner, Washington Irving, Lady Jersey, Lord Kinnaird and his brother Douglas Kinnaird, Henry Luttrell, Lady Mildmay, Lord Rancliffe, Lord John Russell, besides the friend, Dr Williams, who copied the first part, and another voluntary copyist, Dumoulin, as well as a professional one who finished the task after Dumoulin's untimely death.[3] John Murray showed the script to his literary adviser, William Gifford, to William Maginn, and to Lady Caroline Lamb, who alludes to it scathingly in her little-known novel *Ada Reis*. Byron himself lent it to Mary Shelley, and presumably Shelley too was one of the readers. Possibly Samuel Rogers was also among the privileged.

[1] Undated letter, early 1820. Lovelace Papers.
[2] Hobhouse, *Narrative*.
[3] The three men were employed successively on one copy, and there is unhappily no warrant for the idea that several were made. Lady Burghersh was asked to destroy the copy she admitted to having taken, and there is only too much reason to believe she did so.

The delicacy of John Murray in abstaining from looking into the pages must have had a diplomatic motive, because Byron had written to him: '. . . If you like to read them you may, and show them to any body you like—I care not.'[1] The same communication gives a very vivid hint as to the character of the earlier sections of the book:

> The *Life* is *Memoranda* and not *Confessions.* I have left out all my *loves* (except in a general way), and many other of the most important things (because I must not compromise other people), so that it is like the play of Hamlet—'the part of Hamlet omitted by particular desire'. But you will find many opinions, and some fun, with a detailed account of my marriage and its consequences, as true as a party concerned can make such accounts, for I suppose we are all prejudiced.

Such passages must make it plain that the work was not primarily, as it has been called, 'mysterious and scandalous'—unless it is always a scandal for an unhappily married person to give his side of a much canvassed story. That it was to some extent a vindication may be gathered from these lines in Byron's letter offering his wife the perusal:

> You will perhaps say *why* write my life?—Alas! I say so too—but they who have traduced it—& blasted it—and branded me—should know that it is they—and not I—are the cause—It is no great pleasure to have lived— and less to live over again the details of existence—but the last becomes sometimes a necessity and even a duty—
>
> If you choose to see this you may—if you do not—you have at least had the option.[2]

The batch of reminiscences dealing with the post-Separation period must have been a good deal freer with the proprieties than the first; though it is certain that, passed as it was from hand to hand among the English community in Paris, no secret disclosed there could have remained a secret long. Moore showed the new sheets to Lord John Russell who read them through in two visits, but did not begin to investigate them himself till they had been with him a fortnight, when we find in his journal this slightly exasperated entry:

> I see that Byron in his continuation says, that I advised him to go into the details of his loves more fully; but if I recollect right, it was only his adventures in the East I alluded to, as in recounting these there could be but little harm done to any one.[3]

From this it may be inferred that in the original seventy-eight folio sheets 'his loves' were, exactly as he had said to Murray, only touched on 'in a general way'. How unguarded he became as he went on, we do not know because the opinions of the readers are in conflict. At the one

---

[1] *L. & J.* 29 Oct. 1819.
[2] LOVELACE, *Astarte.* 31 Dec. 1819.   [3] 5 Jan. 1821.

extreme there was Gifford speaking of 'eternal infamy', at the other Lord John Russell's assertion that only a few pages contained anything gross.

To plod through the eight volumes of Moore's own Memoirs is a laborious task, and several Byron biographers do not seem to have attempted it, content to accept from Rogers the view that Moore did not bother to read the manuscript entrusted to him. But there is, every now and then, amongst the retailings of the compliments paid him and the amusing chatter he enjoyed with the peerage, a sentence showing that he did not neglect Byron's princely gift, though no word of gratitude for it ever fell from his pen—except when he was addressing the giver. He mentions Byron frequently, and usually in a rather detrimental manner, but nothing in his laconic entries suggests that he was seriously shocked by the contents of the packages he lent about so readily, or that he saw anything in them that threatened to make them unpublishable.

If he could spare the time and space for reporting (twice) that Byron had spoken slightingly of Shakespeare, or that he was displaying bad taste in his controversy with Bowles, or that, according to Rogers, he treated Shelley 'very cavalierly', he was likely also to have expressed his distaste for passages that would make his task of editorship—contingent, of course, upon his outliving Byron—an unenviable one. So far from this being the case, on the only occasions when he enters into any details about the Memoirs, he defends them.

Lord Holland's remark to him that the sale of the book to Murray seemed like 'depositing a sort of quiver of poisoned arrows . . . for a future warfare upon private character', has often been quoted, but without the remainder of the paragraph, which stated that he (Lord Holland) could not remember, when pressed, 'anything that came under this strong description, except the reported conversation with Madame de Staël, and the charge against Sir Samuel Romilly. . . .'[1]

Moore had taken the first step towards annihilating the Memoirs when he was silly enough to confide them to Lady Holland, although, as he told her, he 'rather feared' she was mentioned adversely. It was treacherous to Byron and unkind to her—treacherous to Byron because, when he had so airily given Moore the right to use the book at his discretion, he could hardly have envisaged him handing it straight to the people who figured in it; unkind to Lady Holland because, though she was anything but a sentimental woman, she had a fondness for Byron, and Moore knew it. He had asked her once whether Byron's wife could really have loved her husband, and Lady Holland had given it as her opinion that she could not have done otherwise. 'He was such a lovable person. I remember him sitting there, with that light upon him, looking so beautiful!'[2]

[1] MOORE, *Memoirs.* 4 Nov. 1821.   [2] Ibid. 6 June 1819.

Naturally Lady Holland had said she would not mind the criticism. 'Such things give me no uneasiness: I know perfectly well my station in the world; and I know all that can be said of me.'[1] But indifferent as she had undertaken to be, she did not receive the strictures, whatever they were, with more equanimity than most people feel when subjected to ridicule or detraction. If she and her husband had not been allowed to read Byron's comments, Lord Holland might never have advised Moore to get the book back from Murray; the new contract, which required a pretence that Byron had become doubtful about publishing, would not have been drawn up, and everything might have turned out differently.

In her annoyance, Lady Holland believed she had found in the manuscript what was not there—namely, some admission on Byron's part of his relations with Mrs Leigh. Three reasons may be given for saying it was not there. First, Moore insisted to Lord Holland that it was not, and in terms which, coming from him to a noble lord, were unusually forthright; second, in 1869, Lord John Russell wrote a strong denial to Byron's grandson; and third, even Byron would not have been reckless enough to permit a document to be circulated which, besides grossly injuring his beloved sister, would have been deemed a perfect justification for his hostile wife.

Here are Moore's words, dispatched to Lord Holland on November 5th, 1821:

> What Lady Holland yesterday remarked about Mrs L. is, I find upon recollection, founded entirely on her own suspicions, as Lord B. merely mentions a nameless person whom he calls his 'love of loves' and I never met with but one individual, besides Lady H., who supposed it to allude to the lady in question.[2]

Lady Holland allowed herself at the time to be convinced, and when Moore reiterated the assurance after Byron's death, she wrote to her son:

> We have had little Moore to breakfast this morning. He confirms what I before told you of there not being a line in the suppressed portion of Memoirs by Lord Byron, not a line as far as my memory extends.[3] [i.e. not a line compromising Augusta Leigh.]

In her old age her memory must have become confused, because, according to the ever-gossiping Mrs George Lamb, she then claimed that the Memoirs had been '*full of the attachment*'. Mrs Lamb at once conveyed this information to Lady Byron,[4] and the day after receiving it, Lady Byron passed it on to her daughter Ada with censure of Moore for

---

[1] Ibid. 6 July 1821.
[2] Letter quoted by Strong in his biography of Moore.
[3] ILCHESTER, *Elizabeth Lady Holland*. Letter of 16 July 1824.
[4] LOVELACE, *Lady Noel Byron*. 1 Aug. 1843.

having written a book about Byron as if he were ignorant of his criminality. That censure travelled round the shuddering circle.

But, in assuming that the 'love of loves' was Augusta, Lady Holland had forgotten that there were two other candidates for that title—the Mary Chaworth who had been the unattainable ideal of his youth, and the long-dead 'Thyrza' to whom he had addressed some deeply felt poems, and been wont to refer in a mysterious manner. 'Thyrza', who replaced Mary Chaworth as the object of 'violent though pure' passion, was certainly not Augusta.

Although Moore had considered the Hollands' distaste for his transaction with Murray to be without adequate foundation, nevertheless the smallest doubt expressed by such great social arbiters had thrown him into a ferment of anxiety, and he had set about defending himself more forcibly than he had apparently managed to do in conversation. His letter reminded Lord Holland that Byron had given him a right of editorship over part of the Memoirs, and that he intended to exercise it freely, while, as to the first batch, though he had pledged himself to publish that in the state in which he had received it, he was prepared at one point to break his promise—or rather to interpret it in a special manner:

> With respect to the portion of them [the Memoirs] that is to remain unaltered—except the passage about Madame de Staël and an indecent circumstance alluded to in his last interview with Lady Byron (which, however, interpreting my pledge to extend to facts rather than phrases I shall feel no hesitation whatever in softening down) I know but little in the responsibility which I have incurred, to shrink from.

The passage about Madame de Staël—mentioned elsewhere as 'the reported conversation'—was doubtless concerned with the interview at which Byron had learned of Lady Caroline Lamb's malignant tales to his wife.[1] Brougham, whose nickname was Chronique Scandaleuse, had heard these from Mrs George Lamb, and repeated them to Madame de Staël at Coppet. The 'indecent circumstance' in Byron's last interview with Lady Byron may perhaps be linked up with a piece of information contained in Hobhouse's *Contemporary Account*—that Byron 'had not guessed the possibility of such a measure [as a permanent severance] when Lady Byron left him, she having *lived* with him, as his wife, up to the day of her departure'.

Lady Byron knew that this would have made part of Byron's case if it had come into court and was at pains to account for the surprising fact in some of her Statements. Byron firmly believed, remembering their last hours together, that she could not then have had any serious intention of parting from him for ever, and must have been subjected to pressure by her

[1] See Chapter VII.

parents on arriving home. It may have been to support this contention that he made the disclosure—or possibly he was merely amused at the idea of confronting her with it, having invited her to read and deny if she could.

It is a pity that Moore's letter to Lord Holland, which provides our most immediate glimpse into the irrecoverable book, treats only of what the disgruntled peer and his wife thought objectionable; but as their objections were to have so devastating an effect, it is essential to examine them.

> The alleged misstatement of Sir S. Romilly's conduct [Moore continues] may be easily remedied by furnishing me with the means of contradicting it, and with respect to any charge against Mr Brougham (though I do not remember that any such exists in the work) I can answer for his seeing all that is said about him and thereby having an opportunity of correcting any misrepresentation.

The grievance against Sir Samuel Romilly was that he had been retained by Byron in the Separation proceedings and had gone over without warning to the other side, thereby incurring the poet's most implacable animosity. It was not an imaginary wrong. Byron's solicitor, John Hanson, had given his client in a sequence of letters clear notice that Romilly had accepted his retainer,[1] and it must have come as a profound shock, at a time when all occasions seemed to conspire against him, for Byron to find the celebrated lawyer actually ranged with the opposing forces!

Romilly told Hobhouse, who called on him on March 16th, 1816, that he was not aware he had been engaged by Lord Byron; and admitted, on being shown the retainer by his clerk, 'that he had done a very incorrect thing in being consulted by Lady Byron, but that in the multiplicity of retainers it was sometimes the case that names were overlooked'.[2] To overlook so famous a name as Byron's was extraordinary enough to have appeared deliberate, and Byron, who was little given to the cant of *de mortuis nil nisi bonum*, did not pretend to have mastered his resentment when Romilly committed suicide in 1818. 'I detested him living, and I will not affect to pity him dead', he wrote to John Murray (June 7th, 1819). He attacked him in *Don Juan* and must have launched his charge more specifically in the Memoirs.

It is likely that, despite Moore's forgetfulness of it, they did also contain some indictment of Henry Brougham. Just as the probabilities are all against his convicting himself or his sister of incestuous relations in pages

---

[1] E.g. 'Sir Samuel Romilly had a general retainer for you some time ago, so that he is secured.' (Murray MSS.: 12 Feb. 1816.) 'Doctors Robinson, Adams, and Jenner are retained for your Lordship in the Commons, and you have Sir Samuel Romilly under your general retainer, so that you have a multitude of counsellors.' (Ibid. 22 Feb. 1816.)

[2] HOBHOUSE, *Contemporary Account*.

designed to be seen by some while he and she were still alive, and by many after he was dead, they are all in favour of his relieving himself of the rage which had made him, during the whole period of these writings, treasure the idea of coming to England to challenge Brougham to a duel. What with the breach of professional etiquette by Romilly and the breach of professional honour by Brougham, Byron had felt himself, with more reason than he is usually given credit for, to be the victim of singularly malign influences.

Brougham's position as one of the powerful legal team enlisted for Lady Byron should have imposed discretion, but he had set on foot rumours of a most injurious kind, doubly damaging coming from such a source. On September 21st, 1820, Byron had written to Hobhouse:

> You know that I have never been near Brougham since his insults; and was ignorant of them till long after their occurrence. *Keep this in mind, as you yourself were* one of my informants, and I am sorry to say (though from a good motive) a late one. If I come to England now, I must wait till his trial of the Queen is over before I can have him out. . . .[1]

Byron had not known at the time of the separation how malevolent Brougham's conduct had been. Hobhouse's journal contains such entries as:

> Kinnaird indignant at Brougham, who attacked Byron at Brook's for his *deformity*. Curse him. (25 April 1816)
> Dined at Perry's [the editor of the *Morning Chronicle*] Brougham has been with him, telling him that B. cheated the Duchess of Devonshire of 500£ [the rent of her house]—I said it was a lie out loud, and desired any one present to tell Brougham so for me. Kinnaird, S[crope] Davies, and I all thought something should be done to stop this horrible insolence of Brougham's, who in appealing to Perry did the very thing to which he objected in Byron's friends. (26 April 1816)[2]

Hobhouse did not hesitate to write in the detailed narrative of events which he left to his descendants to be used 'if necessary' that some of the worst rumours about Byron '*were traceable to Lady Byron's legal advisers themselves*', and he coupled this underlined assertion with the name of Brougham. (Politics brought him and Brougham together in later years and his ill feeling was extinguished—though he continued to find his colleague's extreme untruthfulness disconcerting.)

Rogers too was among those Byron complained of. After the statement about Mrs Leigh already quoted, Moore's letter to Lord Holland continues:

> The slighting passage about Rogers' Human Life is in the part over which I have discretionary power, and, at all events, is fully atoned for by the

---

[1] *Correspondence*. The italics are Byron's underlining.
[2] British Museum: Broughton Papers acquired in 1950.

estimation which Lord B, on all other occasions, shows for his works, ranking him indeed, at the very head of all the poets of the present day.

A man whose tongue had an unsparing edge, Rogers had provoked a furious lampoon from Byron in 1818, which Hobhouse described as severe but true; but evidently in the Memoirs there was only a disrespectful remark about one of his works.

That Lord Holland, though displeased with Byron's attitude to Lady Holland, could find nothing worse to grumble at than the matters Moore took up with him is very powerful testimony against the idea that the Memoirs would have proved seriously mischievous. It is to be observed that he had read even the second and less restrained portion, for it was that alone over which Moore had 'discretionary power' at the time.

Lord John Russell, with an eye on Hobhouse, suppressed an account of the burning left by Moore when, in the 1850's, he edited the latter's diaries, and gave this verdict on Byron's Memoirs:

> . . . I should say that three or four pages . . . were too gross and indelicate for publication; that the rest, with few exceptions, contained little traces of Lord Byron's genius, and no interesting details of his life. His early youth in Greece, and his sensibility to the scenes around him, when resting on a rock in the swimming excursions he took from the Piraeus, were strikingly described. But, on the whole, the world is no loser by the sacrifice made of the Memoirs of this great poet.

This has sometimes been taken at face value, but it must be borne in mind that the friends of those who had been blamed for destroying the manuscript had a natural tendency to minimize the loss; and, moreover, that the majority of Byron's contemporaries took a very poor view of his lighter and more colloquial productions. That there were 'no interesting details of his life' is plainly untrue.

A 'long and minute' description of his marriage and the steps that led to it, 'the glimpses of adventures'—so Moore alludes to them—that he met with in Spain, the recollections of his early youth in Greece, the 'amusing account'—also touched on by Moore—of the behaviour of Lady Jersey's guests at the celebrated ball where he was cut, the 'gallery of sketches all personal and many satirical', his picture of Madame de Staël's *entourage* in Switzerland and of the society in Milan where he said he was 'like a ship under quarantine', the 'many opinions and some fun', and the 'passions and prejudices' of which, he told Murray, the work was full—all these in Byron's hands could not have been less than the ingredients of a first-rate book: and even the pages too gross and indelicate for publication in the genteel 1820's might have turned out to have their merits in the judgment of a less squeamish age.

Extract from ' The Times' obituary notice

. . . We know not how many of our countrymen may share the feelings with which the news has afflicted us. There were individuals more to be approved for moral qualities than Lord Byron—to be more safely followed, or more tenderly beloved; but there lives no man on earth whose sudden departure from it, under the circumstances in which that nobleman was cut off, appears to us more calculated to impress the mind with profound and unmingled mourning.

Lord Byron was doomed to pay the price which Nature sometimes charges for stupendous intellect, in the gloom of his imagination, and the intractable energy of his passions. Amazing power, variously directed, was the mark by which he was distinguished far above all his cotemporaries. His dominion was the sublime—it was his native home; at intervals he plunged into the lower atmosphere for amusement, but his stay was brief.

It was his proper nature to ascend: but on the summit of his elevation, his leading passion was to evince his superiority by launching his melancholy scorn at mankind.

That noblest of enterprises, the deliverance of Greece, employed the whole of Lord Byron's latter days—of his pecuniary resources, and of his masculine spirit. It was a cause worthy of a poet and a hero. . . .

15 May 1824

By contrast *John Bull* wrote:

He has . . . quitted the world at the most unfortunate period of his career, and in the most unsatisfactory manner—in voluntary exile, when his mind, debased by evil associations, and the malignant brooding over imaginary ills, has been devoted to the construction of elaborate lampoons.

16 May.

Samuel Rogers and the Memoirs

In Rogers's *Table Talk* he is reported by Alexander Dyce as saying: 'If Moore had made me his confidant in the business, I should have protested warmly against the destruction . . . but he chose Luttrell, probably because he thought him the more fashionable man; and Luttrell, who cared nothing about the matter, readily voted that they should be put into the fire.'

There is a touch of malice in this which is thoroughly typical of Rogers, and he had, as usual, got the wrong end of the stick, Luttrell having opposed the burning of the Memoirs without the precaution of reading them. Moreover, Moore's journal shows that he took the news of Byron's death to Rogers on May 14th, and that the latter advised him 'not to stir at all on the subject of the "Memoirs", but to wait and see what Murray would do; and in the meantime ask Brougham's opinion'. So, very clearly, he was consulted, though not when the destruction was imminent.

Dyce also records this assertion: 'There were, I understand, some gross things in that manuscript; but I read only a portion of it, and did not light upon them.' Washington Irving, however, in his Memoranda for May 3rd, 1824, states that Moore never showed the Memoirs to Rogers, a fact which occasioned the remark: 'I suspect I was harshly handled in that volume.' Rogers's claim to have read even part of the work is also somewhat discredited by his saying that he 'remembered' this story from it:

> On his marriage-night, Byron suddenly started out of his sleep: a taper, which burned in the room, was casting a ruddy glare through the crimson curtains of the bed; and he could not help exclaiming, in a voice so loud that he wakened Lady B., 'Good God, I am surely in hell!'

This seems to be merely an anecdote dressed up out of something Rogers had been told by Washington Irving, whose recollection was that—

> Byron mentioned waking up one morning soon after his marriage and thinking while he looked at his wife and at the red curtains which surrounded him that he was fairly in hell with Proserpine beside him.

Byron's thoughts 'soon after his marriage' amount to something very different from his utterances in the hearing of his wife on the wedding night, and there is strong support from two quarters for Irving's less dramatic version as the correct one. In the first place, Lady Byron never makes any reference at all to such an affront in the statements and correspondence dealing with Byron's intolerable conduct from the wedding day onwards. (Miss Mayne most unfortunately quotes Rogers's *Table Talk* as if she were quoting Lady Byron, just as she gives Hobhouse's extremest example of the lies scandal-mongers told about Byron as if it were to be found in the family records.)[1] In the second place, Theodore Hook, the forger of the Wedding Night chapter in *John Bull Magazine*, introduces the Proserpine incident, which he was obviously basing on something he had heard, directly or indirectly, from one of the readers of the authentic Memoirs.

He narrates a long-winded and rambling dream, in a style the antithesis of Byron's, an attempt at poetic prose, but ends with the memoirist's awakening, saying 'Hail Proserpine!'

> It was a clear January morning, and the dim grey light streamed in murkily through the glowing red curtains of our bed. It represented just the gloomy furnace light with which our imaginations have illuminated hell. On the pillow reclined my wife. . . . She slept but there was a troubled air upon her countenance. Altogether that light—that cavern bed—that pale, melancholy visage—that disordered and dark hair so completely agreed with the objects I had just seen in my slumbers that I started. . . . 'Hail Proserpine' was again upon my lips, but reason soon returned.

Irving's memorandum and Hook's variations on a genuine theme have in common that it was morning, not night, and that Lady Byron seemed like Proserpine—no unflattering similitude—and that hell was simply in Byron's thoughts, not his utterance. The scurrilous Hook would not have failed to use the 'I am in hell' exclamation if he had ever heard it, nor would it have passed entirely from Lady Byron's very long memory.

Rogers is so wide of the mark that we may doubt whether he had any first-hand knowledge of what he was recalling. It is true he visited Paris and saw Moore frequently at the time when the Memoirs were being passed around, but they may have been in the hands of another reader or of one of the copyists.

[1] The story that Byron asked his wife while in labour whether the child was dead. It is from Hobhouse's *Contemporary Account*, and stigmatized as a horrible and groundless slander.

CHAPTER II

BIOGRAPHERS—THE FIRST BATTLE

In every epoch there are people who believe, and others who profess to believe, that there is a kind of indelicacy in publishing anything about the life of a celebrity. On the grounds that to enquire into the personal circumstances and conduct of those whose works have interested us is no better than prying, peeping, tearing aside the veils of decent reticence, they are always as unhelpful as possible to any biographers who may have to make application to them. In acute contrast to the anxious guardians of privacy are those who, when a famous man dies, show an unseemly eagerness to get what can be got, in money or reflected glory, from having something to reveal about him.

Hobhouse belonged to the first category and it came as an infuriating surprise to him that a number of Byron's acquaintances were clamorously, unashamedly, irrepressibly of the second.

Although his friend was famous on such a scale that, even during his lifetime, all sorts of semi-fictitious publications about him had been widely circulated, Hobhouse seriously supposed that, after his death, interest in his personality could be damped down and his renown allowed to rest on a selected body of his poetry alone.

He wanted homage to be paid, but in its most orthodox and formal shape—burial, or at least a monument, in Westminster Abbey.

Lady Byron was more realistic. She too desired that Byron should be admitted to the Abbey (it was one of her many non-conformisms, for she still thought of him as a supremely wicked man); but she knew that a bust or statue would not appease curiosity. There would be a demand for a life story, and her idea was to anticipate it by producing one over which she could exercise some control. On May 17th, when the Memoirs were burned, Hobhouse entered angrily in his journal:

> I should mention that this day I received a curious message from Lady Byron through Captain George (Lord) Byron. It was that she wished me to give out that I should write Lord Byron's Memoirs in conjunction with the assistance of the family, including Lady Byron, as that would stop all spurious efforts and would be particularly agreeable to her. I returned for answer that I had no spirits now nor inclination for undertaking or thinking of any such task.
>
> Poor Byron! Here is his dear friend Tom Moore, his Publisher, Murray, and his wife: the first thing they think of is writing his Life or getting it written. Such are the friendships of great authors!

Hobhouse's indignation was emphasized, not created, by his fear of stirring up old scandals it would be unthinkable to publish. He himself transmitted to posterity scandalous fact and theory which might barely have been heard of but for letters he left to his heirs and comments he wrote gratuitously in the margins of a book; and there were occasions when he hinted in conversation at the things he could tell if he would. Loyal and discreet though he could be, he liked very much to be in the know and to make others aware he was in the know.

The motive of what we might now call his allergy to biographers seems to have been based on the same feelings which, years before, had been so bitterly outraged when Byron's Memoirs were passed round among the friends of Thomas Moore. It was an aspect of his possessiveness. He would, in short, have proved a difficult and touchy executor even if he had not been handling explosive materials.

For several months after Byron's death, the newspapers and periodicals teemed with allusions to him, and numberless special articles were written. So long as nothing was said extolling Moore's self-sacrifice in giving up the Memoirs, Hobhouse bore this on the whole with equanimity. He was accustomed to the great publicity his friend's name always attracted, and he doubtless assumed it would be ephemeral—the last incoming wave of a tide that must recede. Besides, the tone was generally favourable, indeed most laudatory, and that must have been an agreeable change after the vitriolic abuse which had been heaped upon the poet for his later works. In his proprietary capacity, he delighted to hear Byron praised and suffered so much when he was vilified that adverse public opinion could banish all his critical faculty.

Hobhouse has been represented by several biographers as one whose personal devotion was at odds with his incapacity to appreciate genius. This verdict he brought upon himself by his endeavours at various times to stop Byron from writing, but it does him injustice. It was his ardent admiration for a career which he longed to see sustained in untarnished lustre that made him lose his head when risks were taken and hostile critics provoked. He was no Philistine but an enthusiast who had been drawn to Byron in the first place by hearing that he wrote poetry, and was himself a skilful versifier.

It was to be taken for granted that verses in plenty were poured out to commemorate the death of so compelling a figure. Few were on a high level: many could have produced nothing but exasperation or laughter.

> Who can refrain a *dewy* tear to shed
> To see *great Byron* 'midst the silent dead!
> In Grecian bands he took a manly part,
> And when he died, they cried—"Give us his heart!"

The editor of the *Mirror* deemed that worth reprinting from the *Southampton Chronicle*, and this from the *Literary Chronicle*:

> For oh! that his tears with his song could cease,
>   That all was an halo of brightness:
> But ah! he too little has courted that peace,
>   For he thought on his MAKER with lightness.

Admonitory, but how mild compared with the diatribes that had continually assailed the troubled Pilgrim while he lived:

> Vain shallow sophist, arrogant as weak . . .
> Thou reptile form, thou crawling piece of earth . . .
> Thou grand apostate of the scowling eye . . .
> Thou worse than Satan in a serpent's form . . .[1]

The composer of this malediction had gone so far as to invoke (not without results) the offender's death:

> Oh! that an angel's pow'r, or seraph's might
> Would hurl thee headlong from thy topmost height,
> Cast thee confounded on the Stygian shore,
> That all thy blasphemies be heard no more!

After years of vicarious distress through such onslaughts, the charitable regrets of those obituaries that were not pæans of praise left Hobhouse unruffled. Soon a few books were hurried into print, and these too proved not intolerable. Their tone was respectful and distant. None of the authors claimed to be in Byron's confidence. None attempted to use private documents. None had genuine biographical significance.

Sir Cosmo Gordon's tribute to *The Life and Genius of Lord Byron*, which seems to have been produced in two or three weeks,[2] was rapturous enough to atone perhaps for its harmless inaccuracies. The only reference to John Cam Hobhouse was somewhat lukewarm, but it was at any rate free from offensiveness.

Sir Egerton Brydges *Letters on the Character and Poetical Genius of Lord Byron*, begun in May and completed in mid July 1824, were equally innoxious. Here were forty-one elegantly printed short essays in which the author, an amiable baronet of sixty-one, touched on Byron's private life chiefly to elucidate his work. Whether Hobhouse laughed or groaned at such a passage as follows, the fact that we are ignorant of his reaction suggests that he did not rage:

> The fiercer passions seem to have prevailed exclusively over the mind of
> Lord Byron. Tender affection, timidity, sorrow, sympathy, appear to have
> had little influence over him; a love of power and of the unlimited exercise
> of his caprice, and anger and violent resentment at whatever thwarted his
> purposes, were his habitual temperament. It did not seem, that any hold

[1] Lines selected from *A Layman's Epistle to a Certain Nobleman*, 1824.
[2] It was out in June or July 1824, the news of Byron's death having reached England in mid May.

could be made upon his conscience, or the nicety of his regard to the interests and happiness of others. . . .

He took offence without cause; and revenged without bounds, trifling or imagined injuries. Goodness gave him no pleasure as goodness; but only so far as it happened to suit some transient humour.

Or again:

Some minds are cast in so sombre a mould, that they seem naturally disposed to delight in gloom, mysteries, and terrors. There is something in human existence which dissatisfies them, and produces a discontent and ill humour that drive them to seek familiarity with painful emotions. They love 'to enforce the awful, darken the gloomy, and aggravate the dreadful.' No one, I think will deny that this was the bent and ruling genius of Lord Byron.

It was the popular view, a composite portrait of Byron's early poetic hero-villains, so false that his friends could afford to shrug their shoulders at it. And the author was modest, making no pretensions to inside knowledge. The nearest he had approached to his subject was having 'conversed intimately', between his twenty-ninth and thirtieth 'Letters', 'with a gentleman who, at a late period of Lord Byron's life, spent many of his days with him'.

Who this gentleman was will appear in the next chapter. His influence was striking, for it changed a fairly severe critic into a fervent apologist. How different are the sentiments of Letters II and IV, quoted above, from those of Letter XXX, written after conversations with the new acquaintance:

As to his occasional severity and bitterness . . . he had good reason for his discontents and resentments. . . . He was sometimes criticized in the most foul and treacherous manner; and it will hereafter be proved that some of the charges of bitterness and gross abuse which have been heaped most heavily on his name were firstly provoked by *outrageous aggression*.

Letter XXXI amounts to a *cri de cœur*:

It seems to me that Lord Byron's personal character has been frightfully misrepresented and misunderstood.

'Frightfully' was a strong word in 1824.

Reaching Letter XXXIII, we find the opinions expressed in the earlier essays entirely, though unconsciously, repudiated:

. . . Much of that gloom and those bursts of indignation . . . which have been pursued with such tirades of censure had a natural and venial, if not justifiable, cause; and not only do not prove the heartless pride and selfishness imputed to him, but prove, on the contrary, that with all his outward port of haughty and reckless disregard, he had, at the bottom, a bosom of tenderness; a deep, considerate, contemplative mind, intensely sensitive to the sorrows of our nature, a conscience awake, full of regrets . . .

Whether Hobhouse observed the *volte face* or speculated on the identity of the gentleman whose anecdotes and records of association with Byron were said by Sir Egerton to be nearing publication, is not revealed in his journals. Most of his energies were absorbed in his duties as co-executor with the lawyer, John Hanson, of Byron's estate, an office which brought a hundred burdens, sorrows, and annoyances.

There was the will to be proved, there were people who wanted their letters back and delicate decisions to be made as to whether they should have them, the Greek Committee and its pressing affairs to be dealt with, matters set in train for collecting and paying debts, and places to be found for the masterless servants and homes for the favourite dogs.

Byron's embalmed corpse was on its long journey home from Greece, and it fell to Hobhouse to handle the funeral arrangements.

Occasionally the demands that were made on him had a lighter side, but Hobhouse was not in the frame of mind to see it. On June 19th he found that Byron's banker in Genoa had written to his banker in London, Douglas Kinnaird:

> You will excuse my mentioning to you rather a singular request that Lord Byron made me when he was on the point of sailing. The eccentricities of a man of his genius may, I hope, be mentioned to a friend valued by him as you were, without giving offence, or appearing childish or impertinent. He had kept for a long time three common geese, for which, he told me, he had a sort of affection, and particularly desired that I would take care of them, as it was his wish to have them at some future time, it being his intention to keep them as long as he or they lived. I will send them to England, if you please.[1]

These were geese Byron had caused to be fattened for Michaelmas and then had not had the heart to sentence to slaughter, keeping them, as he said, to test the theory of their longevity. Hobhouse was a most humane man, but he had never shared Byron's extravagant fondness for animals, and when it comprised poultry, could hardly believe it sincere. He thought a joke had been played on 'the worthy Barry', and so it seems did Kinnaird, who was writing a month later, 'Tell me what I am to say about the *Geese*? They had better be kept by Mr Barry, I think. . . .'[2]

But Byron had not been joking, though the spirit of pleasantry may have lent a zest to his regard for these unlikely pets.[3] He had gone to some trouble over their preservation long before he had conceived any intention

---

[1] HOBHOUSE, *Recollections*.   [2] Murray MSS. Undated.

[3] Barry kept the geese till late 1827 when, as he was moving, the ever-obliging Countess Guiccioli offered to take care of them. 'I was sending them to her,' Barry wrote to Hobhouse, 'but they only got to Leghorn when her plans were changed, and I do not know if they are still alive.' (Murray MSS. 3 Nov. 1824.)

That is the last news of these birds, which frequently wandered into Byron's villa and were always kindly received.

of going to Greece. There were facets of his character which Hobhouse
and Kinnaird never understood for all their devotion.

A few days later there was another more momentous letter. It was
dated from Missolonghi on April 30th, and began:

Dear Sir,

Both inclination and duty impel me to write to you as the oldest & most
intimate of the late Lord Byron's friends. You perhaps are not ignorant that
for these last four years I have been constantly with him—and his daily
companion. I therefore need not tell you how deeply I am afflicted at his
loss—every one must be moved—for he has left a void, which no man in the
world can fill up—then how heavy & irreparable is the loss to us his chosen
& particular friends. As to the world—you know—how completely they
misjudged his character—which is not perhaps understood by more than
three or four in the world. You knew him best—I have found him the
contradistinction of everything that is said in public or that I had heard or
conceived before I had the pleasure of becoming known to him. . . .

Hobhouse must have looked for the signature long before reaching
the end of the voluminous outpouring that followed. 'E. J. Trelawny.'
He had heard of him, but merely as a member of Byron's Greek expedition. This news of 'daily companionship' for four years could hardly have
failed to come as a rather painful surprise to him, but the tactful references
to his own leading position among the famous man's friends must have
appeased him, and the glowing tribute to the misjudged character was
noted with hearty approval when he wrote his next diary entry.

Too true, it is as Trelawney says, his loss has made a void which nothing
can fill up. I find it so daily.[1]

An honest man does not question the statements of one whom he has
no reason to suspect—especially when the claims that are made have a
boldness which seems a guarantee of their veracity. As Hobhouse read on,
learning more and more about the importance of Trelawny, he may have
wondered why Byron's letters in so long a period as four years had ignored
the existence of this influential man, and he assuredly must have been
astonished at the spelling and punctuation into which, after the careful
beginning, his correspondent subsided; but he thought the communication sufficiently valuable to make known the same day to Byron's sister.

. . . All the charges that have been brought against him are either false—
misstated—or frivilous the real facts have never been stated!

It was long my great object to get him out of Italy—and he was weried of
staying there—excercise & excitement seemed nessesary for both his body
& mind and both seemed declining in his long inactive and secluded way
of living in the south—he became peevish—sickly & indifferent—and dis-
contented with every thing—he acknowleged this—and I continually urged

[1] Hobhouse *Journals*, 25 June 1824.

him with new plans—I built him a yacht for he was always fond of the sea—
he got weried of that—he would then go to South America—& took some
steps for that purpose—then he turned to North America & from repeated
& pressing invitations from there he seemed determined to go there. We
got every thing prepared—though this was much against my wishes—as I
believed it was the country least suited to him! After much delay The
Greeks gaining ground & his strong partiality to Greece—the Interest every
one seemed to feel for its fate & lastly the letters of his friends in England
decided him to go there. You know what followed—and I shall merely
relate a brief detail of his last illness & cause of his Death.

There ensued a narrative, written with an air of authority, of the
poet's last days, with the verdict that his refusal to be bled 'was the sole
& entire cause that so trivial a commencement—was attended with such
fatal consequences'. The particulars had been assiduously collected from
Byron's *entourage*, and many were already known to Hobhouse through
the reports the valet Fletcher had sent to Mrs Leigh and John Murray.
But there was one detail which was quite new. It was in the description
of Byron's last attempts to convey his wishes to Fletcher:

> Nothing but names could be distinguished he "said Tell my sister &
> muttered some minutes, then Ada my child say—& so continued to my
> Wife—Tell Hobhouse—Trelawny—and after thus runing on—evidently
> labouring hard to articulate but in vain—he gained strenth and said "Now
> you know all!

In his accounts of his master's deathbed, Fletcher mentioned various
names which had emerged from the half-delirious struggle for utterance,
but Trelawny's was not one of them. Neither was it amongst those which
Trelawny himself had already repeated to another correspondent after
interviewing Fletcher.[1]

Whether Hobhouse was gratified to find himself, Byron's oldest friend,
coupled at such a moment with this stranger can only be surmised. He
was a somewhat squeamish man, and might have wished to be spared the
next paragraph, a vivid commentary on his friend's internal organs as they
appeared to the doctors on what the writer called 'discection'; but presently he came to a second, less obvious *raison d'être* for the letter:

> I have fulfilled all the last sad duty's . . . His name was a tower of strenth
> to the Greeks. Yet we have to much to do to give way to unavailing regret—
> and honest & independent men are not so abundant here as to be spared—
> Stanhope too our most active & useful member has lost his mother to whom
> he was much attached & is besides in very bad helth—he talks of soon
> returning to Zant—The Committee men & stores—have been either laying
> useless in the warehouse or dribeled away—up to this time nothing done.—

[1] Colonel Leicester Stanhope, to whom Trelawny wrote at great length on 28 April
1824.

There is a violent & general dislike to *Parry* who has gone to Zant. . . .

> This place Missolonghi is a mud Istmus—deservedly cut off from Greece —for nothing can be more dissimilar—every one will leave it I mean Franks —the soldiers are in a state of anarchy—I have visited most parts of Greece and served during the whole winter—but I have seen nothing like this—The fact is Mavrocordato is a weak imbecile tampering character without energy —or any ingredients to form a man to fill a first place, or form a great character he does every thing by intrigue—and is a perfect *Constantinople* Greek—he has tampered with every European power. he is for a foreign *king*—he is a stickler for Legitimacy—and would shine only at a Zenona congress. It is an incalculable injury to *Greece* & *Liberty* that this *man* has shuffled himself into the good opinion & confidence of distinguished foreign powers & particularly England.

Everyone and everything, it would seem, had collapsed except Trelawny. Mavrocordato, the Greek leader in best esteem with Byron and the English Committee, was a feeble and dishonest imbecile, clearly meriting repudiation. Who should take Mavrocordato's place—and who Byron's? Trelawny had the answers.

> Their are some great men hear. I have been serving with a General that is little known—and if eight months spent together in the Camp & I have any judgment, I think him a really *great man*—a Grecian Bolivar. Their are many men here infinitely superior to Mavrocordato—& one is of vital importance to the cause. The soldiers and particularly the pesantry are exceedingly well disposed. I have spent my whole time amongst them & may say so—Odyseus or Ulyses as he is called by the English who commands Attica Livadia Romily, & is now closely blockading Negropont—he is a man of most extraordinary & diversified talents, and out of all comparison the most able soldier, as well as powerful in Greece,—and with such a leader I had little fear of the event of the present campaign even before the present seasonable Loan—now it removes all doubts—that is if it is judiciously expended. . . .

As there will soon again be occasion to refer to this Odysseus, for whom Trelawny was trying to obtain both the official leadership and the large sum of money which Byron was to have administered, it is as well to pause and explain who he was.

Half general, half brigand, in all histories of the Greek War, however they may differ in other respects, Odysseus figures as a cunning traitor, 'false as the most deceitful Greek and vindictive as the most bloodthirsty Albanian'.[1] 'His object in joining the Greek revolt was not to liberate Greece from the Ottoman rule but, if possible, to establish his own authority permanently in Eastern Hellas; and if he could achieve this better by attaching himself to the Turks, it was certain that he would not hesitate to betray the Hellenic cause.'[2]

[1] FINLAY.   [2] GORDON, THOMAS.

This man, handsome, a brilliant athlete, personally courageous, had inspired in Trelawny hero worship in its most adolescent form. Odysseus saw in him a means of going after much bigger game—Byron and his wealth and the astronomical sum the great Milordos's name was reported to have raised in Britain. Mavrocordato, the President of the Provisional Government, stood in his way, and he had laid, it is supposed, a plot to murder him as he had already murdered other opponents, under pretext of a meeting of reconciliation—a plot he had not concealed from Trelawny if we may judge from one of the latter's reckless statements to Mary Shelley:

> He is a miserable Jew, and I hope ere long, to see his head removed from his worthless and heartless body.[1]

Indiscreet as he was, Trelawny could hardly be as candid as that with Hobhouse, so, as he proceeded, he toned down his criticisms—which were written on the same day as the less inhibited sentiment quoted above.

> Mavrocordato has been the chief ingine which has been at work about the Loan . . .—he *writes* to every one—he is of every ones opinion—he is [a] laughing good-tempered & consiliating but nothing more—in his appearance he is a perfect Jew—and his character is not dissimilar to one—If you have interested yourself in Greek affairs—you will be astounded at these bold aspersions of a man—standing so high in the opinion of the English Committee—and I have no inclination to force on you reason's and proofs in support of the charges I have made against him. Mavorcordato has talent—& can be very useful. I only say—he does not employ them usefully—and they are not of first rate quality.

Hobhouse's journal shows he paid little attention except to those passages of the letter that concerned Byron: otherwise, with his almost excessive literal-mindedness, he might have concluded that a writer whose grammar permitted him to talk of Committee men laying useless in a warehouse, and who called Mavrocordato imbecile on one page and talented on another, was a confused and unreliable informant. From a merely superficial reading, he may have been glad that an Englishman, albeit a rough diamond, had arrived to take command at Missolonghi.

> Lord B[s] private papers & manuscripts I have noted you will see he has written very little—but the Zuliotti song & the last thing he composed—written on his birthday is one of his most feeling & beautiful productions and now affectingly so. I scarcely need point out that you and Mr D. Kinnaird had better look over his letters to destroy those which none but a friend's eye should see—& as it was his practise never to destroy even a note there are abundant [*sic*] of such letters!
> Count Gamba takes charge of every thing which has been sealed in my

[1] TRELAWNY, *Letters*. 30 April 1824.

presence. There are about 11,000 dollars in specie. All his domestics accompany his remains to England—the suddenness of his Death has prevented I believe his doing anything for them.[1]

It could not have been agreeable to Hobhouse to be told how to deal with Byron's papers, but the advice in itself was of a nature to win his approbation, and as he remained ignorant till later that Trelawny had copied as well as 'noted' some of the most intensely personal correspondence, the eager helpful letter made something of the impression its author hoped for.

Augusta Leigh, having had it read aloud to her by Hobhouse—'at least such parts of it as concerned the last days and hours'—sent word without delay to Lady Byron:

> There has been a letter received from a Mr. Trelawny of whom I had never heard but it appears that he lived much in poor B's society for the last 4 years—he gives many details of the last days altho he was not there till *one too late*.[2]

Lady Byron wrote back by return of post:

> If you could let me have the perusal of a letter containing details so deeply interesting I would return it immediately.[3]

She did not as yet know that, in his anxiety to establish himself as widely and firmly as possible as the 'chosen and particular friend' of Byron, he had also written to her banker, Samuel Hoare, yet one more account of the death bed, which was duly transmitted to her. Whether by design or a slip of the pen, it was dated April 20th, the day after Byron's death, though he (Trelawny) had not arrived at Missolonghi till a week after.[4]

Trelawny's countless inaccuracies will generally be found to increase his own importance or heighten the drama of events in which he was concerned, and it was not beyond him to bring forward a date to give immediacy to the part he played any more than to pretend that for four years he had been the daily companion of a man with whom he had spent brief periods during a total acquaintance of two years and two months. Nor would he have been in the least troubled by the fear of discrepancy between one letter and another, for his apparent carelessness was part of

---

[1] Murray MSS. A shorter and ingeniously different version of this letter reached Mary Shelley, and is published in *Shelley and Mary*. It had a postscript saying it was intended for Hobhouse but after all not sent, and suggesting that Leigh Hunt should be allowed to pick at it—with a view, of course, to publication. Trelawny did not mention to Mary that the same post conveyed to Hobhouse a much more extensive communication—the one given above, very little of which has hitherto been quoted.

[2] 24 June 1824: Lovelace Papers.   [3] Ibid. 25 June 1824.

[4] Ibid. The Julian Calendar, twelve days behind the Gregorian in 1824, would not account for the difference, and in any case was never used by Trelawny.

his plausibility. It enabled him to seem, in the words of one of his modern apologists,[1] 'entirely devoid of that element of calculation which makes a liar'.

He had written to Colonel Stanhope the day before composing his approach to Hobhouse, 'I am sick at heart that I have lost the friend and companion of many years', and the day before that,

> Your pardon, Stanhope, that I have turned aside from the great cause in which I am embarked; but this is no private grief; the world has lost its greatest man—I my best friend. . . .[2]

But to his more intimate correspondent, Mary Shelley, something of his joy at the death of Byron, whom he rancorously envied and had the folly to believe he could supplant, became unsuppressible:

> I am transformed from the listless being you knew me to one of all energy and fire. Not content with the Camp, I must needs be a great diplomatist, I am again, dear Mary, in my *element*, and playing no *second* part in Greece. . . . No more a nameless being, I am now a Greek Chieftain. . . .[3]

And while the letters to England were still *en route*, he was yet more candid with another friend, Jane Williams:

> I separated as you know from B. at Cephalonia—he was past hope—he trifled four months at that miserable Island, and then went over to the miserable mud bank of Missolonghi—the pestilential air of which together with his languid and exhausted constitution exhausted him so much that a slight attack of fever extinguished his mortality. . . . Could I then longer waste my life—in union with such imbecility. . . ?[4]

This was nothing in comparison with his subsequent disparagements, but enough to have ensured that Hobhouse, had he known of it, would prove hostile, and implacably so if he had dreamed that this adventurer was actually to set himself up as an authority on Byron.

While he resolutely shut his mind against the need for a biography, yet as long as the purpose was vague and unspecified, he was not adverse to the amassing of records. Thus he entered in his diary on June 19th:

> Hanson said that he was putting together a memoir of his recollections of Lord Byron, which joined with his letters, he thought, would be highly creditable to Lord Byron.

But he added:

> Hanson told me he had already had two applications made for his materials respecting Lord Byron's biography; he promised me not to let them go out of his hands.

---

[1] MASSINGHAM.   [2] STANHOPE. 28 April 1824.
[3] TRELAWNY, *Letters*. 30 April 1824.   [4] Ibid. 20 June 1824.

Murray, the bookseller, talked to me yesterday of publishing a volume of Lord Byron's letters, of which he offered me the selection. I told him my objections to having anything to do with memoirs, considering that Moore would then charge me with having wanted to destroy his MSS in order to become biographer myself.[1]

In pressing for the destruction of the Memoirs, Hobhouse had got himself into a pretty impasse as the guardian of his friend's good name. For the reason he noted, he could not become a biographer himself, and neither could he bear to entrust the task to another; so none but those who were prepared to defy him could attempt to commemorate a man of international repute. There were more of these, however, than as yet he had any notion of; and one was to make his intention known before Byron had completed his journey from Missolonghi to the grave.

On a date towards the end of June, he wrote half incredulously:

Murray told me that Dallas, the Dallas, author of Aubrey &c to whom Lord Byron gave his two first Cantos of Childe Harold, had actually made over some letters from Lord Byron to his mother and other letters from Lord B to him, Dallas, to Knight a bookseller in Pall Mall East and that a book of them was to be published immediately.[2]

The same day he saw the book announced in the Press:

PRIVATE CORRESPONDENCE OF LORD BYRON including his Letters to his Mother . . . connected by Memorandums and Observations, forming a Memoir of his Life, from the year 1808 to 1814. By R. C. Dallas, Esq.

Hobhouse had never been more amazed. Robert Charles Dallas was boring and a toady, but quite respectable—an elderly gentleman of moralizing tendencies, and by no means the sort of person one would suspect of the unseemliness of rushing into print, not merely private correspondence, but private correspondence which was not even his own property!

Hobhouse had known him fairly well—who could avoid him?—in the days when Byron was making his great double conquest of the fashionable and the literary world with *Childe Harold*. It was Dallas who had taken the manuscript to John Murray and arranged all the details of publication, and been rewarded for his pains with the gift of the copyright— Dallas, officious and obsequious and given to dropping in on Byron at all hours and on all occasions and preaching at him; but undoubtedly useful to the captivating young celebrity whom he was so proud to claim as a kinsman.

[1] Hobhouse *Journals*.
[2] Ibid. The entry is dated 28 June, but other evidence shows that it should have been 23 June. Hobhouse often wrote up his diary retrospectively, several days at a time. It was this practice which caused him to make an entry about Byron's interment dated four days before it took place.

Dallas's sister had been married to Byron's uncle, so the degree of kinship was not very near, and as this aunt-by-marriage had died somewhere about the time of the poet's birth, Dallas had remained unknown to him until he had introduced himself by a deferential letter expressing his admiration for 'the effusions of a noble mind' which had appeared under the title of *Hours of Idleness*. Byron at nineteen, shy but secretly ambitious, was grateful for the flattery, though mingled with edifying advice, of a man of letters—for Dallas had published several books. He had written back with a great deal of boyish charm and bravado hinting what a depraved fellow he was, and the ensuing correspondence had led to an acquaintanceship profitable to both: to Dallas because he did not scruple to apply for money to this youth who was himself appallingly in debt, to Byron because Dallas was experienced and shrewd in literary matters, and his advice was sound.

Dallas's perquisites as unofficial agent to Byron were ultimately worth many times the value of his services, and it must have been a relief when he went to live abroad shortly after being presented with the copyright of the immensely successful *Corsair*. He conceived himself to have been insulted by John Murray (from whom he had secretly done a little borrowing),[1] and between his testiness and his pious homilies, he had become very weariful. Though he had turned up again before Byron finally left England, the latter's marriage and changed circumstances had loosened the bonds, and he had been able to drop without a quarrel an intimacy which had always had a certain artificiality. Dallas was Byron's senior by thirty years, and never got on to nearer terms with him than calling him 'My Lord' and 'My dear Lord Byron', while Byron for his part always addressed him as 'My dear Sir', and knew him three or four years without being able to remember his full name.[2]

On finding the startling advertisement of Dallas's book, Hobhouse took counsel with Augusta Leigh, and wrote a polite but firm letter:

6, Albany, London, June 23.

Dear Sir,
I see by the newspapers, and I have heard from other quarters, that it is your intention to publish a volume of memoirs, interspersed with letters and other documents relative to Lord Byron. I cannot believe this to be the case, as from what I had the pleasure of knowing of you, I thought that you would never think of taking such a step without consulting, or at least giving

[1] Murray MSS.
[2] In 1811, doubtless because Dallas was one of the very few mature and respectable persons he was acquainted with at the time, Byron had intended to appoint him as one of his executors if Hobhouse and Scrope Davies should die too soon to fill that office. His solicitor left blanks for the Christian names, which Byron filled in, but when he came to Dallas, he wrote on the margin: 'I forget the Christian name of Dallas—cut him out.'

warning to the family and more immediate friends of Lord Byron. As to the publication of Lord Byron's private letters, I am certain, that for the present, at least, and without a previous inspection by his family, no man of honour and feeling can for a moment entertain such an idea—and I take the liberty of letting you know, that Mrs. Leigh, his Lordship's sister, would consider such a measure quite unpardonable. . . .

I trust you will be so kind as to excuse me for my anxiety on this point, and for requesting you would have the goodness to make an early reply to this communication.

Yours very faithfully,
John C. Hobhouse.[1]

Dallas somewhat foolishly made no reply at all to that communication. Hobhouse had refrained from stating that he was an executor because he thought that might seem like 'a menace'.[2] Choosing not to recognize either the claims of the sister or the lifelong friend, and intent only on cashing in on his Byron material, Dallas went ahead with his book. Brisk in business matters as ever, he hurried to Paris where he had been clever enough to make an agreement for simultaneous publication in French, thus averting the risk of piracy.

Both English and French editions were in the press when Hobhouse, accompanied by John Williams, a lawyer and Member of Parliament, called on Dallas's publisher to protest.

I talked quietly to Knight on the impropriety of Dallas's conduct. Knight as quietly replied that he had nothing to do with the indelicacy of Mr. Dallas he looked on his purchase merely as a commercial speculation. I said that the haste in which the publication was to take place was unjustifiable—before Lord Byron was buried. Knight said that he presumed Mr. Dallas was a needy man and knew the intense interest attendant upon everything respecting Lord Byron. What, said I—you mean he wished to strike whilst the iron was hot: Knight smiled—and then said that the work was passing through the press under charge of one of the first literary characters of the day whose name he could not mention and that he as well as himself, would take care that no living characters were compromised—two letters in which Murray the bookseller had been compromised were cancelled and delivered to Murray. I replied that in confidential correspondence individuals might be slightingly mentioned en passant and their feelings most sorely wounded, also that Lord Byron's literary character might suffer. . . .

I then said that as Lord Byron's executor acting for his sister I thought it right to say that unless Dallas could prove his right to the property of Lord Byron's letters to his mother I should step in and move an injunction against the work. Knight replied that he believed Dallas could prove that by a letter from Lord Byron. I said very well if he can—that is another thing but I must see the letter itself. I shall not be contented with a copy. . . .

[1] DALLAS.   [2] Marginal note by Hobhouse in his copy of Dallas's work.

Missolonghi in 1824, from an aquatint by H. Raper

I begged him not to take what I said as a sign of hostility on my part—but merely as a performance of my duty by the legatee of the deceased. . . . We took our leave of Knight who was coldly polite.[1]

After the publisher's several allusions to the very eminent man of letters who was looking after the English arrangements, it came as a surprise to Hobhouse when this gentleman turned out to be Dallas's not particularly distinguished son. The Rev. Alexander Dallas was, in every respect, an intensified version of his father. He wrote even more improving books, he glossed over his sharpness in business with a still richer varnish of piety, and he was so much more sanctimonious—which is saying a good deal—that he worried greatly about his father's spiritual welfare.[2] He had also inherited the paternal irritability and obtuseness which made him suppose such a man as Hobhouse could be brushed aside.

On hearing of the proposed injunction he wrote Hobhouse a letter of rebuke in which he cast doubt on his probity, made light of his power to do what he threatened, and touched, with exquisite tactlessness, on the evil that predominated in Byron's character in his later days.

> There is no man on earth, Sir, who loved Lord Byron more truly, or was more jealous of his fair fame, than my father, as long as there was a possibility of his fame being fair. . . .
> The letters which Lord Byron wrote to his mother were given by him unreservedly to my father, in a manner which seemed to have reference to their future publication; but which certainly rendered them my father's property, to dispose of in what way he might think fit.

No tone could have been better calculated to stiffen Hobhouse's resistance—except, perhaps, that of a letter shown him by Augusta Leigh, who had received it from the older Dallas in France. 'I neither saw,' it stated, 'nor do see any obligation to submit my conduct to the guidance of any relation of Lord B[yron]'s.' This was bad enough, but a still more rash passage followed:

> I own, too, that the MS, as intended for posthumous publication, does contain some things that would give you pain, and much that would make others blush—but . . . I wished as much as possible to avoid giving pain, even to those that deserved it, and I curtailed my MS nearly a half. If I restore any portion of what I have crossed out, shall I not be justified by the insolence of the letter I have received from a pretended friend of Lord Byron, and who seems to be ignorant that a twenty years' companionship may exist without a spark of friendship? I do not wonder at his agitation; it is for himself that he is agitated, not for Lord Byron.[3]

[1] Hobhouse *Journals*, 30 June 1824.
[2] DALLAS, Rev. Alex. R. C.
[3] Hobhouse saw this letter on 3 July 1824.

L.L.B.—F

Hobhouse must indeed have been agitated, for the innuendo was that he would be personally hurt and humiliated by the letters of Byron's in Dallas's possession, and that the friendship which had meant so much to him had meant nothing to Byron. If Dallas wanted to inflict a wound, he had chosen the perfect weapon, but at the same time, in the vanity of his malevolence, he had armed his opponent with a weapon still more effective. Although Hobhouse's first impulse was to withdraw his opposition lest it be thought he feared to see Byron's 'true sentiments' about him in print, he decided on reflection that pride must not outweigh his duty to uphold the rights of the legatee.[1] He now had evidence from Dallas himself on which he could depose that the correspondence about to be published 'contained observations upon or affecting persons now living, and the publication of which is likely to occasion considerable pain to such persons'.[2]

The case for a veto was immensely strengthened, and Hobhouse was no longer content merely to circumvent the publication of Byron's letters to his mother, but determined that even the letters addressed to Dallas himself should not see the light.

On July 7th, five days before the book was due to make its appearance, Hobhouse with Hanson's support, secured his injunction. It was his second victory in the posthumous suppression of Byron's writings and, like the first, was to prove a costly one. The burning of the Memoirs had left Lady Byron as the sole archivist of events as to which she would necessarily be a hostile witness; while the action against Dallas's book was to have repercussions of much unpleasantness.

Reading Byron's letters to his mother, which contribute so entertainingly to our knowledge of his youth, we may wonder why anyone should have striven to keep them from the public, but Hobhouse knew that, unless the executors established their power to restrict, a score of other people who had writings of Byron's would start publishing. No matter how many asterisks and blanks were used, living persons would be identified by readers who had clues to guide them, and there would be scandals and embarrassments beyond telling.

The detached amusement and literary appreciation with which we in the 20th century can enjoy the splendid vivacity of Byron's correspondence, were simply inconceivable to Hobhouse, who was a man of his time with no apprehension of the vast changes that were to take place in moral, social, and religious standards; and who naturally could not feel detached about matters which to him were topical and troublesome. There was also, it must be acknowledged, his emotional entanglement, which often

---

[1] Hobhouse *Journals*, 3 July 1824.
[2] From the Bill in Chancery filed by Hobhouse and Hanson.

deceived him into supposing he was protecting Byron's good name when he was merely exercising his proprietary right.

The week when he won the first round of the Dallas battle was altogether a most harrowing one. He would not have been human if he had not wondered uncomfortably what Byron had written about him long ago that had furnished material for Dallas's spite; and the letter containing the venomous hint was in his hands the day after he took possession of his friend's corpse.

The first news of its arrival was conveyed in extremely characteristic terms by Colonel the Hon. Leicester Stanhope, who had gone to Greece as an agent for the London Committee. Addressing Hobhouse and Kinnaird jointly he wrote:

> *Downs, off Deal, Florida*
> *29th June, 1824.*
>
> Dear Sirs,
>
> The death of your friend Byron occasioned a shock that was felt by every heart in Greece. There, moved by early recollections, and surrounded by classic scenery, the poet's faculties expanded,—his genius glowed, and he wrote like one impassioned and inspired; there, too, with electric sparks, he had roused the dormant spirit of freedom, and had sacrificed to her his comforts, his fortune, and his life.
>
> After so glorious a course had terminated in death, it was good—it was just for Greece to mourn for Byron, and to confer honours on his memory. All this took place. Funeral rites and orations were pronounced, and Athens and Missolonghi contended for the honour of having his remains deposited in the land where he had flourished and sunk. Many, even of Lord Byron's countrymen, thought that his body should be placed in the temple of Theseus. Ulysses was also of this opinion, and desired me to forward a letter, by express, to Missolonghi, soliciting his ashes. I did so; but the body had then reached Zante, and it was determined that it should be sent to England for public burial, either in Westminster-Abbey or in St. Paul's.
>
> On my arrival at Zante, I was requested, by the governor and others, to take under my care the remains of Lord Byron and his papers, and to accompany them, in the Florida, to England. I accepted the charge, and have reached the Downs.
>
> The executors of Lord Byron will now be pleased to make arrangements for the interment of his body, and for the reception and examination of his papers.
>
> With respect to the funeral ceremony, I am of opinion that Lord Byron's family should be immediately consulted; that sanction should be obtained for the public burial of his body; either in the great Abbey or Cathedral of London; that the state barges should be sent down the river to receive the corpse, the principal mourners, and bands for the performance of sacred music; and that the aquatic procession should pass on to Westminster-Bridge. There a hearse should be in readiness to convey the body to its last place of repose.
>
> Britons, who cherish genius and who love liberty, will, I doubt not,

crowd to the banks of the Thames, and to her majestic bridges, to behold the
passing scene, and to sigh for the mighty dead.

I am,

Most faithfully, yours

Leicester Stanhope[1]

Hobhouse had consulted Byron's family several days before this somewhat pompous and peremptory document reached him, and enquiries
were already in train on the question of burial in Westminster Abbey, but
no state barges nor bands of sacred music nor aquatic procession signalized
the return of the exile.

Hobhouse rose very early on the morning of July 2nd and drove
fifteen miles to Standgate Creek; then, being unable to get near the water
in his chaise, he had to walk over the marshes for two miles before he
could board a boat to take him out to the *Florida*. He had a dismal passage
of five or six hours beating up the river, overcome by the sight of Byron's
three dogs playing on the deck and by his undimmed recollections of
Byron himself waving his cap to him from the ship in which he had left
England for the last time.

Besides Stanhope, four of Byron's servants and one of his doctors had
accompanied the corpse, and he was able to hear first-hand accounts of the
lamentable sequence of events at Missolonghi. Almost everyone by this
time believed that Byron had brought death upon himself by refusing for
several days to let the doctors bleed him. His medical attendant, the
highly emotional young Dr Bruno, made this assertion over and over
again, naturally eager to avert a possible charge of incompetence. Another
very youthful physician, Julius Millingen, whom Byron had openly asked
to stay away from him, was yet more determined to lay the blame for
dying upon the patient. Trelawny's statement (which he later repudiated)
in a letter to a friend,[2] expressed the general view: 'He refused to listen
to the advice of his doctors, and resisted the only means of recovery, to
be blooded. . . . On the fifth day he was bled, too late.'

Grief was now tinctured with some exasperation. The poet's death-
bed had been the most disenchanting scene, as far removed from the
picturesque death-beds of contemporary novels and idealizing biographies as the 'mud isthmus' of Missolonghi was from Hobhouse's cosy
bachelor chambers in Albany Court. 'The glorious conclusion of his life'
began to seem rather an empty figure of speech as the grim or dingy
realities were brought to light by the sobbing Fletcher.

[1] STANHOPE. The letter was not received till 1 July.

[2] See footnote p. 79 for particulars of this letter. The repudiation was contained
in an extract from Trelawny's supposed Journal, published in the *London Literary Gazette*,
12 Feb. 1831. In this he stated that from the first he had known the doctors to be in-
competent and had cursed them.

And here was a letter from Dr Millingen[1] giving, for the benefit of the Greek Committee, further particulars and adding that, had Byron lived 'much more', it was doubtful whether his political character, now deserving so much admiration, 'would not have lost somewhat of its brilliancy', because his temper was highly irregular, and he would joke about affairs of importance and burst into a rage about trifles: and Stanhope, who at first impressed Hobhouse as an excellent person, endorsed this verdict.

For all the flowery terms of his written tribute, Stanhope was soon talking about Byron in a style that was regretfully derogatory, and Hobhouse became aware of grievances smouldering under the Colonel's well-bred commiserating manner.

'I premise', he shrewdly wrote, 'that Stanhope has taken a different view of the proper mode of action in Greece from Byron.'[2]

Stanhope had, in fact, been one of the heaviest trials Byron had had to endure at Missolonghi. A deeply earnest man, pretentious and ego-tistical, he had brought out to Greece a dogged determination to propagate the advanced educational doctrines of Jeremy Bentham, to import English schoolmasters, to establish printing presses, to disseminate newspapers, pamphlets, and manifestos, and to promote republicanism. It carried no weight with him that few Greeks could read, that the rulers were semi-barbaric chieftains little interested in Lancastrian schools, and that the country was war-torn, faction-torn, and desperate. He was glowing with the kind of idealism that expresses itself in noble abstractions difficult to confine to any specific meaning, and Byron's down-to-earth realism shocked him profoundly. Byron, for his part, called him the Typographical Colonel.

Before coming to Greece, Stanhope had been what we might now call a Byron fan, able to recite long passages of *Childe Harold* by heart. Having admired the poet enormously, it was no doubt proportionately discon-certing to him to find not the splendid visionary, the ardent hater of kings, the enthusiast for allegorical Liberty, whom he had looked forward to meeting, but an astringent anti-romantic, whose chief horror was cant. There is no one so likely to become embittered as a fan whose idol refuses to live up to the preconceived image of him.

Reading Byron's comments now about the trumpets, lithographic presses, and mathematical instruments, which reached him from England when lack of weapons was causing acute tension, we are struck with his humour and unwonted patience; but to Stanhope this kind of levity was

---

[1] 27 Apr. 1824. It was to John Bowring, but was shown to Hobhouse, who copied it, by Stanhope.

[2] Hobhouse *Journals*. Entry dated 2 July, actually made later.

uncongenial. In a gentlemanly way he did all he could to shake the Committee's confidence in Byron.

At Athens he met for the first time the disaffected Trelawny and Trelawny's hero, Odysseus, who both with great skill set about making a tool of him. In his reaction from Byron, who had tried to reduce his high-flown notions to sobriety, he was easily conquered. Trelawny could coin rich ringing metaphors, and Odysseus, a notorious despot, pronounced himself a complete convert to English liberalism.

> His conversation was of newspapers and schools, the rights of the people, and a museum of antiquities. One morning, while the Colonel and Odysseus were sitting together in the latter's quarters, Dr. Sophianopoulo entered, handed the General a report on the state of the hospital, and answered various questions about it. No hospital existed![1]

Stanhope became so besotted with the influence of the fascinating chieftain and his Cornish henchman that, after Byron's death, he ordered the garrison at Missolonghi to hand over to Trelawny the pitifully few cannon and the sole howitzer the town possessed, with ammunition and other necessaries.

'The departure of these essential objects at the critical moment has rather soured the people,' Mavrocordato wrote in sorrowful remonstrance, 'and I had the greatest difficulty in preventing a tumult which might have had unpleasant consequences.'

Had Stanhope remained in Greece to administer the British loan, the lion's share would almost certainly have gone to Odysseus, whom he tried to thrust upon the reluctant Government, using his anticipated control of the money as a lever. But the bankers who had received the first instalment refused to hand it over, alleging that Byron's decease invalidated the Commission.

The rôle of one about to distribute the long-awaited treasure had heightened his natural officiousness, and he had issued manifestos of the most egregious description: but fortunately he was spared the loss of face that would have resulted from having to announce his impotence. The Foreign Office in London, becoming troubled by the republican propaganda disseminated from the Colonel's printing presses, suddenly and brusquely recalled him; and his being given the charge of Byron's body and possessions invested his departure with a dignity which would otherwise have been wanting.

The Greeks must have been rather astonished when the missionary who had been preaching to them for months about the evils of monarchy began his farewell exhortation with the words: 'The king, my sovereign,

[1] GORDON, THOMAS.

has commanded me immediately to return to England. I obey the royal
mandate. . . .'

He had been about as misguided an emissary as the Committee could
have chosen, but on his return to England, they passed a resounding vote
of thanks to him. It need hardly be said that he was already turning his
attention to the question of publishing his records of the war and his
association with Byron—a fact he refrained from touching upon in his
conversations with Hobhouse.

Not until three days after the arrival of the *Florida* could Hobhouse
bring himself to look at what remained of Byron. Hanson and Mrs Leigh
had told him that the face was unrecognizable, and so it proved. The
autopsy had been ruthlessly thorough. In opening the skull, the forehead
had been damaged and several other injuries inflicted which were not the
consequence of immersion in spirit.[1] To conform to the prevailing custom
in Greece, Byron had grown a moustache, and that increased the dreadful
unfamiliarity.[2]

The crowds that had to be denied access to the body were very large,
but those who had come to pay homage were outnumbered by sensation-
seekers: and the undertaker who emptied the cask of preservative fluid
reported that many tried to purchase small quantities as souvenirs, some
even offering as much as half a sovereign.[3]

Dean Ireland of Westminster Abbey had notified his intention not to
allow the black sheep into the fold—another severe blow for Hobhouse
who, weeks before, had rejected a suggestion from Henry Drury that the
tomb might be in the Church at Harrow where, had he but known it,
Byron had once hoped to be buried.[4] Now there was no alternative but to
arrange for interment in the family vault at Hucknall Torkard, an obscure
little town near Nottingham.

He sought to compensate for the defeat, which was bitter, by ordering
a funeral of uncommon magnificence, counted with satisfaction the forty-
seven carriages that accompanied the banished hearse on the first stage of
its three-day journey, and was gratified by the number who turned out
all the way along the route to see the fine brass-studded coffin, the plumes
and pages and sable draperies. 'He was buried like a nobleman since we
could not bury him as a poet', he wrote at the end of nearly a fortnight
of mournful preparations and obsequies.[5]

[1] See Appendix for remarks on Trelawny's fictitious account of inspecting the corpse.
[2] Account by Hobhouse of the arrival of Byron's body, dated July 5th. Murray MSS.
[3] Murray MSS.
[4] Drury was a friend of Byron's and the son of his old headmaster. Byron's reference
to a wish to be buried at Harrow is in a letter to Augusta Leigh (12 Dec. 1822, Lovelace
Papers).
[5] Hobhouse *Journals*. The entry is wrongly dated 12 July. Byron was buried on the
16th.

There had been some consolation, during that dolorous period, from talks with another companion of Byron's last days—one whose reminiscences were not either openly or covertly destructive; were, in fact, entirely those of a devoted, loyal, and most chivalrous friend. This was the Count Pietro Gamba, younger brother of Teresa Guiccioli, with whom Byron had formed his last, longest, and most satisfactory *liaison*.

He had arrived after Stanhope, and in a different ship, having been told that if he accompanied the body it might cause ill feeling in Byron's family. He was 'prevailed upon to go to England in another vessell', wrote Lord Sidney Osborne to Douglas Kinnaird, '& behaved most exceedingly well'.[1]

Count Pietro always behaved well. His very great delicacy of feeling was combined with a bravery, patience, magnanimity, and honesty which make him the *preux chevalier* among Byron's friends—and incidentally the only person who ever wrote a book on Byron with Hobhouse's blessing.

Though his sensibility was such that he had been obliged to withdraw from the room where the poet was being bled, blistered, and purged to death by distraught and disagreeing doctors of four different nations,[2] he had pulled himself together to take charge of everything at the end. It was he who had sent away the first dispatches with the news that rang through Europe, who sorted the possessions and papers, who arranged with the Greek authorities the lying-in-state and the funeral service in the Church of Missolonghi, who got in touch with Byron's bankers and obtained proper receipts for sums that had been paid locally, who tidied and sorted Byron's effects, and who strove to protect the boxes of dollars which the impoverished Government and many other candidates now tried to sequester. Trelawny later took the full credit of this: he went further and wrote, quite falsely, that Gamba had consented to give away Byron's money.[3] In the reality Trelawny could never bear to face, his was only a very minor supporting rôle; nor was his help disinterested, his object being to circumvent the hated Mavrocordato and obtain for Odysseus anything that might be going.

He would doubtless have enjoyed taking the centre of the stage as he had done with such immense gusto at the exhumation and burning of Shelley, and it must have been galling for him to find that all he could do at Missolonghi was to sign his name as witness to one or two documents,[4] and intrigue against Mavrocordato—whom he had to be cautious

---

[1] 12 June 1824: Murray MSS.

[2] Bruno—Italian, Treiber—German, Millingen—English, Vaya—Greek.

[3] Statement in the *London Literary Gazette*, 12 Feb. 1831; dated by Trelawny in Florence 20 Jan.

[4] He witnessed the handing over of a portion of Byron's remains (the lungs, commonly believed to have been the heart) to the City of Missolonghi on 2 May.

of opposing openly while he still maintained his pose as the intimate friend and ally of Byron. He compensated himself by sending out recklessly fictitious accounts of his activities.

One of his letters found its way to the columns of the *Morning Chronicle*, having been forwarded from Leghorn by his appreciative friend, Captain Roberts, R.N.,[1] the actual builder of Byron's yacht, the *Bolivar*:

> Having left no directions on the point of his funeral, I consented to the wishes of his friends and household, to have his body conserved in spirits, and sent to England. I accompanied it to this island [Zante] to procure a vessel, when General Adam, Lord Sidney Osborne, and Sir Fk. Stoven plotted together, not to allow the body to be sent to England, but even to inter it here in their ill-governed Island that he abhorred. To thus obscurely shove him into a hole, like a dog, I opposed with all my might, as did those interested in his fame. Our expostulations and representations, with the fear of execration obliged them to give up their point. We chartered an English brig to convey the corpse to England.

When he indulged in this invention, Trelawny shared the belief of Stanhope and all the other Englishmen in Greece that Byron would be interred with every honour in Westminster Abbey, and he was thus claiming in advance the glory of having made this possible. But among the Murray manuscripts are quantities of letters from Gamba, Lord Sidney Osborne, and others which show that he had not the faintest influence on the disposal of Byron's remains, that he arrived too late to perform a single important duty, and that the 'plot' between the British officials was as figmentary as his participation in chartering the *Florida*.

The terms of Lord Sidney's first letter to Hobhouse may be set against Trelawny's libellous fantasy:

> To dwell upon the grief I feel at the loss of such a man, by whose friendship I had been honoured for twenty years, or to expatiate upon his numerous excellent qualities, would neither alleviate my grief in writing or yours in reading this melancholy letter; & therefore what I am most anxious to impress upon you is my anxiety to do everything in my power to forward any wishes our Dear Friend may have expressed in his latter moments. . . . With this view it is my intention to sail tomorrow for Zante there to meet Count Gamba & any friend who may have accompanied the remains. . . .
>
> You will see by a letter from Count Gamba to me which I inclose to you that previous to his death Lord Byron uttered some words which were carefully taken down; as soon as I learn what these were I will exert myself to the utmost of my power in order that they may be fulfilled, and should they relate to the disposal of his remains, they shall be a most sacred guide to me. . . .

[1] Roberts had the rank of Commander, but was known as Captain. The letter from Trelawny, published on 28 June 1824, is dated 10 April. It could not have been written before May.

You will perceive that Count Gamba is extremely anxious that the Corpse should be sent to England; but there will be numerous difficulties attendant upon this when it comes to be put into practice, to say nothing of some danger which might attach to the passage of a merchantman under the British Flag; for my own part I should wish it had remained at Messalungi and rested in the land he had already so much benefitted, and would have done so much more for had his life been extended: but as the Corpse will have left Messalungi I should not feel warranted in sending it back, particularly as, though that place is at present quite secure from the Turks, in the numerous vicissitudes of the present war they might gain possession of it, and the sanctity of the grave might not be able to protect our friend's remains from their barbarous vengeance. I should therefore be for the funeral taking place at Zante, where I expect to find the Body, but as I before said any words that Byron may have dropped upon this subject shall dictate the law to me.[1]

When he saw Trelawny's printed letter, Lord Sidney wrote to Douglas Kinnaird saying that it was incorrect throughout. He had no sooner heard from Count Gamba and Fletcher that Byron would have wished his body to return to England than that course was 'immediately carried into effect'—not in spite of himself and Sir Frederick Stoven, but with their perfect concurrence, while 'General Adam was at Corfu the whole time and never interfered in the slightest degree about the matter'.[2]

His only reference to Trelawny by name in the course of several communications to Hobhouse and Kinnaird about Byron's affairs is satirical: 'I have not the honor of any acquaintance with Mr Trelawny who seems to have had charge of the Mule when Count Gamba accompanied the remains of our deceased friend to Zante. . . .'[3]

If Trelawny failed even to meet Lord Sidney and the British Government's other representatives in the islands, while they warmly welcomed Gamba to their counsels, it would go far to explain his attempts to exalt himself at the young Italian's expense.

In his popular and acutely unreliable book on Byron and Shelley, Trelawny implies that not only Gamba but Fletcher and Tita and the steward, Lega Zambelli, failed to perform the most elementary duties towards the dead. He pretends to have found everything in uttermost disorder—'tokens that the Pilgrim had most treasured, scattered on the floor,—as rubbish of no marketable value, and trampled on'.[4] This was

[1] Murray MSS. 25 Apr. 1824. This letter accompanied Gamba's letter in Italian. Lord Sidney Osborne, Secretary and Treasurer to the Senate of Corfu, was the son of the 5th Duke of Leeds by a second marriage. The 6th Duke, his half-brother, was also half-brother to Augusta Leigh, being the son of her mother. Lord Sidney was not related by blood to Byron, but kinship through marriage was held in higher regard than in the present century.   [2] Ibid. 14 Aug.
[3] Ibid. 21 Aug. The mule, valued in an inventory at 'about 80 dollars', had been sent to Byron by Colonel Napier.   [4] TRELAWNY, *Recollections*.

to give colour to his pretext for copying Byron's last letter to his sister, which was that its chance of reaching its destination had seemed slight. The collection of Pietro Gamba's letters deposited among the Murray manuscripts show that the greatest care was observed in gathering together all the possessions of a man whose importance was fully recognized by everyone about him. 'I have had put under Government seal his belongings, which will be opened by Prince Alexander Mavrocordato in my presence and that of certain Englishmen who are here. I have taken an exact inventory of them.' Thus on April 21st, several days before Trelawny appeared, Gamba wrote to Lord Sidney Osborne, and his inventory has been preserved.[1] The papers were reopened in the presence of leading Missolonghi officials in order to make sure that no recent will was amongst them. It may have been then that Trelawny contrived to do his copying.

Considering that Pietro was not above twenty-three years of age when he undertook a load of heavy responsibilities, his conduct reveals him as one of the most intelligent as well as the most sympathetic of Byron's *entourage* in Greece.

With his good looks—for he 'carried the passport of a very handsome person'[2]—his good manners and his perfect lack of pretension, he even succeeded in disarming Hobhouse's possessiveness and making him forget how deeply he had disapproved, less than two years ago in Italy, of the immoral way the Countess Guiccioli's family accepted Byron as her lover.

Augusta Leigh too was favourably impressed, and wrote to Lady Byron after she had received a visit from him:

> I have today seen Count Gamba—which was very distressing for many reasons but quite unavoidable—he is a pleasing, fine looking young man & spoke with great feeling.[3]

The unfortunate Augusta was in one of her worst states of confusion. She had loved Byron, but she had betrayed him, betrayed him not twice, as he had betrayed her,[4] but again and again over a long span of time,

---

[1] Murray MSS. Not until a long while after the death of Gamba and most of the others who could contradict him did Trelawny sketch the grossly improbable scene in which Byron's relics were 'trampled on'. In an earlier document, written for John Murray about 1830, he gave a totally different excuse for copying the letter to Augusta— namely that 'the injunction it contained about the Turkish child induced me to make and keep a duplicate . . .' He did not mention he had also copied a letter *from* her.

[2] MEDWIN, *Life of Shelley*.   [3] 14 July 1824: Lovelace Papers.

[4] Byron does not seem to have disclosed his relations with Augusta to anyone except Lady Melbourne, who proved completely trustworthy, and Caroline Lamb, who broke a solemn oath that she would keep his secret. According to Lady Byron's own statement, she had only 'suspicions' when she left him. After Mrs Beecher Stowe's book came out, Jane Clairmont said she had known all along; but by this time she had become a most mendacious old lady, and earlier evidence contradicts her assertion. The Villiers correspondence shows that Lady Byron laid a trap for Augusta by pretending his indiscretions were yet more serious than they had been.

fawning on his implacable wife, purveying to her in secret the unguarded letters he never suspected any eye but her own would see, feeding the stealthy fires of her animosity: and having betrayed him, she had grown to fear and almost to hate him. She had dreaded his outpourings of affection for her in poetry that he thought would clear her and that only compromised her, and the headstrong folly that tempted him to write on ever more daring themes, teaching the world to guess what repentance and unrepentance preyed upon his thoughts. She had dreaded still more that he might return to England, overshadowing her again with spiritual and social peril.

But this kind of return was what she could never have foreseen . . . that he should come back not voluble but silent, not beautiful but defaced, not in obloquy but with his praises ringing! She could remember now his exciting laughter, his almost filial love for her, her almost maternal love for him. Above all she could remember the anguish of their parting, and how he had been 'convulsed, absolutely convulsed with grief'.[1] So love revived, and in its most sentimental form. While he lived she had lost touch in her perpetual alarms with what was best in him; dead his memory became sacred to her.

She felt almost as strongly as Hobhouse about biographies. Quite apart from the divagations of her 'poor brother'—so she constantly referred to him—there were a hundred reasons why it would be objectionable to have the family history exposed. Whatever latitude she allowed in the warmth of her kindly nature to others—or to herself—she believed implicitly in the moral code she had learned from her good grandmother, the Countess of Holderness, living in a well-ordered Derbyshire manor. She had no desire to see in print that her mother, who was to have been a duchess, had been involved in a scandalous and ruinous divorce,[2] that her father, 'Mad Jack Byron', was a profligate and a bankrupt who had squandered every penny two successive wives had brought him and left the second on the verge of destitution, and that he had died a drunkard and perhaps a suicide, hiding in France to escape his creditors.

It was no more pleasant for the Hon. Augusta Leigh to share this kind of story with the world than it would be for most 20th-century ladies moving in court circles and having children to be settled advantageously in life. She had lived down the rumours which had made the year of the Byron separation a nightmare to her, and she had also succeeded, though with an increasing sense of effort, in persuading her little world to avert its

[1] HODGSON. Her letter of 8 July 1824.
[2] The Baroness Conyers, a peeress in her own right, was first married to the Marquess of Carmarthen, heir to the Duchy of Leeds. After her death Augusta was brought up chiefly by her maternal grandmother and received great kindness from the Leeds family.

eyes from her husband, 'that drone', as Byron called him, whose career of devotion to the turf was reputed to have a certain shadiness. She had earned the right to be left in peace.

Byron's fame was, of course, very wonderful, but it carried with it too many reminders of his terrible indiscretions—the writing of *Don Juan*, which she had never ceased to deplore, his shocking blasphemies like the *Vision of Judgement*, his making friends with the atheist known to her as 'that infamous Mr. Shelley',[1] and his mixing with really low and horrid people such as the subversive journalist Leigh Hunt, whom one would never conceivably meet in decent society.

She was most emphatically opposed to the production of sheer indelicacies, and that was the light in which she saw the proposed book by Dallas. Letters between a mother and a son—a son so outspoken and a mother so far from suitable to be paraded before the public! And brought out by that seedy poor relation, Dallas! Could anything be in worse taste? The ill-mannered man had not even had the common courtesy to write to her about it, but had sent her a verbal message through a niece of his simply informing her that it was his intention to bring out the book. It was a good thing she had Mr Hobhouse to depend on.

There had been a time when she had shared Annabella's detestation of Mr Hobhouse—had agreed with her that he was a bad influence, one of the 'Piccadilly crew' who encouraged Byron to drink and behave outrageously. She was far too diplomatic to have let him suspect the scornful terms in which she was referring to him in her daily letters to Annabella when the marriage was breaking up; and this was fortunate because he had turned out to be a powerful friend to her.

No one had done more to silence the whisperings which connected her, so untruly and unfairly, with the Separation. He was not, after all, the godless debauchee he had once seemed but a serious-minded person who felt exactly as she did about Byron's poetical defiances, and who had the same passionate desire to protect his memory. He was generous too, and although his expenses as a Member of Parliament were heavy and he depended on an allowance from his father, he had renounced for her sake Byron's legacy of a thousand pounds. Hanson, the solicitor, was naturally remunerated for his services, but all Mr Hobhouse's duties as executor were performed without reward. And now there was more trouble brewing with those unbearable Dallases.

Dallas senior was detained in Paris by severe illness, but Dallas junior was full of fight and applying for the injunction to be lifted. He had gone to Byron's cousin, now 7th lord, and had got him to compose an affidavit to the effect that, whereas he had formerly been reluctant to approve the

[1] Letter to Lady Byron, 21 Dec. 1819: Lovelace Papers.

publication unless it had first been examined by the relatives and friends of his predecessor, he had now read the book and was content for it to be issued without that precaution.

There were few things in Augusta's whole life, full of calamities though it was, that hurt her more than this contemptuous slight from George Anson Byron, whom she had loved with an unswerving loyalty, and had looked on as her intimate friend. Moreover, he was without the right to make such pronouncements: he had inherited nothing from her brother but his title, whereas she was not only of nearer consanguinity but the chosen recipient of his property.

These, if she had only known it, were precisely the reasons why her cousin took pleasure in the opportunity of annoying her. Lady Byron did not like Augusta to have intimate friends, and in every instance where the occasion was granted her, she managed to find some excuse for bestowing, in whole or in part, those confidences which never failed to leave her audience agape with wonder at her magnanimity and Augusta's wickedness.

George Anson Byron had seen enough of the poet's atrocious conduct as a husband to be aware that Augusta, so far from being responsible for the collapse of the marriage, had been Lady Byron's greatest support and comfort at the time; but it had been deemed necessary all the same to enlighten him as to the suspicions in the background, and he had repeated them to his newly married wife. Their friendship for Augusta became rather hollow, and the news that Byron had left her practically all his money caused it to crumble to oblivion.

Though Lady Byron knew perfectly well that Byron, as early as the year of their wedding, 1815, had made a will in Augusta's favour, she had evidently not passed on that information; and it came as an appalling surprise to Captain Byron that he had been left without the fortune that would keep up the title. Why he should have cherished expectations it is difficult to see, considering that a nearer relative was poor and in debt, and that he had been on bad terms with Byron since the Separation, in which he had whole-heartedly and with courage allied himself with the opposite side; but that he suffered a shock his letters poignantly show, and the disappointment must have been all the worse because the will was not produced until nearly seven weeks after he had learned of his succession.

'Respecting the will', he wrote to Byron's widow a few days after hearing its contents, 'the very thought of it is painful to me. What Mary has said about it is too true.'

What Mary, the new Lady Byron, had said about it was written on the first half sheet of the same paper:

My dearest Annabella,

The more we consider the most prominent subject in your letter, the more we are convinced of the truth of that dreadful history connected with it. It was a fact unknown to George, that the will was made at so early a period after the marriage, which disproves most effectually the possibility of the disposition of the property being made under feelings of resentment towards him. Though he was ignorant of those circumstances I can confidently assure you he has always expressed the belief, that Ld. B. was entirely influenced by the power of a stronger tie than that of animosity towards him.[1]

It is improbable in a very high degree that Byron had been guilty of deliberately keeping his successor in a state of false hope. His wife had fully assented to the conditions of his will when he had made it, agreeing that Augusta with her small income and growing family had a strong claim upon him, and being quite without reserve in such matters himself, he would hardly suppose his intentions had been kept secret. If he had not provided for his cousin in the days when there was harmony between them he could scarcely be expected to do so after all intercourse had ceased. But the 7th lord concluded that there had been deep-laid scheming by Augusta, and Annabella did nothing to dispel that illusion, which she had gradually come to share herself.

From that time onwards his tone about Augusta became bitter, and to be able to disoblige her was—it may be gathered from extensive correspondence—a satisfaction. He went so far as to urge Hobhouse to withdraw his objections to Dallas's publication.

'Hey day whose mare's dead?' wrote Hobhouse in his diary when he received a note from the new peer beginning distantly 'Dear Sir'. But he consented to receive him, and it was worth while because the uneasiness that had haunted him ever since he had seen Dallas's malicious letter to Mrs Leigh was dispelled:

> He told me that he had read the book—but could see nothing offensive to any body. I was named several times in terms of praise. Once only there was something which he Lord Byron [George Anson] told Dallas might be as well left out—namely, that B. said, 'Hobhouse is going home. I am glad of it, for I am tired of him,' but adding—this is my fault, for I am grown misanthropical.[2]

The actual passage in Byron's letter to his mother in July 1810, of which Hobhouse had this second-hand report, runs: 'I am very glad to be once more alone for I was sick of my companion (not that he was a bad one) but because my nature leads me to solitude.'

Unaware that a more hurtful comment in another letter was being withheld, Hobhouse assumed a tone of indifference.

[1] 9 July 1824: Lovelace Papers.   [2] Hobhouse *Journals*, 26 July 1824.

I told Lord Byron that I did not care what Lord B. had said of me—that it was not the fear of that which had made me stop the letters, but the determination to put a stop if possible to publishing Lord B's private letters, as well as to protect the property—upon principle. . . .

When he showed Captain Byron the insolences of the Dallas correspondence, he secured an admission that an apology was due to him.

I told him that had Dallas come to Mrs Leigh or the executors and shown his MSS no difficulty would have arisen—nay, he might even have been helped, but now he tried to publish surreptitiously even before Lord Byron was buried.

Hobhouse seems to have been generally in a self-deceiving mood at this interview. Nothing is more unlikely than that he would have helped Dallas. It would hardly have been feasible for him to do so when he was resolved not to aid Moore, whose claims were palpably superior, and who had been taking soundings about his prospects.[1] But he was concerned to erase the idea, already current, that he was obstructive: and so made an effort from which a reasonable plan emerged.

After some more conversation I said that I had a proposition to make to him with Mrs Leigh's consent—namely that the book should be looked over by some third person—say Dr Lushington—that if he found any thing he disliked it should be expunged—and that then the work should be advertised and afterwards published with this notice "*by permission of the executors*"
Lord B. said it was a very fair offer and he should recommend young Dallas to accede to it.

Their further talk was of a voyage Captain Lord Byron was about to take to the Sandwich Isles for the purpose of restoring the bodies of the King and Queen who had both died of a mysterious illness on their visit to England; and the young man revealed how much more he was a Dallas than a Byron by telling Hobhouse he would not allow the native members of the King's suite to mess at his table.

Everything appeared to be on the verge of an almost amicable settlement, for Dallas junior announced himself willing, subject to his father's approbation, to agree to Hobhouse's by no means onerous conditions, and Augusta too was satisfied: but Dallas senior was barely appeased:

As to an executor's *veto* [he wrote to his son] shall an executor be allowed to decide on the publication of a work (letters) on general topics, when it may be enough that there is in it a difference of opinion on religion, morality, or politics? . . . I see neither law nor equity in such a *veto*. . . . However, I do not wish to keep up contention, and have no objection (*go which way the*

[1] Hobhouse *Journals*, 6 July 1824.

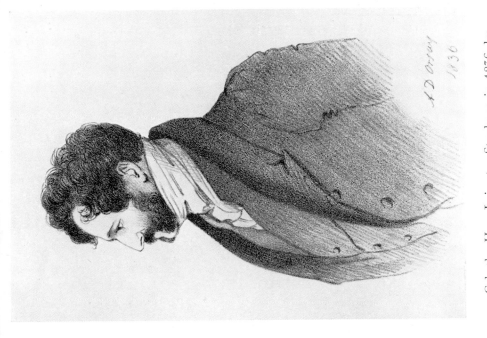

Col. the Hon. Leicester Stanhope in 1836, by
Count Alfred D'Orsay

E. J. Trelawny in 1836, by Count Alfred D'Orsay

Chancellor's decision may) to say, printed with the consent of the executors—
and they will be foolish not to consent, for the circulation of the work would
be but wider if they do not; so act in this as you judge best. But I do not
think the sheets should be shown to him [Hobhouse].[1]

The Rev. Alexander Dallas was unlucky enough at this stage to be
guided by some astonishingly unsound legal advice, the gist of which was
that he ought not to print any statement that the book was published with
the permission of the executors because that might 'seem *to acknowledge a
property* as belonging to the executors, which he does not acknowledge to
belong to them'.

This recalcitrance proved disastrous because Hobhouse still had his
co-executor Hanson up his sleeve, and Hanson took the onus of rejecting
out-of-hand the unwarrantable counter-proposals the other solicitor had
drawn up.

Four affidavits were immediately filed opposing the dissolution of the
injunction. Their purpose was to show simply that Byron had never made
an outright gift to Dallas of the letters he had written to his mother,
and that he had certainly not intended them for publication. Anyone who
has read that boyish correspondence, with its jaunty boastings, its lapses
into peevishness, its frequent emphasis on the financial embarrassments he
assiduously hid from the world's eyes, will feel convinced with Hobhouse
that, whatever view might have been taken by the mature Byron who died
at the age of thirty-six, the man of twenty-six who handed the letters to
Dallas did not for a moment envisage their use in a book.

Dallas averred on oath that the letters were given to him in June
1814 because they touched upon a subject (Newstead Abbey) which they
had discussed together in April 1812—in itself a remarkable instance of
delayed action on the part of one whose youthful character was quick and
impulsive—and that he had said: 'Take them. They are yours to do what
you please with. Some day or other they will be curiosities.' Fletcher, on
the other hand, declared that whatever papers his master had left with
Mr Dallas were deposited for safe custody only.

The other deponents were Hobhouse and Mrs Leigh, who testified
(to show why safe custody was wanted) that Byron had been making preparations to go abroad at the time of handing over the papers; and the
Hon. Leicester Stanhope, who swore that in a conversation with him about
the persons who possessed materials likely to be useful for writing his life,
Robert Charles Dallas was not named, nor did Byron intimate on any
occasion whatever that Dallas was among those whom he would permit
to write or publish anything concerning him.

There was a delay of several weeks in the Court of Chancery while

---

[1] DALLAS. No date.

Dallas junior struggled desperately to have his application heard. His anxiety was intense because, if the injunction remained in force, apart from legal charges, his father, mortally ill, stood to lose the £500 payable by the publisher. On the very last day of the term the cause was still on the waiting list, but the Lord Chancellor, Eldon, whose name recurs frequently in Byron and Shelley annals,[1] was considerate enough on learning the urgency of the situation to take the papers home with him and to hold a private sitting. His judgement was a very important one, and still forms the basis of vital laws relating to copyright.

> . . . The property in letters is . . . that if A writes a letter to B, B has the property in that letter, for the purpose of reading and keeping it, but no property in it to publish it.

By this ruling, Robert Dallas was debarred from printing any of the letters, including those written to him personally. Alexander Dallas was now driven to abase himself. He wrote to Hobhouse offering to submit the manuscript to anyone he named and to expunge anything that was objected to:

> . . . to cut out *two* things that might hurt my feelings—and to put on the title page that the letters were published by permission of the executors. He said that the two things about me could not dwell on my mind a moment seeing that I was mentioned throughout the whole correspondence in terms of great affection.[2]

If he had only stopped there, Hobhouse might have given in, since the victory was on such a scale that he could afford to make concessions, but neither of the Dallases could long suppress a bullying tendency, and the letter ended with a reckless hint that, if the proposition proved unacceptable, his father would publish what he had originally written about Byron before he had curtailed the portions likely to cause distress. 'The poor creature', Hobhouse called him with contemptuous pity.

> I resolved after some consideration not to answer this letter, but I keep it— Had it not been for the sort of menace in the conclusion of it perhaps I might have given some reply to it.[3]

The Dallases made yet one more attempt a month later, sending a letter of appeal signed jointly with the publisher, but the reply, made

---

[1] He was the judge who refused Shelley the custody of the two children of his first marriage (not unreasonably, it would now seem, in view of his desertion of his wife while she was advanced in pregnancy with one child, and looking after the other, a baby in arms). It was Lord Eldon who received Byron from the Woolsack when he took his seat in the House of Lords, who opposed him in his appeal for the Nottingham Framebreakers, who granted an injunction—unsuccessfully—to forbid the theatrical representation of his non-theatrical tragedy *Marino Faliero*, and who refused an injunction to protect *Don Juan* and *Cain* from piracy.

[2] Hobhouse *Journals*, 26 Aug. 1824.   [3] Ibid.

through the solicitors, was a cool refusal and an assurance that proceedings for contempt might be taken if the letters were published abroad as they were told was in contemplation.

This was a threat which Hanson and Hobhouse possessed no power to carry out. Dallas senior had means of proving that he had initiated the transaction with the Continental publisher, Galignani, many weeks before the judgement, nor was the English law for the protection of copyright effective in France at the time.

The French translation of the letters (with Dallas's smug and vindictive memoir) went forward, and soon after a Parisian publication in English followed. Hobhouse and Hobhouse's many personal and political enemies were able to learn what Byron in an irritable humour had said about him when they had parted at Athens after a year's travel together; and all the genial and affectionate comments in a hundred other letters before and after were to lie henceforward under the shadow of this:

> The Marquis of Sligo, my old fellow collegian, is here, and wishes to accompany me into the Morea. We shall go together for that purpose; but I am woefully sick of travelling companions, after a year's experience of Mr. Hobhouse, who is on his way to Great Britain.[1]

Like many men who expect their friends to put up with a good deal of blunt criticism, Hobhouse was himself exceedingly thin-skinned, and the circulation of a remark so derogatory was mortifying in an intense degree. There is perhaps no one strong-minded or dispassionate enough to be able to see in print a friend's disparagement, however fleetingly inspired, without feeling both sorrow and anger; and Hobhouse was vulnerable through his pride in Byron's affection for him as well as his knowledge of the malicious amusement that many would feel to see that pride humbled. The letter, with cruel exaggerations, was constantly brought up against him.

If he had not been so indefatigable in opposing their publication, the Dallases would assuredly have been recommended by Dr Lushington to suppress those few unimportant words, and Hobhouse would not have had occasion to show, years later, how they rankled.

When Moore wrote his biography of Byron, he assumed, and probably with sincerity, that the latter's satisfaction at seeing Hobhouse depart from Athens was due to his 'growing consciousness of his own powers' which made him long for solitary self-communion.

> So enamoured . . . had he become of these lonely musings, that even the society of his fellow-traveller, though with pursuits so congenial to his own, grew at last to be a chain and a burden to him; and it was not till he stood,

[1] *L. & J.* 25 July 1810.

companionless, on the shores of the Aegæan, that he found his spirit breathe freely.

Hobhouse underlined that passage in his copy of the book and wrote in the margin:

> On what authority does Tom say this? [He never called Moore 'Tom' except when writing in a rage] He has not the remotest grasp of the real reason which induced Lord B. to prefer having no Englishman immediately [or] constantly near him.

That Hobhouse disapproved severely of sexual deviation is evident both from what is explicit in his *Travels in Albania*, the book he wrote on his tour with Byron, and what is implicit in the tenor of his conduct; but none the less he was fully in Byron's confidence as to his sudden abandonment to adventures with the youths of the Athens monastery: that is shown by letters now published unexpurgated[1] from which it would appear that his own cherished and admired friend, Matthews, was expected to share sympathetically in the secret. It was a secret he refused to divulge then even to Matthews himself,[2] nor is it imaginable that he would have hinted at it in any form that could have survived for posterity if he had not felt the sting of that wounding allusion.

Dallas and his son were thus the initiators of the long series of mischief-makings by the ill-disposed, the tactless, the careless, the exhibitionists—in short, the horde of second- and third-rate people who were determined to make capital out of their acquaintance with Byron. Against the value of the biographical material they supplied—sometimes dubious and inaccurate—must be set off the immense harm they did to his reputation by raising up posthumous resentments against him.

Difficult as a lover, impossible as a husband, Byron was loyal and generous as a friend, lavish to a fault in his appreciation. It was hard on him that any unguardedly facetious or impatient utterance he made was liable to be turned into a weapon of attack by contending parties. 'Judge me by my acts!' he pleaded, but it was by his words he was judged when his acts could no longer be seen, by his words when he was most incautious; and in certain cases by words he never spoke.

In assessing the weight to be attached to detractions of Byron, it is almost always illuminating to learn what provocation the detractor had received through injudicious or inventive publication.

---

[1] QUENNELL, *Self-Portrait*, and MARCHAND, *Byron*.

[2] 'I sent a letter to you a month ago—in that I told you to keep the *Mendeli Monastery story* and every thing entirely to yourself. I have not opened my mouth to Charles Skinner [Matthews] on any of those branches of learning. I will give you a good reason when we meet.' Hobhouse to Byron, 15 July 1811: Murray MSS. Their friend Matthews died soon after.

Dallas was not one of the liars, albeit a shifty and unpleasant character, as will be seen. His memory was aided by a good deal of authentic documentary evidence, and the part he had played in shaping Byron's early career was not fictitious, though he over-estimated its importance. More dexterously handled, his book need not have been the potent source of trouble it became. Hobhouse's fight against him and his son, exasperating as they had been, was waged with more zeal than prudence.

He was about to learn what a really troublesome book could be.

Trelawny's alleged inspection of Byron's corpse

In Trelawny's much-quoted account of getting rid of Fletcher in order to examine the dead Byron's feet, he stated that the embalmed body of the Pilgrim was 'more beautiful in death than in life', a reflection which enabled him to throw into high relief his description of this Apollo with the legs of a satyr—'two clubbed feet, and his legs withered to the knee'. His admirers, who have tied themselves into ingenious knots explaining away the totally different account of Byron's lameness he published twenty years afterwards, can now absolve him of having lifted the shroud at all.

Not only was it utterly impossible in the circumstances for Byron to look beautiful, but close study of a substantial quantity of published and unpublished Missolonghi correspondence reveals that Trelawny could not have arrived before April 26th, and Byron's temporary coffin had been hermetically sealed on the 25th, as is shown in the official document published in Nicholson's *Byron, The Last Journey*. Owing to the appalling state of such roads as existed, it took eleven days for the news of Byron's death to reach Stanhope (he received it on April 30th from a courier). Trelawny parted from Stanhope carrying a letter for Byron on the 19th, the day of the latter's death. He must have made much better time than the courier even to reach his destination on the 26th.

Hobhouse, in translating Gamba's book, *Lord Byron's Last Journey to Greece*, made several minor errors in dates, possibly because Gamba's writing is excessively hard to read. The day of Trelawny's arrival is given as 'the 24th or 25th' and of sealing the coffin as the 29th. We learn from a marginal note in Hobhouse's copy of Moore's biography that it was he, not Gamba, who composed the passage containing that mistake.

There are many internal evidences that Trelawny read Gamba's book carefully, as well as all other contemporary eye-witness narratives, before writing his own, and this slip was useful to him.

It is noteworthy that, although he had written detailed descriptions of Shelley's corpse and was always full of morbid curiosity, he does not in a single letter of the time say anything about having been led up a narrow stair to see the dead Byron, though it would obviously have been a matter of interest to his correspondents; and to make some comment on the appearance of the deceased was widely customary at the period.

His remark to Stanhope within a couple of days of his arrival is: 'I have been employed in arranging the affairs of my lost friend, sealing papers, and his body is in spirits.'[1]

---

[1] Trelawny's first letter to Stanhope from Missolonghi dated Apr. 28th and beginning 'With all my anxiety I could not get here before the third day', is incomprehensible,

It was strange indeed to circulate all the grim details of the post-mortem that he could pick up from the doctors—they are repeated in several of his letters—and not to make the slightest allusion to having seen the body himself if he had really done so! All 'facts' concerning either Byron or Shelley which Trelawny kept to himself till he brought out his *Recollections* in 1858 are suspect.

He was so coarse-grained a man that he probably had no idea of the disgust he would excite when he made out that he had pretended to need a glass of water so that he might stealthily peep at the deformity Byron had always concealed. He may now be acquitted of any offence except lying.

because, even supposing so rapid a journey through torrents and mountain tracks to have been possible, it would have resulted in his arrival several days before, by any reckoning at all, he came upon the scene.

CHAPTER III

FURTHER ORDEAL BY BIOGRAPHY

While Hobhouse was still battling for his Pyrrhic victory over the Dallases, the gentleman who had met Sir Egerton Brydges in Geneva and had influenced his view of Byron so favourably was hurrying his own book through the press. It was called:

JOURNAL OF THE CONVERSATIONS OF LORD BYRON
Noted During a Residence with His Lordship
at Pisa in the Years 1821 and 1822,

and the author announced himself as Thomas Medwin, Esq., of the 24th Light Dragoons.

Thomas Medwin was at that time a half-pay lieutenant who preferred to call himself a captain, one of the less prosperous distant relations of Shelley, just as Dallas was one of the less prosperous distant relations of Byron. Like Dallas too he combined a genuine taste for literature with a character not very scrupulous and the reputation of being a bore. Unlike Dallas, he was not sanctimonious nor shocked by the atheistical views of Shelley and the daring speculations of Byron. He was tolerant of both and, having a keen eye to the main chance, eager to turn his knowledge of their personalities into cash.

It was too early yet to do more with Shelley than to append a brief Memoir of his life to the book on the more famous poet, but the market for information about Byron had never been better in all the twelve years that had passed since someone had coined the word Byromania.

Nothing would have surprised Medwin's contemporaries, or perhaps Medwin himself at that date, so much as to know that his hasty, opportunist production was to be drawn upon by almost all later biographers, for, as to matters of fact, it abounds in inaccuracies from the title page onwards, while the conversations, he himself admitted (and it is to his credit), were 'the substance without the form'. He states that he used Byron's own words 'so far as my recollection served', but his recollection did not serve him very adequately. He blundered so often that even Lady Byron, who was by no means disposed to judge her husband's character charitably, wrote in a copy of the book,[1] after noting its various discrepancies:

> These & other errors as to times and circumstances, which Lord Byron himself could not possibly have committed, prove the Biographer to have erred so widely in some respects, that it is but fair to Lord Byron to suppose he, Medwin, did so in others.

[1] Presented to the Rev. Frederick Robertson, 1851.

Now that the scandals have no more power to make an impact, the mischievous propensities of the man who extracted profit from them are not immediately obvious. His approach to his subject, unlike Dallas's, is good-humoured, and it requires a strenuous effort on the reader's part to conjecture the feelings of those who were recognizable by name or description in the speeches attributed to Byron.

Medwin himself knew his book would cause trouble. Indeed he set out to cause it.

> I am aware that in publishing these reminiscences I shall have to contend with much obloquy from some parts of his family,—that I shall incur the animosity of many of his friends. There are authors, too, who will not be pleased to find their names in print,—to hear his real opinion of themselves, or of their works.[1]

This catchpenny device was needful because his qualifications for filling a quarto volume about Byron, while not insignificant, were scanty. He had never 'resided' with him, had only been acquainted with him five months—in the very precise reckoning made out by Hobhouse with Pietro Gamba's assistance, from November 1821 to March 1822, and ten days in August 1822—and he had been nearly the outermost member of the small circle of Englishmen who accepted the hospitality of the Palazzo Lanfranchi, Byron's mansion on the Arno at Pisa.

With Shelley's widow, whose help he pleaded for, he did not dare to assume the pretensions which later made him brazenly thrust upon Byron the responsibility for his own misstatements. He wrote frankly of giving the world 'the little I know of him'.

> . . . I shall certainly not publish the work till you have seen it . . . You might be of the greatest possible use to me, and prevent many errors from creeping in.[2]

But Mrs Shelley wrote scathingly to Hogg:

> M. will make many enemies & do no one any good, least himself—unless the yellow coin he receive for it is to [be] considered a good. If he thinks to gain honour by 'I and Lord B' he is mistaken; the world soon divines the secret of such intimacies.[3]

She determinedly refused to co-operate. In her own words to Hobhouse:

> Medwin requested me to correct his MS. I declined even seeing it—he afterwards sent me his Memoir of Shelley [the Memoir given in the book on Byron]. I found it one mass of mistakes—I returned it uncorrected—earnestly

---

[1] Preface.   [2] MARSHALL. Dated only July 1824.
[3] *New Shelley Letters.* 30 Aug. 1824.

entreating him not to publish it—as it would be highly injurious to my interests to recall in this garbled manner past facts at a time when I was endeavouring to bring Sir T[imothy] S[helley] to reason. . . . The book has been a source of great pain to me, & will be more—I argued against the propriety & morality of hurting the living by such gossip—& deprecated the mention of my own connections—to what purpose you see. . . . In times past when a man died worms eat him, now in addition vile insects feed on his more precious memory, wounding the survivors by their remorseless calumnies.[1]

The unfortunate Mary Shelley, who longed for respectability and had all her life been emotionally embroiled with people existing for one reason or another under a cloud, had already begun the course of suppression which was to result in what is now known as the Shelley Legend—the ethereal, emasculated, bloodless projection of the poet so much beloved by the Victorians. She wanted Shelley to be remembered, just as Hobhouse wanted Byron to be remembered, by those of his works which were least vulnerable to moral and religious objection, and she opposed biography strenuously on the grounds that 'the truth, any part of it, is hardly for the rude cold world to handle'.[2]

In disregarding her plea for silence, Medwin did Shelley's fame a real service. He was the first of his admirers to publish biographical details, and the coupling of his genius with Byron's at a time when Byron's stock was at its highest was of great value in calling the attention of the reading public to Shelley's merits. He tried, vainly, to placate Mary Shelley by telling her that this was one of his aims. The world of letters owes much to its less self-respecting and fastidious characters.

Yet the fact remains that Medwin had a bad memory and a mind entirely lacking in precision. Both his short Memoir and his full-length biography of his relative, whom he knew much better than he knew Byron, are full of mistakes, so it is not surprising that he made mistakes everywhere in the reconstructed 'conversations', but only a most curious thing that, even to this day, Byron is often accused of falsehood on the strength of Medwin's muddled, slapdash reporting.

In addition to being careless, he was capable of dense stupidity. The dimness of his perceptions may be gauged from his printing in full, as a work of Byron's, Wolfe's Ode on the Burial of Sir John Moore, because Byron had read it aloud to his guests from a magazine and spoken enthusiastically of it.

I afterwards had reason to think that the ode was Lord Byron's; that he was piqued at none of his own [odes] being mentioned; and, after he had

[1] 11 Nov. 1824: Murray MSS. She had used almost the same closing sentence in her letter to Mrs Leigh Hunt, 10 Oct. 1824.
[2] MARSHALL. Letter to Trelawny, 15 Dec. 1829.

praised the verses so highly, could not own them. No other reason can be assigned for his not acknowledging himself as the author. . . .

There was no other reason, certainly, except that he was not the author! 'B was incapable of praising his own verses', Mary Shelley wrote to Hobhouse in reference to this absurdity, '& was certainly satisfied with the opinion all present had of his talents.'[1] He was sometimes known to defend his latest production from attack, but anything more unByronic than the sly and petty literary vanity imagined by Medwin would be hard to invent.

When reproved for inexactitude, Medwin insisted on having it both ways, pleading that Byron must have been lying to him, but claiming indulgence also for having written the work in only three weeks at Geneva, where there had been no means of consulting reference books.[2]

Byron would have had to be a perfectly motiveless liar to tell Medwin that his mother-in-law's estates were in Lancashire when the county was Leicestershire, that he had inhabited 'a dark street' in London when the house in question was overlooking Green Park, that he parted with Newstead Abbey at a date years before the sale was actually accomplished, that Hobhouse had been present on a tour of Lake Geneva with Shelley, and that his mother had died while he was travelling abroad: nor could there be any conceivable reason for his doubling the few years of his age when he lost his father, saying 'only six' when he meant 'only three', or halving the amount of his wife's dowry, placing it at ten instead of twenty thousand pounds. A certain social status, to which Byron was not in the least indifferent, was signified by the size of a wife's dowry; and an untruthful man would have been more likely to exaggerate than diminish it.

The biographer who could rush into print a pack of discrepancies such as these on matters which could easily be checked is obviously to be read with caution whenever he writes what cannot be checked. Whether he made notes of the conversations immediately after they took place (which, as he informed Mary Shelley, was on nights when they sat up together), or a day or two after, or, in some instances, not till he wrote his book, his slow-moving mind was unequal to grasping and firmly holding Byron's mercurial communications, more particularly as he was not likely to have been very sober when he heard them.

Mrs Shelley's letter to Mrs Leigh Hunt[3] telling her that Medwin was making a book out of Byron's talks with him 'when tipsy' has often been used to explain divagations ascribed to Byron; but Medwin is not to be pictured sitting with a glass of water while Byron drank wine or gin. He

---

[1] 11 Nov. 1824: Murray MSS.
[2] Unpublished Preface intended for a new edition and drafted in a copy of the work now in the Houston Library of Harvard University, Massachusetts.
[3] 10 Oct. 1824.

covered himself by a reference to his own abstemiousness, put into Byron's mouth, but Byron disliked drinking alone[1] and would not have held frequent midnight colloquies with a detached and non-convivial companion. Shelley did not except Medwin when he wrote that Byron's guests made 'vats of claret' of themselves.

Besides misquoting and misreporting, Medwin was not above wilfully misrepresenting, as may be seen by his assertion—especially infuriating to Hobhouse—that his work was the fruit of 'a Residence with his Lordship'. In paragraphs calculated to give great offence to John Murray he stated untruthfully that he had acted as witness to one of Byron's contracts with that publisher. To lend his account of the cremation of Shelley more authority, he wrote as if he had been present at it, provoking Trelawny, who was in every sense the master of ceremonies on that occasion, to call him a 'mesureless and unprincipled liar'.[2]

Unprincipled he certainly was, and it was only from such a source that so irresponsible a flow of gossip could have been poured out.

All the *beau monde* knew of Lady Caroline Lamb's unbalanced behaviour in the days of the furore for *Childe Harold*, but apart from ephemeral paragraphs in newspapers of low repute, nothing had appeared in print about the affair except her own foolish and frantic *roman à clef*, *Glenarvon* (1816), which had almost ruined her socially. It may be imagined with what dismay her much-tried husband and family saw the episode described in terms that provided easy clues to her identity, and were most humliating to her pride.

> The lady had scarcely any personal attractions to recommend her. Her figure, though genteel, was too thin to be good, and wanted that roundness which elegance and grace would vainly supply. . . . She was married, but it was a match of *convenance*, and no couple could be more fashionably indifferent to, or independent of, one another, than she and her husband. . . . I was soon congratulated by my friends on the conquest I had made, and did my utmost to show that I was not insensible to the partiality I could not help perceiving. I made every effort to be in love, expressed as much ardour as I could muster. . . .

Doubtless Byron did describe the amour in some such light—though not in such language—as this, for Lady Caroline had forfeited any claim to be treated tenderly, not only by the exhibitionism of her novel, but by the breaking of the oath of secrecy she had solemnly and repeatedly sworn when he had given her the most intimate confidences it was in his power to bestow. For all the impressive heroics of her letters assuring him she 'would die to save him', she had at the same time been making approaches

---

[1] Hobhouse *Journals*, 3 Oct. 1826, quoting Barry.
[2] Letter to John Murray, 15 Jan. 1833.

of the most consummate hypocrisy to Lady Byron in order to disclose to her
those matters she had vowed not to reveal, and thus to satisfy herself that
the husband and wife would never be reconciled and that Augusta Leigh
would be cast out.[1]

Byron had learned enough of this mischief a few months after leaving
England to convey a warning of it to Augusta.[2] His private account of the
notorious affair years later would therefore not have been couched in the
most chivalrous terms, though he does not seem to have gone as far as he
might. He could have said that Caroline had written to him at least twice
before he was introduced to her,[3] a detail which nowhere emerges in her
own versions of their first encounter, and that he and Hobhouse—like
characters in an Italian opera—had gone to prodigious trouble to get her
out of his bachelor lodgings disguised as a maidservant, when she had
forced herself on him (disguised as a manservant) in the hope of pushing
the already wearied lover to an elopement.[4]

Though Byron had a long memory, and at times liked to portray himself as revengeful, no man was so seldom vindictive in practice. It seems
improbable that he would have spoken even of the treacherous Caroline in
a manner so likely to prove injurious if he had had the slightest inkling
that what he was saying was to be printed—and within two or three years.

Medwin, intent on fame and the £500 he was to receive, spared no one.
The proud families of Gamba and Guiccioli were treated with as little
regard for what they might feel as if they had been characters in a
charade, and Teresa herself alluded to by name in the most explicit
fashion. The portrayal of her, if on the whole flattering, not only added a
year or two to her age but coolly described her as having 'too much
embonpoint for her height', and gave the wounding information that,
though much attached, Byron was not in love with her. Her 'preposterous
connexion' with a husband immensely older than herself was explained
in callous indifference to the fact that she had been obliged to return to
Count Guiccioli's protection and might have to suffer for this distasteful
publicity.

What purported to be a verbatim account by Byron of his marriage as
well as his last love affair was offered to the world without compunction.
The pages concerning Lady Byron, though well stocked with errors, reach
the highest degree of verisimilitude that Medwin attained. On this topic it
is safe to assume that he wrote the communications down soon after they

---

[1] Lady Byron's Minutes of a Conversation on 27 Mar. 1816: Lovelace Papers. It was
on the strength of this interview that she had written to her lawyer, Dr Lushington, to
say her suspicion of Byron's relations with Augusta had now darkened to absolute certainty. See Chapter VII.

[2] LOVELACE, *Astarte*. Letter of 14 Sept. 1816.

[3] In early March 1812. Lady Byron preserved these overtures.   [4] JOYCE.

were made, taking more trouble than usual to discipline his faulty memory. Their effect on Lady Byron when she saw them in print may be imagined:

> She married me from vanity and the hope of reforming and fixing me. She was a spoiled child, and naturally of a jealous disposition; and this was increased by the infernal machinations of those in her confidence. . . .
>
> She thought her knowledge of mankind infallible. . . . She had a habit of drawing people's characters after she had seen them once or twice. . . . Lady Byron had good ideas but she could never express them; wrote poetry too, but it was only good by accident. Her letters were always enigmatical, often unintelligible. She was governed by what she called fixed rules and principles, squared mathematically.

There was enough truth here to disconcert even one who has been called by her biographer 'adept at self-deception'.[1]

It was most unfortunate that so indiscreet a man as Medwin should have come on the scene in Pisa just when, after an auspicious association of nearly ten years, Byron and John Murray were in a state of tension. No doubt Byron did grumble and very volubly: his grievances against Murray were in essence his grievances against all those misguided well-wishers in England who thought to stop him writing disreputable master-pieces by telling him he was losing his hold on the public. Only a Medwin would have filled out page after page with his complaints—some of them ill-remembered and garbled.

Byron's feud with the Poet Laureate was likewise carried on posthum-ously; and Southey's hatred of the greater man was sufficiently deadly without further odium being generated. Leigh Hunt, whose vanity was notorious, would not take kindly to seeing his *Rimini* derided as *Nimini-Pimini* and his *Foliage* mocked as *Follyage*, and the prattle about Samuel Rogers, though probably not rendered unfaithfully, had little prospect of being read with pleasure by that celebrity:

> He is coming to visit me on his return from Rome, and will be annoyed when he finds I have any English comforts about me. He told a person the other day that one of my new tragedies was intended for the stage, when he knew neither of them was. I suppose he wanted to get another of them damned.

Medwin aspired to be a poet, but his career had, up to that time, been obscurity unrelieved, and it must have been most gratifying for him to be able to use Byron as a means of scoring off the writers he envied. 'To bring up a dead man thus to run amuck among the living is a formidable thing', Tom Moore wrote in his diary when the book came out.[2] Medwin's effects were not accidental. He was stupid but knew 'what a fast hold the world takes of anything that disparages'.[3]

[1] MAYNE.   [2] MOORE, *Memoirs*. 18 Oct. 1824.   [3] Ibid. 24 Oct. 1824.

He was later to specialize in disparagement, retracting even his favourable impression of Byron, the one mollifying feature of a book which was otherwise regarded as a shocking and scandalous production. It was issued with the precaution of an announcement:

The Publisher of this Work thinks it proper to state, that he felt desirous of suggesting to the Author, who is abroad, the suppression of certain passages; but finding that these, among various others, had been extracted, with the Author's permission, from the original Manuscript before it came into his possession, and also that they have now appeared in print, he has no longer considered it necessary to urge their suppression in the present Volume.

Medwin had behaved badly to Colburn, allowing the *Foreign Literary Gazette* to print copious extracts in advance, but the publisher was not much more ethical than the author. In subsequent editions, not only were glaring mistakes left uncorrected, but an extremely libellous statement concerning John Murray, which had at first been supplanted by asterisks, was restored to the text, though a proved falsehood.

Colburn did not fail to advertise the 'Conversations' liberally, and Augusta Leigh, who had already been dismayed by the freedom with which her brother was discussed in print, wrote in apprehension to her sister-in-law:

What a worry this Captain Medwin is! At least I feel it so, it really keeps me in a fever—I wonder who and what he is. I heard some time ago very deficient in intellect. He can however *invent*. How sad it is the dead may not rest in peace.[1]

She had not as yet seen the book, for she was staying in Brighton which was a few days behind London in acquiring new publications. Her information about Medwin's defective intellect was obtained from Byron's great friend, Scrope Davies, with whom she was always on affectionate terms. In writing to thank her warmly for the souvenir of a ring worn by Byron, he had added some news about meeting another less intimate acquaintance—

a Mr Hay who was with B. in the affray with the military at Milan [a mistake for Pisa]. He (Mr H.) is a dull but a matter-of-fact man—and as such his information is interesting. He says that the gentleman whose name is in the papers (it begins with an M) as about to become B's Boswell is a perfect idiot, but he suspects Mr M. to be the stalking horse to Mrs Shelley (Godwin's daughter) whom he describes as not perhaps incapable of the task. . . .[2]

Poor Mrs Shelley! It was hard that she should be blamed for doing the very thing she had resolutely set her face against. She was already a successful author, her qualifications for writing about Byron were ten

[1] 25 Oct. 1824: Lovelace Papers.
[2] British Museum: Additional MSS. 31037. 22 Sept. 1824.

times greater than Medwin's or Dallas's, and she might have retrieved herself from all her pressing financial difficulties by doing so. How often it happens that when the near relatives and honourable friends of important men remain silent out of delicacy or refuse to authorize biographies, because they wish to protect the dead, they merely leave a clear field for the guesswork and gossip of those who have no such tenderness!

Hobhouse had also missed seeing Medwin's book, being on a round of visits in the North of England, but he read of it.

> The papers this morning full of Captain Medwin's Conversations of Lord Byron—alas my poor friend! into what society did he fall—but the attaching so much contemptible gossip to his name more than punishes him for that love of low company which I think distinguished him in his latter days. . . . I have not quite made up my mind what to do respecting this shameful publication.[1]

He was already weary of taking measures, or wondering what measures to take, against people who were flaunting their knowledge—or ignorance—of Byron. There were the Dallases, and they were not finished with yet. There was a man called Kennedy, a doctor out in Cephalonia, who had been writing about a project to publish notes he had taken of Byron's views on—of all subjects!—religion: he had been firmly snubbed, but might prove obstinate. There was Edward Blaquiere, a prominent fellow-member of the Greek Committee, who had sent the Honorary Secretary, Dr John Bowring, an account of Byron's last days which Hobhouse had called 'a very vulgar performance'.[2] It contained unbearably revealing things, such as Byron's last little flicker of a joke to his valet, threatening to haunt him if he did not carry out his dying wishes (only no one took it as a joke), and his half-delirious impulse to shoot himself lest he should go mad. Hobhouse had struck these sentences out, but Bowring, without taking any notice of his directions, printed the whole long letter in his paper, the *Westminster Review*.[3]

A few weeks after that, the *London Magazine* had come out with an extensive 'Personal Character of Lord Byron', which gave the impression of being written by someone who knew him, and Hobhouse could not identify the writer.

> . . . He must be a traitor against private confidence. There are falsehoods but on the whole the portrait is a likeness, and the only one I ever saw. It made me very uncomfortable. I was in hopes that no one would have drawn his frailties from their dread abode.[4]

[1] Hobhouse *Journals*, 25 Oct. 1824.   [2] Ibid. 5 July 1824.
[3] Ibid. 3 Aug. 1824. When published in book form, the offending passages were duly cut.
[4] Ibid. 2 Oct. 1824. Hobhouse had as yet only seen extracts in *The Times*. The article is obviously of composite authorship, full of contradictions, and oscillating without

The kind of frailty which rendered Hobhouse especially uncomfortable was perhaps the one which, to judge from some of the letters they exchanged, he himself shared with Byron—a taste for bawdry. The anonymous portraitist had laid stress on it.

While he was still perplexed by this new contribution to the ever-mounting tide of Byron literature which he had no power to stem, he learned that Colonel Leicester Stanhope, whom he had at first set down as an exceedingly good man, was also publicizing his association with Byron!

Stanhope had arrived in England in July and, before the beginning of September, he had handed over his papers to be arranged in book form by an editor, and was now putting in circulation a version of affairs in Greece in which he represented himself as wiser, nobler, more active, diligent, and generous than any other Englishman who had gone to assist the cause. He had done this with all kinds of subtle devices of mock-modesty ('Am I not a swaggerer?' or 'You may see . . . that I do not good by stealth, but that, on the contrary, I take pleasure in making it known'): and he had introduced reports of his arguments with Byron in which his object was to reveal himself upholding the freedom of the press in the face of painful opposition.

> If your Lordship was serious . . . [in contemplating a censorship] I shall consider it my duty to communicate this affair to the Committee in England, in order to show them how difficult a task I have to fulfil, in promoting the liberties of Greece, if your Lordship is to throw the weight of your vast talents into the opposite scale on a question of such vital importance. . . .
>
> He said that he was an ardent friend of publicity and the press; but he feared that it was not applicable to this society in its present combustible state. I answered that I thought it applicable to all countries, and essential here.[1]

Hobhouse could not foresee that, on the strength of Stanhope's own transparently truthful records, posterity would find Byron the better judge (the press was, in fact, most tendentious and provocative). Much more of a Committee man than Byron, Hobhouse was not altogether out of sympathy with the officious side of Stanhope's character: but it was manifestly wrong to have exposed, without consulting him, the evidences of a rift between the Committee's representatives at Missolonghi.

Since his friend's death, Hobhouse had suffered every kind of distress and inconvenience. There had even been a period when it had seemed unavoidable for him to go to Greece himself in Byron's stead. He had made all the preparations for the hazardous voyage, and got passport and letters

balance between applause and disparagement. There is very strong internal evidence that Trelawny, before retiring to the Cave of Odysseus, supplied much of the adverse material.   [1] STANHOPE.

of credit and taken leave of his family before a way out had been found, and he was in a state of considerable emotional fatigue when the first reviews of Medwin's book appeared. A letter from Mrs Leigh in the same harassed strain as that in which she had written to Lady Byron did not at first rouse him from the philosophical calm he had assumed:

> With respect to the 'fusses' you anticipate, always recollect that they cannot be inflicted upon us except by our own consent. For my own part I will endure none—and I advise you to follow so sage an example. Do not bestow a thought upon the comtemptible gossip published in the name of your brother. The world which has an interest in discovering that men of talent have many weak points will encourage and keep alive these shameful records of frailty—but it will only be for a time—and the final judgment of mankind will condemn and consign to oblivion such base and treacherous exposures of private intercourse. So never mind Mr Medwin. He has told three falsehoods respecting myself—but let them pass.

Still stoical, he answered—and with much insight—her comment on 'the Typographical Colonel':

> I perfectly agree with what you say of Colonel Stanhope's publication. He is not a bad man—but he is a weak man and one who follows the new school of *Utilitarions*—that is he is all for being of use to mankind at any risk or expense to the comfort and happiness of individuals. These good folks not only never tell lies, but never omit the opportunity of speaking the truth— and being, moreover, a little vain, they generally prefer those disclosures which include the mention of themselves. Hence the detail of the conversation and controversy with your brother. If I had not expected that all which has happened would happen I should have been grievously annoyed—as it is I bless heaven it is no worse.

There was one matter which he could not pretend either to himself or his correspondent not to mind about. That he should be criticized for his part in the burning of Byron's Memoirs really did exasperate him. Having helped to commit an irrevocable act, he had to believe in its rightness and its needfulness, for his was not the temperament that can admit a folly and repine for it. He became less serene as he continued:

> It does, however, rather vex me that so excellent and honorable and so right-minded a person as your friend Lady Jersey should have had the story of the Memoirs so distorted and so misrepresented her as to entertain the slightest doubt as to the inevitable necessity of destroying those foolish documents.

Lady Jersey was taking Thomas Moore's part and had joined the very substantial number of those who felt he should not be allowed to bear the whole ruinous loss of the two thousand guineas he had repaid to John Murray, a proposition which always drove Hobhouse to fury, for he was absolutely determined to the contrary effect.

. . . I am sure I am not at all concerned [he went on bitterly] at her or or any one else being what you call a 'Mooreite.' If ballad writers had not their admirers heaven preserve us! What would become of us and our national music? The world is wide enough for Tom Moore to range in, and still to leave a corner or two for unobtrusive folks like ourselves. . . .

I am, however, rather apprehensive that the London Magazine and Captain Medwin and Colonel Stanhope and Dr. Kennedy and Mr Bowring and Mr Blaquiere and the Monthly Mirror, and tutti quanti, will rather forestall the great biography which they say is getting up at Longmans.

Poor Byron he is now paying the penalty of his principal fault—a love of talking of himself to any sycophant that would listen to him. That was his real failing and though it looked like an amiable weakness it was a most pernicious propensity inasmuch as it encouraged and fostered that morbid selfishness which was the great stain on his character, and has contributed more than any other to the injury of his fame.[1]

'The great biography which they say is getting up at Longmans' was, at that early stage, a figment of Hobhouse's fears. Moore had certainly shown eagerness to engage in writing Byron's life, but he would not undertake it without the consent of the executors. In doggedly opposing both direct restitution to Moore for yielding up the Memoirs, and the indirect compensation he might derive from producing a book, Hobhouse showed an almost unbelievable blindness as well as want of elementary fairness. Publishers would assuredly have been far less willing to pay large sums to minor authors for their reminiscences of Byron if it had been announced that one of the most famous writers of the time, who had every possible advantage on his side, was about to bring out a full-scale biography; and Moore, unlike the irresponsible outsiders, could have been controlled. It was a point that Hobhouse in his jealousy entirely missed.

Not till his return to London did he realize how impossible it was going to be to live up to his boast that he would endure no fusses over Medwin's book. Fusses assailed him almost from the moment he set foot in the capital. He was summoned to Melbourne House, where Lady Caroline Lamb received him in her bedroom and talked to him for two hours.

She is in the utmost rage at Medwin's Conversations representing her as not having been the object of Byron's attachment and she showed me a very tender letter of his which she wished to publish. She told me that her brother William Ponsonby was not against the publication as he thought with her that no imputation was so dreadful as that of not having been loved by her paramour. . . . She is certainly very mad.[2]

With or without the improbable support of her brother, Lady Caroline had the love letter reproduced by lithography and sent it to Henry Colburn

---

[1] British Museum: Additional MS. 39672. 26 Oct. 1824.
[2] Hobhouse *Journals*, 1 Nov. 1824.

accompanied by a statement about her relations with Byron. It was couched in the form of a letter to Medwin, fulsomely praising his book and only disputing the parts of it that made light of her effect upon Byron, who, she claimed, 'devoted nine entire months almost entirely to my society' and 'loved me as never woman was loved'. (The actual duration of the *liaison* had been about three months.)

Colburn had the decency not to publish this sensational document, though she implored him to do so. 'I am on my death bed, do not fail to obey my wishes.'[1]

If Melbourne House was in agitation, so was 50 Albemarle Street. Hobhouse went there next day, and found John Murray busy with a pamphlet which was to refute the serious calumnies upon him, all appearing as speeches of Byron's. The man who could believe that Byron would not have praised an ode unless he had written it was no fit reporter for a poet with a complicated grievance, but though there were the usual evidences of Medwin's faulty memory and misapprehension, enough remained of authentic exasperation to cast a shadow for a while over Murray's memories of Byron.

Hobhouse took the book down with him to his father's country house, Whitton Park, near Hounslow, where he spent much of his time when he was not in his bachelor chambers; and when he read it, his specious calm broke. The following day, November 3rd, he wrote:

> Employed in reading and commenting on Medwin's infamous publication—which is the most impudent and clumsy fabrication I ever read of—and yet no paper[s] excepting John Bull and the Herald have had the courage to denounce such a scandalous breach of the first rules of society.[2]

On November 4th he was 'employed as yesterday', and on the 5th, it was 'Medwin again'. That day Count Pietro Gamba accompanied Sir Benjamin Hobhouse to Whitton, and Hobhouse enlisted his aid in checking the details of Medwin's various assertions about Byron's life in Italy.

Pietro was himself writing a book on Byron, and with Hobhouse's entire concurrence. More than that, Hobhouse had gone out of his way to suggest publication to John Murray and almost to take upon himself the negotiations, as well as the translation into English. Even Gamba's charm, so generally commended, would not have had this miraculous effect if he had not also had the good sense to consult Hobhouse and make clear his dependence upon him. The latter may have borne in mind too what Stanhope had told him, during their dismal journey up the river in the *Florida*—that Gamba and himself were the two whom Byron had named

---

[1] *L. & J.* Undated letter. She did not die till four years later.
[2] Hobhouse *Journals*.

as most fitted to write his biography, because 'Gamba knew all his latter
years and Hobhouse his early time'.[1]

Hobhouse had shown little regard for Byron's wishes when he pressed
for destruction of the Memoirs, but that object gained, he was ready
enough to do all he thought his friend would have approved and, though
husbanding the estate for Augusta, had given the young count three
hundred pounds out of it in recognition of his many services in Greece.[2]
It was this money which enabled Pietro to take lodgings in Westminster
Bridge Road, and remain in England while he composed his discreet but
very valuable record of Byron's last days.

With his first-hand knowledge of Medwin and of Byron's Pisa sojourn,
it was useful for Hobhouse to have him at hand while he worked furiously
at a pamphlet to show the 'Conversations' up as fraudulent. He had in the
meantime written to Sir Francis Burdett asking his advice, and on the 9th
had a reply urging him not to pay any public attention to Medwin; but he
was in the first fervour of completing his slashing denunciation, and his
diary records:

> . . . I take my MSS with me to London. Arriving there I show it to Murray
> who seizes upon it with great glee and talks of a quarto or octavo impression
> of it. Certainly the exposure is as complete as the nature of the case will
> admit.[3]

The celerity with which printing and publishing were accomplished
at the beginning of the 19th century is a recurring surprise to authors of
the 20th. Hobhouse had the proofs of his pamphlet in his hands next day,
and early enough for him to note:

> Gifford of the Quarterly sees it and approves. Wilmot Horton also writes
> me a letter on the subject, telling me I have damaged the Captain so he will
> never float again.
> I dine at the Literary Fund Club. There the propriety of my noticing
> Medwin was discussed and all said yes, except Mr Croly, the author of Pride
> should have a fall, who used some cogent and worldly arguments which had
> some effect on me.[4]

Hobhouse had received from the ubiquitous Wilmot Horton a lengthy
and officious letter beginning thus:

> I am induced to address you from having heard that it was your intention
> to contradict publicly some of the statements relating to yourself, which have
> appeared in a Work lately published by Captain Medwin, purporting to
> record 'Conversations of Lord Byron'.—If my information is correct, and
> such should be your intention, I have the following propositions to make to
> you.

[1] Ibid. The notes headed 'Lord Byron' written about 4 Aug. 1824.
[2] Ibid. 30 Aug. 1824.   [3] Ibid. 9 Nov. 1824.   [4] Ibid. 10 Nov. 1824.

Captain Medwin states in his preface, that the conversations which he has published would never have appeared, had not the destruction of the Memoirs taken place, by which manifest injustice had been done to the World, and an Injury to Lord Byron's Memory. . . .

I therefore take the liberty of suggesting that the present would afford a convenient opportunity of explaining to the Public that the destruction of the Memoirs of the late Lord Byron was a measure not only highly approved of, but *enforced* by yourself in conjunction with others, and having also the entire approbation of Mr Douglas Kinnaird.

He went on to request that Hobhouse would contradict a number of falsehoods regarding, in particular, the financial affairs of Lady Byron and her husband.

. . . As the confidential and intimate friend of Lord Byron, I am satisfied that you will maintain the impossibility of his ever having seriously given utterance to such misstatements, which, in fact, if it were deemed desirable, could be contradicted at any time, not by assertion balanced against assertion, but by reference to Trustees and parchments and to fifty unprejudiced witnesses.[1]

Hobhouse had already refuted the gross errors Horton indicated, but he would not admit to having 'enforced' the burning of the Memoirs. Although in his diary, within ten days of that victory, he had written 'Nothing but Murray's decisive conduct, backed by my own representations procured the destruction of the MSS.',[2] by November he was less anxious to take his share of the credit, and he replied to that part of Horton's letter disingenuously:

In the note you were good enough to send me the other day I saw a slight misconception on your part regarding those plaguy Memoirs which I think it is as well to rectify.

I did not *enforce*, as you hint, the *burning* of the said Memoirs—what I did enforce, as far as I could, was the performance of Mr Moore's written engagement to put them '*into Mrs Leigh's hands for her absolute disposal.*' I think Mrs Leigh was perfectly right to burn them, and I told her so—but so far from enforcing the burning, I refused to put them in the fire when some one desired me to aid in that pious work—as being no part of my business—But I strongly approve[d] of the burning and do still.

After all it is very idle enquiring who did the deed or who advised or who approved—for the MSS were in Murray's hands and he declared he would not give them up except to Mrs Leigh.[3]

Horton too was perhaps being disingenuous. He had insisted in the course of the letter that the matter was one in which he had no personal concern, and that was correct—there never was a more inveterate busy-

---

[1] Murray MSS. No date. [2] Hobhouse *Journals*, 27 May 1824.
[3] LOVELACE, *Lady Noel Byron*. 23 Nov. 1824.

body—but his further assurance that he had not in the slightest degree been 'authorized' was literally rather than substantially true. There is a great deal of evidence in Lady Byron's correspondence that it was her practice to inspire her friends to take certain steps without actually asking them to do so, thus leaving herself free to deny when it seemed expedient that they had acted with her authority.

Her extravagant cautiousness took at times an inexplicable turn. For no ostensible reason she had decided not to admit to having read Medwin's book, and so the errors respecting her own affairs, which she naturally found most distasteful, could not be contradicted except by the tortuous methods which were customary with her. There was an interchange of letters between her and Augusta on the topic which is quietly characteristic.

> I . . . have been worried and annoyed [Augusta wrote from Brighton] beyond all I can describe. I sincerely hope you may have kept to your wise resolution of not looking at that Vile Book—but from all I hear I rather doubt that you will have been allowed to do so; however I will if possible say no more about it, till I hear from you.[1]

Lady Byron confined her reply to a postscript when she took her guarded pen in hand next day:

> You seem to express some intention of communicating about Medwin *if* I have read it—Don't you think it might be better for us to say we have not discussed the subject.[2]

Augusta was as usual mystified. She had thought they might put up a front together against Medwin.

> I cannot at all understand why in this case we sd act *independently of each other*. . . . Neither do I see what disadvantage cd arise from our having acted in concert.[3]

But Lady Byron was determined never to act in concert with Augusta about anything, and still refrained from any comment which would show she had read the book.

By this time, Hobhouse, having had second and third thoughts about his pamphlet, determined not to publish it except as an anonymous review in the next issue of John Murray's periodical, *The Quarterly*. It was a clear error in tactics, having thrown out such a challenge, to do anything that could be construed into a retreat: but for all his qualities, he suffered from a lack of judgment which is often startling. If only he had made some concession to the Dallases after gaining every point he had striven for, he could have exercised control over their work, but then he had been tenacious in opposition. Now on the other hand, having let it be widely

---

[1] 26 Nov. 1824: Lovelace Papers.　　　　[2] Ibid. 27 Nov.　　　　[3] Ibid. 10 Dec.

known that he was about to show up the spurious or garbled dialogues of Medwin, he foolishly drew back.

Sometimes too headstrong, as in the classic instance of the Memoirs, at others he became diffident and uncertain, going from adviser to adviser irresolutely. Though the majority of his friends favoured publication, Sir Francis Burdett and the Rev. Mr Croly (who could not have forgotten that Byron had satirized him as Rowley-Powley), had not spoken in vain. Hobhouse was no longer the eager rebel Byron had known but an ambitious Member of Parliament with hopes of a career, and 'worldly arguments' had their weight with him.

On November 13th he was in great perplexity:

> . . . I have doubts still what to do. If I publish this, it will be only from a sense of duty for I am not injured—indeed I am on the whole better treated than any one—but then if no one dares to contradict these falsehoods what is to become of biography? What is to become of private life?
>
> At the same time a denial of facts is a very dangerous enterprise especially when you have to do with a rogue who will say any thing and I shall certainly be in a most unenviable condition with all the partisans of scandal yelping at my heels, and the press most probably against me—to say nothing of the efforts which Medwin will make use of to annoy me.

These reflections, with their legal undertone, owed much of their substance to Henry Brougham, who was becoming one of his close friends —which gives the measure of how far Hobhouse had been tamed in the course of eight years, for he had known Brougham to be a detested enemy of Byron's. The rising politician had walked home with him after they had dined at the Beefsteak Club.

> . . . We talked of the Exposure, which he seems to entertain some doubt about publishing though he says it is complete. He promised to give me the meeting at Kinnaird's the next day, and there to discuss the subject.[1]

Kinnaird had from the first approved of publishing, but Brougham, as by a sort of compulsion, did Byron one more injury.[2] If Medwin's book was to be discredited, it ought to have been done before it had enjoyed a wide circulation and while there were still several important critics whose reviews had not gone to press. Instead Hobhouse had the types of his pamphlet broken up and called in the copies that had been privately distributed.

Lady Byron's defenders were disappointed and exasperated. Wilmot Horton wrote to John Murray deploring Hobhouse's decision and quoting

---

[1] Hobhouse *Journals*.

[2] For an enumeration of his curious aggressions against Byron, beginning in the latter's early youth, see Appendix to this Chapter.

a soundly reasoned letter he had just received from Dr Lushington, who was still Lady Byron's legal adviser:

> I am clearly of opinion that Hobhouse will do himself, Lord Byron's memory, and all persons interested, infinite prejudice, by suppressing the publication. That such a publication was preparing, nay, that it was printed, is matter of public notoriety; how it became so I know not, but such is undoubtedly the fact. The suppression will be attributed either to the impossibility of contradiction, or to fear on Hobhouse's part, and Captn Medwin's Memoirs will derive additional claim to evidence. Whatever reasons may have existed against contradiction a priori, none, in my judgment, warrant a suppression at this time, and I deeply regret the resolution taken. I should hope it might be altered.
>
> No publication in the Quarterly can supply its place. A Review is the very worst channel for a contradiction of facts. . . .[1]

As it turned out even publication in the *Quarterly* had been counted on in vain. On December 13th, a month after he had cancelled the pamphlet, Hobhouse went with Pietro Gamba to 50 Albemarle Street and—

> learnt with surprise that now there was some difficulty as to the insertion of my exposure of Medwin in the Quarterly—nay, it is a question whether there will not be an article taking Medwin's stories for granted. Murray stated that Gifford [the editor] was against it—who then is for it?
> I desired to have my exposure back again if it is not to be used—Murray promised a definite answer by the day after tomorrow the 15th. There is no end of the scoundrelism of the writing tribe. I walked about with Gamba.[2]

Hobhouse might well ask—and probably asked many times, walking about with Gamba—why, if neither the editor nor the owner of the magazine wished a contribution to appear, there should be any risk at all of its appearing. He did not wait till the 15th for a decision about his Exposure, but called on Murray a day earlier.

> . . . he again told me that an attempt had been made to induce him to introduce a defamatory article on Lord Byron—but that he and Gifford had resolved against it—they had been frequently taunted with not attacking Byron when alive—they would not assault him now he was gone—but my exposure and article were not to be inserted. . . .[3]

Murray must have been much annoyed by Hobhouse's withdrawal of the pamphlet after he had given him all the trouble of having it printed. There had also been some new unpleasantness about Byron which may have put him still more out of humour.

Murray's own pamphlet against Medwin had contained not only

---

[1] 19 Nov. 1824: Murray MSS.
[2] Hobhouse *Journals*.   [3] Ibid.

abundant evidence that his dealings with Byron had been misreported, but also letters to show that they had been reconciled after the differences which had interrupted their long and brilliant association. But the *Examiner*—the paper formerly edited by Leigh Hunt and now by his brother—had announced that its next number would contain 'an account of the conduct of Mr Murray and an original letter from Lord Byron to Mr Murray of a very different kind from those quoted in the latter's statement'. Hobhouse, at Murray's request, had gone to see Hunt and had asked him to refrain from giving the undeserving Medwin this support, but his efforts to stop the mischief were unwontedly feeble.

> I . . . talked a long time with him [Hunt] and his son but found them exasperated against Murray and could do nothing. The letter is genuine and certainly convicts Murray of a mistake—but it is a pity publishing it.[1]

Murray's various feelings on seeing the hurtful use made of one of Byron's sharp remonstrances[2] were not conducive to his doing anything to oblige Hobhouse or defend Byron, but there was another factor in operation which Hobhouse noted on the day of the bitter final decision about his Exposure (December 14th):

> In this day's paper I see a violent attack of Southey's on Lord Byron—and I presume that the opposition to inserting my article in the Quarterly comes from that quarter.

Southey, the Poet Laureate, was a regular contributor, and his attack, which, though scornful of Medwin, upheld his veracity, was indeed what Murray referred to when he had spoken of having kept out a piece hostile to Byron.

He had judged well, for it was a work of pompous vanity and solemn spleen, which did no credit to the journal that published it, the *Courier*. If Southey had striven for years to prove that Byron's savage and contemptuous remarks about him were well-grounded, he could not have done it better than by this fatuous onslaught:

> It was because Lord Byron had brought a stigma upon English literature that I accused him; . . . because he had set up for pander-general to the youth of Great Britain as long as his writings should endure; because he had committed a high crime and misdemeanour against society, by sending forth a work in which mockery was mingled with horrors, filth with impiety, profligacy with sedition and slander.[3] For these offences I came forward to arraign him. . . .
> It might have been thought that Lord Byron had attained the last degree

---

[1] Hobhouse *Journals*, 12 Nov. 1824.
[2] *Examiner*, 14 Nov. 1824. The letter, written on 22 Oct. 1822, it given in *L. & J.* Kinnaird had been instructed not to deliver it if he thought it 'harsh'.
[3] The work in question was *Don Juan*.

of disgrace when his head was set up for a sign at one of those preparatory schools for the brothel and the gallows, where obscenity, sedition, and blasphemy are retailed in drams for the vulgar. There remained one further shame,—there remained the exposure of his private conversations. . . .

Southey was using a characteristic figure of speech. The 'preparatory school for the brothel and the gallows' was the house of a publisher named Benbow who, having pirated Byron's works, used an engraving of his head for an imprimatur; and had driven the laureate to extremest rage by bringing out an edition of *Wat Tyler*, the 'dramatic poem' he had written in his revolutionary youth and found hideously embarrassing in his Tory maturity. The *Globe and Traveller* pretended to take him literally: 'Somebody, it seems, has set up Lord Byron's Head over a gin-shop with which the Laureate is acquainted.' *The Times*, less flippantly, accused him of being 'inflamed, or raving with malignant jealousy', and the pirate Benbow retorted with a pamphlet which made some crude, rude, and correct prophecies as to Southey's future standing.

The public provocations Southey had received from Byron were not small except in comparison with those he gave, which were rendered more obnoxious by the assumption of omnipotence—as in 1822 (also in the *Courier*):

> I have fastened his name upon the gibbet for reproach and ignominy, as long as it shall endure. Take it down who can!

Fortunately for his self-complacency, he could not foresee that almost the only dicta of his which posterity would easily recall were utterances of an egregious kind about Byron and Shelley, and almost the only verses those which have to be quoted to explain Byron's satires upon him.

Hobhouse, after reading Southey's final outburst, wrote wistfully in his journal:

> I think this day I found a note of Lord Byron's on Southey when he (B) consented to cancel the dedication to Don Juan attacking Southey vehemently. This was done at my request.[1]

Having let prudential considerations govern his arrangements for refuting Medwin, Hobhouse made amends by labouring with redoubled vigour at other means of sustaining Byron's reputation. It was necessary because enemies had grown tired of the truce they had been compelled to observe during the weeks when the news of his death had filled the press with columns of glorification. 'No man ever lived who had such devoted friends', Hobhouse had written, but equally no man ever lived who

---

[1] Hobhouse *Journals*, 20 Dec. 1824. The uncertainty about the day was due to Hobhouse's practice of writing up several days at once.

excited so strong a hatred in a large number of persons who had never set eyes on him.

Certainly, he had given great offence, morally, politically, and poetically, but this was not the entire cause of the strange animus. As a youth of nineteen, at the innocuous outset of his career, he had been selected by a serious journal as the victim of a review ferocious even by the standards then admissible, and all through his literary life, rages had broken out against him which now seem quite disproportionate to the affronts received. The epithets applied to him were on the whole much more severe than those used against Napoleon, the nation's enemy, and after his death there was only a lull before hostilities were resumed.

Medwin's book was widely stigmatized as a breach of the decencies of social intercourse, but from the first, most of the press took the line that the confusions and errors of the author were lies fed to him by Byron. The *London Literary Gazette*'s answer to a protesting correspondent is a fair sample:

> We are aware of the misstatements and inaccuracies in Captain Medwin's *Conversations*; but as we have from the beginning, so do we continue to attribute them rather to his original informant than to his own intention to misrepresent.[1]

Such assertions by strangers were infuriating to Byron's friends, who knew him to be almost tiresomely literal-minded, and given to telling more truth than was seemly.

> . . . I detest all fiction even in song, And so must tell the truth, howe'er you blame it

was on his part a mere statement of fact, and even had it not been so, he was far too well aware of his own fame to speak falsely when every circumstance he touched upon had eager witnesses.

It is profoundly significant that Hobhouse and Byron's other intimate friends never for one moment considered any mistake in Medwin's book as likely to have arisen from inexact communication by Byron. Hobhouse committed himself in print to the statement that 'amongst his other noble qualities [he] was distinguished by a scrupulous regard, even in trifles, to truth'.[2] In the privacy of his diary, he was equally emphatic:

> . . . I saw the Times where indeed I found a scurvy article saying it was more likely that Byron should have *lied* and *garbled* than that Medwin, dull as he is, should have invented, and that Mr H[obhouse] must be a very simple gentleman if he thought to persuade the public to the contrary.

[1] 4 Dec. 1824.   [2] *Westminster Review*, No. 5, 1825.

This is infamous. What does the editor of the Times know of the real character of Byron? I thought of going to the Times and remonstrating and actually walked to Printing House Square. . . .[1]

He had, as was frequently the case now, the ever-sympathetic Gamba with him, whose book provided a useful account of Byron's last year, fond but by no means flowery. Hobhouse was active in translating it, but Gamba wrote it almost entirely without aid, and it is a model of what a straightforward, unpretentious narrative should be.

'. . . It is a pretty book,' wrote Hobhouse, 'but the most interesting part of it is not new.'[2] The criticism seems somewhat unfair since Hobhouse would have been the first to oppose the use of any material either searching or controversial.

Though it has been a source book for everyone requiring information about Byron's Greek enterprise, and was translated into several languages in the year of publication, it excited far less attention in England than the gossiping indiscretions of Medwin, which continued to arouse the scorn of Byron's circle long after the troubles they gave rise to had subsided. (Yet perhaps it would be fair to say that, in a sense, they never did subside, because they set a tone for writing about Byron which was to have many disagreeable echoes.)

Besides his translation, Hobhouse was obliged to devote several days to writing an indictment of Robert Dallas in the form of a review. The incorrigible father and son were not only publishing in Paris their proscribed book of Byron's letters both in English and French, but had also succeeded in overcoming the injunction to some extent in England. They had been advised by the judge himself at the time of losing their appeal that, though Byron's written words were copyright, the substance of them was not; and the younger Dallas had therefore transposed the whole correspondence, quoting almost every detail, but in the form of a third-person narrative.

In losing Byron's words, he lost all the charm and freshness that had given merit to the work, but the compromise saved the bargain with the publisher from being a total loss and enabled the Dallases to vent their indignation against Hobhouse and other opponents by printing their tale of grievances in England as well as abroad. There were in the Preface many deliberately mischief-making pronouncements such as were customary among all the second-rate biographers of Byron, their motive being to annoy or humiliate the living even though it should alienate affection from the dead—an eventuality rather desired by Dallas senior than otherwise.

[1] Hobhouse *Journals*, 21 Jan. 1825.
[2] Ibid.

How base and how ludicrous he could be may be gauged from a specimen of his own composition:

> In the dedications of his [Byron's] poems there is no sincerity; he had neither respect nor regard for the persons to whom they are addressed; and Lord Holland, Rogers, Davies, and Hobhouse, if earthly knowledge becomes intuitive on retrospection, will see on what grounds I say this, and nod the recognition, and I trust forgiveness of heavenly spirits, if heavenly theirs become, to the wandering poet with whose works their names are swimming down the stream of Time. He and they shall have *my* nod too on the occasion. . . .

The meaning to be unravelled here seems to be that in heaven, if they should happen to go there, the friends to whom Byron had dedicated works would learn that he had not really cared about them, but would nevertheless not snub him on that account; and Dallas himself would benignly nod his recognition to them all, not excluding Byron himself.

The critics did not give a very warm reception to Dallas, for his mean motives were palpable. In the words of one of them:

> The object of Mr Dallas . . . is to show that while Lord Byron enjoyed the benefit of his society he was a much better man than after their intercourse ceased; and for this purpose he does not hesitate to speak in very harsh terms of his Lordship's conduct.[1]

Both loyalty and his ardent passion for victory brought Hobhouse swiftly back into the fray, and with an absolutely devastating weapon. On November 25th he had written:

> Employed on a critique of that rogue Dallas's Recollections of Lord Byron—fortunately Murray has got a long letter sent by Dallas to Byron on which B. has made some comments—they will completely upset this vilainous [*sic*] performance.[2]

The letter of Dallas's which Byron had forwarded to John Murray was of a much later date than those the writer had made public. It was a most unpleasant kind of begging letter, half maudlin, half minatory. Its object was to make the recipient feel how much his career owed to Dallas's guidance, and to press him to express his gratitude in some negotiable shape. Byron was asked for 'fresh materials'—i.e. further gifts of copyright—'which may justify or conciliate', because 'there are circumstances which not only palliate, but call upon men to show that, however they may pass it over, they are not ignorant of what is their due'.

Dallas furthermore declared that 'I was chiefly instrumental, by my conduct in 1812, in saving you from perpetuating the enmity of the world, or rather, in forcing you against your will into its admiration and love;

---

[1] *New Monthly Magazine*, Dec. 1824.   [2] Hobhouse *Journals*.

and that I afterwards considerably retarded your rapid retrograde motion from the enviable station which your genius merits'.

'*When did this happen? and how?*' Byron had scribbled against that passage, and there were protesting comments upon several other claims. He denied that Dallas had saved him from 'the enmity of the world' by persuading him to suppress *English Bards and Scotch Reviewers*; and as for the remark that it was 'not in the power of money to satisfy or repay' the agent for his literary services, and the hint that six or seven hundred pounds had been entirely inadequate as a reward, all his Scottish blood rose and he struck back without quarter:

> Two Hundred pounds before I was twenty years old. Copyright of Childe Harold £600 Copyright of Corsair £500 and £50 for his nephew on entering the army: in all £1350 and not 6 or 700 as the worthy accountant reckons.

At the end he added wryly:

> Here lies R. C. Dallas
> Who wanted money and had some malice,
> If instead of a cottage he had lived in a palace
> We should have had none of these sallies

. . . The letter has remained and will remain unanswered. I never injured Mr R. C. Dallas but did him all the good I could, and I am quite unconscious and ignorant of what he means by reproaching me with ungenerous treatment; the facts will speak for themselves to those who know them—the proof is easy.[1]

Thus invincibly armed, Hobhouse fell upon Dallas with gusto:

> . . . We do not intend to permit the notice of this trumpery volume to draw us into a general comment on the character of the extraordinary person whom it was meant to defame. . . . We shall not introduce any more facts respecting Lord Byron than may be just sufficient to portray, in their proper colours, the author and editor of these Recollections. . . . It appears on their own showing that Mr R. C. Dallas, having made as much money as he could out of Lord Byron in his life time, resolved to pick up a decent livelihood (either in his own person or that of his son) out of his friend's remains when dead. . . .
>
> But it appears that Mr R. C. Dallas could not wait for his money so long as was requisite, and that in the year 1819 he became a little impatient to touch something in his life time: accordingly in an evil hour, he writes a long, long letter to Lord Byron, containing a debtor and creditor account between R. C. Dallas and his Lordship; by which, when duly balanced, it appeared that the said Lord Byron was still considerably in arrears of friendship and obligation to the said R. C. Dallas, and ought to acquit himself by a remittance of *materials*. . . .
>
> Lord Byron, however, seems to have entertained very different notions

[1] Murray MSS.

as to the nature of the account between the parties; he sent no *materials*; and Mr R. C. Dallas . . . consoled himself with the notion that his manuscript would be worth something at some time or other, and that either alive or dead, Lord Byron would still be forced to furnish some hundreds of pounds to him and his heirs. . . .

The booksellers . . . were so active as to be prepared to bring their goods to market before Lord Byron's funeral. Nay, more . . . they contrived to announce it for publication on the very day that the remains of Lord Byron were carried through the streets of London, on their way to the family vault in Nottinghamshire. Certainly, no scheme short of arresting the body itself could seem better imagined for discharging Lord Byron's debts to Mr R. C. Dallas.

Those were spacious days for reviewers, and Hobhouse could take his time in disposing of his victim, mounting up in paragraph after paragraph examples of his meanness, ingratitude, and 'malignant bigotry'. The task was one it gave him considerable satisfaction to perform.

When the *Quarterly* had refused his Exposure of Medwin, he had been obliged to turn elsewhere for a publisher, and Bowring of the *Westminster Review* agreed to take the article on Dallas with it; so the two counterblasts appeared together, with some polemics against Southey for good measure. Most unluckily for Hobhouse, Dallas managed to evade the crushing defeat prepared for him. He died while the number was in the press.

Hobhouse did not withdraw his denunciation—there was no reason to spare Dallas, who had not spared Byron—but he was now at the disadvantage, in the eyes of the world, of attacking a dead man. Though it was doubtless agreeable to harass Dallas junior—the scoundrel parson, as he called him[1]—it was not the same thing as bringing down alive the real antagonist. He might have taken comfort, and gloried in fresh contempt, if he could have seen a letter the parson, whose literary style might have given Dickens a hint or two for Mr Chadband, wrote to his vicar:

> My book! Oh, my dear friend, what a hard, hard trial that unhappy book is to me! I cannot tell you half that it has brought upon me. . . . There is a most unwarranted attack upon me in the Westminster Review. The writer has misquoted and misstated my book. Pray for me, my dear friend. I need your prayers much, very much. . . .
>
> Nevertheless, the book sells; 1300 copies were sold the first day. I hope they will continue to sell, for the loss upon the other book is most ruinous, upwards of £500. . . .[2]

[1] British Museum: Additional MSS. 31037. Letter to Augusta Leigh, 1 Dec. 1824. Dallas senior was already dead at this date, but Hobhouse was unaware of it.

[2] DALLAS, Rev. Alex. R. C. The book he refers to as his was the English edition, in which the text of the letters was paraphrased. 'The other book' was the one with the injunction upon it.

Alexander Dallas had found 'his father's spiritual state a heavy burden on his heart'. On his death-bed, Robert Dallas had uttered despairing expressions 'which could only be met by argument and prayer', but before the end his son's ministrations had been effective. 'He is deeply impressed with the tardiness of his awakening . . . his strivings are awfully vehement.'[1] There was nothing he had striven for more vehemently than the publication of the Byron work, which he laid as a sacred charge on his heir, and the pious rancour of which would have made him an easy target for Hobhouse's wrath.

The Medwin exposure also had disappointing results. For all the stings he had inflicted, the half-pay lieutenant was, or at least appeared, a very light-weight adversary, and the ponderous blows that Hobhouse rained on him had the effect of arousing sympathy for the victim. Hobhouse would have served his cause much better if he had not assumed the whole work to be fictitious. In solemnly indicting each blunder as a wanton deception, he provoked the inevitable retaliation that the deceiver was Byron, and even the far-fetched theory that Byron was purposely hoodwinking Medwin because he recognized in him a would-be Boswell.

To mislead a future biographer on matters of fact would have been quite out of character in Byron (though not out of the character of the person who first put forward the idea, Edward J. Trelawny); and the topics he discussed showed that he was not talking for publication. His marriage, for example, had already been dealt with fully in the Memoirs John Murray had purchased.

Hobhouse might have shaken the reader's confidence by proving that Medwin's memory was defective and his understanding of Byron poor; instead he brought defenders to his side. Anonymity was also a handicap. His respected if not popular name, his open attestation of long familiarity with one whom Medwin had observed superficially, could not have failed to carry weight. Withholding his identity suggested weakness.

Lady Byron told her friend, the Rev. Frederick Robertson, that he had done so because Medwin threatened to fight a duel with him.[2] Persistently underrating Byron and everyone who was attached to him, she always attributed unworthy motives to them. When Medwin did, in fact, send a challenge, it was not Hobhouse who flinched.

On September 2nd, 1825, Hobhouse had occasion to write a very long journal entry. First there was the interminable and depressing business of the war in Greece. He and his friends on the Greek Committee had been rash enough to engage, for an immense fee, the mercenary and dilatory Admiral Lord Cochrane to attack the Turks with steam boats. The boats

---

[1] Ibid. Letter of 19 Sept. 1824.
[2] Robertson's Notes on a Conversation with Lady Byron, Jan. 1851: Lovelace Papers.

were not yet built, and it sometimes seemed that they never would be built. Moreover, Cochrane had been speculating in Greek script and advising others to do the same, which was imprudent to say the least in one who had already been involved in a financial scandal.

Then the morning mail had brought a letter from a Mr Humphreys at Zante stating that Trelawny was

> shut up in a fortified cave on Parnassus having under his charge the family and treasures of the late Greek chieftain Odysseus who was killed attempting to escape from the citadel at Athens—that a Scotsman tried to assassinate him and did wound him severely, and that he (Humphreys) having visited him in his cave was afterwards arrested by the Government at Napoli [di Romania]
>
> Trelawny remains blockaded in the cave and is afraid to give himself up either to Greeks or Turks as he has a good deal of money with him.

'He has married a sister of Ulysses', Hobhouse added without comment. Not being aware of what he soon afterwards learned—that Odysseus had abandoned the war against the Turks and Trelawny with him—Hobhouse at once wrote to the latter's uncle, Sir Christopher Hawkins, and suggested measures for getting the British Government to interfere.

> I had also this morning a letter from the scoundrel Thomas Medwin dated 22 August, stating that the Westminster Review of his *work* had only *just* reached him, that he had heard from unquestionable authority I was the author—that it was a tissue of lies and calumnies—and that if I would give him the satisfaction that would enable him to wipe the stain of [*sic*] his *character* he would come to England.
>
> Burdett advised me not to answer or notice this billet doux—the time which the fellow had taken to make up his mind to this step—for I am sure the review had reached him long ago (Mrs Shelley told me so by letter in April last)—the nature of the charge, and the character of the accuser would have fully justified my silence—but after some reflexion I thought it would be the shortest way to let the infamous defamer know that I was ready to be met with whenever he might choose to enquire after me, so I wrote to him thus.

Sept. 2   1825

Sir,
   You must know that your letter admits of no answer, but if you have any thing to say to me personally I shall remain in England for the next six months and am always to be heard of at No 6 Albany Court Yard in London.
   I am

Your obdt hble sert
J. C. H.

It would not have been right to acknowledge that he had the right to fasten an anonymous publication on me, or even to ask me if I was the author, for the interests of society require that folly and impudence and villainy should be chastised by anonymous criticism. If, however, the rogue does come to me I will tell him in good set phrase what I think of him and his *work*, before I let him have a shot at me. It will be a sad thing if I should be forced to put myself on a level with such a miscreant. When one does fight one likes it to be with a man of character—but whatever happens I have the consolation of thinking that I interfered in this instance merely to do good to society by the exposure of a base fraud and to rescue my late friend's character from the hands of an impostor.[1]

Hobhouse was getting on for forty, and even in his ardent and rebellious youth he had never been much of a duelling man. It is apparent that he took up the challenge reluctantly, but he did take it up. It need not have disturbed him. Medwin's bluff was called, and though he attacked Hobhouse again and again with all the venom that was in him, he did so on paper—and from a safe distance.

In his two-volume Life of Shelley, he not only vilified Hobhouse, but turned on Byron, who, on his own showing, had never done him anything but kindness. Though it was published as late as 1847, Hobhouse was still playing a King Charles's Head rôle, having at one point upwards of seventeen consecutive pages of abuse devoted to him, quite disconnected from the theme of the book. Every conceivable material that could injure his affection for Byron's memory was introduced.

Thomas Moore was also insensately attacked, and Byron's cruel lampoon on Rogers was dragged into the text though it was completely irrelevant and had not even the merit of a first appearance, having already been published in Fraser's Magazine.[2] The satirical remarks on 'the Beau, the Bard, and the Banker' (Campbell, Moore, and Rogers, poets whom Byron, sharing the taste of his time, had admired) were of the grossest kind, and demonstrated that the puerility of the author's talent was only less than the vulgarity of his spite.

Earlier, in the 1830's, he had squeezed a little further revenue from Byron by introducing him into his two discursive volumes called *The Angler in Wales*, but the new conversations were almost candidly bogus, a feeble imitation of the Noctes Ambrosianæ of *Blackwood's Magazine*.

After a brief phase of prosperity through his marriage to a woman with money, Medwin had become a seedy drifter, trading tirelessly on anecdotes of Byron and Shelley, the latter by this time as highly honoured as before he had been denigrated. He had developed the most grandiose notions of the importance of his book on Byron, exaggerating audaciously the number of editions it had appeared in and the sums the publishers had made out of it, and demanding a word for word credence quite at variance

[1] Hobhouse *Journals*.
[2] The copy was secretly supplied to the editor by Lady Blessington, another writer who used Byron as a weapon against those who had aroused her resentment.

with his original statement that the conversations were 'the substance without the form'.

Although his name had never been missing from the title page, he seems to have entertained some confused belief that he had brought the book out anonymously. Thus, when in 1849 or 1850 he decided to revise and reprint it, he composed a new preface which began:

> More than 25 years have elapsed since the publication of these Conversations—which have past [sic] through half that number of Editions. A friend of mine many years ago told me that I had thrown them on the world like a bastard child. The time is arrived for patronising the offspring, and that parental Duty I now perform.

If this does not mean that he was at last putting his name to a hitherto anonymous production, it cannot mean anything, and yet it was written on a Contents page of the printed volume![1] The thought of Hobhouse and Moore came over him with all its old bitterness, and he continued: 'Though the wounds I received no longer bleed the scars remain.'

But he crossed out that admission and resumed his blustering style:

> The difference between my remorseless enemies and myself is that they endeavoured by falsehood that they thought could not be detected as such and through the medium of a venal press and the influence of the God Almighty of publishers to injure the fame of one who stood single and was therefore a fair mark for calumny and to suppress a book which will be wanted as long as the name of Byron endures.
>
> The real question before the World is whether I had an opportunity of seeing Lord Byron and reporting his Conversation, whether I took notes of what passed between us and whether the result is not a lively and faithful picture of the ordinary mode of passing his time, and habits of that very extraordinary man.
>
> If I had underrated his line of conversation or given a false colour to his character, or misrepresented his estimate of contemporary talent, or taken away the life and spirit of an interesting anecdote by the way of telling it the public would have had reason to complain—nor would the work be in the repute it is abroad—have been translated into German several times— into French and often reprinted in France and Belgium. When I met Lord Byron in Pisa I had just returned from India. Many of the topics of his Conversation were new to me, most of his contemporaries unknown. It is monstrous to suppose that I could have had any Interest in libelling them.

This was dust thrown in the prospective reader's eyes, for the book was not written when Medwin had newly come from India, but more than three years later, when there had been plenty of time for him to learn about the famous men of letters whom he had formerly discussed; and the preface to the first edition, as well as his correspondence with Mrs Shelley, explicitly referred to the trouble he knew he would be causing.

[1] In the Houston Library of Harvard University.

He grew sillier and sillier, claiming that his sketch showed Byron *en déshabille* whereas 'with Messrs Moore and Murray knowing that all he wrote them would appear in print after his death he was playing a part'.

The idea that Byron revealed himself unreservedly to Medwin—a man he had received simply as a friend of Shelley's—while playing a part with Moore and Murray whom he had seen or corresponded with intimately for more years than, in the other case, there had been months, could only have occurred to a mind which had become impenetrable.

> If my work had no pretensions to authorship it occupied scarcely 3 weeks and was taken literally from my Diary.

Here even Medwin must have perceived that he had entered upon dangerous ground, and perhaps that realization was why the projected new edition never appeared. If the conversations were literally copied from a diary, why had he never so much as hinted at producing it? What better method of refuting Hobhouse could there have been than to confront him with the daily dated records of Byron's utterances? How carefully would so powerful a means of self-defence have been hoarded! The fact that the diary has never come to light suggests that he dared not let his critics see the flimsy scaffolding on which he had raised his structure.

No doubt in the first thrill of conversing familiarly with a great celebrity, he did write down with diligence what he remembered, but as the novelty wore off, the entries must have grown less expansive and, judging from results, slovenly recollection was the sole source from which the substance of a couple of magazine articles was padded out into a quarto.

His opportunities too had soon diminished. An undated letter from Augusta Leigh to Hobhouse, in the Murray archives, quotes a statement by Fletcher which the latter was willing, and indeed anxious, to publish. It described Medwin as:

> . . . A mean, despicable, low Villan, [sic] whom my Lord has so repeatedly sent from his door & moreover said "if he calls a thousand times I will never see him"—"if I see him it shall be when I ride, but *no time* else & never alone" ! ! ! ! ! My Lord has said to me more than twenty times "I will not see him & send him to — — — —" ! — — — —

Medwin must certainly have exaggerated greatly the number and length of his *tête-a-tête* sessions with Byron.

Nevertheless something emerges which has biographical value—something comparable with a distinct likeness achieved by a bad draftsman. Even in drawing grotesquely wrong conclusions, Medwin gives a glimpse of Byron which brings him vividly before us. His eager praise of the anonymous ode in a magazine, his hurrying away from the dinner table to find his copy and read it to the company, are brush-strokes in a realistic portrait, though the artist casts shade instead of light.

We can see when the subject is smiling though the artist does not—as when somebody told him that the English plum pudding he had ordered was not good. 'Not good,' said he (and Medwin gives it as an example of his avarice), 'why, it ought to be good, it cost fifteen pauls.' It is almost incredible that such a remark was taken seriously by one who was a guest, so he tells us, at a weekly dinner party at which the miser provided 'every sort of wine, every luxury of the season, and English delicacy. . . . I never knew a man do the honours of his house with greater kindness and hospitality.'

We can tell too, the difference between the frown of anger and the frown of pique. Medwin thought Byron insincere in his assertion that his tragedy, *Marino Faliero*, had not been written for the stage, and that his disclaimer was due solely to its failure. Any sensible observer would have recognized that a dramatist with practical experience of Drury Lane management would not have composed a play bristling with theatrical difficulties if he had destined it for performance, and that to get an injunction against performance is an odd step for a man to take when he has been writing for the theatre.

Medwin is invariably incapable of reckoning by any measure but a personal and petty one, so that his opinions and interpretations are worth little; but his very surprise at finding himself dining at Byron's table or sharing his nocturnal musings, sharpened his vision for the registration of appearances, if not facts, and in the beginning at any rate he did seek to convey what he had seen.

Hobhouse, with his meticulous accuracy, naturally despised Medwin. He was disgusted by his impudence and his lack of reticence, and ashamed that a man of Byron's stature should have had the smallest association with him. The book also brought upon him annoyances which we can only gauge by imagining how we ourselves should feel if some half-informed stranger were to put in circulation foolish and embarrassing views about persons and topics of the greatest moment to us.

Yet, though we may sympathize with his resentment—which was lifelong—we cannot but wish that he had fought his battle more adroitly. Medwin's production was irresponsible but it was not written with the express object of defamation. There were books to come which were much more deserving of being held up to obloquy, but Hobhouse squandered his rage and energy on small fry and was almost exhausted when it came to contending with Byron's dedicated enemies.

Brougham's conduct towards Byron

Brougham's first assault on Byron was the sledge-hammer blow delivered at the unpretending little volume brought out when the poet was nineteen, *Hours of Idleness*. It was an incomprehensible attack for a lawyer of thirty to make upon a youth whose work had been out for months, barely noticed. The secret of authorship was well kept, and Byron attributed it for many years to Francis Jeffrey. Whenever Brougham was suspected, he was firm in denial, and it was not till long after Byron's death that he admitted the truth.[1]

No doubt Byron's brilliant and effective rejoinder had been an embarrassing surprise, and when he became famous, Brougham's animosity must have been heightened by the consciousness that, if found out, he would be deemed to have made a singular fool of himself. He had facetiously and arrogantly counselled the literary aspirant that he should 'forthwith abandon poetry' and turn his talent to better account,

> . . . We must beg leave seriously to assure him, that the mere rhyming of the final syllable, even when accompanied by the presence of a certain number of feet . . . is not the whole art of poetry. We would entreat him to believe that a certain portion of liveliness, somewhat of fancy, is necessary to constitute a poem: and that a poem of the present day, to be read, must contain at least one thought.[2]

Another kind of man might have owned a blunder, laughed over it, and become friends with Byron, as Byron himself became friends with several whom he had unfairly aimed at in *English Bards and Scotch Reviewers*; but this was not in Brougham's nature. He was delighted when the victor again became the victim.

Hobhouse's diary for 1816 contains many examples of his spite against Byron during the period of the latter's fall from society's good graces.[3] As one of Lady Byron's legal advisers, Brougham was in a position to do great harm, and his whisperings about a reason for separation 'too horrid to mention' were probably second only to the gossip of Caroline Lamb as a cause of ostracism. Byron ascribed Brougham's hatred, when he learned of it, to his having made some unlucky remark about Mrs George Lamb, unaware at the time that Brougham was in love with her.

The next occasion to do injury was provided by the two Separation poems, 'Fare Thee Well' and the 'Sketch' of Mrs Clermont. By passing on copies privately obtained from John Murray to the unscrupulous editor

---

[1] DUFF.   [2] *Edinburgh Review*, Jan. 1808.
[3] See Appendix 1 to Chapter I.

of a Sunday newspaper, the *Champion*, he was able to ensure publication and a storm of resentment, most especially bitter on the part of Lady Byron's family.[1]

An equally fruitful opportunity of inflicting misery occurred in Switzerland, when Brougham was able not only to circulate evil stories wherever Byron was kindly received, and particularly at Mme de Staël's, but also to make certain that any attempt at reconciliation should fail in a humiliating manner. The following letter is so full of artful malignance that one cannot but compassionate the man who, however wrongly he had behaved, had such deep machinations in train against him:

Geneva Augt 23. 1816

Dear Lady B.

I hesitated for some time before I resolved to write to you—for I thought it could serve no other purpose than to open wounds hardly yet healed— But I cannot take upon myself the responsibility of not writing, and therefore I must run the risk of giving you pain—

You are probably aware that Lord B. is living in this neighbourhood— avoided by the numerous English who are here—and associating with hardly anybody—I have met him two or three times without taking any notice of him—but I have heard of his speaking of me to one or two persons in a way to shew that he wished to meet me—However, I have carefully shunned him, and should continue to do so were I to remain here—I came about seven weeks ago & go to Milan tomorrow.

The language he holds upon all occasions to such as will listen to him, is that of despondency; and he says (at least to those who are likely to repeat it to me or one or two other friends of your's who are here) that he has no blame whatever to impute to you—in short he says, to those persons, every sort of good of you—and only accuses you of being unforgiving—You may easily imagine how much pains I have taken to undeceive them & to shew that forgiveness was impossible—

But of late I have been assailed in another manner—He is, or at least expresses himself very sollicitous [*sic*] of a reconciliation—and in such a manner as to shew he is desirous his professions should come round to me— I have said that whoever thought this possible knew nothing of the story— Nevertheless—you must judge & not I—Therefore I tell you exactly what I have heard—

I shall now give you my opinion—I think it very possible it may only be another device to put you if possible in the wrong & make people believe the separation rests with you—But it is also possible that he may be feeling the annoyance attending his situation—& may wish to regain some footing of esteem in Society—He may find reports spreading & wish to give them a refutation, by having once more your countenance—

Whatever his motive may be, I cannot fancy for a moment that it is a good one—especially considering the life he has been leading here—But I must beg you to consult your own feelings & your own judgment—premising

[1] See Appendix 1 to Chapter IV.

that whatever answer you may give me, I shall of course entirely obey your instructions. . . .

I have let my own clear & decided opinion appear perhaps too plainly—but you will of course lay it quite out of your view—

. . . I assure you no one takes a deeper interest in your welfare & happiness—I know too well what misery is not to feel for my fellow sufferers—even were they far less interesting than you—

Believe me your sincere & faithful friend

H. Brougham[1]

Lady Byron wrote back a letter of bitter severity against Byron, empowering Brougham to communicate whatever he thought proper from it to those who concerned themselves with the matter. This crossed with another from Brougham telling her he had now learned that Mme de Staël had sent an overture of reconciliation from Byron through Lady Romilly:

Had I known of it I should have tried to prevent it—as such a thing *can* only give you annoyance—

. . . I trust and hope that this new attempt against your peace (for such only I can consider it) will fail & that you will not take any notice of it—[2]

Hobhouse knew that Brougham had been Byron's enemy, but had no idea of the strength and extent of his ill will, or he might not have consulted him about publishing the pamphlet against Medwin and Dallas. It would have been reasonable for Brougham to advise him to modify his too vehement tone and to use a lighter touch; but his recommendation to suppress the rebuttal altogether was very unfortunate. If Hobhouse had come out under his own name as one prepared to deal openly and fearlessly with opportunist productions about Byron, he might have prevented much mischievous publishing.

[1] Lovelace Papers.   [2] Ibid. 12 Sept. 1816.

CHAPTER IV

WIDOW, SISTER, AND FORTUNE

The year of Byron's death was an exceedingly chequered one for Augusta Leigh. Her grief was real and overwhelming, but it must have been tempered to some extent by the knowledge that what he had left her would relieve her ever-pressing monetary difficulties.

The determination to make Augusta the villainess of a drama has fostered such misunderstandings as to her inheritance from Byron and her financial affairs in general that some plain figures will be serviceable. Byron left about £100,000, of which a portion was used to pay debts, substantially more than £64,000 was spent on securing Lady Byron's jointure, and £16,000 (four-fifths of Lady Byron's dowry) was placed in trust for his daughter, Ada.

'. . . When I married you—I settled all I could—& almost all I had upon you', Byron wrote to his wife in one of the letters his grandson did not see fit to publish, 'and though strongly advised & justified in demanding a settlement of your father's disposable property—I would not—& did not—solely from delicacy to you—& to your family.'[1]

Indeed the arrangements in her favour were far beyond the means he then had, and beyond what her carefully tied-up and only partly paid dowry of £20,000 entitled her to, according to the materialistic code of the day. As shown in a paper drawn up by Byron's solicitor for legal consideration when a separation was demanded:

> Lord Byron did not possess a Shilling with Lady Byron. All the Fortune which her Ladyship had, was 16,000£ provided by her Father's Marriage Settlement. . . . And her Father entered into a Covenant to add £4000 to it in three years, making £20,000.
>
> This £20,000 was settled on Lady Byron and her issue—Sir Ralph Noel did not settle any other Part of his Estates or fortune on his Daughter, whilst Lord Byron settled £60,000 of his Property on Lady Byron and her Children. Out of this £80,000 Lady Byron has a Pin Money of £300 a Year during Coverture and will take a Jointure of £2000 a year for her Life in case she survives his Lordship.
>
> Lord Byron on the Proposal for a Separation, to which he was averse, was advised to object to the Admissability of any Arrangement respecting the Wentworth Property now in Contingency.[2]

[1] 11 Mar. 1816: Lovelace Papers.

[2] Ibid. and Murray MSS. Copy of Hanson's Statement of Mar. 1816. The reason why £60,000 produced only £2000 a year was partly that there was a mortgage to be repaid and partly that the money was very badly invested in Government Funds. Byron repeatedly appealed for reinvestment (there was also capital depreciation) but this was refused by the Trustees.

This Wentworth property was what his mother-in-law, Lady Noel, who was Lord Wentworth's heiress, was bound by entail to leave to her only child. But Lord Wentworth's will was so worded—though this was not known till after his niece's marriage and his death—that Byron would ultimately control the estate, a perfectly normal state of affairs in those days when husbands commonly had the property of their wives in their power. At the time of the Separation, great pressure was brought to bear upon him to renounce this legal right, but—as Hanson's Statement shows —he was advised against it.

In his own words, from the letter last quoted:

. . . The Wentworth property is no part of present consideration—it may never be the subject of consideration at all:—*You* may survive me (I hope you will) Lady Noel may survive you—or both—If I survive you it ceases to me. When the time comes—if it does come—I will do what is right—you have no reason—at least no just one—to doubt me on such points. . . .

If however you doubt me—in the event of the succession to the W. estates—you will *then* have the means of redress should I seem to you reluctant in making proper arrangements:—but in the present case—whatever your success might be in the probable cause which may ensue—*possessions* & not *reversions* are under the cognizance of the Courts.

At all events—I shall not submit to such measures as may lead to further misconstructions of my conduct. . . . If the W. property falls in—I will make what shall be fully allowed to be fair & liberal arrangements—but I will not be menaced—nor forced into any present stipulations—nor deprived of the pleasure of acting of my own accord towards yourself—at least as liberally as the law would desire for you—supposing (for it is but a supposition) that you carried it all before you. . . .

P.S. As I do not write with a lawyer at my elbow—I must request a fair construction of what I have written.

Lady Byron did write with a lawyer at her elbow, and was warned that the best that could be done was to persuade her husband to agree to an arbitration when the contingency arose. As she herself admitted—'it was at his option to make a provision for me out of it [the Wentworth Estate] or not'.[1]

The arbitration was consented to, and when Lady Noel died in 1822, Lord Dacre was appointed for Lady Byron, Sir Francis Burdett for Byron. Their decision was that the income should be shared equally between the two, an award based on the marriage settlement and the extent to which Byron had thereby placed his own fortune out of his reach. Those critics who have described him as living on his wife's money are wanting either in fairness or in information.

In her statements touching their financial situation, Lady Byron gave

[1] Letter to Mme Mojon, 10 May 1841: Lovelace Papers.

utterance to conflicting views. She naturally did not care for it to be said
that the poet had married her because she was an heiress, and so was at
pains to point out that the disposition of her uncle's property was quite
uncertain at the time. On the other hand, the story of her ill usage would
not have been complete without mercenary motives. Hence she would
convey the idea that, though he had not exactly married her for money,
he had had her money and made free with it. For example, in a letter to
Mme Mojon, wife of one of her many medical advisers, she wrote:

> My fortune (dot) given by my father on my marriage was £20,000,
> which was entirely at Lord Byron's disposal.[1]

This, in any less favoured witness, would have been called falsehood.
Four-fifths of that dowry, as has been shown, was settled on her daughter,
and of this not more than £6000 had actually been made available before
the Separation. The remaining fifth was not paid at all during Byron's
lifetime, only the interest on the capital being produced. The rate was 5
per cent. Out of the total income of £1000 which the £20,000 yielded,
Lady Byron received £300 for the year 1815, and £500 per annum
afterwards.

> Lord Byron bequeathed all his property to his sister Mrs Leigh, and her
> family for ever [she further explained]—Ada inherited nothing from him:
> but £16,000 had been settled upon a daughter by the marriage settle-
> ment.
> The amount of property bequeathed to Mrs Leigh in present and in
> reversion was more than £100,000.

There is no hint in this that two-thirds of the purchase price of
Newstead Abbey had gone to provide the jointure, that Ada's portion was
the bulk of her own dowry, stated to have been 'entirely at Lord Byron's
disposal', or that Mrs Leigh could not receive 'all his property' unless
Lady Byron and Ada pre-deceased her, and was only in possession of a
fraction of the £100,000 described as having been left to her. It was this
arrangement of the facts which was presented to all sympathizers and
particularly Lady Byron's susceptible grandson, the author of *Astarte*.

Acrimony about money matters is the usual accompaniment of matrimonial disasters, and the Byron separation and its aftermath provided a
great deal of it—less on Byron's part than on that of his wife and mother-
in-law. Their grumblings—natural and human, but not heroic—were
never quoted in Lord Lovelace's writings.

By the time Lady Byron became a widow, her mother was dead, her
father, aged seventy-seven, was hastening to his end. The sole owner now
of the Wentworth property, which Byron had only encumbered for two

[1] Letter to Mme Mojon, 10 May 1841: Lovelace Papers.

years, she was richly provided for, and had no occasion to grudge Augusta a legacy of, at the most, about £25,000.[1] But Augusta seems to have sensed that she would take umbrage, if not on her own behalf on that of George Anson Byron, whose means were insufficient for his elevation to the peerage.

She wrote apologetically both to Lady Byron and the new lord, begging to know what she could do to assist him, making suggestions about insurance policies for his children: but he would not be appeased, and soon, as has been shown, he annulled all her good-will by virtually sponsoring Dallas's objectionable book.

Whatever lofty motives Lady Byron may have had when she had first set herself up as Augusta's 'guardian angel', she could be satisfied with nothing less than absolute subservience from one who was, as she saw it, completely at her mercy. She had made Augusta abject and had then luxuriated in being magnanimous towards her, but she desired the penitent to wear sackcloth and ashes for ever. At any sign that sackcloth was discarded, she became profoundly annoyed.

Money inherited from Byron by Augusta was a reward for wickedness. She felt an extravagant sympathy for George Byron and his wife, and under its influence decided to let them have the income from her marriage settlement. They were thus much better off than they would have been if Byron had left them all he was free to leave—and proportionately devoted to their benefactress.

Somehow the good deed got into the newspapers. It was just when Byron's body had arrived in London, and not guessing Annabella was still implacable (for she herself could never be) Augusta was telling her what she thought would be flattering and comforting:

> . . . I hear that Col. Stanhope (who has offered to come to me) says that he talked latterly *much* of *you*—& in very kind terms & of his child with the greatest affection—I mention this because I think it will give you pleasure. . . . I treasure up for you all that I hope & think can give you a particle of satisfaction. . . .
>
> If I understand you rightly dearest A, I fear you have been annoyed by the concluding sentence of the Paragraph in the Newspaper giving an account of the Will. I mean that which states your having given up yr Jointure to G. B—as '*a proof at least*' &c &c &c. . . .

[1] Hanson, Hobhouse's co-executor, gave £15,377 as the sum from the trust fund available for Mrs Leigh, but there were also £8312 in personal assets of Byron's, and later a few thousands from the sale of copyrights. Some outstanding debts, and numerous gifts of money to the servants, to the doctors and Count Pietro Gamba, depleted the total amount. There was also the payment of costs and fine for Leigh Hunt's brother. What with these and normal legal charges, £25,000 is probably an optimistic estimate for Augusta's legacy. It was increased in 1828 by £4000, the part of Lady Byron's dowry which Sir Ralph had been unable to produce in his lifetime, and which was not settled on Ada.

I am very sorry you have been annoyed by it,[1] & you may be sure it does not originate with Mr Hobhouse—My wishes & feelings on this point must be so well known to *you* that it is needless to repeat them—it is a most painful subject to me—but at the same time it is my duty I am sure to be grateful for the very unexpected blessing (& the *very* undeserved one) of thinking that my Children will not be Beggars—

Your mention of the arrangements you have *so* kindly made with G. B—— is the *first* communication *I* have had on the subject except from public report—I think it *Most* extraordinary that he has never named it to me or to his own sister.[2]

Augusta's humility was having its customary soothing effect, and Lady Byron wrote the same day—the letters may have crossed—in a strain that was not ungracious, but was not ingenuous either:

It has occurred to me that since the contents of the Will are public, *my* authority for opinions concerning it may be falsely alleged by some. I assure you that I have not given any opinion which could possibly be quoted respecting the dispositions of the property. I am very far from wishing to deny now what I have more than once said to my husband—that it was his duty to provide for you and yours—how far *exclusively* is a question which I am relieved to be under no necessity of discussing—and therefore certainly shall say nothing about the matter, whatever may be said for me.[3]

The implied criticism of the 'exclusiveness' of the will related not only to George Byron, but to what was to be a theme full of bitterness in the years to come. In default of a male heir, Augusta's children were to have the reversion of the capital settled in trust for his widow. Augusta herself, contrary to what some biographers have supposed, never had this money, having died nine years before Lady Byron. Lord Lovelace wrote of the 'spoliation' of Lady Byron's daughter and of George Byron, of Augusta's 'grasping covetousness', and of her 'robbery' of the family,[4] but it is to be remembered that the will was made when Lady Byron was pregnant in 1815, and Byron fully expected to have sons, and had not the slightest anticipation that his marriage was to break up after the birth of the expected child. Whatever he may have said in black moods about wishing all he had could go to Augusta (there are depositions from Mrs Clermont to this effect) the will was fairly and thoughtfully drawn up and Lady Byron given a chance to approve its conditions.

It must have seemed to the young man of twenty-seven a remote contingency that his money would pass away from his own descendants, and hardly needful to provide for an heir-presumptive who had so little

[1] The *Morning Chronicle* had incomprehensibly mentioned Lady Byron's sacrifice of her jointure as a proof that she must have approved of her husband's 'dispositions to the female branch of his family . . .'

[2] 7 July 1824: Lovelace Papers.   [3] MAYNE, *Lady Byron*.

[4] Lovelace, *Lady Noel Byron*. Miss Mayne takes her tone on this, as on most other topics, from Lord Lovelace, though in more restrained terms.

prospect of coming into the title as his cousin George. Later, when he realized there would be no son, the defection of his cousin and the liberal expectations of his daughter combined to discourage any change in the 1815 arrangements. But weeks after his wife had left him, he was still persuaded that they would be reunited and that she would give him an heir, and in the belief—by no means groundless—that his mother-in-law had helped to sever them, he wrote to her with an impudence which staggered her:

Feby 27th
1816

Dear Lady Noel—
    Augusta has communicated your account of my little girl.
    I am glad to hear that it is so fine a child—& I hoped that I could have contrived another for you still finer—had it so pleased Lady Byron (& yourself) to have continued encreasing our antient & respectable families—

Yours very truly
Bn[1]

That Augusta, aged thirty-two, had plotted to inherit the fortune of a brother five years younger than herself,[2] married and awaiting the arrival of his first-born, is so far-fetched an idea that only a very acute sense of injury could have conceived it.

Byron's legacy of more or less £25,000 did not go far because she was deep in long-standing debt when it was put in trust for her. She lived without ostentation but was a bad manager, and her husband had always had all he could lay hands on of whatever money she could raise. The feckless blood of the Byrons was uncorrected in her and her children by the canny Gordon strain which had been the salvation of her half-brother. Her sons were expensively educated to follow their father's far-from-gainful profession as officers, or to wait till some influential friend should provide them with sinecures. So far as the struggling mother could manage it, her daughters had to be equipped and dowered for the marriage market. One of them, her namesake, was mentally unbalanced, and was looked after away from home at a cost of £200 per annum—fully as much as the fees of a boy at Eton.

Whatever the economic difficulties might be, Colonel Leigh never dreamed of doing without his manservant and his creature comforts, while Augusta, who moved in the most exalted circles, was obliged to keep up the appearance expected of an attendant upon royalty. It needed no blackmailers to account for the shifts and straits to which this cornered victim of heredity and a preposterous social system was reduced.

---

  [1] Lovelace Papers.
  [2] Lord Lovelace erroneously gives the difference as four years. Augusta was born in 1783, Byron in 1788.

The conjecture that Augusta had been impoverished by paying black-mail money was suggested to Lord Lovelace by Lady Wilmot Horton, one of the longest-lived of Lady Byron's confidantes, in a letter of January 1870.

> . . . It has always appeared to me to be the most conclusive Evidence against poor Mrs Leigh, the state of abject poverty to which she was reduced—with *no expensive* habits, and no doubt in consequence of the claims made upon her by those who threatened disclosure.[1]

A more reckless speculation could not easily be cited as 'conclusive Evidence!' Only one attempt at pecuniary blackmail is known—a singularly feeble one—and on that occasion, as will be seen, Augusta turned to Hobhouse, John Murray, and her solicitor. Blackmail of another kind, however, found her an easy prey, for her softness of heart was accompanied by a distressing want of moral courage.

Only a fortnight after Sir Francis Burdett had broken to her the news of Byron's death, there was an unpleasant little interchange of letters between her and Mary Anne Clermont, known by a courtesy accorded to superior servants as Mrs Clermont though she was unmarried. Annabella and her parents appear to have addressed her as 'C'. She has come down to posterity chiefly as one who was 'Born in the garret, to the kitchen bred . . .'

May 30th (?), 1824

Dear Mrs Leigh—

I would not willingly have intruded upon your attention at this time, but that my character is again so shamefully traduced in various Newspapers—such Calumny *must* not continue uncontradicted.

You are the person most fully acquainted with *all* that caused and *all* that passed at the separation of Lord and Lady Byron—my chief reason for not before taking any public measure for my own justification was a determination not to injure the Interests of another, as I must inevitably have brought you forward—*all* apprehensions on that account are now removed and I trust you will not hesitate to act towards me as every principle of Justice and your own inclination I have no doubt equally demand, the Measure least annoying to all parties would be that you should give merely a Simple *Declaration of my being entirely innocent of the charges brought against me in the affair of the separation*, this I am certain you can conscientiously give—such a Measure will probably put an end to the unfounded Calumny without any further Proceeding, at least I shall consider it a sufficient vindication of my Character.

This should be done as speedily as possible for reasons which it is un-necessary to mention.

Your Humble Servant,
M. A. Clermont.

[1] LOVELACE, *Lady Noel Byron.*

St. James's Palace, June 1st, 1824

My dear Mrs Clermont,

In answer to the letter I have this Morning received from you, I must beg to assure you how very sorry I am for the annoyance you are now feeling, owing to the Calumnies revived against your character in the Newspapers.

I have—whenever any opportunity has presented itself—not only contradicted them, but also done justice to the kind forbearance I have invariably observed in you—upon occasions most trying to any friend of Lady Byron's—and you may depend upon my continuing to do so.

You are quite at liberty to shew this letter to any of your friends and to express my entire conviction of your being perfectly innocent of the charges brought against you—in any way most satisfactory to yourself, *except through the Channel of a Newspaper* in which it would on every account be extremely painful and unpleasant to me to be brought forward. . . .

Ever my dear Mrs Clermont
Augusta Leigh[1]

The explanation of Mrs Clermont's ability to command this servile response calls for a backward glance into the first months of 1816, when Byron, in a fever of misery, wrote his furious 'Sketch' of her.

While it would be absurd to suppose that it accurately portrayed this privileged retainer of his mother-in-law's house, it is equally ridiculous to accuse him of an unprovoked attack on a defenceless woman. 'C', a character at once pitiful and sinister, played the part of an eager go-between and inveterate mischief-maker at the time of the Separation, and if she had not as much influence as Byron supposed in bringing it about, her letters show that she laboured indefatigably to prevent a reconciliation.

She had been in service in the Milbanke household from girlhood, and had earned the station—more comprehensible in the 18th century than now—of humble domestic confidante, allowed to enjoy certain familiarities and even to criticize and rebuke, but always obliged to be on guard against being ousted from favour, or losing any inch of ground gained, and perpetually conscious of the unspoken admonition: 'So far and no farther shall you go.'[2]

According to her own account:

I was born in the House of my Father a respectable Tradesman the same in which He had lived with a former Wife my Mother being a second Wife my Father died when I was an Infant and my Mother lived in the same until her Death twenty six Years after leaving me and my Brother property to the amount of about a thousand pounds.[3]

---

[1] Ibid.

[2] These are her own words in a letter complaining of Lady Byron's coldness towards her, dated 24 Nov. 1829: Lovelace Papers.

[3] Statement of March 1830, intended for publication but not used.

L.L.B.—K

Lady Byron with a deft touch or two gave her background a more romantic colouring, for it had been most distasteful to see publicized the vulgarity of a woman known as her companion.

Mrs Clermont was the daughter of a French Emigré. She accepted at an early age the situation of Lady's Maid to my Mother, never having left her own family till then—Her education was continued by my Mother, & she was considered fit for the charge of me when I was 7 years old. When Mrs Clermont came into possession of her Family property some years afterwards, she consigned it to my Father, who was then embarrassed, for an Annuity.[1]

Mrs Clermont's fitness to have charge of Miss Milbanke from the age of seven could not have depended on her qualifications as a governess. That must have been, like 'Mrs', a courtesy title. Contrary to Byron's notion—

> She taught the child to read, and taught so well
> That she herself by teaching learned to spell—

Mrs Clermont never learned to spell, at least not reliably, and her grammar was uncertain; but she held some position near enough to make the relationship a most emotional one on her side. In several of her letters she expresses a devotion she herself recognized as obsessive.

It has been my Fate through Life [she wrote in later years] to suffer under the constant effort of repressing feelings, not in themselves wrong, but too strong for the circumstances in which I have been placed. . . . It is no pleasant thing to have none to love or be loved by—upon *you* alone in the days of your infancy and Childhood I could lavish fondness & indulge my affection unrestrained, & I loved you with all the intensity likely to result from undivided affection.[2]

And earlier, after she had first learned that the price of her too successful intervention was exile:

. . . In the present state of your feelings towards me, to address you as formerly would perhaps be considered as presumption on my part—but I cannot refrain from telling you the state of my feelings to you whether credited or not—my affection for you was formed at the time of life when I believe they are most strongly engaged. I have loved you from the Age of eighteen *do* & ever shall it is not even in *your* power to prevent it. . . .[3]

It may easily be imagined that any husband who had won her idol would have come under a somewhat jaundiced scrutiny; but such a husband as Byron—without one domestic virtue except devotion to his sister! She embraced with zeal the duty of dispossessing him.

[1] Notes on Mme Belloc's Life of Byron written for Mme Mojon to transmit to the author, c. 1841: Lovelace Papers.   [2] Ibid. Postmarked 24 Nov. 1829.
[3] Ibid. No date, probably 1816. If she was eighteen at the time of Annabella's birth, as may be assumed from this letter, she was forty-two when she became the subject of Byron's 'Sketch'.

Yet she must have had the manners of an amiable woman to have won so many confidences. Even Byron perceived the quality, for in calling her the 'general spy', he also said she was 'the genial confidante'. Augusta was one of those who played into her hands. She communicated much—how deeply shocked she was by her brother's conduct to his wife, how apprehensive for the violence of his temper, what cruel threatening things he had been saying about his marriage.

All was stored up in 'C's' retentive and dramatic mind to be brought out in the statements furnished for her beloved Annabella's lawyers. The darkest and most desperate of his words (usually uttered, though this does not appear in the depositions, when he was under the effects of heavy drinking) we have only at third-hand—Mrs Clermont's recollections of what Augusta had passed on to her.

The impression she claims to have derived from all she heard was 'that he was likely to put her [Lady Byron] to Death at any moment if he could do it privately. I told Mrs Leigh such was my opinion—she replied I will never leave him alone with her until she is brought to bed, and then you must stay always with her.'[1] What was Augusta up to, adding fuel to the fire that was almost to incinerate Byron? Was she, as Lady Byron afterwards believed, deliberately manœuvring to get him suspected of insanity so that his rash hints might then appear to be mere raving? Scheming so villainous was almost certainly beyond the compass of Augusta's brainless good nature. Look wherever we will among hundreds of her letters, covering a long span of her life, and we shall find only a silly but intensely kind person, treacherous because she was complaisant rather than because she was cunning.

She talked no doubt for a mixture of reasons. The atmosphere was nerve-racking and the personality of the listener inviting. Perhaps she hoped by indignation against Byron to dispel any idea of an excessive affection between them. Perhaps her fear that he would commit some murderous act was genuine, wrought up by her being advanced in pregnancy.[2] She may not have been above enjoying the importance it gave her to be the protector of the wife and the pacifier of the husband. But the anger and dismay at his behaviour which she announced so freely to others did not inspire her to risk any serious quarrel with him. There were sometimes remonstrances, but not to the extent of causing a rift. Otherwise he would not have written those impassioned verses on her loyalty which are pathetic when read beside the Clermont Statements,

---

[1] Ibid. Mary Anne Clermont's Statement, 22 Jan. 1816.

[2] In a letter to Mrs Clermont, 13 Feb. 1816, Lady Byron says Byron never threatened her personally. All the terrors that were complained of can be sifted down to tones of voice and 'expressions of countenance'. In later statements she claims to have been frequently menaced.

and which must have brought very wry smiles to the faces of those who knew what part she had really played.

It is to Lady Byron's credit that Byron was never told of this much-lauded sister's betrayals of him. To Mary Anne Clermont, held up to obloquy in celebrated verse, the undeserved praise bestowed upon Augusta was bitter. As long as she lived she lost no opportunity of reiterating that it was 'a near Relation and most intimate Friend of Lord Byron's who spent several Weeks at different times in his House' who had '*volunteered*' the information about his ill-treatment of his wife:[1] and in her latest years, she remembered that Augusta had pressed her to stay for the confinement, saying she feared that he might injure his wife or even his child.[2]

The difference between the two confidantes, however, was that Augusta went to great lengths to avert the final catastrophe, which she seems not to have realized she had been helping to bring about, whereas Mrs Clermont seized with both hands the chance to keep the tormented couple apart. She had a sanction for her obduracy, Lady Byron having written to her a few days after leaving him:

> I never must see him again—I shall wish otherwise when I am less sane —but let me be preserved from it by every means.[3]

'C' not only busied herself with parents, lawyers, and partisans, but fortified the emotionally torn fugitive almost daily with artful letters:

> . . . Now from all I have been able to collect ever since your departure it does not appear he has any desire that you should return which I confess when you left I thought he would he seems to wish to have letters from you *only* because when asked about you he does not know what to say and constantly declares his dislike to being a Married Man & that he has always felt.
>
> I am now convinced that he first sought you because you took no notice of him when all the Women were fooling him the first morning you met & pride which began urged him to continue the pursuit—the same feeling may now perhaps make him dislike your leaving him but I have not the smallest doubt his real wish is that a separation should take place at the same time he would chuse that you should remain attached to him.
>
> . . . He must feel himself a free man again and he will do it by some means or other even though he should break your heart & have that upon his conscience ever after.
>
> . . . Great powers have been given you by God and you will be criminal in allowing them to be destroyed (which had you continued with him they soon would have been). . . .[4]

---

[1] Statement of March 1830: Lovelace Papers.

[2] Ibid. Physician's Statement, 11 Oct. 1846. She was then about seventy-two. Lady Byron gives the date of her death as 1850.   [3] Ibid. Letter of 21 Jan. 1816.

[4] Ibid. 2 Feb. 1816. 'I hope you don't deceive me and represent things any *harder* than is just', Lady Byron wrote rather pitifully on the 4th.

It would be hard to contrive any exhortation better calculated to stiffen the resolution of a very vain and spoiled girl who undeniably had been given plentiful cause for complaint: and it was succeeded two or three days later by:

> I find *he* wrote to you on Saturday for the sake of your feelings I wish he had not but trust you will not send any unguarded answer as you know he is very capable of taking advantage of them.[1]

This incessant interference came to the knowledge of Byron through Mrs Fletcher, his valet's wife, who was with Lady Byron as personal maid, and also through his housekeeper, Mrs Milward, who had worked in the Noel family and was the wife of Sir Ralph's butler.

> Mrs Milward, together with every other servant in the house, attributed the principal share in the attack upon his Lordship to Mrs Clermont, of whose influence many scandalous stories were told. . . .
> He was aware that this woman had been busily employed in procuring, or rather searching for every proof which might tend to the condemnation of the husband in his suit with his wife.[2]

So wrote Hobhouse, who believed that the incest suspicions had been nurtured by her; but there he was wrong. They had been formed at an early period of that brief married life through Byron's own preoccupation with the theme of guilt, and Lady Byron had with little delay imparted them to Mrs Minns,[3] another personal servant, wife of one of the footmen, and the very first of the army of confidantes who sustained the 'Policy of Silence'.

'C' was, of course, not kept in the dark, but at this time, as Lady Byron herself asserted over and over again, suspicion was all she had to go upon. (A legend, which still circulates, that one night she found Augusta and Byron in *flagrante delicto* is contrary to all the evidence, and would make nonsense of Lady Byron's contemporary letters and other writings.)

For the first few weeks of acting as emissary to all those officially or unofficially concerned on her employer's side, Mrs Clermont spoke well of Augusta, believing they had in her an ally, though admittedly one whose feelings were too favourable to the enemy. Augusta remained with her brother at 13 Piccadilly Terrace, and, being encouraged to regard herself as the close and trusted friend of her 'dearest Sis', sent daily reports of his sayings and doings. These Lady Byron secretly dispatched to her solicitor's office to be certified.

---

[1] Ibid. 5 Feb. 1816.   [2] HOBHOUSE, *Contemporary Account*.
[3] Lady Byron's undated Narrative, written late in life, and designated 'Q' by Lord Lovelace. Lovelace Papers. '. . . I told her I was sure there had been something most dreadful between him & his Sister which he never could recover—I imposed a silence which has been strictly kept.' This was true: Mrs Minns never revealed anything even when very hard pressed.

Augusta had no ability to see below the surface of either of the characters she was dealing with. She failed to perceive either that Lady Byron was cast-iron rather than tempered steel, and incapable of flexibility, or that Byron was only to be taken literally when stating facts, never when giving vent to his intensely variable emotions. It seems simply not to have occurred to her that, though he had spoken resentfully of the ties of marriage, he would be shattered by the departure of his wife; or that Lady Byron, while longing to be back in his house, if only 'in the coal hold',[1] would nevertheless insist on irrevocable estrangement.

When she had before her the spectacle of his suffering, which, whether due to love, remorse, or wounded *amour propre*, was desperate, she regretted her many indiscretions and wrote imploring Annabella not to desert him.

Annabella turned to Mrs Clermont:

Pray don't let me have his death to answer for—if there should be *danger* things must not be pursued too hastily—You *must* consult Le Mann on this.[2]

Mrs Clermont, more implacable at this time than her pupil, replied at once:

I find Lord Byron has his dinner and goes to the Play as usual. . . . Pray do not be so weak as to mind Mrs Leigh's Oh's and Ah's. . . . [it] is quite decisive as to its being his Pride that is affected & not his tenderer feelings.[3]

It was soon apparent that Augusta was no ally at all, and not to be depended on as a witness against Byron. She painted an agonizing picture of his desolation, she represented the private and public ruin that must ensue if, by refusing a reconciliation, Lady Byron confirmed the appalling rumours that were current about him.

'. . . He is sometimes charged with having done even worse things than is true', Mrs Clermont reported with satisfaction after an interview with the lawyer, Dr Lushington. '. . . Were it possible which I think it is not that you should return to him again I would go to the most unlikely place for hearing of you that I could devise & never if I could help it hear of you again.'[4]

In the face of so extensive a series of letters loaded with malice and containing indisputable proofs of all the mischief Byron suspected, it is curious that anyone who ever had access to the documents should have subscribed to the theory that he did a gross injustice to one who never

---

[1] *L. & J.* Lady Byron to Augusta, 20 Jan. 1816.

[2] 4 Feb. 1816. Lovelace Papers. Le Mann was the physician who had been investigating Byron's sanity.

[3] Ibid. 7 Feb. 1816. The following day she was obliged to admit that Byron had gone, not to the Play, but to visit his lawyer.　　　　[4] Ibid. ? 18 Feb. 1816.

gave him cause for animosity. The verses were a piece of invective in the manner of Pope, whose style he more than once resorted to when composing to relieve rage. Their publication, with the famous 'Fare Thee Well' lines, was not only unsanctioned by him, but was, in fact, a dire calamity, for it was accompanied by virulent abuse of his conduct, and extended the hostilities against him from a small society to the world at large.[1]

Byron's baleful prophecies of retribution to be exacted from Mrs Clermont were soon in a considerable measure fulfilled, and partly through the instrumentality of his own verses. It was deemed desirable, after the Separation, that Lady Byron should not be seen to associate too freely with one who had been publicly accused of having a malign influence over her. Arrangements were made to keep her at a distance for a while. At the same time, Lady Byron's feelings underwent the revulsion commonly experienced by those who have allowed themselves to be swayed by advice torturingly at variance with their wishes. The company of the devoted 'C' became unwelcome, and the intimacy which had been the proud happiness of her life declined to the point where she wrote her sad words about 'having none to love or be loved by'.

Her letter of veiled menace to Augusta certainly does not suggest lovable qualities, and all Augusta's weakness both of spirit and position is visible in the prompt reply exonerating this nefarious meddler from having deserved any reproach. Augusta had no courage to ask why she should be held responsible for newspaper paragraphs with which she had not the remotest connection. Her swift gesture of conciliation was doubtless made with an eye upon Lady Byron, to whom she immediately wrote uneasily:

My Dearest A,

   I do not like to worry you with every little circumstance that occurs— but you might think it odd in me not to tell you that I have heard from Mrs Clermont on the subject of the Newspaper paragraphs concerning her— and if she does not communicate with you, you shall have her note and my answer from me—But I am afraid of tormenting you with a *twice told tale.* . . .

Yr. most affec.
A. L.[2]

She was requested, it would seem, to supply the letters, and in doing so abased herself still further:

   I will enclose Mrs C's note, which *pray return*—& my answer which you may burn. I only hope she approved as I have not heard since & I hope you will think I said *all* I *could*.[3]

[1] See Appendix 1 for accounts by Hobhouse and Benjamin Haydon of how the 'Sketch' came to be published.
[2] 3 June 1824: Lovelace Papers.   [3] Ibid. ? 5 June 1824.

Lady Byron did not burn Augusta's letter. Even in the days of their ardent friendship, she had made a practice of keeping letters Augusta had earnestly begged her to burn, and now that she regarded her with disfavour that steadily intensified, she quite systematically amassed evidences against her.

It is painful to watch a young, attractive, and in many ways gifted woman allowing herself to be consumed with vindictiveness passing itself off as righteousness. The pedantic, legalistic tone of many of Lady Byron's letters has tended to obscure the captivating personality which from youth to old age, exercised a powerful charm over all kinds of morally aspiring persons. She had no need to dwell on the past counting over her injuries, for her position, her intelligence, her wealth, and her remarkable ability to command friendship gave her advantages that should have placed her above so destructive an occupation.

Her biographer[1] has made great play with Lady Noel's warning: 'Once more take care of X [Augusta]—if I know anything of human nature she does and must hate you', quoting the passage at least four times, as if it were oracular truth. But she fails to indicate a single episode in which Augusta behaved as an enemy towards her sister-in-law. One could almost wish she had been an adversary worthy of all the precautions she inspired, instead of the timid, slavish, and affectionate creature for whom compassion is blended with contempt.

Among the records Lady Byron handed down are many which may reasonably lead to the conjecture that she gave a colour of high, even quixotic honour to actions dictated sheerly by some rather ignoble form of self-interest or self-indulgence. In a number of these, such as the attempt to achieve Augusta's salvation by inflicting misery on her, she probably deceived herself as much as anybody else; but in others she knew what she was doing.

There are, for example, certain papers relating to the disposition of Byron's correspondence, most of which was being dealt with by Hobhouse. Byron was under the impression that all his wife's letters had been returned,[2] but it would seem that he had left with Augusta a batch of documents amongst which some from Lady Byron were unexpectedly found. Augusta wrote offering to withdraw these before the collection was put in the hands of the Executors.

On August 15th, she received this self-abnegating answer:

The MSS & letters which belonged to B.—not having been specifically bequeathed, I believe, on consideration, that it is right they should be com-

---

[1] MAYNE.

[2] *L. & J.* 3 May 1823. He wrote to Lady Blessington '. . . I have no picture, or indeed memorial of any kind of Lady B., as all her letters were in her own possession before I left England, and we have had no correspondence since—at least on her part.'

mitted to the hands of the Executors in order to be disposed of to the best of their judgment for the interests of the deceased—and such being the case, I should particularly object to have my letters withdrawn from the collection which is to be so considered by Mr Hobhouse. Will you therefore surrender to him, by my desire, such writings of mine as were B.'s property?—I am nevertheless very sensible of your kindness in wishing to reserve them.

With her copy of this she wrote on the same day:

> Mem. of my reasons for deciding against receiving back my Letters to B.
> 1. Had I done so, I should have felt myself under an honorable obligation to restore certain letters in my possession which others may wish to have restored.
> 2. By accepting those letters, I might afford some ground for supposing that I feared their publication.
> 3. By the same measure, I might have incurred the appearance of collusion with A. L. for my own interest.[1]

Hobhouse would not have been taken in for a moment by the lofty pretext. 'The coldness and calculation of this person . . . are quite unaccountable', he had written in his diary a few weeks before. 'It would be impossible to live with such a woman.'[2] This last comment was omitted, together with numerous others that might give pain to Lady Byron's descendants then living, when Hobhouse's daughter, Lady Dorchester, edited his journals.

In one of his best and most vivid writings, his 'Contemporary Account of the Separation of Lord and Lady Byron',[3] Hobhouse left some observations on Byron's wife which are wonderfully supported by a variety of evidences that were and remained unknown to him. At a time when Byron still regarded her as a paragon of truth and only 'lacking one sweet weakness—to forgive',[4] Hobhouse committed these much more authentic opinions to paper:

> Miss Milbanke may have been deceived in the expectations she formed in uniting herself with Lord Byron, but she was not deceived by Lord Byron, she was deceived by herself.[5]

[1] Lovelace Papers. Miss Mayne erroneously attributes this correspondence to 1834 instead of 1824, and therefore misinterprets completely Augusta's offer of the letters, adding that Lady Byron 'had learnt her lesson . . . that Veracity could not always be entirely adhered to by the heroine of the Byron Separation-Drama'. But unless Veracity *was* adhered to by that heroine, much of Miss Mayne's biography, leaning so heavily on her *ex parte* statements, has a very frail foundation.

[2] Hobhouse *Journals*, 25 June 1824.

[3] Written in 1816, privately printed in 1870, and reprinted with his 'Recollections' in 1909.

[4] Cf. '. . . His Estimate of me was beyond measure favorable; the turn of his Imagination being to picture *me* all Angel & *himself* the Opposite.' Narrative of March 1854, designated FF by Lord Lovelace.

[5] Cf. '. . . I had given my deepest sympathies to the *ideal* man on whom I had dwelt *in absence* so absorbingly.' Narrative of 1854.

. . . Her mind was perpetually in the balance between an adherence to what she had said, and a feeling for that which she wished really to do.

. . . To the accident of knowing nothing of mankind [she] joined the misfortune of imagining that her assiduous studies had made her a very competent judge of human character.[1]

. . . When she thought Lord Byron's character was not a little depressed in the world, she could show that she had magnanimity enough to spare him, but when she found that there was, at least, a division of opinion in his favour, she could not allow the least chance of any the smallest portion of blame being attached to herself.

(This was extraordinarily astute. As long as it was palpable that she was exercising generosity and forbearance, it was in her nature to do so, but to the end of her life, a word in praise of Byron was always taken as an attack upon herself, and awakened all her brooding indignation.)

. . . She appeared, as far as could be at all made out by Lord Byron's friends, to be angry that he should have any chance of being forgiven by the world.

They [Byron's friends] thought they saw and could prove, even from her own letters, such signs of weakness and perversion and even of duplicity, to say nothing of inveterate attachment to her own opinions, as would invalidate all she should say from her own knowledge only. They were aware that they had to deal with a singular character, who trusted rather to some rule of action and the attainment of a proposed end, than to any of the feelings and inclinations of her sex, both for a motive and a justification of her conduct.

He had a moment of unusual prescience when he foresaw something of the wreck she would make of her future.

The flutter of resentment or pride, the exhortations of zealous companions, and the very agitation of those troubled waters on which she is now borne, may, for the moment, keep her buoyant: but when there shall be no longer any cause for anger, nor occasion for self-commendation, when decency itself shall prescribe the silence of friends, when the struggle is past, what is to preserve her from sinking in that dead calm that must succeed the tempest of her passions and her griefs?

Hobhouse knew more about her passions and her griefs than the world at large because he had read letters from Mrs Fletcher to her husband describing her mistress's terrible agony and despair after she had committed herself finally to dissolving the marriage; and in his capacity of official friend and adviser to Byron during the proceedings, he had also been shown those letters—some of them deeply touching, many of them based on a deceit he never forgave—by which she had drawn from Byron his fatal second proposal.

[1] Cf. 'Her belief in her own powers of discernment was unbounded.' William King, 1st Earl of Lovelace (her son-in-law), in an undated paper probably written for Abraham Hayward. Nottingham Central Library.

He was right in his guess that a dead calm would succeed so heavy a tempest, but it was a surface calm only. She herself has depicted it better than anyone in what she called her Auto-Description, written in early middle age:

> ... When I withdrew from the conflict, convinced that my duty imperatively enjoined that step, I felt appalled at the desert which seemed spread before me—At first indeed I felt relief from breathing an atmosphere of innocence —but it was not for long. There was a burning world within me which made the external one cold. . . . In this state I had a singular degree of insensibility to *the real*. The touch of every hand seemed cold. I could look on tears without sympathy—and I returned kindness heartlessly & mechanically.[1]

Thus far she saw what had happened to her clearly enough, but she was persuaded that philanthropy, a system of self-control, and 'the pleasure I derived from self-approbation in these respects', had ultimately turned the specious calm into reality. There is eloquent testimony to the contrary from her own pen. The cultivated air of tranquillity concealed storms and stresses which abated little during year upon year of constantly hearing the name, the disgraces, and the glories of the man whom she had left while she was still in love with him.

They could never have made each other happy: sooner or later, even if she had been a far softer and less egotistical character, Byron would have driven the marriage on the rocks. But that 'clean break' by which young and inexperienced lovers hope to abolish their problems does such violence to nature that it cannot result in anything but weak recantation or lasting embitterment. For most ill-assorted couples there are many capitulations, many groping efforts of adjustment, before, with comparatively mild pangs at last, the bonds are loosened and dropped. Not yet twenty-four years old, brought up by worshipping parents to believe herself infallible, sustained by a large circle of bosom friends before whom she dared not avow her desire to return to a husband whose wickedness she had un-stintingly disclosed, and having in her temperament a decided vein of what we now term sado-masochism, Annabella was under a compulsion to take the way hardest for both.

And, like her shrewd critic, Hobhouse, she could not admit that in a vital matter she might have made an error. She looked incessantly for justifications; she came to depend more and more for them on her scape-goat, Augusta.

By 1824 she had all but forgotten her own explicit declarations of eight years before that Augusta had not been the cause of the separation; she no longer felt indebted for the quick and keen sympathy with which

---

[1] MS. on paper watermarked 1831. Probably written somewhat later. Lovelace Papers.

—so unfortunately for Byron—Augusta had supported her through the dismal scenes at Piccadilly Terrace. All that had come to seem part of a plot against her.

The progress of her delusions is illustrated unmistakably by her private memoranda. First there is a genuine and sensitive attempt to see the best in Augusta:

A—— is formed to feel for all—yet from the nature of her situation must not feel as she could—and otherwise circumstanced *ought*—The moment her heart softens, its tenderness returns to one from whom it should be banished for ever——

'Had I been happy, I too had been gentle' —— She has all the unamiable & unendearing duties of life to perform—She must spare the feelings of others—and sacrifice her own— — —[1]

Next there is the combination of sympathy with appreciation of her own merit and a certain uneasiness:

Kirkby, Octr. 5th. 1816

. . . I have sacrificed self-justification in a great measure to A's salvation— or the hope of it—and am now considering it more than anything else—to save her from the dangers around—I do believe her sincerely penitent—I have *found* her so—and my truest friend—and I feel that whatever the world might judge, I owe her more friendship than I have shown—that in some respects I have been actuated by personal considerations—or distant fears for my child, to regard her welfare less than otherwise I should—& than in any case I ought.

All this I am now determined to compensate for—if possible—[2]

The meaning of this was that her conscience was troubling her for having deposited with her lawyers—in secret, of course—a case against Augusta, using the not very convincing excuse that she must be armed lest Byron should claim the custody of his child. It was an odd way of behaving to her 'truest friend', and she shows in recognizing this that her sight was not yet so distorted as it later became.

About four months later, there is a change of tone.

Duty to A. L. It is my unalterable belief that she has never meant to do me harm, and that she has often incurred personal vexations to fulfil her conception of acting as my friend—moreover she has placed confidence in me— I cannot prove its motives to have been altogether selfish; nor altogether sincere, but I am not to presume the *Evil* only.

It is in her power to give the most important evidence against Lord B.— & in case of a contest respecting my maternal guardianship, I consider her bound to afford it to the utmost—excepting only the confession of her guilt—

---

[1] One of the fragments of writing designated DD by Lord Lovelace. Lovelace Papers.
[2] Ibid. Remarks in a Commonplace Book.

Were she to refuse what I conceive to be just, I should think myself at liberty to proceed against her personally—but in no other case.[1]

Annabella was going to the length, when this was written, of having her child made a Ward in Chancery without Byron's knowledge, in order to nullify the paternal rights which were then so all-embracing. It did not, after all, prove necessary to put Augusta up as a witness against him, but as the Memorandum shows, she had been perfectly prepared to do so, and even to 'proceed against her personally' in the event of refusal. Had the danger that Byron would seriously attempt to deprive her of the infant been more acute, this willingness to thwart him by ruining one who had befriended and trusted her would evoke more sympathy.

Communication between the sisters-in-law had cooled a little after Augusta's astounding, though doubtless terrified, defiance of January 1820, when she had dared to say that, if Byron had come to England, she could not have positively refrained from setting eyes on him. The scare had occasioned a renewal of correspondence with Mrs Villiers, who was treated solely as an outlet for stimulating news about the iniquities of Byron or the temptations of Augusta, and an audience for sublime sentiments on those topics.

'I am reluctant to give you *my* impression of what has passed between A— and me respecting her conduct in case of his return', she wrote. Nevertheless 'to converse with you at this moment would be peculiarly satisfactory to me'. But a new 'aggression' by Byron eclipsed the other subject. He had sent her a letter announcing

> plans which are so insidiously adapted to injure me, and provide sorrow for Ada that I fear I shall be under the necessity of appealing to a public tribunal. Contrary as such opposition is to my perhaps too yielding nature, I will not shrink from it, if it becomes a duty.[2]

The menace referred to was the composition of Memoirs for posthumous publication of which 'he has the audacity to offer me the perusal'.[3]

On the news of his death, Mrs Villiers sent condolences giving utterance, it would seem, to some pious hope, on the strength of a report by Augusta, of his redemption at the end, but Lady Byron made short work of that:

> . . . The *only* satisfaction which you can discover in the circumstances, is in my opinion unfounded. It has been fondly inferred by Augusta from what cannot justify the inference to any rational mind. No—the only consolation for those who *once* loved him is to reflect that with his physical peculiarities

[1] Ibid. Undated Memorandum, designated EE by Lord Lovelace. It may be ascribed by internal evidence to January 1817.
[2] Ibid. 26 Jan. 1820.   [3] Ibid. 28 Dec. 1819.

& ruinous education, his responsibility is not to be estimated by any human eye—

She had had a premonition of his death and had been 'arranging all the papers which ought or ought not to be in existence after that event', and knew the moment she saw Captain George Byron's chaise what he had come to tell her. It was a relief, she said, to her father who believed the term for which he could protect her (presumably from Byron) would be short; and she reported with complacency that

> . . . With respect to all pecuniary arrangements I am now completely independent—& I trust that years of comparative privation will have taught me how to do more good to others.[1]

Four weeks later the report of how Byron had left his money enabled her to take up her pen and draw attention to fresh wrongs:

> I write now because I will not leave you ignorant of what appears to be the final disposition of Lord Byron's property as no later Will is to be found than that to which a Codicil was added in 1818. The property is bequeathed to the Leighs; *Hanson* & Hobhouse the Executors. The amount will be upwards of £100,000 in the end. On this subject I shall inviolably adhere to the determination of making no remarks.[2]

The settlement of much more than half the fortune upon herself for life is left unmentioned here, as in her later statements, and no one could have gathered that the Leighs were not presently—or indeed ever—to enter into possession of £100,000.

From this time forwards, her preoccupation with her grievances became, if not more intense, at least more candid, until as the years went on, she felt obliged to excuse herself for having shown mercy to the sinner, and gave as one of her explanations 'That the publicity of atrocious crimes is injurious to society'.

> . . . Her subsequent proceedings [she added in a postscript] have shown me that the love of money was her ruling passion, & I believe she was actuated by it to disunite Lord B—& me—I also think she may have *feigned* resistance to his wishes *before me*, & permitted them *in private*.[3]

No doubt her hostility has been correctly attributed to jealousy. The undertaking she had imposed on Augusta to produce all Byron's letters for her inspection had thrown a darker shade over her own unhappiness not less than over Augusta's treachery. She herself had never received

---

[1] 18 May 1824: Lovelace Papers. She had been in receipt of a personal income of about £4000 per annum during the period when Byron had shared in the Wentworth Property.

[2] LOVELACE, *Lady Noel Byron*, 15 June 1824.

[3] 'The Circumstances connected with the Birth of E. Medora Leigh.' An undated MS. c. 1841.

from him such outpourings of unguarded love. And the adoring verses—
she had been so wrought upon that she had actually interfered to prevent
John Murray from publishing them, had asked him not to let Augusta see
them![1]

> For thee, my own sweet sister, in thy heart
>   I know myself secure, as thou in mine;
> We were and are—I am, even as thou art—
>   Beings who ne'er each other can resign;
> It is the same, together or apart,
> From life's commencement to its slow decline
>   We are entwined—let Death come slow or fast,
> The tie which bound the first endures the last.

There was something even in the way he told Augusta about his other
love affairs which showed a warm and smiling assurance of mutual understanding wholly absent in his marriage.

Social jealousy too may have had its influence. Annabella was so ill-
adapted to the world of fashionable people like her aunt, Lady Melbourne,
that from early youth she had been on the defensive against it with sneers
and moralizings; whereas Augusta, steeped in 'atrocious crime' though she
was, remained quite at ease among leaders of the *ton,* such as the intimidating Lady Jersey, had relatives of her own who were of the highest
rank below royalty, and would write unthinkingly (or was it thinkingly?)
in this mode:

> I am the *worst* person to consult about Brighton visits. . . . I should not
> have visited anyone—but *some* wd visit me—Jerseys, Hollands, Ly Stanhope
> and so on. I think Ly H. Blaquiere was ye only person I went near voluntarily
> & that was for ye D[uches]s of Leeds's sake *her* sister but I was obliged to be
> *civil.*
>   . . . The *first* in rank ought to visit *first.*[2]

Though the advice had been asked for, Augusta being a mistress of
etiquette, the tone was potentially exasperating. From one who held her
position in society solely on the other's sufferance, nonchalance was merely
provocative.

It may have been an additional cause for envy that it was Byron's
sister, not his widow, who received the tributes paid to the dead poet
during the weeks when his fame had glittered again with all its old
lustre. Retiring as she imagined herself to be, Lady Byron took considerable pleasure in having attention focused on herself. This was recognized
by several who knew her well, and is apparent in the copious poetical

[1] Lovelace papers, Murray MSS. Correspondence of Sept. 1816. The Epistle to
Augusta, quoted above, was suppressed through Lady Byron's intervention, and did not
appear till 1831.   [2] 28 Oct. 1825: Lovelace Papers.

works which were the vehicle of expression for her frustrated longings. To bask in reflected glory might not have been as good as having a glory of one's own, but it perhaps appeared better than remaining obscure at Beckenham while Augusta, in St James's Palace, was honoured as the great celebrity's next of kin.

Stanhope, Gamba, and others who had known Byron in his last days, all made their visits of condolence to Mrs Leigh, but Lady Byron was precluded by her dignity from seeing anyone but the valet.

Fletcher had been sent for to give her Byron's dying message, on which she seems to have based some mysterious and unwarrantable hope, but she learned that hardly a word had been articulate. She was, so Fletcher told Mrs Shelley, 'in a fit of passionate grief, but perfectly implacable, and as much resolved never to have united herself again to him as she was when she first signed the separation'.[1]

The idea of his speaking her name and what it might have been meant to convey had a softening effect, however, at least while the description of his death-bed was fresh in her memory; and she found it necessary to relieve her feelings in verse:

> In a far foreign land did he breathe forth that soul
> Which had reign'd like a God, and had own'd no control
> And no lov'd ones were near him to bless and be blessed,
> Or to read ere it faded each wish not expressed!—
>
> But far from the scenes of his birth and his youth,
> That breath of sweet song died away in the south.
> And silent and lone was the vale of the grave;
> There were none to divine the last tokens he gave!—
>
> The dying desire that he long'd to impress,
> The one truth then reveal'd, that might save and might bless,—
> That hallowed last link 'twixt the living and dead,—
> 'Twas all speechless and void;—and that word was not said.
>
> The effort was made, but all, all, was in vain,
> And dark is that page which he sought to explain.
> For the voice tho' it strove, it could bring forth no sound,
> And the heart tho' it heav'd, had no rhythm nor bound.
>
> That eye which had gleam'd as in flashes from Heav'n,—
> Whose glances by angels and demons seem'd given,—
> It anxiously gaz'd, but its language and lights
> As they faded were seal'd from mortality's sights.[2]

---

[1] Mary Shelley to Trelawny, 28 July 1824. I cannot find any source in the Lovelace Papers or elsewhere for Miss Mayne's account of her walking about the room, shaking with sobs, etc.   [2] Lovelace Papers.

Lady Byron, from a water colour by W. J. Newton

The Hon. Augusta Leigh, a drawing by Sir George Hayter

Lady Byron's carefully preserved poetry has a pathetic eloquence as to what she termed the Causes of Disunion generally lacking in the statements she wrote with the intention of wringing the heart. It reveals also, better than any of the more studied documents, the painful ambivalence of her feelings about Byron, an ambivalence which had existed from a period shortly before the marriage (which she went into, if her reminiscences are to be trusted, 'with the conviction that I had linked myself to Misery, if not Guilt', and 'prepared to suffer the worst I could then imagine')[1] and ended only with her life. In one mood, his death is obviously regarded with something approaching satisfaction—a relief to her father, a means of attaining to her property free from encumbrance: in another she weeps because she has missed the 'hallowed last link 'twixt the living and dead'. Now she is sitting calmly down to write the most lacerating recollections of his villainy, leaving him with not a shred of goodness in his nature, finding base motives for his every action: while on another occasion she is bitter against Augusta for having come between them.

It is commonplace, of course, for unhappy love to leave behind intensely variable sentiments, but when these vacillations continue over several decades, and result in self-contradictions on matters of fact, as well as being accompanied by delusions of persecution from the world at large, we may wonder how their victim came to be regarded as a reliable witness.

Augusta was not aware in 1824 how far she had fallen out of favour. In whatever tone Lady Byron wrote *about* her to lawyers and friends, when writing *to* her she invariably began 'My dearest A'—it was a reciprocal endearment—and ended with some such phrase as 'Yours most affectionately', and her professions of friendship were often renewed: but the other seems to have known at all times that it was necessary to go carefully with Annabella, to take a humble and propitiatory tone, and especially now when herself being treated as next of kin had something of irony in it.

She sent bulletins to her of all that was going on, making a point of consulting her, or appearing to consult her, although it was really under Hobhouse's guidance that she did everything.

> On the subject of *Biography*—I am very nearly mad [she wrote when the first wave of public interest was running high]—You do not tell me what *you* wish about Mr Hodgson, & *I* have no wish to interfere . . . I should be so sorry to vex *him*—or the other *H*![2]

The other H was Hobhouse, with his vigorous determination to repress every biographer, even when he should be an old friend like the Rev. Francis Hodgson, who was given to moralizing but would not have made

---

[1] Ibid. Narrative of 1854.   [2] Ibid. 28 (?) May 1824.

an unseemly disclosure for any reward, and whose memories of Byron were most affectionate and creditable. (But Hobhouse in any case did not like Hodgson, whom he still saw as the dissipated young man who had fallen in love with oyster wenches, washerwomen, and common strumpets, rather than the highly respectable clergyman and ripe classical scholar time had made him, and he was horrified to discover how much money he had had from Byron.)

Augusta, with her terrible cowardice about vexing anyone, sometimes forgot she had set her face with Hobhouse's against biography.

> . . . There is another friend started up with the same proposal—[she continued feebly] one whom I think wd do it well & to whom it might be of *real* & essential service! You will feel my perplexities—Why should they not *all* write! Pray my dearest A tell me what you think & wish on this subject. . . .

Hobhouse, who always spoke gently of Augusta and acted generously towards her, would have suffered a shock if he could have seen that 'Why should they not *all* write!' It was the kind of silliness which had earned her the nickname of Goose, and it meant nothing whatever. Two days later she was fluttering round the subject again:

> I think I *must* write to Mr Hodgson—or he will be hurt—& what to say of the Biogy I do not know. It is impossible for me to sanction any one in particular—as I could not bear to hurt the feelings of *any*, by expressing a preference.[1]

Who was the new candidate for the post of approved biographer? Nothing more emerges about him, but it is not impossible that it was Scrope Berdmore Davies, Fellow of King's College, Cambridge, who, though living in France to avoid going to a debtor's prison, was in touch with Augusta and a sufficiently devoted partisan of Byron's to be trusted with his reputation. His letters to her, like Hodgson's, are full of the uncomplicated fondness that soothed her troubled spirit.

> Pray do give me the history of the ring which poor B. wore—When did he get it? what is the stone? On which hand and on which finger did he put it? These are all trifles but what is not interesting about the departed when they are such as he was. . . .?
>
> Your account of the last moments of B. has been more interesting to me than all the letters, papers, conversations, declarations, and affidavits the world had produced.[2]

Scrope Davies's qualifications were such that he might have written a most valuable book. He had known Byron extremely well from his Cam-

[1] 30 May 1824: Lovelace Papers.
[2] British Museum: Additional MSS. 31037. 22 Sept. 1824. In Gronow's *Reminiscences* there are several derogatory opinions about Byron attributed to Scrope Davies, but the book contains so many errors that it is safe to assume some error or exaggeration here.

bridge days onwards, and had, in fact, lent him the sum of £4800 that took him on his Grand Tour with Hobhouse in 1809. He had seen him often during the years of fame in London, had been nearest to him, after Hobhouse and Augusta, in the wretched weeks succeeding the collapse of his domestic life, and had stayed with him afterwards at his villa in Switzerland. He was thoroughly acquainted with the fashionable world which, to men like Medwin, was uncharted land; and being admired by Byron for his ready wit, was unlikely to have taken seriously the poet's jests and half-jests.

His pressing need of money would explain Augusta's remark that it might do him 'a *real* and essential service' to be allowed to produce the book. But the project—if project there was—fell through. He would probably not have had sufficient application for a regular biography, but he is known to have set down, in his latter years, very voluminous recollections of his friends which have never come to light. It may be that in some French library, some village or provincial town, a delightful verbal portrait of Byron by one who saw him both in grief and gaiety remains to be discovered.

What Lady Byron wrote to Augusta about the various biographical projects can only be guessed, for most of her replies of this period are missing except when she herself took copies before dispatching them. That they were guarded and equivocal goes without saying, because this was the character of all her letters to her 'dearest Sis' ever since she first deemed it advisable to save her soul and at the same time to build up a case against her and Byron which could come into court if Byron should prove refractory.

At no time did Augusta realize how very precarious was that immunity which she had purchased by being so true to Annabella and so untrue to her brother. She was indeed, in her disarming way, a most obtuse woman.

The notion that George Byron would unforgivingly resent acquiring his cousin's title without his money seems not to have crossed her mind, and though she was apologetic, she hardly suspected that he and his wife and Annabella would draw together in aggrieved alliance. When Dallas's distasteful book came out with what amounted to George Byron's blessing, she wrote imagining she would find in Annabella a sympathizer:

> . . . I wish too I had never loved G B, sufficiently to make me more than angry at his late conduct—I think his sanctioning Mr Dallas's Book is an *outrage* to the living & the dead—such a production *I* never saw—putting aside what is said of myself by his Relation Mr Alexander [Dallas].[1]

[1] 28 Nov. 1824: Lovelace Papers.

And again:

[I] am quite *sick* of the sight of myself *in print* in Mr Dallas.[1]

What she had singled out for complaint was an attack on Byron's will, spitefully suggesting that Hobhouse had obtained his injunction against publishing Byron's letters as '*a matter of property*' only—

. . . to add a few hundreds to the hundred thousand of pounds that Lord Byron has stripped from an ancient and honourable title which they were meant to support—not to give to his daughter, which would have put the silence of feeling upon the reproach of justice, but to enrich his sister *of the half blood*, . . .

This was assuredly to curry favour with Lady Byron to whom the Rev. Alexander sent 'the very first copy' from the press, with a fulsome letter.[2] It was followed by another paragraph, equally severe and intended to flatter the new lord, in which, having claimed (quite inaccurately) that his father had been the means of bringing Byron and Augusta together, he affirmed:

The result of this union, *so produced*, has been that Lord Byron, against all *moral* right, has applied the money procured by the sale of Newstead Abbey, to enrich his half-sister, and left the family title without the family estate which belonged to it. . . . He leaves a title and a name distinguished in almost every generation, from the conquest, without any of the rewards which were given to the successive bearers of that name, to support its ancient honours.

This sort of thing was undeniably offensive to Augusta, but by no means so to Annabella.[3] She may or may not have recalled that her marriage settlement had rendered the sale of Newstead Abbey an unavoidable necessity, and that it had been urged, with what Hobhouse thought indecent avidity, by her mother. What was congenial was that attention had been drawn to the usurpation of the estate, whether in lands or moneys, by Augusta. She could not very well openly defend Dallas, but she did the next best thing by defending George Byron, pointing out that he had never seen the Dallas book—he having sailed for the Sandwich Isles before it was issued.

She received back one of the few but striking letters in which Augusta spoke her mind with little of the 'damned crinkum-crankum' which was her usual style:

G. B. never saw the work entitled 'Recollections &c'—let *that* pass. . . . No one I think wd *dare* to affirm that he had given his sanction to the *Preface* & other parts of the 'Recollections' which are not only offensive, but as I'm told *actionable*—if contempt was not what they best deserve—

[1] 2 Dec. 1824: Lovelace Papers. [2] Ibid. 16 Nov. 1824.
[3] She calls approving attention to Dallas in one of her Statements.

but to come to the point—What business had Mr Dallas to publish letters of the *late* Lord Byron's? (omitting all that relates to the *Manner* in which he wd have done it)—and what right had the *present* Lord Byron to Sanction such a publication which he did in the original Book—which original Book I have read, now published in French. . . .

Such letters too! those of a Son written confidentially in the fullness & openness of heart to his Mother & de *tout* ce qui lui passoit par la tete—The *least* that can be said of G B's upholding his Uncle in such a measure was that he was weak & good natured enough to wish to put a little Money in his pocket—& considering that Uncle's past obligations to my Brother, I think he might have had the *delicacy* to have *tried* at least to have prevented his adding to those obligations by such very *indelicate* & improper means— to have *protested against* it, if he could have done nothing more effective.

Such is my opinion on *that* point. The *present* Book may be more or less objectionable than ye *original* one—but what I contend for is, that it was *wrong* in George to listen one moment to the publication of *any* letters— at *such* a moment too! . . . You may say this was an error of judgement, & perhaps it was—I am *grieved* at it let it be what it would.[1]

She ended with the exact and unhappy prophecy that it was her peculiar lot 'to mourn over the living loss of all I best loved'.

Annabella did not care for Augusta to have grievances of her own. Siding wholly with George Byron, yet not admitting that she had received and read the objectionable book, she wrote a remonstrance on his behalf; but Augusta, though affectionate as ever, held her ground:

You seem to have misunderstood in some way or other my feelings towards George Byron—You know I am not given to Quarrel *for quarrelling's sake*—& had I done so, I think *he* wd have been the last *Victim* I sd have chosen! It is impossible you can understand me *quite* if you have never had the Dallas books—& I'm sure I do not wish you to do so—but if you did I think you wd understand why for the sake of *the Dead* I never can again speak to him or be on terms of friendship unless he takes the step which wd be right.[2]

No such step was ever taken. The 7th Lord Byron spent from September 29th, 1824, to May 4th, 1825, sailing to the island to which he was returning the bodies of the South Sea King and Queen, and an equivalent period on the return voyage. It was 1826 before he was accessible again, and Augusta, with a tenacity rather exceptional in her, wrote him a stern letter saying it was a duty incumbent upon her to explain the painful cause of her changed feelings towards him—

in the anxious hope that you may be induced to participate in the conviction I entertain of how imperative it has become, for the credit & honor of the

[1] Lovelace papers. No date. Probably early January 1825.
[2] Ibid. No date. Presumably a few days later.

name you bear, & the title to which you have succeeded, to endeavour by every means in your power to remove the stigma which most unquestionably has been cast upon them by Mr Alexander Dallas' 'Recollections of the life of the late Lord Byron.' In this production Mr A. Dallas has not rested satisfied with *basely* attacking the character of the *Deceased*, but has most unjustifiably attempted to Implicate the *Living*. . . .

It is almost unnecessary for me to condescend to add that both Mr Alexander Dallas & his Work (including his *amiable* opinions of myself) would have passed unheeded and *unfelt*, but for his so cruelly placing on record, & so artfully endeavouring to incorporate with his own malignant insinuations the approval & sanction of that person, for whom I entertained, and would have wished to continue to entertain, so sincere an affection.[1]

It was a most stupid blunder to blame her cousin for unpleasant features of the Dallas book of which he was altogether ignorant, but even in its obstinate illogicality, the letter has a certain pathos, as showing how recklessly she had placed her faith in Annabella's perfect trustworthiness. She had no vestige of suspicion that George Byron knew the 'malignant insinuations' to be well-founded, nor that there would be an immediate exchange of correspondence between himself and her 'guardian angel' on the subject.

Mary [his wife] has sent you a copy of her letter verbatim a more artful and insulting production I shd think she has not before composed.[2]

The tone of Lady Byron's reply may be gathered from what he wrote back to her:

Bath   Apl 29th

My Dear Coz—

Many thanks for your kind note, it delights me the more as it is exactly the feeling & opinion I entertained of that studied production; you e'er this will have rec^d the copy of my answer in which I trust I have forborne to do more than answer her unjust accusations, her conduct deserves pity— instead of resentment but I must own tis a great struggle within me to adopt the better and more Xtian part. *I could have been severe*, but it wd have been unmanly and unwise. I hope my answer will meet with yr approbation. . . .

Ever My Dear Coz

> Your sincerely Afft
> friend
> Byron[3]

It is alarming to surmise how he might have written if he had not been in such a Christian frame of mind, because what he did write was scathing enough:

The 'open' & 'honourable' measure which you acknowledge you have taken in the disclosure of your 'altered feelings' towards me which awaited

[1] 19 Apr. 1826: Lovelace Papers.   [2] Ibid. 25 Apr. 1826.   [3] Ibid.

my arrival in Bath, would have met with the indifference your letter deserved but that I consider it right to inform you that I hold myself in no manner responsible for any misunderstanding which may exist between you and an author for whose publications & sentiments I can in nowise be accountable.

. . . I might consider myself exonerated from that delicacy which you have failed to observe towards me & I might reasonably consider an apology necessary. . . . Feeling however that there is a determination on your part to divide that intercourse which has hitherto subsisted between us, & from what motive is best known to yourself, I shall merely observe that I have, so far from being accessory to Mr Alexander Dallas's publications, never read the work to which you allude. . . .

From the time I saw Mr A. Dallas in August 1824 I have never had any intercourse with him, but what I then told him I still maintain, that the original letters of the late Lord Byron intended by Mr Dallas for publication & shewn to me were not calculated to reflect discredit either on the late Ld B's character or that of any other person.[1]

He ended with a word of 'compassion for those bitter feelings which can alone be the result of your own imagination'.

Thus crumbled even the façade of friendship between the successors to Byron's title and to his fortune. Both had behaved provocatively. The new Lord Byron had done his utmost to enable his uncle to publish the late Lord Byron's letters despite Augusta's objections—a fact well known to her through Hobhouse. Augusta for her part had been rash to tax him with complicity in the offensive remarks he could truthfully deny ever having seen.

It is not likely that she was deliberately seizing an excuse to quarrel with him, as both he and Lady Byron believed; she had no advantage in the world to gain by that. The presumption is that, glad as she was to inherit money from her brother, she was troubled by the fear of revived scandal that it might give rise to, and in her sense of insecurity, became truculent. She had for many years been expected to submit her very soul to the will of her sister-in-law, and to have a relative whom she could, as she thought, stand up to, may have proved too much for her discretion. She was very much in error. Sustained by Annabella's money and encouragement, privy to the secret of Augusta's alleged 'crime',[2] he could afford to be on bad terms far better than she could. He returned her next letter unopened.[3]

Augusta did not suffer from the 'moral idiotcy' Annabella so complacently ascribed to her: the desire to be a good woman is revealed in a multitude of her letters and many of her actions, and made her more than

---

[1] Ibid. 27 Apr. 1826.
[2] Incest with a brother or half-brother was not then a criminal offence in law, but the term was constantly applied to Augusta's case.   [3] Murray MSS.

commonly responsive to appeals to conscience, exhortations to do penance, and (possibly) pleas for confession. Weak as her conduct was, there is no reason to doubt the sincerity of her religious faith, and those who have sneered at her giving away Bibles or speaking the language of Anglican piety would seem to be assuming that the sinner has no right to repent.

But whether or not she was supported by spiritual wisdom, her judgment in worldly affairs was perpetually at fault. She stumbled and groped her way through life in a state of desperate myopia, and was never more pitiable than when she prided herself on plans of extraordinary sagacity. It was one of these plans that led to the catastrophe of her daughter Georgiana's marriage to a young Cornishman, her third cousin, Henry Trevanion. When he proposed in the year succeeding Byron's death Georgiana had just turned seventeen.

In promoting this match—as fatal in its way as that of her equally ill-judging brother—it cannot be said that Augusta was governed by any prudential considerations whatever. If she had been either ambitious or mercenary, she could have done a good deal better. Georgiana was related to several great families, and she had a share in the reversion of the £60,000 which was settled for life on her aunt-by-marriage. Lady Byron regarded herself as an invalid, and had been so regarded by all her friends for a number of years, and no one could foresee that she would outlive almost everyone connected with her. Henry Trevanion was only a second son, and though his family were landed gentry, they did not belong to that high sphere of society into which Augusta, a member of the royal *entourage*, might expect her daughter to marry. Moreover, the immediate financial obstacles were great.

In the absence of a single inducement except her belief that Trevanion was an attractive and deserving person, it may reasonably be affirmed that her intention was the one she professed—to bring happiness to two young people. Seventeen was a favoured age for marriage; Trevanion was extremely presentable, Augusta incurably romantic.

The ill-omened subject was first introduced to Lady Byron in a communication written towards the end of 1825, containing a large assortment of news and voluble comment. There was Ada's birthday, for which Augusta sent her best and most affectionate greetings. There was Lady Byron's health which always occupied much space in the letters of both correspondents. ('I do so wish you could give me better accts of yourself . . . it seems, you are always doomed to suffer in *some* way.') There was John Murray's illness—he looked dreadfully altered—and an angry argument, which she had been hearing about from Hobhouse, still raging over the business of the burned Memoirs. Moore was determined on writing 'a *Quarto* about poor B' and was 'a little Villain'—the 'little' underlined three times. Four of her children at home had been ill with influenza, her two boys at school with measles; the governess ill too.

(She could be very boring on such topics. Though she had not lost the silliness Byron had found so endearing, she had retained little of that gaiety which had been part of its charm.)

At last she reached what had 'really absorbed the greatest portion of my thoughts of late'.

> You will perhaps be much surprised to hear it is a *proposal* of *marriage* to Georgey! The Proposer is a Relation, his name *Trevanion*. . . .
>
> The young Man is studying the Law & has talent to make the most of his Profession—exceedingly clever & in other respects the only person I know *worthy* of Georgey—I had known his Family as relations before my Marriage, but that event banishing me from the opportunities of continuing our intimacy, we renewed it, only about 2 years ago—& I asked after the *Hero* of my present tale among a groupe of other Children forgetting how years must have made them into men! he was introduced to me in that character by his Father about last July twelvemonth & I've seen much of him since from liking him & finding him so far superior to the *common herd*, but without the slightest idea till lately that Georgey was likely to attract him or indeed any body—She is such a *quiet* being—with very sound & excellent sense & good judgment, but not brilliant in any way, & I sd have said too *awkwardly* shy to be admired. The present state of things is that the Father at a distance of 300 miles, is approving in ye kindest & most flattering manner but doubting whether there will be *de* quoi to enable to marry at present.
>
> I (who from experience) have a *horror* of long engagements & who see little Chance of delay bringing any speedy material improvement, am strenuous for the thing being brought to pass as soon as possible. They are young—but they are both very steady, & have any thing but extravagant notions.[1]

So she rambled on for pages, 'afraid of thinking of its being brought to pass, as of something which wd make me *too* happy. . . . As far as one can judge, it promises all the happiness *this* world can give—& in case of any thing happening to me, it wd ensure a sort of protection to her sisters.' Words more ironical were never set on paper.

A few weeks later the difficulties were predominant. Colonel Leigh opposed the match, Trevanion's father was thinking of taking a second wife and wanted to settle his own affairs before settling his son's. Augusta's object was to raise £2000 for immediate purposes.

> I cannot at this distance describe to you the sort of *unheard of Misery*. *The Lovers* are both looking like Ghosts, & as for *the Law* there will be no studying of that while this state of things lasts. . . .[2]

[1] 9 Dec. 1825: Lovelace papers.   [2] Ibid. 12 Jan. 1826.

An aged aunt of Henry Trevanion's, from whom he had expectations, had turned out to be in her dotage and not manageable as to any ready cash—and there is something coarse in Augusta's manner here, even allowing for the callousness of the time towards old people with property. But Annabella had offered help.

> I did not understand *how* you thought you could be of use in facilitating what I might wish to do & it never occurred to me I could raise any thing till you kindly suggested it.   ≡

This hardly strikes a convincing note. Augusta had been only too well accustomed to raise money by all sorts of measures, and she tackled the details in anything but the language of a novice.

Her conduct in money matters never commands respect. There is a want of pride in her so readily accepting Lady Byron's offer of assistance that betrays a mind of little delicacy. It is but a slight extenuation that she did not initiate the proposal, and that money was due to her from the part of Lady Byron's Marriage Settlement which had never been paid. Pride would barely have allowed her needs to become known in that quarter.

Yet there are two distortions in the usual description of her transactions with Lady Byron which must be corrected. First, their number has been much exaggerated. Second, the most careful arrangements were made—and with good reason—for securing repayment. The impression which has been given that she had recourse to her benefactress again and again for loans which were never repaid is false. There is voluminous correspondence, but it relates to very few transactions.[1] The debt in this instance was cleared in little over two years.

To look for motives in Lady Byron beyond generosity and the promise she had given Byron 'to be kind to Augusta' would be hypercritical if she herself had not provided so many grounds for believing that she was seldom without some *arrière-pensée*. Generosity there was, and the pleasure of smoothing the way for the young lovers, but perhaps there was also some satisfaction in increasing Augusta's obligations, which were never long absent from her mind.

Whatever her purpose, she could not have even vaguely dreamed that in making the marriage possible, she had taken a more exquisite revenge on Augusta than if she had plotted her ruin.

Despite Colonel Leigh's resolute hostility, the wedding, which he did not attend, took place at St James's, Piccadilly, within three months of the proposal. Colonel Henry Wyndham gave Byron's favourite niece away, and the only members of her family present were her mother and her

---

[1] See Appendix 2 for Horton's estimate of her income, etc.

sister Libby, later to be known as Medora. After the ceremony Augusta
wrote one of her few cheerful letters:

A Line—dearest A to tell You our Marriage thank God! is happily over
& in parting with dearest Georgey I feel that I could not to anyone in the
world with such perfect confidence *as* to Henry Trevanion. I have seen him
daily hourly for 3 months—in Moments of Sickness, Sorrow, anxiety
and suspence—all most trying predicaments to the Lords of the Creation—
& which Shew the *real* Character—& his has only *risen* in my estimation!
    I cannot express *all* I feel to you for your kindness on this occasion to
which we owe *so* much! but indeed I *am* grateful—so are they—[1]

To raise all the money required not only for dowry but for trousseau
and incidental expenses, Augusta had drained her resources for years to
come; and when it turned out that Henry was too delicate in health for
the legal profession, and that his father allowed him only £450 a year and
not £900 as promised, she crippled herself still further to maintain him
and his wife, and the grandchildren who soon made their appearance.

The awful helplessness of well-bred young men and women in an
epoch when to work for money usually entailed complete loss of caste
now seems almost despicable, but it was accepted then, even by the most
critical, as one of the necessary evils accompanying birth and station. No
one regarded it as in the least odd that Mrs Leigh, endlessly juggling with
credit, should help to support her son-in-law's idle establishment.

Despite his lack of any tangible asset, she remained for several years
delighted with him and with the match which was eventually, in her
own words, to bring 'disgrace, misery, and embarrassment in every shape
upon my family and finances'.[2]

[1] 4 Feb. 1826: Lovelace Papers.
[2] British Museum: Additional MSS. 31037.

The publication of the 'Separation Poems'

Augusta Leigh wrote to the Rev. Francis Hodgson just after Byron left England, 'You have probably *read* and *heard* of the *Newspaper War* which was very sad—Mr Murray writes me word it was entirely owing to the Villainy of Mr Scott Editor of the Champion—who inserted (basely) some verses of B. in his Journal. . . . *Great* was the irritation on *all* sides —the last time I saw poor Ly B. I observed great harshness in her towards B— and all about him . . . several things she said I wd not *for worlds* he ever heard. . . .'[1]

The 'Newspaper War' blazed out of the publication of Byron's two Separation poems and of the defence attempted by the *Morning Chronicle*. The episode began with Byron's asking John Murray to have some copies printed for private use. (It was one of these printed copies of the 'Fare Thee Well' lines that was sent to Lady Byron.) According to Hobhouse's *Contemporary Account*, 'by the indiscretion of his Lordship's publisher' they were 'handed about in print more generally than the circumstances of the case seem to justify'.

Both poems—'Fare Thee Well' and the 'Sketch from Private Life'— came into the possession of John Scott, a specialist in the curious cant which typifies the journalism of the period. Scott did not receive the copies from Murray direct, for he was by no means in favour with that publisher, having recently procured from him as a kindness advance copies of Byron's *Siege of Corinth* and *Parisina* and used the privilege to launch abusive criticism at the two works prior to their publication. It was from Brougham, whose animosity towards Byron had an almost obsessive quality, that Scott secured the domestic verses surreptitiously—a fact which seems to have been unknown to Hobhouse, but which emerges from the account written by Benjamin Haydon, who knew Scott intimately. Haydon tells the story thus, writing in his diary immediately after he first heard of Byron's death:

> Scott attacked him from mere spite, because he met Byron at Hunt's table when he was in Prison, & Byron took no notice of him. When his 'Farewell' was privately circulated, Scott called on Brougham by chance, and Brougham had one; he gave it to Scott, & Scott published it the Sunday following. It was highly dishonorable, but Scott's paper lagged in circulation, and he would have availed himself of any circumstance, even to calumniating his Father, if it would have added a dozen papers to his sale. This was the private History of all that noise that took place at Byron's separation. The Champion was the first paper that had the 'Farewell,' & the 'Attack' [on Mrs Clermont] and it became public instantly.

[1] Murray Copies: 28 Apr. 1816.

After this, Moore breakfasted with Scott, & I heard Rogers say to Sir W. Scott that he was very angry with Moore for doing so. Scott called on me on his return from Brougham & shewed me the 'Farewell' & told me his intention of printing it, which I disapproved.[1]

The *Champion* naturally accompanied the piracy of Byron's verses with an onslaught on his character, and from that date (April 14th, 1816) the London press felt released from any obligation to preserve reticence, and there were columns of sanctimonious denunciation in nearly every newspaper. When James Perry, the editor of the *Morning Chronicle*, made a gallant though incautious attempt at a defence, saying that there was a 'conspiracy against his Lordship's domestic peace', Lady Byron's father, accompanied by Colonel Doyle, called on him and demanded public retractation. As Hobhouse saw it:

His Lordship had never interfered with the editors of any of the papers which had attacked him; he had made no effort to defend himself in any way that could possibly implicate Lady Byron; but the instant that a single paper steps forward to say a word in his favour, Lady Byron's family will not allow of any defence being made for him.[2]

Sir Ralph, not receiving the apology he required, became most pressing that the *Chronicle* should publish a letter from himself containing the following statement, actually composed by Lady Byron:

. . . The step taken by Lady Byron was the result of her own unbiassed judgment, and . . . her parents and friends interfered only when called upon by her to afford her their support. In the necessity of this step, indeed, her friends fully concurred; but in the suggestion of it they had no concern.[3]

Lest his command should be disobeyed by Perry, Sir Ralph made sure of publication by sending, on the same day, a copy of his lengthy letter to a rival paper, the *Courier*, which readily printed it. A society scandal had been turned into a public sensation.

The effect of the celebrated 'Fare Thee Well' lyric on Lady Byron was the clean reverse of what its author must have anticipated. Far more sensitive to public opinion than she would ever acknowledge, she felt it was a bid for sympathy which might make the world suppose she was in the wrong; and even before the verses appeared in the Press, they had caused her the greatest annoyance and uneasiness. She had written to Dr Lushington suggesting that she should publish something to stem the tide of feeling that was turning against her. His reply was dated April 13th, the day before the *Champion* had fired its broadside.

---

[1] POPE, Haydon's *Diary*.
[2] HOBHOUSE, *Contemporary Account*.
[3] 18 Apr. 1816.

You will pardon me saying that for once I must distrust your information—'The Tide of feeling has been turned against you.' Indeed I do not believe it. Nay, I am perfectly satisfied, that it cannot be so. When I left London the feeling of all, (with the exception of a very few who have no feelings at all) was unanimous in your favor, & I must doubt the magical effects you attribute to the 'Fare Thee Well.'

I think also that in point of character & credibility your friends are as likely to obtain credence as Lord Byron's, & that in fact there are not twenty persons in London, who, tho' ignorant of the particulars, are not satisfied that the Separation has arisen from Lord B's gross misconduct.

You must forgive me therefore for not being able to see so clearly as yourself the necessity of shewing the world that the measure you have adopted was called for by imperious circumstances; and I greatly question the propriety of your making use of the Declaration even if some avowal of your reasons were requisite.

Until that Declaration be given to Mr Hobhouse, . . . the contents should not be made known by you, & if afterwards used, it should be with great caution—The impression that you gave a declaration, which did *not* clear up Lord B's character & that you afterwards used it *against him* . . . ought I think to be avoided for perhaps such conduct might be distorted into a species of double dealing.[1]

'That Declaration' was the skilfully worded paper in which Lady Byron denied that she or those most nearly connected with her had spread any injurious rumours. It baffled Hobhouse's plea for a refutation of the serious allegations against Byron while appearing to grant it. Byron's advisers at first failed to notice the loophole—that there was no denial of the truth of the rumours.

Begging her not to take any step that would allow an unprejudiced person 'a shadow of ground for impeaching the candour of her conduct', Lushington continued, alluding no doubt to the accusations against Byron of having done 'even worse things than are true':

That all persons should think exactly as they ought of you is not possible, but surely it is infinitely better to be deemed by some 'Righteous over much' than for any to believe you could have endured without disgust & horror scenes even remotely connected with those iniquities which are so widely circulated, believed in their full extent by some, to a certain degree by a very large proportion.

An indifference to right and wrong is a much more serious imputation than even an affected abhorrence of venial Errors. — — You must be satisfied if by a very few, the less important deviation from the right line should for *a very short time* be imputed to you.

Lady Byron, however, took most seriously the aspersion that she had been 'righteous over much', and the word 'unforgiving' in the farewell

[1] Lovelace Papers.

verses was regarded by her as an imputation of extreme gravity. It gave her an excuse for setting aside the spirit, if not the lettter, of Dr Lushington's advice, and when Sir Ralph Noel and Colonel Doyle called on Perry, they brought with them a self-justifying explanation of her actions addressed to Doyle, which Sir Ralph expected Perry to insert in the *Chronicle*.

> To put such a communication in the hands of an editor of a paper [Hobhouse wrote indignantly] and so to prejudice the opinion of the public against his Lordship by reference to an authentic document from his wife must be pronounced *inexcusable* in Lady Byron. It was just as inexcusable as it would have been to have communicated Mrs Fletcher's deposition [in Byron's favour] to the Editor of the 'Champion' or the 'Times' . . .

Lady Noel was much embittered against Hobhouse by her guessing, correctly, that he had prompted the defence of Byron. (It is impossible not to accord a measure of sympathy to Byron, however disgraceful his conduct as a husband, on seeing how much it shocked and angered those on the other side to find that, in the greatest calamity of his life, he had a single friend to stand by him.)

It was Hobhouse who had the last word in the Newspaper War.

> If Sir Ralph Noel began this epistolary contest, it was ended by Mr Perry —partly, it may be conjectured from the persuasion on the part of the worthy Baronet that there would be nothing very gainful to him in the continuance of such a warfare; and partly owing to the direct assurance conveyed to him from Lord Byron, through Mr Hobhouse, that the inevitable consequence of any further appearance of Lady Byron's father as an advocate against Lord Byron would be the publication of the whole correspondence.[1]

In 'the whole correspondence' Hobhouse meant to include the letter Lady Byron most dreaded that the world should see, the first written by her after her arrival at her parents' home—the only act of hers, Dr Lushington said, which required explanation. Since Hobhouse's threat ended her part in the newspaper controversy, Dr Lushington promised to go much further than a lawyer normally would in setting her in the right by private measures:

> I shall consider it my duty without detailing the particulars of the past to establish as far as I can to the world a complete justification of your conduct, & to prove that your resolution of finally separating was a measure dictated by imperious necessity. . . . I feel not a shadow of doubt but that the opinion of all, whose opinions you could esteem, will in a very short time be unanimous in reprobating the injuries you have received & in approving the conduct

---

[1] HOBHOUSE, *Contemporary Account*. It is written, like all his more deliberate records, in the third person.

you have followed. As far as I can have any weight, be assured, I will suffer no misstatement to pass without the most direct contradiction.[1]

The extent to which Dr Lushington admitted talking about Byron's private affairs, as part of his duty of protecting his client from the least breath of criticism, is somewhat extraordinary, considering that he was dealing with a matrimonial dispute which had been kept out of court; nor did he scruple to pass on to Lady Byron in his letters pieces of gossip it might have been more discreet for a lawyer to keep to himself.

John Scott, whose malice sowed the seeds of all the public rancour which made it virtually impossible for Byron to live in England, was in touch with him just two years later in Venice, and most kindly treated. He died in 1821 as the result of wounds received in a duel, and Byron under the pseudonym of N. N. sent thirty pounds, when asked to subscribe ten, for his widow. He is sometimes called a school-fellow of Byron's, having attended the same school in Aberdeen, but as he was nearly five years older, it is not probable that this association formed much of a link between them. Haydon describes him as an entertaining and knowledgeable man, and that was the likeliest reason for the undeserved clemency he received from Byron.

[1] 25 Apr. 1816: Lovelace Papers.

A Sketch from the Private Life of Lord Iron. One of the numerous caricatures sold in the print shops at the time of the Separation

Augusta Leigh's income

Writing to Kinnaird, one of the trustees of Byron's money, on December 13th, 1827, Horton states that Augusta's income was £1934, made up as follows:

£984 *NOW* received from the Executors of Lord Byron

£350 Interest of her own fortune
    [she had £7000 held in trust by the Duke of Leeds. The source may have been her maternal grandmother Lady Holderness.]

£300 Received annually from Colonel Leigh, out of £1000 which forms a separate income from him

£300 Pension[1]

Nearly £2000 a year was a handsome revenue in the 1820's, but she had only been entitled to so much for a very short time. (The pension, which was from the Royal Family, was granted in September 1819, but not paid till 1820 or later.) In any case, she was paying £250 per annum to liquidate one debt, and £380 towards clearing another. Worse still, she seems to have concealed from Horton, to whom she had painted her situation as favourably as possible, that her receipt of £300 a year from Colonel Leigh was actually most precarious.

She also owed at this time £500 to Douglas Kinnaird, secured by an insurance policy, £250 to Horton himself, £20 cash to Lady Byron[2], and some tradesmen's bills. He thought the total of all debts, great and small, was £3457, but he was mistaken, because she had not had the courage to tell him everything. What was left of her income when she had coped with her creditors was committed down to the last guinea for the school fees of her sons, the maintenance of her mentally abnormal daughter, and the claims of the Trevanions. The consequence was that her liabilities became more and more entangled, and she had recourse to money-lenders.

[1] LOVELACE, *Lady Noel Byron*.
[2] The money for Georgiana's dowry was lent under the name of Lady Byron's companion, Miss Chaloner. This was doubtless one of the two larger debts which were being paid off at so much per annum.

CHAPTER V

DISCORDS FROM GREECE

Every epoch has its own forms of idealization in which awkward reality is so habitually veiled that its appearance without that softening disguise seems like an indecency. The neo-classical modes that followed the French Revolution established a taste for a noble kind of smoothness. In paint, in prose, in marble, in music, what the frequenters of good society thought estimable was refinement. Everything fashionable was given a gloss and rendered graceful and symmetrical. It is true that high drama flourished —on the stage, on canvas, or in print—but only if it conformed to the romantic yet very carefully contained lines prescribed by fashion. Portraits were expected to be flattering. Biographies abounded in anecdotes which were false in colouring but shapely, and their lack of authenticity gave little concern.

When the Marquis de Salvo, who had never known Byron and had not troubled himself with inconvenient research, wrote—in French—a book about him, the *London Literary Gazette* quoted at three columns' length a story almost wholly fictitious about his adventures with a heroine named Celina, and praised the work because it contained no private knowledge![1] The author's indifference to private knowledge disarmed even Hobhouse who, on being tactfully visited, had presented him with a page of Byron's manuscript for reproduction.[2]

Yet only a few days before he had recorded, as an example of the man's ridiculous ignorance that 'Count Salvo—or Marquis Salvo' (he had an Englishman's disregard for foreign titles) had told Gamba he had 'met Lord Byron in a diligence in France and that after some talk, Lord B. had said You see before you the author of the Corsair!!!'[3] Byron had never been in France, and his declaring himself in a public conveyance to be the author of *The Corsair* was so eminently a fabrication that Hobhouse doubtless felt he could afford to smile at such nonsense.

Books and magazine articles by people who could not claim to have known the poet, or even those whose claim was a blatant lie, gave him a comparatively mild annoyance.

> I see that someone has published an account of a voyage of Byron's to Sicily with Shelley mentioning names &c and the New Times believed it because Shelley was said to have been afraid in a storm! ! !![4]

---

[1] 19 Apr. 1825. [2] Hobhouse *Journals*, 27 Nov. 1824. [3] Ibid. 12 Nov.
[4] Ibid. The fraudulent work in question professed to be by a Captain Benson, R.N., Master of Byron's yacht. Extracts from it were widely quoted to show, as one journal had it, 'the conduct of the *Atheist*, Shelly [sic], whose literary labours were devoted to the subversion of all right feeling and the inculcation of principles equally abominable and blasphemous with his own'. Shelley was represented as grovelling with terror 'imploring

There was no need to waste words on disproving an out-and-out invention. What he resented was not being able to dismiss an offender with brief contempt.

The Hon. Mrs Leigh was more concerned that whatever was written should be in the correct style of approved euphemism—not rough, not coarse, not vulgarly revealing. She had suffered much from unfeeling publications of every species, and had received in her drawing-room at St James's Palace a procession of persons connected with her brother, scarcely any of them the kind of company she was accustomed to, when there came, nine or ten months after the news of his death had brought these trials upon her, the most uncouth, the most unpresentable of them all.

A *Mr Parry* [she informed Lady Byron] who was in Greece called here the other day—& not knowing the *sort of Animal* he was I saw him—*much* to my annoyance—he is among the Biographers I fear—a most *vulgar rough Bearish* person—he desired me to say if you had any *wish* to see him he wd go to you—I did not encourage him to expect you *wd* wish it & I sd advise you not from what I felt myself.[1]

At the time when William Parry paid this unwelcome visit, he was writing *The Last Days of Lord Byron*, the best, most vigorous, most convincing account by any eye-witness of Byron's final struggles in Greece, his personality in sickness and despair, and the personality of his plausible adversary, Colonel the Hon. Leicester Stanhope. There was no man more deserving the kindness of Byron's friends, and no man who received less of it.

It was Parry's misfortune not to be a gentleman—very obviously not a gentleman; and it seemed outrageous to friends and critics alike that a peer and a peer's son should be written about by a common fellow who had been a firemaster in the Navy. The book was scornfully handled by most reviewers and its author rejected everywhere.

In the 18th century the lines of demarcation had been so emphatically drawn that nobody bothered very much about keeping people who were not gentlemen in their place: they seldom attempted to come out of it. But with the rise of the prosperous middle classes, and the upheavals of Revolution in France and war all over Europe, the station to which each man had been called by God no longer seemed unquestionable—except to those who had been called to a station of high privilege. Each class

---

the protection of the Being whose existence he affected to disbelieve'. He had, in truth, been with Byron in a storm (though never with Captain Benson) and had displayed singular courage. Hobhouse, though not attracted by Shelley, told Moore he was 'as brave as a lion.'

[1] 2 Mar. 1825: Lovelace Papers.

had more power than in previous times to intrude upon the class immediately above it, and thence arose a new self-consciousness which brought the word 'gentleman' constantly to people's lips.

'Quite the gentleman', 'the perfect gentleman', 'conduct unbecoming a gentleman'—such phrases were not, as now, old-fashioned and even suggestive of the speaker's own insecurity, but were reiterated by well-bred tongues and aristocratic pens; while respectable society of all grades was united in rebuking—with what seems to us a brutal harshness—low persons who took liberties.

Leigh Hunt, in the book written to show what a very objectionable character Byron was, pointed out that his principal friends were 'of humble origin; one, of the race of booksellers; another, the son of a grocer; another of a glazier; and a fourth, though the son of a baronet, the grandson of a linen-draper'.[1] Hunt, who just squeezed into the ranks of gentility by having a clergyman for a father, was retorting upon the Press, which had accused him of being an impudent Cockney. This sort of accusation and counter-accusation, so antipathetic to our present feelings, was the daily fare of readers in the eighteen-twenties: and if it seemed shocking that Byron had consorted with Hunt and Medwin, whose education had not taught them how to address a lord,[2] it may be imagined how much more derogatory it was for the 'Noble Bard' to be portrayed by one who was little better than a manual worker.

It was thought that an ex-firemaster must be incapable of producing a book, the more so as he was reputed to be addicted to drink; and even those who were impressed by the information he gave, were of the opinion that the writing had been done for him. It is probable that some editorial corrections were made, his grammar being as rough and ready as his person, but he published the letters he had addressed to Bowring and Stanhope, and would at once have been exposed by those indignant men if there had been any falsification of his text, which is in the same direct and trenchant style as the book itself. The grammatical lapses are no worse than Trelawny's, whose works likewise had to be edited and corrected for publication.

Parry made his apologia bluntly and in prose wonderfully free from all the circuitous and strained elegance characteristic of the minor authors of the period:

[1] HUNT, *Lord Byron*, 2nd edition. The bookseller was, of course, John Murray, the grocer's son, Moore, the baronet's son Hobhouse, whose grandfather was a rich Bristol merchant. The glazier's son was William Gifford, who was not, however, among Byron's friends though Byron admired him as a critic.

[2] Medwin, 'the vulgarian', was taken to task for saying that a letter from Sir Ralph Milbanke to Byron had begun 'Sir'. Leigh Hunt had caused almost a sensation by opening his dedication of *Rimini* with 'My dear Byron', reckoned a gross familiarity in any form of public inscription, even between equals.

The only object I have in view, in sitting down to write a Preface, is to tell the reader why I have written a book. . . . Lord Byron's conduct in Greece has been attacked, in the book which Colonel Stanhope published on that country; it has also been attacked in the London Magazine, for October 1824; and as I was with him at the time, or immediately afterwards, when the coolness existed betwixt him and Colonel Stanhope, I may hope, by publishing an account of what I saw and know, not only to furnish the reader with some curious details relative to the latter days of Lord Byron, but also to vindicate his memory from some unjust aspersions.

During the last two months of his existence, there was no person in whom he placed more confidence than in me. I was employed by him to carry his designs into execution: I was intrusted with the management of his funds, and made the depository of his wishes. I lived under the same roof with him, was his confidential agent, and was honoured by being made his companion. As far as I have seen the accounts which have been published of his situation in Greece, there are some inaccuracies and many omissions in them all. The people of Great Britain have never been told, as it appears to me, of the numerous privations, the great neglect and the endless vexations to which Lord Byron fell a victim. Neither his physician, who should have guarded against many of these evils; his personal friends, who should have shielded him from others; nor that particular person, who was the cause of much of his perplexity, has described, or is ever likely to describe, all the circumstances of Lord Byron's situation in Greece. They fell under my observation, however, as well as under theirs; the reasons for their silence do not apply to me. . . .

There was nothing false in his claim to have been Byron's principal support during the last two months of his life. 'A fine fellow,' Byron called him, 'extremely active, and of strong, sound, practical talents . . .'[1] He had endeared himself at once by complaining of the 'enthusymusy' part of the Greek Committee, which included Stanhope and his Philo-Muse Society, his lithographic presses, and his determination to give the Greeks Lancastrian schools with English schoolmasters and to convert them from 'the mummery' of their religion.

Parry . . . sorely laments the printing and civilising expenses, and wishes there were not a Sunday-school in the world, or *any* school *here* at present, save and always excepting an academy for artilleryship.[2]

Thus he had made exactly the right start with Byron, who thought the Committee's special emissary, Stanhope, a good and honest man, but knew him for an extreme type of prig. It was a comfort to him to have an intelligent down-to-earth factotum at his command, fatherly and protective (he was twenty years Byron's senior) yet deferential too, a good companion over glasses of brandy and water, a humorous man who could give a lively imitation of Jeremy Bentham and laugh at the idealists in

---

[1] MOORE, *Byron*, Letter to Charles Hancock, 8 Feb. 1824.   [2] Ibid.

London bent on winning the war with Bibles, bugles, and the Bentham political doctrines—three commodities they were lavish of dispensing when everything else was wanting.

Parry himself, whose coming had been eagerly looked for because he was to have brought out Congreve rockets, had arrived instead with 'an elect blacksmith, intrusted with three hundred and twenty-two Greek testaments'.[1] No one was more unhappy at being unable to provide the expected missiles than he, no one more conscious of the Committee's ineptitude; but there is a natural comedy in the situation of a man so frustrated and frustrating, and especially when he is irascible, eccentric, and a toper. In the *London Magazine* Parry had been described, with scant regard for his feelings, as Lord Byron's butt—the very expression used about him by Stanhope himself conversing with Moore and Rogers several months before the article was published.[2] Contemporary writers took their tone from that, but it would have been just as valid to say that Stanhope, Gamba, or any other coadjutor was Byron's butt. No one was proof against his love of mockery.

When John Murray was seeking pictures of Byron's friends for the book of Finden engravings he brought out in 1834, Hobhouse, on being asked for his portrait, wrote banteringly of collecting around the poet—

all those whom he has cursed and quizzed and laught at and lampooned a hundred times. Take care that some wag does not illustrate your illustrative portraits with suitable inscriptions either in prose or verse from the hand of the Master himself.[3]

Byron might sometimes laugh at Parry, as he laughed at everyone, but he seems more often to have laughed with him. Stanhope, with his perfect mania for Bentham, whom he called 'the finest genius of the most enlightened age',[4] and 'the greatest civilian of this, or, perhaps, any other age',[5] could not but inspire satire in such a man as Byron. The anonymous and probably composite author of the magazine article had bestowed paeans of praise on Stanhope, from whom he very clearly derived some of his material. He contrasted his enlightenment with Byron's erring judgment, gave him the credit of having been infinitely more valuable in Greece and said that he aroused deep jealousy in Byron; all of which was infuriating to one who had been on the spot and had seen the doctrinaire Colonel at his follies.

Until Parry's book came out with its forthright denunciation, Stanhope had been able to have it all his own way in representing himself as

[1] MOORE, *Byron*, Letter to Charles Hancock, 5 Feb. 1824.
[2] MOORE, *Memoirs*, 14 July 1824.   [3] 11 Sept. 1833: Murray MSS.
[4] STANHOPE, Letter to J. Bowring, 23 Dec. 1823.
[5] Ibid. Article in the Greek Chronicle, 1824.

the wise man of the Greek War, the public being very ready to believe that a trained soldier must have more aptitude for warfare than a poet. Combining his criticism with generous-sounding eulogium, he was ingenious in belittlement of Byron. No one could hear him without being soon persuaded that Byron's financial contribution to the Greek cause had been enormously exaggerated, that his policies were misguided, and his genius of so wild and excessive a type that he was not suited to command.

Being a republican, he had been alarmed lest Byron should accept the Crown of Greece, which was almost certainly offered to him.[1] He also objected to his assuming command of the army by a commission from Mavrocordato, leader of the Provisional Government. He himself sets out his position thus:

> Lord Byron was for shining as a hero of the first order. He wished to take an active part in the civil and military government of Greece. On this subject he consulted me; I condemned the direct assumption of command by a foreigner, fearing that it would expose him to envy and danger without promoting the cause. I wished him, by a career of perfect disinterestedness, to preserve a commanding influence over the Greeks, and to act as their great mediator. Lord Byron listened to me with unusual and courteous politeness, for he suspected my motives—he thought me envious—jealous of his increasing power; and, though he did not disregard, did not altogether follow my advice. I was not, however, to be disarmed by politeness or suspicions; they touched me not, for my mind was occupied with loftier thoughts.[2]

Those lofty thoughts were shrewdly interpreted by Parry:

> Colonel Stanhope carried in his head plans for organizing the army, regulating the government, establishing schools, setting up newspapers, forming utilitarian societies, running mails, instructing the people, reforming the rulers, changing the religion, framing codes of law, regulating judicial proceedings, and, in short, for doing every thing. He had a constitution ready cut and dried; and he set about all these mighty projects without any of that previous acquaintance with the Greeks which one might expect would at least be possessed by any man who proposed to legislate for them. . . .
>
> In addition, also, to his being a visionary and a theorist, he was a soldier — a man bred up in habits of severe command and rigid obedience. He was a sort of Mussulman legist, ready to thrust freedom down the throats of the common herd of mankind at the point of the sword, and ready both to expound and enforce his theories.

Parry, ignorant and vulgar though he might be, was able to furnish support for everything he said, from the Colonel's own published letters.

[1] A hitherto unpublished passage in Hobhouse's *Journals* (18 Aug. 1825) speculates on the possibility that Admiral Lord Cochrane, in whom Hobhouse placed a quite unwarranted confidence, might 'establish himself in the sovereignty of Greece', and he adds, 'The Deputies told me over and over again during the discussion that had Byron lived he would now have been at the head of Greece'.

[2] STANHOPE, 1825 Edition.

Stanhope was incensed beyond measure. He hurried to bring out a new edition of his book, with a deceptive vindication:

> Among the numerous Calumnies which have been industriously circulated in this country relative to my conduct in Greece, is that of my having acted in factious opposition to Lord Byron. The degraded quarter from whence the mass of these charges proceed, and their total want of truth, absolutely precludes me from replying to them in any manner whatever; but I cannot forbear quoting the testimony which his Lordship himself bears in my favour.

Reproduced in facsimile was a passage from a letter of Byron's to John Bowring:

> I am happy to say that Colonel Leic.[r] Stanhope and myself are acting in perfect harmony together—he is likely to be of great service both to the cause and to the Committee—and is publicly as well as personally a very valuable acquisition to our party on any account.

Beneath these lines were appended Byron's initials, without any indication of omission, but Stanhope had left out the rather important continuation of the paragraph:

> He came up (as they all do who have not been in the country before) with some high-flown notions of the sixth form at Harrow or Eton, etc: but Col. Napier and I set him to rights on those points, which is absolutely necessary to prevent disgust, or perhaps return; but now we can set our shoulders *soberly* to the *wheel*, without quarrelling with the mud which may clog it occasionally.

Also missing from the quotation was the date—December 10th, 1823, when the writer had known Stanhope little more than a fortnight. That he was trying to overcome misgivings he had had from the beginning is at once apparent when we see the whole postscript—for such it is, an afterthought to a communication about other matters: and we cannot but wonder whether, if Stanhope had been so honest a man as he always seemed, he would have chosen to use what amounts to doctored evidence in his own favour.

There is something very artful too in his flattery of Hobhouse while subtly besmirching Byron in such a declaration as this:

> Mr John Cam Hobhouse was his long-tried, his esteemed, and valued literary and personal friend. Death has severed these; but there is a soul in friendship that can never die. . . . Mr Hobhouse has given many proofs of this, and among others, I saw him, from motives of high honour, destroy a beautiful poem of Lord Byron's, and, perhaps, the last he ever composed. The same reason that induced Mr H. to tear this fine manuscript will, of course, prevent him or me from ever divulging its contents.[1]

[1] STANHOPE, 1825 Edition. Hobhouse may have destroyed the poem in front of Stanhope but he had taken a copy of it. The verses beginning 'I watched thee when the

If 'high honour' had caused the poem to be destroyed, honour on quite an elementary plane might have precluded the incident, as well as the nature of the poem, from being 'divulged'.

Stanhope, being a truly committee-minded man, had a public attitude to Byron quite different from his private one. Formally, he passed as it were his vote of thanks, writing in a strain of homage, and with an air of chivalrously indulging the eccentricities of an extraordinary character, the little damaging touches being introduced as under a compulsion to do impartial justice. Privately, he undermined.

When Moore breakfasted at Sam Rogers's for the express purpose of talking to Byron's confrère, Stanhope told him the poet had been 'a mere puppet' in the hands of Mavrocordato, that the story of his giving thousands of pounds to assist the cause in Missolonghi was not true ('a little money goes an immense way in Greece') and that it was injurious to the dignity of the Greeks for Byron to have accepted the command of troops. All this was laced with back-handed tributes to his physical courage ('he was always for rushing into danger' and would laugh at himself afterwards') and to his good nature and genius.[1]

In private with Hobhouse, he was yet more bent on despoiling the hero of his laurels. 'Stanhope told me one or two truths too true I am sure about Byron's last career in Greece.'[2] So Hobhouse wrote in his journal only a few days after he had received the grandiloquent letter about the 'glorious course' that had 'terminated in death'. The things he had then learned were exactly such as would most disturb and distress him.

There was among Byron's followers a boy who figures variously in the annals as Lukas, Luca, or Luke, according to the nationality of the writer. He was handsome, haughty, and much spoiled by Byron, whose habitual nostalgia for the past invested him with the charm of a time of happiness long lost. On his first visit to Greece more than thirteen years before, he had spent a winter 'most social and fantastical' living in an Athenian monastery, surrounded by youthful students, and giving rein to 'hoydenish spirits'.[3] The glamour of this era in his life, when he himself had been carefree and captivating, writing for fame without any of the burdens fame brings, had always irradiated his memories of Greece, and Lukas had come upon the scene when he was in an especially susceptible and sensitive frame of mind.

There were no women about—none, at least, who could exert that

foe was at our side' refer to events so near the end of Byron's life that they are almost certainly his last, and were so described by Hobhouse, who suppressed but preserved them. They appear in *Poetry*, Vol. VII, and have been frequently reprinted. See MARCHAND, Vol. III.

[1] MOORE, *Memoirs*, 14 July 1824.   [2] Hobhouse *Journals*, 8 July 1824.
[3] QUENNELL, *Self-Portrait*. Letter to Hobhouse, 19 June 1811.

'softening influence' he valued them for. His paternal feelings, which had grown very strong, were never gratified. The child whom he described as 'my poor little natural baby'[1] was dead; and of his daughter by Lady Byron he could know nothing except what Augusta's now rare letters were permitted to convey. He had redeemed this boy's family from a harrowing plight as refugees in Ithaca, and was able, through him, to indulge the love of being patron and protector which had always been one of his most rooted characteristics. He requested Count Gamba to see the protégé supplied with all the finery a Greek whose family had once been rich could wish to wear. The account was rendered on the day of Byron's death by Lukas himself, laboriously writing somewhat baffling Italian. It was, of course, evidence of his good background that he could write at all, especially in foreign characters:

> To his excellency Signor Count Garba [*sic*] according to his orders from Milord N. Bayron for certain expenditures I have made

There were various garments including a jacket magnificent with gold, and another fine jacket for riding; there were also a saddle and a saddle-cloth with silk cording, and 'my pistols which I had gilded'.[2] These items had cost nearly a thousand drachmas.

At about the same time Byron had equipped another child in like splendour, a little Turkish girl named Hatajè who had been brought to him with her mother by the English doctor, Millingen.

> . . . He became so much struck by Hatajè's beauty, the naïveté of her answers, and the spiritedness of her observations on the murderers of her brethren, that he decided on adopting her. . . . He immediately ordered more costly dresses to be made for them, than those I had given them; and sent to Hatajè a necklace of sequins. Twice a week I was desired to send them to his house. He would then take the little girl on his knees and caress her with all the fondness of a father.[3]

Hatajè, like Lukas, became spoiled and Byron had to scold her because he was told she had grown pert and forward. He thought sometimes of sending her to England to be brought up with Ada, and sometimes he wondered if Teresa would have her in Italy.

Stanhope too had adopted a child, Mustapha Ali, a Turkish boy whom he brought back to England in the *Florida*. The rescue of children was a constant preoccupation of humane participants in that barbarous war, because it was the practice of both Greeks and Turks to slaughter whole families, excepting, by an untender mercy, only the youngest who were

---

[1] Letter to Augusta Leigh, 12 Dec. 1822: Lovelace Papers. Byron always masked his affectionate feelings towards Allegra from his worldly friends; and they were at first complicated by his neurotic revulsion against the mother.

[2] Murray MSS.   [3] MILLINGEN.

then left helpless and destitute. Mustapha Ali, though he had seen his nearest relatives murdered, was resilient. His gay disposition asserted itself, and he was given to 'singing, dancing, mimicking, and laughing'. Stanhope placed him as a day boy in a Utilitarian school in the Borough Road, and he often succeeded in bringing home a card for good conduct. He had a disconcerting habit of firing off pistols while dancing, but otherwise gave little trouble.[1]

It was far otherwise with Lukas, who was neither cheerful nor responsive. To Byron it was a strange experience to feel an affection that was not returned, and doubtless, in the deplorable circumstances in which he found himself, it heightened his emotion. He felt, as Parry said, 'forlorn and forsaken', and he grieved because it seemed that the last vestige of his youth was gone.

Like most outstandingly fascinating people who have known their looks to be part of their attraction, Byron was intensely conscious of what a later poet, his great admirer, called 'the cruel dishonour of time'.[2] Hair thinning and greying, and possibility (so menacing in those days of primitive dentistry) of not being able to keep one's teeth, the threat of corpulence, of inactivity—these are matters that, perhaps, give no serious concern to those whose beauty has never been a strong asset, but they worried him who knew that the world would watch the symptoms of Don Juan's decline with no charitable eye. In his typical self-destructive way, he constantly drew attention to his age, and even to his being older, through the pace at which he had lived, than his actual years.

He was aware that, turning thirty-six, oppressed with ill-health, disappointment, and anxiety, he could appear to his attendant of fifteen or sixteen no more than the outworn being he had often pronounced himself to be. He, whom so many had loved, had no other attraction for Lukas than his ability to send him out in the cavalcade with troops to serve under him, gold-embroidered clothes, gilded pistols, and money in his pocket. And in the sadness of this realization, he wrote:

> 'Tis time this heart should be unmoved,
>   Since others it hath ceased to move;
> Yet, though I cannot be beloved,
>   Still let me love!

[1] STANHOPE. There was a curious flowering of romance between Byron's Hatajè and Stanhope's Mustapha. A means was found of restoring Hatajè to her father, and she left Missolonghi on the ship that carried Byron's body to Zante, where she had to stay some weeks. There she met Mustapha Ali, who was waiting to sail with Stanhope in the *Florida*, and they played together in the quarantine house where Byron's body lay in its temporary coffin. Mustapha became deeply attached to her and was 'very sorrowful and disconsolate' when her father took her away, and 'wept for her absence for several days'. What became of these interesting children in later life is so far unknown.

[2] RODEN NOEL.

My days are in the yellow leaf;
    The flowers and fruits of love are gone;
The worm, the canker, and the grief
    Are mine alone!

The fire that on my bosom preys
    Is lone as some Volcanic isle;
No torch is kindled at its blaze—
    A funeral pile.

The hope, the fear, the jealous care,
    The exalted portion of the pain
And power of love, I cannot share,
    But wear the chain. . . .

Tread those reviving passions down,
    Unworthy manhood!—unto thee
Indifferent should the smile or frown
    Of Beauty be.

If thou regret'st thy youth, *why live?*
    The land of honourable death
Is here: up to the field and give
    Away thy breath! . . .

Stanhope had been one of the first, if not the very first, to read that striking lyric when Byron had produced it on the morning of his thirty-sixth birthday. Whatever 'those reviving passions' were—and most complex they must have been—Byron had striven to tread them down. He had deferred to the wishes of the leaders whose policies he was most inclined to trust, and had stuck it out in Missolonghi, with neither privacy nor comfort, when he could at any time have betaken himself and the members of his suite whom he favoured to a more agreeable environment.

Stanhope himself was nowhere near Missolonghi in the last months of Byron's life. He had removed to the more congenial atmosphere of Athens, where he could disseminate freely, with no satirical eyes watching him, the newspaper propaganda he so passionately believed in. (His journal was estimated to have a circulation, throughout all Greece, of forty). He had become an advocate for the robber chieftain, Odysseus, and his correspondence with Byron had been extremely scanty. Yet he did not scruple to give Hobhouse the most disillusioning account of Byron's activities and to say that 'he did little—but shoot pistols—and ride—and drink punch with Parry . . .'[1]

[1] Hobhouse *Journals*, the Notes headed 'Lord Byron' written about August 4th, 1824. Hobhouse was evidently ill at ease about Stanhope's motives in making such communications, and noted cautiously: 'I have heard from others that Stanhope tried to get him to approve of some of Jeremy Bentham's Reviews and Byron laught at them'.

Anyone who had sat down and worked out the dates would have discovered that, since Parry had not reached Missolonghi till the afternoon of February 5th and Stanhope had left on the morning of the 21st, all the idleness and dissipation reported must have been observed within a space of fifteen days, and that Stanhope could be no authority for anything that had taken place afterwards. But Hobhouse, who had never been on the scene or followed the movements of the protagonists, and was morbidly touchy on the subject of his friend's fame, allowed himself to be worked upon. His proprietary care for Byron's reputation was linked in this case with his resolve, as executor, to round up every remnant of Byron's property for the needy Augusta, and there were moneys which had not been adequately accounted for. Such, at least, was his excuse for putting pressure on Pietro Gamba. Angry curiosity must also have played its part. Towards Byron he was like a fond but stern parent who is always wanting to know the worst.

Pietro, usually most courteous and respectful to the imperious gentleman fourteen years his senior, suddenly found his patience wearing thin. In a handwriting even more tormentingly cryptic than usual, he sprang to Byron's defence and at the same time revealed an incident so full of sorrowful irony that it has never before been allowed to cloud the story, already sufficiently melancholy, of the poet's death.

As I have explained to you in other letters, as I have told you more than once by word of mouth, the credit which Mylord had with the city of Missolonghi for the sum of 2600 dollars[1] was legally transmitted to Lukas Andrizano.[2] Moreover it was within my knowledge and that of the steward of the house and Fletcher that more than thirty Spanish doubloons and 200 francesconi in silver ought to have been found in possession of Mylord.

After the death of B there was a search for this sum, about 700 [? dollars] —but in vain. It was suspected that Lukas had it. I questioned him skilfully and he declared that Lord Byron had given him some doubloons to assist his family. We did not wish to press the matter, because to recover the money appeared hopeless, and after all it might have been a cause of gossip damaging to the reputation of our friend. Every friend of Byron must desire that this *mischievous topic* should be buried if possible.

I always took every precaution that ever seemed prudent to prevent its being talked about in any way, and this I shall still do. But if you and Colonel Stanhope warn me that by reason of some mischance[3] there might be some rumour, I wish to inform you of all that is known to me of this miserable business, so that in any worse supposition, you have weapons in hand to confound the malignities and the calumnies of his and your enemies.

---

[1] The word used by Pietro is 'talleri' here translated as 'dollars' rather than 'thalers', dollars, either Spanish or American, being the currency chiefly used by Byron in the Greek War.

[2] The name was actually Chalandrutsanos.

[3] The word is illegible, but the context makes the meaning clear.

Pietro in his naïveté had no idea that those rumours which Stanhope professed to fear emanated from himself, and that he had passed them on to Hobhouse as truths. Simply, loyally, and, as to facts, conclusively, the brother of Teresa Guiccioli unfolded the little history of the very last and saddest of all Byron's attachments; and yet one in which he had behaved far better than in the triumph and egoism of his youth.

In August last year Lord Byron and his suite made a journey from Cephalonia to Ithaca. Many unhappy families from Patras and from Chios had sought a refuge there. Mr Knox the Resident in this Island begged Mylord to accord some succour to the refugees, for the most part women, old men and children, and he recommended to him particularly a family formerly rich in Patras, flung into poverty by the Revolution. There was an old infirm mother, with three very young daughters—Mylord gave 50 pounds sterling as help to the refugees and caused the family to be transported to Cephalonia giving them a monthly allowance of about 30 dollars. The three daughters were very young and not displeasing, but the conduct of Byron in regard to them could not have been more disinterested and more generous. He scarcely saw them [more than] once or twice in the house of Signore Corialegno.

Two of their brothers were in the Morea, one (Lukas) in the service of Colocotroni. On hearing of the generosity of Byron towards their family they both hurried to Cephalonia and begged Mylord to take them into his service. Lukas spoke Italian—he was about 15 years old—of a well-bred manner and person.

He did not wish to degrade him to the rank of a servant. Many a time he had said to me that, going to Greece, he would need many young people to serve as pages. We were then on the eve of our departure for Missolonghi, and thus he took Lukas in the quality of page.

During the voyage and the residence at Missolonghi he watched with [such] particular care over this youth that one might call it a weakness. He gave him splendid clothes, arms, and money; and he passed some half-hour every day with him reading Modern Greek. He took him with us in the cavalcade, and in the end he gave him the command of 30 irregular soldiers of his own brigade. On one occasion when this boy had a somewhat dangerous illness, Mylord was pleased to give up his own bed and slept in the common room with us on a Turkish divan for 3 or four days. This should not appear so strange, however, when you remember that the illness required a bed, and that no other was to be found in the house—and that on another occasion, when I was ill he made me the same offer; and that in the passage from Cephalonia to Missolonghi, Fletcher having a severe chill, Mylord gave him the only mattress on board and was pleased to sleep, himself, on deck.

Whatever suggestion was made to you that M—— [Mylord] could have slept in the same bed is absolutely false. The donation of 3000 dollars was given in consideration of his poor family.

If the conduct of Mylord towards that youth might seem to imply weakness, these facts and these few observations will suffice to prove to you that this weakness rose only from a noble source and a generous aim—his pity for the innocent unfortunate.

Tenderness to the memory of our friend has induced me to write this letter privately.

Please believe me,

Your devoted s[ervant] and f[riend],

Pietro Gamba[1]

The letter was marked Private, and addressed ceremoniously to 'Mr. J. C. Hobhouse,M.P., Executor and Personal Friend of Lord Byron'.

None of the accounts of Byron's death written by persons who were in the house includes any mention of Lukas visiting the sick-room. Byron would not have wished to be seen, his forehead covered with leeches, his pillows bloodstained, his body tortured by the remedies of the terrified doctors. In what was thought to be delirium, he often mentioned sums of money. Was he trying to exonerate the boy, to explain that he had given him the golden doubloons and silver francesconi his faithful steward would soon miss? Or was Lukas using the opportunity provided by the disruption of the household to steal from his dying patron?

Perhaps he took what he was sure was meant to be his, for Hobhouse heard from Fletcher that, when almost inarticulate, his Lordship had 'expressed an anxiety to do something for his favourite *chasseur* Tita and his Greek boy Luca—but Fletcher told him to speak of more important concerns'.[2] The inmates of the house would have had reports of what was going on.

Lukas disappears from the story for several years. Then, in February 1831, the *London Literary Gazette* printed some diatribes by Trelawny purporting to be an extract from an unpublished journal, and here we find a version of Lukas's tale. It was used as a means of attacking the hated Mavrocordato. Forgetting that in 1826 he had been in ecstasies over the heroic defence of Missolonghi, and had had letters in *The Examiner* about the necessity of it printed at his own especial request, he reverted to his earlier view that the place was 'a miserable mud bank' which ought never to have been held.

That Mavrocordato and the Mesolonghiot Primates should have done their utmost to detain Lord Byron and his chest of dollars amongst them was not to be marvelled at: besides his name was powerful as the mountain of loadstone mentioned in the Arabian tales, drawing all that approached it to their destruction; for, though they were lost, their dollars remained, which was all the Greeks wanted. So exclusively had Mavrocordato appropriated, in imagination, to his own use Byron's dollars, that not content with constituting himself his heir, he had extracted a considerable sum from him while living.

[1] 11 Aug. 1824: Murray MSS.
[2] Hobhouse *Journals*, the Notes headed 'Lord Byron'.

Lord Byron had, at Ithaca, undertaken to maintain a family of exiles from Patras. The eldest son he took to Mesolonghi, and made him his chibookghee; when partly for himself but chiefly as a provision for his family, he made over to him on several occasions, between three and four thousand dollars. Mavrocordato was commissioned to send a portion of the money to the family, then residing at Cephalonia, and the remainder he undertook to place in the hands of Lord Byron's agent at Zante, Samual Barff, Esquire, for safe conduct. I have only to add that Mavrocordato retained the entire sum for his use. The family was left in utter destitution at Byron's death, and the young man died six months after, in want of the necessaries of life. So much for 'honest, honest Iago.'

This article, though some of it, according to the author's claim, was written on Byron's coffin,[1] abounds in such gross misstatements that the parts relating to Mavrocordato must be read with reserve; but the information regarding Lukas's death and the destitution of the family is accurate.

It is certain too that there was a debt of some thousands of dollars due from the civic authorities of Missolonghi to Byron and that he legally empowered Lukas to receive that sum, or a portion of it, for the use of his family; and it may well be that the bankrupt city, desperate for money, with Byron dead and the Greek loan from England frozen, did not fulfil its obligations.

The confirmation of Lukas's early death comes from an unexpected quarter—a letter in Greek dated December 9th, 1832, and forwarded by the British Consul at Patras—

To the respected lady,
Noble daughter of Lord Byron.

It was an appeal for money from the three sisters of Lukas, the girls whom Pietro had described as very young and 'not displeasing'—but they were nearly eight years older now. They spoke with reverence of 'the great Philhellene Lord':

The moment he set foot on our soil he showed his philanthropy to all suffering Greeks, generally and particularly. Among those who were thus charitably treated was one of our brothers named Lukas, who was very much loved by the unforgettable Lord Byron, but who died in the midst of the war and in the midst of the happiness which Byron had procured for him. . . . In Greece many families have had to mourn such losses and many have shed tears for that. But our misfortune is the worst . . . three girls, poor, abandoned, we do not know where to turn, and the only thing that remains for us is to address ourselves to you who, born of a Philhellene father, will

[1] 'At the house of the Primate Apostoli Arestoli in which he died, Mesolonghi, April 29th 1824.' The surname of the man who owned the house where Byron died was Capsali. One might suppose even Trelawny would have managed to get it right if really using so portentous a desk to make a most deliberate record.

pity our misfortune. You will complete a good work which, unfortunately your unforgettable father to our misfortune did not manage to fulfil. . . .[1]

'Lukas, very much loved by the unforgettable Lord Byron. . . ' It would seem from this that he had been proud to give his family the tidings of the Generalissimo's regard for him; nor is there any reason to doubt that Byron had hoped his bounty would bring relief to them all. Trelawny arrived in Cephalonia in September 1825, and it may have been there that he heard of Lukas's lamentable end, as it was in that island that Byron had temporarily settled the boy's dependants.

Hobhouse, possibly a little ashamed of having lent such a ready ear to the insinuations of one who was almost a stranger, never again seems to have touched on the subject; and by the time the books by Parry and Gamba came out, he knew Stanhope rather better than in those first few tense and nervous days after the arrival of the *Florida*. He even allowed Pietro to make one or two gentle thrusts at the Colonel in the 'Narrative' which he translated.

Parry's work was less dignified than Pietro's but livelier, and it came as a wholesome counterblast to all disparagement disguised as gentlemanly concern. Hobhouse had not liked the idea of its being written, but when it came out he was silent—almost a testimonial in view of his express resolution to challenge biographers who published falsehoods. He may even have felt some satisfaction that Stanhope's pomposity had been deflated. No doubt he would have preferred that it had not been one of the 'low company' Byron had so perversely cultivated who came before the public to defend him; but the recollections in themselves were both creditable and convincing—not the less so because the author was modest in his professions:

> I must here observe that I make no pretensions to repeat his Lordship's exact words; they were so well put together, that it would be impossible for me to imitate them; but his sentiments I cannot forget, for they made a deep and lasting impression.

Parry fell into occasional errors of judgment (to him the future historian, Finlay, was a frivolous young man who wasted Byron's time), but his estimates of most of the persons, situations, and events he discussed have been substantiated. In some respects he was in advance of his time. He had to swim entirely against the current of opinion, for example, when he firmly condemned the bleeding of a patient 'low, and weak, and half-starved as Lord Byron was, and debilitated beyond measure'. Such a view was utterly unorthodox among both doctors and laymen.

Parry's book contains the most moving of all descriptions of Byron's

---

[1] Lovelace Papers. There is no sign that this letter was answered, or even translated.

L.L.B.—N

death-bed. Avoiding the bland anti-realism with which it was customary to treat such a theme, he sets the harrowing scene before us in all its sordidness:

> As there was nobody invested with any authority over his household, after he fell sick, there was neither method, order, nor quiet in his apartments . . . There was also a want of many comforts which, to the sick, may indeed be called necessaries, and there was a dreadful confusion of tongues. In his agitation Dr Bruno's English, and he spoke but imperfectly, was unintelligible; Fletcher's Italian was equally bad. I speak nothing but English; Tita then spoke nothing but Italian; and the ordinary Greek domestics were incomprehensible to us all. In all the attendants there was the officiousness of zeal; but owing to their ignorance of each other's language, their zeal only added to the confusion. This circumstance, and the want of common necessaries, made Lord Byron's apartment such a picture of distress and even anguish during the last two or three days of his life, as I never before beheld, and wish never again to witness . . .

> There was the gifted Lord Byron, who had been the object of universal attention, who had, even as a youth, been intoxicated with the idolatry of men, and the more flattering love of women, gradually expiring, almost forsaken, and certainly without the consolation which generally awaits the meanest of mankind, of breathing out his last in the arms of some dear friend.[1] His habitation was weather-tight, but that was nearly all the comfort his deplorable room afforded him . . . The pestilent *sirocco* was blowing a hurricane, and the rain was falling with almost tropical violence. In our apartment was the calm of coming death, and outside, was the storm desolating the spot around us. . . .

> On the 16th he was alarmingly ill, and almost constantly delirious. He spoke alternately in English and Italian, and spoke very wildly. I earnestly implored the doctors not to physic and bleed him . . .

> On the 17th, when I saw him in the morning, he was labouring at times under delirium. He appeared much worse than the day before; notwithstanding this, he was again bled twice, and both times fainted. . . . Those conversations which Count Gamba reports, as heard by himself and others, are all of that rambling character which distinguish [*sic*] delirium. It is particularly necessary to make this observation, because a great degree of importance is sometimes attributed to death-bed speeches. In Lord Byron's case, whatever may be reported as said by him, must be taken with the consideration that he was frequently delirious, for the last five days of his existence.

The unskilful young doctor had bound his head up so tightly that he was in agony, crying to himself 'Ah Christi!' and when Parry loosened the bands, he shed tears of relief.

[1] Pietro Gamba wished to go to him but, unhappily, 'had not the heart. Mr Parry went, and Byron knew him again, and squeezed his hand, and tried to express his last wishes.' GAMBA.

I encouraged him to weep, and said, "My Lord, I thank God, I hope you will now be better; shed as many tears as you can, you will sleep and find ease." He replied faintly, "Yes, the pain is gone, I shall sleep now," and he again took my hand, uttered a faint good night, and sank into a slumber; my heart ached, but I thought then his sufferings were over, and that he would wake no more.

Parry had known the rough life of a seafaring man in Nelson's fleet, he had served in the Navy under Congreve, yet he showed what is called a woman's tenderness to the dying poet, and he left a picture of his last days in an almost literal sense. The four illustrations to his book were done by Robert Seymour after sketches which Parry supplied. The original of the frontispiece here reproduced is in the Gennadius Library of Athens.[1] In a bare-looking room where Suliote soldiers are selecting weapons from rows hanging on the walls, or seated on the floor playing cards, Byron in his peaked cap, with a blue surtout almost to his ankles, an open-necked shirt and long, loose trousers, playfully waves a cane at an enormous Newfoundland. The sketch of him in a late stage of his illness establishes that he died on a reasonably commodious bed and not on the low folding pallet shown in the Athens Ethnological Museum.[2]

It is unlikely that Parry's book will ever be reprinted in full, much of it being devoted to controversies from which he long ago emerged victorious (though it was victory he did not live to see). No one has been able to deal adequately with Byron's last struggles in Greece without drawing upon it, yet thanks to Trelawny rather than the direct antagonist, Stanhope, several biographers, even while using the narrative, have taken a scornful or patronizing view of the narrator.

Trelawny describes him as 'a rough burly fellow, never quite sober, but he was no fool, and had a fund of pot-house stories. . . . All he did, however, was to talk and drink.'[3] This last aspersion is completely exploded by the authority of Byron and Gamba, and others who were at Missolonghi when Trelawny was enjoying his hunting expeditions with Odysseus far from the vexations of the 'mud isthmus': Parry could not produce Congreve rockets without coal, which the Committee had not seen fit to send, but he displayed phenomenal energy in every direction where he was not thwarted, nor is it unthinkable that his drinking was

---

[1] The inscription on the back runs: 'This sketch of Byron and his favourite dog, Lion, with his Suliote guards, was made by Robert Seymour of London from a sketch and description furnished by Major Parry in my presence. May 20, 1825. Henry Lacey.' Lacey was one of the publishers of Parry's book.

[2] Sir Harold Nicolson stressed this point in *The Last Journey*, published as long ago as 1924, but it is a slow business getting an ungenuine specimen withdrawn or properly labelled once it becomes a favourite exhibit in a Museum. Byron never seems to have used his camp-bed, though it was considered luxurious by a young man to whom he lent it, Thomas Smith.   [3] TRELAWNY, *Recollections*.

exaggerated by Stanhope, who was to become an ardent temperance reformer.

Trelawny's habitual air of omniscience prevented any investigator from noticing that the scene in which he introduces Parry could not conceivably have taken place. Parry's statement that he left Missolonghi on April 21st is supported by contemporary letters from Gamba. Trelawny had not yet arrived there: nevertheless, this is what he reports in his *Recollections*:

> On hearing a noise below, I went down into the public room, and found Parry with a comrade carousing—. . . .
> I said, "Well, major, what do you think was the cause of Lord Byron's death?"
> "Think? I don't think anything about it; I am a practical man, not a humbugging thinker; he would have been alive now if he had followed my advice. He lived too low: I told him so a thousand times. Two or three days before he slipped his wind, he said: 'Parry, what do you think is the matter with me, the doctors don't know my complaint?' No, I said, nor nothing else, my lord; let me throw them out of the window. . . . Brandy, my lord; nothing but brandy will save you; you have only got a chill on an empty stomach; let me mix you a stiff glass of grog. . . .'

The dialogue, substantial in length, is sheer fantasy; and yet this libel-writer is constantly quoted as evidence for the most improbable utterances by Byron.

Parry was on the verge of collapse at Byron's death, and was confined to his room at Zante in a state of nervous breakdown[1] during the brief halt Trelawny made there before rejoining the 'glorious being', Odysseus. That was the only time they were ever within a mile of each other.

His word is the sole authority for the subsequent career of Parry, who, he said, 'was three months in Greece, returned to England, talked the Committee out of £400 for his services, and drank himself into a mad-house'.[2] Every derogatory assertion from this quarter demands investigation. Parry left England in the service of the Greek Committee on November 10th, 1823, and did not return till about July 1824, having been recalled through Stanhope's complaints of him. His salary was to have been £400 a year, and he had been obliged to pay a high proportion

---

[1] Hobhouse says in his *Journals* (5th June 1824) 'Parry is mad at Zante', but though he must have had this information from some quarter, it is not confirmed by correspondence with Gamba and others who were on the spot, then or later. Gamba speaks respectfully of Parry in several letters. Parry himself says: 'My constitution is naturally a good one, but it was worn down by the climate of such a place as Missolonghi, and the fatigues I had latterly undergone.' Dr Millingen was also severely ill, and so were many others.

[2] TRELAWNY, *Recollections*. Gordon, in his information about Parry, is merely quoting what he heard from Trelawny.

of the expense of the outward voyage, which it was proper for the Committee to refund him. Had he made any claim beyond what was reasonable, it had little chance of remaining unrecorded by Hobhouse.

It is true that he fell under an affliction of mental illness and died in an asylum. It may or may not be true that the illness was caused by drink, but if it were, then he was a better witness drunk than Trelawny sober, since his work is full of details which—as to what came under his own observation—have never been faulted after much more than a century of research, whereas Trelawny's swaggering accounts generally fall to pieces when examined.

If the payment of £400 was made, it must have been before April 1825, when the book, with its vehement onslaught on some of the leading Committee members, came out. He would hardly have dared to ask for the money after! And as he was still at large in April 1826, when he was the subject of a furious attack in the *Examiner*, he was drinking himself into a madhouse at a very measured pace.

Stanhope must have forgotten how he had declared that he was 'absolutely precluded from replying in any manner whatever' to the aspersions of the plebeian firemaster when he let the editor (Leigh Hunt's brother) publish a letter that had been written on May 14th in the previous year.

> Sir,
>   I this morning read your historic work, entitled the Last Days of Lord Byron. From the fictious [*sic*] libels it contains, you should have called the romance *Parry's Slanders.* . . .
>   As you were a sort of Caleb Quotem[1] about Lord Byron, in your medical capacity you prescribed brandy to him on several occasions, and especially after an epileptic fit.[2] You remonstrated against bleeding Lord Byron though the doctors thought that early bleeding would have saved his valuable life.
>   You seem to be sore at having, in consequence of my representations, been recalled and dismissed by the Greek Committee. To be revenged you represent me as the enemy of Lord Byron. The reverse is the fact. Such was my respect for Lord Byron that I solicited the Greek Committee (though in vain) to be allowed to act under his Lordship. You are right in stating that I occasionally differed from his Lordship; but upon this fact you graft a heap of misstatements. I should explain Lord Byron was a friend to the Freedom of the Press, but he feared its dangerous influence in Greece. . . . I was, however, far more alarmed at the early efforts made to shackle the Press. I had experience in British India, of the safety and usefulness of free discussion in checking the licentiousness of the people and their Government; in destroying superstition the growth of ages; and in removing by degrees those evils which produce discontent, military mutinies, civil rebellions, and foreign wars.

---

[1] A jack-of-all-trades in a play by Colman, *The Review*.
[2] On 15 Feb. Byron had a seizure which was mistaken for an epileptic fit.

To recur to Lord Byron, I am bound in justice to his memory to state that he was the friend of the Free Press. It is true that I occasionally differed with Lord Byron on this and other matters, and that violent discussions ensued. I never saw anything equal to the starts of his passion. The flash of his eyes, the thunder of his voice, the convulsion of his frame, were like a frightful hurricane; but the storm soon subsided, and sunshine followed. These altercations never affected the private friendship or public esteem I entertained for Lord Byron. . . .

Your whole book is full of accusations against me. You certainly had a good opportunity of judging my conduct, from having long lived in my room and at my table. Your intimacy indeed was so great, that you even broke open one of my letters addressed to Mr Hodges. . . .[1]

This repetitive and undignified letter—abbreviated here—was written not by an untruthful man but one whose mind was confused and self-deceiving. The schoolboyish admirer of Byron's poetry may have asked in London to serve under him, but in Greece he not only opposed and argued with him incessantly, but sent critical and disturbing opinions about him to the Secretary of the Committee. As for his 'private friendship', we have seen what that amounted to from the samples of his conversation with Hobhouse. His taxing Parry with having 'long lived in my room and at my table' persuades us that all his statements must be tested for exaggeration, because the utmost period of their contact was a fortnight. The house they occupied in Missolonghi had so few rooms at the disposal of the English party that Parry would have been obliged to use those of Stanhope, who had taken the best for himself before Byron arrived, leaving the lame man only the top floor to accommodate his suite as well as himself.

His open letter was accompanied by an abusive footnote ostensibly from the editor:

This man *was* a caulker in the dockyards, and *is* (not to repeat the worst of him) a slanderer, a sot, a bully, and a poltroon. Who wrote the book to which he has prefixed his name we cannot exactly say; but he himself cannot write ten words of English.

A week after the publication of this unseemly *argumentum ad hominem*, the Colonel attacked again, and the letter, illuminating though full of childish spitefulness, appears never to have been reprinted:

My dear Sir,

Lord Byron passed many of his idle hours with Mr Parry and his Greek page. Mr Parry christened Lord Byron Hal, and himself Falstaff. His Lordship used to turn all poor Parry's plans into ridicule and fine his sharp wit on him. For instance, Lord Byron one night made Parry act Richard III. His Lordship repeated all the other parts from memory. Lord B. kept his

---

[1] Hodges was an artificer serving under Parry, and superseding him by Stanhope's orders.

countenance, but the company laughed outright. In the middle of this performance Mr P. said he would show how he presented a petition to the Admiralty from the shipwrights of the Thames. He rushed up to Lord B., flung himself down upon one knee, spread out both his arms, and began repeating some bombast slang written by the hard-handed gentry.

His attitude, his figure, his vulgar English, and his great conceit at length overcame even Lord B.'s gravity, and all burst out into a loud chorus of laughter.[1]

Such anecdotes merely prove that Byron was on terms of considerable jollity with Parry; and whatever made him laugh, the slang of a shipwright, the vulgar English of a sailor, would not have been unacceptable to the author of *Don Juan* and grandson of 'Foulweather Jack'.[2] Had Parry been the sottish buffoon Stanhope tried to depict, it is improbable that Gamba, a young man of good breeding, would have consulted him and placed him among 'le persone più rispettabili' who were about Byron when he died,[3] and renewed his friendly relations with him in London.

Parry had complained in his book that he was kept out of the sickroom when Byron became ill, on the grounds 'that he was asleep, or quiet, or had better not be disturbed', and yet that he was always summoned when the doctors required someone to exert influence over the patient—and he was able to point to Gamba's 'Narrative' for support. Stanhope, with a cruelty suggestive of some state much less mature than 'the sixth form at Harrow or Eton', informed the public that—

> Latterly, Lord Byron was quite jaded with Falstaff's swaggering and intrusions. . . . The simple fact is that Lord Byron though he did not wish to hurt the gentleman's feelings, took measures with his friends and servants to get rid of his companion. Lord Byron complained much to Mr Fowke of Mr Parry's intrusions. "If," said he, "I send you down a book, or a piece of paper with nothing written upon it, will you invent some excuse to draw Parry out of my room? No matter what excuse so that you can make him bolt."
>
> On another occasion, Mr Parry complained that he could not find time to do anything. Lord B. in a start of passion, exclaimed: 'How the devil is it then, that you can find time to sit with me every day for nine hours?'

As Stanhope was not present, he presumably heard this gossip from Edward Fowke, one of the young men 'of a light and frivolous cast'

[1] *Examiner*, 9 Apr. 1826.

[2] William Girdham, coxwain of the *Salsette*, in which Byron took his longest sea voyage, said he was 'a great favourite with the sailors, both on account of his liberality and the frankness of his intercourse with them'. (FIELD.)

[3] E.g. 'I believe myself obliged by reason of the full and long confidence I enjoyed from the noble Lord during his life, and by the advice of Prince A. Mavrocordato, Mr Parry, and all the most respectable persons who are to be found, here, to take everything into my care.' Letter to Samuel Barff, 20 Apr. 1824. Murray MSS.

whom Parry seemed to dislike. On the other hand, Fowke's surviving remarks about Stanhope are not in a respectful tone. Writing to Hobhouse to thank him for presents which were souvenirs of Byron, he added:

> I received a curious letter from Stanhope demanding from me sans ceremonie whatever papers I might have concerning Greece Lord Byron and Parry. Offering to publish it anonymously in his second edition, recommending me to follow his order and style &c.[1]

It may be gathered that Fowke, who was greatly attached to Byron,[2] would not have been very pleased to see himself quoted in print as the source of the humiliating gossip about Parry—though it is probably true that Byron had wearied at times of the old firemaster's company, as he wearied of all company, cramped and lacking in privacy as his days in Missolonghi were.

Stanhope's assaults, whatever effect they may have had on the readers of the *Examiner*, never succeeded in disposing of Parry. If he was originally a dock labourer, this makes it the more remarkable that he managed, by whatever means, to present so lively, touching, and penetrating a survey of a most intricate scene. If he really was common, illiterate, intemperate, then his winning the trust and esteem in a crucial hour of such a man as Byron shows some quality in him bigger than Stanhope and his friends could recognize.

Among the many recipients of Stanhope's protests was Augusta Leigh, to whom he wrote:

> Mr Parry has published a book of slanders against me in which he has most falsely represented me as the enemy of your lamented Brother Lord Byron.[3]

Doubtless he received a very civil reply, but when, some months later, he brought out the new edition of his own work, enlarged by further material, she was intensely annoyed.

> I think Leicester Stanhope's production *most uncalled-for* and *in bad taste* [she wrote to Lady Byron]. I sd think Hobhouse will be in a rage at the mention of him.[4]

Hobhouse could not be openly at loggerheads with Stanhope because they were both prominent members of the Greek Committee. They had to see a great deal of each other and make a show of working in unison, but for all the mutual compliments they published, there was no liking between them. The allusions in Hobhouse's diary show that, though he made a conscientious effort to recognize his merits, he saw Stanhope's

---

[1] British Museum: Additional MSS. 36461. 6 May 1825. Stanhope had plainly read Parry's book before the date on which he said he had done so.
[2] KENNEDY. [3] Letter without date: Lovelace Papers. [4] Ibid. 12 Jan. 1826.

weaknesses clearly. In one passage he mentions him as 'the poor be-praised Colonel . . . plotting to set up schools in Tripolitza in the heart of Ibrahim's camp'. (Ibrahim was the Turkish enemy.) 'Nevertheless,' he adds, 'Stanhope is a good man—jusqu'à la vanité.'[1]

Stanhope's letters he characterized as 'absurd' or 'most silly'. When he and Sir Francis Burdett were accused by Stanhope of being 'torpedo struck' in their lethargic movements on behalf of Greece, Hobhouse was very angry,[2] but they patched up their differences in the face of public criticism.

However he may have regarded it when it appeared, in his old age he spoke highly of Stanhope's 'Sketch of Lord Byron' which he called, with Finlay's 'Reminiscences' in the same book, an excellent picture of his friend 'just as he appeared to me during our long intimacy'.[3] They are certainly both most percipient pieces of writing, but it is possible that Hobhouse was not uninfluenced by their agreeable references to himself: he very much liked that 'long intimacy' to be acknowledged.

The publication of letters about Byron by Finlay and Hamilton Browne and Stanhope's own 'Sketch' was one of the many good results of Parry's book. After having been accused of acting with hostility to Byron in Greece, Stanhope was on his mettle to show that, whatever their divergencies on matters of policy might have been, he was not without appreciation of the greatness of the man he had been dealing with. But his valedictory lines can hardly be considered gracious:

> Lord Byron's constitution was broken by excesses; by the workings of his own mad genius; by his wild and racing career, and by the capricious systems of abstinence and of eating and drinking which he had at times adopted. . . . Medicines had become part of his daily food; without them he could not have existed. Under all these circumstances . . . it is next to impossible that he could have been long-lived. His bodily functions were in reality destroyed, and his youthful and 'burning thoughts' were every instant preying upon his existence.

Praise for so frank a verdict from the man who had once thought that all facts about Byron's volcanic life should be concealed testifies eloquently to the effect of the several decades of pitiless revelation.

As for Finlay, Hobhouse was generous to speak so highly of his veracity, or else he had never come accross what Finlay ultimately wrote of him. In his famous *History of the Greek Revolution*, published in 1861, he came out boldly with the opinion that—

> Lord Byron was . . . a far wiser counsellor than the Typographical Colonel, and had he lived, might have done much to arrest factious madness

---

[1] Hobhouse *Journals*, 24 May 1826.
[2] Ibid. 24/25 Nov. 1826.   [3] HOBHOUSE, *Recollections*.

and shameless expenditure which rendered the English loans the prize and the aliment of two Civil Wars.

... The persons principally responsible for this waste of money and delays were Mr Hobhouse, now Lord Broughton; Mr Edward Ellice; Sir Francis Burdett; Mr Hume; Sir John Bowring, the Secretary of the Greek Committee; and Messrs Ricardo, the contractors of the second Greek loan.

The folly of these misguided well-wishers was 'purchasing the services of Lord Cochrane to command a fleet for the sum of £57,000, and setting apart £150,000 to build a fleet which he was hired to command'. The first vessel did not arrive till after the battle of Navarino!

Many pages of Hobhouse's diary are occupied by the almost incredibly ill-judged bargain he and his Committee made with the grasping admiral, whose numberless postponements of action are a curiosity of naval history. Cochrane had contravened the Foreign Enlistment Act by taking service, on a purely mercenary basis, with the Brazilian Government. He still had —or considered he had—unsettled claims amounting to £50,000 against Chile, and he stipulated that the Greek Committee should guarantee him this sum, which was tantamount to sacrificing it, and pay him as well £4000 a year, with a pension of £2000 a year after his retirement, to be continued to his widow. So inordinate were his demands that when the proposed appointment was set before the Greek Committee in Paris, the financial terms were diplomatically left out of the paper.

Hobhouse admitted that the Greek Deputies, Orlando and Luriottis, were frightened at the extent to which, against their own judgment, they had committed the means left at their disposal.

> Should they exhaust all their funds upon the appointment of Cochrane and any accident should happen, they will inevitably be ruined. They feel the rope about their necks, particularly Orlando who has a wife and five daughters in pledge at Hydra. Burdett and I told them to be of good cheer they had saved their country. . . .[1]

The Greeks tried more than once to retreat from their onerous agreement, or at least to get Cochrane to give some definite undertakings in their favour, but he refused, and they were firmly held to the terms by Hobhouse and Burdett, who again and again overruled them.

> Certainly without our intervention the arrangement would never have taken place. . . . The sacrifice of so large a sum to Lord Cochrane would have been an invincible obstacle unless persons of character and judgement had recommended it.[2]

The tone is exactly that in which he congratulated himself on having, with Murray's aid, got Byron's Memoirs destroyed, and the two incidents

[1] Hobhouse *Journals*, 15 Aug. 1825.
[2] Ibid. 18 Aug. 1825. The capital sum ultimately set aside for Cochrane, apart from salary, was £37,000.

were closely parallel. Hobhouse watched Byron's reputation suffer every kind of onslaught as the direct and indirect effects of that blunder, but he could never bring himself to acknowledge he had erred. In the same way, he saw Cochrane's plans for the steamboat fleet progress only from one delay to another, so that, just two years after Byron's death, Missolonghi had fallen with frightful carnage before a single ship's engine, let alone a ship, had been constructed: but though his own diary must be the best record in existence of the ineptitude of the whole organization, he was still, in his old age, justifying the measures taken.

The Greeks were certainly very curious people to deal with, and exasperating to Englishmen—who could not understand their mixture of fiery patriotism on the highest plane and financial opportunism on the lowest. Hobhouse had a good deal of trouble with Orlando and Luriottis, who were discovered by one of their own confrères, a third Government representative in London, Spaniolachi, to have indulged in peculation to the extent of £40,000.[1] Yet when Missolonghi was first—prematurely —reputed to have fallen, Luriottis 'burst into an agony of grief, crying and sobbing most bitterly. . . . I could scarcely appease him.'[2]

The patriotism of the Deputies was not less real than their opportunism, but their situation in London was demoralizing in the extreme. Not only were they forced to stand by impotently awaiting a steamboat fleet in which they had little faith, but they were obliged to bow their heads to disgraceful waste of the funds subscribed for their cause. The bankers Ricardo sliced a commission of £64,000 off each of the two loans of about a million pounds, and over and above this, an intrusive Mr Bonfil took £4800 a time for brokerage. A remittance of £155,000 went to an American shipbuilder for two frigates which showed no sign of ever making an appearance. The futile services of General Lallemand for one year cost £12,000. Cannon to the value of £20,000 were purchased in England, and remained in England: and Stanhope, with his feet on the ground for once, protested at a bondholders' meeting that Cochrane's chosen engineer, Galloway, had been paid £80,000 for four 50-horse power vessels which were unfit to use and 'rotting in the river'.[3]

It was small wonder that, where all this jobbery and squandering were going on, the Greek Government officials should have felt inclined to put something in their own pockets. Byron, with his international prestige and the vigour of his pen, would never have been subjected long to such impositions: but Hobhouse had only one remedy, the very worst where decision and forcefulness are needed—'to keep matters quiet'.[4] It

---

[1] Hobhouse *Journals*, 12 Jan. 1826. They admitted only to £14,000 or £15,000.
[2] Ibid. 6 Apr. 1826.
[3] 10 Sept. 1826. He was taken to task for this disloyalty by Hobhouse and Hobhouse's supporters later.   [4] Hobhouse *Journals*, 6 May 1826.

was the principle he acted on in all scandals—'no squabbling in public'.[1] He could be as firm as a rock in personal transactions, but whenever he became a committee man, his concern for presenting a smooth front resulted in feeble compromise and yielding of ground.

The sums subscribed in France and England to assist the Hellenes, though trifling compared with the cost of even a minor war on the modern scale, were vast in proportion to the normal revenues of Greece and had been raised largely on the strength of Byron's name. When he had learned of the mismanagement on one side and rapacity on the other, he had worried about recommending the loan and prophesied gloomily to Finlay that 'many honest English families' would lose their money through his Philhellenism.[2] So shockingly was the contribution misused that the very flower of the foreign volunteers, among them the chivalrous young Italian, Count Pietro Gamba, had followed Byron to an early grave before a single gesture of the high-minded but unrealistic organizers in London had become effectual. Had the money been properly administered, and used as an instrument for ending instead of promoting faction, it is inconceivable that the ruthless slaughter could have been prolonged for eight years after Byron's death.

[1] Hobhouse *Journals*, 24 May 1826.
[2] FINLAY, *Greek Revolution*. When Byron undertook to go to Greece, Bowring, the Committee Secretary, wrote to him (Murray MSS. 22 July 1823): 'I cannot easily communicate the delight which your Lordship's letter of the 7th July has given us all. Its contrast to nine tenths of the epistles I receive on this subject is as bright as a sunbeam. We have dispatched more than two thousand letters, which bring in a few driblets, but there is no important result, no congregated mass of efficient sympathy.' It was Byron's personal identification with the cause that brought that.

CHAPTER VI

TRIALS OF AN EXECUTOR

It is rather a curious fact that Byron took it for granted the principal members of his household would accompany him on a hazardous adventure to a country in the throes of a violent revolution, and equally, that they took it for granted they were to go. Even Fletcher, who had been in Greece before and grumbled all the time, did not put up any resistance beyond grumbling again. It thus fell to the executors' lot to provide for a number of extremely miscellaneous dependents from foreign parts, ranging from an unfrocked Italian priest, who had been steward and major domo, to an American negro described as a courier, whose privilege it had been to address his Lordship as 'Massa'.

The steward and the valet were given gratuities sufficient to set them up as small tradesmen, and Augusta presented Fletcher with the whole of Byron's wardrobe, which filled five trunks. As he had been a most faithful servant for twenty years, she undertook additionally to pay him the then substantial annuity of £70.[1] But a man who, during the whole of his adult life, has been directed and looked after like a little boy, is not likely to learn the ways of prudent and independent business management in his middle forties; while Augusta, for her part, overwhelmed with the calamities arising from her daughter's marriage and the extravagances of her sons, only kept up the pension for a few years.

Lega Zambelli, the ex-priest, joined his resources to Fletcher's to open a macaroni factory, but it failed. The negro, Benjamin Lewis, was also liberally dealt with by Hobhouse, and was easily able to find new employment, but, whether from accident or illness, he met with an early death in 1825.

Giovanni Battista Falcieri, known as Tita, who from being a gondolier, had become a chasseur, was taken into Hobhouse's own employment as a valet. After a year in this service, he had communicated, both by word of mouth and in a formal letter, addressed to the Rispettabile Signore Hobhouse Esqre M.P., his determination to return to Greece. Though his new master's political life was full of fights and crises, his private life, which was all Tita saw, must have seemed very humdrum compared with that of the renowned milord who had perpetually raised up storms, and Tita went eagerly back to danger. His plan seems to have been to serve the young Count Gamba. It was highly inconvenient to Hobhouse, but he gave his blessing and in tangible shape.

Soon after Pietro's death at Metana in spring 1827, Tita was found at Malta in great want. He entered the service of another lively young man,

[1] Murray MSS.

Mr Benjamin Disraeli, who was wholehearted in admiration, not to say imitation, of Lord Byron, and proud to employ the tall black-bearded Venetian whose fine appearance caused a stir wherever he was seen.

Hobhouse had done his best to take on as many of Byron's personal responsibilities as he could handle. These included dogs. Two were adopted by Henry Drury at Harrow, but the favourite, Lion the young Newfoundland, was a gift to him (Hobhouse) from Augusta. Here too something went wrong. Lion, whose gambollings were the only sure source of pleasure Byron had known at Missolonghi, died within a year of arriving in England. 'Poor fellow. He is buried under the willow-tree near the water at Whitton,' Hobhouse recorded.[1] Among the voluminous dossiers of his correspondence is an aggrieved letter from the veterinary surgeon, Mr Youatt, who ran 'a new and commodious hospital for dogs' and always headed his advertisements with the lines:

> . . . Casts round the world an equal eye
> And feels for all that live.

Mr Youatt had been told that Hobhouse had called him 'a fool, an ass, and a dolt'.

> The associated names of Byron and Hobhouse [he wrote in sorrowful protest] rendered that animal most interesting to me. . . . My best and warmest feelings were identified with the recovery of that dog. . . .
> You, sir, know that it was a complicated case. You know the disadvantage under which every veterinary Surgeon labours, whose patients can tell neither the nature, degree, nor seat of the pain. I knew that he was not well, but I suspected not that he was so near his end. I dreamed not of so speedy a death. . . .
> This *an ignorant man* might say proves me to be the fool, ass, the dolt which you describe. From you I expected a more liberal and juster decision.[2]

Denying the reported insults, Hobhouse sent Mr Youatt a donation to the Western Philanthropic Institution—benevolent, presumably, to dogs—which quickly brought back an acknowledgment of 'unfeigned pleasure' and an admission that the writer had been visited by many misgivings after dispatching his remonstrance.

Besides touchy vets, there were troublesome doctors. Who was to be paid, for instance, for embalming what Augusta always delicately called The Remains? Bruno, the young Italian medical man who had been engaged by Byron to accompany the expedition, claimed to have performed that work, Treiber, the German, shared in and received a payment

[1] 5 June 1825: Murray MSS.
[2] 26 June 1825. British Museum: Additional MSS. 36461.

for it, but there was also a demand for £100 from the Englishman, Julius Millingen.[1] As, despite the absence of facilities, the embalming and autopsy were completed the day after Byron's death, doubtless all the doctors were active, but Millingen's avidity for remuneration outstripped even his diligence, £100 being several times his annual salary from the Greek Committee. Dead or alive, Byron represented cash to a large number of his associates.

Bruno, like all the *entourage*, received a keepsake from Mrs Leigh and also a present of money from Hobhouse and Hanson acting in her name. On July 23rd he wrote to her in terms of the deepest gratitude,[2] but on the 29th such scanty peace as she enjoyed was broken by an entirely different kind of letter. Addressing her in groping yet percussive French, he poured out an elaborated grievance:

Very honourable Madame Leigh,

Yesterday I had a dispute with Mr Hobbouse [*sic*] that perhaps you will already know about. . . . He asked me into his room to notify me of your very respectable intentions, and those of Messieurs the Executors. I was very satisfied and very happy with all the arrangements they had made on my account, and above all with the kindnesses you yourself wished to honour me with. I was on the point of leaving with consolation in my heart when I understood the Servant Battista to say they had made him a present of 100 pounds sterling, which was double what you gave me. Then it came into my thoughts that they would do the same in regard to Lega, and the servant Benjamin, so that I was persuaded they considered me beneath the servants, and that it would have been much more honourable for me if they had given me nothing rather than treat me as inferior to the servants.

I went into Mr Hobbouse's [*sic*] room, I told him that I was very dis-satisfied at their conduct towards me, and with what they wanted to give me as a present. I did not wish to receive it except as a recompense for the surgical operations I did upon Milord,[3] which I was in no way obliged [to do], and I would not accept any present lower than that of the servants.

Mr Hobbouse is astonished at my so swift change from a state of the liveliest satisfaction to that of the greatest discontent; he tells Mr Hanson that he finds in my action a motive of interest so as to obtain more. I reply that I had no view to my interest at all, but that I behaved in that manner for the sake of my own honour not wishing to be considered either lower than, or on the same level with, the servants. Mr Hobbouse repeats that he believes it is self-interest that actuates me in this instance. I reply to him that if interest in money had actuated me, I should have made more than two hundred pounds sterling by selling the story of Milord's medical life from the beginning of his youth, and an infinity of other moral things[4] about him;

[1] One of Gamba's 'Spiegazioni' for Byron's Executors. Murray MSS.
[2] British Museum: Horton Papers.
[3] This is probably a restrained allusion to the embalming.
[4] 'Choses morales.' The doctor's meaning would probably be rendered now as 'psychological observations'.

but as they had judged it proper to burn the story of his life written by himself, I should not have published my work even for a million pounds sterling. . . . That all the time I had had the advantage of being with Milord I had never desired to receive any present from him, not even when he offered me precious ones several times, that those in Milord's suite know that he had offered to a very feeble surgeon at Genoa double what he gave me who have qualified in medicine and surgery, and besides, this surgeon, after promising Milord to go to Greece with him, refused some time before the departure from Genoa. Having been informed of all this, I reproached the surgeon for his bad conduct, and for having been willing to accept money for serving so great a man.

Having myself been asked by the English Dr Alexander if I would go with Milord to Greece as his doctor, I insisted[1] for several days that I wished for absolutely no pay, although I knew that Milord could not have found either at Genoa or at the University of Pisa a doctor to accompany him to Greece at any price for fear of dangers. I on the contrary abandoned my mother who is alone, and whose consolation I was, my goods in the hands of strangers, and my profession in my own country which yielded me double what Milord gave me.

Dr Alexander, who would be better suited to the profession of merchant than that of physician profited by my enthusiasm for Milord and for Greece, and made this written contract which is almost humiliating on my side. Your very honourable brother knew my character so well that he said several times he had seen various phenomenal things in Italy and among others, his physician Dr Bruno, who was Genoese and nevertheless disinterested: and a thousand other proofs which, to be briefer, I will pass over in silence. But Mr Hobhouse would not change his opinion and persisted always in saying that such an instantaneous change from satisfaction to discontent sprang from pecuniary motives to obtain more. Then I sent back to him the four hundred crowns I had received three weeks ago as part of my pay as Lord Byron's physician, and I promise you that I will not accept a liard, either of money which is due to me as my salary, nor of that repetition which was so generously offered me by you, unless Mr Hobhouse assures me of being mistaken in his judgment and of renewing the honourable opinion of me which he had before.[2]

It is not to be wondered at that Hobhouse suspected some mercenary design behind an outburst of jealous rage so unreasonable. Tita had been devoted to Byron through six years—a service which at one time had landed him in prison.[3] His gift from the estate was proportioned not to his station in life but in his deserts. To lessen it for the doctor's appeasement was out of the question, and it would have been almost equally ridiculous to add to an amount the doctor had at first accepted with delight.

Bruno's purpose, however, in writing his long *cri de cœur* to Augusta

---

[1] The French here is almost unintelligible. The verb is '*j'ai contrasté* '—possibly a slip for '*insisté*'.

[2] Murray MSS.   [3] After the Pisa affray in 1822.

must have been to arrive at some mode whereby he might undo without loss of face the effects of his gesture, and after an apology for distressing her with the 'unhappy affair', he admitted that 'It was an error on my part that gave rise to it, an error that Mr Hobhouse made worse'. He was now convinced by 'very sound reasons' that she did not after all rate him lower than the others, and he hinted that a few words which it would not be difficult for Hobhouse to pronounce would restore the former status.

As we hear nothing more of Bruno's mortification, though he was in England for some little time to come, and indulging in public controversy about the treatment of his illustrious patient, we may assume that he was induced to receive back the four hundred crowns he had impulsively surrendered, and perhaps also to swallow his pride and accept the gift of fifty pounds.

His letter disposes of one of the most quoted of all the anecdotes told about Byron by Trelawny. In its first form it appears thus:

> The Genoese doctor whom we brought from Italy was a student under twenty. When I remonstrated with Byron against engaging an unpractised boy, his answer was,—"If he knows little, I pay little. I have got the fellow for twenty pounds a year:—Is it not a good bargain?"[1]

Trelawny's respectful tone in letters that Byron preserved nowhere suggests that he was on such a footing as to be able to indulge in remonstrances. Bruno was not a student of 'under twenty' but a young man highly recommended as having qualified with distinction. He had received from the executors a hundred pounds as a part only of his salary. Moreover, if he spoke the truth—and it was a matter easy to verify since Hobhouse was then in close and constant touch with Gamba and the steward Lega—he had repeatedly offered his services for nothing, and had also refused presents of value from Byron.

The origin of this tale of meanness may be traced to the fact that Trelawny, on July 3rd, 1823, had written to Byron deferentially urging him to take a certain Dr Wilson to Greece, who, he said, was rich and would pay every expense himself.[2] Byron had disregarded this advice, and preferred an Italian—a 'mercenary Italian'—and the resulting annoyance had its aftermath in a compensatory invention.

Why anyone should have believed it is mysterious since Trelawny eventually published a letter addressed to none other than himself containing the terms Byron was willing to offer to a doctor:

> I want a surgeon, native or foreign, to take charge of medical stores, and be in personal attendance. Salary, a hundred pounds a year, and his treatment

---

[1] *London Literary Gazette*, 12 Feb. 1831.   [2] Murray MSS.

at our table, as a companion and a gentleman. He must have recommendations, of course. . . . Perhaps you can consult Vacca, to whom I have written on the same subject. . . .[1]

Though Vacca, head of the school of surgery in Pisa, had no qualified man available, and Bruno was ultimately engaged through the English physician, Alexander, nothing could be clearer than that he was paid something upwards of a hundred pounds a year and his full maintenance, a liberal rate at that time, and that the dialogue in which his employer congratulates himself on getting him for twenty is a fiction.

The letters Trelawny sent off in all directions when he was posing as Byron's chief mourner in Greece had succeeded perhaps almost beyond his own expectations in establishing him in people's minds as the intimate of the famous poet, and a person of importance in the Greek campaign. He owed a great deal of this ready credence to Colonel Stanhope whom he had flattered to the top of his bent, writing to him, for example, on Byron's death:

> The greatest man in the world has resigned his mortality in favour of this sublime cause. . . . I call on you, in the name of Greece, to do all you can to fill his place. . . . You must not leave us; you are public property. . . . I have ascertained that you are legally and indisputably now in full possession and full power.[2]

Stanhope had not been able to accept the resounding invitation, but he had brought back to England a high opinion of the man who had thus addressed him, and being the first person of any standing to come from Greece after Byron's death, his praise of the picturesque Cornishman who had thrown in his lot with General Odysseus commanded attention. The period of Stanhope's acquaintance with Trelawny and Odysseus had been a few weeks between the beginning of March and April 19th, but they were weeks of such great comfort after the laughter and cynicism of Byron that they made a most pleasing impression. It seemed there was nothing Odysseus wanted for Greece so much as newspapers and schools, while Trelawny, if his letters are a criterion, spoke to the Colonel in noble abstractions perfectly attuned to his ears.

Gratefully Stanhope had called on Mrs Brereton, Trelawny's mother, a woman who devoted her life, with a stagey and extravagant insistence, to social climbing and trying to marry her daughters to men of fortune. Mrs Brereton had always been out of sympathy with her unhelpful younger son, but he had now redeemed himself somewhat in her eyes by

---

[1] TRELAWNY, *Recollections.* Letter without date. What Byron wrote in Italian to Vacca has also been published, confirming these terms: 'He [the surgeon] would be maintained in lodging and board, at my own table, with a salary of a hundred louis d'or annually, and I will guarantee him a year for certain.' *L. & J.* No date.

[2] STANHOPE, 29 Apr. 1824.

becoming associated with an eminent peer: for he had written to tell her
—and he did not often write—that he had the command of a fine ship, the
Hypernea, belonging to Lord Byron.[1] (The ship in which they had sailed
for Greece was actually the *Hercules*, commanded by Captain John Scott,
and in Trelawny's own much later words 'a collier-built tub'.) Being
rather sceptical at first of Stanhope's glowing account of the black sheep,
she had caused a friend to question him confidentially, and had found that
his good report of her son was not diminished behind her back.

Next, Stanhope published Trelawny's letters to him, containing statements about his association with Byron which the public naturally supposed to be true.

> . . . He is connected with every event of the most interesting years of my
> wandering life. His every-day companion,—we lived in ships, boats, and in
> houses together,—we had no secrets,—no reserve, and, though we often
> differed in opinion, never quarrelled. . . .
>
> I was absent from him in Rome when he wrote to me from Genoa, and
> said 'Trelawny, you must have heard I am going to Greece, why do you not
> come to me? I can do nothing without you. . . .'[2]

How could anyone suspect that those years of shared existence could
be sifted down to the very fortuitous intercourse of a few months in Italy
and six weeks from the time of sailing for Greece? The bluff was so
audacious that, unless it was promptly called, it was certain of success. It
appears to have been, on Trelawny's part, quite coolly calculated; in
several instances he wrote to persons with influence on the Press and suggested that some publicity should be given to his expedition with Lord
Byron and his views of Greek affairs.

The slow and uncertain communications of those days, when newspapers had no trained reporters hurrying to the scenes of war and revolution, allowed little scope for checking any assertions that might be made
by a man on the spot, and it was proportionately easier to set up as an
authority. Yet even allowing for these conditions, it seems an odd thing
that hardly any one noticed, then or later, how little Trelawny's conduct
squared with his fine phrases.

'I would coin my heart to save this key of Greece', he said of Missolonghi, and the grandiloquent words were published approvingly in the
Westminster Review, and reprinted at the back of Medwin's popular 'Conversations'; but Stanhope's own volume contained evidence as solid as
evidence can be that, so far from trying to save Missolonghi, Trelawny had
caused every available weapon in the town to be removed for Odysseus,

---

[1] HILL, *Trelawny's Strange Relations*. The information is from a letter by Mrs
Brereton to her brother.
[2] STANHOPE. 28 Apr. 1824.

and that Mavrocordato had protested against his endeavours to take from the garrison 'the whole brigade of artillery'.

Recent researches into Trelawny's early life[1] have shown his tragi-comic inducements to take refuge in that world of fantasy in which he was a deserter from the Navy, a corsair, a man who, unwitnessed, swam the rapids of Niagara Falls—and afterwards rowed a clumsy boat upstream with heavy oars! His money-obsessed father, his grotesquely snobbish mother, had made him a rebel; and the withholding of maternal love spurred him on, it would seem, to try to move her wonder and admiration. It may have been at his own request that Stanhope had called on her.

Medwin's book was issued in Paris by Galignani and circulated almost as widely there as in England: and the reprinted *Wesminster Review* article contained Byron's letter inviting Trelawny to go to Greece, the copy evidently having been made from the original by someone who had seen Trelawny while he was at Zante.[2]

> T——. You must have heard I am going to Greece; why do you not come with me? I am at last determined—Greece is the only place I ever was contented in—I am serious—and did not write before as I might have given you a journey for nothing:—They all say I can be of use in Greece. I do not know how, nor do they, but at all events let us try.[3]

When Trelawny published this note in his *Records*, it had in it a sentence missing in the first and almost certainly more accurate copy: 'I need your aid, and am exceedingly anxious to see you', words which, when quoted to Colonel Stanhope, had appeared as, 'I can do nothing without you'. The original of one of his few letters from Byron, in the Keats-Shelley Memorial, Rome, shows, when compared with his printed version, subtle and skilful alterations, and even sentences inserted into the text to make Byron seem less curt and more familiar with him,[4] so it is

[1] By Lady Anne Hill.

[2] Probably Blaquiere, who supplied much of the material in this article. It was written by Bowring, and has been mistakenly attributed to Hobhouse, who objected to it.

[3] 15 June 1823. Trelawny did not hurry to Byron's side as he represents, but lingered five weeks before joining the expedition, a fact which may have some connection with his pretence, less than a year later, that he had received the summons in Rome. He was actually in Florence, and wrote from Leghorn on July 3rd, 'I pray your pardon for being so dilatory.' (Murray MSS.)

[4] 21 Nov. 1822. E.g. in the genuine letter, Byron wrote 'I was just going to send you down some books of yours.' By leaving out 'of yours' Trelawny makes it appear that Byron was volunteering a friendly attention instead of merely returning possessions left on the *Bolivar*, and the next sentence is adjusted to support this. After some discussion about dealing with the disbanded crew of the yacht—part of which is omitted without indication—Byron is quoted as writing: 'But I hate bothering you with these things.' No such apology is in the letter. There is also a remark about the ominous absence of news from England, which Trelawny explains as an allusion to the threatened prosecution of the *Vision of Judgement*. It was actually an interpolation of his own, and its object must have been to give an air of being in Byron's confidence.

not presuming too far to suggest that one or both of the flattering addenda
might be of his own contrivance.

Even as first printed, the letter put up his stock considerably with his
mother, and she wrote proudly about his strange and wonderful new
address, which was in the care of General Odysseus in a camp at the foot
of Mount Parnassus.[1]

But the romantic General was doing his best to get out of the fighting.
He found it more profitable, now that he had lost all hope of Byron's
money, to enter into an arrangement with the Turks. He had already
been making a good thing out of releasing Turkish prisoners for large
ransoms and keeping the money, and was also notorious for extorting
tribute from his compatriots by cruelties he had learned as the minion of
Ali Pasha of Janina: and he had laid up a hoard of wealth in a cave of
Parnassus, which he fortified. Part of his armament was what Trelawny
and the gullible Stanhope had stripped from Missolonghi. All his positions
from Livadia to Athens were left without defence while he and Trelawny
prepared what was meant to be an impregnable retreat and treasure house.

In December 1824 Odysseus made a private peace with the Ottoman
Government, which guaranteed him the Captaincy of East Hellas.
Trelawny had sworn brotherhood with him and taken as 'wife' his
twelve-year-old sister, Tersitza,[2] an alliance the wily chieftain had no
doubt intended to further his interests in the acquisition of British money,
for his avarice, according to Finlay who had been acquainted with him,
was boundless. As Trelawny spoke no foreign languages and Odysseus is
said only to have known, apart from Greek, a few words of French, their
close companionship must, while it lasted, have been a somewhat taciturn
affair; but Trelawny's hero worship was undiminished after several
months.

It was very slowly and confusedly that the news of his defection
filtered into the English Press, and the situation was too obscure for more
than a few tentative lines to be ventured, but they were enough to re-
awaken the disapproval of his family. 'John you have of course heard of,'
one of his sisters wrote to their uncle Sir Christopher Hawkins, 'as it was in
the papers his marrying Ulysses's daughter, [*sic*] and gone over to the
Turks; it is thought the most extraordinary thing, and not much to his
credit.'[3]

Few, if any, in England were as yet aware that Odysseus (Ulysses) had

[1] HILL. 28 Jan. 1825.

[2] Trelawny, in a letter to Claire Clairmont (23 Mar. 1836), said she was *now* twenty-
two, which would make her ten at the time of their union in 1824; but he was probably
miscalculating. She had two children by him, one of which died. In no Greeks did he
leave greater bitterness than in the family of his sworn brother.

[3] HILL. July 1825.

already been defeated, fighting his own countrymen at Daulis on the side
of the Turks. Treason had lost him most of his followers, the Turks distrusted, and were not disposed to protect, him and on April 25th, a year
and a week after Byron's death, he surrendered and was imprisoned in the
Acropolis. Trelawny meanwhile stayed ingloriously in the cave on Parnassus where he had been more or less immured for months, blockaded by
the Greeks, despised by the Turks.

Odysseus could hardly expect clemency after a career of treachery and
atrocity which had left him without a friend among his own people, and in
June or July he was killed by Ghouras, who had once been his lieutenant.
It was said that he was trying to escape. At any rate, he was flung down
brutally from the height of the Acropolis.

The attempted assassination of Odysseus's English brother-in-law was,
in the circumstances, not a very surprising eventuality. 'There have been
several conspiracies to get possession of the cave on the part of the Greeks',
wrote Trelawny's friend, Humphreys, when he was urging Hobhouse to
arrange a rescue; but Parnassus and its cavern belonged to the Greeks
much more than to Trelawny, and so did the money amassed by Odysseus's treason and brigandage. It was not conspiracy for the Greeks to try
to dislodge a most troublesome intruder; but that they—or a handful of
them—chose to do so by suborning companions of his to shoot him was
discreditable.

On hearing of his plight Humphreys with much courage went to his
aid:

> An Englishman at least a Scotsman who was with Odysseus also and
> blockaded with Trelawney [*sic*] attempted to assassinate him (nearly *at the
> same* time Odysseus met his death at Athens). He is severely wounded. I was
> at the camp opposed to the Turks then at Salona in Roumelie when I heard
> of it and immediately hastened to the cave, found Trelawney better than I
> was led to expect, and after staying a day with him went immediately to
> Napoli di Romania to procure a surgeon for him.
>
> I was there in a most unauthorized and infamous manner arrested by the
> Govt for having attempted to aid my countryman; and only owing to the
> arrival of English men of war did I owe my liberty.[1]

While respecting Humphreys for his bravery and good nature, we
cannot but smile at 19th-century British arrogance which so deeply resented the interference of foreigners, acting, in their own territory, as
men under provocation have always acted in the stress of war. Had he
been a Greek he would have been given much shorter shrift.

---

[1] Humphreys to Hobhouse, 24 July 1825. British Museum: Additional MSS. 36461.
Trelawny rewarded Humphreys for his exertions, which were indirectly successful, by
publishing, without comment in his friend's defence, a letter which sought to connect
him with the attempted murder.

Trelawny received great credit for having spared the life of one of his would-be assassins. (The other was killed by a shot from a bodyguard in the cavern.) By his own account, he had the assailant, a youth of feeble intellect, kept with hands and feet in irons, chained to a wall for five weeks—or twenty days according to the version he published—subsisting only on bread and water, 'mad with terror', and under such threats as being roasted over a slow fire or hung from a beam and beheaded. But he reprinted with complacency this report of his own forbearance from Thomas Gordon's *History of the Greek Revolution*:

> In the midst of his agony, he had the magnanimity to dismiss, unhurt, the unhappy youth who fired at him.

Gordon was Trelawny's next-door neighbour at Zante after the latter had withdrawn from the war, and had this information direct from the only witness available, Trelawny himself.

Hobhouse, without straining every nerve, made efforts to extricate him from the cave, corresponding with Sir Christopher Hawkins, the Greek Deputies and others for some weeks about the means of getting assistance. Sir Christopher's idea was that the Greek Government should be asked to give him a safe conduct out of the country, and protection for Odysseus's family, on condition that he handed over the chieftain's hoarded wealth. Hobhouse seems to have pointed out to Trelawny's uncle that it was rather difficult to work up much enthusiasm in the Greek Deputies for the well-being of one who was reputed to have betrayed the cause. He received a remarkably naïve exculpation from Sir Christopher:

> Whatever insinuations may have been made with respect to Odysseus and my nephew going over to the Turks I have reason to believe the only reason for withdrawing their services was the difference of opinion they held as to the future Government of Greece.[1]

The family were evidently individualists of no common temerity, but they exerted themselves with an entirely conventional loyalty in striving to send aid to their relative.

After a few weeks, Sir Christopher wrote again:

> . . . Mr Canning [the Foreign Secretary] has been so good in a very full answer to my letter to regret his inability to interfere for my nephew without giving the Turkish Government reason to complain of the assistance given by British Subjects to the Greeks and sanctioned by the King's Government, and without endangering the lives and the prosperity of other British Subjects in the Turkish Empire. Mr Canning seems to consider this line of conduct his public duty, which it undeniably is. . . .

---

[1] 6 Sept. 1825. British Museum: op. cit.

Mrs T. Brereton has written to Sir F. Adam, [the Lord High Commissioner of the Ionian Isles] but she is unacquainted with the naval commander and I take the liberty to suggest what might be a mode of bringing under the Greek Government Mr Trelawny and party who either never were inimical to the Greek Government, or who cannot now injure them, and by this means of benefiting the Greek Government and of enabling them by pardon and protection to show an act of generosity and humanity that could not but be creditable to them.[1]

What Mrs Brereton did not know or had forgotten was that her son had accused General Sir Frederick Adam of conspiring to 'shove' Byron's body 'into a hole, like a dog' at Zante, although that officer had been at Corfu at the time.[2] He was therefore not disposed to be helpful.

Trelawny took great pride in his ultimate deliverance by the British Navy, their care of his 'shattered hulk' for two months, and his arrival at Cephalonia in a man-of-war. It may be assumed that he was not posing at this period as one who had deserted from the Navy to become a privateer on the side of the French!

He had scarcely settled again on neutral soil than he resumed his career of bluffing his way into the limelight. As if his spoliation of Missolonghi and his prolonged adventure with Odysseus had never been, he became a zealous letter writer to the British Press, expatiating on the glories of the Greek cause and, in particular, the necessity of standing firm at Missolonghi. Bitter as he had been in his private abuse of Byron for remaining in that pestilential spot, he now gave the most cogent and excellent reasons why it must be held.

... A mud bank stretches out seven or eight miles on the three sides by which Missolonghi is encompassed by the sea, the depth of water varying from an inch to a foot. ...

Thus it is that the Turks have never succeeded in blockading the town by sea. ... A boat drawing six inches of water must before she can approach the town at a distance of five miles, pass within ten feet of this strong fortification [the island of Vassiladi].

... Its great importance was so obvious that even the careless Greeks put a strong garrison in it. The buffle-headed Turks saw very early the necessity of reducing this fort (as apparent as the necessity of killing the guard at the door before we can enter the enemy's quarters), and every successive year of the revolution there have been repeated attempts to reduce it ... but to the honour of the Missolonghiotes, they were hitherto repulsed.

... There are general fears prevailing that Missolonghi, if not speedily succoured by the fleet, will capitulate ... it has cost them much blood and treasure, and kept four successive armies in check that would otherwise have reduced Eastern Greece. ...

If Missolonghi is lost, the Turks and Arabs will be excited to phrenzy and

---

[1] 24 Sept. 1825. British Museum: op. cit. [2] See p. 79.

the Greeks will hang their heads. The Arabs will, in conjunction with the Albanians, overrun, unchecked, Eastern and Western Greece!

. . . Greece, the land of Socrates, Phidias, Themistocles, Alcibiades, Aristides &c &c will be covered with the tents of the dusky Arab, the natives of Ethiopia, and the savagery of Barbary and Morocco.[1]

Trelawny knew no more of Alcibiades or Aristides than he knew of Sophocles or Aeschylus—authors whose names he confused when he palmed off on Shelley's son a spurious relic.[2] The words are rhetoric only, and it was always either rhetoric or to violent invective that he resorted when trying to throw dust in the eys of the public—a practice in which he enjoyed unparalleled success. How could anyone give a second thought to Mavrocordato and his protests against the removal of Missolonghi's defences by Stanhope and Trelawny when reading such words as these?

. . . We are sunk in gloom and despair [at the thought of Missolonghi]. The heroic resistance for five years, insulated, unaided and alone, standing in a position against a mighty empire, of a paltry fishing town, floating on a mud bank—inhabited by petty traffickers—banked in with mud, and defended by a few almost useless cannon—has kept a succession of immense armies in check.

But man is not omnipotent—heroes are not immortal, and the heroic bosoms that for years have stood the bulwark of their country are now cold as the heroes of Marathon and Thermopylae.[3]

In a private letter to Mary Shelley sent a few days after this one, he referred with the utmost contempt to the Greeks and ended: '. . . Their only hope is that the bloody Asiatic may do by their other Cities as he has by Ipsara and Missolonghi—exterminate. . . .'[4]

*   *   *   *   *   *

One of Hobhouse's major activities in 1826 was the inauguration of a project for a monument to commemorate his friend. He had been bitterly hurt at Dean Ireland's refusal to allow burial in Westminster Abbey, and above all at his being given the opportunity of refusing. John Murray had made the approach, or so at first he angrily thought, but he was told later that the letter was dictated by Douglas Kinnaird.[5] Still, the overture had gone from Albemarle Street, and he himself would have taken his bearings very carefully before risking a rebuff. He decided to bide his time and try the Abbey again, and meanwhile to raise money for a statue. He

---

[1] *Examiner*, 8 May 1826. Letter dated 18 Mar. from Cephalonia.
[2] He presented Sir Percy Shelley with a brine-soaked book which he said he had found on Shelley's corpse. Professor Marchand (*Keats-Shelley Memorial Bulletin IV*, 1952) gave reasons for concluding this to be a 'hoax'. The relic has since been withdrawn from the Shelley exhibits in the Bodleian Library. The Sophocles Shelley had in his boat was not this one.   [3] *Examiner*, 4 June 1826. Letter dated 27 Apr. from Zante.
[4] TRELAWNY, *Letters*. 6 May 1826.   [5] Hobhouse *Journals*, 5 July 1824.

was encouraged by an unsolicited subscription of 500 rupees (about forty pounds) from a Mr Paternoster of Madras.[1]

The first step was to form a committee, a matter he was discussing with Augusta at a time when her daughter's marriage to Henry Trevanion had been arranged. His letter begins in an unwontedly playful vein:

> Dear Mrs Leigh,
>
> First and foremost I must congratulate you and yours on the approaching event, and tell your daughter that if any accident should break off the match I shall be very happy, if she will condescend, to marry her myself.
>
> I have got almost all the names you mention—and have had favourable answers—Lord Clare, Lord Jersey and the Duke of Devonshire write yes by return of post. I think of writing to Agar Ellis and to Mr Wilmot Horton. This last I have been told I ought to apply to.
>
> You may depend upon it that the thing will do credit to all parties concerned. Otherwise I shall drop it. . . .
>
> Best compliments to the bride
>
> > Ever yours truly
> > John C. Hobhouse[2]

His spirits were soon dashed by a 'very cold, unfeeling' refusal from Lord Delawarr, to whom he had been particularly recommended by Lord Clare, another old school-fellow of Byron's. He took this slight so much to heart that he sat down and wrote indignantly to the Duke of Devonshire about it, forgetting that Byron and Delawarr had parted in early youth to go in the most precisely contrary directions. This was the only instance, however, of the defection of a friend once loved, and in a few days he was able to report that the committee consisted of William Bankes, one of Byron's Cambridge cronies, Sir Francis Burdett, Thomas Campbell, Thomas Moore, Samuel Rogers, Sir Walter Scott, Lord Clare, Colonel Wildman the purchaser of Newstead Abbey, the Duke of Devonshire, Lord Holland, Lord Jersey, Lord Lansdowne, the Hon. Douglas Kinnaird, Lord Sligo, Lord Tavistock, and Mrs Leigh's new son-in-law, Trevanion.

With such a group of famous writers, Whig noblemen, and eminent persons in general, there should have been no difficulty in making a flying start. Events in Greece were justifying Byron's policies. He was still a figure of prodigious public interest, and at the time of the fall of Missolonghi, an appeal for contributions might have had a very wide response. But having, in one of his spells of energy, built up his Committee, Hobhouse slackened and missed his moment. His personal and political affairs were beginning to encroach on his old preoccupations, and indeed, it is extraordinary that with his numerous activities as a Member of Parliament, a leading figure on the Greek Committee, a man who frequented a

---

[1] Hobhouse *Journals*, 22 Dec. 1825.
[2] No date. About 23 Jan. 1826. British Museum: Additional MSS. 31037.

large and distinguished social circle, and an affectionate son and brother, he managed to give so much attention to what he conceived to be his duty to his friend's memory.

For months on end the monument scheme, so auspiciously launched, disappears from his diary or is a subject of desultory reference. In September 1826 he was in Milan and asked Pindemonte and Monti, the Italian poets, to be honorary members. (The former refused.) In November he discussed it in Paris with Benjamin Constant, complaining that Mme de Staël's son would not consent to subscribe; and was told that both Staël and his sister, the Duchesse de Broglie, had become Methodists.[1] After this the matter dropped almost into abeyance until 1828, when he suddenly spent a Sunday in March 'writing letters about Byron's monument'.[2]

With the Abbey always in his mind, he may have had some policy in waiting, but it seems more probable that simple lassitude had overcome him, and the exigence of important private affairs. In 1827—encouraged, possibly, by the courtships of his half-sisters, the children of his father's second marriage—he made for the first time in his life a proposal of marriage himself. His choice fell on one of the daughters of Sir Francis Burdett; but though he had the fullest parental approval, the young girl did not see the forty-year-old colleague and companion of her father as an eligible suitor, and, to his distress, he was rejected. A few months later, he was having a love affair which was necessarily of the most clandestine kind with a married woman of position and repute: and before he had quite broken off this attachment—so worrying to a man of his innate respectability—he had become engaged to another lady, a sister of the Marquess of Tweeddale. Inevitably, therefore, the energy he usually consecrated to Byron was a little depleted.

In April and May, however, before committing himself to matrimony, he was busy again with the Monument Committee, and had made it much larger and less manageable than before. He had had the belated good sense to invite the support of John Murray, who became a useful co-adjutor, but he had also roped in the painters, Archer-Shee and Thomas Phillips, the Orientalist W. M. Leake, the diplomat Sir Robert Adair, the man of many parts, Sir James Mackintosh, and a score of others: and Thomas Moore had annoyed him by saying he had better have Jackson the boxer as well.[3]

His object was, of course, to assemble all the most impressive 'names'

---

[1] Hobhouse *Journals*, 3 Nov. 1826. Constant had been Mme de Staël's lover. There was a reaction in Byron's favour when her granddaughter, the Comtesse d'Haussonville, became an ardent admirer and one of his biographers.

[2] Ibid. 30 Mar. 1828.

[3] Ibid. 11 Apr. 1828. 'Gentleman' Jackson had taught Byron boxing.

directly or indirectly connected with Byron; but so large a committee was a slow and unwieldy instrument for getting anything done. Hobhouse, with his extensive experience, and the disasters of the Greek Committee still oppressing him, might have guessed that he was merely encumbering himself with clerical work and petty annoyances; but he reported the first meeting with satisfaction,[1] even though there was an argument, started by Lord Lansdowne, to the effect that 'monument' was not a sufficiently explicit word, and the term had to be changed to 'monumental statue'.

This quibbling would have amused Byron but it might have pleased him to know that Lord Clare, whom he declared he had always loved 'better than any (*male*) thing in the world',[2] was in the chair. Within ten days of his last illness, he had written to Clare: 'I hope that you do not forget that I always regard you as my dearest friend and love you as when we were Harrow boys together.'[3] And it seems likely that the name he pronounced in the hearing of Fletcher when he was dying was 'Clare' rather than 'Claire', as the valet supposed and passed on to Mrs Shelley. Hobhouse had certainly suppressed many of his long-standing jealousies to cast his net as wide as possible.

The members of the committee, who were for the most part rich, readily agreed to his suggestion that they should give £1000 towards the 'monumental statue' without announcing their individual contributions, and a sub-committee was formed to make a semi-public appeal. '. . . So far the project looks well,' he wrote, 'and I trust I shall have to congratulate myself on having done something to show my attachment to my friend.'[4]

Only a few days later, however, his not unjustified complacency was shattered by an amazing open letter addressed to him in *The Times*.

Sir,

. . . Ashamed at length by the stigma of such neglect as you have shown to the memory of your friend, at the expiration of four years, you come forth under cover of a committee of 50 great names to propose (what was long since proposed, and strongly supported in purse and person from the furthest corners of the earth) the measure which, but for your indifference and even opposition, might long ago have been carried into effect. Nothing then was wanting but the smallest portion of zeal and energy in you to produce a monument worthy of him and you, which might have become by this time the admiration of the world. How indignantly must the spirit of that mighty genius look down on the man who, after such apathy, now presumes, as his friend, to offer this tardy and unwilling tribute to his fame.

I shall not be sparing of your peace in estimating either your motives or your deeds: you have brought it on yourself, and are entitled to no mercy.

[1] Hobhouse *Journals*, 7 June 1828.   [2] *L. & J.* Letter to Moore, 8 June 1822.
[3] *L. & J.* 31 Mar. 1824.   [4] Hobhouse *Journals*, op. cit. 7 June 1828.

The author of this outburst, who signed himself 'Byronicus', continued for some paragraphs to castigate Hobhouse not more for neglecting than for promoting the memorial, and also to attack in pungent terms 'the self-constituted committee, who come forth with such impudent arrogance and claim the honour, as personal friends of the illustrious deceased, of directing the monument and appropriating the large funds which no doubt will soon be raised for it, to the exclusion of those kindred admirers of the poet, who, professing the same opinions, conceive themselves to be his disciples, and are infinitely more deserving of the distinction'. He blamed Hobhouse for having refrained from advancing the project from the fear of offending persons in authority and members of Lady Byron's family, and hinted in the most scurrilous manner that he would find it all rather too troublesome an undertaking 'without being paid for it'.

I am sorry indeed to say [the astounding libeller went on] that the names of the committee now published are a poor guarantee that any further steps will be taken this time, to however large a sum the subscriptions may amount; and that unless voluntary subscribers . . . shall appoint an efficient committee of their own to carry into effect their wishes, the affair may be deferred for another *lustrum*, and for another particular friend of Byron to execute.

Let us examine the qualifications of these elect more minutely. Of all the opulent members of it, who in the time of Byron's distress, of his domestic troubles, and his severe trials, when, as he himself expresses it 'Reason half forsook her reign'—who ever assisted him with the value of a shilling, or afforded him any of that solace which is 'as balm to the wounded soul?'

Wildly, the anonymous accuser proceeded to hold the Duke of Devonshire up to obloquy for having allowed 'the harpies of the law' to seize Byron's property, 'when out of his superfluous myriads, he might by one word have prevented the catastrophe'. The heartless Duke had not even given shelter to Byron's carriage, which had had to be kept at quite a distance from the house.

No, not one helping hand was stretched out to him in time of need, and no one kindred heart bled in sympathy with his own!

Worse than anything, all these perfidious associates had continued to pay him 'useless and importunate visits up to the very hour of his departure, with vain and unmeaning professions of friendship. Out upon such d——d hypocrisy, then . . .!'

Of the whole fifty, Leicester Stanhope is the only man—(I speak it with pride) who, on the arrival of Lord Byron's remains in this country, proposed to give him an honourable funeral, and to attend him to his last home with every demonstration of honour and respect. . . .

I confine myself for the present to objecting *in toto* to the plan proposed . . . and shall in another letter state more specifically my objections; and, should the present plan not be altered, shall take the liberty of detailing the obligations the noble poet was under to each of those fifty . . . thus impudently inviting censure.

Hobhouse might well feel staggered, both by the letter and the fact of its publication.

The whole bearing of the charge is that I deserted my friend when alive and neglected his fame when dead. Now what can be said for the editor of a paper like the Times for admitting such an accusation against any man without the slightest attempt to inquire into the facts . . .?

The indistinctness of the imputation renders it irrefutable, and to defend oneself against such an assault it would be necessary to tell how one had behaved towards one's friend, which would be almost equally indecent with publishing how well one had conducted oneself to a wife. . . .

I thought of answering it, but determined to be silent, and to labour on in pursuit of my project, so I went to the sub-Committee of the Byron Monument.[1]

Although this was a time full of private drama for him, when he was successfully wooing Lady Julia Hay and unsuccessfully trying to reconcile his other love to the prospect of his marriage, he set himself to identify the obnoxious 'Byronicus', and found that he was no other than the Mr Paternoster who had turned the monument idea from a vague wish to a solid intention by sending 500 rupees from Madras. This enthusiastic gentleman was now in England, bearing a palpable grudge because his munificence had not brought him any invitation to serve on the committee. And there were hints that he might prove a somewhat unsavoury character.

He has been trying to purchase Byron's letters to Rushton at Newstead, so Wildman tells me.[2]

Robert Rushton had been Byron's page on the first stages of his foreign travels in 1809, and had been shipped home from Gibraltar with a letter to his father saying he was too young for the rigours of the journey about to be taken, and arranging for him to be sent to school. Byron's letters to him are usually in the patriarchal tone it was his habit to adopt with his male servants (even those older than himself claimed that he had been 'a father' to them), and two or three refer to the Newstead housemaid Susan Vaughan whose infidelity had given him a bitter shock just before his spectacular rise to fame. But Caroline Lamb had circulated a rumour that Rushton was a favourite in a stronger sense of the word than Byron had used when recommending the boy to his mother's care;[3] and

[1] Hobhouse *Journals*, 19 June 1828.   [2] Ibid. 2 July 1828.
[3] 'Pray show the lad kindness, as he is my great favourite.' Letter of 11/15 Aug. 1809.

Paternoster may have been hoping for something to gratify a prurient curiosity.

Though he might reasonably have wondered what had happened to the subscription sent two and a half years before, the unfairness of his newspaper onslaught was grotesque: but Hobhouse was painfully learning that anyone who had a grievance connected with Byron was sure to make a sortie against himself. There was something about his personality which seemed to have a provocative effect.

Hobhouse's marriage, his travels abroad, his political career, loomed very large for the next year or so, and almost nothing was done to augment the sum already acquired for the monument. In 1829 Chantrey was approached in the hope that he might be persuaded to make a statue for £1000, but he refused.[1]

Hobhouse then acted on Kinnaird's much better idea of putting the same proposal to Thorwaldsen, the Danish sculptor domiciled in Rome, and learned that he would not only perform the work but would add a relief to the pedestal. Whereas Chantrey would have had nothing to go on but the portraits of other artists, only two of which were in three dimensions—and one of these a bad one[2]—Thorwaldsen had already done from life a bust said by Hobhouse, who was the owner of it, to be a first-rate likeness. He knew too the way his subject moved and the attitudes he assumed. Accordingly, he received a definite commission, and was informed—very much too optimistically as it turned out—that the statue's destination was Westminster Abbey.

During all this time the executorship continued to pose its problems. Many of these were financial, and Hobhouse had Hanson and Kinnaird to assist him in dealing with these. He did, however, take upon himself the investigation of the Rev. Francis Hodgson's business with Byron. He had been shocked to discover, amongst letters concerning old transactions, that Hodgson had received on various occasions no less than £1400 which he had never attempted to repay. When enquiry was made, he had at first repudiated any indebtedness whatever, and then, being told there was an acknowledgment under his own hand, had come out with what Hobhouse considered 'a very lame story indeed'. It must have been the true one—namely, that Byron had given him most of the money to pay his father's debts which stood in the way of his own much-desired marriage.

The lawyer they consulted was a cousin of Hodgson's, and Hobhouse

---

[1] Hobhouse *Journals*, 2 July.

[2] The Bartolini bust now in the National Portrait Gallery. Byron said it made him look like 'a superannuated Jesuit', and Teresa Guiccioli, in her unpublished book, remarks that they were 'afflicted' when they saw it.

The original of the Thorwaldsen bust is now in the Royal Collection.

told him that he thought Byron's old friend had acted shoddily in not being more open.

He said the whole forte of the case lay in the *spot* in which the letter was found—if amongst letters of business than it was against Hodgson. I told him how the fact stood—he expressed himself pleased with my behaviour to his relative on this occasion but I was not pleased with myself in appearing to be friendly towards a person who I think has behaved so ill.[1]

Hobhouse himself had once owed Byron nearly as large a sum, but it had been scrupulously paid back; and Hodgson's denial of the obligation rankled deeply with him—as well it might, for the clergyman had at one time become distinctly sententious about the poet's morals, and had also criticized his maturer work severely in a pamphlet called *Childe Harold's Monitor*.

In his last days Byron had made a friend of his banker in Genoa, an Englishman named Charles Barry, who grew warmly attached to him. (He always had the happiest relations with bankers.) Barry was in touch with Kinnaird and Hobhouse from 1824 onwards about a hundred details of assets and effects left in Italy. The furniture was sold at a valuer's appraisal; Barry, for sentimental reasons bought some of it himself, but the rest was dispersed, including, presumably, the sofa associated with Shelley which Byron had bought in Pisa and refused to give up to Mrs Shelley, saying he could not bear the idea that anything Shelley had used should be 'within the same walls with Mrs Hunt's children . . . dirtier and more mischievous than Yahoos'.[2] (He had sent her another sofa in its stead, but of course his high-handed manner gave grounds for resentment.)

There were three carriages, including the splendid one fitted with all sorts of comforts and luxuries which he had had copied from Napoleon's, but it was now eight years old, and the highest offer received for it was a thousand francs, about forty pounds. Nine snuff-boxes, a watch, and some other personal treasures were sent to England, together with five cases of books. Among the snuff-boxes was a fine musical specimen assessed by a Leghorn jeweller at 2240 francs, and a very valuable one with a portrait of Napoleon in it, and Marie Louise and her son on the double lid. The others together were worth about 1600 francs.[3] Some of these bibelots may have been presented as keepsakes to Byron's *entourage*.

Barry was also trying to cope with a troublesome outstanding debt on the *Bolivar*—the schooner which had been built at the same time and place as Shelley's ill-starred yacht, known now as the *Ariel*, but never

[1] Hobhouse *Journals*, 12 Jan. 1825.
[2] *L. & J.* 6 Oct. 1822. The sofa which Trelawny presented to William Michael Rossetti as Shelley's is possibly another of his spurious relics. He told contradictory stories about it, and its provenance is doubtful. See p. 442.
[3] Barry to Byron, 12 Nov. 1823: Murray MSS.

Bust of Byron at the age of 30, done in Rome from life by Albert Thorwaldsen

referred to by any member of the Shelley circle except as the *Don Juan*. Trelawny had taken upon himself with delight the ordering of both pleasure boats, which were built by his friend the naval commander, Daniel Roberts. Nothing pleased Trelawny more than being in charge of things and relied on as an expert; and in his excitement at what must have been one of the most enjoyable assignments of his life, he had given Roberts almost *carte blanche* as far as Byron was concerned. The result was that a plaything on which Byron had expected to spend 'a hundred or more',[1] actually cost a thousand or more. After the death of Shelley, Byron had little heart for the *Bolivar*, and it was left at Trelawny's disposal for several months, until the expensive crew and running costs at last caused it to be laid up.

In 1823, the Blessingtons and their cortège arrived at Genoa in all the extravagant panoply that was to lead to the ruin of a great estate. Lord Blessington was possessed, in Byron's words,[2] by a 'headstrong wish to purchase' the sumptuously equipped and almost unused schooner, and he got it for four hundred guineas, very much less than half what it had cost. It has been thought extremely parsimonious of Byron to wish to remove the guns, which he required for Greece. Lady Blessington touches on his meannness in one of the two highly profitable books in which she made use of her acquaintance with him, telling how he offered only eighty pounds for a horse of hers which had cost a hundred, and which he had 'repeatedly and earnestly' begged her to let him buy. Her account is not borne out by the correspondence.

Lord Blessington wrote to Byron that, having his wife's permission, he would comply with Byron's wish to have the horse. 'I gave for him 2400 francs. I thought that it had been 2000 but I remember and Alfred [D'Orsay] tells me that it was Louis not Napoleons.'[3]

Byron's rejoinder was: 'I fear that I can hardly afford more than two thousand francs for the steed in question, as I have to undergo considerable expenses at this present time, and I suppose that will not suit you.'[4] This is a simple affirmation that, though he had been willing to pay the price originally named for the horse, he would not go higher, and his brevity— coupled with an apology for not accepting a dinner invitation—by no means suggests that he had 'begged and entreated' to have the privilege of making the purchase. What Lady Blessington did not mention was that,

---

[1] *Correspondence.* Letter to Kinnaird, 23 Feb. 1822. Shelley also found that the expense of the boat-building had been enormously under-estimated. A letter to Trelawny (6 May 1822) speaks of Roberts's £50 growing into £500.
[2] *L. & J.* Letter to Barry, 9 Apr. 1824.
[3] 22 May 1823 (dated only 'Thursday evening'): Murray MSS.
[4] *L. & J.* 23 May 1823. In the same letter he said he must not forget to contribute to Blessington's fund for assisting the Irish peasantry. We may be very sure that, if he had forgotten, the malice of the reporter would not have overlooked it.

L.L.B.—P

whereas Byron paid promptly for Mameluke, Lord Blessington could not be induced to settle for the *Bolivar*—an eventuality Byron had foreseen and prophesied to Barry.

The draft on Blessington's bank was dishonoured,[1] though Barry had pretended that he personally would be the loser. 'He thinks I have paid you and perhaps it is as well for you that he should, as I know he thinks you are not in want of money & he can't know whether I am or not.'[2] After Byron's death the bill was presented again and again. 'I had a letter from Lord Blessington the other day but not a word about payment of the bill for the Boat', the banker wrote to Douglas Kinnaird on July 12th, 1824. 'I hope however to get it settled with him when he comes this way.'[3] But many weeks later he was telling Hanson the solicitor that he had tried in vain to obtain the money, and could not get an answer from Lord Blessington about it. The cost of the ostentatious parade by which Lady Blessington compensated herself for exclusion from the society she hankered after was mounting into debts of tens of thousands; some few of which were staved off for a while later on by her joining the substantial ranks of those who set up as authorities on Byron's character on the strength of a few weeks of propinquity.

In the pretended diary of her travels, *The Idler in Italy* (based on a real diary, but containing quantities of observations which show evidence of later composition), she took her revenge for having been dunned for the cost of the *Bolivar* by writing that Byron had asked what Barry thought an unfair price for the boat, but an ample correspondence shows that, on the contrary, Barry had persuaded Byron against his judgment to deal with a man he distrusted.

Both the *Bolivar* and the salvaged *Don Juan* got back into the hands of their creator, the rather shady Commander Roberts, who professed to be a spy for the British Navy; and at different times the two vessels were wrecked—the *Bolivar* in 1828 or 1829 on the rocks off the coast a few miles from Ravenna.[4]

*   *   *   *   *   *

In 1827, the last remnant of Byron's library was disposed of by the auctioneer Evans in Pall Mall. It was one of Leigh Hunt's almost number-less criticisms of Byron that he had only few books and most of them modern. He did not choose to remember that a very enviable collection belonging to the poet had been forcibly sold to meet the demands of creditors in 1816, and that his life as an exile in foreign countries had

---

[1] Barry to Byron, 19 Nov. 1823. Murray MSS. 'I wrote this day week to inform you of the dishonour (as we Merchants call it) shewn to Lord Blessington's bill for four hundred guineas, the price of the boat. . . .'

[2] Ibid.   [3] Murray MSS.   [4] MEDWIN, *The Angler in Wales.*

hardly been conducive to accumulating bulky property. After the sale of certain volumes in Italy, there were two hundred and thirty-three left for consignment to the London auction room.

A report which seems to have been written for John Murray states that 'the principal purchasers were Mr Hobhouse M.P., Mr Moore, Mr Rogers, Colonel Stanhope, and Mr Longman the Bookseller'. There were about a dozen presentation copies, and another dozen, more or less, which contained Byron's autograph.

These are the only books which brought higher prices than if the leaves had not been turned by the mighty poet's fingers. The Presentation Copy of Sir Walter Scott's Kalidia Hill with inscription on the fly leaf 'Right Hon. Lord Byron, from his sincere and affectionate friend the Author' sold for £2.7.

Biblia Sacra Armenia with his Lordship's autograph thus 'Byron Venice, Dec. 3rd 1816' on the fly leaf and the title page brought £3.8 A copy of Bysshe Shelley's Prometheus, unbound, [sic] £1.7 after a struggle. The Greek Tragic Theatre and English Translation in 7 Vols. by different authors. Lord Byron has occasionally pencilled some of the most striking passages in these volumes which sold for £6. 0. 0.

Coleridge's Biographia Literaria with Lord Byron's autograph—13/6.

Atherstone's presentation copy with this inscription 'To Lord Byron with much deference' by the author sold for 11/-

Anacreon Greek and Latin with the autograph of Percy Bysshe Shelley £1. 2.

Anslar, a Bedineen Romance by Hamilton £3

Butler's History of the English Catholics 16/- Lord Holland's Life and Memoir of Lope de Vega presented to his Lordship by the noble author £2. 15. Ossian Neuve Canti da Leoni, with Lord Byron's autograph bought by Mr Hobhouse for 5½ gs. The Poetic Mirror for 1816, with his Lordship's title in the first page, written by Lady Byron, sold for £1. 0. 0.

Taciti Opera Notis Variorum 2 Vols. Elzevir 1672 bought by Mr Hobhouse for 3 gs.[1]

Although it was 'a struggle' to get £1.7. for the 'Prometheus', which was thought to be unbound, the fact that two Shelley items are singled out as amongst the most important lots in the sale shows the upward trend of that poet's reputation. Greek and Latin texts of Anacreon were common enough, but already Shelley's signature, even in a work not his own, had a monetary value.

After this, there was only one more public sale of Byron property, that of the copyrights, which took place by auction—a rare method of transacting such business—at Hodgson's on February 20th, 1830. They were purchased by Murray—all except *Don Juan*—for 3700 guineas. Hanson and Hobhouse were well satisfied with the result, although *Don Juan* had to be withdrawn at 310 guineas, the most any publisher would

[1] 7 July 1827: Murray MSS.

then pay. A week later, Hobhouse learned that they might have got 4000 guineas or more if the auctioneer had only trusted his instructions from Murray's rival, Colburn, 'who gave him carte blanche to exceed Murray's biddings till he stopt him. However, we have got a large sum,' Hobhouse added, self-consolingly.

Murray had paid during Byron's lifetime for the use of the copyrights £15,455,[1] on which he admitted having made a most handsome profit. This sum did not include anything for *English Bards and Scotch Reviewers*, which had gone through several editions in other hands, or Byron's earnings from a number of major works published by the Hunts, amongst which were *The Island, Heaven and Earth*, and eleven cantos of *Don Juan*. With nearly £4000 for the copyrights bought by auction, the amounts ultimately given for *Don Juan*, and a further sum paid in the 1840's to extend the period of the monopoly, it seems likely that Byron, who printed his first work at his own expense under the unassuming title *Fugitive Pieces*, remains, in the materialistic sense, the most successful poet who ever lived. He, Kinnaird, and Murray were also very good business men, and if Hobhouse was somewhat ungifted in that line, he made up by conscientiousness what he lacked in ability.

The beneficiary of all this talent and good management was Mrs Leigh, described by the long-suffering Kinnaird as 'I think half-witted',[2] but what with debts, money-lenders exacting ferocious rates of interest, ne'er-do-well husband, sons, daughters, and son-in-law, and her own incapacity, her entanglements were beyond unravelling, and she was soon selling Byron's manuscripts and discussing plans for making money out of some of his letters.

Her original intention was to have a selection of them published by Trevanion. It was a notion Hobhouse deplored[3] but there was no plan for publication that could ever have won his approval. Not only did he passionately desire to keep even the most innocuous aspects of the celebrity's private life unprofaned by the eyes of the public, but he was also of the opinion that Byron's letters were entirely without literary merit and likely merely to lower his reputation.

He had therefore been much annoyed when John Murray did what he looked upon as a most damaging thing:

> The Representative—Murray's new paper, has quite failed—To bolster it up Murray has been making extracts from Lord Byron's letters and publishing them under the title of the Byron Papers—They are sad trash and do no honour to Byron even as confidential communications.

[1] MURRAY, *Pamphlet*, 1824.
[2] Letter to Hobhouse, 8 Mar. 1829. British Museum: Acquisitions of 1950.
[3] Hobhouse *Journals*, 9 July 1829. The entry is transferred to 20 Nov. by the editor of the *Recollections*.

I remonstrated with Murray on their publication, and he said his paper was such stuff something must be done—he said, however, that he had not yet come to his own letters—by which I suppose he meant to hint that he had hitherto been using Caroline Lamb's. At any rate the man shows himself not trustworthy.[1]

Murray can scarcely be blamed for having been less than candid with Hobhouse, since he too had certain proprietary rights, and was determined not to let this fanatical executor deprive him of them. The 'Byron Papers' which were appearing in the newspaper he had so misguidedly launched in collaboration with the young Disraeli, were not letters at all, but passages from the 'Detached Thoughts' Byron had jotted down at Ravenna in 1821, and might almost have been called a surviving fragment of the Memoirs.

On June 8th, 1822, Byron had written Murray:

. . . I have sent you by my earliest and dearest friend, Lord Clare, a commonplace book, about half-filled, which may serve *partly* hereafter in aid of the Memoirs purchased by you from Mr Moore. There are parts which have no reference to, nor will answer your purpose; but some others may do perhaps.[2]

Had Hobhouse known of this, his already warm resentment would have passed all bounds. The words 'my earliest and dearest friend' were alone enough to have embittered him, for he had not as yet seen any of Byron's sentimental allusions to Clare; and he would have thought them most unfair. Had Clare ever had his friendship put to any test or his loyalty tried by any strain? He had moved in so different a world that Hobhouse himself had never encountered him until nearly a year after Byron's death.

As it was, even without knowing that this 'sad trash' of Byron's was material that had escaped the holocaust, he got the series suppressed.

I told him [Murray] I would never quarrel with him but he really ought to reconsider his conduct.

Murray had long-term plans which could not be carried out if Hobhouse was in opposition, and he must have resolved not to jeopardize them. From the day of the remonstrance, no 'Byron Papers' appeared in the *Representative* for a month, and after only two more selections, of very much reduced length, the series petered out.

There was still a collection of papers in Italy—those which Byron had given to Charles Barry. Hobhouse called on Barry when visiting Genoa in 1826, and found him in the large villa at Albaro where Byron himself had spent the very last of his Italian days. The banker had renewed the lease

---

[1] Ibid. 8 Feb. 1826.   [2] *L. & J.*

in readiness for the tenant's return and, after that hope failed, had kept the house on at his own expense, leaving everything so far as possible as it had been before.

> Lord Byron gave 25£ a year. Barry rents it for 20—there are two acres about of garden and pleasure ground, an old summer house, and an alley of trees, ilexes, I think under which Byron used to read. Barry who speaks with an affectionate veneration of him showed me the little round table at which he (Byron) used to dine, and the spot where he placed his chair—We dined in Byron's bedroom. . . .
>
> Madame Guiccioli's apartments and those of Gamba father and son are at the other side of the house or great hall. Barry told me that Gamba the father seemed to live amongst the servants of the family—
> He showed me a letter from Madame Guiccioli in which she expressed a sort of intention of writing something about Byron—and in which she confessed there was foundation for some things in Medwin's book—but that others were *absolutely false*. Byron was certainly tired of her, yet in a letter to Barry from Cefalonia he said he had left his heart in Italy.
> At and after dinner Barry showed me a great many papers of Byron's both prose and verse, some published, some I think unpublished.[1]

Hobhouse afterwards made 'an imperfect list from memory', and it is so remarkable a feat in its enumeration of a large quantity of correspondence and a score of literary items, some of which are described, that it strengthens the confidence his records cannot fail to engender. The accuracy of his quotations after a single reading is most striking. But he was mistaken in his supposition that certain stanzas headed 'The Bitch patronizes a charity ball' were inspired by Caroline Lamb. It was Lady Byron who had touched off that burst of temper, with its acrid refrain, 'The Saint keeps her charity back for the ball'. He read, with gratification, a long letter addressed to Byron by Walter Scott, and then, in furious disgust, one from Thomas Moore.

> . . . In this he calls Byron 'my dear fellow' and tells him he has now got the MSS memoirs all his own by cancelling the original deed and putting the MSS into Murray's hands merely as a pledge for the repayment of 2000 guineas, so, says Moore '*Write on as they will be all for me.*'
> He tells Byron that some *not of the finer order of spirits* had objected to the original transaction as if he (Byron) 'had wished to purchase a biographer.'

These words were, of course, those he himself had used in complaining of Byron's gift of the Memoirs to Moore.[2] He knew that the light and

[1] Hobhouse *Journals*, 3 Oct. 1826.
[2] See Chapter I, p. 39. This passage from Moore's letter abundantly proves that Cordy Jeaffreson, Mayne, and several other biographers were mistaken in their belief that the revised arrangements with Murray were the consequence of a decision on Byron's part to regain possession of the Memoirs because he himself had second thoughts about publishing them.

jocular comment, so different from his own earnest style, was made at his expense, while the easy familiarity of the Irishman's manner drove him to his very worst state of umbrage—the one in which he called Moore 'Tommy'.

> Well done, Tommy Moore. 'The finer order of spirits' indeed! The fact is he knew that I had objected to the transaction, and this was only a poor fling at me—but he told me that Lord Lansdowne and Lord Holland had also objected to the transaction, and poor little Tom would hardly call them not of the finer order of spirits.
>
> His exhortation to his friend to write on is very *fine* indeed. The next thing would have been to tell him to die in order that Moore might make the MSS into money. Moore signs his letter 'affectionately.' Now in all my intimacy with Byron I hardly ever did this—nor do I to any body but my own family—it is sad slobbering work.

At this point Hobhouse must have remembered that only a page or so before, he had mentioned with pride that Scott, whom he deemed one of the first men of the age, had signed himself 'affectionately' to Byron, and he added: 'Scott might do it—he was older and had a great character.'

Moore was also older and famous on a scale very little below that of Scott, and he bore a character for the highest integrity; but Hobhouse was not jealous of Scott, had never up to that time seen him in fact, while Moore's convivialities with Byron and such figures as Sheridan and Colman, their meetings in houses which were as yet *terra infirma* to Hobhouse, must have been a thorn in his side on many a day and night. And he had behaved so ruthlessly to Moore over the Memoirs and everything connected with them that, being fundamentally a humane man, he could not but feel guilty towards him, and this guilt, since he could never bring himself to acknowledge it, was converted into feelings of injury.

The more he was reproved for his memoir-burning folly, the more determinedly he strove to convince himself and others that he could not have been wrong. On one occasion there was 'an unpleasant scene' about it. He was criticized during a social evening by the Comtesse de Flahault, who, as an English, or rather Scottish, heiress on the grandest scale had in her own right the title of Viscountess Keith and would later hold the Barony of Nairne. In the years when Byron, as a very prepossessing and sought-after bachelor, had moved from one country house party, one London rout, to another, this lady had been Miss Mercer-Elphinstone, stepdaughter of Dr Johnson's Queeney Thrale, immensely rich, immensely eligible, the intimate friend of Princess Charlotte of Wales, and known as the Fop's Despair for the enormous list of her rejected suitors.

Byron and she had flirted, and he had gone to Tunbridge Wells to see her, and given her the Albanian costume he had worn for his portrait by Phillips, with directions how to don it for a masquerade. (It had cost him £50, a sum he might have had some difficulty in laying hands on at the time, but of course she could not guess at that.)

A lesser heiress, Miss Milbanke, had looked on her with disapproval, finding her assuming and rough-mannered,[1] but her letters to Byron are those of a charming, lively, worldly-wise young woman; and there is something agreeably free from affectation in her reply to his reminder that 'any apparent anxiety on my part to cultivate your acquaintance . . . would have been attributed by others to a motive *not* very creditable to me'. 'I am but too well aware of all the *désagréments* of my own situation', she responded simply. '. . . With regard to our acquaintance, I can only say I must ever think of it with pleasure, and trust that all the nonsense that has been said, or may be said, will not prevent its continuance.'[2]

She was one of the last persons he wrote to on leaving England. He could never forget that at the ball given by Lady Jersey, when he, so recently the darling of society, had been cut by almost every woman in the room, she had come up to him as he stood alone plumbing the depth of his ruin, and had said, with the teasing geniality of a friend: 'You had better have married me. I would have managed you better.'

Perhaps, if he had ever really set about winning her, she would have married him, and his whole history, and some of ours, would have been different. No one can suppose he was fitted in those years of immaturity to make a comfortable domesticated partner, but with a wife less critical of the world, less analytical and self-consciously righteous than the one he chose, the inevitable frictions might have been no worse than those a hundred high-spirited couples managed to endure without catastrophe. He wrote at last, in his most modest strain, to hint, but not too wistfully, at why he had never paid her his addresses:

> . . . *Now* no motive can be attributed to me with regard to you of a selfish nature—at least I hope not.
>
> I know not why I venture to talk thus, unless it be that the time is come when, whatever I may say cannot be of importance enough to give offence, and that neither my vanity *nor my wishes* ever induced me at any time to suppose that I could by any chance have become more to you than I now am.[3]

Several decades later, in the 1860's, when Mme d'Haussonville, the granddaughter of Mme de Staël, was working on a book about Byron, she asked the Comtesse de Flahault, long resident in France, for her recollections. 'I am very proud', wrote the aged *grande dame*, 'of the friendship

---

[1] QUENNELL AND PASTON.
[2] Ibid. Byron's letter is dated 3 May 1814, and hers is doubtless a day or two later.
[3] QUENNELL, *Self-Portrait*. 11 Apr. 1816.

that he always showed me, and above all I appreciate the last and sad proof he gave me of it, in sending me this touching letter of farewell at the very moment when he was leaving England for ever.'[1]

In the days when she taxed Hobhouse with his wrong-headedness about the Memoirs, and caused him to record the fact of the 'unpleasant scene' in his diary,[2] she was still red-headed and bright-eyed as Byron remembered her. The terseness of Hobhouse's journal entry conveys that he did not feel he had had the best of the argument.

[1] QUENNELL AND PASTON. The letter is here translated from the French.
[2] Hobhouse *Journals*, 16 Jan. 1827.

CHAPTER VII

THE BLACKMAIL CANARD

The writing of begging letters was one of the gainful occupations of the 18th and 19th centuries. The Mendicity Society had a special department with long lists of persons who subsisted entirely on the proceeds of addressing tales of want and woe to skilfully selected recipients. Dickens who, as a national celebrity, was besieged by all kinds of impostors, made begging-letter writers the subject of one of his essays, entering with his customary zest into the details of their methods. One of these was to make sure of enclosing something—'verses, letters, pawnbrokers' duplicates, anything to necessitate an answer'.

Hobhouse, as a Member of Parliament of known humanitarian principles, received numbers of such approaches, but, unlike Byron (who had to live up to the reputation of giving a nobleman's largesse), he was generally unresponsive. The enclosure of verses was frequent, but left him unmoved; and he was cautious too of tributes to the memory of his famous friend. In consequence of this hard-heartedness he received, on February 3rd, 1826, one of the many irritating communications that postmen and messengers had been in the habit of bringing him ever since Byron's death:

Sir,
      It is now upwards of a month since I addressed a packet for your perusal —containing a copy of my last published Poem—The Destroying Angel— and a manuscript tribute to the memory of Lord Byron—accompanied by a statement of my situation and an appeal to your generous sympathy. I also mentioned having in my possession extracts from the confessions of a Lady of Rank relative to Lord Byron—which certainly do not set his private life in a very amiable point of view—and which I could dispose of to almost any publisher to advantage—did not my veneration for the departed Bard resist the suggestion of Calamity—at least until I have exhausted every other means of alleviating my distress. I am at this moment Sir, labouring under every privation concomitant to unfriended talent—destitute of a meal—a fire —of everything! with an aged parent dependent on my exertions—and the companion of my sufferings—
      If you have done me the honour of reading the contents of my packet— I trust you will consider me deserving of a better fate—and I appeal to your enlightened and powerful intellect as well as to your humanity—a very trifle would save me from perishing—and for that I am ready to give up those papers—being now the only copies in my possession—which I must otherwise be compelled to give up to some unfeeling and mercenary bookseller.

I entreat the favour of an *Immediate communication*, and trust you will pardon the intrusion.

I remain, Sir, With the highest respect,
                         Yr ob. and H. Servant
                              J. Wilmington Fleming.[1]

39 Great Andrew Street,
      Seven Dials.

Hobhouse disliked publicity, he was a believer in hushing things up, but he always rebounded strongly against anything resembling a menace. He had, moreover, the wit to see that a man who had somehow obtained a private document involving a Lady of Rank, and was capable of threatening to sell it to a publisher, would have sold it in any case if it had been such as a publisher would pay for. He therefore left this second letter unanswered like the first, though perhaps not without a mild tremor of curiosity. Were the 'confessions' genuine or the work of some fiction writer? If genuine, which Lady of Rank?

Lady Oxford, dead two years? Lady Frances Webster, whom he had last heard from soon after Byron's death, asking anxiously though not ungracefully about her letters and the Memoirs?[2] The Countess Guiccioli whose letters ('a cartload') he was to regret having returned?[3] Or Lady Caroline Lamb, now an addict of the brandy bottle and separated at last from a husband who had endured a martyrdom? Lady Caroline had a mania for showing off and had already tried to publish an account of her affair with Byron. She was by far the likeliest to have committed an indiscretion, but her stock stood so low that Hobhouse could have cared little for what she might have confessed. He did not even mention the matter in his *Journal*.

In less than three weeks the pertinacious writer made, so far as Hobhouse was concerned, his final attempt, and being obviously without professional qualifications as a blackmailer, he naïvely showed his hand. The third letter is postmarked February 22nd.

Sir,
        I have waited long and anxiously in the expectation of hearing from you on the subject connected with my appeal to your benevolent feelings—at the time I enclosed my manuscript verses on Childe Harold—and a copy of my last published poem The Destroying Angel.

        I considered from some passages in the papers to which I alluded—(copies of which I subjoin) that you would not wish them to become the property of a mercenary publisher—to which nothing but the extreme misery of my

---

[1] British Museum: Additional MSS. 36461.
[2] QUENNELL AND PASTON.
[3] Hobhouse *Journals*, 5 Oct. 1827. She annoyingly made a contribution to Moore's biography.

situation could induce me to consent—and I hoped that you would generously bestow a trifling sum in lieu of their possession.

If I have been deceived I beg pardon for the intrusion and trust you will return me the manuscript poem as I have no other copy.

I remain Sir

Your Obt Servant[1]

Hobhouse must have recognized Lady Caroline in the first five lines of the extracts quoted, and summed up at a glance the weakness of the lever by which the author of *The Destroying Angel* had tried to move him.

Extracts from a Journal

It is a pity that the *Memoranda* has been destroyed yet I think a copy still exists—in the possession of either Moore or Hobhouse—

Hobhouse writes that if I will give up Lord Byron's letters—to be destroyed!—he will return mine: he says that Byron should only be known to the world by his great talents and noble death and that it is the business of a friend to draw a veil over his errors.

His behaviour had changed my heart and when he informed me of — — — — — I shuddered even at his presence.[2]

The first time Lord B—— said that to me which he should not &c

The first time he saw Miss Milbanke (now Lady B.) was at M[elbourne] House and he did not like her—and he was formal and stiff etc.

The evening before the execution of Bellingham—he came to me *pale* and exceedingly agitated and said he must see him die, he was silent and restless and I liked him less on that evening—he departed early and appeared at breakfast next morning—calm and tranquil. I have seen him suffer (he said) and he made *no confession*.[3]

It was *me* and no general that introduced Lord Byron to the King—it was at etc. etc.[4]

He used to lament the mischief he had occasioned—saying that he and W[illiam] L[amb] were like Hamlet's two pictures!—&c.

It has been reported that I visited Lord B.'s Lodging in the disguise of a Page. Jonny Green was my page at that time.

Whether or not he returned Mr Fleming's 'last published poem' and the verses on 'the departed Bard', Hobhouse took not the slightest notice of the letter. He had reason to know the journal had been written for

[1] British Museum: op. cit.

[2] We may assume that the row of blanks reproduces similar blanks in the original, because Fleming's own method of indicating the incompleteness of a passage is by *etcetera* signs.

[3] Bellingham assassinated the Prime Minister, Spencer Perceval. Byron with two friends attended the execution. It was the first time he had seen that then very popular spectacle. Though he must have felt it to be part of the experience of a man of the world to witness a public hanging, there is other evidence that he was extremely nervous beforehand, and his change of mood the following morning may have been the reaction after having got through the ordeal.

[4] Byron was presented to George IV, then Prince Regent, in June 1812.

publication (what private diarist would have needed to remind herself that Miss Milbanke was 'now Lady B'?) and buying up the few and feeble extracts that had been copied could not effectually prevent their circulation. On November 1st, 1824, after recording in his own diary his talk with Lady Caroline about Medwin's *Conversations*,[1] he had continued:

> She gave me a ridiculous account of the attempt lately made to confine her as a mad woman, and mentioned that she had sent 16 volumes quarto of journals kept by her since 1806 to Godwin, the author, to do what he would with. She also opened a communication with the newspapers. This frightened Mr Lamb and the family. She said Godwin returned the journals. I saw the first volume: it was funny enough.

Although her husband and family had apparently succeeded in bringing pressure to bear against publication, nothing would stop that dissolute and *déclassée* woman from showing her journals to anyone who would read them. This was one of the occasions when Hobhouse shrugged his shoulders, thankful doubtless that he had refused to let her have her letters when she had played one of her dying scenes with him about them. It was the only guarantee, he said, 'against her making a novel out of Byron's letters'.[2]

The needy poet turned elsewhere. On March 8th, without troubling to enclose a copy of *The Destroying Angel*, he approached the lady in St James's Palace. Since a false legend has been spun out of this letter, it is necessary to quote it, like the others, in full:

> Madam,
>
>   I have to crave your pardon for this intrusion, the more as it is connected with a subject dear to your feelings, and sacred to your memory; and I beg most solemnly to assure you that nothing but the extreme urgency of distress and wounded feelings could urge me to draw your attention to the subject.
>
>   As a literary man—I became acquainted with Lady Caroline Lamb, who, with her usual eccentricity of mind (though at that time I knew it not), flattered my talents and encouraged my hopes—in short, Madam, she deceived me by false promises—and afterwards treated me most ungenerously. Previous to this, she gave me her utmost confidence and the possession of her private journal and Confessions relative to Lord Byron—and his Lady—from which I have extracted the most interesting passages—not at the time with any other view than the possession of a highly valuable and entertaining manuscript. But my feelings, my situation and my views, are altered. I am now perishing—with a mother dependent on me for support—without a friend in the world—and in the hourly expectation of being turned into the streets. At this moment then, Madam, of desperation—and misery—I can dispose of the manuscript I mention to a *publisher*—who of course will make an unworthy use of them—which would also wound the feelings of those individuals who are blameless.

---

[1] See p. 105.   [2] Hobhouse *Journals*, 22 May 1824.

Now, Madam, I apply to you. Within a few days I must part with them
—without indeed you benevolently condescend to feel for my situation, and
take them into your own possession. A comparative trifle will obtain them—
and relieve me from the direst necessity—and I beg the honour of an immediate communication on the subject.

The Manuscript relates Lady Caroline's first interview with Lord Byron
—his subsequent approaches—his attacks upon her weakness—his opinion
of Lady Byron—and that Lady's account of the usage she received from him
on her last visit to Lady Caroline previous to her separation—with other
subjects painful to a relative's feelings and interesting to the Public.

I could, Madam, as you may well conceive, dispose of them immediately
—did not my feelings of respect for the memory of the Author of 'Childe
Harold' prevent me until I had made the present offer to one who was so
dearly connected with him.

An immediate answer will oblige.

Madam &c[1]

Augusta reacted with good sense and comparative calm by writing at
once to Hobhouse. The letter did not contain the smallest hint of a
menace against herself: the topics named were of no direct concern to her
other than as all evidence of Byron's misbehaviour must be 'painful to a
relative's feelings', and if the blackmailer knew anything to give him a
hold over her personally, he was singularly reticent about it.

Unfortunately for herself, she followed her customary practice of con-
fiding in Lady Byron. They were on terms of the warmest friendship just
then, for besides having recently provided financial aid which had enabled
Georgiana Leigh to marry Henry Trevanion, Annabella had sent Augusta
a draft for £20 to help her out of the difficulties left by wedding and
trousseau expenses, and had also offered her the loan of her house in
Brighton during a long trip abroad for which she was preparing. In a letter
thanking her, and expatiating on that perennial problem, how to raise
money, she observed without any sign of nervousness on her own behalf:

Mr Hobhouse has not written nor answered a note I sent him last night,
enclosing a most extraordinary letter I had received, offering me the refusal
of a *publication* of Extracts from Ly C. Lamb's Journal ! ! ! ! ! ! ! ! ! ! ! I cannot
think what he is about.[2]

Hobhouse was about the business of the country, speaking and voting
in the House of Commons against flogging in the Army, a cause most
important to him, though he was later—most unfairly—to be nicknamed
Flogging Jack. He had in any case been out of town on the evening when
her messenger called: but the attitude of impatience because she did not

---

[1] LOVELACE, *Lady Noel Byron*. The name was copied by Lady Byron as Washington,
instead of Wilmington, Fleming, a mistake repeated by Miss Mayne.

[2] 9 Mar. 1826: Lovelace Papers.

receive an instantaneous reply was becoming only too typical of her. She had grown extremely expectant, and if those who had been Byron's friends did not drop everything else to respond to her appeals, considered herself ill done by.

Her next reference to Fleming is a mere postscript to a letter wholly about other matters, and by repeating more or less what she had already said, she shows a forgetfulness incompatible with terror.

Ly Caroline L. has been shewing her *Private Journal* to a man who *took the opportunity* of copying from it! & now upon being ill treated by her, & very poor, is going to *publish* it ! ! ! & offers it to *me* for any small sum *my benevolence* wd bestow ! ! ! ! ! I wish that Woman could be sent to the Tread Mill as well as that shame*less* Man her husband![1]

This comment on William Lamb was tactless because he was Lady Byron's first cousin and an ally of hers. However, the reply seems to have been amicable, even sympathetic, and Augusta could have had little idea of the report that was about to be spread when she wrote again to her 'dearest A' as follows:

As for *the Copy*—I sent a person—merely to say that I could have nothing whatever to do with any such things. I thought this more civil than *total silence* & I wd not on any account write—& I could not help pitying anybody in such a sad state as the letter represents & which from his appearance when he was visited with my message appeared to be quite true—since this I have had another letter & I enclose *both*, for I think it probable *you* may also be attacked—Of the truth of the Statement concerning the contents of the Journal *I have not the least doubt*—from all I *know* from those who have read it—& I believe it is shewn a qui voudra lire! That Woman is a perfect *Demon* & one of the few I never can be charitable to.

I cannot believe her *mad*—but excessively bad, & as any body might become by giving loose to ungoverned passions—in short I have a perfect *horror* of her from what I know—& it was a happy moment for me to meet her last night ! ! ! when coming away with ye Dowr D[uche]ss of Leeds from Ly Salisbury's. We were waiting for the Carriage in the *Cloak Room* [when] she suddenly jumped before us like *Beelzebub* mad or drunk! accosted the D[uche]ss to *her* horror! & to my dismay! for the last 10 years & more (ever since the publication of Glenarvon) I have never acknowledged an acquaintance with her & all but turned my back—Imagine after that, her accosting me & absolutely thrusting her hand almost into my face! I believe I *just* touched it & made her the most profound Curtsey! then she made off somewhere—thro' a trap door I believe—for the whole apparition was to me like something from the lower Regions! & I half expected like the man in Der Freichutz to find the *Fiend's Mark* on my hand—not my brow!—

[1] Ibid. 14 Mar.

I *have* not & *shall* not answer or take *any* notice of this last letter—the *honorable* proceeding of Copying what was shewn (I *suppose* in *soi-disant* confidence) speaks for itself—pray return them to me—[1]

Lady Byron took copies of one, or more probably, both of Fleming's letters before she returned them, but the second has not been found. It would almost certainly not have supported the case which has been built upon the first—namely, that Augusta was alarmed lest the secret of her own sinful love should be exposed. It is to be observed that on receiving the second letter, she resolved not to answer it; that she thought it likely Lady Byron might also be 'attacked' (i.e. troubled by the begging-letter writer); and that, like Hobhouse, she was aware of Caroline's habit of allowing anyone to read the journal who might wish to, and thus had no motive for paying hush money.

The proposal that hush money should be paid emanated wholly from the person who afterwards represented Augusta as the victim of blackmail.

Lady Byron had her own reasons for feeling uncomfortable. Whatever may have been in the second of the two Fleming letters forwarded, the first, as has been shown, specifies a copy of her own confidences about her husband to Caroline. It was true that she had seen Caroline shortly before the Separation became legal, and had exchanged deep confidences with her, and thenceforward indeed had allowed the discarded mistress aching for revenge to guide her policy. Collusion with a woman of the most tarnished reputation, whom she had disliked intensely from girlhood, did not fit in at all with the accepted picture of her conduct—believed, even by those who regarded her as cold and obdurate, to be based on principles of the loftiest dignity.

* * * * * *

That the immense influence of Caroline Lamb on Byron's matrimonial disaster may be understood, it is necessary to recapitulate certain facts that are known and to introduce a number that have hitherto been suppressed. Byron's liaison with that unbalanced but very plausible and, for a time, seductive personality was brief only on his side. She remained absolutely obsessed by him, and for years after the end of the amour, was performing antics of every kind to regain his attention. As late as 1821, nine years after he had passed from her to Lady Oxford, her wild and disjointed novel *Ada Reis*[2] was full of little barbs aimed at this demon lover.

So far from being the frank, impulsive, and fundamentally generous spirit some biographers have depicted, she was guileful, tenacious, and

---

[1] 16 Mar. 1826: Lovelace Papers.
[2] The Ada of the book is an Oriental male character satirizing Byron. Ada was his daughter's name, but violations of good taste were irresistible to Caroline Lamb.

Lady Caroline Lamb, from a portrait by Thomas Phillips

vindictive in no common degree. Her trouble-making propensities had been the bane of cousins, aunts, and relatives-in-law years before she met Byron. She made generous gestures, but they were perfectly empty. She professed moral views verging on the sanctimonious but was intensely carnal. No guesswork could have been more wide of the mark than that of Rogers who thought her infatuation over Byron was without a physical basis.[1] Letters of hers survive, unpublished, which suggest that Byron, with his libertine's admiration for purity, may have been repelled by her abandon.

She had put herself in the way of being humiliated by him, and like her cousin-by-marriage, had ended with feelings that were cruelly ambivalent. Jane Clairmont looked back with nothing but hatred, Teresa Guiccioli with nothing but love: Lady Byron and Lady Caroline were tormented with love and hatred entwisted together.

When the news that the marriage was breaking up first reached her, early in February 1816, Caroline seized the opportunity of renewing her advances to Byron by writing him heroic letters about her anxiety to serve him; but he suspected, correctly, that she had played some part in circulating the very stories she clamorously deplored, and left her overtures unanswered. Thus again rebuffed, she resolved to ally herself secretly with the other side and do him all the injury she could. An excuse was necessary, since her professions of friendship towards the husband might have reached the wife's ear, and she fixed upon a very ingenious one—a rumour that Byron intended to press for the custody of his child.

Shortly after the middle of March 1816—the letter has no date—she sat down and devised an approach of consummate artfulness:

Lady Byron
It is not for me to write to you or in any way to appear in this most melancholy scene—God protect & preserve you through it—trust in him & in your own good heart & in yr Parents who still remain to watch over and save you—What I could say I will not—my lips are forever seald & all interference on my part either way must be misrepresented—Yet I will never be so mean as to deceive you—in the first moment of surprise & regret when I heard with every gross & shameful misrepresentation of yr departure & his dispair [*sic*]—I wrote to him with all the kindness and affection of a friend imploring him to follow you to seek you & to regain you — — I even spoke more bitterly in my letter of yr Parents who I was informed had forced you to this act. Such letter I am miserable at having written—if for one moment you or *he* or any other can think me base enough & false enough to every feeling of humanity & the commonest principle—as to take His part against yours—Lady Byron whatever may be my fate—from this hour nothing on earth shall tempt me in word or thought to have the Slightest communication or friendship for one of *his* character—

[1] DYCE.

I have suffered Many *deserved* griefs through his Barbarity & my own innexcusable [*sic*] & criminal conduct thank God I have suffered them as in part perhaps they may attone [*sic*] for my weakness & crime, but I can assure you that never till this hour did I feel Disgust & indifference for one who deserves no other sentiments—so different is the feeling which arises from the blow given to ourselves When we feel that we deserve it from the hand of God—& the unmerited cruelty exercised on one—not only innocent —but by *his* own account exemplary noble—& all that ought to have been prized & loved—[1]

This preamble was pitched in exactly the right key for Annabella, who liked sinners to express remorse and submission, and was particularly susceptible to flattery on the score of her own virtues. Before hinting further at the revelations she had it in her power to make, Caroline went on solemnly to enjoin her never to let any human being learn that she had written:

. . . Your name at this time must not be coupled with mine—You must not even speak of me with the generous kindness you ever have—

Annabella had never spoken of Caroline without severe distaste, but to achieve her determined purpose the latter was set upon running the whole gamut of flattery, both in its subtlest and its frankest forms.

. . . There may come a time when I shall prove in more than words how I esteem & love & feel for you—but for God['s] sake Hold no sort of communication with me now—only were I to die for it tonight—I will not suffer another hour to pass without telling you—that I would stand by you not him were the whole world & every thing in it—in his favour—& if he has the cruelty to tear the child from You I will tell you that which if you merely menace him with the knowledge shall make him tremble—

Lady Byron badly needed evidence against her husband. Depositions as to drunkenness, cruelty, and infidelity were not enough to secure a woman a legal separation from a man who resisted and claimed restitution of conjugal rights. The laws of the time, which permitted divorce to males for unfaithfulness alone, were heavily weighted against any attempt by wives to get rid of husbands. Enormous latitude was allowed for the moral weaknesses of the masculine sex, and if Byron persisted in putting up a fight, badly as he had behaved, the upshot of a trial in the Ecclesiastical Courts was by no means a foregone conclusion.

On March 11th Byron had written to her, after receiving a message to say she was not to be intimidated by legal measures:

The words 'legal measures' were first used by your father in a letter to me (ready for production when necessary) and all that has been said or done by

[1] Lovelace Papers. Far from imploring him 'to follow, to seek, and to regain' his wife, she had begged him most strenuously to assent without demur to the separation (*L. & J.*, II, p. 449).

me since that amounted & amounts only to a determination to resist such proceedings by such lawful defences as truth & justice permit & prescribe to the accused as well as the accuser. These measures have not been of my seeking—& whatever the results may be—I am not aware of any impropriety in declaring that I shall defend myself from attacks which strike at the root of every tie—& connection—of hope—and character—of my child's welfare—& it may be—even of your own.

I am prepared on such points—& being so—should not have alluded to them—had I not conceived that you have either misconceived—or been led to misconceive me—by attributing to me 'legal measures' which I merely resolved to resist.[1]

It seemed inevitable then that the case would come to court. To strengthen her hand, she had told her lawyers all her suspicions relating to Augusta, but they had informed her in effect that, though this was a first-rate card to hold, it could not be played until such suspicions were capable of most positive proof. It may be imagined that she rose with eagerness to the hope held out: '*I will tell you that which if you merely menace him with the knowledge shall make him tremble—*'

Never was bait dangled more enticingly; and there were sly warnings, too, against Augusta, opening a prospect that the needful proof might be forthcoming:

Think of my situation when I saw you an innocent unsuspicious sacrifice to his selfish & cruel vanity——do not fancy that I stood by coldly & calmly to see it——he made every promise of amendment Man could make——but still I reproach myself that I did not fly before you & tell you all I knew—— all I had sworn never never to reveal——to keep such oath was more scandalous than to have broken it—but I still loved Byron even then—& had he behaved to you as he said—I could not have hated & despised him as from my soul I now do & will——

Lady Byron though you are spotless & pure & I am all that is fallen & worthless yet hear me—it is on my knees I write to you—your friendship your protection can be nothing to me—don't then think I say what I now say for any purpose or to flatter you—but for yr dear child's sake for yr poor Mother's——trust no one—there are serpents round you who can smile on you & bite you to the heart — — — all will tell you that some have taken yr part but do not believe them——perhaps they have a motive for their behaviour—oh beware even of your own Shadow——keep all at a distance— be cold to his friends & relatives——they are more *his* friends than yours—— above all mistrust those who tell you *he* is *ill* & unhappy——I will let you know if he is really so——I took the allarm [sic] upon false reports——but he is only crafty—double mouthed that he may the better deceive you—to Lady Melbourne & Hobhouse he holds the proudest language—speaks of you however as you deserve—but asks repeatedly if you were not Happy—lays the change on yr Parents & false friends——says he knows you love him & shews some letter with tender expressions from Kirby in proof

[1] Ibid.

> Mrs Lee [*sic*] too espouses yr part—it is *not natural how much* she takes it —oh mistrust even her—keep all at a distance. . . .

Having said everything that could be said on paper to isolate her former successful rival from friends and to render it certain that husband and wife would never be reunited, she now, for the first but not the last time, gave the advice which set the tone for Lady Byron's subsequent occult manner of hinting at wrongs shrouded in dark mystery:

> . . . Above all intimate to *him* that you have the knowledge & proof of Some secret which nothing but dispair shall force you to utter.
>
> Do not think me cunning & crafty because I thus write to you but you are so innocent so good you can not be aware of their arts——truth & virtue will find its way in Heaven & God will preserve & protect you—but to spare you a scene of horror to spare you the agony of having yr child taken from you & consigned to such hands—I urge you to follow my counsel it is from the heart I write it — — & urge it——there is a secret—he dares not face that[.]
>
> I would sooner die I think than reveal it—but if he thinks that you know it—if he feels he is in yr power he will not dare to push matters to extremity ——he will not face a public trial——or if he does—he will yield to all such demands as you must insist on——

Lady Byron would have been superhuman if she had long resisted this invitation to learn the secret the other was so palpably burning to tell. It was transparent that Caroline could hardly restrain herself. All she wanted to be sure of was that Byron would never be enlightened as to the name of his betrayer, so that she could go on proclaiming to him and to the world her undying friendship for him. Over and over again, here and in later letters, she stressed, in dire and dramatic terms, the need of silence.

> *Now* Lady Byron I have done for you what I would not for myself or any other——I have placed my life my honour in yr hands——& acted a shabby part by one I thought once I had died merely to please——yet so strong are my feelings for you—so great my indignation—that I will run any risk sooner than not do my utmost to save you——
>
> One word more I wish to say—to no one living not even to Caro [Mrs George Lamb] who loves you as if you were her sister tell that I have written this letter—burn it for God['s] sake—& do not answer it upon any account whatever—if questioned by Lady M[elbourne] I wish to be able to say that I have not ever heard from you.

Lady Byron was more than willing to accede to the request that the usual coolness and distance between them should ostensibly be kept up. To be in possession of the secret and yet free from any appearance of alliance with one who had long been an object of disapprobation in society was in perfect accord with her wishes. At the same time, it must have been gratifying to find she had a friend in the camp of the enemy—for

Lady Melbourne, in whose great house Caroline lived, was so regarded by Annabella and her devoted mother.

They resented her most inveterately both for having promoted the unhappy marriage, and for not coming out strongly on the side of her brother's child when it broke up. On this Caroline had something to say—something which, while it seemed for an instant to be a defence of her mother-in-law, was actually the first step in a systematic campaign to deprive Byron of one of his staunchest and most valuable friends:

> . . . Lady Byron if some indignation Springs up in yr mind at finding yr own Aunt less warm in your Cause than others——oh remember that he who can make friends & relations think whatever he pleases—has blinded her not now alone but long long before — — & it appears to me that kindness & attention may perhaps bring her round from her infatuation — — —
>
> When guilt remorse & a barbarity little expected from one who had appeared so kind so good to me—drove me to acts of insanity & dispair ————Lady Melbourne even at that time espoused Lord Byron's cause—& her doing it added to the bitter agony I endured—Farewell my Dearest & much honoured & loved Cousin—God support & bless you—& pardon me
>
> ever yrs
Caroline Lamb

'Lord Byron's cause', at the time when Caroline was committing acts to which she herself gave the name of insanity, was nothing more sinister than to be left in peace by one whose importunities had become disturbing and farcical. The efforts of Lady Melbourne, whose son was married to this spectacular scene-maker, to detach her from a very jaded lover would not have seemed unkind or unreasonable to a normal person.

The portentous letter ended with a postscript requiring operatic language:

> Prego in Dio a lei di Brucciare questa lettera e che niente vi fa scrivere a me[1]—but if you are not offended & feel kindly—when next you see Caroline [Mrs George Lamb]——send me a message—such as yr remembrance——but even to her do not say I have written as I wish her to be able to say that she does not know of our having had any communication whatever——
> Believe me at this moment it is of consequence for were you to adopt my advice & hint at some secret—if it were to be known to have come from me ——it would seem I had acted the part of a King's evidence—& God knows what — — therefore I stake as it were my life in yr hands — — — —

Lady Byron took no notice of the appeal to burn the letter any more than if Caroline had been Augusta—and in this case, there was little reason why she should, because she had not asked for the confidence, and though the repeated note of homage was mollifying, she probably had a very good idea of the motives actuating the writer.

---

[1] I pray you for God's sake to burn this letter and let nothing make you write to me.

Whether she would send the desired message through William Lamb's sister-in-law, Mrs George Lamb, Caroline did not wait to learn. Within a few hours she had dispatched another frantic yet wily missive. Its principal object was to press home all the points in the first; but in the course of writing that, it must have occurred to her that the possibility of winning the influential Lady Melbourne away from Byron and thereby dispossessing him of a powerful support, was worth taking more trouble about, and she expounded this topic at some length.

> After the long letter I wrote to you at 3 oclock last night—you will be surprised at my again intruding——but I must say all that is on my mind & that done—I shall persevere in my resolution & till the whole of this is settled one way or other—hold no Sort of communication with you—but my Dear Lady Byron—I am Situated in a manner that seeing all things & Knowing much more than any *unless yourself* — — I cannot but be allarmed [*sic*] — — — in the first place you wish this amicably settled—& who would not provided your interest & dignity & child are left you——now in such case do you not perhaps think it were as well to conciliate in some measure yr Aunt—to write her a kind & frank letter—perhaps in Some such manner as this—saying
>
> ['] My Dear Aunt you will no doubt be surprised & hurt that at a moment of great affliction like the present I have not written openly or seen you—— but I too have been deeply wounded—& have thought by all I have heard that you have rather taken part against me than with me—there are things which I will never communicate to any—which are wholly my own but in all else I wish to shew you confidence ['] ——it is not possible for me exactly to say *how* I wish you to write yr own good feelings may dictate this—but be assured when I tell you that Lady Melbourne is of that warm nature that if she thought you dealt openly with her she would be touched——& is it a moment for anger—is it indeed worth it—[1]

Lady Melbourne had evidently complained that, when she had made a well-meant attempt at mediation, she had received from Annabella only a few glacial lines keeping her firmly at a distance.[2] She was hurt, for she had conducted herself with anxious sympathy towards all, and had tried in several letters to her brother, her brother's wife, her niece, and Byron himself, to represent each party favourably to the other and to undo the work of mischief-makers—no easy task with such daughters-in-law as hers.[3]

---

[1] Lovelace Papers.   [2] Ibid. 20 Feb. 1816.

[3] 'Caro George' and 'Caro William' were the two sources whence all the more serious rumours about Byron first emanated. Lady Byron was obliged to write to Mrs George Lamb and ask her to be less free-spoken, to which the latter answered: 'Indeed I cannot agree with you in the propriety of being silent, as to your wrongs. I cannot bear that vice should triumph, or that conduct so perfect as yours has been, should be in the slightest degree blamed or misunderstood. . . . Great God can I sit by and hear him defended when I know him to be the greatest villain on earth . . .?' Lovelace Papers, about April 1816.

Lady Caroline's seeming compassion for her mother-in-law was not without an infusion of malice, and under its cover she was able to go on sowing distrust of others.

> I will not deceive you or say You should trust her—but recollect my Dearest Lady Byron How artful *he* is & what a manner he has of turning things & pity rather than hate those whom he deceives — — I can assure you too that himself and M[rs] Leigh & Hobhouse though they all keep repeating—*She* is faultless—oh she is generous good kind noble — — say every now & then a Word—that makes the more impression from this apparent candour — —
>
> Now God forbid I should Judge anything——I believe M[rs] Leigh is your sincere friend—but recollect also that she is his sister & that she may feign this warm defence of yr conduct for some purpose——for is it probable also that she should be against *him*—there is a difficult game to play & they are playing it skilfully—
>
> I write not in enmity but merely to put you on yr guard—some affectionate letter of yours has already been much misrepresented & made a vast deal of use of against you——

Lady Caroline, though she was utterly perfidious, had that sort of sincere, cosy, and good-natured manner when in *tête-a-tête* conversation, that loosens the tongues even of the most cautious. Her pretence of an affection for Byron so magnanimous that no unkindness could impair it was the means of her being kept well-informed about his affairs long after she had become his indefatigable enemy. She maintained the character of one who was benevolent at heart by the secrecy she managed to impose on the recipients of her confidence.

> . . . Lady Byron you will ruin me forever if you tell one word of this even to yr real friends and what is worse you will do yourself incredible harm — —
>
> Remember the situation in which I stand——were it but thought that I espous'd your cause would it not hurt it — — so she has joined with Lady C. L. against him will be said—the cast-off Mistress & the Wife make common cause—

This was entirely Lady Byron's own view, but the argument was hammered home with more words than can be quoted.

> . . . If *you* want to hear anything if my seeing you or Mrs Claremont [Clermont] can serve any end—I could ride at 8 oclock in the Morning——or go out at 7 or 8 in the Evening——to any 3rd place you might know of. . . .
>
> William Lamb desires me to say all that is kind from him—he thinks if you could try & conciliate yr Aunt it were well—but it requires consideration — — & be assured that a cold letter or reserved manner will only further irritate—She is infatuated about Lord B—— she ever has been—& she is now more willing to think him Mad at times than wicked——besides which

she has an idea that you have a *cold* character — — — & certainly as the story has been represented to her it is singular—it is thus — — —

He says ['] I have now lived with Annabella upwards of a year—we have had disputes it is certain I make no one complaint against her——

I hear she makes every complaint against me——her Virtue & my want of it must make it Natural that all should side with her — — I wish it not otherwise——yet to be left thus is hard & my child too—& not one word to prepare me [']—then he appeals to his sister & Hobhouse—'I know I have been rough at times—but Augusta have you not seen me go to her—Kiss her and sooth[e] her——have we not been more fond than most married people are before others — — — that she has been led to this by her Mother who is my enemy—that I feel sure of — — — ['] & much more than this he says—for Lady M repeated it all to me—& I can tell you that at the first I felt furious against Lady Noel & you—& thought him most cruelly used—but it was only one day I laboured under this illusion—Murray whom I went to the next at once undeceived me—

Therefore Dearest Lady Byron feel for yr Aunt—but never whilst you live let her think I have had any communication with you—burn these letters pray——

In the previous communication she had asked Annabella to declare to Byron himself that she had knowledge of a secret that would make him tremble, but now she went further and proposed that others too should receive this intimation, Lady Melbourne in particular, and Lord Holland, who was endeavouring to bring about a reconciliation.

. . . When sufficiently calm try & see her & say you will not for *his* sake tell—but that it is no puerile reason—above all let Lord Holland imagine that you know something which nothing but dispair will tempt you to tell—but seem assured of this—& it may do much good.

. . . Remember that Lord Byron's real character is known to but a few—perhaps 40 or 50 Victims may rue the hour they saw him & heard him but he wears a mask to all others——and Hobhouse himself though a good hearted man in reality is utterly blind — — —

Murray—of all his friends is the one who has the most warmly espoused yr cause—but even he is imprudent & his situation inclines him to talk—

Fletcher loves Lord Byron he is not absolutely bad—he blames his Master but I fear he is not to be trusted [i.e. not to be trusted to give evidence against Byron, which it was proposed he should be asked to do]. . . .

In your conversation with Lord Holland—appear frank & kind—for he has a good heart—but do not trust him as he tells all to Lady H—though he may promise not — — — do not strive however to hide that you feel deeply —as they have it now all over the Town that you are cold . . . .

. . . Part with yr Maid she is Fletcher's Wife! Pray remember that!

Seem to hint to Lord Holland that you know something very bad—but that dispair alone & the loss of yr child shall tempt you to reveal it say however that if Driven to the last extremity if yr generous forbearance is not understood—if ye family instead of supporting you joins with & supports him

—if the causes you can & will name are insufficient—oh say that you will come forward yourself & bring such accusations against him that he dares not stand—

For God['s] sake speak thus to Lord Holland—you have no conception of the good it will do—you have no thought how much it will tend to facilitate an amicable separation & believe me Lady Byron were it to come to the worst were I to see your Child taken from you—I would appear myself against him in Justice & call on the humanity of Strangers to prevent so wicked so barbarous an act — — —

Fare well——burn this for God['s] sake.

Within a day or two came a third outpouring. Caroline had had a talk with Lady Melbourne and was more than ever convinced that Annabella must 'either write to her or do some thing kind'. She was blinded by 'prejudice art & flattery' on Byron's side, 'coldness & distance' on Lady Byron's.

Be secure that at bottom she has a kind & generous disposition—& it appears to me that were she to think that you had the means — — if driven to necessity of ruining him & abstained from generosity—she would admire & love you. . . .

. . . Do hear me—& try & conciliate yr Aunt———

Lady Byron thereupon took Caroline's advice and wrote Lady Melbourne the conciliatory letter recommended. She explained the grounds of her coldness, and elicited some straight speaking and the promise of a visit the following day, March 25th;[1] but the immensely sophisticated, worldly-wise aunt with her 18th-century laxity of morals never really got on well with the niece who was already groping out to the Victorian Age, and despite the unpleasant things she could not avoid hearing, Lady Melbourne retained a good deal of fondness for Byron.

Lord Holland too was duly interviewed and had the bones of the skeleton rattled at him from the cupboard. A note from him to Lady Byron shows that he called on her by invitation, and afterwards (March 29th, 1816) he wrote to her in respectful and subdued terms. The only guess he could make was that Byron must have attempted to subject his wife to some sexual practice deviating alarmingly from normality. This he passed on to Lady Holland, and also, many years later to Hobhouse, who, marvelling that Lady Byron remained implacable even in widowhood, began to wonder if there had been some grain of truth in it.[2] Thus

---

[1] Letter of 24 Mar: Lovelace Papers.

[2] As is well known, in a marginal note to a conjecture in Moore's biography that Lady Byron may have taken in sober seriousness some 'dimly hinted confession of undefined horrors' by her husband, Hobhouse wrote: 'Something of the sort certainly unless as Lord Holland told me, he tried to —— her.' The manner in which Lord Holland arrived at that conclusion is now not difficult to conjecture.

Lady Caroline's plot was attended with a success which must have given her exquisite satisfaction.

Her adjuration that not a word should be breathed to the Hon. Mrs George Lamb was a kind of window-dressing to keep up the air of a secrecy hitherto unviolated. The other Caroline[1] was completely enlightened as to all her relative could tell her about Byron—except, of course, what might lead to grave self-inculpation. It was at her house, it would seem, that the meeting so schemed for duly took place. Lady Byron could not call at Melbourne House in total obscurity, nor could she entertain as conspicuous a figure as Lady Caroline Lamb at Mivart's Hotel where she was staying. A morning call upon 'Caro George', however, was quite in the normal course. It may be assumed from Lady Byron's 'Minutes' that the hostess discreetly retired but returned before her visitor left the house. We may judge too that Caroline had followed up her three letters, not with the promised silence and distance, but with a note appealing for a meeting.

Minutes of Conversation with Ly C. L. March 27th 1816

Ly C. L's purpose in requesting the Interview appeared to be to require the burning of her letters to me—I told her I should seal them up, and write on them that in case of my death they should be returned to her—

I then desired to know to what those letters alluded—She became greatly agitated—and told me she would constitute me the judge of what she ought to do—having been bound by a solemn promise not to reveal these secrets— yet having felt it her duty to have done so before my marriage in order to save me from so dreadful a fate, and moreover that it had been her intention, but his protestations that he would never renew such crimes had prevailed upon her to be silent.

I then said that I conceived *her* promise was released by the infringement of *his*, and that she might now redeem all by giving me this knowledge if as important as she signified to the preservation of my Child—that, neither on earth, nor in Heaven would she, in my opinion, have cause to repent so disinterested an action.

All these preliminaries were a mere ritual, since Caroline had already confided in John Murray and others, had no evidence at all that Byron had infringed his undertaking not to renew 'crimes', and was clearly bent —hell-bent does not seem too strong a word—upon disclosure. However, the parade of scruples satisfied two consciences that were both in their different ways pliable, and the interview proceeded according to Caroline's plan.

The reader must be reminded before continuing that he is hearing the narrative of a woman who inspired this warning: '. . . The only safe

---

[1] Known as Caroline St Jules before her marriage, she was the daughter of the 5th Duke of Devonshire by Lady Elizabeth Foster whom he subsequently married.

method is to believe not one word she says',[1] and who, two or three weeks *after* the treacheries here recorded, was again writing to tell Byron she would die to save him.[2]

> She then confessed as follows, with an unfeigned degree of agitation— That from the time Mrs L— came to Bennet St. in the year 1813—Lord B— had given her various intimations of a criminal intercourse between them—but that for some time he spoke of it in a manner which did not enable her to fix it on Mrs L— thus—"Oh I never knew what it was to love before—there is a woman I love so passionately—she is with child by me, and if a daughter it shall be called *Medora*"—that his avowals of this incestuous intercourse became bolder—till at last she said to him one day, "I could believe it of *you*—but not of *her*"—on this his vanity appeared piqued to rage, and he said "Would *she* not?"—assured Ly C. L— that the seduction had not given him much trouble—that it was soon accomplished—and she was very willing—that in their early years they had been separated by Lady Holderness on account of some apparent improprieties—

This last reminiscence may safely be deemed fictitious. Byron and Augusta had little opportunity of meeting in childhood, when in any case her being a most painfully shy girl,[3] five years older than he, would have tended to rule out unseemly conduct. Their separation was due partly to their living far asunder, and partly to the mutual dislike of their adult relatives.

It is conceivable, of course, that he was employing a desperate measure to get rid of Caroline by shocking and scarifying her, but—inexcusable as his conduct was in making any avowal that would compromise Augusta— the boast of an easy seduction is quite out of keeping with his customary eulogistic manner of referring to her, and quite *in* keeping, on the other hand, with Caroline's jealous desire to paint her as black as possible.

She was fully capable of inventing, and indeed must have invented, the dialogue about the unborn child to be called Medora.[4] There seems no occasion when it could have taken place, because they had no communication except by letters, frequent on her part, few and reluctant on his, from July 1813, when Augusta's pregnancy began, until after the infant's birth. A programme of their movements as well as an immense amount of correspondence from and about them, show that they were not in personal contact for nearly a year after what Byron called 'our summer

---

[1] LEVER, p. 133. Letter from the Hon. George Lamb, her brother-in-law.
[2] *L. & J.* No date, but internal evidence proves April.
[3] Murray MSS. 1798. A charming sketch of Augusta at the age of fifteen by her kinswoman Lady Mary Osborne, who describes her as 'Shy to a degree beyond all the shynesses I ever saw before.'
[4] There is no other source for this detail which was quoted in *Astarte* with the admission, in a footnote, that the informant (left unnamed) was 'not in all respects trustworthy'.

fracas'—that is to say, the violent scene when Caroline had made a feint of stabbing herself at Lady Heathcote's ball (July 5th, 1813).

After a long period of troubling him only with letters and messengers, she suddenly began a new series of scenes when she heard he was paying court again to Miss Milbanke in 1814, certainly a situation to arouse her jealousy at its worst: and his enraged letters to Lady Melbourne show that there were perpetual nerve-racking intrusions. But he spoke of her with bitterness and detestation and asked Lady Melbourne to let her see what he had written, so that credence is strained to picture him sitting down to confide the dread secret of Medora's paternity to her!

The 'Minutes' of the meeting continue:

> Ly C— L— still declining to believe,—Ld B— called Fletcher to give him his portfolio (at the Albany) and threw from it to Lady C L a number of letters from Mrs L— in which were expressions that must refer to such a connection, amidst much foolish levity—but occasionally there appeared feelings of remorse, and she particularly remembered this—"Oh B— if we loved one another as we did in childhood—then it was innocent" —but these feelings apparently become less frequent—and there were crosses + + in such positions as could not be mistaken. Ld B— positively declared this crime—and his delight in it—and Fletcher appeared to Ly C— L— to be conscious of it—
>
> Since *that* avowal—Ly C— L— never suffered any intimacy with Ld B— though she had been prevailed upon to forgive "other & worse crimes"—

Before proceeding with the 'worse crimes', it would be as well to consider the general probity or improbity of this passage.

The reminder of innocent love in childhood scarcely supports the statement that Byron and Augusta had then been separated on account of their 'improprieties', nor is there anything but extravagance in the presumption that, because Fletcher brought in a portfolio when ordered to do so, he was privy to the contents. He lived to be more than eighty years old, fell into great poverty, had every reason to turn against Mrs Leigh who dropped the payment of the annuity she had promised him, but never was known to say a single word in confirmation of the scandals.

It is to be observed that Lady Byron has a parenthesis recording, with an air of not letting a material fact escape, that the portfolio was produced 'at the Albany', distinguishing this address from Bennet Street, where Byron had lived before. He moved into Albany Court on March 28th, 1814, and on the 30th wrote to Lady Melbourne about all the 'hammering' and general bustle that were still going on about him. On April 2nd he left London to go to his sister, whose confinement was very near, and did not return till the night of the 7th. Elizabeth Medora Leigh was born on the 15th. Whatever foolish confidences he may have made much earlier to

Caroline, it is of all things the most improbable that any were imparted 'at the Albany', in the period when he had grown to distrust and loathe her. The object of postdating them may have been to avoid admitting that her attempts to win him back, so widely known, had taken place after the disclosures which, she always pretended, had been mortal to her love.

Her assertion that she 'never suffered any intimacy' with Byron after learning of his feelings for Augusta was true; she had no chance of suffering intimacy because he was perpetually in flight from her, but there are several of her own letters showing that she not only continued to pursue him, but even tried to pander to the passion she regarded as criminal. Two months after Medora Leigh's birth she was writing to ask if she could see him at Watier's masquerade, adding:

> . . . Tell your sister to try & not dislike me—I am very unworthy of her I know it & feel it but as I may not love you nor see you—let her not judge me harshly—let her not pass me by as Lady Gertrude Sloane does—& Lady Rancliffe—tell her I feel my crime sooner—but try and make her forgive me—if you can—for I love that Augusta with my heart because she is yours and is dear to you.[1]

Either she had invented his confession or, as is more likely, was trying to use it then as a means of retaining some hold over him. The further revelations must be examined in the light of the witness's character.

> Of these [the 'worse crimes'] she gave the following account—that he had (after touching distantly on the subject at various times, by allusions which she did not understand till subsequently) confessed that from his boyhood he had been in the practice of unnatural crime—that Rushton was one of those whom he had corrupted—by whom he had been attended as a page, & whom he loved so much that he was determined Ly C —L— should call her page Rushton—which she owned with shame she had done.
>
> He mentioned 3 schoolfellows whom he had thus perverted. (N.B. two of their miniature pictures were burnt with a curious remark).

Here was a labyrinthine complex of truth, falsehood, and exaggeration. Byron may have had some homosexual experience at Harrow: that is very possible, but since he was on excellent terms with old school friends and even masters after leaving, and many of the most respectable were on the Monument Committee, it would not appear that he had left a bad reputation. Lady Byron had little knowledge of the behaviour of adolescent boys, and was perhaps more appalled by what Caroline told her than the headmaster of Harrow would have been.

That Byron asked Caroline to call her page after his own is an incredible suggestion for it would have been tantamount to advertising the very fact that, according to her, he was in trembling anxiety to keep dark. Nor,

---

[1] Murray MSS. Undated. The masquerade referred to was in June 1814.

even allowing that there had been physical relations between him and this boy—a doubtful supposition—is there any reason to believe that romantic feeling about him persisted till 1813 or 1814. Since taking him abroad (with two other servants, a courier, and John Cam Hobhouse) in 1809, his amatory life had been crowded with experiences, each one emotionally supplanting the other. Caroline presumably had dressed herself in page's livery hoping to stimulate some response from him—that was conformable with the depravity of her love letters—and she may have named one of her own pages after Rushton to embarrass him at the time when her pursuit amounted to a veritable persecution, but his desiring her to do so is far-fetched.

What she had told was much more than Lady Byron expected and exactly what she needed. Homosexual practice was regarded as the vilest crime in the calendar, and in its extreme form was punishable by death, the culprit being hanged on a separate gallows so as not to contaminate robbers and murderers. If anything of this nature could be proved, or even convincingly alleged, against Byron, he had not the remotest hope of succeeding in court against her. She was very busy in the afternoon of March 27th sending off a letter to her lawyer[1] and composing her Minutes.

> Ly C. L— did not believe that he had committed this crime since his return to England, though he practised it unrestrictedly in Turkey—His own horror of it still appeared to be so great that he several times turned quite faint & sick in alluding to the subject—
>
> He concluded by threatening her in the most terrific manner, reminding her of Caleb Williams, and saying that now she knew his secret, he would persecute her like Falkland[2]—he then endeavoured to regain her affection, whilst she sat filled with dread—and when he said 'but you love me still'—answered 'yes' from terror—he thrice obliged her to take the most solemn vow never to reveal—
>
> Mrs W. Webster has since mentioned to Ly C. L— Lord B's strange partiality for Rushton in former years—and told her the circumstance of Ld B's never sleeping without having R— in the adjoining room.
>
> I almost disavowed the belief of Incest—appeared so much [struck through] agitated by the other subject that I suspect Ly C L— discovered her statement to be only a confirmation of my own opinions. I told her Rushton was now with Lord B—

---

[1] Lovelace Papers. In this letter, Lady Byron writes: 'The result of my interview this morning was, I am most concerned to say, to change my strong impression relative to the 1st and 2nd reports, into *absolute* certainty.' Dr Lushington replied the same day: 'I hardly know what to say of your interview this morning, except most cordially to congratulate you upon your final escape from all proximity to or intercourse with such contamination.'

It is particularly desirable to note that Lady Byron spoke of *reports* that were now confirmed, not of knowledge to which she could personally have testified.

[2] Falkland, in the melodramatic novel by William Godwin, relentlessly pursues Caleb Williams who has discovered him to be a murderer.

Before I went I repeated in presence of Mrs G. Lamb that I had declared *no* belief.[1]

Lady Byron '*almost* disavowed' her belief in incest, but not quite, and it was one of those cases where a miss was as good as a mile. On the other grave allegation she said enough to allow her informant to discover that she already held an opinion derogatory to Byron. Repeating in the presence of Mrs George Lamb that she had 'declared no belief' was just one more part of the ritual, like the pretence that Mrs George Lamb knew nothing about the interview.

Lady Caroline had undoubtedly enjoyed herself very much, and wrote one of her long letters to Annabella before the day ended giving her, among many other religious counsels, the assurance that—

Hypocrisy may succeed a few years longer—but God is just—& the mask cannot long hide such deformity——

I did not like to tell you this morning what I thought might seem like a desire to appear over zealous—but now that you are going to let me tell you— that Wm Lamb—spoke to his Father & Mother [Lord and Lady Melbourne] & moreover has stated to Lord Holland his sentiments on this occasion & his disgust at any conduct which appears lukewarm—& doubtful with respect to you.

. . . Remember my own Cousin & I never felt so proud of any thing as of that name—do remember that you have to oppose 2 of the greatest Hypocrites & most corrupted Wretches that were ever suffered to Exist on this earth . . . there will fall a vengeance upon them for their treatment of you—soon or late—you do not wish it I know—you are too good & too kind but I do—I have forgiven too much already. . . .

. . . I have no doubt of your goodness——& would trust my life in yr hands at any time——Make any use of what I have told & will stand by— that is good for you——think of your own & your child's interest—and even if the generous desire of sparing him should seal your lips let it not prevent respectable & numerous friends from being acquainted with part of his atrocious conduct——

Recollect that such Hypocrisy will gain a Host around him & that you may perhaps be left with your child in some degree unprotected——

. . . You have a subtle foe to contend with——& virtue & generosity against him are only so many victims——

. . . I have followed your advice & not written to that vile woman [Augusta Leigh]—in all things I will follow your advice but don't be deaf to mine—for I can feel & think of nothing on earth but you & your injuries. . . .[2]

Caroline now tasted revenge in its fullest sweetness, and was able to imagine she had ruined Augusta and been the principal cause of Byron's

[1] Lovelace Papers. Only an expurgated version of this document was seen by Miss Mayne, Sir John Fox, and M. André Maurois, when they wrote their respective books on Byron and Lady Byron. The original was deposited in Coutts's Bank in the early 1920's before any of these three authors began their books, and remained there till 1957.
[2] Lovelace Papers.

retreat from the battle to regain his wife. This was indirectly true, inasmuch as the scandals she had been assiduously circulating on every side must have proved a very disturbing factor; but he had already decided to give up the struggle. On March 25th, two days before Lady Byron was assured of what she had hitherto only suspected, Byron wrote to tell her she was mistaken in supposing he had ever spoken 'harshly or lightly' of her.

If in the violence & outrageous latitude of accusation which has been indulged beyond all example and all excuse in the present case by those who from friendship to you or aversion from me—or both—have thought proper to proclaim themselves assailants in your cause—any few (and but few they must have been) of those who have known me and judged less severely of me —have been provoked to repel accusation by imputation—and have endeavoured to find a defence for me—in crimination of you—I disavow their conduct—& disclaim themselves. ——

I have interfered in no such proceedings—I have raised no party—nor ever attempted it—neither should I have succeeded in such an attempt— The world has been with you throughout—the contest has been as unequal to me as it was undesired—and my name has been as completely blasted as if it were branded upon my forehead: this may appear to you exaggeration— it is not so—

There are reports—which if once circulated not even falsehood—and their admitted and acknowledged falsehood can neutralize—which no contradiction can obliterate—nor conduct cancel—such have since your separation been busy with my name——

You are understood to say—'that you are not responsible for these— that they existed previous to my marriage—& at most were only *revived* by our differences'—Lady Byron, they did not exist—but even if they had— does their *revival* give you no feeling?—are you calm in the contemplation of having (however undesignedly) raised up that which you can never allay? & which but for you might have never arisen?—Is it with perfect apathy you quietly look upon this resurrection of Infamy?[1]

It is pitiable, with Hobhouse's diary and Byron's own wretched, agonized, and almost incoherent correspondence of this time before us, to read the sentiments attributed to him by his wife, her lawyers, parents, and confidential friends. Everything he did and wrote was ascribed to deep and wicked calculation. The 'Fare Thee Well' verses were said by her (to Lushington) to have been written only so that he might get his publisher to show them round,[2] the lawyer thought his tortured letters were 'frivolous pretexts for other objects',[3] her mother maintained it was all a 'deep game' played with 'Pecuniary Motives',[4] and friends were

[1] Lovelace Papers and Murray Copies.
[2] Ibid. 27 Mar. *op. cit.* Caroline Lamb wrote on the same date 'His beautiful verses I consider as a cowardly attempt to make you appear barbarous & himself injured.'
[3] Ibid. 28 Mar.
[4] Ibid. 6 Feb. to Sir Ralph Noel, and several variants of the same terms on other occasions to correspondents including Mrs Clermont.

united in using every synonym for villainy.

But Lady Melbourne, nagged daily by both her daughters-in-law and sometimes by her sons, managed to stand firm.

> I request you to take most particular care what you say to Lady M. [Caroline wrote to Annabella]—you may ruin me if you chuse by showing anyone on earth this letter. . . . Take a high tone— Seem sure of everything but tell her nothing — — — — and for God sake [*sic*] do not name me—
>
> I think it perfectly useless to trust her—his influence over her is such that I feel sure *now* nothing can shake it — — Pray take care—above all let her not imagine what you know — — —[1]

She was angling for Byron's attention again with a letter imploring him not to publish a poem to Augusta and denying that she had ever given utterance to any report against him, and must have dreaded lest he should learn what a liar she was. But it was never known to him through Annabella.[2] That was the one secret that, until old age, she told to none outside her father's house and her lawyer's office.

If Caroline had expected to be rewarded for turning suspicions into certainties by the friendship of the 'cousin' for whom she professed so lively an admiration, she was to have an icy awakening. She had served her turn and, like Mrs Clermont, was henceforward to be kept at arms' length. Requests for further interviews were met with polite but firm refusals; nor was this surprising after the unrestrained exhibitionism of *Glenarvon*, the novel about her affair with Byron which she had published soon after he left England.

On September 7th Lady Byron had occasion to write to her:

> My dear Lady Caroline,
>   I thank you for your note which came when I was particularly engaged. There are perhaps some reasons why *at this moment*, it might be better we should not meet, and I tell you so openly, trusting to your expressed desire that I should do so, instead of deceiving you by pretended excuses.
>   If Mr Lamb should be inclined to call upon me, I shall be happy to see him.
>   Pray give my thanks to Lady B[essborough] for her kind offer—which it is not in my power to accept, and believe me to remain
>   Yours very truly obliged
>   A. I. Byron[3]

[1] Ibid. No date, but obviously after the revelations of 27 Mar. and before Byron's departure from England.

[2] It was through the channel of Mrs George Lamb that Byron found out, the same year, about Caroline's complicity in the slanders. 'Caro George' told the story to Henry Brougham, who repeated it to Mme de Staël when he was at Coppet. Mme de Staël well-meaningly passed it on to Byron at the time of trying to bring about a reconciliation.

[3] Lovelace Papers. Copy kept by Lady Byron. Lady Bessborough was Lady Caroline's mother, and in her confidence.

Caroline actually agreed in the humblest terms to allow her husband to call instead of herself, begging Annabella never to turn harshly from her, though she might and must condemn her. We might suppose she had wished to explain away the indiscretions of *Glenarvon*, in which the former Miss Milbanke figures as Miss Monmouth and herself, Caroline, as an erring but injured heroine named Calantha: but her approaches had two other motives.

The first was to keep animosity active against Mrs Leigh:

> . . . Let me hope that at some future period you will of yourself see me—I shall never speak or allude to any subject that is past & indeed I think you may have confidence in me in this respect—Yet to you before whom I opened my whole heart so entirely & for whom I broke so solemn an engagement I must yet relieve myself from one painful doubt——they say you live almost wholly with Mrs Leigh.
>
> It astonished me & William—yet promise me—that even if your better judgment—kindness—or any further investigation have altered your opinion of her entirely—promise me to open my eyes also—to say to me 'You were deceived—he deceived you—& I know it [']—for that secret rests on my heart & makes me miserable & I would give anything never never to have heard or thought it—
>
> One thing more——Mrs Leigh's manner to me is that of hatred——I never for one instant suffered myself to believe you had betrayed me—— but I am sure if she did not think I had spoken she durst not & would not thus look on me no not if I were black with every sin—for how should she judge me. . . .
>
> I would give half I have to know that I wronged her & that I had been most cruelly deceived——*You* should you ever think this ought to tell me— you should not let me die in the belief of crimes such as this——& when you remember that for you I broke every engagement—you cannot let any consideration move you to deny me what I ask—[1]

Lady Byron was deep at this date in arrangements with the Hon. Mrs Villiers to save Augusta's soul by getting her to confess all her sins, and all her brother's sins, to show his confidential letters, and to make herself 'comfortable' by 'utter and entire submission' to her (Lady Byron's) directions,[2] so it was not a favourable time for Caroline's machinations. But the latter had another delicious topic to engage her histrionic powers. The person whom she called her 'dearest friend', Caro George, was in moral danger!

> Caro is as good as pure as innocent as yourself—but perhaps her mind & principles are less strong . . . it is my constant dread that we shall lose her— if kind & good friends do not write & urge her to sacrifice every feeling to what is right.

[1] Lovelace Papers ? 8 Sept. 1816.
[2] Ibid. Letter from Mrs Villiers, 17 Aug. 1816.

... Perhaps you have not heard the reports to which I allude & do not know the circumstances — —

The truth of it all is this—the D[uche]ss does not think Caro happily married—she herself may possibly be brought to believe that George does not care for her which however he does. . . . Mr Brougham seeing how she was circumstanced & being much more attached to her than he ought—has so wound himself into her society that all believe he is resolved to die sooner than not gain upon her to go with him—

She went abroad——all wished her to do so but me——all advised it— I knew at least I guessed what would happen—he has followed her—[1]

Lady Caroline was again longing to take the situation in hand. Her plan was that Annabella should write Caro—

a kind a warm & open letter as if you felt interested for her & eager to see her again—as if you knew nothing of reports & ill thoughts concerning her— but wished to see her—& considered her as a comfort to you—do you know that such a letter might do a great deal & where many are engaged in advising ill—a few good natured words from a person we esteem & admire have a great effect . . . indeed you might save her without even seeming to do it—will you then permit yourself to refuse what I ask—

Lady Byron was interested in Caro's moral danger; she wrote to her parents about it; she also sent off the letter to Italy as recommended;[2] but she was not to be drawn into further association with Caroline Lamb.

The following year that tireless traitor was pleading again even for 'one moment's interview' ('I could I think be of use to you at this instant') but met with a very determined negative, though she was assured that 'the conduct I may for various reasons have thought it right to pursue has not been actuated by any motives personally unkind towards you'.[3]

This was too much even for Caroline's sycophancy. She tried to re-establish contact with Byron—any sort of contact, benign or malevolent. She wrote to him announcing in one and the same letter that she was suffering greatly from having sinned against him and that she had always been his sincere friend.[4] She showered attentions on his publisher and succeeded in seeing his works before they came out and even in reading his Memoirs; she wrote praises and criticisms clearly intended to be

[1] Letter of ? 8 Sept. The Duchess was Mrs George Lamb's mother, now married to the Duke of Devonshire.

[2] 'Caro George' heartily disliked her would-be rescuer, the other Caroline, and wrote in answer to whatever Lady Byron may have said to her: 'I was glad that you refused both the offers made you by Caro and the Melbournes, the first because she has ruined herself so completely in public opinion by her *impudence* that it does not work upon one's compassion to protect her, and that in your situation it would be said you listened to slanders occasioned by disappointed pride and pique. As for the others, though I am not a mischief maker, I must always say to you, that I do not think their cordiality sincere . . .' Lovelace Papers. 4 Oct. 1816.

[3] Ibid. Early May 1817.   [4] QUENNELL AND PASTON. Late 1818.

conveyed to him; she went to a masquerade as Don Juan, making her entrance with a troop of devils; she found excuses for seeking out his friends.

She opened his secrets to Michael Bruce, a friend of his and Hobhouse's, and then pretended to have a fit of agonizing remorse.

> . . . How could I tell you those things which I ought never to have said their name—it is little comfort for me to feel that you are honourable. I ought to have been so too—nothing can excuse my breach of promise.
> Fare thee well. Come here. Remember that I am always at home & alone from nine till eleven. . . .[1]

And again:

> . . . My hearts in torture & my whole soul the same—it is as if there was a sword run through me—or a fire burning in my brain—no ship that ever was lost on a strange sea without daring to anchor anywhere—or in immediate fear of being lost—ever yet was so distressed as I am. . . .
> . . . If this is what is called remorse how can people say there is no Hell. What burning flames can be worse. I shall die very soon & when I do—do you remember it and tell them that I suffered enough—tell it Byron—but I only accuse myself not him. I have no excuse none & my hearts depraved & my whole mind corrupted.
> . . . If a wretch has murdered his benefactor & Master the remembrance must go with him to the grave. . . .[2]

But when her correspondent said something in favour of Byron, she quickly dropped the penitent pose, and wrote back that he (Byron) was mean, selfish, grovelling, and base.

> . . . He will live to make more people miserable—to wring other hearts & to prove that the brightest & most beautiful talents added to every charm of person & mind & every art of seduction to give them force—are but so many curses & causes of degradation if misapplied. I am unhappy. . . .
> . . . Write everything you hear of Lord Byron. . . .
> He has the curses of hearts that are broken of souls that are torn from virtue & peace on him by night & day, he is wicked, cruel—mean coldly cruel—& most barbarous. . . . He has no honour—no faith in any transaction. Do tell me why you say he is ill—after all I trust in God he is not ill.[3]

Constantly announcing her impending demise, she outlived Byron by nearly four years. His death gave her an opportunity for fresh agitations, and some of them may have been genuine, for the knowledge that such letters as hers were held by Hobhouse in a spirit of frank precaution must have been worrying. Once more she began begging to see Lady Byron. She was relentlessly informed that her strong feelings would have an unfavourable effect on one who was obliged 'to avoid every fatigue or

---

[1] BRUCE. Undated letter, early 1817.
[2] Ibid. 3 June 1817. [3] Ibid. Undated letter, 1817.

excitation', and that she had no reason to feel alarm (Hobhouse was paid this tribute) respecting any manuscripts of hers which might have come into the executor's hands.

> . . . Dare to consider the worst as in one respect a relief—from the misery of acting a part & thus circumstanced, believe that you may experience a peace and consolation. . . .[1]

From now on, Caroline's *degringolade* became complete. She got drunk in public, committed extraordinary insolences, and was all but ostracized by society. Unable to exist without an audience, she cultivated people to whom her noble rank was a wonder, and showed off to them till they too wearied. Her soiled and untidy clothes distressed her family. Her lovers likewise became less and less presentable. She had a well-deserved hallucination that Byron's ghost came and gazed at her,[2] but the terror this caused did not prevent her from surrounding herself with mementoes of him and talking about him by the hour, far from truthfully. She was, according to her sister-in-law, 'always muddled either with Brandy or laudanum',[3] yet she held out till she had made the most mercenary bargain before she would agree to separate from her nerve-racked husband.

As Caroline grew giddier and wilder, Lady Byron became ever more sober, her never very ebullient youth suffocated under a pall of respectability. From the day of leaving her husband at the age of twenty-three years and eight months, she had lived in celibacy and self-elected exclusion from fashionable company; and as a widow she devoted herself to education and good works of what seem today—and seemed to many people then—a conspicuously frigid type. She knew she was a figure of interest, and cared very much indeed for the world's opinion. To be right, to be acknowledged to be right, to be unruffled by the faintest breath of criticism—perhaps no young woman ever lived whose writings show so intense a preoccupation with her own rectitude.

*   *   *   *   *   *

The news that a man was threatening to publish a journal which contained a record of her intercourse with a person whom she herself called one of 'the worst women in London'[4] must have given her a very unpleasant turn. For one thing, it was a reminder of what she had tended to forget more and more as the years went by—that she had told her lawyers *two* stories of the monstrous immoralities of Byron. There were a few very

---

[1] 31 Oct: 1824. Lovelace Papers. Copy kept by Lady Byron.
[2] LEVER. Letter from Caroline to William Lamb, 8 Sept. 1825.
[3] Ibid. Letter, 15 June 1825.
[4] Letter to the Hon. Mrs Villiers, 12 May 1816: Lovelace Papers.

close friends who had heard from her about 'the other propensity', and, of course, she had spoken about her suspicions a good deal to Augusta, who was horrified: but, in general, it had proved much more satisfactory to let the onus of evil fall quietly on Augusta's own shoulders.

In an infinitely more restrained way than Caroline, Lady Byron was likewise given to dramatization. 'She was', says her biographer, 'prone to gaze upon a Narcissistic vision of . . . herself,' and 'unconsciously impelled by the vanity of suffering.'[1] Constantly applauded by a circle of friends, she cast herself in the rôle of the 'Saint'[2] who rose above every human weakness to forgive Augusta her sins, to reform her character, and, by not withdrawing her countenance, to preserve her position in society.[3] This was a much more satisfactory and shapely drama than guesswork about indecencies at Harrow and crimes in Turkey which, as she had heard from Byron's own lips,[4] were not called crimes in that benighted country.

In the long hours when she lived over the past, searching out meanings in a hundred things he had said and done, and even in the remembered expressions of his face, and writing down her conclusions, Augusta occupied immeasurably more of her thoughts than his guilty doings in the East. 'The vanity of suffering' could focus on Augusta with a keenness not to be experienced over unknown youths in foreign lands: and as for the story about Rushton, after the first momentary credulity, it lost its reality for her. She could recollect clearly that during her last attempts to remonstrate with him on all his misdeeds (January 3rd, 1816) he had said: 'I have not done an act *that would bring me under the power of the Law—* at least on this side of the water'[5] and she believed that on matters of this kind, he was truthful. Much as she wanted to establish iniquities that would justify her, she must have seen on reflection how implausible it was that, after binding Caroline under a triple oath of silence, he would then persuade her to invite curiosity (and in the house she shared with Lady Melbourne!) by absurdities about his page's name.

By 1826, when Wilmington Fleming's two letters were sent to her, a rather peculiar situation had arisen. Augusta thought the sole secret charge Annabella had made against Byron was that he had committed sins

---

[1] MAYNE, *Lady Byron*, pp. 401 and 404.

[2] '. . . It requires more than ordinary exertion to keep up the character of a Saint', she wrote somewhat smugly to Mrs Villiers. (LOVELACE, *Lady Noel Byron*. 19 Sept. 1816).

[3] 'Having taken all the care I could of her character *in the world*, I have now only to attend to her character in more material respects.' Ibid. 28 July 1816.

[4] Lovelace Papers. Various statements. E.g. 'He laboured to convince me that Right & Wrong were merely conventional, & varying with Locality and other circumstances. . . . He stated such facts as that Morality was one thing at Constantinople, another in London.' Statement designated FF by Lord Lovelace. '. . . He has sought to make me smile at Vice . . . attributing the condemnation of such practices merely to the manners of different Countries.' Statement designated U.

[5] Ibid. 'Remarks on Lord B's letter of Feb. 8th' (1816). Lady Byron's underlining.

which, however anyone might look on them in barbarous places like Constantinople, were a hanging matter in England. She had never had the least notion that she herself had figured in that indictment. Annabella for her part could scarcely remember anything else. The aberration she had most relied on to win any case against him, comprised in '*three words* that might annihilate him for ever',[1] had become as it were merely a technical offence. She looked back and thought that if his sister had not lived, her lot might have been almost tolerable.[2]

It did not seem to her dishonest to turn Augusta into a scapegoat because she was unaware that she was doing so; nor could she distinguish between serving an end of her own and doing something out of charity. Her motives had for more than ten years been confused inextricably, and 'she could not follow her own windings and turnings, her own flight from self-recognition'.[3]

She wanted Caroline Lamb's journal suppressed, but it must be done under the guise of one more philanthropic deed for Augusta. The two letters of Fleming's which Augusta forwarded were received on March 17th: she took immediate measures without waiting for the blackmailer to repeat his demands. First and by return of post, she sent some advice to Augusta; next, she wrote to Mrs George Lamb, asking her to impart the facts to Caroline's husband.

> I cannot think myself justified in withholding the following circumstances from Mr W. Lamb, as they so nearly concern his interests, as well as those of *other connections of mine.*
>
> A person of the name of Washington [*sic*] Fleming, to whom Lady Caroline Lamb imparted the contents of a Private *Journal*, took a copy of some very objectionable parts of it, as a matter of curiosity (according to his own representation) but is now impelled by extreme poverty to turn these extracts to profit, though he would prefer disposing of them to some member of the Family, instead of selling them to a *Publisher*—a very small sum, he says, would induce him to do so.
>
> I am averse, for myself, to all transactions of this nature—but considering what [might] be the consequences of such a disclosure, I think some measures should be taken by the parties most nearly concerned, and I therefore beg you to make Mr W. Lamb acquainted immediately with the address of Mr W. Fleming. . . .[4]

Both William Lamb and his sister-in-law, Caro George, had been behind the scenes in 1816, and they were on her side, but even with them there could be no admission of self-interest. Yet it is evident from letters to be quoted that the 'objectionable parts' of the Journal were concerned

---

[1] Ibid. The phrase was used by Mrs Villiers, who knew both charges. Lady Byron replied agreeing that she had the power, but saying she doubted if Byron knew it. 26 Sept. 1816.   [2] Ibid. 'Sketch for a Memoir'.

[3] MAYNE.   [4] LOVELACE, *Lady Noel Byron.* 19 Mar. 1816.

with her own confidences to Caroline rather than Caroline's confidences about Augusta, and that the suggestion of negotiating for the purchase of the document originated from her: and if the sample sent by Fleming in his second letter to Hobhouse be compared with his description of the manuscript in his first letter to Augusta, the emphasis will be seen to be all on matters likely to embarrass Lady Byron alone.

Though Augusta's letters are always boring and repetitive, to make an end of suppression every word material to the theme is here given:

Monday [20th March 1826]

My dearest A,

I found Murray at *last* yesterday about 5—& explained the business & told him what you suggested—

On reading the Man's letters when he came to the part which enumerates the *heads* of the facts (!) mentioned in the MSS & that which states your account to *Ly C L* of the treatment you had met with, he said Oh—yes— "that is exactly what I heard from Ly Caroline herself"! ! ! !—the end of it all was however that he said he wd send a person to this Mr Fleming today to see what he could make of him—but wanted *much* to offer the £5 from *me*—as he says if he goes in his character of Publisher he wd ask *more* & be exhorbitant—

I told him I wd rather *re*pay him the 10 or 20 £ after, than have my name mentioned at all & charged him not to do so—He began by saying Ly Caroline had told him the man "*was the Greatest Scoundrel*" She had given him her Papers & some [? other] papers & he had Sold two of her works to Colburn for £10—& Colburn being *Another Scoundrel*! won't now give them back tho' Wm Lamb has been to him ! ! ! ! She will of course *now* try to cover with some falsehood what she has done for some of her Demoniacal views of the moment![1]

The letter ends with several pieces of family news, and has the air of annoyance rather than apprehensiveness. The specified sum of five pounds is apparently what Lady Byron had proposed should be offered to Fleming through the agency of John Murray. Augusta, who had not intended to answer his second letter at all, was naturally unwilling that the offer should be made in her name.

Tuesday [21st March]

My dearest A.

I saw Murray after I wrote to you yesterday—he had been twice at *the Man's* but did not find him & enquired the most likely hour to do so today.— However—he seems *very averse* to have to do with it, as he says he will never let *him* have the MSS for 10£ he thinks—& he says it will be endless for he is sure that in a short time there wd be others—& that *this man* has *copies*—that he is a Scoundrel & I'm sure I wish I knew the *feminine* of that Name in English for it wd be highly applicable to his Employer—

[1] Lovelace Papers.

For my own part I am quite convinced She is in league with him or *has* been—& now finding herself in a scrape, tells all possible falsehoods to extricate herself! I am to call on M——today again—because he wished me to *consider* about it—but after all my consideration I can only come to the same conclusion—one does not like to urge M—— to purchase what he is averse to do—

Pray let me have a line with your opinion—[1]

In a final paragraph she tells of her worry over failure to raise a mortgage, and the inadequacy of Hanson, the solicitor.

The undertones throughout this series of letters, having regard to her usual febrile style, are altogether more suggestive of her sympathetically reporting her endeavours to do an obliging thing for Annabella than her appealing to Annabella for help in a desperate dilemma of her own.

> *Wedy* [*22nd March*]

My dearest A,

I have made every effort to see Murray *today*—but in vain—yesterday (*after* writing to you) I saw him—& he accosted me with the 2 letters in his hand, to this effect——"I don't know what the result of your deliberations [may] have been but that of mine is that it is quite useless to do anything in this business—it is vain to try to stop it—depend upon [it] the Man has copies—the disgrace must be Lady Carolines!" & with all this he seemed in great haste & to wish to get rid of me—and he added "Ly Caroline assured me that the Man had nothing of hers but the Novels she sold to Colburn"—

which *inclines* me to think that she is quite aware he *has* *these* things!

What shall I do my dear A? I will try to see Murray before tomorrows post—but it is difficult to press him to buy what he is so evidently disinclined to—& as he is not *Mercenary* I cannot help thinking he has reasons to think this *Fiend* is in league with the Man.

After all Wm Lamb is the only person to act if he would! but no hope of that, from so contemptible a character who cares not for any disgrace to himself or his nearest Relations—

I know a person to whom Ly Caroline has shown her Journal & who told me there were things that could not be *named*, scarcely *thought of*!![2] No doubt there are others to whom she has been equally liberal & who have copied them & we know that Notoriety is her Idol & that Shame is a feeling unknown to her! I will try to see M & talk to him again——[3]

The remainder of this letter is devoted to news about various persons, and some firm words on her 'deep cause for being hurt & grieved with George Byron' (who had returned her last letter unopened but whom Lady Byron defended). It is noteworthy that in her outburst against

---

[1] Ibid.

[2] These unmentionable things did not necessarily relate to Byron. Caroline had several other lovers.   [3] Lovelace Papers.

William Lamb she speaks of his not caring for disgrace to himself or his nearest relations. She herself was in no way related to him; Lady Byron was. Obviously she was very unwilling to go on badgering Murray.

The next communication is unmistakably a reply to an urgent request that she would not fail to induce Murray to see Fleming and secure the manuscript. The last paragraph places that beyond conjecture. About half-way through, the letter rambles off on to other topics, and it is assuredly not in the strain Augusta uses when in personal fear:

> *Thursday Mar 23rd*
>
> Dearest A——
>
> After much pressing, urging writing & *messaging* I've got Murray to say he will see me about 5 in Whitehall Place—he had not an earlier moment—so I begin this foundation of my letter that I may have all the time left I can for what he determines—you wd receive my despairing letter of yesterday [i.e. the one quoted above]—& I do grieve that in your state of health you sd be subject to *such worry*—on *such* subjects—from *such* a source—Even my iron nerves & Elephant constitution s'en ressentent—I certainly do today *fully* understand your propositions & see the expediency of Murray (as a Publisher) securing the MSS & Copyright—& hope I shall persuade him—but never saw him so averse or reluctant to any Subject in my life—
>
> I think *your* having made a communication to Wm. Lamb may do good —& induce Murray to comply—& I am truly obliged to you for *not* mentioning *me*—& for your determination to remain & *face the Enemy*. You are the only person on earth to cope with her—& certainly it may be termed 'warring with the powers of darkness'—. . . .
>
> Just seen Murray—he will make a point (as you wish it) of seeing the Man tomorrow & seeing me after. He feels sure he won't let *him* have the *MSS*—& he says it being Ly C L's Work or Journal, & this Man having only *cribbed* bits from it, gives *no* Copyright at all or the least security that there May not be other *copies* or Scraps & moreover *this Woman's* being at the bottom of it—you can have no security in *any* way—
>
> You shall hear tomorrow[1]

The penultimate 'you' is Lady Byron. Augusta never on any occasion uses that pronoun in a generalized sense. There is no conceivable meaning for the letter except that Lady Byron was very much worried, so worried that Augusta, though she deemed her nerves much stronger, felt with her and for her; that she claimed to understand fully 'today'—not having quite grasped them before—propositions the other had made as to getting Murray to buy the copyright of the blackmailer's manuscript, and she promised to try and persuade him; that she thought Lady Byron had done

[1] Lovelace Papers.

well to approach William Lamb and esteemed her for her determination to put off her journey and face the enemy. Finally, she had just learned from Murray that purchasing a copy was not the same as purchasing a copyright and warned Lady Byron that she could expect no security from such a step.

Her belief that Fleming was acting in collusion with Caroline fully accounts for her being glad not to be mentioned in a letter to William Lamb that might reach that malignant woman's knowledge. (She could not guess that, though not mentioned, she had been very decidedly hinted at.)

Anyone who recalls the habitual effusiveness of her language when expressing gratitude will perceive at once that, if Lady Byron had actually undertaken to postpone her first travels abroad to 'war with the powers of darkness' for Augusta's sake, her thanks would not have been conveyed in such few and temperate words as 'I am truly obliged to you'. Giving so much trouble, she would necessarily have been apologetic, but there is not the faintest tone of apology in one line of these letters.

Whatever communication she sent on March 24th is, like the second Fleming letter, missing or mislaid. It must have contained the information that Murray, by reason of illness, had done nothing as yet and was inaccessible that day, for on Saturday, March 25th, she wrote saying: 'Murray is still confined to his room so nothing *can* I say till Monday on that subject.' She had left word that she would call the following day on the chance of his being better and able to see her.[1] The greater part of this note is a continuation of the discussion about George Byron, and it ends: 'And now dear A—— you won't fancy I bear malice hatred or any *uncharitableness*—but that in Truth I have been most unfortunate in all the dearest & nearest ties. God bless you.'

On Monday, March 27th, she had a letter from Lady Byron to the effect that William Lamb had refused to interfere, and asking her to consult Wilmot Horton, which she did. The next day she reported:

> I have just seen Murray who is better—but we of course can *do* nothing & *think* little more about the matter till your next suggestions arrive. The Lamb is just what I expected he would prove—& you & I seem to be singularly gifted in Relations of *that* degree of Consanguinity [first cousin-hood]. . . .[2]

She went on to speak of her financial affairs and of Murray's 'indulging in *panegyrics* upon Hobhouse respecting that detestable *little* M[oore] till my heart is sick and my head turns'. Her letters had been growing successively shorter and more casual on the subject of Fleming, and at this stage the correspondence appears on the verge of petering out. There was

---

[1] Ibid.   [2] Ibid.

no reason for continuing it since he had made no further appeal and Murray, with his explanation of the copyright law, must have shown that the chance of finding a publisher to print the extracts was remote. To buy the begging-letter writer's copy would be locking the stable door after the horse was gone, seeing that Caroline had been so free with the original.

The whole incident would have passed into oblivion if Lady Byron had not taken it into her head to write a most extraordinary letter to the Hon. Mrs Villiers, that friend who was seldom called upon except to play the role of admiring spectator to noble deeds.

My dear Mrs Villiers,

. . . I have again had occasion to try to be useful to A—— on a very unpleasant business—which I will confide to you——

It seems that Lady CL has allowed some very material facts which were learnt from her intercourse with Lord B—— to get into the hands of a villain—who is trying how much money he can get for them—and she has vainly endeavoured to reclaim her 'Journal'———Information of this was given to A—— and she applied to me——I thought the proper person to take measures on the subject was William Lamb—and I accordingly apprized him of it—He will do nothing——

I cannot so far place myself in the situation of a guilty person as to stop any publication—nor should I advise *her* to do so without obtaining more security than appears possible against copies—because her appearing to regard it would add to the credibility of the imputation—In short I don't know what is to be done, having no experience in such matters—& all the people I should wish to act upon have their heads or hearts quite wrong—still I tremble, and think I cannot go abroad and leave her to such impending danger, if my presence can protect her——

It may be fortunate that I have never denied any thing *for myself*—— so that my silence (if such aspersions should be circulated) can bear no un-favourable Construction, particularly when my countenance in other ways is considered. A promise of kindness, *sealed by death*, must ever bind me.[1]

The paragraph which follows criticizes Augusta for her 'implacable' sentiments about the Byrons, George and his wife—although no shadow of an allusion to his wife is to be found in Augusta's letters—and completes the picture of her own magnanimity with 'All I can do therefore is to persuade Lord B—— not to resent her strangeness'. (That was exactly what she did not do.)

The innuendo of this utterly gratuitous act of tale-bearing is false throughout. Fleming's list of objectionable passages in the Journal, as furnished for Hobhouse and sketched out for Augusta, does not comprise one item which threatened her. Augusta had not 'applied' to Lady Byron, but, thinking it probable that he would seek to involve her, had forwarded his letters with a remark that she herself should 'not answer or take any

[1] 29 Mar. 1826: Lovelace Papers.

notice'. It was Lady Byron who had wanted to buy the copy and Augusta who had given warning that no 'security' was obtainable by that measure. The sequence of misrepresentations and suppressions is so striking that it must reflect seriously on the validity of a mass of evidence dependent solely on *ex parte* statements.

Since Augusta's final decision, doubtless on the advice of Hobhouse, was to place the matter in the hands of her solicitor, Lady Byron was hard put to it to keep the drama from falling flat, particularly as she was, after all, going abroad and leaving Augusta to the 'impending danger'. She managed, however, to give even the precaution of taking legal advice the colouring of a stealthy and culpable act, writing again to Mrs Villiers a week later:

> I have been obliged to leave Lady CL's documents to chance. After asking advice, which was in the first instance 'Treat the matter with contempt' A—— has only half adopted it by taking the half-measure of sending Hanson to the Man—Most unadvisable! thereby establishing the discreditable & suspicious fact of an authorized communication from her—
>
> What errors always seem to be entailed by a radical one!—I regard all these proceedings but as inevitable *consequences* and therefore feel that the pardon of the original cause should include the subsequent aberrations— but it is very vexatious to have one's wisdom frustrated—I took the advice of an enlightened professional man on the subject——and his opinion concurred with mine—viz—that as Mr Lamb could not, or would not take any measures, all appearance of communication with any part of the Byron family was to be most carefully avoided.
>
> I believe Lady CL has *allusions* of a striking nature in his handwriting— She is very miserable, I believe, about these effects of her imprudence.
>
> A's account of the scene at Lady Salisbury's in a letter to me, was that she was *compelled* to *touch* Lady CL's hand—not very like *cutting* in appearance. Half-measures will always be her bane.[1]

Every insinuation in this second bulletin, as in the first, is a piece of misdirection. There is not a single letter of Augusta's which could by any stretch of its meaning be an answer to one which had told her to 'treat the matter with contempt'. Indeed Lady Byron had written to Mrs George Lamb to quite the opposite effect, advising that 'measures should be taken. . . .' She herself had been very anxious that Murray should call on 'the Man', and why it should be a discreditable and suspicious 'half-measure' for Hanson, the legal representative of the family, to do so is not to be accounted for other than on the theory that every move Augusta made had to be represented in such a way as to support the tale of her guilty fear. After telling that story it must have been disconcerting to find her acting independently and sensibly.

[1] Ibid. 6 Apr. 1826.

It is not a convincing presumption that the solicitor went so far as to visit Fleming. Nor is it likely that he would have found that unappreciated poet at home if he had called. 'In the hourly expectation of being turned into the streets' several weeks before—a statement which has the ring of truth—he must by now have passed from the neighbourhood of Seven Dials. Hanson being Hobhouse's co-executor, they looked after Augusta's interests together, and some record would have been left, either among his own numerous papers or in Hobhouse's diary, if there had been any further trouble with him. A debtor's prison may have been his next retreat.

It is not easy to believe that what was imparted to Mrs Villiers in writing was withheld from nearer confidants seen much more frequently. The rumour that Augusta was paying a blackmailer developed over the years into a belief that she was paying several blackmailers, until, as has been told,[1] Lady Wilmot Horton informed Byron's grandson in 1870 that this was the reason for her poverty. Lord Lovelace later had all the correspondence here quoted before him, and also knew that the extent of the fortune Augusta inherited from Byron had been tremendously overestimated; but he printed nothing that would not bear out the case presented by his grandmother.[2] The intervention of Caroline Lamb was never revealed by him, though he made use, without naming her, of her accusations against Augusta.

Whether Lady Caroline was 'very miserable about the effects of her imprudence' or not, she would not have stinted words of contrition. She had always made a speciality of demonstrative penitence, a characteristic noted with asperity by Miss Milbanke in the year of their both meeting Byron:

> She tries to disarm the condemnation of her friends by unreserved confession of her errors, and the generosity of the hearer may at first be duped by that proceeding; but its frequent repetition destroys all esteem for the *motive.* . . . Our confidence in her integrity is also diminished by perceiving a delicate attempt at self-justification, through the apparent candour of self-reproach.
>
> . . . She *manages* every feeling as she sees it rise to the mind of those whom she would persuade.[3]

[1] See p. 134.

[2] Miss Mayne based her information on his book, *Lady Noel Byron and the Leighs*, and gave an account of the episode which is erroneous throughout. The lack of further reference to the subject in Augusta's correspondence is due, not to concealment, but to Lady Byron's being abroad from April 1826 to December 1828. It is not true that 'everywhere she went, Augusta's long screeds pursued her'. For several months there was a gap in their correspondence, which was reopened not by her but by Lady Byron.

[3] '*Character.*' November 1812: Lovelace Papers.

Caroline died in January 1828, aged forty-two. Lady Byron who in youth had seen through and through her with a merciless eye, describing her as one who had 'almost forfeited the *power* of self-command', and had continued to write of her with contempt after their covert understanding of 1816, changed her view as the years went by, and lived to say that 'Lady Caroline behaved nobly'.[1]

On her death-bed, according to the Rev. Frederick Robertson, Caroline gave Byron's 'presents and jewels' to his widow. Those who attended her last illness do not seem to have left any record of this bequest, nor is there a mention of it in Lady Byron's contemporary correspondence: whereas there exists a letter showing that Caroline returned Byron's few gifts in a grand gesture when he married.[2] The clergyman who wrote down Lady Byron's conversations in 1851 encouraged her to be a rather imaginative witness. For example:

> Ly Car: Lamb knew the dreadful secret—Ly B. heard that he had forborne with her, & acted generously. She did not know that her virtue was gone—this generosity was one of the motives wh[ich] led her to the marriage. . . .[3]

Reading over the pathetic series of letters by which she drew him into his ruinous second proposal in 1814, one cannot but wonder if self-deception could go further. If she had been the sort of woman who could have admitted that she had married Byron because he was attractive and sought-after, because his fame, his looks, his manner, had a fascination for her, and not because she was deluded into believing him virtuous, she might have spared herself forty-five years of recrimination and misery.

[1] Ibid. Rev. Frederick Robertson's *Conversations with Ly B.* January 1851.
[2] No date. Murray MSS.
[3] *Conversations with Ly B.* Lovelace Papers.

CHAPTER VIII

THOMAS MOORE
VERSUS SEVERAL ANTAGONISTS

It was hardly to be expected that, when people from the outer fringes of the Byron orbit were selling their real or pretended recollections for good round sums, Thomas Moore was going to remain for ever in unrewarding silence. He had put in his claim to be biographer even before Byron's own manuscript was burned, saying, after he had so rashly consented to give it up to Mrs Leigh: 'I hope after this sacrifice that if any Memoirs are to be written the family will give me the preference.' Kinnaird had replied: 'I think they ought,' but Hobhouse had protested, 'Why, that must be for consideration.'

'Here was a specimen of a poet's friendship!!' Hobhouse wrote afterwards in his diary. 'It was like Rousseau's consoling himself for Claude Anet's loss by thinking he should get his old coat.'[1]

Moore did not see it as so contemptible a thing to be the chronicler of a great poet whom he had intimately known, and, being deep in debt to his publisher for the part Hobhouse had forced him to play in the drama of the Memoirs, he looked to recouping himself by writing about his friend.

Medwin's unworthy book afforded him, as he thought, an opportunity to win family authority for his own, and before the end of 1824 he had approached Lady Byron's friend, Colonel Doyle, asking for his good offices with the two ladies. He did not guess that Mrs Leigh positively hated him —how could he, seeing she had never met him?—and that she would take council with Lady Byron in the most hostile spirit:

> I am routed from my silence today by receiving thro' Wilmot from Col. Doyle a letter of Mr Moore—which I conclude has in the first instance been forwarded to you—I am anxious to know what you do and answer on the subject—I *detest* his very name—but then we are to remember that *he reserved to* himself the power of saying what a *noble* sacrifice he has made to me, in putting the Memoirs into my hands! It really torments me to death and as if this letter was not enough, I have one from Lady Jersey from Bowood (Lord Lansdowne's) saying she hopes I will allow Ld. L. to call upon me 'when he will convince me in a few minutes *how nobly Moore acted* and that Murray only *wanted* ye money—and asked Moore for the interest of the £2000!' She 'is sure I cannot like the poor little man to be a sufferer by what my Brother meant him to be enriched' and she thinks if he does not like to take the money, it ought to be given into some *Trustees* hands for the benefit of *the Boy* [Moore's son]. *That* he could not refuse and that it

[1] Hobhouse *Journals*, 15 May 1824.

wd be, she wd think, pleasanter than to feel that he who is so poor should be really in *distress* from his generous consideration to my feelings and those of others (! ! ! !). . . .

I have no patience with it—as for giving Mr Moore information I've very little to give and certainly should bestow that little on another if I gave it at all—but *what* to say or do I know not—and Wilmot is so ill judging and makes such messes that I will not say a word to him about it—it is entirely owing to him that Murray ever took ye money at the moment—But pray consider all this *confidential* at least for the present—and pray tell me what *you* have said in answer to Moore—at least if I am not asking an indiscreet question.[1]

Augusta had intertwined in her bemused fashion two distinct subjects, and they remained in confusion. The first was Moore's request for a blessing on his biography—to which Lady Byron replied that she had informed Moore she would not participate in *any* biography;[2] the second was the question which now increasingly filled the letters of those who had been concerned in any way—and several who had not—ought Moore to be compensated for what he had lost on Byron's Memoirs?

The intricacies of the correspondence to which this problem gave rise all but baffle human understanding, and therefore little of it has been published, though it loomed large in the mind of several persons—particularly the unfortunate Moore—long after the Memoirs themselves were ashes. Wilmot Horton, whether or not he was answerable, as Augusta thought, for Moore's having repaid Murray two thousand guineas when he had no need to do so, had endeavoured earnestly to get some restitution for him, but both Hobhouse and Murray had opposed him, Murray holding that reimbursement of Moore would be an imputation against himself.

Lady Byron, who at first had been very willing to supply half the sum required, had grown less so as the months passed, partly, it may be, because of her increasing dread of doing anything of that kind 'in collusion' with Augusta; partly because she considered Wilmot Horton was throwing some of the responsibility for the burning upon her. She had once contemplated going to law to suppress the Memoirs, she had certainly received with immense relief Horton's special messenger carrying the news of their destruction, but she remained able to say that the decision was not hers, and paying compensation might, after all, look like an admission that she had wished to get rid of the book.

Augusta was torn between upholding Hobhouse and giving Moore fair play. She wrote to Lady Byron (on June 6th, 1825) in an even more than usually excruciating muddle to explain her point of view. There had

---

[1] 26 Nov. 1824: Lovelace Papers.
[2] Ibid. 27 Nov.

been criticism of Murray for accepting the money from Moore, and
Augusta took it upon herself to speak in his defence:

> I think he *can*—& that he *ought* to explain to you, about his having kept
> the Money—or ever taken it—it was *not* his fault—& *there* I think Moore
> behaves shamefully & makes himself out a swindler—in appropriating what
> he has no right to, by refusing to take the Money from Murray *back*—when it
> was fully proved he was in equity bound to take it. . . .
>
> With respect to Mr Hobhouse the points on which we differ refer wholly
> to *myself*—but might possibly stand in the way of his being a good person to
> negotiate or meddle—& then *he* thinks I believe that there is no need of *any*
> *remuneration* . . . but then Surely, as Mr Moore was intended to benefit by
> the Gift, we cannot rest Satisfied with his remaining *un*benefitted.[1]

But Moore did remain unbenefited, at least by any form of direct
restitution. The pretext was that he had said, or his friends had said for
him, that he would receive nothing from the hands of Murray (wherein,
according to Augusta's bewildering asseveration, he was 'making himself
out a swindler'), and those who were to provide the cash ungraciously
decided that he was to have it through that channel or not at all.

A letter from Horton to Lord Lansdowne gives the gist of the story
and its not very creditable ending.

> . . . I always thought that Mr Moore should not have insisted upon Mr
> Murray receiving the money, knowing, as he did at the time when the
> money was paid, that the property in these Memoirs was in Mr Murray, and
> knowing, also, that his representations, (however unintentionally) had mis-
> led those parties who were originally consentient to the payment of the
> money by Mr Moore. . . .
>
> However, as the fact is that Mr Moore did offer the money to Mr Murray,
> and that Mr Murray accepted it, I have thought and do think, that the most
> simple course was, for the family of Lord Byron to pay to Mr Moore, or to
> some Trustee on the part of Mr Moore, the sum paid by him to Mr Murray;
> and your Lordship is aware that I assented to this view of the case. . . .
>
> It is, however, necessary for me to explain that Lady Byron, Mrs Leigh,
> and Mr Murray himself, entirely differ from that opinion, and that they
> think that the money ought to be paid to Mr Murray, and to Mr Murray
> alone, and that it will be for Mr Murray then to induce Mr Moore to accept
> it, or to appropriate it as he may chuse, in the event of Mr Moore's con-
> tinued refusal.
>
> I understand your Lordship, as the friend of Mr Moore (though in no
> degree whatever authorized by him upon the occasion) to object strongly
> to that arrangement. . . .
>
> Under these circumstances my interference is worse than useless, and I
> therefore beg to terminate all such interference with this letter.[2]

[1] 6th June 1825: Lovelace Papers.
[2] Ibid. 17 Aug. 1825 and Murray MSS.

Quibbles about the manner in which Moore should be refunded, and the endeavour to impose humiliating conditions upon him, were symptoms of an ultimate desire to let him bear the loss. All the money Augusta could lay hands on had soon been swallowed up in her husband's debts and her domestic obligations, while Lady Byron had come round to thinking that not Moore but Murray should be recompensed. At any rate, he ought to have some handsome acknowledgment for having sacrificed his interests as a publisher by surrendering the Memoirs 'for the very inadequate compensation of the purchase-money, at a time when their value was at least quadrupled by the power of immediate publication'.[1] She toyed with the idea of giving him a present of plate or a marble bust of Byron.

Everyone complained of Horton's tactlessness, and it is manifest in his literary style that he was fussy and self-assertive; but for the second time in this business of the Memoirs, he had produced, though vainly, ideas of decency and common sense. It was he who had suggested that Byron's manuscript should be placed in a bank and examined at leisure, and he who had again and again urged that those who had approved of destroying the Memoirs owed Moore something for having forfeited them, even if technically they belonged to Murray.

Though Augusta and Lady Byron had all too readily been persuaded to set aside Moore's claims, a passage in Hobhouse's diary discloses that the ultimate obstacle to restitution lay in Albemarle Street:

> This day I saw Murray and in consequence of a promise I made to Lord Lansdowne on Friday made to him a communication respecting Moore. It seems Lady Byron and Mrs Leigh will not consent to pay over the 2000 guineas to Moore without Murray's consent. Murray says that Moore has ill-used him—that this payment would be an acknowledgment that Moore deserved a recompense—and that he will never be a party to such an acknowledgment. Lord Lansdowne desired me to tell Murray that he does not think ill of his (Murray's) conduct and that he had told me so before, and that he hoped that such a false impression would not be the cause of Murray's objecting to the arrangement with Moore.
>
> Murray requested me to let Lord Lansdowne know that his objection did not arise from that circumstance but from Moore's ill conduct, and that he would not consent to the proposed repayment to Moore's children, so it looks as if the money would never be given—and Heaven knows there is not the slightest reason for giving it.[2]

Moore himself, lest his pride should be wounded, was kept in 'official' ignorance of Lord Lansdowne's intervention, and that of Lady Jersey, Horton, and others, until all their attempts had proved futile. Several months later, having been advised by Sir Walter Scott that he should seek

---

[1] MAYNE. Quoted from a letter to Joanna Baillie, November 1825.
[2] Hobhouse *Journals*, 18 Aug. 1825.

Lord Lansdowne's help in overcoming the continued resistance of 'the family' to his biography project, he consulted that great nobleman and learned what had been going on, which 'threw me into a state of nervousness and depression on my return home, from which it required all the efforts of my natural cheerfulness to recover me'.[1]

Moore's 'natural cheerfulness', while it endeared him to hostesses and the poetry-reading public, had entirely the opposite effect on Hobhouse and Kinnaird, who perceived that it was such a sparkle as plays only on very shallow waters. Byron had over-rated Moore in every possible way. He thought him an immortal poet and a most reliable friend, and if he remarked with laughter that 'Tommy loves a lord', the foible was one that could hardly have escaped anybody's observation. Moore was much less whole-heartedly attached to Byron.

In his diary, his tone about him during the three or four years preceding the latter's death was usually critical and lacking the warmth that Byron's generosity and hospitality might have been expected to kindle in him. Famous as he was himself, there were many ways in which he could not but see Byron as a rival, and twinges of jealousy coloured his feelings.

Thus in 1819, conversing in a mail coach with a Frenchwoman who did not know his identity, he had called English 'une langue épuisée':

"*Comment*," she answered, "*une langue épuisée*, when there are such poets as Byron and Scott alive?" This silence about me I bore very philosophically. . . .[2]

People do not boast of bearing things philosophically without a consciousness that they have cause for grumbling.

A few months later, he was remarking:

. . . It is somewhat discouraging now to write, when the attention of all the reading world is absorbed by two writers—Scott and Byron; and when one finds such sentences as the following in the last Edinburgh Review, 'These novels (Scott's) have thrown evidently into the shade all contemporary poetry, except, perhaps, that inspired by the genius, or demon, of Lord Byron.'[3]

Jealousy was scarcely disguised the following year when he professed to see a self-interested design in Byron's depreciation of 'the present school of poetry'.

Lord B. willingly surrenders the skirts of his poetical glory rather than let any of us poor devils stick in them, even for ever so short a time. The best of it is, too, that the wise public all the while turns up its eyes, and exclaims, 'How modest!'[4]

It had been one thing to be magnanimous to an up-and-coming young man—a lord to boot—in London when one could enjoy the pleasure of his

[1] MOORE, *Memoirs*. 12 Dec. 1825.   [2] Ibid. 28 Dec. 1819.
[3] Ibid. 8 Apr. 1820.   [4] Ibid. 3 May 1821.

company in the best society; it was another to endure his still shedding his eclipsing light from the other side of the Alps. But even without the element of rivalry, Moore could never have cared as much for Byron as Byron for him, because the one was a deeply emotional temperament, the other primarily sentimental.

His journal entry the day Byron's coffin left London gives his character in epitome. He went to church reluctantly, having always avoided funerals, and he felt a nervous trembling come over him which lasted throughout the ceremony. When he saw a lady crying in a barouche, he said to himself, 'Bless her heart, whoever she is!' Noting that there were 'few respectable persons among the crowd', he 'left the hearse as soon as it was off the stones, and returned home to get rid of my black clothes, and try to forget, as much as possible, the wretched feelings I had experienced in them'.

While in the coach he had listened to Stanhope talking about Byron's strange mixture of avarice and profusion. Stanhope never lost an opportunity of detracting from Byron, sometimes using methods of quite feline delicacy, but he was still suffering from having been obliged to play second fiddle in Greece; one would have supposed that Moore, who had been by no means troubled with Byron's avarice, might have found another topic, riding behind his hearse. Afterwards he walked with Rogers, and met a soldier's funeral, 'which, in the full state my heart was in, affected me strongly'. He dined with a publisher, talked business, and then decided to pay one or two social calls and—

> found Lady Morgan half-dressed, and had the felicity of seeing the completion of her toilette; looking however much more at her handmaid (Morgan's pretty daughter) than at herself. From thence went to Mrs Story's and supped with her. I and the girls went to Vauxhall: a most delicious night.[1]

After the cremation of Shelley, Byron and Leigh Hunt had drunk wine and driven through the darkness singing wildly; and Hobhouse, while they were removing Byron's body from the chest in which it had travelled from Greece, had 'felt like a person intoxicated or in a state of feverish excitement without the power to think distinctly. . . .' Having forced himself through the dreaded and postponed ordeal of inspecting the corpse, he had gone to dinner at his father's house and been so strangely high-spirited that 'I believe they must have thought me tipsy'.[2] Such violent reactions are not unusual in impressionable persons affected by nerve strain. But no one who reaches Volume IV of Moore's Memoirs will

---

[1] Ibid. 12 July 1824.
[2] Hobhouse *Journals*, 5 July 1824. These illuminating glimpses were censored from the published extracts of the diary.

doubt for an instant that his 'delicious night' with the girls at Vauxhall can really be taken at face value.

For Hobhouse, with his much more tenacious affections, Moore's privileged place among Byron's friends was a sheer exasperation, and he worked himself up into a rage whenever he thought of the Memoirs having been passed round among all sorts of people, while he himself had never seen them. When spurious Memoirs began to appear purporting to be copied from the real ones, both he and Murray blamed Moore bitterly for having allowed the MSS. to be read instead of blaming themselves for the destruction which had paved the way to fraud.

> The MSS were sold as property [Hobhouse wrote, when John Bull Magazine produced what were said to be Byron's recollections of his wedding night]—they were not property for Moore showed them about so as to permit them to be copied—so that, in fact, besides the gross indelicacy of the original transaction—we have a direct deception practised on a tradesman. And yet Tom Moore—honest Tom Moore—merry Tom Moore, clever Tom Moore—will get over this.
> Holland House, Lansdowne House, and Barnes of the Times will push and puff him through whilst those who declare against such a nefarious dealing will be run down and reprobated. So goes the world—but never mind—go on—[1]

Poor Moore, who loved to be on genial terms with everyone, would have been horrified if he had dreamed what loathing he inspired. Kinnaird, according to Augusta, was ten times more 'furious' than Hobhouse[2] —a difficult degree of fury to achieve; and Augusta herself never mentioned him without expressions of disgust. This odium was certainly not diminished by her talks with Hobhouse about him, but originally it would appear to have had no other motive than to oblige Lady Byron, who was in the same position of never having met him,[3] but who took it for granted that Byron's friends were reprobates. (Perhaps nothing would have afforded so much surprise, if a premonition had been granted her, as the very respectable careers almost all of them were destined to attain; even the object of her especial aversion, Hobhouse, being created a peer and shown much personal favour by a monarch far more moral than George IV.)

Charming as he was, Moore was unable, when at last he did meet Augusta, to overcome her prejudice, though he was not allowed to suspect it, for she was too well-mannered and too badly afflicted with moral cowardice to be other than agreeable in a fashionable drawing-room. She described the occasion sarcastically to Annabella:

[1] Hobhouse *Journals*, 3 July 1824. See Appendix 1 for an extract from fraudulent Chapter.
[2] Letter to Lady Byron, 6 June 1825: Lovelace Papers.
[3] Marginal comment in her copy of Medwin's *Conversations*.

. . . A very *pleasing* little circumstance occurred to me last night—I was invited to Holland House—& in ye sort of way, that it wd have been difficult for me to refuse going there—So with a heavy & I think *foreboding* heart I set out—& who should be there but *Mr Moore* ! ! ! whom I had been thanking My Stars for the last year & ½ that I did not know (even by sight). I am convinced it was a planned thing of My lady's in one of her malicious mischief-making moods—we were introduced of course—but I flatter myself that as far as it has gone *I have been even* with her!—I never felt myself so *satisfactorily* placed in any Scrape before—perhaps it is that my Spirit is roused, by the *plot* which is now quite evident to me.[1]

Lady Holland, who was one of Moore's patronesses, may have hoped to do some good by presenting him to Augusta, but the 'plot' was not malicious and he himself had no part in it. How it appeared to Moore his journal shows:

In the evening, to my great surprise and pleasure, Mrs Leigh appeared. Could not help looking at her with deep interest; though she can hardly be said to be like Byron, yet she reminds one of him. Was still more pleased, when, evidently at her own request, Lady Stanhope introduced me to her: found her pleasing, though (as I had always heard) nothing above the ordinary run of women. She herself began first to talk of him, after some time, by asking me 'whether I saw any likeness.' I answered, I did; and she said it was with strong fears of being answered 'No', that she had asked the question. Talked of different pictures of him. I felt it difficult to keep the tears out of my eyes as I spoke with her. Said she would show me the miniature she thought the best, if I would call upon her.[2]

Unless he deceived himself as to the cordiality of his reception, Augusta's politeness must have amounted to duplicity. A few weeks afterwards, she was writing, 'Thank Heaven I did not see him when he called!'[3] And he remained in her letters 'that detestable little Moore'.

Lady Byron spoke of Augusta's 'smooth way of making mischief', but this was part of the obsession she developed as she brooded over her wrongs. If there had ever been any deliberate attempt by Augusta to cause trouble, it must have come to light by now, among the numberless letters she wrote, those written about her, and those she received from Byron himself, many of them showing that she had spoken with emphatic kindness of his wife. It would be hard to find one instance where she set out to make mischief, but it cannot be denied that she had an amiability which was often insincere and sometimes bordered on deceit.

Several painful factors had contributed to it. She had had to bow and scrape at the disagreeable court of a disagreeable queen.[4] Her domestic

[1] 4 Sept. 1825: Lovelace Papers.   [2] MOORE, *Memoirs.* 4 Sept. 1825.
[3] 28 Oct. 1825: Lovelace Papers.
[4] Charlotte, Consort of George III and mother of the Regent.

life had been harassed and miserable beyond words, and she chose to
conceal its wretchedness from the world. Timid and conventional in outlook, she had been born in the shadow of scandal and threatened for many
years with personal or vicarious disgrace. Between her husband's money
troubles and her own repented follies, dignity had been drained from her
spirit. Judgment she had never had.

She belonged to an age which has rarely had its equal for snobbery,
artificiality, and cant, and she honoured its standards—the standards her
brother, to her despair, had tried to shatter. Her letters about his later
works, on which his reputation as a major poet now largely rests, are of a
tragi-comic absurdity.

In mitigation it must be said that her view was fervently shared by his
publisher and all the friends of his she had ever met, several of whom had
kept her informed of his literary misdemeanours before they had a public
audience. In 1819 Hobhouse had called on her 'vexed and worried to
death' after reading the first cantos of *Don Juan*, and had said, 'I would
not hesitate to burn it before his face but I can't behind his back'.[1]
Scrope Davies had told her she 'could not have an idea of the *improprieties*
with which the poem abounded',[2] and this had been more than confirmed
by Mr Murray, whose decision to publish it (without his imprint) had been
solely because it might otherwise 'be transferred to those who will not
have ye same regard for the consequences'[3]—a rewarding altruism
because he did very well out of it. He had begged her earnestly not to read
it, but, though she had assured him she would not, she had found it
necessary to know the worst, and it was 'as bad as possible—ruin to himself—disgrace to his family—triumph to his enemies'.[4]

'Imagine my horror', she groaned, 'at this horrid thing appearing ye
day of the Carlton House fête where I was in *duty bound* to go.'[5] She had
written to Byron to protest. Everyone had written to protest; and Mr
Gifford had sent such an affecting letter to Albemarle Street on the subject, that, when Mr Murray read it to her, she had shuddered to hear it.[6]
With scarcely any support except from 'that infamous Mr Shelley'—
the self-same epithet she had used five years earlier—and under
such a barrage from the critics as no other except Mr Shelley himself
could have survived, he had gone on from one shameful production to
another.

But now he was dead, couldn't such derelictions be forgotten? Couldn't
every error of his life be buried away? Why, if books must be written
about him, could they not be like the books that were written about other

[1] Quoted in a letter to Lady Byron, 9 Apr: Lovelace Papers.
[2] Ibid. 5 Mar.   [3] Ibid. 9 Apr.   [4] Ibid. 12 July.
[5] Ibid. 20 July. The Carlton House fête was given by the Prince Regent.
[6] Ibid. 6 July.

famous men—works of good taste in which hardly a fault, an indiscretion, was allowed to be guessed at?

No doubt if her son-in-law Trevanion had been able to carry out the project of publishing letters, they would have been edited into something most refined under her supervision, but Hobhouse was successful in dissuading her.

Thanks largely to his quiet intervention, Moore too met with so much discouragement and resistance that only his anxious need of money impelled him to press forward. He was middle-aged and his poetical energy was declining, yet he was dependent wholly upon earnings, in debt, and full of touchy pride that forbade him to reduce his responsibilities. He and his family had lived for some time on the proceeds of a Life of Sheridan, and as he did not know that it was widely considered even by his friends to be a literary failure, he could not but see in the Byron biography a source of revenue to which he had a fair claim.

His diaries do not show any such animus against Hobhouse as Hobhouse felt against him; and it is as probable that he was not so good at hating as it is certain he was not so good at loving. Still, considering all he had borne from the other's obstructiveness, it must have gone hard with him to write twice running, in January 1826, to ask 'how far his approval of my undertaking, or his duty as executor, would allow him to assist or co-operate with me in such a work'.[1] The answer was what he expected:

> Says he sees no good in a life of our late friend, and he sees many objections to it. He also puts into the following form the opinion which I understand he has lately held in company, whenever my talent for biography, as exemplified in the 'Life of Sheridan' was the topic. 'You will write, there can be no doubt, a very clever and very saleable book; but I shall be agreeably surprised, if you should accomplish those higher objects which you must propose to yourself in writing the life of a man like Lord Byron.[2]

The beautiful and rare exactitude of both Moore and Hobhouse makes it always a pleasure to check one diary by another. Hobhouse's account runs:

> I refused being a party to any such work, saying I saw no good end that could be produced by it. I told him he would make a clever and a saleable work, but not answer any of the higher ends of biography. I know that by taking this line I expose myself to the censures of my lady ———— [? Holland] and to the gentlemen of press with whom Tom is in league, but I know I do right.
>
> I asked Burdett's advice and he gave it distinctly that I should say no shortly.[3]

---

[1] MOORE, *Memoirs*, 15 Jan.   [2] Ibid. 17 Jan.
[3] Hobhouse *Journals*, 18 Jan. The published version is, as in many cases, garbled as well as abridged.

'I know I do right' was a frequent refrain of Hobhouse's when he was acting in a drastic and an unreasonable fashion; and on such occasions he became not only defensively complacent but also callous. He was happy to hear Sam Rogers being malicious about Moore a few days afterwards.

> . . . He deprecated T. Moore's writing the life of Byron—and said he was a wretched fellow—was 47 years old with three children and worse than nothing—yet he refused a small pension which Lord Wellesley offered to settle upon his mother. Rogers said he had no right to do this.
> R. said he hoped I was going to write Byron's life. I said no by no means. I knew nothing more to be told about him.[1]

Moore had just tried flattering his way into Hobhouse's good graces by writing to thank him for the frankness of his negative, adding:

> Though you make me doubt whether I ought to impose such a confidence on you, I will nevertheless confess my opinion as to the objections against writing a Life of Lord Byron is very much the same as your own, and that if I can possibly avoid the task, it has all along been my intention to do so.[2]

He owned that his necessities alone compelled him to undertake it, and said he trusted this admission to Hobhouse's confidence. 'Of course, I shall not tell', Hobhouse remarked irritably in his journal, 'but I wish he would not make a confidant of me.' Yet the seeming reluctance of Moore must have had a mollifying effect, and Hobhouse wrote saying he had a plan to propose which would enable him to 'abandon the design'.

What this plan may have been is not clear. The discussion of it was postponed till they should have a meeting, and that did not take place for several months—by which time Moore was able to delude himself that he found Hobhouse 'full of kindness, and inclined much more to assist than to thwart me in my designs of writing "Byron's Life" '.[3]

Though this was altogether too roseate a view, there was on Hobhouse's side, a decided yielding of ground. It may have been partly due to belated and fitful glimmerings of justice, but there was also the realization that if he remained obdurate he might find things going on without him —a situation he could never abide. It was true that he had power to prevent Moore from using some of Byron's unpublished writings, but he could not stop him from producing a book. It therefore seems to have occurred to him that it might be best after all to make some concessions and thereby win a measure of control.

> I told him I wished it was not *necessary* for him to write such a thing— but the next best thing to *no* life was a short life.

---

[1] Hobhouse *Journals*, 26 Jan. 1826.
[2] MOORE, *Memoirs*, 23 Jan. 1826.   [3] Ibid. 14 May 1826.

I then told him I had thought he might get together a volume of letters and prefix a memoir on Byron's life and genius. I suggested that he might read the letters sent by B. to Lady Melbourne—and that I should have no objection to his making extracts.

I told him that I did not know how I could write a life if I had chosen to do so—I could point out the faults of other biographers, and if any man in authority wrote falsehoods would do so—but a regular life I could not write.

He owned to me that he was under the same or worse difficulties, and he said that had I intended to write, he would have 'veiled the bonnet to me.'

He said there were things in the Italian journal of B. that ought to be destroyed—he told me what they were. I agreed with him, and he promised to do so and to write to me when he had done it.

He then said that he would show me what he had written and ask me to correct dates &c. I told him I would do anything short of participating in a work which I did not approve and which except to get rid of encumbrances, he did not approve. He said he perfectly understood me and was much obliged.[1]

Moore's show of deference, his parade of difficulties, were obviously meant to curry favour with Hobhouse, and so too, it may be supposed, was his offer to go on destroying Byron records. (One would have thought both men would have had enough of that, but the journal in question was duly subjected to excision, published as 'Extracts from a Diary' and then apparently demolished altogether.[2] Surely no great writer has ever been so unlucky as Byron in his choice of literary guardians!)

Hobhouse now ingeniously suggested that Moore should seek a reconciliation with Murray. He himself had not been on very good terms with Murray since the rejection of his exposure of Medwin in the *Quarterly Review*, but he knew he could end the slight estrangement at any time, and he would be able to exercise more influence in Albemarle Street than with Moore's own publisher, the Longmans, strangers to him. His willingness to allow the use of correspondence sprang not from any change of mind about Byron's defects as a letter-writer but from the belief that not a paragraph could be published without his own consent.[3] He therefore hoped that carefully edited letters would form the bulk of the text.

It seemed to give him some curious satisfaction to think of Moore's

[1] Hobhouse *Journals*, 14 May 1826.

[2] A journal from 4 Jan. to 27 Feb. 1821. The portion where omission is explicitly indicated is where Byron is about to tell of the 'violent, though pure love and passion . . . of the most romantic period of my life'. This was almost certainly his ardent friendship for the chorister Edleston, about which it would be invaluable to have his own retrospect.

[3] Moore claimed that Byron had given him rights over correspondence in constituting him editor of the Memoirs with full discretion to use additional material. Hobhouse considered such rights had been cancelled with the destruction of the Memoirs. They arrived at a compromise. Murray MSS.

book as an entirely mercenary proceeding, and in that light he refers to it again and again:

> Moore owned very frankly to me that he would make a book to get the money he wanted, but not a book of real merit as a life of Lord Byron.
>
> On the whole I think he looks at the subject fairly—except that he believes he has some claim on account of his share of the destruction of the manuscript which he has not. . . .
>
> I told him that there was a very general feeling against life-writing as unfair and unprofitable. He agreed with me there ought to be—this was when we were talking of his Byron. . . . We parted he agreeing to give me his answer about Murray in a day or two.
>
> I am sorry that circumstances have made this interview necessary, but as I feel that Byron certainly intended a benefit to Moore I cannot but assist him in some degree to gain his 2000 £ out of Lord Byron's memory. That is his motive—he has no other.
>
> I write this journal just after his visit.[1]

Such was the spirit in which the nearest approach to an official biography was undertaken on the one side and grudgingly sanctioned on the other.

Moore bowed to Hobhouse's proposal that he should make peace with Murray, and Rogers offered to mediate between them, but on May 22nd, 1826, two years after the breach, Moore happened to see Murray in the street.

> . . . It occurred to me that, as the thing was to be done, the shortest and manliest way was to do it at once myself, without any intervention. Accordingly sallied out after my man and accosted him. He seemed startled at first, but on my saying, 'Mr Murray, some friends of yours and mine seem to think that you and I should no longer continue upon these terms, I therefore proffer you my hand, and most readily forgive and forget all that has passed;" he soon brightened up into smiles, and we walked on together very amicably. On our parting at Charing Cross he shook my hand, reiterating, "God bless you, sir! God bless you, sir!"

The end of Moore's quarrel with Murray meant, as Hobhouse had foreseen, that there was soon a treaty between them for the biography, and the Longmans, on the promise of being repaid the large sum they had lent to Moore, behaved very generously in setting their author free. Murray considered that the life of Byron was 'his birthright', and cheered Moore greatly (who had supposed material would be scanty) by telling him that he alone possessed enough to fill nearly a quarto. They both concurred in hoping that Hobhouse would not be 'too fastidious' as to what he would let them use of all this.[2]

Hobhouse, convinced that by getting Moore and Murray together he

---

[1] Hobhouse *Journals*, 14 May 1826. [2] MOORE, *Memoirs*. 29 May.

could impose his own scheme on them, now, in another interview, put it to Moore:

> I . . . told him that the best thing he could do would be to edit Byron's works and prefix a memoir like Mason's Gray—he agreed and I promised not to throw any impediment as executor—but rather to assist him as far as looking over his book went.[1]

Had this plan been followed, the biography would have been a mere extended preface: and to give the key in which he would have liked it pitched, he spoke highly of the impeccable volume by Count Gamba.[2] The very next day, however, Murray informed Moore that he would publish the 'Life' altogether separately from the Works.

Of this fact Hobhouse was not apprised for a long while to come, because the project now began to hang fire for reasons in which he was not concerned. Moore left London, having taken on an assignment to write for *The Times* as well as other literary labours. Murray himself was in ill-health and dilatory, and he started to toy with an idea of using his copious Byron papers in a publication independent of Moore. At this Moore took umbrage, and their relations became so strained that, nine months after their apparently happy *rapprochement*, they had another quarrel.

Murray had been advised by Canning and the ever-vigilant protector of morals, Gifford, that Byron's letters to himself were unsuitable for print, and he told Moore he now intended to leave them unpublished as a legacy to his children. For a quarto volume of Moore's own materials he offered £2500 to be paid in instalments, and not until publication. (He was feeling the effects of having lost £28,000 on his newspaper *The Representative* in the previous year.) Moore, angry on many counts, declared he would return forthwith to the Longmans.

> In the course of our conversation I said, "Well, I don't see how I shall be able to make out a 'Life,' and I think you had better take *any* materials off my hands, and let them go to your children with your *own*." At this hint he seemed eagerly to jump, and said he should be very happy to enter into such an arrangement with me, but I answered (what was true) that I had spoken without thought, and that, as to parting with a paper of Lord Byron's (except to put it in the fire) there was nothing more remote from my thoughts.[3]

The Longmans received Moore back with open arms and begged him to lose no time in getting the book written, but he was busy on a novel,

---

[1] Hobhouse *Journals*, 28 May.   [2] MOORE, *Memoirs*. 28 May.
[3] Ibid. 26 Feb. 1827. The second parenthesis evokes gloomy speculations as to what private acts of destruction Moore may have engaged in; but in any case, after his death, a large quantity of Byron material which he had published in bowdlerized form disappeared totally, having been either lost or demolished by his executor, Lord John Russell, or his widow.

The Epicurean, and it was nearly midsummer in 1827 before he set to work seriously collecting biographical data.

He began with Mary Shelley, who had read all or most of the Memoirs and who promised to write out for him her recollections of them, much more vivid than his own: her memory had the advantage of being eighteen years younger and not subject to the distractions of life as an almost professional diner-out and drawing-room entertainer. After Shelley, Byron had impressed her far more than any man she had known, as may be seen from his recurring appearance thinly disguised in several of her novels, and, scarcely disguised at all, as Lord Raymond in *The Last Man*. The help she gave was extensive and varied. She secured for the book Byron's correspondence with Dr Bowring of the Greek Committee, and also a memoir by the Countess Guiccioli which Moore described as 'perfection'.

> . . . It is all told with such a beautiful unconsciousness of there being anything at all wrong in any part of the proceeding. I should delight in printing it exactly as it is, but I suppose I must not.[1]

Other contributors were tutors and schoolmasters of Dulwich and Harrow; school-fellows, amongst whom were the beloved Clare, the Rev. William Harness, now a popular preacher, and Colonel Wildman, who was assiduously preserving relics of Byron at Newstead Abbey; early friends such as the sensible Miss Pigot of Southwell and her mother; the Rev. John Becher at whose instance Byron had obligingly destroyed practically the whole of the first issue of his poems, and the once worshipped Mary Chaworth; companions of undergraduate days, including the Rev. Francis Hodgson, from whom Moore extracted a letter in which he acknowledged—after at first trying to be vague about it—the handsome treatment he had received from Byron; men like Michael Bruce and Lord Sligo who had known him in the Near East; and, of course, the friends Moore himself saw often in social life—Lord and Lady Holland, the none-too-veracious Sam Rogers, Lady Jersey and many others.

It was not until he had worked some months at interviews and the copying of correspondence, that he wrote to Hobhouse asking to see the Melbourne letters and reminding him of promised help. The effect was by no means what he anticipated. Since their comparatively amicable meeting Hobhouse had resumed all his old intransigent attitude. He had read and been enraged quite unduly by the letter in which Moore had gently poked a little fun at him.[2] He had heard that Moore named him among sympathizers and supporters—presumptuousness which set him writing disclaimers as indignantly as if he had never for an instant abated

---

[1] 15 Apr. 1828: Abinger Papers.   [2] See pp. 220-1.

his hostilities. Then several people whose assistance to Moore he had tried to circumvent were being won over by the little Irishman's dexterous handling and also (though Hobhouse could never grasp this point) by the soundness of his case for writing an adequate biography. And after all, the book was going to the Longmans, not Murray's.

Moreover, he had now read Byron's letters to Lady Melbourne, which, when he had agreed to Moore's using them, had still been in the keeping of her daughter, Lady Cowper; and although his comment on them was mild enough—merely 'Very extraordinary productions, such confessions' —he had no intention of allowing them to be quoted, and had already told Moore so, encountering him at a dinner party months before.[1]

Perhaps he did not then know that it was Byron himself who had desired Moore to see those letters, writing about them to Murray in a communication expressly devoted to the topic of documents that might be helpful for his biography;[2] but in any case he was never disposed to let Byron's wishes stand in his way when he deemed it his duty to protect him from his own indiscretions. (He did not penetrate the mysteries of this correspondence as interpreted in the 20th century. Had he regarded it as a confirmation of the rumours about Byron and Mrs Leigh, he would have had no hesitation in destroying it, whereas he preserved it intact and left it to his daughter: but even without recognizing all the dramatis personae of the period when Byron had so unhappily cast—or mis-cast—himself as Valmont with Lady Melbourne in the rôle of Mme de Merteuil, he could see that he was handling the sort of materials he called 'combustibles'.)

> After a great deal of deliberation I wrote to *repeat* that I could not be a coadjutor in his work, and that he could not consult the letters to Lady Melbourne. I added that if I found any more of his own letters he should have them. I told him that I found Barry and Me Guiccioli had been told I was assisting him, and that I was piqued at it.
> Moore answered my letter in proper terms. . . .[3]

Hobhouse did not perceive the underlying irony in Moore's response, quoted thus in the latter's journal:

> Wrote to Hobhouse, saying that if I had been (which I feared very much) unfortunate or troublesome to him on the subject of Byron, I begged he would forgive me, and I would plague him no further; that it was possible some expressions of mine relative to his kindness, &c might have been construed by Barry and others into a boast of his sanction and co-operation, but that it was by no means my intention to produce such an impression,

[1] MOORE, *Memoirs*. 3 July 1827.
[2] 28 Sept. 1821. See Appendix 2 for what may be deduced from this suggestion.
[3] Hobhouse *Journals*, 29 Nov. 1827.

and that I would do my utmost to remove it; that, indeed, the simple fact
of my work being likely to appear without a single contribution of either
paper or anecdote from any one of Lord B.'s immediate friends or relatives,
would, of itself, sufficiently absolve them from any share of the responsibility
attached to it.[1]

In sending back, on request, the letters Byron had received from
Moore in Italy, Hobhouse could not resist the opportunity of revenging
himself for having been laughingly classed as 'not of the finer order of
spirits'. After telling him 'half jocularly' (Hobhouse's half-jocular tone
was, if anything, more intimidating than his blunt one) what he thought
of him for having written that letter, he went on

> However, I forgive you; but in the true spirit of the Gospel, I will heap
> coals of fire on your laurelled head, by telling you an anecdote. Gamba's
> Memoir of Lord B.'s last residence in Genoa [*sic*] was put into my hand and
> therein I found it recorded that when Lord B. was in Cephalonia, he received
> a letter from you, in which you said something that incensed him very much;
> so much that, after various threats, he said he would write a satire against
> you. I struck my pen across this story, and requested Gamba not to let it
> appear.[2]

Moore, who had put up with a great deal, now fell into the temptation
to have revenge in his turn, and Hobhouse, infinitely more vulnerable,
could no longer pretend to be even half jocular.

> At home all morning, answering a letter from T. Moore in which he
> tells me he had done me the same service as I had performed for him—by
> expunging something against me in one of Byron's letters to him—and
> offering to open a new account with me. . . .
> I beg'd him to venture the expunged passage. I concluded by telling him
> what I thought of my association with Byron—he [Moore] had all the praise
> I all the knocks. . . . T. Moore's letter to me was in the true Irish style, very
> malicious—he reminded me of my early poems. I confessed I was ashamed
> of them, and burnt them wherever I found them. Our correspondence is
> likely to have an ugly termination.[3]

While all this foolish and childish sparring was going on between two
men whose fundamental decency has never been called in question, a man
with no decency at all was able to take advantage of their disunity and
spring upon the literary world an attack on Byron compared with which
the homilies of the Dallases were a display of loving kindness, and even

[1] MOORE, *Memoirs*. 30 Nov. 1827.
[2] Quoted by Moore, 11 Dec. 1827. The word Genoa must be a misreading for Greece.
Byron had been annoyed by a letter from Moore saying he had heard that 'instead of
pursuing heroic and warlike adventures, he was residing in a delightful villa continuing
Don Juan'. He wrote Moore a straightforward protest.
[3] Hobhouse *Journals*, 14 Dec. 1827. Hobhouse's early poems are rather improper.

Thomas Moore, from a contemporary engraving

the anonymous scurrilities of the *John Bull Magazine* mere noisy, smoky squibs, too crudely intended for mischief to succeed in effecting it.

Moore, whatever his shortcomings, was better qualified than anyone Byron had known to write an authoritative biography, and had he only been encouraged instead of meeting with obstacles and frustrations at every turn, he would easily have forestalled the malignant Leigh Hunt's production *Lord Byron and Some of His Contemporaries.* It is too much to say that Hunt would never have discharged the venom which must for years have been seething in him, but a magazine article might have sufficed to relieve him. If Moore and Murray had got in first with all the wealth of documents at their command and the immeasurably higher standing Moore then had in the literary world, the market for full-length reminiscences by Hunt would have been too small to tempt the publisher from whom he had borrowed.

His agreement with Colburn was not for a book on Byron but a selection from his own writings, and he spent the money (£200) two years before doing the job. The delight of finding himself, he said, in England again after his years of discomfort in Italy (where he had remained against all advice, and entirely by his own desire) conspired with his 'bad habits of business and the sorriest arithmetic' to make him avail himself of the open-handed treatment of his publisher 'and indulge in too long a holiday'. He was middle-aged but inclined to write of himself in a whimsy style as if he were a fey little child, slyly watching the effect of its own lovable and amusing naughtiness and easily bursting into tears or tantrums if the grown-ups were unresponsive.

> . . . Time crept on, uneasiness returned, and I found myself painfully anxious to show my employer how much I would fain do for him. The worst of it was, that the sick hours which I dreaded on a renewal of work, returned upon me, aggravated by my not having dared to encounter them sooner; and my anxieties became thus increased. I wished to make amends for loss of time: the plan of the book became altered; and I finally made up my mind to enlarge and enrich it with an account of Lord Byron.[1]

Hunt never explained how or why he could make up for lost time better by writing an original work than arranging the already existing materials the publisher had paid for; he was merely seizing upon any excuse he could think of, knowing that excuse was going to be necessary.

> I must even confess, that such is my dislike of these personal histories, in which it has been my lot to become a party, that had I been rich enough and could have repaid the handsome conduct of Mr Colburn with its proper interest, my first impulse on finishing the work would have been to put it into the fire. Not that I have not written it conscientiously, and that it is not

---

[1] HUNT. Preface.

L.L.B.—T

in every respect fit to appear; but it has long ceased to be within my notions of what is necessary for society, to give an unpleasant account of any man. . . .

I could not conceal from myself on looking over the manuscript, that in renewing my intercourse with him in imagination, I had involuntarily felt an access of the spleen and indignation, which I experienced as a man who thought himself ill-treated. With this, to a certain extent, the account is coloured, though never with a shadow of untruth; nor have I noticed a great deal that I should have done, had I been in the least vindictive, which is a vice I disclaim. If I know any two things in the world, and have any two good qualities to set off against many defects, it is that I am not vindictive, and that I speak the truth.

Here we have the keynote of this fearful book, compounded of vanity calling itself modesty, deadly and tireless malice, whining apology, and half-truths and concealments dressed out as irrepressible frankness. An obbligato of self-praise accompanies almost every disparagement of others. Introducing his pages overflowing with hatred, he disclaims vindictiveness. He partakes 'none of the ordinary notions of merit and demerit with regard to anyone'. Flattery is impossible to him, otherwise he might have got on better with Byron. He is not captious; he has often been remonstrated with for not showing a stronger sense of enmity and ill-usage. He could not think without regret of the picture he had drawn of Byron's infirmities: he regretted speaking disagreeable truths of any man.

The Preface to the second edition provides a further catalogue of his virtues. He is a humanist who speaks the truth with zeal and candour, and all that he has suffered from his critics will not hinder him from being sincere. 'I shall remain so to my dying day, knowing what an effect one strenuous example has upon society.' He is sorry his sincerity has taken a splenetic turn but—the reader may smile at his simplicity—in the sharpest things he has written, he only thought to have awakened the remorse of his adversaries. (The dead poet was presumably expected to be remorseful in the shades.) Byron's defenders are unprincipled calumniators and convicted cowards, while he himself is 'hampered by the humanities'. Mr Moore in particular ought to be ashamed of himself—and here Hunt's characteristic whining note grows shrill—because 'he knew what a situation I was in; what a family I had; what struggles I had gone through, for the sake of freedom; and how openly I had ever behaved to himself, both in what I ventured to praise in him and to differ with'. Moore has aimed a blow at him 'as the father of a family'.

The cant and cunning with which this champion of domestic sanctities grovelled for public sympathy inspired him to refer touchingly to Byron's wife as 'the woman who had lain in his bosom', though at the time when he was fawning on Byron, no one had been more adhesively on his side.

On and on flows the tide of bitterness, not only against Byron but anyone who had spoken a word in his favour: on and on the stream of compliments to himself, until the display of hysterical rage leads to an announcement that he hardly dares tell the reader 'how little even the grossest abuse affects me, in the angry sense of the word, when I think the writer a sincere person'.

His own sincerity and the 'openness' he thought it meritorious to observe towards Moore had encouraged him, in the first edition, to make some personal remarks on Moore's acceptance of Byron's Memoirs. Shelley had been disappointed, for the sake of the financial advantage, that Hunt himself was not the recipient: Hunt doubtless felt the same, and we may regret it too since it is certain that no pride, false or real, would have influenced him to renounce so lucrative a gift. But his criticism of Moore's conduct in the matter fails to evoke sympathy because it is obviously the outcome of spite, Moore having cautioned Byron against any business association with him. Moore's warning had, of course, been conveyed in private, but Hunt's come-back was a public one, and inserted with much artifice into an ostensibly flattering verbal portrait. (He had a style of flattery so oily and at the same time back-handed, that his praise often makes more uneasy reading than his detraction.)

He took Moore to task not for the destruction of the manuscript but for his declaration concerning his unwillingness to be reimbursed by the family:

> The meaning of this is, that Lord Byron presented Mr Moore with the Life for the purpose of turning it into money; that Mr Moore did so, and got two thousand guineas for it (a poor sum, by the by, if it was all he was to have): and that although he had no objection to receive money in this way, he had in any other. . . .
>
> Mr Moore, on this and other occasions, has been willing to give the commercial British public to understand, that he has a horror of pecuniary obligations, though, it seems, he has no objection to pecuniary's worth. This, I confess, is a splitting of hairs, which I do not understand. If a friend is worth being obliged to, I do not see how a man is less obliged, or has less reason to be so, by accepting his manuscripts than his money. . . .
>
> The truth is, Mr Moore's notion in this matter is a commonplace; and I used to think him higher above commonplaces than he is. I should look upon myself as more tied, and rendered more dependent, by living as he does among the great, and flattering the mistakes of the vulgar, than by accepting thousands from individuals whom I loved. When I came to know Lord Byron as I did, I could no more have accepted his manuscripts than his money, unless I could prove to myself that I had a right to them in the way of business. Till then, I would as soon have taken the one as the other, if I took any.

He had taken both manuscripts and money, being perfectly well able to prove to himself that he had 'a right to them in the way of business' just as he had had a right to thousands from Shelley in the way of friendship. (Besides smaller but by no means minor 'borrowings', he had allowed Shelley, who was eight years his junior, to raise £1400 from money-lenders for him by post-obit bonds at an interest of at least a hundred per cent.) To Moore, who was in the same position as to maintaining a wife and several children without private means, but who refused help far oftener than he accepted it, Hunt's sly attempt to bring him down to his own level as a hanger-on of Bryon's must have been provoking; but to do him justice, it was not for himself that he blazed up in anger when he read that meanly malevolent book. He was shallow but not petty, supple but not feeble, and if his affection for Byron had failed at certain crucial moments, it nevertheless retained sufficient force to protest against so unseemly a betrayal of hospitality.

In a fine and rare flash of indignation, he dropped his gentility, his drawing-room graces, and recapturing the courage of his youth, the courage to make enemies, he published under a pseudonym that took nobody in, *The 'Living Dog' and the 'Dead Lion'*:

Next week will be published (as 'Lives' are the rage)
    The whole Reminiscences, wondrous and strange,
Of a small puppy-dog, that once lived in the cage
    Of the late noble Lion at Exeter 'Change.

Though the dog is a dog of the kind they call 'sad,'
    'Tis a puppy that much to good breeding pretends;
And few dogs have such opportunities had
    Of knowing how Lions behave—among friends.

How that animal eats, how he snores, how he drinks,
    It is all noted down by this Boswell so small;
And 'tis plain from each sentence, the puppy-dog thinks
    That the Lion was no such great things after all.

Though he roared pretty well—this the puppy allows—
    It was all, he says, borrowed—all second-hand roar:
And he vastly prefers his own little bow-wows
    To the loftiest war-note the Lion could pour.

'Tis indeed as good fun as the cynic could ask,
    To see how this cockney-bred setter of rabbits
Takes gravely the Lord of the Forest to task,
    And judges of Lions by puppy-dog habits.

Nay, fed as he was (and this makes a *dark* case)
    With sops every day from the Lion's own pan,
He lifts up a leg at the noble beast's carcass,
    And—does all a dog so diminutive can.

However, the book's a good book, being rich in
Examples and warnings to Lions high-bred,
How they suffer small mongrelly curs in their kitchen,
Who'll feed on them living, and foul them when dead.[1]

Hunt's retort to this was exceedingly ineffectual. In verses entitled *The Giant and the Dwarf*, he attacked Moore for his small stature and his low Irish birth, and for accepting Byron's Memoirs while pretending to keep his independence. In order to make Moore seem culpable, he had to suggest that the Memoirs were unfit to have been sold, which took him over to the side of the suppressors; and, as the money had been repaid in full to the purchaser, the taunts were pointless. To throw on Moore the ridicule of being, mentally as well as physically, a dwarf, he was obliged to stress that Byron was a giant, and this was contrary to the whole thesis of his book.

As that book and certain events that led to it must be reverted to in another chapter, it is only necessary here to convey enough to account for the events it immediately set in motion. *Lord Byron and Some of His Contemporaries* came out in January 1828, while Moore was on a tour to Newstead Abbey, Southwell, and other places where he could interview the friends and servants of Byron's youth. On the 29th he received a letter from John Murray, forwarded from his home, saying that Leigh Hunt's work had induced him to change his mind with respect to the publication of his Byron papers, that he had been discussing with Rogers a new proposition for Moore, and was willing to visit him in the country if they could not meet in London. Moore had several engagements to fulfil— one of them being a lively public dinner in his honour at Derby, another a 'rather dull' private dinner with Mrs Musters (Mary Chaworth) at whose house near Nottingham he stayed one or two nights, and consented to romanticize her story by rounding it off on the sentimental chord of her last meeting with Byron[2] and not making any allusion to her subsequent reopening of correspondence. (Mrs Musters, who did not allow music in her house on Sundays, begged Moore to let her have the pleasure of sending him a copy of Chalmers's *Devotional Exercises*, symptoms which seem to rule out the popular presumption that she was the woman with whom Byron could have been happy.)

On February 7th, while his long-suffering wife waited outside in Albemarle Street, Moore called on Murray and listened to proposals on the very handsomest scale. Murray, infuriated by Hunt, was willing to place all that was publishable of his papers at Moore's disposal, and to pay him four thousand guineas for the biography.

[1] *The Times*, 10 Jan. 1828. Signed 'T. Pidcock'. Pidcock was a man who kept a menagerie.   [2] MOORE, *Memoirs*. 3 and 5 Feb. 1828.

Told him that I considered this offer perfectly liberal, but that he knew how I was situated with the Longmans, and that I certainly could not again propose to take my work out of their hands without having it in my power to pay down the sum that I owe them.

"They would, I suppose (he said) be inclined to give some accommodation in the payment?" "I cannot at all answer for that, Mr Murray (I replied). I must have it in my power to offer them the payment of the debt." "Very well, sir (he said) you *may* do so."

Once again the Longmans behaved with the greatest generosity, saying that, although they were very sorry not to have the book, and that the public would be apt to think they were 'rather slightingly treated', Murray was the right publisher. Murray, for his part, agreed to pay them at once £3000 that Moore had borrowed, and 'nothing indeed', as Moore wrote, 'could be more frank, gentleman-like, and satisfactory than the manner in which this affair has been settled on all sides'.[1]

Hobhouse now withdrew his opposition. He had not read Hunt's book, only some extracts from it in a review, but these were enough to convince him that it was 'a most villainous production', though on the strength solely of the passages quoted, he thought there might be 'a great deal of truth' in it.[2] Bowring invited him to criticize it in the *Westminster Review*, but he had worn himself out on minor offenders, and could not at first even bring himself to look at it. He was intensely busy as Member for Westminster and he may have felt, too, that he was no match for such a vitriolic fighter as Hunt, who descended to depths of abuse in which he spared no infirmity or misfortune.[3]

On February 5th Hobhouse noted:

I saw Murray on Friday last. He told me he had offered Moore 4,000 guineas for his Life of Byron, and the use of all his papers. I told him he was right. His motive evidently is Leigh Hunt's infamous book, in which I presume Murray cuts a poor figure.

Moore wrote to me the other day a good-natured letter, which I answered good-naturedly—also Hodgson wrote to me on the subject of Moore, and his Life—he had been helping Moore and says the book will be well done.[4]

A few days later he saw Moore and managed to refer afterwards to the arrangements for the biography without any expression of acrimony.[5] Leigh Hunt, in defiance of copyright, had published more than a dozen of Byron's letters, and after this, permission could not, with any show of justice, be withheld from Moore and Murray.

[1] MOORE, *Memoirs*. 11 Feb.   [2] Hobhouse *Journals*, 20 Jan.
[3] E.g. his attacks on Gifford contained cruel reminders that his victim was a cripple and had originally been a cobbler.
[4] Hobhouse *Journals*. Hobhouse had made one of his mistakes of date through entering a number of days at once; Murray's proposition was not put to Moore until Feb. 7.
[5] Ibid. 13 Feb.

Hobhouse must have thought often in those days of all his warnings to Byron against association with a dangerous man. Although he maintained his refusal to review the squalid performance, he consented to assist whomever might be doing so by answering a questionnaire. This has been preserved, hitherto unpublished, and is endorsed in his writing:

Questions from Bowring relative to Leigh Hunt's Lord Byron.[1]

Many of these questions, twenty-seven in number, are left without an answer. It would seem that he had only jotted down a few tentative remarks when Bowring decided that it would be best after all to ignore the book. Here are the points Hobhouse did deal with, some of them in a manner which may be found surprising:

Bowring (quoting Hunt)—Lord B. could receive some very strange and small favours, such as made people wonder over their wine. *Is there any truth in this? And what does it mean?*

Hobhouse—*I do not know.*

Bowring—What *completed* the *distress* of his connection with the Countess Guiccioli was his want of generosity in money matters. *Is this true?*

Hobhouse—*Totally untrue. He was the most munificent man I ever knew, but he had a very proper dislike of being cheated.*

(Hunt had dwelt again and again on Byron's avarice, which Hobhouse recognized as a reaction against years of being imposed upon, both by tradesmen—whose prices automatically went up for a nobleman—and by several of his friends. Hunt himself did very well indeed out of Byron.)

Bowring—He had no address [even in the ordinary sense of the word . . . he hummed and hawed and looked confused on very trivial occasions]. *Is this true?*

Hobhouse—*A monstrous falsehood.*

Bowring—He talked of Mrs L. Hunt as being 'no great things' called L. H. a 'proser' and the quiet and respectable children 'impracticable.' *What did he really think of them all?*

Hobhouse—*He talked to me very kindly of the wife and children and said he could not bear to think of doing any thing which might distress them.*

(Byron's constantly quoted remark that Mrs Hunt was 'no great things' was a piece of tittle-tattle Hunt accepted at second hand. Byron may never have said it, though it would have been the gentlest of indictments if he had, judging by her diary, her son's description of her character, and some recently published comments on her personal habits by Benjamin Haydon.[2] Hobhouse's talk about the Hunts took place on his

---

[1] Murray MSS.　　　　[2] POPE, *Keats-Shelley Journal*, Autumn 1959.

visit to Byron at Pisa, which began on September 5th, 1822. In the very first hours of their reunion after several years—Byron being, as Teresa records, overcome with emotion on hearing Hobhouse's name announced[1] —Leigh Hunt most tactlessly joined them.)

Bowring—Dedication of Rimini. Did not Lord B. write 'familiar coxcomb' or some such phrase in the margin of his copy, which was sold for two guineas in consequence?

Hobhouse—'*Impudent varlet.*'[2]

Bowring—Mr Hobhouse rushed over the Alps (to put a stop to the Liberal).[3]

Hobhouse—*Quite false—for the Liberal had not appeared in 1822 Septr nor did Mr H[obhouse] know it was about to appear.*

Bowring—Lord B. was afraid of Mr Hazlitt . . . [he admitted him like a courtier for fear he should be treated by him as an enemy].

Hobhouse—*He was afraid of no living being.*

Bowring—He was jealous of the smallest accomplishment.

Hobhouse—*I never detected him in any jealousy of any accomplishment.*

Bowring—His superstition was remarkable . . . petty and old womanish.

Hobhouse—*He had no superstition but used to talk sometimes as if he had.*

Bowring—He had no conversation . . . [He could not interchange ideas or information with you, as a man of letters is expected to do.]

Hobhouse—*Quite false—and L. H. has told me to the contrary himself.*

Bowring—It is insinuated in several places that he had no courage and that he died of fear. Any remark on this?

Hobhouse—*One of the most atrocious falsehoods in the whole book—Count Gamba's work may be relied upon as true—ask Colonel Stanhope who saw him when he had his first fit.*

What were the foibles of Stanhope compared with the perfidy of Hunt, whose final conclusion about Byron was that he ought not to have been born?[4] But at least the odious production reconciled for a time some of the jarring friends of Byron. Some but not, unfortunately, all.

It was Murray's anxious desire to gain the support of Mrs Leigh who, apart from being able to make a tangible contribution of manuscripts and

[1] *La Vie.*

[2] This must have been one of the books seized by Byron's creditors in 1816. Hunt's dedication was in a style of free and easy familiarity unheard of in polite circles at the time: 'My dear Byron—You see what you have brought yourself to be by liking my verses. It is taking you unawares, I allow, but you yourself have set example nowadays of a poet's dedicating to a poet; and it is under that noble title as well as the still nobler one of friend, that I now address you,' etc.

[3] The question implied here is upon a passage about the enemies of the Hunt-Byron partnership: 'This man wrote to him, and that wrote, and another came. Mr Hobhouse rushed over the Alps, not knowing which was the more awful, the mountains, or the Magazine.'

[4] He was, said Hunt, 'an excessive instance of what we see hundreds of every day; namely, the unhappy consequences of a parentage that ought never to have existed'.

letters, could give the work official status by her approval. About February 23rd he wrote to her:

> You may probably have heard of the re-junction of Mr Moore and me in publishing Memoirs of Lord Byron—I withheld my papers because I thought it indecorous as his Lordship's publisher to print any, during my life time— but since Leigh Hunt's infamous book—I felt it to be a duty which I owe to
>
> Lord B's memory to assist as much as is in my power, in the removal of the odious impression, which this villainous work is otherwise calculated to leave —I therefore sent for Mr Moore and told him, that if he could dissolve satisfactorily to both parties his agreement with Messrs. Longman, I wd give him all my papers which could be published at this time, and Four thousand guineas besides, to write a Life of Lord Byron as it ought to be.
>
> In a few days I was glad to find that my proposal met with the approba- tion—entire approbation of the friends of both parties—and Mr Hobhouse in particular.[1]

He went on to point out to her with pride that in his transactions with Byron during his life he had avoided even the appearance of being mercenary, and 'after his death I destroyed his Memoirs because they wd have proved injurious to his memory'. He hoped that she would do all she could to further his great object, 'that of conveying a favorable and durable character of your Noble Brother'.

Augusta liked Murray very much, but her abhorrence of Moore was still greater. She thought it absolutely insufferable that he had been in- vestigating her brother's early life, and seemed rather disposed to let Hunt have the last word than to do anything to promote a book based on re- search. She wrote at once to Hobhouse and, having had his reply, which appears to have been less enthusiastic than Murray would have wished (for though he was no longer obstructing Moore, he would not become his ally), proceeded to consult Annabella.

> I answered this [Murray's letter] so as to avoid the shadow of an appear- ance of *Sanction* to the *measure* of *writing at all* at present—but, if it *was*
>
> to be so as to convey to *our* M [Murray] that the 'rejunction' (inasmuch as *he* was concerned [)], was *all I* trusted to for its being well conducted—in short so as Not [to] bestow a word of approval or any thing approaching it to the other *M*—who besides ransacking all *Nottinghamshire*, had even before I
>
> received M's communication beset *Fletcher* who came down in such a *fluster* to me! to ask *what to do?* & puis a 2nd time after an interview with the *little* Monster—who said the design or the work had *yours* & *my* entire approba- tion ! ! ! ! ! ! & then, complained of *how* he was *Minus* 2000 Gs! for which he was Now paying interest ! ! ! ! F——*naively* replying he could not under- stand that, since he had only *repaid* What he had conjointly *received* ! ! ! ! he

---

[1] Copy made by Augusta: Lovelace Papers.

(nasty little M) then desired F. to meet him at Rogers's—F. said he sd *not* till he had seen me!

I told him he had better go to Murray & see what was to be done,—for I knew Nothing about it—only—that his work *Moore's* certainly had no sanction of *mine*—& I *thought, not* of yours—! — — What is to be done my dear A?—Murray's conduct *from first to last,* appears to me (beyond every thing) beautiful.

Moore has even been visiting the Musters's (Chaworths) & the poor little simple woman did not seem to see *a bit* his project—he also went to South-well, which was the residence during the Minority or part of it—when poor dear Newstead was let—

. . . Hobhouse answered kindly—tho bluntly—I think he was in bad humour as he is often during the Hse of Commons days—that the Exrs had nothing to do with the business in question—he wd have written sooner but waited for Hanson's opinion—who has not ansd at all! which means I do not know what—I wish it was all finished for it wears My spirits![1]

What Lady Byron replied to this hysterical vapouring is not known, but a week or two later Captain Lord Byron called at Albemarle Street to protest on her behalf. The harassed publisher committed himself very far to avoid antagonizing her, and was anything but loyal to his author.

My dear friend [George Byron wrote]
    I had a long conversation with Mr Murray today, he declares that he would have nothing to do with the work if there was one word in it that could give offence or in any way wound the feelings of any individual, more especially yourself, and as to Mr Moore having stated that he had yr sanction to the publishing the work, he believes it to be a most determined falsehood for his words were—'how[eve]r bad Mr M. might be he did not believe him base enough to spread or make such a report,' and as to any mention of it in the work he says that he will be answerable not only for that not being the case, but for all that is in it, as *He* is to be the publisher. He Mr Murray said that he had intended to have written to you on this subject & *beg'd me to* do so *for* him, he says that had he not joined Mr Moore an offensive work might have appeared, but he told Moore that if such a work did appear there were persons who might reply in a manner that he Moore might not be aware of, and d—n Ld B——s character and those of his friends for ever.
    Such was Murray's conversation this morning with these opinions and remarks, if Mr Murray is to be believed, the forthcoming work is to exalt the genius of Ld B. & put him as a public character in as favorable a light as possible—his Murray's last words were '*his Moral* character you know *I can-not defend*'
    . . . Murray said that on speaking to Moore of the *memorable* Memoirs,

[1] 24 Feb. 1828: Lovelace Papers. It is not surprising that on the 21st, Moore, in his Memoirs, said he could scarcely get anything out of Fletcher but blustering. The servant, dependent on Mrs Leigh for his pension, was evidently echoing her tones.

that Moore owned they were of such a low *pot-house* description that he cd not have published them, nor cd he recollect a page if he was to try,—by which nice mess, he, Murray, continued, I am minus £10,000! I how he makes this out I know not, but he blames Wilmot Horton for most of it or I believe all.[1]

It was an extraordinary feat on Moore's part to produce out of all this timidity, opposition, interference, and faction, a biography which, if not among the greatest, is certainly among the most delightful, in our language. Of course, he had Byron to support him, the letters, five hundred and sixty-one of them, the great majority entirely new to the public, the journals and Detached Thoughts, so unpretentious yet so curiously evocative and persuasive, the verses and 'versicles' thrown off like sparks from an unquenchable fire—all these combined to make the book richer and livelier than any Life which had appeared since Boswell's Johnson.

But Moore himself rose to the occasion with tremendous verve. Though there are suppressions and tamperings, there are also frank and sometimes fearless disclosures, and a portrait emerges which has not been invalidated by the scores of new and searching lights that time has cast upon it. We are conscious that we are seeing the sitter at his best, yet there is no lack of realism. Faults are dealt with indulgently, but not ignored or dismissed with a pious platitude or two as was the widely accepted practice of the age. The absence of sanction from near relatives or any active aid from such close friends as Hobhouse and Kinnaird was a positive asset to the author, since it gave him a much freer hand than if he had been under the necessity of deferring to the sentiments and prejudices of obliging helpers.

Moore, though he had not the genius his contemporaries ascribed to him, was gifted with talents of a high order, and a subtlety of understanding which had raised him from what Leigh Hunt called 'the bogs of Clontarf' to a place of eminence among the wits, poets, and social *élite* of the British Isles. His judgments have the sagacity we would expect in a man who had so skilfully exploited his own personality; and his interpretations of Byron's responses to various kinds of experience are extremely sensitive. Even Hobhouse, who had begun to read in the most sceptical spirit, accorded a qualified admiration.

Although the need of a counterblast to Leigh Hunt had compelled Hobhouse to adopt a position of neutrality, his animosity to Moore had

[1] Ibid. 15 Mar. Moore's comments on the Memoirs are not in conformity with this version, either in his diary or his biography of Byron. He found 'coarse things' only in the second and much briefer portion. Murray must have been speaking very loosely, because if the work had been really unpublishable he had lost nothing and was lucky to have recouped his original expenditure.

been felt, if not displayed, on numerous occasions during the two years that elapsed between his surrender and the appearance of the first volume. One of his journal entries early in that period is:

> Kinnaird showed me a letter from Tom Moore in which he talked of the dignified silence of Lord Byron's friends, naming me, which he did not hesitate to call *faithlessness to the memory of their common friend*. Now this comes from the man who is always soliciting my kindness, and who wrote to me only a month ago saying he hoped I would receive him kindly. He supposes that these hard words go for nothing. Words do go for nothing with him. Kinnaird had refused to help Moore before I saw his letter.[1]

At another time he refers to Moore's coolness towards him whenever there was 'nothing to gain by caresses'.[2] It did not seem to cross his mind that his own attitude might have contributed something to Moore's.

> By the way I have seen Tom twice lately at Murray's and he was very cool indeed, and all for why? I have lent Murray my portrait of Byron by Saunders to be engraved for Tom's book. I prevented Mrs Leigh from publishing her brother's letters which would have hurt Tom's book . . . in short I have done him no injury—on the contrary much service—but then I did not contribute to his book, and besides he feels I know him—he is a poor creature.[3]

There was no pleasing him where Moore and his biography were concerned, and when Murray suggested that Byron's 'real friends' ought to be giving more material for it, he wrote ungraciously saying he looked on the whole enterprise as 'one of money and for money'.[4] When the book was on the verge of publication, he had a fleeting notion of stealing a march on Moore by printing a 'character' of Byron that he himself had written,[5] but 'dignified silence' prevailed and his admirable sketch did not see the light for many years.

When Volume I of the *Life, Letters, and Journals of Lord Byron* at last made its appearance, it assumed for several days a more important place in his diary than the political records which were gradually taking precedence of all other topics. At first his tone was contemptuous:

> This morning the Times announced that Moore's Byron was out and puffed it in the leading article. Jerdan of the Literary Gazette who was at the Club had read some of it and praised it, but disapproved some remarks on

---

[1] Hobhouse *Journals*, 29 Feb. 1828. Hobhouse had been making his views about assisting with biographies of Byron perfectly clear to Kinnaird for the past three years and more. He was greatly annoyed when Kinnaird allowed some of Byron's most innocuous letters to appear in the *Anniversary*, and said they did 'no credit to the writer or to the publisher'. (20th Nov. 1829.)   [2] Ibid. 7 June 1828.

[3] Ibid. 14 June 1829. The Sanders painting of Byron at the age of nineteen, standing beside a rowing boat with his page Rushton in the background, is now in the Royal Collection.   [4] Ibid. 18 Sept. 1829.

[5] Ibid. 31 Dec. 1829. Hobhouse's 'Character' may be read on pp. 503-4.

Byron's early scepticism on religious subjects—so do I—besides I doubt the
fact which is chiefly founded on the authority of that scoundrel old Dallas and
his more scoundrelly son.[1]

The following day, January 14th, 1830, he received the book as a gift
from Murray, and though at first his observations were in the same key,
there is a decided change as he progressively jots them down:

> I turn over some of the pages and see two or three inaccuracies at once—
> but am struck by the information collected as to Lord B's early days. I called
> on Murray and told him what Jerdan had said—aye replied Murray—'well,
> let Lady Julia read the book and hear her opinion." This I took to be a clever
> mode of letting me know the book is written for the women.

'I walked about', he added. He always walked about when his
emotions were disturbed, and this graphic picture of his friend's youth
stirred in him all sorts of old fondnesses, jealousies, angers, and griefs. It
stirred also that deep sense of proprietorship which made him half-
scornful of those who did not know the things he knew about Byron, and
half-alarmed in case they should. Next day he was again held fast by the
book.

> Reading Moore—he has managed with much adroitness to make such
> mention of me as I can hardly quarrel with even though the general result
> is rather unsatisfactory than otherwise—as to Byron's character, he has on
> the whole, portrayed it fairly. The most unjust of his conclusions is that B's
> singularities both in conduct and opinion are chiefly to be ascribed to college
> associates. Certainly B had nothing to learn in the way of depravity either of
> mind or body when he came from Harrow nor was his Southwell recreation
> such as Moore pretends them [sic] to have been. I have Byron's own word for
> his *innocent* amusements there.
> A great deal of stress is laid on the influence of Matthews (Charles) on
> Byron's opinions—I do not believe he had any—if he had that influence
> related more to practical debauchery than to metaphysical conjecture.
> Moore has dilated on B's unequal friendships such as for Ed[d]lestone and
> Rushton. He little knows the ground he treads.[2]

Once more Hobhouse walked about; and again the next day's entry
begins tersely 'Moore—walk'. The churlishness with which he expresses
himself not merely about Byron but also about the beloved lost companion
of his own youth, Charles Skinner Matthews, must have arisen from an
intricate entanglement of feelings. Perhaps the hand of the detested outsider Moore laid publicly on the two most sacred friendships of his life
seemed to sully them both and he had a mood of almost wanting to spurn
them. In his growing conventionality he took unnecessary umbrage too at
Moore's statement that Byron 'had not a single friend to whom he could

---

[1] Ibid. 13 Jan. 1830.   [2] Ibid. 15 Jan. 1830.

look up with respect' during his Cambridge days, though this appeared in a context where he had little right to resent it, an apology—somewhat savouring of cant—for the undergraduate's want of religious principles. (Hobhouse himself had been not less irreverent in those days.)

Then his agreeable certainty of his own omniscience on all matters relating to Byron must have been distressingly undermined. He had to admit that he and Hanson, who could remember his famous client as a ten-year-old child, were surprised at how much Moore had managed to find out.[1] This had the effect of setting him delving, as if for reassurance, in regions where he still believed himself to be the sole repository of know-ledge. Recklessly, he scattered over the wide, inviting margins of the splendid quarto[2] a series of remarks by which he sometimes seems to have been unconsciously getting his own back on his friend for having so often preferred Moore to himself, a fact which Moore had not scrupled to exemplify in several quoted letters.

For a man who despised indiscretion, those marginal comments are a strange performance. A diarist, even though he may believe Byron's dictum that 'everything written is written for the purpose of being read', will allow himself latitude because a journal is recognized as essentially a private document; but to hint, and more than hint, at secrets on the pages of two large printed volumes is an imprudence by any standards, and that Hobhouse did so is an evidence that he was shaken out of himself.

He began with a mere wanton desire to argue, to express his scorn for the author. In the brief Preface, Moore praises the 'vigour, variety, and liveliness' of Byron's letters, and ends by saying that in him 'the literary and the personal character were so closely interwoven, that to have left his works without the commentary which his Life and Correspondence afford, would have been equally an injustice to himself and to the world'. *'Which, however,' Hobhouse scribbled, 'T. M. would [not] have done if he had not wanted 3500 £.'*

Moore stated in his opening paragraph: 'In the character of the noble Poet, the pride of ancestry was undoubtedly one of the most decided features', on which Hobhouse remarks *'This may be true, but I never perceived it'*, an interesting rebuttal of an accepted idea—if it was not made in the spirit of contradiction. A few pages later, it is Byron whom he contradicts. Writing of 'the complication of only children' in his family —which was indeed a rarity in those days of unrestricted parenthood— he had declared that 'the fiercest animals have the fewest numbers in their litters'. *'There was nothing fierce in Ld. B'*, Hobhouse asserted, unmind-ful of certain furious lampoons and rages.

---

[1] Hobhouse *Journals*. 16 Jan.
[2] Formerly in the possession of the Hon. Sir Harold Nicolson.

The description of Byron's father as a profligate draws a far-fetched reproof: '*Moore seems to have forgotten that this unmanful (?) personality had a daughter living to read his character.*' But soon afterwards Moore's scepticism as to whether the 'wildness and grandeur' of Scottish mountain scenery really had much effect in awakening Byron's poetical talent is greeted with the approbation Hobhouse could never withhold from exposures of romantic and high-flown ideas: '*Extremely judicious observations*'.

By page 18 the story is beginning to interest him for its own sake. Dealing with Byron's love at eight years old for the little girl Mary Duff, Moore had a footnote about the early sensibilities of genius. To this Hobhouse supplied a note of his own which has the air of personal reminiscence: '*At a still earlier age —— felt the same passion—he was sitting on the knees of a very pretty woman and suddenly flung his arms round her neck. The lady started and the company laughed which so frightened the young lover that he burst into tears. Yet —— is not a genius.*'

And again, at the end of Byron's memorable description of this passionate affection: '*With respect to the early development of these propensities in Byron I am acquainted with a singular fact scarcely fit for narration but much less romantic and more satisfactory than the amour with Mary Duff.*' This was no doubt Byron's distasteful sexual initiation at the age of about nine by the Calvinist nurse whose devotion to the Bible did not prevent her being cruel and corrupt. Hobhouse had learned of that most injurious experience not from Byron but from Hanson,[1] and it shows a lack of sensibility in him that he should have supposed it 'satisfactory', for Byron never did. To him it was associated with the profound melancholy of having 'anticipated life'.[2]

Some of Hobhouse's comments were erroneous and some unreasonably contentious. Moore writes that the chance of succession to the title was at first uncertain, and Hobhouse jots down: '*At his birth there were six lives between him and the title.*' There were in fact only two, his father and his father's cousin, the grandson of the 5th lord who then held the title. Moore says that 'such an early elevation to rank would be but too likely to have a dangerous influence on his character', and Hobhouse retorts: '*This elevation to rank was not earlier nor more lofty than that of a thousand young heirs to titles*'—dissent apparently for the sake of dissenting. Peers of ten years old are at all times few and Moore was perfectly justified in assuming that succession so young might have been fraught with some peril for an unwisely brought-up boy. That Hobhouse

---

[1] Hobhouse *Journals*. The Notes headed 'Lord Byron'. Afraid or ashamed to confide in his mother, there had been no one for the boy to unburden himself to but the family solicitor.   [2] *L. & J.* 'Detached Thoughts.'

knew it to be so he showed there and then by his own anecdote about the event:

> Byron himself told me that he was sent for by the master of the school, who gave him some cake and wine and told him that his great-uncle was dead and he was now a lord. Byron added that the little treat and the respectful manner of the master gave him at once high notions of his own dignity.

Throughout his commentary Hobhouse displays a tendency to belittle all his friend's physical and mental accomplishments—which may explain why Moore inspired more affection.

'*I am confident Lord B. could not repeat twenty lines of poetry in any language,*' he says at one point.[1] Doubtless Hobhouse was not one of those with whom he let himself go 'spouting', in Medwin's word, the *Khubla Khan* and *Christabel*. When Moore cites Dr Drury, Byron's former headmaster at Harrow, as a witness of his pupil's early promise, Hobhouse counters: '*But Lord Byron did not leave Harrow or at least did not come to Cambridge with any reputation for superior attainments or extraordinary talents.*' Drury's praise for Byron's ready eloquence in declamation is put down with: '*He had nothing of this talent afterwards—his parliamentary speeches were written by himself or J. C. H.*'[2]

Moore touches on the addiction of various poets to sports and games and says Byron was 'pre-eminent in all sorts of exercises', to which Hobhouse rejoins: '*Not at all, except swimming*', and he notes in another place: '*A very bad horseman*'.

'*Certainly he had not read these books*', he snaps, when Moore speaks of the range of the poet's early reading; but his unwavering respect for Byron's veracity caused him, when he came to an actual list, to concede: '*As Lord Byron says he read these books I am inclined to believe the fact, but it is certain he never gave any sign of this knowledge afterwards.*'[3] Byron's letters, poems, and notes to poems are sprinkled everywhere with allusions which reveal an exceptionally catholic taste and memory, but culture was then measured by familiarity with the Greek and Latin classics, and ability to illustrate with correct quotations from antique authors, and by that criterion, Byron fell far short of Hobhouse.

[1] This is in flat contradiction to what he had stated in his review of Medwin's book about the accuracy of Byron's memory when quoting poetry.

[2] Byron only made three speeches in the House of Lords, and Hobhouse certainly over-estimated his own contribution to them.

[3] At nineteen years old, when he composed his list, he was less literal-minded than he became in maturity, and his claim to have read 'above four thousand novels' cannot be taken except in the sense indicated by the reviewer of the *Westminster* (Thomas Love Peacock), who wrote: 'Few young men at College, Mr Moore thinks, had read so much: we think so too: we may make large deductions from it and still think so. There is, however, a way of scouting through books, which some people call reading, and we are much afraid the reading here set down was of that description.'

Catherine Byron, mother of the poet, from a portrait by Thomas Stewardson

On another page we learn that he was 'totally ignorant of any question of politics'. His attempt to appear unshaken by the attack on his youthful poetry in the Edinburgh Review is shown up with: 'He was very near destroying himself.'

Often Hobhouse's argumentativeness made him incredulous on topics about which Moore was better-informed than he: for instance the recollection of a passage in the burned Memoirs recounting Byron's anguish on overhearing Mary Chaworth say to her maid: 'Do you think I could care anything for that lame boy?' Hobhouse's pencilled exclamation is: 'I do not believe this story.' But Moore had questioned Mrs Musters before writing it, and had her admission that she had probably said some such words—words so unpleasant that surely they would have been repudiated if that in honesty had been possible.

Again, at the beginning of the second volume,[1] Moore speaks of Byron's humiliation in 'betaking himself to an exile that had not even the dignity of appearing voluntary, as the excommunicating voice of society seemed to leave him no other resource'. Hobhouse's dogmatic assertion is: 'There was not the slightest necessity even in appearance for his going abroad.' If he had not been wilfully shutting off remembrance, he would have bethought him of the bailiff's distraining nine or ten times on Byron's possessions in a few months, his own precautions to save the very carriage in which he had driven with his friend to Dover, the party at Lady Jersey's where, great as her influence was, she had been unable to prevent many of the guests flocking from the room as Byron entered it, his sister on his arm—a débâcle it would have taken years to live down—the tirades in the Press, and the caricatures on sale in the print shops.

It is true Hobhouse did not suspect all the communications Lady Byron had made to sympathizers whose whisperings would never have subsided if they had continued to meet the culprit in society; nor had he the least vestige of an idea that Augusta had made a confidante of her sister-in-law, nor even that she had anything destructive to confide. When Moore wrote that the storm of invective raised around Byron over the Separation was 'utterly out of proportion with his offences', Hobhouse's marginal protest was: 'What offences?'

He was irritated by Moore's obsequious tone towards Lady Byron; and beside a paragraph conveying some regret because Byron had not had the fortitude to refrain entirely from touching her fortune, he broke out: 'It would have been absurd as he had given all his fortune to her.' (He had assisted with drawing up the Marriage Settlement, and advised Byron against acceding to the large demands then made on him.)

---

[1] The second volume did not come out till a year after the first, but for the sake of continuity the whole work is dealt with here.

There was a piece of sycophancy which must have annoyed all the poet's friends. During his last days with Moore in Venice, 1819, he had expressed a belief that his wife felt 'a fixed hostility' towards him which would not rest, he thought, even when he was in his grave, and he had begged Moore 'not to let unmerited censure settle upon his name, but, while I surrendered him up to condemnation where he deserved it, to vindicate him where aspersed'. As Lady Byron's papers have since disclosed, his forebodings were, of course, perfectly right, and it is a pity he was not equally prescient in regard to the man to whom he was entrusting his Memoirs. Moore, however, whether sincerely or to ingratiate himself, affirmed that his apprehensions were 'groundless and wrongful'.

> . . . By none, I am inclined to think, would a generous amnesty over his grave be more readily and cordially concurred in than by her, among whose numerous virtues a forgiving charity towards himself was the only one to which she had not yet taught him to render justice.

'*False and base*', Hobhouse proclaimed with, for once, much greater percipience than the pliable biographer. How false it was, if not how base, Moore was very soon to learn.

From time to time his characteristic vanity goaded Hobhouse to exhibit his equally characteristic jealousy. Moore's parade of compliments paid to himself by Byron stimulated several sardonic reflections, and when, very tactlessly, 'the young pilgrim' was depicted suffering from a 'total want of friends and connections' before the publication of *Childe Harold*, Hobhouse jeered: '*In fact he had no friend till he knew Tom Moore.*' The introduction of some flattering remarks from one of Moore's own early letters to Byron[1] provoked a quite childish explosion of palpably jealous anger: '*This shows the sort of intercourse which Moore and Byron kept up. "What a commerce was yours when you got and you gave."*'

But despite the all too evident combativeness the reading induced in him, there were moments when he drew an approving line beside some judgment of Moore's and moments, better still, when he forgot about Moore altogether. '*He was fond of singing*', he recalled, at the description (obtained from Mary Shelley) of Byron's voice sounding over the lake at Sécheron; or, against one of the protesting and agitated letters:[2] '*This shows the way in his anger he would say any thing to anyone.*' Or '*Excellent!*' '*True!*' '*Admirable!*' '*Quite right!*' beside apt self-analyses of

---

[1] 'Though I have not written, I have seldom ceased to think of you; for you are that sort of being whom everything, high or low, brings into mind. Whether I am with the wise or the waggish, among poets or among pugilists, over the book or over the bottle, you are sure to connect yourself transcendently with all, and come "armed for *every* field" in my memory.' No date.

[2] 20 Jan. 1821—to John Murray in connection with the performance, against his wishes, of his first tragedy.

Byron's addressed to various correspondents, who had been getting, as he gradually began to see, no such 'sad trash' after all.

'*This is the man*', he wrote delightedly when Moore quoted: '. . . My turn of mind is so given to taking things in the absurd point of view, that it breaks out in spite of me every now and then.' Against Byron's claim '. . . My first object is truth even at my own expense', he put '*Very true*' —a valuable tribute where the general spirit is so far from laudatory. And at one of Byron's denials of being anything like the Byronic legend,[1] '*See the sense and truth of this. It is the man himself.*'

As he approached the end of the second volume there were more reminiscences than criticisms, until at last, in the final pages, he read for the first time a reverie from the little journal Byron kept at Ravenna:

> It is singular how soon we lose the impression of what ceases to be *constantly* before us; a year impairs; a lustre obliterates. There is little distinct left without an effort of memory. *Then*, indeed, the lights are rekindled for a moment. . . .
>
> Let any man try at the end of *ten* years to bring before him the features, or the mind, or the sayings, or the habits, of his best friend. . . .

For Hobhouse the lights were rekindled. '*Of all the peculiarities of Byron his laugh is that of which I have the most distinct recollection.*'

---

[1] 5 July 1821—to Moore, regretting that he had probably been a disappointment to a young American visitor: '. . . I suspect that he did not take quite so much to me, from his having expected to meet a misanthropical gentleman, in wolf-skin breeches, and answering in fierce monosyllables, instead of a man of this world. I can never get people to understand that poetry is the expression of *excited passion*, and that there is no such thing as a life of passion any more than a continuous earthquake, or an eternal fever. Besides, who would ever *shave* themselves in such a state?'

A spurious extract from the Memoirs

The salacious wedding night chapter is the unpleasant apex of the anti-Byron campaign conducted by Theodore Hook in *John Bull* and the short-lived *John Bull Magazine* issued under his editorship. This campaign was sustained with extraordinary virulence and had a political motive, Hook's vehemently Tory paper having been launched originally to combat the enthusiasm for Queen Caroline at the time when the King was endeavouring to divorce and discredit her. The Whigs and Radicals, being supporters of the Queen, were all objects of perpetual abuse by Hook; and Byron inspired a ferocious animosity, which persisted after his death and manifested itself in passages of jocular scurrility about his funeral, his embalmed remains, and the loyalty of his friends.

If Hobhouse had stayed to read the 'chapter' in question, he must at once have recognized it as a forgery without the benefit of any copying facilities. The style was not remotely like Byron's and the pretended Memoirist refers to his bride either as Miss Noel or Anne. She was, of course, Miss Milbanke and Byron called her Bell. (The forger was unaware that the bride's parents had not assumed the name of Noel until several months after the wedding.)

A broad hint was thrown out that the 'copy' emanated from either Lady Caroline Lamb or Lady Burghersh, but although there is here and there a touch suggesting that Hook had heard snatches of gossip from one or two who had actually read the Memoirs, he was wildly out about all the circumstances of the marriage, as the following sample will show:

> It was now near two o'clock in the morning, and I was jaded to the soul by the delay. I had left the company and retired to a private apartment. Will those, who think that a bridegroom on his bridal night should be so thoroughly saturated with love, as to render it impossible to yield to any other feeling, pardon me when I say, that I had almost fallen asleep on a sofa when a giggling, tittering, half-blushing face popped itself in at the door, and popped as fast back again, after having whispered as audibly as a *suivante* whispers upon the stage, that Anne was in bed. It was one of her bridesmaids.
>
> Yet such is the case. I was actually dozing. Matrimony soon begins to operate narcotically—had it been a mistress—had it been an assignation with any animal covered with a petticoat—any thing but a wife—why, perhaps the case would have been different.
>
> I found my way, however, at once into the bedroom, and tore off my garments. Your pious zeal will, I am sure, be quite shocked when I tell you I did not say my prayers that evening—morning I mean. It was, I own, very wrong in me, who had been educated in the pious, praying kingdom of Scotland, and must confess myself—you need not smile—at least half a Presbyterian.

There were no bridesmaids at the wedding and no company at Halnaby when the young couple arrived there attended only by servants on a freezing winter day. According to the real Memoirs, the marriage was consummated on a sofa 'before dinner'. Moore told Hobhouse that this was the only objectionable disclosure in the first part of the manuscript, and Hobhouse was shocked beyond words by his having shown it to Lady Burghersh and others.[1]

Influenced no doubt by the description of Lady Byron as 'serenely purest of her sex', Hook depicted her as shrinking under the embraces of a satyr-like husband; and having written as obnoxious a piece as he could get into print, he used it as a means of rebuking Byron's low morals, running a copious correspondence on his depravity. It was very widely believed to be genuine. Lady Holland must have been referring to this forgery when, a week or two after its publication, she wrote to her son: 'I forget whether you read his own account of the marriage. I send you the vile thing.'[2] (On several occasions she gives evidence of a very vague memory, and perhaps she had only skimmed over the parts of the real Memoirs that did not concern herself and her circle.)

[1] Hobhouse *Journals*, 15 May 1824. See p. 28.
[2] ILCHESTER, *Elizabeth, Lady Holland*, 16 July 1824.

APPENDIX 2

Byron and the Melbourne correspondence

Byron wrote to John Murray on September 28th, 1821:

> I add another cover to request you to ask Moore to obtain (if possible) my letters to the late Lady Melbourne from Lady Cowper. They are very numerous, and ought to have been restored long ago, as I was ready to give back Lady M[elbourne]'s in exchange: these latter are in Mr Hobhouse's custody with my other papers, and shall be punctually restored if required. I did not choose before to apply to Lady Cowper, as her mother's death naturally kept me from intruding upon her feelings at the time of its occurrence. Some years have now elapsed, and it is essential that I should have my own epistles. They are essential as confirming that part of the 'Memoranda' which refer to the two periods (1812 and 1814) when my marriage with her niece was in contemplation, and will tend to show what my real views and feelings were upon that subject. . . .[1]

He was unaware that, on April 7th, 1818, the day after Lady Melbourne's death, and weeks before he himself, in Italy, heard of it, Hobhouse had made a very blunt and tactless application to Lady Cowper (Lady Melbourne's daughter) for the letters. The Hon. Mrs George Lamb wrote of it to Lady Byron saying that it was an unfeeling demand with 'no expression of sorrow or kindness to the family—I always had the worst possible opinion of that man but I can believe they are all in a great fright; I do not know that she kept any, indeed the probability is that they were all burnt.'[2]

They were, of course, preserved and given to Hobhouse after Byron's death, and were published in full in 1922. After his first headlong request, Hobhouse was content to wait substantially more than six years for the letters, and initially consented to let Moore have the use of them for his biography, so the theory of his 'fright' (or Byron's) does not hold good.

His seemingly officious intervention was due to an urgent letter from Augusta Leigh:

Monday 4 o'clock [6th April 1818]

Dear Mr H.

> You will think me the plague of yr life—but I can't help it —Since we met this morng, & having a visit to make at Whitehall I call'd at Lady Melbourne's door to enquire after her & really was quite shocked to hear she was *dead*! Now—B's message to you was, that *in case of such an event he desired you would apply to her Son George*, [the Hon. George Lamb] for *his* B's letters to Ly M—which contain what he does not wish Ly C. L. '*to lay her paws upon*'—this is the *substance* & as near as I can recollect the *words* of his message & I think it right to lose no time in

[1] L. & J.   [2] 8 Apr. 1818: Lovelace Papers.

giving it to you—as there are many hints besides of *her having been his confidante & 'acquainted with all his intricasies'* [sic.]

Pray let me hear you receive this & let me see you when convenient.

Ever yrs

Augusta Leigh [1]

It is odd that Byron was content to deal with so important a secret by a message to Hobhouse through a third party, and of all people, Augusta, from whom it might be thought he would be determined to conceal these letters, and odder still that, not obtaining them, he dropped the matter for three and a half years.

The Melbourne correspondence contains the only documentary evidence—or what has been accepted as such—that exists (if we exclude Lady Byron's 'Minutes' of what Lady Caroline Lamb told her) that Augusta Leigh's third daughter, Elizabeth Medora Leigh, was Byron's own child. His apparent willingness to submit such a revelation to the scrutiny of his future biographer deserves more consideration than it has been given. Byron always believed he would die young; he was most anxious to make provision for Augusta and her children, and it is not to be supposed that it was a matter of indifference to him whether, once he was dead, ruin and disgrace befell them. To the end of his life she had his profoundest affection, and the remorse which not seldom haunted him may be traced more to his sense of having cast a shadow over her than to his sorrow for having wronged his wife.

There seem to be only two possible explanations of his paying so little heed to the inferences that Moore or any other intelligent person would draw from the Melbourne letters. The first is that he had forgotten the secret they disclosed—which may well be thought a most unlikely lapse on the part of a young man with a phenomenally good memory writing only a few years after events vital to his life story. To have been on terms of such singular and astonishing confidence with the mother-in-law of Lady Caroline Lamb and the aunt of Miss Milbanke was hardly the kind of thing that would slip from his mind. His willingness to let Lady Cowper have Lady Melbourne's letters to him—which was duly done— is also surprising: for they contained, according to Lady Byron's remembrance, such admonitions as the one which told him he was on the brink of committing crime 'for which there is no salvation in this world whatever there may be in the next'.[2]

The second explanation is that the famous lines of April 25th, 1814, 'Oh! but it is "worth while", I can't tell you why, and it is *not* an "*Ape*",

---

[1] Murray MSS.

[2] Statement headed 'Reasons—' March 1816: Lovelace Papers. There is no record of this often-quoted letter except Lady Byron's memory.

and if it is that must be my fault' are not what they seem. Written ten days after the birth of Elizabeth Medora, they have been thought to refer to some medieval superstition that the child of incest would be a monster. They could conceivably, however, bear other interpretations. Even though there was no question of his being the father, Lady Melbourne might have warned him, in the not too solemn tone she always used with him, that his obsession with his sister might have an evil influence on the child. (It was an epoch when the appearance and character of an unborn child were believed to be affected in the most drastic manner by anything untoward that happened to the expectant mother.)

It would be hard to dispute that he was carried away by ardent though intermittent passion for Augusta, but there is little except this one letter, Lady Caroline's report, and Lady Byron's retrospective suspicions, to sustain the hypothesis that Augusta bore a child by him.

This is not to say that his relations with her were innocent but merely that his 'confessions' did not include the paternity of one of her children. As for the rest of the allusions to Augusta, he may have thought them too cryptic ever to yield up their secret.

The 1st Earl of Lovelace, Lady Byron's son-in-law and at one time close confidant, came to disbelieve the Medora story emphatically, and he was much nearer to the events than the 2nd earl, having at one time been quite embroiled in them. His son, the author of *Astarte*, seemed to think Lady Byron was proving her case merely by writing to Augusta accusing her of having had a child incestuously, and this at a time (1841) when she had involved the daughter, Medora, in litigation against her mother. But an accusation without opportunity of defence for the accused means little, and Lady Byron returned unopened the letter in which Augusta tried to reply.

CHAPTER IX

LADY BYRON'S 'REMARKS'

For all his general perceptiveness, there was a vein of fatuity in Moore which allowed him to believe every compliment that was paid to him. His journal sometimes becomes little more than a register of the effect of his singing upon drawing-room audiences (it must have had extraordinary charm, for once even Hobhouse was delighted) and all the fine things he heard about his literary works.

On February 2nd, 1830, soon after the first volume of his Life of Byron came out, and while the second was in the press, he had a conversation with John Murray and John Croker about 'the letter Davison, the printer, had from Bland, Lady Byron's solicitor, in which he says that Lady Byron was highly pleased with the "Life"'.[1] Even Moore must have found this difficult to swallow, and he goes on, 'Murray assured me that Bland is not the man to have said this, unless he had good grounds'.

Within the next few weeks, they were abruptly disillusioned. Lady Byron had issued, and was circulating privately but on a very considerable scale, a pamphlet which expressed the reverse of admiration for the book. It began with the contemptuous words:

> I have disregarded various publications in which facts within my own knowledge have been grossly misrepresented; but I am called upon to notice some of the erroneous statements proceeding from one who claims to be considered as Lord Byron's confidential and authorized friend. Domestic details ought not to be intruded on the public attention; if, however, they *are* so intruded, the persons affected by them have a right to refute injurious charges. Mr Moore has promulgated his own impressions of private events in which I was most nearly concerned, as if he possessed a competent knowledge of the subject.

Disclaiming any spirit of self-vindication or accusation, professing extreme reluctance to advert to her marriage, she declared that the conduct of her parents had been 'brought forward in a disgraceful light, by the passages selected from Lord Byron's letters, and by the remarks of his biographer', and that she felt bound to defend their characters from false imputations. Byron had said and Moore had let his readers believe that her mother had exercised undue influence upon her, and that Mrs Clermont had played the part of a domestic spy.

She set about a denial of both aspersions, and in doing so, found it necessary to make unmistakable references to Augusta. Explaining

---

[1] MOORE, *Memoirs*. John Davison Bland was a trustee of part of Lady Byron's fortune.

how she had left Byron in the belief that he was insane, she pointed out that—

> This opinion was derived, in a great measure, from the communications made to me by his nearest relatives and personal attendant, who had more opportunities than myself of observing him during the latter part of my stay in town.

Byron as an adult was not rich in relatives: none had been near him at the time of the Separation but his half-sister and his cousin George Byron. To make certain of being understood, she added in italics: '*With the concurrence of his family*, I consulted Dr. Baillie. . . .' Not till she was persuaded by the result of the enquiries that the notion of insanity was an error, had she authorized measures to secure herself against ever being in his power again; and to support these various assertions she printed a very recent letter from Dr Lushington (January 31st, 1830), saying that, whereas when he was visited by Lady Byron's mother alone, he had not deemed Byron's offences of such an 'aggravated' nature as to make a separation indispensable—

> When you came to town in about a fortnight, or perhaps more, after my first interview with Lady Noel, I was, for the first time, informed by you of facts utterly unknown, I have no doubt, to Sir Ralph and Lady Noel. On receiving this additional information, my opinion was entirely changed: I considered a reconciliation impossible. I declared my opinion, and added, that if such an idea should be entertained, I could not, either professionally or otherwise, take any part towards effecting it.

The pamphlet ended with some regrets from its author for being compelled to break the silence she had always hoped to observe and an appeal to the readers of Lord Byron's Life to give impartial consideration to the testimony which was 'extorted' from her.

Dr Lushington's statement, it may now be said, was based on lapse of memory. During the period when Lady Noel was consulting Sir Samuel Romilly and himself, she had written home daily accounts of their colloquies. From these and other letters of hers it is apparent that, on the information he had been given, he never for a moment considered a reconciliation possible, but, on the contrary, had confirmed Lady Noel's unswerving view that it was out of the question.

Furthermore, he was mistaken in supposing that Lady Byron's parents had been in the dark about anything whatever. Though she had not at first told them her doubts about her sister-in-law, but, on the contrary, had written that Augusta had 'ever been the truest of friends' to her,[1]

---

[1] 'I very much fear that She may be supposed the cause of the separation by many, and it would be a cruel injustice.' 25 Jan. 1816: Lovelace Papers.

she thought better of this *before* her initial consultation with Lushington
on February 23rd, 1816.[1] The whole remainder of her case—such as she
believed it to be—had been opened to them at an earlier stage. So many
horrifying complaints had she let fall against Byron that she herself had
felt obliged to withdraw a few of them.[2]

Whether in 1816 Dr Lushington had been more appalled by the suspected incest or the suspected homosexual adventures—both suspicions
confirmed to his and Lady Byron's satisfaction by Lady Caroline Lamb—
in 1830 the second offence had receded into a shadowy background.
Augusta had become all that was needed in the way of a culprit.

It is so much easier to blame a woman than a vague 'propensity'. And
Augusta in middle age, tense with insecurity, her laughter extinguished,
her letters perpetually filled with lamentations, had become a trial even
to those who were well disposed to her. Shortly before the appearance of
Moore's book, the façade of Lady Byron's good-will had crumbled.

Since the production of the pamphlet was closely connected with this
loss of favour, a brief account of the estrangement—which was absolute—
must be given.

Towards the end of 1829, there had been an imbroglio about a mortgage, in which Augusta considered that Douglas Kinnaird had behaved
without regard for her pressing needs. (She was very prone nowadays to
become aggrieved.) He was one of the trustees of her inheritance from
Byron, and, after enduring much from her muddle-headedness and im-
providence, he suddenly decided to resign his office. Being mortally ill,
he could no longer struggle with her vagaries.

On the strength of representations made to her on Augusta's behalf,
Lady Byron wrote to Lushington saying that Kinnaird had been 'guilty of
the greatest misconduct', and had resigned in case the business should
'come to light', and she cast grave reflections on his honour.[3] As usual,
she was too harsh in her judgment of one of Byron's 'Piccadilly crew'.
Kinnaird's probity in money matters was so unquestionable that, on
an occasion when he wished to raise £50,000 from five friends in an

[1] 'I have been *perfectly* confidential with Dr Lushington who was far from thinking
that the suspicions are any good to me—but deprecates beyond anything the slightest
intimation of them as having the appearance of Malice—and altogether most injurious
to *me* in a social view—. . . Dr Lushington *insists* upon your writing in a kind manner to
Mrs Leigh as being most essential to my justification *whatever she may turn out*—and that
she should be spoken of by us in a friendly manner. . . . At the same time precaution will
be used against her weakness.' 23 Feb. 1816. Ibid.

[2] E.g. 'A spirit of animosity on my part cannot tend to my justification— The
temperate are always believed. . . . I wish very much to have altered part of my Statement. . . . That "unintermitting principle of Revenge" was not a justifiable assertion. . . .
Nor can I think there has been any *design* or *cunning* in the business—far too much
incoherency.' Letter to Lady Noel, 22 Jan. 1822. Ibid.

[3] 28 Nov. 1829: Lovelace Papers.

emergency, he had not the slightest difficulty in rallying Hobhouse, Burdett, and others instantly to his aid.[1]

He was an exceedingly chivalrous man, but hot-tempered and suffering from the pain of cancer. Doubtless Augusta had annoyed him, according to her usual blundering manner, by appointing strangers to deal with the mortgage; but when Hobhouse taxed him with abandoning her, he wrote back, offering to see him at his own hour:

> . . . I am very anxious to make you at least accurately acquainted with what my conduct and feelings have been throughout this extraordinary business. It will be a great weight off my mind—and I hope I need not assure you that I should consider it one of the greatest misfortunes of my life that you should feel a difficulty in justifying any part of my conduct towards Mrs Leigh. . . .[2]

And again:

> I have never had an angry word with her in my life—and I am quite ready to call upon her—for God knows I only *pity* her and have no resentment against her for being a dupe. It has occurr'd to me you might have the means of giving me, from your intercourse with her, a hint how to act. Should I leave a card?[3]

In January 1830 Kinnaird's illness grew acute and he was known to be dying, so it is improbable that he ever saw her again. On March 12th Hobhouse called at Ransom's Bank and found that he had lost one more dear friend:—'Vernon—Matthews—Byron—Kinnaird—all are gone—there seems a fatality attending my friendships.'[4]

Whoever was in the wrong (and Hobhouse attributed much of the trouble to Kinnaird's 'intemperate language')[5] the appointment of a new trustee was thus inevitable. Byron's fortune, which Kinnaird had administered jointly with Bland, was apportioned, it may be remembered, as follows:—£16,000 settled upon Ada; £60,000 settled upon Lady Byron during her lifetime[6]—the income of which was, however, paid by her desire to the 7th Lord Byron; the remainder, to the extent of about £25,000, Augusta's own property but tied up so that the capital would descend to her children.

Until this time, one of the trustees had stood in friendly relation to Augusta, the other to Lady Byron: but now it was arranged that Kinnaird should be replaced by Lushington. This to Augusta was a most painful decision. Though she had never guessed at her 'dearest A's' willingness at one time to 'proceed against her personally', nor dreamed of all that

---

[1] 17/19 Dec. 1825. Hobhouse *Journals*.
[2] Undated letter, end of Nov. 1829. British Museum. MSS. acquired in 1950.
[3] Ibid. 7 Dec. 1829.   [4] Hobhouse *Journals*.   [5] Ibid. 22 Nov. 1829.
[6] See p. 128.

Lushington and his wife, a very close friend of Annabella's, had heard to her detriment, she could not have forgotten that he was the lawyer who had acted against her brother; and, as he had the lowest possible opinion of her, it is not likely that he had been very gracious when, on at least one occasion, they had come face to face.[1] With financial exigencies so far from normal—her husband constantly threatened with arrest for debt, her married daughter and son-in-law falling back on her for support—the trustee would require a tolerance and sympathy emphatically not to be found in the new nominee.

On November 28th, 1829, she had the courage to make a protest:

My dearest A——
    I do not like to detain your servant, and was unable to answer your letter the moment I received it. As regards your nomination of Dr. L. as trustee, I have to observe that he is a perfect stranger to me; that in a matter where my own individual interests are concerned it is of the highest importance to my comfort that I should be on terms of friendly intercourse and even intimacy with the Party; and that possessessed as you are already of a Protector to your interests in the person of Mr Bland, I had not thought it unreasonable to hope that you would allow me a similar advantage in the appointment of some individual personally known to me, and in whom I could confide entirely.
    Had I been consulted I should naturally have preferred a friend of my own, but as you have not considered that step necessary, I hope I may be permitted to request that in any event Mr Capron may be named as solicitor to the trust for my Protection, as with him I can communicate on all occasions. . . .
                    Ever yours affectionately,
                                    A. L.
Sunday Morning. P.S.—Under all the circumstances I have stated, I cannot help thinking that Dr Lushington himself would not wish to accept the Trust, and I hope it is not asking too much to request you to put him in possession of this letter before anything is finally concluded.[2]

Everything had already been concluded before Lady Byron had sent her servant with the announcement, and on Dr Lushington's own advice. She had, in fact, written to him saying that Mrs Leigh's nominee was Colonel Henry Wyndham, and that perhaps it was not to be expected that *both* trustees should be friends of her own, but asking what he thought about it. His reply was a rejection out of hand of the idea that Augusta had the smallest say in the matter, and the immediate acceptance of the nomination.

The news that the decision was unalterable was broken not by Lady Byron but her solicitors, Messrs Wharton and Ford. Augusta now became

---

[1] Bathurst Statement. Lovelace Papers.
[2] LOVELACE, *Lady Noel Byron*. Capron was the solicitor dealing with the mortgage business which had so much annoyed Kinnaird.

speechlessly indignant. Annabella waited some days, then not receiving any such submissive letter as was customary, she herself wrote in the strain of a kind governess addressing a sulky child:

> Am I to conclude from your silence that reflection has not yet made you sensible of all the consideration which has been shown for your interests?—or am I rather to suppose that your mind is preoccupied by "the distracting state of affairs" to which you alluded?
> If so, can my advice or sympathy afford you any comfort—for I am,
> Your faithful friend
> AINB[1]

Augusta now broke her silence, but only to give vent bluntly to what she called the honest expression of her wounded feelings.

> I will not be so unjust to myself as to affect an acknowledgment with reference to late events which I cannot feel.—on that subject I *never can have but one opinion*—and no future advantage I may ever derive from the late nomination can compensate to me for the appointment itself—the manner of communicating it—or the misery harassment and vexation which all the measures connected with it have occasioned.[2]

What Dr Lushington thought of this—for it was of course at once forwarded to him—may be gathered from his comments to Lady Byron:

> . . . Frankly speaking, no one but the most ignorant or most selfish of our species could entertain such feelings—and to this is to be added the base ingratitude to yourself who have shown every disposition to aid and assist her wishes to your own great trouble and annoyance.
> A Trustee of Mrs Leigh's nomination might injure you and Ada for her advantage. A Trustee of your selection could not injure Mrs Leigh for your interest. . . .
> You have already extended your forgiveness to Mrs Leigh to so un-paralleled an extent that I must in candor say that all she can feel write or say in this transaction is comparatively of no moment. Any personal contact with her is I think a degradation to you and I shall think if her ingratitude to you on this occasion be the means of preventing it in future, all the anxiety you have had will be well repaid by the cessation of such intercourse.[3]

Lady Byron, half-resolving to accept the counsel implied, sought sympathy from Mrs Wilmot Horton:

> I have had a good deal to annoy me lately. Think of Mrs Leigh's having, after all my endeavours to serve her, accused me of the most unfriendly conduct! . . . She cannot, I think, believe what she says, after all the reason she has had to know how sacred I have held the promise to be 'kind still to

---

[1] Lady Byron's copy. Undated, about 10 Dec. 1829: Lovelace Papers.
[2] Ibid. 12 Dec. Quoted by Lady Byron in a later letter.
[3] LOVELACE, *Lady Noel Byron*. 14 Dec. 1829.

Augusta.' I grieve that she deprives me of opportunities of *acting* up to it in future. It is impossible for me to admit of personal intercourse with her after such wilful misconstructions.[1]

On January 13th, 1830, she wrote Augusta a sternly reproachful note saying that only one painful course was open to her to avoid future occasions of 'injurious misconstruction', but leaving the door a little ajar by undertaking to send accounts of Ada's health 'when desired'.[2] Augusta replied on January 15th with none of that humility which would have placated her co-heiress. Instead she gave utterance to some angry surmise that Lushington had made a prior agreement with Kinnaird to take over the trusteeship. She had grown quite intransigent and plainly something drastic was needed to bring her back to the sense of her real situation.

Meanwhile Moore's book had been issued and, though its references to Byron's wife were few and respectful to a degree which made Hobhouse's gorge rise, there was a suggestion in it that Byron had not deserved all the abuse heaped upon him through the collapse of his marriage, and that 'the charitable influence of time' was already softening those harsh judgments. If ever Hobhouse had a moment of almost preternatural insight, it was when he arrived at the verdict that, though Lady Byron was capable of generosity towards her offending husband, it was only when he was completely out of favour with everyone else: that she could not allow the slightest risk of a shade of blame falling upon herself and seemed 'to be angry that he had any chance of being forgiven by the world'.[3] Not only did Moore prophesy the world's forgiveness but he mentioned her 'last words of playful affection' and Byron's own high praise of her as a proof that—

> . . . At the time of their parting, there could not have been any very deep sense of injury on either side. It was not till afterwards that . . . to the party which had taken the first decisive step in the strife, it became naturally a point of pride to persevere in it with dignity.

The 'last words' were the genial letter she had written Byron *en route* to her parents' house, and the positively facetious one beginning 'Dearest Duck' and signed 'Pippin . . . Pip . . . Ip' dispatched on her arrival. This lively communication, with its joke about the W.C., the '*sitting*-room and *sulking*-room' he would have all to himself if he joined the family party, had been a source of the greatest anxiety to her ever since it had left her hands, because she knew it had gone much further than was needful to fulfil Dr Baillie's instruction that, while her husband's sanity was being investigated, she should 'avoid all but light and soothing topics'. It was in a style that could not but mislead, and, being one of the points on which

---

[1] Ibid. 30 Dec.   [2] Lovelace Papers.   [3] See p. 144.

she felt herself open to criticism, she was touchily defensive about it.[1] The influence ascribed by Byron to his mother-in-law was another such point. None could be better aware than Annabella, with bundles of corresponding dence in her possession, that she had placed herself in her mother's hands and allowed her and Mrs Clermont a perfect latitude to do exactly as they thought best for her.[2] Mrs Clermont too was a source of discomfort, having been employed exactly as Byron supposed.

In short, like most people who take up weapons, her object was to defend herself not where she felt strong but where she inwardly knew her case to be weak. But though the paper she wrote was ostensibly a vindication of her parents, no one with any inkling of the inside story could doubt that it also amounted to a veiled attack upon Augusta. The 'additional information' she had imparted to Dr Lushington at that first interview was indeed nothing but the charge involving Augusta. That there had ever been another charge was a fact unknown to any but the inner circle of her confidants, and even they had tended to let it lapse in favour of a scandal more rewarding to eyes and ears alert for symptoms of guilt. The odious Turks were very far away, but Augusta was to be seen frequently in London society.

To publish Dr Lushington's letter touching upon a secret reason why reconciliation had been impossible must inevitably be a reminder to everyone who was in the know, and a confirmation to those who had only heard rumours, of Mrs Leigh's wickedness. It is very doubtful whether Lady Byron would have struck this blow at her erstwhile 'truest friend' if she had had an early apology from Augusta for her outburst, with proper acknowledgments for 'all the consideration' she had shown. No such gesture being made, she devoted herself to the composition of her paper, and began to canvass the members of her consultative council: but the course she followed indicates that she had no notion of taking their advice unless it was in accord with her wishes.

The first to be approached was Dr Lushington who did not like the prospect of her going so far as to publish anything, but was swiftly overruled. The second was Sir Francis Doyle, now a baronet, who with his sister Selina had been unreservedly in her confidence from the beginning, even seeing by her request the letters she had written to her mother when

---

[1] She had confessed to Mrs Clermont: 'My agony is about that second letter—of Jan. 16. I must have been mad to write so—for it contained an expression of regret to be away from him—and compromised my parents by the mention of kind wishes on their part towards him—But I was distracted between Law and Medecine [*sic*]. . . . However what can it appear but a proof of my tenderness—? though by the bye it may seem like hypocrisy in conjunction with subsequent proceedings.' 21 Jan. 1816: Lovelace Papers.

[2] 'Take care of me amongst you in this most difficult & delicate case—I would willingly resign my judgement into anybody's hands, and be found non compos myself'. To Lady Noel, 21 Jan. 1816. Ibid.

legal proceedings had first been in question. He told her that he thought Moore's book did not call for an answer of any kind from her, and that she would be reviving the whole controversy by publishing her statement.

> However natural and just your feelings on the subject, I do not think the observations respecting your parents contained in the passages you have noted would now justify a disclosure of the facts which at the time . . . you thought it right to conceal. I have some kind of an impression that there was an understanding that upon one contingency only, namely, the taking from you of your child and placing her under the care of a particular individual— would that disclosure be made. . . . It rests on my mind that there was something like a voluntary engagement to that effect. . . .
> Precisely the same sort of attacks on your parents, though stronger, were made at the time of your separation. . . . I do not think that the reproduction of these insinuations on the present occasion, in the manner in which Mr Moore has introduced them into his book, is a sufficient ground for your employment of that full defence of yourself to which you would not then resort—or for the publication of facts now Lord Byron is dead—which you declined to bring forward when he was living.

He referred to Ada and said it would be agonizing for her to have such matters brought to her knowledge, and, moreover, that he was convinced the world would never understand the magnanimous reasons which had permitted the continuance of affectionate intercourse with 'the person to whom these matters relate'.

> Nothing but a case of paramount necessity could justify your now removing the veil. . . . Certainly not, I think, the passages, however painful to your feelings, which you have noticed. . . . I am convinced that you ought to take no notice whatever of the book. . . .
> I offer this advice and opinion, dear Lady Byron, with the most anxious solicitude for your happiness and that of your daughter.

Finally, he pointed out in a very sensible manner that Byron's reference to 'my mother-in-law—or rather *at* law' was not a serious innuendo but 'a flippant quibble merely'.[1]

A day or two later came Robert Wilmot Horton's letter agreeing, somewhat reluctantly, that she should abide by Dr Lushington's opinion (of which he seems to have been given a misleading impression) but adding:

> I advise you *very strongly* to let A. L. have a copy of your Manuscript, or at least to inform her, or have her informed, of *its cause*, nature, and *tendency* —before it is actually published. It is, I think, desirable that she should know she is not directly *alluded* to, and only *indirectly* as one of the 'nearest *relations*' who suggested doubts as to *his* sanity. . . .

---

[1] LOVELACE, *Lady Noel Byron*. 7 Feb. 1830. This mother-at-law joke must have been in one of the sentences he specifically asked her to cut out. It does not appear in the publication.

I think also that she should be told that this Publication leaves the cause of the separation as doubtful as ever. . . .

You will perhaps say—*what* is the use of informing her?—Will she not form the same conclusions, when she reads it in print?

She ought to do so, but as she does not appear to be *too much* under the influence of sound judgment—she *may* construe it into an overt act against herself.[1]

Lady Byron took no notice of Sir Francis Doyle's endeavours to restrain her, nor did she show the manuscript to Mrs Leigh as recommended by Wilmot Horton. She issued it in pamphlet form and through two firms of printers simultaneously.[2] As she planned to have it read by everybody whose opinion was of consequence to her from George IV downwards, and yet to send out each copy as a private document, it is not an extravagant conjecture that she thought it politic not to let anyone, even the printer, know the full extent of the edition.

Before broadcasting it, she called twice on the ever-receptive Mrs Villiers, but being unable to see her, sent a letter which began with a flattering but not very accurate assurance that she wished *her* to know before others about the measures she was taking to oppose 'this ungenerous attack on the dead'. (She referred of course to her parents. None of the persons ranged against Byron ever seemed to realize that *he* was dead.)

I *ought* not to be silent.

Still it is my earnest desire to avoid anything which could be injurious to the living, and as *my own* justification is not the object, I trust that no such consequences are likely to ensue—Certainly not unless there should be the greatest imprudence on the part of *another*.

The alternative which I am forced to adopt is a painful one—particularly to a person who has never *voluntarily* been brought into notice—but I see no expedient by which it could be avoided.[3]

About the same day a letter came from Augusta, with an enquiry as to Ada's health, and some expression of a desire to know Annabella's sentiments and to rectify her own mistakes, but it was too late. She was commanded in imperious terms to give 'an unqualified assent' to the truth of four numbered assertions:

First, that she (Augusta) had no sort of right or claim to interfere in the nomination of a trustee or a solicitor,

Second, that she had no reason to doubt Lady Byron's readiness to promote her and her family's interests, or to take offence at the manner in which the nomination of Dr Lushington was arranged or announced,

Third, that there was no ground for her absurd suspicion that Dr

---

[1] LOVELACE, *Lady Noel Byron.* (?) 11 Feb.
[2] Richard Taylor, and March & Miller.
[3] LOVELACE, *Lady Noel Byron.* 21 Feb.

Lushington had a preconcerted plan with Kinnaird, and no cause whatever to suppose his conduct would be prejudicial to her interests or unfriendly to her personally. (Those last words, considering the terms in which he had spoken and written about her were rather uncandid, but Augusta had put herself in the wrong by voicing what could be construed as a slur upon him.)

Fourth—and this was a redundancy—that it was unreasonable to complain of being notified of legal decisions by a solicitor.

> If after full consideration you can't admit that my assertions are perfectly well founded, I must beg you to signify your dissent by silence on the subject.[1]

Possibly if Augusta had acceded to this request, much of her subsequent dismal history might have been different. The one thing Annabella had never been able to bear long from her protegée was silence. Whenever there had been any likelihood of their losing contact it was she, not Augusta, who took steps to reopen communications. Silence would almost certainly have evoked a wish to restore a *status quo* which was not without psychological advantages for the party who could derive a keen sense of superiority from the relationship. Unluckily, Augusta chose to be voluble. She wrote back at length and anything but humbly:

> *Feb. 24th 1830*
> I dissent essentially from the contents of your letter, but I will not do so 'in silence' lest that silence should be misinterpreted.

Her not having any legal right to nominate a trustee, she said, dealing with the first of the numbered headings, only gave her an additional claim to a right by courtesy.

> . . . All I requested was that you would not fix upon a person who was a total stranger to me, but if you did, that you would enable me to communicate with such a person directly through my own solicitors. . . .
> 2nd. I never doubted your disposition to promote the interests of 'myself and my family by any just means'—and even when most hurt by the nomination I never expressed such an idea.
> 3rd I did regard the Nomination in question and the mode of communicating it (through your solicitor) as extremely unkind of you after my letter of the 28th of November, and calculated to give me extreme pain, however upright your motives might have appeared to yourself.
> 4th . . . I did say, in a moment of irritation, that the whole thing appeared to me preconcerted, but I do willingly and entirely acquit Dr L. of all such intention as you would make me ascribe to him. . . .

She was grateful for his exertions but was still astonished that he should have accepted the trusteeship in despite of her objections, and she could not admit that she had taken umbrage at 'imaginary offences'.

[1] Ibid. 22 Feb.

Either you made the nomination in direct opposition to my earnest and respectful entreaty, and without even the form of explanation or regret for its necessity, or you did *not* . . . if the latter, then indeed I am under a complete delusion to this hour. . . .

It was this and this total apparent absence of all consideration for my feelings at that moment that I complained of. I was dreadfully hurt and I expressed myself so without reserve, but I did not on that account refuse myself the hope of being reconciled, still less did I attempt to put any limits to explanation or correspondence. This has been your doing. . . .

If she had finished there, it might still have been well, or at any rate, not calamitous; but driven on by a Byronic instinct for fatality, she added some last words:

I can forgive and do forgive freely, all and everything that has agonized, and I may say almost destroyed me. I can believe that you have been actuated throughout by a principle which you thought a right one, but my own self-respect will never allow me to acknowledge an obligation where none has been originally conferred, or to turn my own self-accuser by admitting imputations which my heart has uniformly disclaimed.[1]

Forgiveness! Forgiveness from Augusta Leigh! A boast of self-respect! Repudiation of benefits conferred! At once a letter was dispatched to Mrs Villiers:

I told you that I had given her one more chance of repairing her misconduct in this Trustee business. The consequence is that I have received a letter to which I can only apply the term 'insolent'. She bestows her *forgiveness* upon me for all my unkindness!—It appears to me that she expected I should apologize for having exercised a right vested in myself only. . . .

The wish to meddle in the appointment of Trustees was in itself an imputation upon me. . . .

I have no resentment on the subject of her present proceedings. She will, I fear, injure herself by them. I have not yet determined what to do in reply to these accusations.[2]

With Mrs Lushington, who was not, like Mrs Villiers, one of Augusta's closest friends, she could be less restrained:

Feb. 27th 1830

My dearest Sarah,

I think it advantageous to me that Mrs L. should have written a letter which so absolutely precludes my holding any intercourse with her—She might have left herself a loophole—but I never can pass over her insolence in offering me her forgiveness. . . .

The copies [of the pamphlet] I wish to have presented first, or at the same time with those to the Relatives, are the Royal ones—and this requires arrangement.

Yours most affcy.

AINB[3]

---

[1] Printed in the *Athenaeum*, August 1883.
[2] LOVELACE, *Lady Noel Byron*. 25 Feb.   [3] Lovelace Papers.

From this it will be seen that she was bent upon a course of publicity, and such a one as might do great harm to Augusta, who was dependent upon the Royal bounty for rent-free apartments in the palace, a pension of £300 a year, and a social status it would be disastrous to lose. While the Queen Dowager was still alive, Lady Byron had been fully conscious of what it meant for her to have discountenanced ill report by keeping up 'a limited intercourse'.[1] George IV and the Royal Dukes were not in a position to be censorious, but there was a point beyond which tolerance must not be stretched; and the wife of Colonel Leigh, a far from popular courtier, could not afford a revival of the old whisperings.

Augusta had used a phrase in her rash letter which showed she was at last beginning to understand the character by whom she had once been completely subjugated—'however upright your motives might have appeared to yourself'. Annabella's voluminous archives are unremittingly analytical, inquisitorial even, yet there is scarcely an instance—perhaps not so much as a single one—where she questions the perfect purity of her own motives even when her decisions were occasioning dark misery to others.[2]

Her quarrels became devastating, they laid waste the lives of those who were involved in them, but she seemed absolutely blind to the possibility that either fault or error could lie on her side (except by reason, as she sometimes admitted, of too much generosity); while her belief in her 'undeviating rectitude'—the phrase is hers—made her certain at all times that such weaknesses as ill temper, jealousy, or spite, could only affect the behaviour of others.

In her own certitude, she must have been uncommonly persuasive. It was many years before Mrs Villiers, for example, failed to respond, sympathetically outraged, to the tales of horrid ill usage with which she was from time to time regaled. The latest development was especially shocking, and she wrote about it by return:

. . . That a person so encompassed by misfortune as poor Augusta is on all sides should add to the many evils of her situation by the indulgence of a perverse temper is really melancholy.

I had considered her saved as far as this world was concerned by your extraordinary kindness and I had hoped that the feelings she expressed some time after your separation from Ld B. would have dwelt upon her mind for her future benefit. . . .[3]

---

[1] 'What does the Queen think I wonder?' she asked Mrs Villiers during one phase of the scandal. 16 July 1817: Lovelace Papers.

[2] E.g. 'When I am *forced* into positions of Antagonism one of the greatest pains I suffer, & the least understood, is the suppression of kind feelings.—I am so sorry, even grieved, for those who are suffering from false visions of relative facts. . . .' Letter to the Rev. F. W. Robertson, 5 Feb. 1853: Lovelace Papers.

[3] LOVELACE, *Lady Noel Byron*. 26 Feb. 1830.

Lady Byron had sent her Augusta's letter of eight years ago exonerating Mrs Clermont from having done anything but show 'kind forbearance' at the time of Byron's matrimonial crisis, and Mrs Villiers thought a few lines from Mrs Clermont herself should be printed and circulated with the pamphlet, and that 'Moore and his adherents *should* see it'. (This was as yet a doubtful point.) 'My means of circulation are so very limited. . . . Have you determined upon sending the paper to Ld. Holland—I find that Moore is so much the habitué of Hd. House that I conceive there can be no better channel of communication.'

Lady Byron was waiting for the opinion of her very important cousin William Lamb, now Viscount Melbourne. Since Caroline's death two years before, this seemingly languid, unemotional man, who had seldom raised a finger to check his wife's follies, was becoming capable and ambitious, and making himself felt in politics. Liberated from domestic turmoil, the social charm and worldly wisdom inherited from his mother grew potent at last. He was currently Home Secretary and soon to become Prime Minister. Lady Byron now regarded him as the head of the family, and had once or twice approached him—unsuccessfully—to get preferments for other relatives of hers, including the clergyman who in an evil hour had married her to Byron. She had shown him the pamphlet, but he had not as yet given his view, and on March 6th she sent him a reminder.

My dear Lady Byron [he replied with that curious formality which must have made the use of a Christian name in the upper classes a rich endearment], I find your note upon my return from the Country, whither I went early this morning—I am truly sorry to hear of your being so unwell—

The more I think of the matter, the more I am anxious that it should be settled if possible, by Moore's making such a retractation as would render any publication upon your part unnecessary. I come to this conclusion disinterestedly, and solely upon consideration of what appears to me would be the best for all parties, and particularly for you—for as to myself, tho' I do not care much about the matter, yet I own I feel so much remains of resentment as would make me rather glad than otherwise of any thing which should tend to unmask his real character and shew it in its true colours.—

I do not know any better way of effecting the above object, than that of communicating with Moore through Ld. Holland, and for that purpose if you approve it, I will ask Ld. H to go down to see you, which I have no doubt he will readily do, or if you feel yourself unequal to such an interview, I will speak to him upon the matter myself, tho' I think it would be better that you should see him, because you can explain and impress upon him your own particular feelings more strongly, than I should be able to do.

Let me know which of these courses you prefer.

Yours faithfully and affectionately,
Melbourne[1]

[1] Lovelace Papers.

Lord Melbourne's honesty blows refreshingly through the fog of self-deception that pervades this correspondence. Instead of saying that he bore no resentment against Byron but felt it his duty to see that evil was exposed, he actually acknowledged that he did bear resentment and could have wished the worst might be told: nevertheless, he did not think it judicious to publish any paper. He had not yet been informed that it was already printed and arrangements well advanced for sending it to very high places.

Wilmot Horton too was ignorant of the full extent of Lady Byron's plans when he gave her some further well-meant suggestions, couched in his usual style like the minutes of a committee meeting:

> That a copy of this MS should be placed in Moore's hands by Dr Lushington—and that he should be told that it would be instantly published unless he was prepared to say in a passage to the second Volume that from communications which he had received, he felt himself called upon in honor to retract all the charges and inferences without exception, which were to be found in his first Vol. against Lady B's parents, or anybody belonging to them, as having been directly or indirectly the cause of the separation.
>
> He must also add that he Mr Moore was now satisfied that this case of Separation was one of those unfortunate cases which were unavoidable, and which were considered at the time as unavoidable not only by Lady B, her legal advisers Sir S. Romilly and Dr Lushington, but also by the nearest relations of Lord Byron. . . .[1]

('Male', Lady Byron inserted before 'relations', remembering how Augusta had at first refused to deliver to Byron the letter announcing the finality of the parting.)

> Such a Statement would leave the case where it ought to be left—in *mystery*—. . . .
> I may regret that you feel it necessary to publish at all, but if you are irrevocably decided to publish, I think this suggestion may be worth your attention.

His gentlemanly advice against keeping Augusta in the dark as to what was being done had so far been disregarded. Her copy was dispatched the same day as Lord Holland's, and not direct but under cover to Mrs Villiers. With it went two letters, one of which was marked 'Private'. The other, which was meant to be shown to Augusta, said:

> Will you have the goodness to deliver the enclosed paper to Mrs Leigh, as soon as it will not appear a want of consideration for her present distress to do so—I am desirous to put her in possession of one of the first copies so that she may not receive any false impression from others—
> She will see that my *object* is such as cannot be painful to her feelings,

---

[1] Ibid. Undated.

and that in my endeavour to accomplish it, I have refrained as far as possible from making any allusion to herself.

The 'Remarks' are unpublished, and I have not yet determined on the extent of their circulation.[1]

In the note which was not intended to be passed on, she speaks of having had an intimation that Moore was saying something she interpreted as 'a *threat*' against herself, which 'renders my line of conduct more *decided*'. This is somewhat at variance with the air of tentativeness in the last words of the communication Augusta was to read. Within a few days copies had gone out far and wide.

Moore had not uttered any threats against Lady Byron. He was at work in his country cottage and not even aware as yet of the existence of the brochure;[2] but friends brought her these tales, and, with a positive eagerness to be persecuted, she believed and elaborated upon them. The tendency to estimate anything less than ardent praise as denigration and insult, which is manifest in scores of her letters at the age of twenty-four, was now at thirty-eight a deeply rooted neurosis. Her self-enforced retirement, generally in extremely uninteresting neighbourhoods, her excessive leisure, the celibacy she had with so much anguish embraced and persisted in, had all acted detrimentally upon an habitually mistrustful temperament.

Though she slept soundly and her appetite was excellent, she had since the Separation regarded herself as one broken in health and nerves. She was perpetually in the hands of doctors, and inclined to insist upon the most drastic treatments. She kept for years an 'issue' (a small open wound) in her left arm. The application of leeches was frequent; cupping and even emetics were used with satisfaction; and the medical men who were prepared to advise such remedies were the ones who inspired confidence. She was thus of a wraith-like appearance, and subject to feelings of weakness and lassitude; but there was so much semi-invalidism among the more prosperous gentlewomen of the time, free as they were from the necessity of exertion, that her friends accepted it as the natural sequence of her conjugal sufferings, and did not perceive that enormous vitality, driven to find an outlet, was overflowing sometimes in good works but oftener in irritations, animosities, and embittering retrospections.

It was not delicate of Moore to publish letters of Byron's showing his distaste for his mother-in-law, but there was nothing in his book to justify a counter-attack taking the form of this pamphlet from one who spoke of

---

[1] LOVELACE, *Lady Noel Byron*. 8 Mar. The 'present distress' may have been a bereavement. It was about this time Augusta lost the daughter named after her.

[2] Moore states correctly in his diary that he received the 'Remarks' a few days before he left home, which was on the 18th March. They were posted to him on the 10 March.

herself as pledged to silence. If she had really had no other wish than to uphold the character of her mother, she had only to address a few lines to any newspaper saying that Byron had been entirely mistaken, and she would doubtless have commanded credit. There was no call for a letter from her lawyer hinting at secrets too dire to have been disclosed to her parents—especially when on that point she knew full well the writer was forgetful or misinformed.

In 1816, Lord Holland, much as he had liked Byron, had been disposed to take her side; but in 1830, asked again to mediate, he became convinced she was a grievance-monger and grew less respectful. Receiving the 'Remarks' with a suggestion that he should pass them on, as if spontaneously, to Moore, he replied with firmness:

9 March
1830

Dear Lady Byron,

Mr Moore is in the country & I do not think I am likely to see him before his second Volume appears. . . . If however you wish me to send him your printed statement I will do so, with any further explanations or suggestions you may wish—but in that case it would be idle to attempt to conceal that it is at your desire that I communicate with him—

I should at the same time in justice to him add that I am perfectly satisfied that he is quite incapable of having conveyed to you any thing like a threat & I am equally so that he is not actuated by any unkind or hostile feeling towards you or yours—Indeed how or why should he be—

In the letters he has published the expressions respecting Lady Noel & Sir Ralph would I am satisfied have been suppressed if the feelings & opinions which dictated them had not already in various & even more offensive shapes, been obtruded on the publick both by the writer & by those who at the time took upon themselves unasked the task of defending or attacking him—It is now too late to erase them & it is I fear impossible to deny that such were the feelings or at least the language of the person whose life & character Moore has undertaken to delineate—

With respect to your letter mentioned in 651[1]—I have no doubt that Moore was ignorant of the impression & intention with which you wrote it —he would not I should hope have drawn the inferences he does from it so strongly & as his own, if he had been aware of what passed in your mind at the time—If therefore you think any explanation of that matter an object it may not be impossible to make him see the propriety of adding in a note to the second Volume your account of that letter—But of course the facts as he relates them will remain the same & as far as his inferences relate to what passed in Ld Byron's mind, they will probably be unaltered also—

Such My Dear Lady Byron is the utmost that one can reasonably expect, or indeed that a common friend can well ask of an author who has, I am convinced, sincerely endeavoured according to the best of his judgement, to

[1] The playful letter beginning 'Dearest Duck'. Moore touches on but does not quote it.

give the most favourable account of those unhappy transactions, he could consistently with truth & Justice—& who would have gladly abstained from all mention of them if he had not imagined that his silence would have implied a censure on his deceased friend much stronger than he could conscientiously sanction—I can assure you that he felt & feels the indelicacy of such topicks, & though he thought himself compelled not to omit them altogether, was very desirous to pass them over in the manner least offensive to any one & above all to you. . . .

From all this I submit to your judgement & discretion the advantages of inviting more publick attention to matters which it cannot but be painful to all parties to discuss in print—In the second volume there is not likely to be any allusion to that period of Ld Byron's life & indeed I know that it is Mr Moore's intention to avoid it—Excuse the hurry & the length at which I have written & believe me
    Dear Madam,
                    Your obedient & devoted
                            Vassall Holland[1]

Lady Byron could not have liked this tone, and she was not deflected by it. Only one day later he had occasion to write to her again:

I will obey your instructions & send your remarks to Mr Moore—without any request or suggestion which he can suppose originates with me.

If he consults me I confess I should to him as to you be disposed to deprecate all discussion or controversy.[2]

Lord Melbourne had, like Lushington, withdrawn his opposition, and was now telling her, not only that she was right to communicate with Moore through Lord Holland, but also that he would forward 'any more' of her papers that she cared to send him.

I suppose you contemplate ultimately a more extended distribution. This appears to me necessary to make your measure effective.[3]

She had not waited for this encouragement. Day after day copy after copy was being sent out. Some went to bishops, some to peers and peeresses, many to the middle-class friends and acquaintances who were beginning to form an increasing element in the society she drew about her, and were eventually to outnumber the members of the aristocracy many times over.

There were copies for the Southeys—Dr Southey and his brother, the Poet Laureate, Byron's loathed enemy, who expressed his deep approval, a copy for Mrs Bowdler, a relative of the great expurgator, who thought Moore blackhearted and even 'fiendlike' for renewing and aggravating the pangs of that 'wounded bosom'; copies for celebrities like the young Fanny Kemble, whose cool reply is in the third person though she had been a friend and admirer, and copies for obscure people with names

[1] Lovelace Papers.   [2] Ibid. 10 Mar.   [3] Ibid. 13 Mar.

unknown. There was also a copy presented through Lord St Helens to George IV.[1]

The King, very soon to die, was too ill to take an interest, and the response from that quarter was disappointing; but letters poured in from less exalted recipients. Many were persuaded that they had been favoured with a mark of distinguished confidence and returned such assurances as—

> You may rely upon the secrecy you have enjoined upon us being preserved in regard to the paper of your Remarks. (William Eden, March 18th)

> I will strictly obey your injunction not to let your paper go out of my own hands, but I will not neglect a proper opportunity of imparting its contents. . . . (Fanny Bowdler, March 18th)

The peculiar knack of ensuring a secret would be imparted and yet convincing the hearer that it was being kept had been attained by much practice. In several cases she sent packets of the pamphlet for discreet distribution.

> I had the honor to receive your Ladyship's letter this morning, and also a parcel of the Remarks on Moore's late work.

So wrote John Hill of Leicester with a promise to circulate copies among the subscribers to his library. (March 23rd.)

How briskly the document passed from hand to hand may be gauged from such extracts as the following:

> Before I received Miss Montgomery's letter I had given one of your Publications to Lord Cleveland for the perusal of himself & his family with the request that he would not at present part with it & I had written to the same effect with one to Miss Shafto.
>   (G. B. Wharton, Lady Byron's solicitor, March 21st)

> I do not know whether you will say I have done right, but as you were so kind as to express a wish that Mrs Courtenay should have one of the papers . . . I thought it best to send the one you had sent to me, hoping that you would allow me to have another Copy.
>   (Harriet Courtenay, March 30th)

> I have had great pleasure in showing Lady Byron's Remarks to Mr Whishaw who thinks them extremely satisfactory. . . .
>   (J. L. Mallet, March 15th)

> Lord Rosslyn has the honor to return to Mrs Ellison the little publication which she had the goodness to lend him . . . & which appears to do great honor to Lady Byron   (March 21st)

---

[1] Ibid. Letter to Lushington, 16 March. Acknowledgments for or on behalf of all the other correspondents referred to are in the same collection. Miss Mayne says: 'Only a few copies were printed and privately circulated by her!'

The mother of Mr Bland, the trustee, had been reproved for her son's admiration of Moore's book, and sent an explanation and apology with her thanks on March 15th.

Lady Byron and her nearest friends had never doubted that the vindication would fill Moore with dismay, and it may be imagined with what provoked feelings she read a polite offer tranquilly conveyed by Lord Holland:

14 March 1830

Dear Lady Byron,

I received a letter from Mr Moore yesterday acknowledging your 'remarks' which I had enclosed to him. He adds—'Pray say to her that I am obliged by her attention in sending me the Remarks & that it is my intention, if she has no objection, to subjoin them to the second edition of my first Volume.'

This is entirely his own notion unsuggested by me, & I hope it will satisfy you that if he has committed any mistake or betrayed any want of judgement it has not proceeded from any unkind feeling to any person living or dead & still less from the slightest wish of reviving unpleasant recollections & dissensions. It will give me great pleasure to find that all parties are satisfied & that any thing like hostile controversy is avoided.

I am, Dear Madam

Yours obliged & devoted

Vassall Holland[1]

Lady Byron was upset. Writing to Mrs Villiers to know what she thought of this proposal, she said, 'I am not obliged to answer immediately and am indeed too unwell to *think*'.[2] To Dr Lushington, however, the same day she expressed her thoughts with perfect coherence:

. . . I will tell you what strikes me—

1. That the sentiments I entertain with respect to Moore's principles and conduct make the appearance of any alliance with him, and still more of receiving any obligation from him inadvisable—

2ndly. That I should in reality confer an advantage upon him by promoting the sale of his 2nd Edition—and this I am not particularly disposed to do—

On the other hand it may be argued that if it be sincerely my wish to show the falsehood of his representations, the mode suggested by him would be most effectual—

I am of opinion however that *I* could ensure as wide a circulation as I might think desirable.

My inclination is therefore to reply very civilly to Moore—that is Lord Holland—declining his offer, as I prefer to direct the circulation of the tract myself—as well as for other reasons which it is unnecessary to enter upon.[3]

But Dr Lushington gave his opinion by return that she could not well refuse Moore's proposition, and she was obliged to yield to his verdict.

---

[1] Lovelace Papers. [2] Ibid. 16 Mar. [3] Ibid.

March 18th   1830

My dear Mrs Villiers

The result was, that I wrote to Lord Holland, acquiescing, but in such a manner as to make it apparent that I conferred instead of receiving a favor—and I think Lord H. must feel bound in honor to see that a proper expression of Moore's sentiments shall accompany the paper. If the case be properly represented I expect that public opinion will demand a retractation. . . .

Till I have been able to send copies to all who have a claim to such attention from me, I should regret the appearance in the papers—

I am miserably ill.

Yours very affecy,

AINB

The more the real motives of my conduct are spoken of the better—there will be misrepresentation of the transaction with Moore.[1]

Over and over again in her numberless letters, Lady Byron gives her friends little nudges to remind them of the turn their conversation with others ought to take. One may wonder whether Mrs Villiers was as deluded as her correspondent about 'real motives', because the principal topic between them, taking an easy precedence of Moore's ill doings, was the iniquities of Augusta. And in this connection another little nudge had been given.

Augusta had a friend, a Colonel D'Aguilar, who had been essaying the hopeless task of setting her to rights financially; it was he who had suggested lending out her capital on mortgage to get a higher rate of interest, and had fortified her in her attempt to be represented by her own solicitor.

A—— is acting under the influence of Col. D'Aguilar [Lady Byron had written to Mrs Villiers]. . . . I found that he had a totally mistaken view of her real position, and from a sort of chivalrous feeling, was urging her to measures quite inconsistent with it. Of course *I* was obliged to leave him in error—but it is a pity that someone should not moderate his Quixotism a little.[2]

That underlined 'I' is eloquent. She, with her noted beneficence, was not the person to tell him how Augusta was beholden. She could not recognize that for someone else to do so on a hint from her was the same morally as if she had spoken herself.

Nor did she see that scattering so many copies of her half-revelations that they got into the bookshops and were reproduced in all the principal newspapers throughout the kingdom was little different from open publication.

[1] Ibid. 'The Remarks' did not have to wait for the 2nd Edition but were bound into the 2nd Volume of the 1st Edition.
[2] Ibid. 1 Mar.

You will see how people torment me by publishing on all sides [she wrote] as if *I* had put myself in the shops to be sold for sixpence.[1]

Nevertheless that was where the pamphlets now were, and it was in a bookseller's window that Hobhouse for the first time saw a copy. It was on the day of Kinnaird's funeral, which he had attended with a sorrowful heart. Thence he had called at John Murray's and learned that there had been a letter of serious remonstrance on Lady Byron's behalf from Captain Lord Byron. She was very angry with Murray because he had promised in that expansive interview with the 7th Lord, two years before, that Moore's book would not contain a word that could offend her.

Hobhouse did not bother much about anyone's complaints of Moore, being still far from well disposed to him; but he was filled with rage, pausing at another bookseller's, to see the Remarks exposed so that they could be read from the street. The pages that were open contained a statement that, though Byron had at first rejected the proposals for a separation, yet 'when it was distinctly notified to him that if he persisted in his refusal, recourse must be had to legal measures' he had given in. Hobhouse had been Byron's mainstay during the whole of that searing struggle, and he always, as long as he lived, maintained that it was not out of reluctance to go into a court that his friend had surrendered. His journal did not mince words.

I . . . saw enough to convince myself that the woman is either crazy or totally indifferent to truth.

I doubt much whether I ought not to tell what I know on the subject and so I told Wilmot Horton in the lobby of the House of Commons, mentioning at the same time how indignant I felt at Lady Byron's behaviour—and informing him that I should appeal to W. H. himself against certain of the assertions made by Lady Byron—e.g. that Lord Byron was compelled to sign the separation by threats of legal proceedings.

It was quite the contrary. Lord Byron was with difficulty persuaded by myself to sign the separation and he it was that threatened legal proceedings against the parties who detained his wife from him.[2]

The matter was still much on his mind during the ensuing weeks, and he discussed with Lord Lansdowne his idea of writing a refutation.

Lord L. said that if I interfered the better the case I made against Lady B. the more I should be blamed. He said he thought Lady B. had not gained by her publication.[3]

Still he could not overcome the feeling that he ought to do something. The publicity the statement was receiving had grown to be tremendous, there had been nothing equal to it since the Separation itself; and a new

---

[1] Ibid. To Mrs Villiers, 24 Mar.
[2] Hobhouse *Journals*, 19 March 1830.   [3] Ibid. 4 April.

protagonist had come into the arena with the distressed lady's banners flying, a popular magazine at his disposal, a genius for what we now call sob stuff, and a grudge against both Byron and Moore.

In the first volume of the biography, though his name was hidden by asterisks, Thomas Campbell had been perfectly recognizable in a passage from Byron's 1813 journal:

> C—— last night seemed a little nettled at something or other—I know not what. We were standing in the ante-saloon, when Lord H. brought out of the other room a vessel of some composition similar to that which is used in Catholic churches, and, seeing us, he exclaimed, "Here is some *incense* for you." C—— answered—"Carry it to Lord Byron, *he is used to it.*"
> Now this comes of 'bearing no brother near the throne.' I, who have no throne, nor wish to have one *now*, am at perfect peace with all the poetical fraternity. . . . What does it signify who is before or behind in a race where there is no goal?

Byron had probably interpreted as sarcasm a remark meant pleasantly enough; his position, at the age of twenty-five, among the seniors he had outstripped in popularity, was a delicate one, and may have made him hyper-sensitive. On the other hand, Hobhouse, in much more mature years, described Campbell as 'a very envious and vain and testy man'.[1] In whatever spirit he had pronounced the words, he had been displeased to see the comment on them in print; and though many of Byron's references to him were of the most flattering character, and one of his now forgotten poems described as 'perfectly magnificent', he had subjoined to the review of Moore's 'Life' in his magazine, *The New Monthly*,[2] a letter denying that he had ever envied Byron, and insisting that the younger poet had always been far too affectionate and too kind a friend to him to inspire anything but affection in return.

But seemingly the introduction of those idle words had rankled, and on receiving from Lady Byron a copy of her pamphlet, he decided to change sides. He announced this himself in the next number of his magazine:

> Among the literary notices in the New Monthly, I consented to the insertion of a laudatory account of the work [Moore's biography]; nay, more, I expunged a portion of the manuscript critique in which Mr Moore was censured for unfairness towards Lady Byron. This I did from unwillingness to blame Mr Moore, and from having scarcely dipped into the censured parts of the book. Besides, I did not *believe* Lady Byron to be so perfectly justifiable in the separation as I now know her to be.

On closer inspection, he continued, he found that Moore had produced 'one of the most injudicious books ever published'. It was hardly a very

[1] Ibid. 17 Mar. 1827. [2] 1 Mar. 1830.

close inspection; he conceded that he had not actually read the book 'for I
hate to wade through it', but people told him that Moore had 'warily
depreciated Lady Byron', and this was more than he could stand.

> . . . The state of circumstances has wholly changed. Lady Byron has now
> spoken out. As her friend, I could not keep my mind quiet about her feelings
> under this ill-starred resuscitation of the question concerning her.[1]

In terms curiously insulting to Moore and going far beyond what his
argument required—so much so as to astound even sensational papers like
John Bull—he proceeded to castigate the unread book, to condemn Byron,
and to praise Lady Byron as even she had never been praised before,
showing all the while that he was privy to her secret wrongs, and that
what had not been opened to him by herself could easily be learned from
her friends—which was true.

She had sought his aid, he told Lord Dudley, to defend her against the
'attack' that was being made on her.[2] On March 21st he visited her at
Hanger Hill. A day or two afterwards she wrote to Mrs Villiers as if she
had been approached by him first.

> He came to make a frank acknowledgment of the impressions which my
> Statement had removed, and offered me his services unreservedly. . . . He
> pressed me very closely on one point but evidently from good and generous
> motives. He said that as a friend 'a sincere and devoted friend,' he could
> not but represent to me that my silence respecting the causes of my Separa-
> tion left a stigma, not on my own character so much as on that of another,
> and of an innocent person—that my motives for such reserve were liable to
> misconstruction. I replied—I *submit* to that misconstruction.[3]

This was all very fine, but the journalist's curiosity had been set going
not by her silence but by her Remarks. 'I trust he did not penetrate the
truth', she added, but she was fully aware that he did. Before sending her
letter to Mrs Villiers she had received one from Mrs Lushington, who had
driven back to town with Campbell after the interview.

> . . . He pushed me hard on Mrs L[eigh] and said he had *Hobhouse's
> authority for the fact.* I was not as good as you, nor as bad, but did not do a
> quarter what I should have liked.[4]

Mrs Lushington, wife of Lady Byron's lawyer, would not have had to
do much to afford full confirmation of what Campbell had been allowed
to suspect: the mere absence of a denial was sufficient.

---

[1] 1 Apr.
[2] ROMILLY. Letter misdated by the editor 25 November 1830. It can only belong to
about the same date in March. Lord Dudley had formerly been well known to Byron
under the name of John William Ward. Campbell was very gay about the matter and
wanted Dudley to drink some champagne with him when discussing Lady Byron's
pamphlet.   [3] LOVELACE, *Lady Noel Byron*. 23 Mar.
[4] Ibid. No date. Almost certainly 22 Mar.

He was after a scoop for his paper, and was prepared, it would seem, to tell any lie to get it. Hobhouse had so hearty a contempt for Campbell that he would not have made a disclosure about Byron even if he himself had believed 'the fact'. 'I have heard Byron say he could make Campbell miserable by praising anyone', is a typical comment in his journal,[1] and he knew Campbell was no friend to Byron's fame because, in 1828, *The New Monthly* had liberally puffed Leigh Hunt's book. On terms of complete cordiality with Augusta, Hobhouse had recently invited her to meet several interesting guests at one of his wife's dinner parties,[2] and was incapable of speaking in so ruinous a manner about her.

But Lady Byron, with her deep detestation of him, gave ready credence to Campbell's falsehood, repeating it to Mrs Villiers:

> . . . He asserted that he had Hobhouse's authority for *that fact*! This is not inconceivable to me. H—— would not object to its being supposed the prominent cause, and it will be well if certain friends do not make her *their* victim.[3]

This is one of her rare sidelong references to the other charge against Byron that Mrs Villiers knew, contained in 'three words' that might have 'annihilated' him.[4] It was going rather far to suggest that friends of his would implicate Augusta rather than have any other deviation suspected, and Campbell later asserted many times that it was Lady Byron herself who had told him of this second obliquity! Certainly from his *New Monthly* article more than one surpassing immorality may be inferred: but when she wrote to him the day after his visit, there were still only grounds for guesswork on his part.

> *Hanger Hill*
> *March 22ᵈ*

Dear Mr Campbell
On taking my pen to point out for your private information those passages in Moore's representations of my part of the story which were open to contradiction, I find them of still greater extent than I had supposed—and to deny an assertion *here and there*, would virtually admit the truth of the rest.

If on the contrary I were to enter into a full exposure of the falsehood of the views taken by Moore, I must detail various matters which consistently with my principles and feelings I cannot under the existing circumstances disclose.

I may perhaps convince you better of the difficulty of the case by an example. *It is not true that pecuniary embarrassments were the cause of the disturbed state of Lord Byron's mind, or formed the chief reason of the arrangements made by him at that time.* But is it reasonable for me to expect

---

[1] 17 Mar. 1827 *op. cit.*   [2] Ibid. 23 Jan. 1830.
[3] LOVELACE, *Lady Noel Byron.* 23 Mar.   [4] See p. 253.
L.L.B.—Y

that you or anyone else should believe this, unless I shew you what *were* the causes in question?

I believe that the most judicious & friendly part towards all concerned is to mark clearly to such persons as may attend to the subject the real object of my statement—tho' I can scarcely suppose it possible to mistake it—

My object is *not* to prove myself right or Lord Byron wrong, but to exonerate from all blame those parties who were involved merely *in consequence* of my determination—Having done this act of justice, my mind is at peace.

I have other documents besides *that* letter of Lord Byron's corroborative of parts of my statement, should such evidence be required by you.

Believe me, & c

A. I. Noel Byron[1]

Campbell must have written at top speed to have his lengthy contribution finished and printed within the week. Since the ice of reserve was broken, he explained, by Byron's biographer, someone had to say for Lady Byron what she could not say for herself.

A female friend offered to do this, and she would probably have done it better than I can. But I could not be such a craven as to let a woman come forward in my place. . . .
My interest in a suffering woman needs no apology. . . . I claim to speak of Lady Byron in the right of a man, of a friend to the rights of women, and to liberty, and to natural religion.

She had been brought out by Moore's book, he said, 'from the shade of retirement where she hid her sorrows', and compelled to defend her friends and parents from being 'crushed under the tombstone of Byron'.

Nay, in a general view, it has forced her to defend *herself*, though with her true sense and her pure taste, she stands above all special pleading. To plenary explanation she ought not, she never *shall* be driven. Mr Moore is too much of a gentleman not to shudder at the thought of that; but if other Byronists, of a far different stamp, were to force the savage ordeal it is her enemies and not she who would have to dread the burning ploughshares. . . .
If indelicacy be charged upon me, I scorn the charge. . . . I look with wonder and envy at the proud purity of her sense and conscience, that have carried her exquisite sensibilities in triumph through such poignant tribulations. But I am proud to be called her friend—the humble illustrator of her cause . . . nor is she to be suffered, when compelled to speak, to raise her voice as in a desert with no friendly voice to respond to her.
. . . To throw the blame on her parents is proved ridiculous by Dr Lushington's letter, for it shows that the deepest cause, or causes, of the separation, were not imparted to her parents. . . .
You speak, Mr Moore, against Lord Byron's censurers in a tone of indignation which is perfectly lawful towards calumnious traducers, but which will not terrify me, or any other man of courage, who is no calumniator,

---

[1] Lovelace Papers. Printed here in full from Lady Byron's copy. The italics represent her underlining.

from uttering his mind freely with regard to this part of your hero's conduct. I think your whole theory of the unmarriageableness of genius a twaddling little hint for a compliment to yourself. . . . I repudiate your morality for canting too complacently about 'the lava of his imagination,' and the unsettled fever of his passions being any excuses for his planting the *tic douleureux* of domestic suffering in a meek woman's bosom.

These are hard words, Mr Moore, but you have brought them on yourself by your voluntary ignorance of facts known to me. . . . If the subject was too delicate for you to consult Lady Byron's confidential friends, you ought to have had nothing to do with the subject. But you cannot even have submitted your book to Lord Byron's sister, otherwise, she would have set you right about the imaginary spy, Mrs Clermont.

Hence arose your misconceptions, which are so numerous, that having applied to Lady Byron (you will please to observe that I applied not for facts against Lord Byron, for these I got elsewhere, but for an estimate of the correctness of your statements), I received the following letter from her Ladyship.

Therewith, to Lady Byron's sheer horror, he produced the letter from her already quoted, and although he was merciful enough to leave out the final sentences showing that she was cognizant of his intention to produce the article and had been willing to supply evidence for him, it still remained palpable that they had been engaged in intimate discussion together.

Only on the eve of publication had he submitted the piece to her, and she had written to him quite desperately:

I beseech you, if it be possible, omit *that note of mine*.—You *shall* have my reasons but I claim this as the greatest proof of your friendship for
Yours & c
AINB
Let no consideration of expense prevent the alteration of the impression.[1]

His reply was that the impression was already issued. She had been hoping to be able to disclaim any part in his polemics against Moore on her behalf; and even as it was she did her best to dissociate herself, hurrying off at once a letter to Lord Melbourne, the purport of which may be gathered from his reply:

Your letter found me this morning at Holland House and very opportunely it came; as it had been said there yesterday evening that the article in question was written in concert with you—I said then that I did not believe it, but your note enabled me this morning to contradict it authoritatively.[2]

---

[1] Ibid. Lady Byron's copy. (30 Mar.) Miss Mayne mistakes the appeal for a reference to the 'Dearest Duck' letter, which Campbell had never had any opportunity of seeing and had not even touched upon in his article.

[2] Ibid. 1 Apr. Moore's Journal for the same date says that Melbourne allowed him to see Lady Byron's letter, and that she expressed great regret for the 'injudiciousness' of Campbell's article.

To Mrs Villiers, with whom she had now temporarily resumed her close alliance of 1816 and whom she was seeing frequently, she gave one of her nudges:

> If any one should suppose that I concurred in it, pray state that I was entirely ignorant of its nature and contents, except that I believed some notice would be taken of Mrs Clermont's letter.
>
> Surely *my* letter must speak for itself as to its *private* character—and it also proves that I refused all specific information to Campbell. . . . . . . Do you think Moore will consider himself attacked by *me*?—And that he will feel called upon to take any measures.[1]

There is a note of alarm in this. After having for so long been lauded for what Fanny Kemble had called her beautiful gift of silence, it was anything but agreeable to have it plainly revealed that she had 'confidential friends' who had been perfectly ready to communicate 'facts against Lord Byron', and the eulogies of herself that ran parallel with every condemnation of him were in a strain of such fulsome cant that they could not have been much consolation.

> Excellent woman! honoured by all who know her. . . . I will believe her on her own testimony.

She felt obliged to excuse herself to Mrs Villiers by explaining: 'I consider it quite ascertained that Mrs Leigh is employing every power she can command to injure me.' Although it contained an express injunction that it was not to be used 'through the channel of a newspaper', she had given Campbell a copy of Augusta's self-abasing letter to Mrs Clermont, and he had made a quotation from it that was not even accurate.[2]

That she had spoken very familiarly with this vulgar defender was embarrassingly manifest throughout the article.

> It is a further mistake on Mr Moore's part, and I can prove it to be so, if proof be necessary, to represent Lady Byron, in the course of their courtship, as one inviting her future husband to correspondence by letters, after she had at first refused him. She never proposed a correspondence. On the contrary he sent her a message, after that first refusal, stating that he meant to go abroad and to travel for some years in the East; that he should depart with a heart aching but not angry; and that he only begged verbal assurance that she still had some interest in his happiness. Could Miss Milbanke as a well bred woman, refuse a courteous answer to such a message?

---

[1] Lovelace Papers. 31 Mar.

[2] The letter appears whole and entire in the *Edinburgh Observer*, furnished, according to an editorial note, by one of Lady Byron's friends—together with many reckless falsehoods. One of these was that the Rev. William Harness had been unable to remain with Byron at Newstead Abbey because 'his conduct was intolerable and disgusting in every respect'. Harness wrote an angry contradiction, saying that he had never found Byron other than kind, generous, and amiable, and that his conversation had usually been literary and never indelicate.

She sent him a verbal answer which was merely kind and becoming, but which signified no encouragement that he should renew his offer of marriage. After that message, he wrote to her the most interesting letter about himself —about his views, personal and religious, to which it would have been uncharitable not to have replied.

This was the most complete misrepresentation of the beginning of a correspondence which she had unluckily set going by a letter to Byron, several pages long, expressing a wish to establish 'unreserved friendship' with him, and arriving ten months after the rejected proposal of marriage that Lady Melbourne had conveyed. The mistake was not Campbell's, for on several later occasions she gave the same version of events. But though she may have told herself many times over that she had heard from Byron first and answered out of charity, there must have been a certain discomfort below the surface of her mind when she thought of all Augusta knew—who had once been the cherished confidante of both.

It is more for Lord Byron's sake than his widow's [Campbell went on] that I resort not to a more special examination of Mr Moore's misconceptions. The subject would lead me insensibly into hateful disclosures against poor Lord Byron. . . .
The most universal impression produced by his book is that Lady Byron must be a precise, a wan and unwarming spirit—a bluestocking of chilblained learning, a piece of insensitive goodness. Who that knows Lady Byron will not pronounce her to be everything the reverse?

Here he burst into a veritable pæan. He said she had written poetry that would do no discredit to Byron himself, that she had brought to him 'beauty, manners, fortune, meekness, romantic affection, and everything that ought to have made her to the most transcendant man of genius— *had he been what he should have been*—his pride and his idol'. He proclaimed that the most gifted women of the age would agree that they had scarcely ever in their lives met a being so intellectual. She was cool on first acquaintance, he agreed, but only because her beauty and large fortune had attracted such numbers of suitors that she could not otherwise have kept them at a distance. But then he undid some of the effect of the rhapsody by admitting that, compared with the fascinations of Byron, who had 'suborned the favour of almost all women by the beauty of his person and the voluptuousness of his verses', she had nothing to offer but truth and justice!
He apostrophized Moore again:

Keep off your sentimental mummeries from the hallowed precincts of the widow's character. . . . You said, Mr Moore, that Lady Byron was unsuitable to her Lord—the word is cunningly insidious. . . . They tell me . . . that you have described a lady that would have suited him . . . . as if in mockery of that forlorn flower of virtue that was drooping in the solitude of sorrow. . . .

A woman to suit Lord Byron! ! ! Poo! Poo! I could paint you the woman that could have *matched* him, if I had not bargained to say as little as possible about him.

This word 'matched', with its connotation of resemblance, was 'cunningly insidious' indeed. Everyone who had known the gossip recognized a pointer towards Byron's sister.[1] The diatribe drew to an end with:

Let me tell you, Mr Moore, that neither your poetry nor Lord Byron's, nor all our poetry put together, ever delineated a more interesting being than the woman whom you have so coldly treated. This is not kicking the dead lion, but wounding the living lamb, who was already bleeding and shorn even unto the quick.

No wonder the article made Mrs Villiers 'feel the full force and justice of the old prayer that God would protect us from *our friends*—we could defend ourselves from our Enemies. . . . What a production,' she exclaimed in one of her sympathizing letters, 'even as a matter of writing, for a literary man or a Gentleman!' She and her family, she assured Lady Byron, were saying whenever and wherever they could that the publication was unsanctioned.[2]

Whether or not it came to Campbell's knowledge that such denials were made by Lady Byron and her friends, after she had so warmly received him and shown him at least one of Byron's letters and a statement by Mrs Clermont which she had wanted him to use,[3] he turned his coat again very soon. On January 2nd, 1831, he wrote a profuse and handsome apology to Moore for 'the over-vehemence of manner in which I addressed you on the unfortunate subject which divided our opinions',[4] and the year after that he was paying gallant attentions to the pretty and charming Countess Guiccioli,[5] who was visiting England for the first time and whom Lady Byron regarded as a most shameful person. He seems to have been a man altogether without emotional stability.

[1] *John Bull* did not fail to draw their reader's attention to the probable 'writhing' of Byron's relatives under these 'dreadful allusions'. Most other periodicals took up the theme, some defending, some attacking his memory.

[2] 5 Apr. Lovelace Papers.

[3] 'I will mention to *you* in confidence that Mrs Clermont has sent me something which she wishes to publish—indeed she is I believe determined to do so, and I have no right to prevent her. . . . Campbell may do much for her, if he adverts judiciously to the exculpatory letter—You will of course see the New Monthly.' Letter to Mrs Villiers written on March 27th, after his visit to her and while she was still hoping his article would be on the lines she had indicated. Lovelace Papers. Her reference in the next communication, 31 March, to having believed 'some notice would be taken of Mrs Clermont's letter' must refer to the *self*-vindication and not the 'exculpatory letter' from Augusta, which he had in fact noticed. The Clermont Statement is quoted briefly in Chapter 4. [4] BEATTIE.

[5] Invitations, verses, etc., in the Gamba Papers, Ravenna.

Hobhouse, whose loathing of the flowery style would have made him despise the effusion in *The New Monthly* even if it had been in praise of Byron, was in every way disgusted.

Lord Holland had a long conversation with me at Brookes as to the propriety of my answering Lady Byron & Tom Campbell's defence of her. He agreed with me that Dr Lushington had no right to allow Lady B. to publish his letter on a professional opinion formed on ex parte statements, when the disputants had agreed to adjust their differences by a quiet separation. He told me that he had spoken to Lushington the other day in the House of Lords, & that Lushington thought it best to hush up matters.

I said that was very well, but the Doctor and Lady B. had struck their blow & it might be too late for them to preach forbearance to others.

Lord Holland confirmed my statement as to Lady B.'s friends *not* having used menaces to compel Lord B. to separate quietly—and told me that when applied to by Lushington and Wilmot Horton at the time to persuade Lord Byron to consent to terms, he stopt the Doctor who was making use of strong language and said if there was anything like a threat Lord Byron ought not to consent to a separation & he would not advise such a step.

Lord Holland recommended silence saying that Lady Byron would feel more if no notice were taken of her & [she] were treated with contempt by Byron's friends than if she were to figure in a controversy—this is true.[1]

The Hollands had from the first been of the opinion that she was really trying to stir up the trouble she pretended to deprecate; and while Lord Holland was waiting for Moore's reaction to the pamphlet, Lady Holland had written to her son:

Your Papa is doing his utmost to quell her restlessness, but in vain. I am afraid she is a cold obstinate woman.[2]

She said Moore had it in his power to publish many things that would be painful to Lady Byron which he had considerately omitted from letters; and perhaps that was what Lady Byron herself feared when she asked Mrs Villiers whether he was likely to 'take any measures'.

But even without Lord Holland's dissuasions, Hobhouse met with a check when he contemplated refuting Lady Byron:

I forget whether I have recorded that I have seen Mrs Leigh who although she denies some of Lady Byron's assertions, still requests me not to publish any answer.[3]

That was, of course, the complication. Augusta's position *vis-à-vis* Annabella was too precarious for her to allow a word to appear that might provoke reprisals. What with her obsequious letters and the loans of

---

[1] Hobhouse *Journals*, 8 Apr. 1830.
[2] ILCHESTER, *Elizabeth, Lady Holland*. 12 Mar.
[3] Hobhouse *Journals*, 8 Apr. *op. cit.*

money and the treacheries she had committed against Byron, she could only pray that her friends and his would lie low.

It does not speak well for Mrs Villiers that she repeatedly called on Augusta during the period when she was receiving frequent hostile letters about her from Lady Byron. What motive could she have had, shocked as she professed to be by all she had heard of Augusta's ungrateful behaviour, but to see—and possibly report—how the pamphlet and the consequent new outbreak of scandal were affecting her? In this she was unsuccessful.

> I am persuaded that Mrs Leigh is determined not to see me, I called 3 times in one week, was told she was not at home, after long waiting, and have heard nothing from her—I shall perhaps make one more attempt—but if she has really taken the line you have heard she did she is of course right in not admitting those who she knows to be of a contrary opinion.[1]

Lady Byron replied, 'You and I have *served our purpose*, and are to be discarded it seems!'[2] She forgot that she herself had resolved to discard Augusta and had told Mrs Lushington so.

It was very annoying to her that Wilmot Horton disapproved of her not warning Augusta before publishing the Remarks.

> I find that Mr W. H. does not yet see completely through the nature of Mrs L's conduct—indeed, without the longest and most intimate experience, who would not be deceived.[3]

He had also expressed a fear that she had put herself in the wrong by not giving Moore a genuine chance of correcting the offending passages before starting to distribute the pamphlet. Endlessly bent upon the self-justification she always claimed to have renounced, she wrote him one of her casuistical letters saying she had sent Moore a copy 'before I circulated any other (except to Mrs Leigh)', and that she did not '*suggest* to him to retract or rescind (for this would have been a *threat* or a petition) but had he *offered* to do so', she had been prepared to withdraw the refutation.[4] Since a substantial number of copies had already gone out, that would have been an impossibility. As for the statement that the copies for Moore and Augusta were the first to be circulated, it was mere untruth.

Comment among Byron's admirers was naturally adverse, and Lady Byron, who had thought the Rev. Francis Hodgson the only respectable and enlightened friend he had ever had, would have been grieved if she could have seen the letter he dispatched from his Bakewell Vicarage in response to a groan from Henry Drury at Harrow:

---

[1] 5 Apr. Lovelace Papers.
[2] Ibid. 7 Apr.   [3] Ibid.   [4] Ibid. 8 Apr.

I have indeed fully seen the late wretched matters about poor Byron and his ruined memory!

My God, how cruel, how utterly revengeful is the letter of his widow! Do you for a moment give her credit for being actuated by regard for her parents' memory? If so, that would have been the most prominent part of the letter, and dwelt upon most, but it occupies most inadequate space; and the rest shows the real reason for her breaking silence: *pique* at being described as so ill-suited a wife for Byron. Doubtless this was provoking enough; and one could hardly have wondered at her resenting it on the spur of the moment. But when this is so evidently the real cause of her speaking out, her laying it all on filial feelings is as shallow as hypocritical.

But alas! I fear the evil has only commenced.[1]

He was a friend of Augusta's, but did not know the inside story of her offences and her punishment.

Augusta wrote to him:

I am always afraid of the impetuosity of my feelings on such occasions (of which I am fully aware) making me uncharitable. God forgive *her* if she has made me what I never was before, or believed I could be; but I will not dwell on my feelings; you can guess them. If it was not my own dear brother whom it concerned, I do think I should still feel disgusted at such unfeeling conduct.

I agree with every word you write on the subject. . . . What has she to gain now that he is powerless to injure or oppress her in any way? I do think nothing, were it ever so bad, could possibly justify anyone defaming the dead.[2]

Later, when the second volume of Moore's work came out, she dared a still more unrestrained—and disingenuous—expression of her long pent-up resentments.

I long to hear what you think of this book. I have been dreadfully annoyed at certain passages. . . . What will Lady B. do or say? What can she? And yet if she is quiet she must *writhe* under the torture! But she may thank herself either for her own sufferings, or the contumely which will rest on his memory! A few *gentle* words, instead of that despicable tirade on the last volume, would have secured her the esteem and pity of all the world, and prevented what *has* and what may follow. . . .

On the 10th December (Ada's birthday) I could not resist sending her some little token of my remembrance. I selected a Prayer-book (the Book of Common Prayer in two volumes, with the lessons bound up with it). I had them nicely bound, and *Ada*, in old English characters, engraved on the back, and wrote her name and the date inside, put them up directed 'To the Hon. Miss Byron, with every kind and affectionate wish,' and wrote over this, 'With Lady Byron's permission.' In another outside envelope directed them to Lady B . . . and . . . have never heard one word since.[3]

But whether from weakness of spirit or from good nature, Augusta was quite incapable of nursing a grudge relentlessly, and the day came

---

[1] HODGSON. Quoted without date.   [2] Ibid.   [3] Ibid.

when, bowed by the many disasters of her children, she entreated that Annabella would see her. It was in vain.

Never again, despite repeated humble appeals, were the two women to meet, except on one grim occasion—an interview at the White Hart Inn of Reigate, when Augusta was sixty-six and Annabella fifty-nine. The sister Byron had so rashly but so faithfully loved was within six months of death, and she had 'rather suddenly become a very sunk and aged person'.[1] She had been invited to Reigate chiefly to confess that she bore the responsibility for Byron's bitterness against his wife. He had been dead twenty-seven years, he had been parted from her thirty-five years, but still Annabella brooded, still she was obsessed by the belief that he could, he should have loved her—should have forgiven her own refusal of forgiveness to him.

> I told her I had become convinced that it was not in human nature for any one to keep up such animosity as Lord Byron had shown towards me, unless it had been *fed*—that for *his* sake, that he might not be blamed more than he deserved, I sought to know the truth about this. I said emphatically that I referred *only* to correspondence subsequent to 1816 when he left England . . . he could not have continued to feel bitterly *so long*.

Augusta defended herself, denied that she had contributed to ill feeling, swore that his irritation had owed nothing to any word of hers. She could not see how much it would have soothed and calmed her questioner to believe he had been alienated by some mischievous intervention and not by the vain folly of her own implacability.

Her memorandum of the interview, dated April 8th, 1851, gives a harrowingly vivid picture of the sufferings it was her nature to feel and to impose on others. She had asked Augusta to trust her unconditionally, but she gave no trust in return, and after the desired communication had been made, she could only cry tormentedly: 'Is that all?'

> Had I spoken I must have said "false—false"—There appeared to be no motive on her part but *Self*. . . . After this she expressed her extreme gratitude to me for kindness to herself and her family. My feelings then broke loose from all control and I said something about its having been all in vain—I felt utterly hopeless—and asked to be left alone to compose myself. . . .
> . . . There was a mingling of indignation with the intense pity I had before felt—and I was afraid of myself—I said, I believe, that I should always wish her the blessing I could not give her, or something of the kind if my tears did not prevent my uttering it—but, the strongest desire to be out of her presence took possession of me lest I should be tempted beyond my strength.[2]

[1] LOVELACE, *Lady Noel Byron*. Letter of Lady Byron (wife of the 7th lord), 14 Apr. 1851.   [2] Ibid.

It would be hard for a writer of fiction to invent a more macabre scene between two old women, or a more pitiful contrast than that of their circumstances, the one ill, poor, bereaved, disgraced, indebted; the other rich, esteemed, and attended wherever she went by assiduous friends—sustained even at this meeting by an admiring clergyman whom she had brought with her as witness.

Augusta went home and strove with pen and paper to prevail over Annabella's unbelief. Once again she denied, and truly, that she had ever encouraged Byron in any bitter feeling.

> I can as solemnly declare to you as if I were on my oath or on my death-bed that I never did so in any one instance, but that I invariably did the contrary. I have letters from him, and of my own to him (and returned to me after his death), which would bear out this assertion, and I am ready at this or any other moment to make the most solemn asseveration of this, in any way that you can devise.[1]

The clergyman, the Rev. F. W. Robertson of Brighton, to whom Lady Byron had confided all her wrongs in many verbal and written communications, returned the letter at her request, unopened and with a message to the effect that she considered the correspondence to be entirely at an end. Augusta wrote again—this time to him, imploring him, since he had been made a party to the interview, to see her, to let her show him the proofs she had in her possession that never, in her letters to Byron, had she done any injury to his wife.

He consulted Lady Byron and refused. 'The proofs which you desire to give could only be given in Lady Byron's presence, and she will never consent to another meeting. The last was final.'

And he informed her that if she knew herself to be clear in her conscience of having done harm to Lady Byron, then the sense of her innocence in God's sight would make the opinion of any human being of no consequence to her, but if, on the other hand, she had some sorrowful acknowledgment to offer which she had missed her last and final opportunity of offering at that meeting, the whole matter would be heard 'very, very soon' when she met God face to face.[2]

[1] Ibid. 26 Apr. 1851.   [2] Ibid. 21 May 1851.

CHAPTER X

TROUBLE FROM TWO SCOTSMEN

If Hobhouse had treasured any fond hope that, by withdrawing active opposition to Thomas Moore, he would at least discourage other friends, acquaintances, or enemies of Byron's from publishing, his disillusionment must have been lamentable. Scarcely had the enormous wave of speculation which followed the appearance of Lady Byron's 'Remarks' ebbed away than John Murray had the temerity to bring out Dr James Kennedy's

CONVERSATIONS ON RELIGION,
with
LORD BYRON
and others,
Held in Cephalonia, A Short Time Previous to
His Lordship's Death

There had been so much horror in orthodox circles about Byron's alleged blasphemies, that his friends were particularly sensitive on the topic of his religion. An injunction against the piracy of three cantos of *Don Juan* had been dissolved, and one against the piracy of *Cain* had been refused, on the grounds that the works were of so flagitious a tendency that no protection ought to be granted to them and therefore anyone at all must be allowed to publish them! (The pirate, Dugdale, had pleaded most eloquently and successfully the shocking nature of the poetry from which he had been making a profit, and its unworthiness to be dignified by copyright.)

Unbridled cant was the fashion in discussing religion (the evangelist movements of the next generation were largely a reaction against it), and Hobhouse, unable to conceive of a book about Byron's sceptical opinions that would not raise a storm of protest, had scotched Dr Kennedy's effort, as he thought, six years before.

The Doctor, a military physician stationed in Cephalonia—then under British rule—had stated his aims a few weeks after Byron's death, writing to Douglas Kinnaird whom he mistook for one of the executors:

> My object is simply to give a faithful account of the conversations which took place between his Lordship & me & all such facts as may illustrate his character & opinions during the last six months of his life, & my motive for doing so is a belief that such a relation will neither be discreditable to his memory, injurious or offensive to any one, nor perhaps useless to the Public.[1]

Kinnaird had passed the letter on to Hobhouse, who, then or at some time later, had made enquiry about Kennedy of the man on the spot, Lord Sidney Osborne. The answer seemed conclusive:

[1] Murray MSS. 26 May 1824.

When I see that Mr Kennedy, thinking that he made considerable progress in what he conceives converting Lord Byron is expected to publish something on the subject, I am anxious to let you know the estimation in which certainly two months previous to his departure from Cefalonia Byron held the gentleman; he mentioned to me the visits paid him by this gentleman, which he confessed amused him a little, chiefly by flattering his hopes of making a proselyte of him, & then disappointing him. This is the account Byron gave me himself the end of last October of his communications with this gentleman whom he always used to term Saint Kennedy in contradistinction to a very pleasant young man there whom he called Sinner Kennedy.

I have not the honor of being known personally to the former of these characters, whom I saw for the first & last time at Metaxata the first visit I paid Byron, who instantly said to me, "My dear Sidney you came just in time to my relief for I was dreadfully bored with the Saint." . . .

I understand he is a man of some talent & a great deal of cant, & therefore he will very possibly endeavour to persuade the world that he carried conviction upon important subjects to the powerful mind of our friend. . . .[1]

If Hobhouse had glanced again at the Doctor's letter he would have seen that this was exactly what he did not pretend.

Though I failed in convincing him of the soundness of those views of Revealed Religion which all Orthodox Members of the Protestant churches entertain yet he expressed many sentiments which if known will tend to remove part of that obloquy which is attached to his name in the minds of most Christians.

Such had been his modest claim; but Hobhouse, on seeing Lord Sidney's letter, had determined to take measures of discouragement, and had sent direct to Kennedy a polite remonstrance. On receiving a further most courteous, though certainly long-winded, explanation of the literary plan, he had answered only with stony silence. But as books on Byron poured from the presses, he remained nervous, and early in 1825, another enquiry went to Lord Sidney, who replied:

Dr. Kennedy is at Cephalonia still, and I have heard nothing more of the intended publication, nor am I likely to do so from himself, for I do not know him, my character for chastity not standing high enough to entitle me to that honor. I believe him to be a gentlemanlike man, but led by the desire of converting others, and establishing his own superior claims to sanctity.[2]

This was less disquieting than the warning of the previous year; and Kennedy proved his right to be described as gentlemanlike by refraining from publication. In 1827, however, he had died of yellow fever on service with troops in Jamaica, and now in 1830 his widow had somehow

[1] Ibid. 14 Aug. 1824. 'Sinner' Kennedy was Private Secretary to Colonel Napier, the Resident.   [2] Ibid. 7 Feb. 1825.

prevailed on Murray to publish the work he had sadly put aside.

Hobhouse's judgment, and that of Byron's other intimates had, as usual in such matters, been much at fault. Kennedy's book, by far the least popular of any that was based on personal knowledge, would seem to be as literally true an account of Byron's talk and demeanour as ever was written, and he was perfectly right in believing it would do no discredit to its subject. Yet Lord Sidney was equally right in reporting that Byron was 'woefully bored' with him. Only his zest for accuracy and the vividness of what he had to tell saves him from being unreadable; and as a conversationalist it is easy to see that he must have driven his companions almost to despair.

Byron esteemed him, trusted him, and probably came to dread his approach. He never led Kennedy seriously to suppose he was within reach of conversion; and therefore could not have had any notion of playing such a cruel trick as to flatter his hopes and then disappoint him: but with his men-of-the-world friends, like Lord Sidney and the laughing officers of the garrison, he might pretend to a cynical attitude, finding it difficult to explain the mixture of kindliness and curiosity and respect for sincere belief, coupled perhaps with a desire to air a knowledge of the Bible on which he prided himself, which had brought him and this earnest Scotsman into their strange conjunction.

Kennedy's description of Byron's effect upon the islanders starts his book off with a splendid impetus :

> His arrival at Argostoli excited a great sensation among the Greeks and the English. The former were eager to behold a wealthy English nobleman, and a celebrated poet . . . on his way to join their country, to add the whole weight of his name, influence, talents and fortune to the cause of freedom. The latter felt a still greater curiosity to behold a countryman not less interesting by his unrivalled talents, than by that mystery and awe thrown over his character by his faults and misfortunes; but, above all, by the daily rumours of his misanthropy, profligacy, and infidelity, and by the warfare which he had so long carried on against many of the most distinguished literary characters, as well as against the government and religion of his native country.
>
> He was viewed by us all as an object of wonder and astonishment; and as one whose talents, character, and sentiments separated him, as it were, from the rest of mankind. All alike were anxious to view his person and watch his proceedings, and none but a spectator of the scene could conceive the vague and unrestrained wonder which he occasioned.

Unlike several more pretentious reporters, Kennedy is not concerned to show how superior he was to the general impression, and thus is able to conjure up in a few words that sense of 'awe and mystery' which Byron's reputation created about him wherever he went, and which must have

weighed intolerably at times on the consciousness of a man who was fond
of laughing and also rather shy.

> Hitherto I had seen his lordship only on horseback, as he took his evening
> ride with his friends; and while I often listened to the details of his sayings
> and actions, which formed the subject of general conversation, and which,
> for the most part, were only interesting because they were said or done by
> Lord Byron, I had no anticipation that circumstances were preparing the
> way for affording me a near and an intimate intercourse with him.

To Dr Kennedy a magical thing was about to happen. Spending the
evening with four friends, all Scotsmen like himself, he proposed to
attempt to convert them from the 'free and deistical' ideas they were
expressing by giving them—provided they did not interrupt him—'a full
and correct explanation of the doctrines of Christianity'. On hearing that
an appointment had been made for the session at the house of Dr Muir the
following Sunday, Byron suddenly signified a desire to be present.

> On the next day M[uir] communicated to me his lordship's wishes, and,
> though I had never spoken to his lordship, and little anticipated such a
> hearer, I readily consented to his being present, notwithstanding my fears
> that a consideration of his reputation and rank would embarrass me. . . .

Despite his tremors on that score, it must have been disappointing to
receive a message next day to the effect that this exciting person would not
after all be present, having decided to embark his horses. There could not
have been any real need for Byron to embark the horses himself when he
had a steward, a groom, and other servants to see to it. Perhaps he had
heard for the first time that Kennedy insisted on twelve clear hours to
expound his theme!

The Doctor had a gratifying idea that he was ultimately indebted for
the honour of Byron's company to Captain Scott's refusal to have such
'heathenish and outlandish doings' on board his ship as the embarkation
of horses on a Sunday; but it is more likely that Byron was prevailed upon
to change his mind by the officers who wanted the fun of seeing the
author of *Don Juan* at grips with a Methodist. At any rate, yet another
message came saying he would be present. 'The rumour of the meeting
now spread through the town. . . . This produced some uneasiness in the
minds of my friends, lest they should be branded as infidels and enemies
to religion.'

Kennedy prepared himself for his marathon discourse by sending a
quantity of religious books to Muir's house. The informal gathering of
fellow-Scots was being turned by the expectation of Byron's arrival into a
notable occasion, and Kennedy, who was only thirty and quite unused to
public or semi-public speaking, must have felt some dismay when the

Resident himself, Colonel Charles Napier, turned up, and Byron came accompanied by Hamilton Browne and Count Gamba. Just before this, another officer had been refused admission, but when he stated that he had come because he was a believer and 'not influenced by a mere desire of seeing Lord Byron', the objection was waived.

The gentlemen settled themselves, the young doctor began to preach, urging them to give him their undivided attention and to regard themselves for the first hour not as disputants but as persons obliged to divest themselves of prejudices.

A huge tract of print is occupied by what he could remember of his preliminary outline. It was plodding, dull, and badly organized; wanting in every quality likely to hold an audience. The mercurial Byron, the incisive Napier, the active, restless Hamilton Browne, and the bewildered Pietro, understanding only one word in half a dozen, must have been almost crushed under their boredom. 'To relieve their attention' Kennedy decided to read to them 'part of the works of John Newton'.

> I had, on a different occasion, found them productive of much utility to two persons of excellent understanding and of great candour; but on the present occasion I was disappointed. Whilst speaking, I was listened to with attention; but I had not proceeded far in reading, before I observed signs of impatience in some of them, especially in N[apier] and his lordship. I endeavoured to obviate this, by saying I would soon finish; but I had proceeded a short way further, when I was interrupted by his lordship asking me, "if these sentiments accorded with mine?"
>
> I said "they did, and with those of all sound Christians, except in one or two minor things, which I would point out as I went along." He now said "that they did not wish to hear the opinions of others, whose writings they could themselves read at any time, but my own."

Stubbornly Kennedy continued to read, and Byron to interrupt, saying:

> "What we want is to be convinced that the Bible is true; because, if we can believe this, it will follow, as a matter of course, that we must believe all the doctrines it contains."

Everyone joined in, trying to speed Kennedy up by begging him to keep in mind what they were seeking, a demonstration that the Scriptures were the word of God.

> They had violated their engagement to hear me for twelve hours, for which I had stipulated, entirely with the view of giving them, as far as the time permitted, useful and necessary instruction; and yet, under these circumstances, they desired, and seemed to expect, that I should convince, or attempt to convince, them in a short period.

He renewed his dogged attempts at reading, this time from the Preface to Scott's *Commentary on the Bible*, but they had not undertaken to

listen to a book, and Byron struck in again before he had got to the end
of a paragraph, asking if he believed in miracles.

> I immediately shut the book . . . his lordship's patience was evidently
> at an end.

The sermon thus terminated, Kennedy and Byron spoke on religion
for more than an hour. There is no doubt that the Doctor was on his
mettle to remember with exactitude the most interesting conversation he
had ever had occasion to record, that he lost no time in getting it down,
and that he was writing what most of those who had been present would
be able to read and criticize. Except for brief speeches here and there in
letters and diaries, there cannot be anything nearer to a precise and immediate sketch of Byron talking. The occasion had become serio-comical.
He knew the officers were laughing at the preacher's grave admonitions
and painful lack of capacity for the task he had set himself. On the other
hand, he realized that Kennedy was possessed by a genuine conviction
and that cant was not his weakness, and so he would not give his friends
the pleasure of watching him score too roundly off the Doctor.

We see him in that conversation, and in all his subsequent conversations related by Kennedy, clear as in a sharply defined photograph. He is
delightfully affable—the adjective constantly applied to him by new
acquaintances who expected to meet 'a misanthropical gentleman in wolf-
skin breeches'—but his affability does not extend to falsifying his
opinions or concealing beyond a certain limit his impatience with topics
that bore him. He has developed authority and is skilful at steering the
talk in a direction that suits him. He is adroit in setting his associates at
ease, yet too outspoken in contradiction to be termed a tactful man. But
having sat from eleven till three o'clock engaged in a debate in which he
has courteously had the best of the argument (his remarks being 'heard
by the others with apparent approbation and applause'), he has the grace,
on rising, to enquire flatteringly of his opponent, 'Why do you not print
your thoughts on these subjects?'

> He then said, that they were much obliged to me for the trouble I had
> taken with them. I replied, that "I was sorry I had been able to do so little
> good after so long a meeting." He smiled and said, "We must not despair,
> as we can meet again." He then departed, accompanied by his friends.

With mingled relief and regret Kennedy waited in vain to see his
agreeable challenger at future meetings, relief because the company had
not been slow to tell him that Byron was better versed in theological books
than he was himself, regret because that soul had seemed so worthy of
salvation.

L.L.B.—Z

I rather wished to converse with his lordship alone, than in mixed society, as from what I had observed, his presence would have had no good effect upon my military friends, nor would he himself have been benefited, as he would have been incited to speak for the sake of impression and effect, and what he said would, by some at least, have been listened to with equal avidity and credulity.

He met Byron again at a dinner party, and found him 'polite, lively, and facetious', saying of the Pope, 'I like his holiness very much, particularly since an order, which I understand he has lately given, that no more miracles shall be performed.'

Charming but elusive, Byron retreated from Argostoli to Metaxata several miles away. The officers used to ride out to visit him, and one of them, Hesketh, told Kennedy that Byron would be glad to see him there. He longed to go, but drew back as from a temptation.

. . . I wished not to appear forward in visiting Lord Byron, as I knew that my motives would be misrepresented, and I was not previously assured that his lordship wished me to come. I thought also that if he were in earnest to hear religion explained, he must have been aware that the least hint from him would induce me willingly to comply with his desire. I was besides deterred a little by the consciousness that there was often a secret, ambitious desire of making such a convert, and though I immediately repressed such vain desires, yet I knew that others would readily enough impute to me these motives: thus I had convinced myself that it was more proper not to go near him, but to be ready, should he at any time invite me.

With this view I was diligently employed in preparing myself for these possible interviews. . . .

Poor Kennedy! He was humourless, but he was honest, and he looked back as he wrote his book and saw that he had been studying and cudgelling his brains on points 'which were not in the least interesting to Lord Byron'.

He called at last, when he heard from Count Gamba that they would leave for Missolonghi in a few days, and as he was made welcome and offered refreshments, he told his host how he had been engaged in preparations to meet him. What intricate web of theology he spread out we do not know, but Byron amiably brushed it aside with 'These certainly are things I do not trouble myself with at present', and asked him what had drawn *him* to Christianity and whether he had made progress with his conversions. Kennedy found himself telling the famous poet how difficult his toil was, how intractable were the young men he was striving with, how hard it was to get a patient hearing from them, and how they lay in wait to turn what he said to ridicule. Kind and sympathetic, Byron seemed to understand what it all meant to him, and Kennedy insensibly went on to plead and struggle for his soul.

It is the longest verbatim, or near verbatim, report of Byron's conversation existing; and ranges, as he flitted this way and that like a will-o'-the-wisp, from the conception of God, the Gospel and its commentators, the literal truth or otherwise of the Bible, the works of Gibbon and Warburton, and the hypocrisies of society, to the sublimity of *Faust*, his personal apathy towards Milton, his scepticism about the British idolatry of Shakespeare, his admiration for Pope's character as well as his works, and his own failure to write tragedy.

Kennedy, released, chided him soundly for the vice and impiety of his writings, and Byron justified them in terms we cannot doubt he used, for the arguments are too good for the Doctor, whose disapproval was profound, to have given gratuitously to the other side; nor could he have contrived the twists by which the mischievous poet baffled him.

It would be all but impossible, certainly, for a man, even in a state approaching exaltation, to remember accurately every phrase of a discussion that must have lasted an hour; but there are speeches as to which it is reasonable to be persuaded that we are hearing something near Byron's very words.

"You seem to hate the Socinians."[1]

"Not the individuals," I replied, "but their principles. I believe their system a terrible delusion, and that there is more hope of a deist, than of a Socinian, becoming a real Christian."

"But is this charitable?" he asked; "why would you exclude a sincere Socinian from the hope of salvation?"

". . . If any of them are sincerely seeking the truth, God will in due time teach them, and bring them out of their Socinian delusion; but those who die believing it, die, as far as I can judge, unregenerated, and consequently, according to the Scriptures, die in a most dangerous state."

"Their religion," said his lordship, "seems to be spreading very much. Lady B. is a great one among them, and much looked up to. . . ."

I said I was exceedingly sorry to hear that her ladyship was among such a set. . . .

"I should have been pleased," said Lord B. "that you had known Shelley. I should like to have seen you argue together. You very much remind me of him, not only in countenance, but in your manner of speaking. He was to have been my companion in Greece, poor fellow! had the unfortunate accident which deprived him of life not taken place."

I replied, that I should indeed have been pleased, were he here now: not that I might argue with him, but that time might have been given to him to change his sentiments, and amend his life. "I never read any of his writings, but I have seen some extracts from them in the 'Quarterly Review', and most certainly it would be no honour to resemble him in his opinions, whatever it might be to do so in other respects. From what he says there, he

---

[1] The Socinians believed that Jesus was a prophet of God's word, but not God, and that the sacraments had no supernatural powers or origins.

appears to me to have been a man totally destitute of common sense. His poetry may perhaps be fine and sublime, but to me it is perfectly unintelligible; unless so far as it appeared that the poor man was a virulent hater of Christianity, and ascribed all the evils and miseries of life to its introduction."

"I do not mean to defend his sentiments," said Lord B., "nor to approve of the mode in which he published them; but Shelley possessed many virtues, and many excellent qualities, and you would have liked him as a companion. He was cool in his manner; yet impassioned, animated, and eloquent in his conversation. . . ."

"I wish . . . [it is Kennedy speaking] that Shelley had been alive, that the wanderings of his imagination had subsided, and that he had become a sober, sensible man, a good Christian, and an honest member of society."

"He possessed," said his lordship, "one of the first Christian virtues, charity and benevolence. His benevolence was universal, and his charity far beyond his means."

But Kennedy denied sturdily that benevolence in Shelley could be a Christian virtue. His fate was tragic, he agreed, but he had died with his sins unrepented, a striking warning to others of the necessity of preparing for death and judgment.

"I see," said Lord B., "it is impossible to excite in your mind sympathy, or obtain a proper degree of allowance, for an unfortunate man of fine genius and imagination."

That dialogue assuredly took place almost word for word as repeated by Kennedy, because he died before Shelley was famous enough to inspire invention and could not have seen Byron's letters about him. It must have been ironical to Byron, since Kennedy resembled Shelley physically and in manner, and was about the same age, to observe his entirely different style of fanaticism, and he may at first have been glad to see the Doctor for the sake of his memories of much more brilliant conversations tending in precisely the contrary direction: but ultimate boredom was inevitable.

The younger man came away from that encounter thinking of all the things he might have said better, and troubled lest he had been wearying Byron by the length of his arguments. He was not as fatuous as the onlookers imagined, and realized that he had made little or no progress towards the longed-for conversion.

There was nothing in his manner which approached to levity, or anything that indicated a wish to mock at religion; though, on the other hand, an able dissembler could have done and said all that he did with such feelings and intentions. . . . I am perfectly uncertain what impression was made on Lord B's mind.

He questioned other people who knew Byron as to the effect they thought he had had, and on the whole they were discouraging.

The wits of the garrison made themselves merry with what was going on, and passed many jokes on the subject. Some of them affected to believe,—I know not on what ground—that Lord B's wish to hear me proceeded from his desire to have an accurate idea of the opinions and manners of the Methodists in order that he might make Don Juan become one for a time, and thus paint their conduct with the greater accuracy and fidelity: some of them did not hesitate to tell me that this was the case, and that, if I were wise, I should let his lordship alone.

To these gibes Kennedy very justly replied that, if his lordship had any such intention, he was not playing the part of a gentleman. Byron's dealings with Kennedy prove a considerable unwillingness to hurt his feelings, and, by the time he left the island, a reliance on his good and honourable qualities; but it was not in his nature to refrain from savouring the comedy of the situation, and the joke about making Don Juan a Methodist for a canto may easily have started with him. Nor was it possible that the discussions should continue in a strain of perfect solemnity on his side. We detect the note of raillery, though Kennedy did not, in such passages as the following:

"How does S. get on? Is he in a fair way still?"

"He continues," I replied, "to read the Bible, and to reflect on these subjects. . . . Though he is not convinced, his progress hitherto is so far pleasing. Has your lordship," I said, "read any of the books I took the liberty of sending?"

"I have looked into Boston, but have not had time to read far. I am afraid it is too deep for me."

"Be not afraid," I said, "but continue, and you will find it easier than you imagine. . . ."

"I have begun," he said, "very fairly; I have given some of your tracts to Fletcher, who is a good sort of man but still wants, like myself, some reformation, and I hope he will spread them among the other servants, who require it still more. Bruno and Gamba are busy reading some of the Italian tracts, and I hope it will have a good effect upon them. . . . We must have patience, and we shall see what has been the result."

Kennedy asked him if he had begun to pray that he might understand the Bible.

"Not yet," he said, "I have not arrived at that pitch of faith yet . . . you are in too great a hurry. Remember how long you have been with S. and M. and the others, and consider what progress they have made."

He produced a book which he had put aside for Kennedy, *Illustrations on the Moral Government of God* by E. Smith, M.D., explaining that in it 'the author proves that the punishment of Hell is not eternal—it will have a termination'.

Kennedy feared that so evil a belief could only be maintained by one of the Socinians, and Byron grew a little sharper.

. . . "The arguments he uses are strong. He draws them from the Bible itself, and by showing that a time will come when every intelligent character shall be supremely happy, and eternally so, he expunges that shocking doctrine, that sin and misery will for ever exist under the Government of a God whose highest attribute is love and goodness. . . ."

Kennedy had no intention of being deprived of hellfire and put up a stout fight. He was afraid, he said, that the author would find himself miserably mistaken in a future life. He thought the Roman Catholic doctrine of purgatory, which appealed very much to Byron, was utterly absurd; he could not conceive how any soul could expiate sin by suffering.

"But why are you," said his lordship, "so anxious to maintain and prove the eternity of hell punishments? It is certainly not a humane doctrine, and appears very inconsistent with the mild and benevolent doctrines of Christ."
"I maintain it," I said, "because it is revealed in the Scriptures, and because a disbelief in it renders the whole of the doctrines of Christ perfectly unnecessary . . . It appears nothing else than a delusion of the devil to persuade men to continue in sin here. . . ."

They came to a deadlock. Byron was obstinate in denying that eternal punishment could be compatible with the principle that God is love, and all Kennedy could do was to undertake to write down his reasons in favour of Hell in the hope that his opponent would examine them at leisure. That morning he was very dogmatic and persistent in uncongenial theories, so it is not surprising that when Lord Sidney Osborne turned up, Byron should have said he was 'dreadfully bored with the Saint', but it was hardly fair of him not to keep his love of mischief in check on hearing his new guest arriving on horseback in the courtyard below. 'Do stay and we shall have dinner immediately,' he said to Kennedy. 'Your conversation will be useful, perhaps, to Lord S[idney].'

We then walked to the door, and as we descended the stairs, Lord B. was standing at the head, and called out, "I really wish you could convince this wild fellow of a lord, he has as much need of it as I have."
I smiled, and said, "You see my task is sufficiently heavy with you. Let us wait till we finish your conversion. . . ."

Kennedy was not a gifted writer, but such was his zeal for truth and the impact of the experience, that he was able to differentiate with extreme clarity Byron's mode of speaking from his own, a feat in which several much cleverer recorders failed, and some, like Lady Blessington, quite abysmally. Who can doubt the literal exactness of this little interchange, written after an occasion when he stayed to dinner at Byron's house with Pietro, Dr Bruno, and others?

Lord Byron . . . said "he was particularly struck with a remark of Bishop Beveridge, in one of the tracts, [sent by Kennedy] 'that in our best actions we sin.' Do you remember the passage?"

"No," I answered, "I did not observe it."

"You are a fine fellow to give me tracts for my conversion, without knowing yourself what they contain. . . ."

S. had been saying something at the corner of the table while he was sitting next to Count G. which did not appear to be very orthodox: his lordship called out to me, "Do you hear what S. has been saying? Why, he has not advanced one step towards conversion. He is worse than I am!"

That is surely authentic reporting, and if only Kennedy had not been even more eager to set down his own speeches, which are nearly interminable, than Byron's, his book might have sold as well as Medwin's. As it is, it has never been reprinted.

The talk that day was going rather gaily when something unfortunately directed Kennedy's attention once more to the heresies of the deadly Socinians, so that he was led rapidly back to hellfire and the small hope of salvation there was for people with such 'damnable opinions'. He held forth at a merciless length against the idea of purgatory, saying there was no warrant for the belief that the wicked could be cleansed of sin and raised to Heaven. It was not the will of God. 'If it depended on me,' he acknowledged, 'judging by mere feelings of humanity, I would have all saved. . . .'

"Nay," exclaimed some of them, "I would not save all."

"I would save," cried his lordship, "my sister and my daughter, and some of my friends,—and a few others, and let the rest shift for themselves."

"And your wife also," I exclaimed.

"No," he said.

"But your wife, surely, you would save your wife?"

"Well," he said, "I would save her too, if you like."

Lady Byron read Kennedy's book with interest, but what she thought of that dialogue we do not know. Perhaps, as she believed, in advanced years, that 'it was not in human nature to keep up such animosity as Lord Byron had shown' towards her,[1] she took it seriously. She seems to have missed the whole point of Byron's arguments, for she told Henry Crabb Robinson:

'Strange as it may seem, Dr Kennedy is most faithful where you doubt his being so. Not merely from casual expressions but from the whole tenor of Lord Byron's feelings, I could not but conclude he was a believer in the inspiration of the Bible, and had the gloomiest Calvinistic tenets. To that unhappy view of the relation of the Creature to the Creator, I have always ascribed the misery of his life. . . . Judge then, how I must hate the creed which made him see God as an Avenger, not a Father.'[2]

[1] See p. 336.   [2] Robinson: Letter of 5 Mar. 1855.

Her own character was fixed and reveals no change from girlhood to old age, only an intensification of traits already strongly marked in youth, whereas his was immensely resilient and capable of development; and there was little or nothing left of his early Calvinist fears when he steadfastly refused to accept the doctrine of eternal damnation.

It was evidently some psychological stress that made Lady Byron adhere to her theory of his inhuman hostility, because she was able to read the evidence of several sound witnesses that, at the end, he had revived his desire to be reconciled to her. Kennedy was most explicit on this point, and, as he quoted things which were true and which could not have been known to him unless he had heard them from Byron, she might have given credence to the rest of his report.

"If I said anything disrespectful of Lady B., I am very much to blame. Lady B. deserves every respect from me, and certainly nothing could give me greater pleasure than a reconciliation."

"With such sentiments, how is it possible that a separation has taken place, or how is it that a reunion cannot be effected?" . . .

"Lady B. left me without explaining the cause. . . . What could I have done? I did everything at the time that could be done, and I am, and always have been ready for a reconciliation."

". . . Before I tell you what you might have done, let me ask you what you would not have done, when you were paying your addresses to Lady B?. . . Would you not have compassed sea and land, and gone to the uttermost parts of the earth, in order to obtain her hand?"

"I would," said his lordship.

We may presume that Byron, whose courtship had been anything but fervent, was to some extent playing up to the romantic attitude of his innocent and good-natured mentor; but his wish for reunion seems to have been as sincere as it was ill-founded.

It came upon him after leaving Italy. At thirty-five, he was tired of being uprooted, and would have welcomed a settled and domesticated life, the pleasures of fatherhood, a return to his country, and a truce in his war with society: and since none of these aims was attainable while the scandal of his broken marriage still hung over him, he allowed his longings to expunge all but deluding memories of his wife—a woman whose tastes were ascetic, whose habits were restless, and who was by inclination far less domesticated than himself.[1]

Divorce and remarriage would, in our own age, doubtless have solved the problems of both parties, but under the laws of that time no grounds

[1] She was constantly changing both her residence and her servants, and there is an almost total absence of references to household gods of any kind in her letters. She was a fond mother and grandmother, but not otherwise interested in children except as material for educational projects. She had little feeling, as her writings show, for animals, and never kept a pet.

existed, and Byron was doomed to be for ever disreputable unless he could win her back. The need was father to the wish, and the wish was father to the thought: and it may be that the very realism he could never surrender in his dealings with the Greeks left him the more susceptible to the illusion fostered by his nostalgia for England. Considering the many humiliations his wife had inflicted on him, his hopes were pathetic and unworthy—though the reports he had from Augusta may have led him to believe he was still loved.

He was too moody a creature, however, to entertain any dream except intermittently; and there was also a modifying characteristic which the Doctor did not fail to note: 'His conversation and manners varied according to his company.' With sober and earnest men like Kennedy and Stanhope, and fatherly men like Parry, his response, unconsciously histrionic, would be to enter fully into the sympathetic rôle of erring husband anxious to be forgiven. Livelier and more worldly company saw him under another aspect.

> With some of the young officers, whose chief pleasure consisted in excitement and amusement, he was among the first for wit and repartee, and according to accounts I have heard, he was not on every occasion scrupulous in refraining from indelicacy, and even infidelity. . . .
> When he visited one of the officers with whom he seemed pleased, he was accustomed to jest, laugh, smoke, drink brandy and water, and porter, with the best of them. I never saw him guilty of any such actions.

Byron was careful of Kennedy's feelings, just as he had been careful of William Harness's, who had found his talk 'uniformly delicate' in the old Newstead Abbey days. We can tell the disposition of his correspondents— the gossiping, the ribald, the sententious, the sentimental—merely from his style of writing to them.

Kennedy came as near as anyone could to making Byron solemn.

> I have heard him say several witty things; but as I was always anxious to keep him grave . . . after allowing the laugh to pass, I again endeavoured to resume the seriousness of the conversation, whilst his lordship constantly did the same. Those sayings to which of course my attention was not directed, I have forgotten. . . . My impression from them was, that they were unworthy of a man of his accomplishments: I mean the desire of jesting.

What Byron thought of Kennedy we know directly from one of his letters to Augusta:

> There is a clever but eccentric man here, a Dr Kennedy, who is very pious and tries in good earnest to make converts; but his Christianity is a queer one, for he says that the priesthood of the Church of England are no more Christians than 'Mahound or Termagent' are. He has made some converts, I suspect rather to the beauty of his wife (who is pretty as well as

pious) than of his theology. I like what I have seen of him, of *her* I know nothing, nor desire to know, having other things to think about.[1]

There are also a few words about him to Charles Barry in Genoa:

I have recently seen something of a zealous Dr. Kennedy—a very good Calvinist, who has a taste for controversy and conversion, and thinks me so nearly a tolerable Christian, that he is trying to make me a whole one.[2]

It is thus plain that, though he saw, as did everyone else, the ludicrous side of the young man's perpetual expostulations, he was very far from regarding him as a butt.

George Finlay sketched their relationship as it seemed to an irreverent onlooker:

I own I felt astonished to hear Lord Byron submit to lectures on his life, and his vanity, and the uselessness of his talents, which made me stare. The conversation was excessively amusing. Dr Kennedy had given Lord Byron some silly tracts, which, to my utter astonishment, I found Byron had read. He flew to his room to show a passage of Sherlock, quoted in one, which was in opposition to something urged by the Doctor, and forced Kennedy to own he had not read them himself, though he had given them to Lord Byron for his conversion. There was no argument, for though Lord Byron was extremely fond of conversing on religious subjects, he seldom argued; single objections he would start, and strive to raise perplexities, and lead his adversary into contradictions, but I never heard him enter the field as a professed deist.

. . . Few people were better acquainted with the Scriptures. . . .

Before the end of the conversation with Kennedy, however, he grew very warm—talked a little too violently but calmed again—asked Kennedy if he could not be a good Christian without believing in eternal perdition; and said he knew few he could abandon to such a fate. . . .[3]

It was often observed of Byron that he disliked and avoided argument, but what Finlay describes sounds distinctly like one. Perhaps he meant that Byron did not press for victory.

Kennedy tells that when they parted he made Byron a little speech saying that he would pray for him, and the other, taking his hand, replied, 'I shall always feel myself indebted to you.'

About two months later the Doctor received a letter in the almost undecipherable Italian of Count Pietro Gamba, telling him about the little Turkish girl of eight whom Byron had adopted.[4] While deciding upon her future, he wanted to send her for safety to one of the Greek islands and Pietro, acting as private secretary, had been instructed to enquire whether the Doctor and his pretty wife would take her for a few months, 'it being

---

[1] *L. & J.* 12 Oct. 1823.   [2] Ibid. 27/29 Oct. 1823.
[3] Stanhope: Letter of 31 May 1824.   [4] See p. 176.

well understood that the expenses for her maintenance and education be placed to the account of my lord'.[1]

The letter was presently followed by one from Byron himself saying that the child, 'your future convert', appeared to him to be 'lively, and intelligent, and promising', and that she had 'an interesting countenance'.

> . . . My idea would be to send her to my daughter in England (if not to respectable persons in Italy) and so to provide for her as to enable her to live with reputation either singly or in marriage, if she arrive at maturity. I will make proper arrangements about her expenses through Messrs. Barff and Hancock, and the rest I leave to your discretion and to Mrs K's, with a great sense of obligation for your kindness in undertaking her temporary superintendence.[2]

Did he see in this destitute infant a means of repairing certain omissions in his conduct towards his dead child, Allegra? Or did he, at least momentarily, fancy that in providing an exotic little companion for Ada (now in her ninth year) he might make a conjugal *rapprochement*?

Soon there was a complication. He wrote to Kennedy again:

> There is a slight demur about Hato's [Hatajè's] voyage, her mother wishing to go with her, which is quite natural and I have not the heart to refuse it; for even Mahomet made a law, that in the division of captives, the child should never be separated from her mother. But this may make a difference in the arrangement, although the poor woman (who has lost half her family in the war) is, as I said, of good character and of mature age, so as to render her respectability not liable to suspicion.[3]

Mrs Kennedy was now faced with the problem of either having to withdraw from her undertaking, or take into her small household an adult woman as well as a child: 'but', she says in a footnote, 'as Lord B. had put us to the test, as Christians opposed to Mahometans; although highly inconvenient, we consented to receive both.'

Byron's death spared the Kennedys the necessity of fulfilling so generous a promise, nor was Lady Byron ever called upon to decide whether she would educate the little Turk with Ada. On account of the respect for her character which was implied, she was by no means displeased when she read of that project, and was known to refer to it with complacency in the years to come.

The papers on the Kennedys' side relating to this episode, as well as Dr Kennedy's special arguments for Byron on the state of damnation, and several other documents—of which he had no copies—were high-handedly impounded by Hobhouse with the intention of frustrating the book. The polite applications for them made first by the Doctor himself, then by his

---

[1] Kennedy: Appendix. 24 Feb. 1824.
[2] Ibid. 4 Mar. 1824.   [3] Ibid. 10 Mar. 1824.

widow, were ignored—a discourtesy which was remarked, not very surprisingly, in the Preface and a footnote. If Hobhouse had had his way, an
invaluable and exceedingly creditable account of Byron on his last
adventure would never have seen the light.

On January 21st, 1831, a querulous entry appears in the diary:

> A letter from Mrs Kennedy, widow of Dr. Kennedy, whose religious
> conversations with Lord Byron have been published. A most insolent epistle
> indeed and likely to add to the thousand and one squabbles which my
> intimacy, and I may add, my honest and disinterested friendship for Byron,
> have entailed upon me.
>
> The woman is angry with me for discouraging her from publishing the
> catch-penny conversations above-mentioned: I knowing from Lord Sidney
> Osborne that Byron was playing upon Dr Kennedy. . . . Query Shall I
> answer the widow! I should not like to hurt her feelings although she has
> shown no care for mine—she is a woman and a widow, moreover I can say
> nothing on the subject which might not lead to an inference injurious to
> Lord Byron.[1]

A few days later he was writing:

> Finished the second volume of Moore's Life of Byron, and am now more
> pleased than ever with the resolution taken by me, of not contributing to that
> work. Nevertheless, it presents a tolerably fair picture of Lord Byron's real
> character, and some of Moore's observations are exceedingly just and con-
> veyed in appropriate language. That the letters and journals raise Lord
> Byron in public estimation as a man of talent no one will be foolish enough to
> assert. What then has this publication achieved? It has put £3,500 at least
> into the pocket of T. Moore.[2]

It is difficult to form any idea of what kind of material, according to
Hobhouse's judgment, *would* have raised Byron in public estimation. Anything in a high-falutin or romantic vein would have been at least as ill-
received by him as the colloquial and easy writing the most eminent critics
of the day had at once acclaimed. Had it been left to Hobhouse, we should
have had no memorial of Byron but a marble statue and a set of his works
—expurgated.

Not that he was without many causes for grumbling, had he kept his
indignation within bounds. There were frequent uncalled-for attacks upon
himself in books and articles about his friend, and he had every reason to
know that a number of them were political in origin. It is difficult to see
that staid personage, whose fundamental instincts all led him towards
conformity, as a hot-headed rebel striving to subvert to social order, but

---

[1] Hobhouse *Journals*. Mrs Kennedy cannot have done well out of the book because it
did not sell, but she drove a very hard and canny bargain with Murray. He agreed to give
her two-thirds of the profits, having at first offered half. Murray, like Hobhouse, found
the tone of her letters unconciliatory.   [2] *Ibid.* 31 Jan. 1831.

such he was considered during his brave days as a Radical and Reformer.

Such he certainly appeared to the Ultra-Tory Scot, John Galt, whose conduct towards Hobhouse entirely revives our sympathy for him just when his purblind prejudice against Kennedy has alienated it.

That Galt of all people should have elbowed his way to the forefront of the army of biographers was in itself irritating enough.

> . . . I knew him [Hobhouse wrote] when Byron and I used to laugh at him as the most absurd of coxcombs, scarcely responsible for his conduct, for he had a touch of crazy folly about him.[1]

Besides being ill-informed and conceited, he was also ill-mannered and publicly insulting—and this after Hobhouse had broken his strict rule against assisting any of the invaders of privacy. Galt had met Hobhouse in the lobby of the House of Commons, and announced to him that he was writing a book on Byron (in reality, he had all but finished it) and would call on him about it. When he did call, Hobhouse was absent, and Galt the same day sent a note to ask whether he could enable him 'to contradict a story that has been reported to me'.

> viz. that he left 'the Guiccioli in destitute circumstances after having promised to leave two thousand pounds for her until he sent for her. . . . I shall be content with a brief note to settle the point.[2]

Hobhouse could not let his friend lie under such an aspersion. He had written saying he knew Byron had offered to give her a sum of money outright, or to leave it to her by will, and that she would not hear of any such provision being made,[3] and he added that he had in his possession a letter in which Byron extolled her for her disinterestedness.

Having requested the means of contradicting the story and received them, Galt had not contradicted it, but had given it prominence with a footnote of incredulity respecting Hobhouse's version: 'My friend says . . . that Mr Hobhouse is not correct.' To make matters worse, he had printed the whole of Hobhouse's letter, meant to set him right but not to be published, and called attention to it in his Preface with the words: 'I could not expunge from my text what I had stated, having no reason to doubt the authority of my information.'

The impertinence of this, after having so explicitly appealed to Hobhouse as a competent authority, gives an immediate notion of the character of the man whose book drew Hobhouse back to the heat of

---

[1] Hobhouse *Journals*, 6 Oct. 1830. In a letter to Hodgson, asking him to give a favourable review to one of Galt's early books, Byron called him 'a cock-brained man.' (*L. & J.*, 21 Feb. 1812.)   [2] Murray MSS. 28 July 1830.

[3] Moore quotes in his 2nd volume, published after Galt's work appeared, a letter from Barry (12 June 1828): 'When Lord Byron went to Greece, he gave me orders to advance money to Madame Guiccioli; but that lady would never consent to receive any.'

controversy, and wrung from him the poignant cry: 'This fellow annoys me as much as if he was the first of the biographers.'[1]

There was something egregious about Galt, some element, over and above his impenetrable self-complacency, which, despite a vein of talent, made almost his whole life a series of abortive projects, and caused even his few successful enterprises to collapse before yielding their reward. But vexatiously enough, his *Life of Lord Byron* was not, as to popularity, one of his failures. On the contrary, it went through four editions in as many months, and, being much cheaper, was read by more people than Moore's, which it claimed to correct.

Moore's 'compilation', Galt said in his Preface (and the word came ironically from him who had taken much more than half his book from other sources) had not proved satisfactory. He had evinced too eager an anxiety to set out the qualities of his friend to the brightest advantage.

> I respect the generosity with which he had executed his task. I think that he has made no striking misrepresentation; I even discern but little exaggeration, although he has amiably chosen to paint only the sunny side: the limning is correct; but the likeness is too radiant and conciliatory.
>
> . . . Perhaps I ought to state that I never stood on such a footing with his Lordship as to inspire me with any sentiment likely to bias my judgment. I am indebted to him for no other favours than those which a well bred person of rank bestows in the interchange of civility on a man who is of none. . . . I am gratified with the recollection of having known a person so celebrated, and I believe myself incapable of intentional injustice. I can only regret the impression he made upon me, if it shall be thought I have spoken of him with prejudice.

All this had a very candid air, but it amounted to no more than an argument that not knowing Byron well was a specially good qualification for writing about him. The patronizing near-approbation of Moore was provocative from a man so scantily equipped to pronounce a verdict, and when, in a later Preface,[2] he felt obliged to answer those who had pointed out how much he himself was indebted to Moore's research, he took refuge in arrogance: 'When a book has been published, its contents become public property. . . . His documents have been occasionally referred to, and his opinions also controverted. . . .'

He threatened to depart from his 'quiet habits', and to let the critics—'the nettles of Parnassus'—feel his hoofs and his teeth. He seems to have been unconscious that the metaphor made an ass of him.

Galt's book was written soon after his release from a debtor's prison, at headlong speed and in desperate need of money. It consisted of some personal remembrances stretched as far as they could go, and whatever he

---

[1] Hobhouse *Journals*, 6 Oct. 1830.   [2] To the Third Edition.

chose to lift from Dallas, Medwin, Gamba, Parry, Stanhope, Leigh Hunt, Moore, and even Kennedy, whose work came out only a few weeks before his own. Partly because of the visible padding, and partly because he wanted to make as much as possible of the few occasions where he could speak from his own knowledge, it is of crudely unbalanced proportions. He devoted more than a third of his space to Byron's tour of the Near East between 1809 and 1811. Even on that ground, his want of material induced him more than once to stray widely from his subject and tell his own adventures when Byron was nowhere near the scene:

> . . . It will not be altogether obtrusive here to recapitulate what happened to myself during a visit to Velhi Pasha, the son of Ali, and whom his Lordship afterwards visited.

Or:

> As I soon after passed along the same road, I shall here describe what I met with myself in the course of the journey. . . .

Galt was a novelist, a vivid writer when able to sketch a scene he had observed; but if his capacity to portray makes up for some defects, his taste for portraying discomfiture frequently imparts an unpleasant and a vulgar savour to what he depicts. He belonged to that class of 19th-century authors whose humour turns on the oversetting of someone's pretensions to status, on social uneasiness and humiliation, not on a grand but on a petty scale. Dickens began at that level with his *Sketches by Boz*, but genius and compassion enabled him soon to rise above it. Galt could not rise above it: he had no other standards at all for the interpretation of character than those of a class-conscious provincial who is rejoiced whenever he sees pride take a fall.

As biographer, he follows his bent as fiction writer, and makes use of every device for poking fun at his subject. Though his admiration for Byron's poetry is unbounded, he seldom fails to attribute a contemptible motive to his conduct, sometimes going to extraordinary limits to find one. Pointing out, for example, that Byron wrote nothing in *Childe Harold* about Malta, he remarks:

> . . . The silence of his muse on a topic so rich in romance . . . persuades me that there must have been some specific cause for the omission. . . . I should be inclined to say, notwithstanding the seeming improbability of the notion, that it was owing to some curious modification of vindicative spite.

When an eloquent poet's spite expresses itself in total silence, it must indeed be curiously modified.

Galt, thirty years old to Byron's twenty-one when they met, was travelling on the same sailing packet from Gibraltar to Malta. It would seem to have been the first time he had ever had the opportunity of studying a young nobleman, and his tense inverted snobbery made him watchful for signs of presumptuous aristocracy. But we discover this only from his book. The letters he wrote to Byron, in which he was generally asking or thankfully acknowledging a favour, are most assiduously deferential, and there was no one who found it a greater honour to be—'with the most respectful regard'—his Lordship's very obedient servant.

He opened, or tried to open, a correspondence after they had parted at Malta by writing from Palermo to say he could engage a painter there if his Lordship wanted to take one on his Eastern travels.[1] Four months later he ran across the two companions in Athens, and within a few days was asking Byron to use his influence in getting a firman for him to enter territory under the rule of Ali Pasha.[2] As he arrived in Athens on February 20th, 1810, and left for Smyrna on March 4th, their meetings could not have been numerous, but no doubt they had the delusive conviviality that travellers assume when their paths cross in remote places; and Athens was then a very remote place for most Britons.

At Smyrna a month or so later they had another and much briefer encounter, and perhaps Galt's peculiarities, which left him at times almost friendless, were beginning to grate; because he remarked that Byron was less cordial, more opinionated, more lordly, and was altogether the sort of man who could never become an object of esteem. This did not prevent him from applying again for a firman, which Byron procured for him.[3] In after years he could remember nothing of his deference. His attitude throughout his book is that of one on a higher plane of wisdom who had been diverted and sometimes repelled by the posturings of an absurd though undeniably impressive young man.

He usually saw Hobhouse as well as Byron in a ridiculous light: (he says in his autobiography that their acquaintance 'was not very cordial at any time'); and his recollections of them both are commonly in this key:

> Having landed the mail at Girgenti, we stretched over to Malta, where we arrived about noon next day—all the passengers, except the two friends, [Byron and Hobhouse] being eager to land, went on shore with the captain. They remained behind for a reason—which an accidental expression of Byron let out—much to my secret amusement; for I was aware they would be disappointed, and the anticipation was relishing. They expected—at least he did—a salute from the batteries, and sent ashore notice to Sir Alexander Ball, the governor, of his arrival; but the guns were sulky, and evinced no respect of persons: so that late in the afternoon, about the heel of the evening, the two magnates were obliged to come on shore, and slip into the city unnoticed and unknown.

[1] Murray MSS. 23 Oct. 1809.
[2] Ibid. 25 Feb. 1810.   [3] Ibid. 17 Sept. 1810.

. . . The merchants were truly hospitable and few more so than Mr
Chabot. As I had letters to him, he invited me to dinner, along with several
other friends previously engaged. In the cool of the evening as we were
sitting at our wine, Lord Byron and Mr Hobhouse were announced. His
Lordship was in better spirits than I had ever seen him. His appearance
showed, as he entered the room, that they had met with some adventure,
and he chuckled with an inward sense of enjoyment, not altogether without
spleen—a kind of malicious satisfaction—as his companion recounted, with
all becoming gravity, their woes and sufferings, as an apology for begging a
bed and a morsel for the night. God forgive me! but I partook of Byron's
levity at the idea of personages so consequential wandering destitute in the
streets, seeking for lodgings from door to door, and rejected by all.

How clearly we understand Galt, how vaguely Byron, from such a
narrative! Galt tells us he has had great pleasure in seeing a lord and his
friend taken down a peg, and we believe him; but what can we make of
Byron's feelings—the combination of high spirits and spleen, the 'malicious satisfaction' in being without food or lodging? A person who was not
persuaded that spleen, malice, and vindictiveness (three words Galt constantly applies) influenced almost everything he did, might suppose that
his youthful high spirits rose to the adventure of being so stranded in a
foreign land, while, on the other hand, his body wanted food and repose,
and that he was therefore as pleasant as he could be to the mercantile party.
It must have been annoying for Galt to have to end the story: 'Next
day, however, they were accommodated by the Governor with an agreeable house. . . .'
Though he admits he could not overcome a certain prejudice against
Byron, he got in touch with him again in England, and one of his letters
is a request for 'the favour of an order' to hear a debate in the House of
Lords. In another, he thanks him flatteringly for a pre-publication copy of
Childe Harold.[1] But, however eagerly he may have sought the young
poet's company, he was still observing him with a jaundiced eye.

Long before Childe Harold appeared, it was generally known that he had
a poem in the press, and various surmises, to stimulate curiosity, were
circulated concerning it: I do not say that these were by his orders, or under
his direction, but on one occasion I did fancy that I could discern a touch of
his own hand in a paragraph in the Morning Post, in which he was mentioned
as having returned from an excursion into the interior of Africa; and when I
alluded to it, my suspicion was confirmed by his embarrassment.
I mention this incident not in the spirit of detraction . . . but as a tint of
character indicative of the appetite for distinction by which, about this period
he became so powerfully incited, that at last it grew to a diseased crave, and
to such a degree that were the figure allowable, it might be said, the mouth

---

[1] Ibid. Both undated.

being incapable of supplying adequate means to appease it, every pore
became another mouth greedy of nourishment.

How a young man who had in the press a book on his travels through
Portugal, Spain, Turkey, Greece, and the *terra incognita* of Albania
(though spitefully leaving out Gibraltar as well as Malta), could benefit
himself by getting it announced that he had been to Africa, is a question
that is left to bewilder the reader.[1] Despite his 'diseased crave' for distinction, Byron was troubled, in Galt's own words, by 'the fears, the timidity,
and bashfulness of the young', and his embarrassment, if any, on being
asked about an erroneous paragraph in the *Morning Post* may have been
due to his perceiving with discomfort the suspicion in the mind of his
questioner.

'Lord Byron had his faults, many faults certainly,' Hobhouse wrote to
Galt in almost pitiful protest, 'but he was not the mean tricky creature
you have represented him to have been.'[2]

Galt was less dispassionate than he supposed himself when he set about
challenging Moore's favourable portrait of Byron. He had taken deep
umbrage at a remark Moore had published from Byron's journal of
December 10th, 1813:

> Galt says there is a coincidence between the first part of 'The Bride' [of
> Abydos] and some story of his—whether published or not, I know not, having
> never seen it. He is almost the last person on whom any one would commit
> literary larceny. . . .

This detraction quite cancelled out the pleasure of seeing in print, a
few pages earlier, that Byron had received him on a day when he had
been 'not at home' to a duke, and had afterwards written:

> Galt called—Mem.—to ask someone to speak to Raymond in favour of
> his play. We are old fellow-travellers, and, with all his eccentricities, he has
> much strong sense, experience of the world, and is, as far as I have seen, a
> good-natured philosophical fellow. [5 Dec. 1813]

In a chapter with the heading, *Plagiarisms of his Lordship*, Galt
revealed how much Byron's casual disparagement of his work had stung
him. He said the comment showed 'the excoriating sensibility with which
his Lordship felt everything that touched or affected him or his', that he
was obviously offended and excited, and that it was 'amusing' on his part
to deny pilfering the thoughts of others when there was so much evidence
that it was 'an early trick of his Lordship to filch good things'. He thought
Byron's *Curse of Minerva* was plagiarized from a poem of his own called

---

[1] 'The interior of Africa' was probably a mistranscription for 'interior of Albania'
into which Byron and Hobhouse had penetrated more deeply than any other Englishmen
up to that time.   [2] Murray MSS. 2 Sept. 1830.

The Atheniad, and that some lines from *The Giaour* were inspired by other verses of his, which he quoted.

It can only be considered as one of Lord Byron's spurts of spleen, that he felt so much about a 'coincidence' which ought not to have disturbed him. . . . Perhaps, when some kind friend is hereafter doing as indulgently for me the same kind of task that I have undertaken for Byron, there may be found among my memoranda notes as little flattering to his Lordship as those in his concerning me.

So much for the 'good-natured philosophical fellow's' impartiality!

(Writing his autobiography three years later, his rancour about the supposed plagiarisms surged up again and, after reverting to Byron's journal entry, he became unmistakably extravagant.

When the Life of Byron was written, I entertained a higher opinion of his originality than I do now, for I am reduced to the alternative of considering him as one of the most extraordinary plagiarists in literature.

He had formed a theory that a novel by Joshua Pickersgill, published when Byron was fifteen, had provided 'the incidents, colouring, names, and characters, of his most renowned productions',[1] and he had set going an investigation for the *New Monthly Magazine.* The editor, Thomas Campbell, bore a similar grudge, believing Byron had stolen certain of his own ideas, and he had very readily given space to it.)

Hobhouse was disgusted with the new biography on Byron's account, and even more so on his own, for Galt had not only introduced him into undignified anecdotes, brushed aside his refutation of Medwin, and given further currency to the tales of Leigh Hunt, but had conjectured that he (Hobhouse) had discouraged Byron from publishing *Childe Harold.* Since this was the work in which he took the greatest possible vicarious pride, he could not restrain himself from sending an indignant letter.

. . . There is not the slightest foundation for this supposition—nor is it true, as you state, that I 'was the only person who had seen the poem—as I was with Lord Byron whilst he was writing it.' I had left Lord Byron before he had finished the two cantos and, excepting a few fragments, I never saw them until they were printed. My own persuasion is that the story told in Dallas's Recollections of some person, name unknown, having dissuaded Lord Byron from publishing Childe Harold, is a mere fabrication, for it is at complete variance with all Lord Byron told me on the subject. At any rate, I was not that person—if I had been, it is not very likely that the poem which I had endeavoured to stifle in its birth should . . . be dedicated to me.

---

[1] This book, *The Three Brothers,* had been acknowledged openly by Byron as the source of his theme for *The Deformed Transformed.* He also adopted the name 'Manfred' from one of its characters. No doubt, like John Moore's *Zeluco* and Godwin's *Caleb Williams,* it had contributed to his adolescent outlook and attitudes, but as an inspiration for all his major works it is, to say the least, ludicrously inadequate.

I must therefore request you to take the earliest opportunity of relieving me from this imputation which . . . cannot fail to produce a very prejudicial effect. . . .

You have fallen into many other errors both as to facts and inferences, chiefly as it appears to me, from relying too implicitly on the catchpenny compositions of your predecessors, some of whom you know to be very good-for-nothing fellows.[1]

He reminded Galt that Byron's foibles when 'almost a boy' could not fairly be regarded as belonging to his mature character, by which a man had the right to be judged, and he chided him for his gossiping stories and for having helped himself to copious extracts from his own book, *Travels in Albania*.

Galt's performance had given so much cause for complaint that only a profoundly apologetic tone could have mollified a more patient man than Hobhouse. He chose instead to be surprised that any offence had been taken; said he had written nothing that he had not meant to be considered kindly, and that he had condemned Byron for his conduct to Leigh Hunt on his own showing, as he had 'not *then* seen Hunt's work'—a strange excuse when he had used many direct quotations or paraphrases from Hunt's book. He offered to correct in the *New Monthly Magazine* the mistake about Hobhouse's condemnation of *Childe Harold*, and either to correct or to defend other errors likewise, provided they were pointed out before the 20th of the month; and he maintained that he had not aided the propagation of anything to Byron's disadvantage.

The measure of Hobhouse's rage at this air of injured benevolence may be gauged by a single excerpt from Galt's chapter about Byron's relations with Hunt.

> There is no disputing the fact, that his Lordship, in conceiving the plan of the Liberal,[2] was actuated by sordid motives, and of the basest kind. . . . Being disappointed in his hopes of profit, he shuffled out of the concern as meanly as any higgler could have done who had found himself in a profitless business with a disreputable partner. . . . Whether Mr Hunt was or was not a fit co-partner for one of his Lordship's rank and celebrity, I do not undertake to judge, but any individual was good enough for that vile prostitution of his genius, to which, in an unguarded hour, he submitted for money.

'The puppy', wrote Hobhouse. 'I do not quite know what line to take with him—he has not got the sense or feeling to make correction effectual.'[3] Tactically, as has been shown many times in this book, Hobhouse, for all his courage, was a very bad fighter. He swung between indecision and

---

[1] Murray MSS. 2 Sept.
[2] *The Liberal* was the short-lived periodical which Leigh Hunt edited and Byron and Shelley planned. See Chapter XII.   [3] Hobhouse *Journals*, 5 Sept. 1830.

impetuosity, sometimes losing his temper too soon, sometimes letting opportunity slip through keeping it too long. Galt's conduct in the subsequent battle precludes any possibility that he could ever have been a chivalrous antagonist, no matter how delicately handled; but Hobhouse was unwise to give him a pretext for new insolences.

It was one of the occasions when he could not hold his anger in check, and he wrote back hotly:

> . . . A more attentive perusal of your book convinces me, that nothing which it contains is likely to affect me or anybody else permanently. You may, for aught I know, have written your *Life of Byron* with the good intentions professed in your letter to me; but I am sure that any one would suspect from the work, that you care not what you say. . . .
>
> I wonder that even common policy did not induce you to be more cautious in making statements which might be so easily disproved, and which have, indeed, already been incontrovertibly refuted. The very conversation, which you have judiciously selected from Medwin, as one of those parts of his trumpery book to the truth of which you can speak, I know to be a lie: for I never went on the tour of the lake of Geneva with Lord Byron.
>
> Still more surprised am I, that you should think it possible that your mode of treating your subject should be '*kindly considered*'. . . .
> . . . Your plan ought certainly to have compelled you to make yourself thoroughly acquainted with his [Byron's] poetry, and to quote him just as he wrote. Nevertheless, you have misrepresented him at least nine times in the ten stanzas of that poem which you call the last, and which was *not* the last, he ever wrote.[1]

He refused the offer Galt had made him of 'mending' the work, which was beyond repair in the short time allotted, but he would have no objection, if they should happen to meet, to mention two or three of the grosser blunders, 'for, in spite of your ill usage, I should wish to part in peace'. Galt defended himself at every point. He said he had no control over his first edition, implying that the blunders had been made by his publisher. At the same time he reminded Hobhouse—'all my statements are founded on the works and reports of others, except what I speak from my own knowledge', as if an author had no responsibility in passing on as truths what might be falsehoods. He blamed the publisher for cancelling a list in which he had acknowledged his sources, and the printer for making nine errors in one lyric—though these errors were not misprints; and he said Medwin, in a pamphlet not published, had refuted fifty of Hobhouse's criticisms of him. With crazily exasperating cocksureness, he remarked:

> It may be true that my esteem for Byron and yourself, was not an adoration so great for either as you could have wished, but still it is 'good respect', and the book does justice to both, for it reflects my opinion.[2]

[1] Murray MSS. 7 Sept.   [2] Ibid. 9 Sept.

Since the Medwin controversy six years before, Hobhouse had never been so goaded. It was beyond human endurance to let audacity on this scale go uncastigated.

Though sneering at him (he sneered at most of those who provided his materials), Galt in his book had stated his belief in Medwin. Hobhouse now wrote:

> Such a decision against me upon points on which I spoke of my own knowledge, was, of course, in itself sufficiently offensive, but . . . you tell me, I am refuted in upwards of fifty statements . . . Not one of all the statements contained in the article . . . is capable of refutation. Contradicted they may all be—for the man who utters one falsehood has of course another at hand to support it. . . .
>
> You justify what you say of me in your book in a manner that convinces me that all remonstrance must be thrown away on you. What ground—what possible pretext can you have for saying that I wished for adoration for Lord Byron or for myself? This is but a poor recrimination in reply to a charge of absolute misstatements respecting both. In fact it is one misrepresentation more and shows the spirit in which your book was written. But the drollest part of your justification is that in which you say ' *My book does justice to both of you, for it reflects my opinion.*' There may have been before your time many men with the same happy confidence in their own infallibility—but those who have been unwary enough to proclaim it have generally been laughed at for their pains.[1]

In Galt's next letter he said loftily that facts which Hobhouse might 'possibly make out' before the 20th (the press day presumably of the *New Monthly*) would be admitted and the others would be 'answered'. With a kind of fatuity all his own, he explained: 'As to "adoration"—I used it because I felt no anger, and to give our correspondence the appearance of less asperity. . . .'[2]

Determined this time not to vouchsafe a reply, Hobhouse optimistically recorded the close of the correspondence, but there was an unpleasant surprise in store for him. Galt did not let the matter drop, but published in the October number of the magazine a letter spitefully calculated to belittle him. Under the pretence of righting a wrong which he had done him when he had named him as the adverse early critic of *Childe Harold*, he said that he had spoken under the impression that Hobhouse had his Lordship's confidence. Suggesting that he now knew better, he dealt with Hobhouse's assertion that he had left before the two cantos were finished by pointing out that the manuscript was endorsed 'Concluded Canto II, Smyrna March 28, 1810, Byron', and that Mr Hobhouse had been with his Lordship long after that date.

However anxious to stand on his dignity, Hobhouse could not pass over

[1] Murray MSS. 10 Sept.   [2] Ibid. 11 Sept.

an insinuation that he was a liar palmed off on the public as an act of 'personal consideration' for him. His journal for October 8th registers that he had been writing remarks on Galt's 'vile letter—what a loss of time!' He was still at this troublesome task on the 12th; and on the 21st he called on Colburn, the publisher.

> . . . Saw Bentley, his partner. I complained to him of Galt's conduct and he agreed with me. I settled with him to write a letter in the next New Monthly Magazine.[1]

On October 22nd he dispatched his letter to Campbell, noting that it was 'about the 10th of the sort that I have written and torn up'. It was one of those dismal days which he signalized by the words 'Walked about'.

The vindication, which appeared in the November *New Monthly*, cannot be said to make short work of Galt, because, except as a diarist, brevity was not Hobhouse's forte, nor did the magazine readers of the day expect or desire it: but it did effectually prove the bad faith of his antagonist. Anyone who read *Childe Harold* with more attention than Galt, he pointed out, would have observed that additions had been made to the canto by Byron, according to his practice, after he had at first thought it finished.

> Mr Galt's attempt to refute a private statement of mine by a public reference to my friends autograph memorandum, will, I trust, hardly change the opinion which may be entertained as to our respective authority on matters connected with Lord Byron.

Among the many drafts of that letter which Hobhouse wrote and rejected there was one he did not destroy. It is much longer and more revealing than that which appeared in the *New Monthly*, and it contains one or two details about *Childe Harold* and other topics that seem not to have been quoted:

> The truth is . . . that the fragments of Childe Harold which were written during our journey through Albania to Attica were shown to me by Lord Byron previously to Mr Galt's arrival at Athens—and that I did not see the poem afterwards until it appeared in print—although Lord Byron frequently spoke to me on the subject—
> . . . I may add that of the portions shown to me at Athens there were two to which I objected—they were the stanzas relating to the Convention of Cintra and to the citizens' aquatic excursion. It is just possible that Lord Byron may have mentioned this circumstance to Mr Dallas—if he did there is some small excuse for the absurd tale told in the Recollections.[2]

[1] Hobhouse *Journals*. Galt's publisher was also the proprietor of the magazine which Campbell edited.   [2] Murray MSS.

It is now known that Dallas was deceiving himself or others when he took the sole credit for having 'discovered' *Childe Harold* and caused *Hints from Horace* to be laid aside, and that he was assisted in his judgment by one Walter Wright, a friend of his who had been Consul-General of the Ionian Islands.[1] It made, of course, a much better tale for the young poet to be depicted as enthusiastic for the wrong poem and being prevailed upon against his will by his bold kinsman to bring out the right one. And what is more likely than that the man who had shaped this popular anecdote inflated what he had heard of a friend's objection to a few stanzas into a general condemnation, frustrated by himself?

> I would ask Mr Galt how he has '*authenticated*' the stories copied from Medwin and Dallas [Hobhouse demanded in the letter he did not publish]. . . what does he know of Lord Byron's residence at Milan which enabled him to 'authenticate' a narrative written by an author called by him 'M. Stendal' but who is in truth a certain Mr Beyle, writing under the name of Count Stendhal. As Lord Byron and myself were living together at the only time my friend ever visited Milan I can speak positively to the fact, that Mr Beyle's narrative is all but a romance from beginning to end—and that the honest Count, who did see Lord Byron about four times in the October of 1816, has so far forgotten even the year of that fortunate event, that he has transferred the Milanese visit of the poet to the summer of 1817.

It would have piled Pelion upon the Ossa of Hobhouse's grievances if he could have foreseen that, when Galt's own compendium of errors had fallen, except for some twenty or thirty pages, into the near-oblivion he prophesied, the still less authentic reminiscences of Henri Beyle, introduced to pad out Galt's volume, would retain an apparently unshakeable status in Byron annals. This was but one, however, of Stendhal's several accounts of Byron, which are divergent and imaginative enough to deserve a chapter to themselves.

Hobhouse's lengthy uncorrected draft gives a glimpse of his own relations with Byron so unguardedly intimate that he could not but suppress it. Indeed, it would have made him a laughing-stock to all the enemies he had managed to raise up for himself. Yet perhaps today it will serve to show an aspect of him which explains something of the warm and lifelong affection of his friends. It concerns the prose part of the epitaph on Byron's Newfoundland dog Boatswain which had been quoted in Galt's book, and held up by some critic as a sign of the 'bitterness of spirit' which inspired the poet.

> . . . Another fact is that the epitaph was written not by Lord Byron, but by myself—Lord Byron had shown to me his verses on the death of Boatswain—which your readers will recollect conclude thus—

---

[1] MARCHAND, p. 279.

'To mark a friend's remains these stones arise
I never knew but one—and here he lies.'

On reading them, I suggested an alteration which I told my friend sub-stituted worse grammar but better sense—it was to insert '*I*' for '*he*' in the last line—on which Lord Byron burst out laughing & exclaimed—"why you are not jealous of the dog are you?" My rejoinder was—"Perhaps I am a little—but I can praise him in prose and match your misanthropy"—accordingly I wrote the epitaph and Lord Byron directed it to be engraved together with his own verses on the monument now in Newstead gardens.[1]

I should not think it worth while to trouble your readers with this trifling anecdote did it not afford a striking proof, as it seems to me, of the incompetence of mere compilers to write the memoirs of illustrious con-temporaries.

It is an astonishing testimony to Hobhouse's overmastering love of truth that he should have set down, with even a momentary notion of publishing it, that little confession of his jealousy.

As for the more reserved communication that was printed, his reputa-tion for obstructing all comers made it ineffectual, while his hope that he might be allowed the last word in the controversy, was shattered the following month in the most lacerating manner.

Galt, who was a passionate believer in the institution of slavery, was writing a series of articles against the Abolitionists, to whose activities he applied such epithets as fraudulent, despicable, humbug, imbecile, and sneaking, making particular reference to 'Mr Macaulay and his friends' as 'active as fleas and venomous as gnats'. He did not see any way to prevent the West Indian planters being forced to liberate their slaves—the efforts of fanatics like Wilberforce had gone too far—but he considered it essential that generous compensation should be paid them for sacrificing their property. These appeals he was publishing, with applause from many British investors, in the reactionary magazine, *Fraser's*; and thus, when the *New Monthly* had allotted as much space to the contestants in the Byron dispute as seemed reasonable, he was able to find a new forum where nineteen columns of print were placed at his disposal.

Under the heading 'Pot *versus* Kettle', which brought Hobhouse down to his own level, he reproduced the entire correspondence, both the public and the private letters, and added a commentary of his own.

The coarse and vulgar vituperations of Mr Hobhouse were no doubt indulged in, by supposing I should not have the fortitude to publish them. He will see that the craftiest—in his own conceit—may sometimes be mistaken.

---

[1] The epitaph composed by Hobhouse and attributed to Byron runs:

Near this spot are deposited the remains of one who possessed Beauty without Vanity, Strength without Insolence, Courage without Ferocity, and all the Virtues of Man without his Vices. This praise, which would be unmeaning Flattery, if inscribed over human ashes, is but a just Tribute to the Memory of BOATSWAIN, a Dog.

It was a time of great scurrility in newspapers and periodicals, and Hobhouse was accustomed to abuse, but seldom had it been on so mean a plane as this. The charges against him were shifted from literary to political grounds, and were so far-fetched as to disclose—though perhaps not to the readers of *Fraser's Magazine*—the weaknesses of the accuser's hand and the real cause of the rudeness with which it had hit out. To keep his contributor's colours flying as high as possible, the editor furnished for the same number an article on Galt as one of the most 'Illustrious Literary Characters' of the epoch, and faced it with a picture of him standing beside a bust of Byron supported by a pile of books. The names of Medwin, Dallas, Hunt, and Moore appear on the spines, and, topping them all, of Galt himself!

If Hobhouse had not been a man of very high honour, he could at any time in this controversy have scored a total victory over Galt. As executor he had in his keeping a number of those letters in which the other had sought to ingratiate himself with Byron, and few would have been likely to quibble at his publishing them.

How it would have delighted the conclave of *Blackwood*'s—which had already given Galt's book a slashing review—to know that to Byron's face he had denied all accusation of plagiarism, writing: 'You are the father and founder of a school. You may rely upon having many imitators;'[1] that he had called at Newstead Abbey in the hope of seeing the owner, and preened himself on being asked by one of the servants if he was a member of the family;[2] that he had solicited his Lordship's good offices in trying to secure for himself a Consul-Generalship at some Mediterranean port;[3] and that, nearly nine years after their last meeting, he had sent a letter to Italy saying, 'I cannot but remember with pleasure many incidents of my "Voyages and Travels" nor feel without pride the advantage of having known your Lordship so intimately', adding a diffident commiseration for 'the envy and malice and all the uncharitableness which your Fame and Genius have so mortified and provoked'.[4]

Hobhouse never put to vindictive use any of the countless Byron papers that had been consigned to him. Had he been less scrupulous he would have made a much better defender.

It must have been gloomy for him, in this losing battle, to have almost no one now who had belonged to Byron's circle in the old days with whom he could discuss his tribulations . . . Kinnaird dead, Scrope Davies permanently exiled by reason of his debts, Murray, if anything, on the other side, having recently helped to get Galt appointed to the editorship of a

---

[1] Murray MSS. 11 Dec. 1813. Galt himself was one of them. He wrote a plagiarism of *Manfred* called *The Star of Destiny*.
[2] Ibid.   [3] Ibid. 25 Sept. 1814.   [4] Ibid. 20 July 1822.

Tory newspaper, the *Courier*—a step he was destined to repent. Even Moore might have been a congenial ally in such a war.

Moore was in Ireland, and had published what he called a 'squib' against Galt's book, which, he said, 'that wretched thing richly deserves'.[1] His touch was as usual much lighter than Hobhouse's, but then he had a great deal less to bear. The squib was in verse, and took Galt to task for his very bad grammar and his turgid metaphors—'that dark diseased ichor which coloured his effusions', 'that gelatinous character of their effusions', 'the poetical embalmment, or rather, amber immortalization'. He laughed at the most famous passage in his book, the description of Byron as he appeared at night on the ship:

> . . . When the lights were placed, he made himself a man forbid, took his station at the railing between the pegs on which the sheets are belayed and the shrouds, and, there, for hours, sat in silence, enamoured, it may be, of the moon. . . . He was often strangely rapt—it may have been from his genius; and, had its grandeur and darkness been then divulged, susceptible of explanation; but, at the time, it threw, as it were, around him the sackcloth of penitence. Sitting amidst the shrouds and rattlings, in the tranquillity of the moonlight, churming an inarticulate melody, he seemed almost apparitional, suggesting dim reminiscences of him who shot the albatross. He was as a mystery in a winding-sheet, crowned with a halo.

At twenty-one this was doubtless just the impression Byron liked to make, and Galt was for once playing up to, instead of pulling down, his subject; but Moore would have none of it.

> What his meaning exactly is, nobody knows,
>   As he talks (in a strain of intense botheration)
> Of lyrical 'ichor' 'gelatinous' prose,
>   And a mixture call'd 'amber immortalization.'
>
> *Now*, he raves of a bard he once happen'd to meet,
>   Seated high 'among rattlings,' and churning a sonnet;[2]
> *Now*, talks of a mystery, wrapp'd in a sheet,
>   With a halo (by way of a nightcap) upon it.

Galt replied to Moore in some embarrassingly poor verses called 'Tit for Tat', in which he was reduced to the hackneyed device of mocking the other's small stature.

Though he always pretended to feel only sardonic amusement, Galt never forgot or forgave a criticism. He had another fling at Moore in his

---

[1] MOORE, *Memoirs*, 19 Sept. 1830.

[2] Galt used the word 'churming' in all editions of his book, and it was not a misprint as Moore evidently thought, because it appears again in his autobiography. It seems to relate to the twitterings of birds.

autobiography, and attacked the loathed Hobhouse afresh with ingenious malice. He praised his own book on Byron heartily, saying:

> . . . It is a memoir which says all the good which can be said of that extraordinary man, written by one who had some opportunities of observing his qualities, and who shut his ears and his heart alike to the flatteries of his friends and the detraction of his enemies.

Not for an instant did it ever seem to occur to him that one whose slight contact with Byron had ended in 1813, soon after the outset of his career, and who normally moved in an entirely different world, might not have been fitted to set up as the final arbiter on his whole life and personality.

Unable to believe that anyone could have found fault with his work except through personal hostility, he ascribed Hobhouse's objection to having been unfavourably mentioned in his novel *The Ayrshire Legatees* some years before. He tells a sniggering story of how he was in a back room of Fraser's bookshop, soon after his onslaught on Hobhouse appeared in the magazine, when he heard a person with a 'cold, iron clanking' voice remonstrating with the bookseller. After this man had gone, Fraser, full of mirth, informed him that Hobhouse had called—

> in a towering passion about my publication of Pot versus Kettle . . . which led Fraser to mention that I was in the back room, and he had no doubt would reply to anything he had to say. Mr Hobhouse, however, chose to go away, expressing magnificently something about considering me a bookseller's hack, too insignificant, of course, for his high mightiness to notice. I was exceedingly glad to have nettled him so much.

Galt's book which, like so many others, contained enough good material for one magazine article, long remained a 'standard work'. In protesting against it, Hobhouse had done what was proper both for himself and Byron, but he might as well have saved his temper and his ink. There was no winning against an opponent protected by perfect obtuseness, blindly pugnacious, for ever laughing at others and never at himself, a man who could not even begin to understand what it meant to have earned the dedication of *Childe Harold's Pilgrimage*:

> . . . To one, whom I have known long, and accompanied far, whom I have found wakeful over my sickness and kind in my sorrow, glad in my prosperity and firm in my adversity, true in counsel and trusty in peril—to a friend often tried and never found wanting;—to yourself.
> . . . I wish to do honour to myself by the record of many years' intimacy with a man of learning, of talent, of steadiness, and of honour, . . . to thank you for an indefatigable regard, such as few men have experienced, and no one could experience without thinking better of his species and of himself. . . .

Wishing you, my dear Hobhouse, a safe and agreeable return to that country whose real welfare can be dearer to none than to yourself, I dedicate to you this poem in its completed state; and repeat once more how truly I am ever

Your obliged

And affectionate friend

BYRON

CHAPTER XI

AN IMAGINATIVE FRENCHMAN

Stendhal was by far the most gifted of the authors who wrote false or highly embellished accounts of their dealings with Byron, but he was by no means above the weakness so many of them shared, a desire to score off his subject—a desire which augmented in inverse ratio to the degree of truth to which they aspired. The reason in general is not difficult to find. If our contact with an eminent man has been brief and slight, we are obliged to stretch our material very far to write anything about him that will create an effect: the most must therefore be made of flaws and eccentricities, which in skilful hands fill space so entertainingly. Moreover, it places us at an advantage to appear critical, detached, not to be influenced by fame. Stendhal became more critical and more detached, the further he got, in time, from his actual experience of Byron.

The three accounts he published of that fleeting association—elaborated by him into the frequent intercourse of a season—contain numerous discrepancies, but nobody seems to have troubled much to compare them with one another, let alone with extraneous sources of information;[1] and the third, entitled *Lord Byron en Italie, Récit d'Un Témoin Oculaire*, though full of things demonstrably contravertible from his own evidence, is one of the most quoted of 'eye-witness' narratives. It is described by Hobhouse, who was present at each encounter, as 'a tissue of fictions'.[2]

When Byron had arrived in Milan with Hobhouse in October 1816, Stendhal was merely Monsieur Beyle, a deeply dissatisfied man of thirty-three, whose life had been a series of brilliant false starts. He had held a post in the *entourage* of Napoleon, whom he professed to worship, and was full of bitterness against the English for their unchivalrous usage of the Emperor. At least, that is the position he chose to assume for literary purposes. He represented himself as behaving towards Byron with icy coldness because he was a member of the legislative body that had sent Napoleon into exile, but in reality he had been determined to meet him, and had written to his friend, Louis Crozet, to say that he was going to be presented at the first opportunity.[3] Nor, when that occasion came, had he indulged in anything resembling the cool appraisal he afterwards set forth. On the contrary, he had been tremendously excited and attracted.

I have dined [he wrote again to Crozet] with a handsome and charming young man, [who has] the face of an eighteen-year old, although he is

---

[1] Doris Gunnell in *Stendhal et L'Angleterre* (Paris, 1909) recognizes—in footnotes—the disparities, but nevertheless accepts the general truth of Stendhal's statements. She had not seen any part of Hobhouse's diary, a vital document in the case.

[2] Murray MSS.   [3] STENDHAL, *Correspondance*. 1 Oct. 1816.

twenty-eight, the profile of an angel, the sweetest manner. . . . He is the greatest living Poet, Lord Byron.[1]

He did not mention that there were present nearly a dozen other persons. He himself, it would seem, was not at first sight prepossessing. Polidori, who had recently been Byron's travelling physician, set Beyle down in his journal as 'a fat lascivious man, . . . He related many anecdotes—I don't remember them.'[2] Hobhouse, who had brought out a book of considerable merit about Napoleon's Hundred Days and was therefore more interested, said in his diary that, though he believed him trustworthy, 'he has a cruel way of talking, and looks, and is, a sensualist'.[3]

If his talk was anything like his private letter-writing and his journal, this vein of cruelty would reveal itself in a feline and wanton mordacity. Even when he was announcing his admiration of Byron, his impatience to see him, he added: 'He travels accompanied by an excellent pimp, an Italian doctor',[4] a statement entirely unwarranted by the nature of Polidori's employment: while later, when he was dispatching gossip to Paris about Byron's affair with Teresa Guiccioli, his tone was so coarse and ribald that personal spite against the Countess might be suspected, yet he did not know her name and had never set eyes on her.

Struggling to gain a foothold in literature, Marie-Henri Beyle, like many another beginner before and since, solicited the attention of established writers by presenting them with copies of his works: but he went further than others, asking the recipients to accept copies not only for themselves but for their friends, and his flatteries were more fulsome and at the same time less related to his real opinions than any more temperate individual would have ventured. Begging Thomas Moore to read his *Histoire de la Peinture en Italie*, he sent him an order on a bookseller for three copies, and informed him that he had just read *Lalla Rookh* for the fifth time—a statement which takes a good deal of believing.[5] To Byron, offering *L'Histoire de la Peinture* and also *De L'Amour*, he wrote: 'When I read Parisina for the first time, my soul was stirred for a week. I am happy to have occasion to thank you for this lively pleasure.'[6]

But his remark in a letter to Baron de Mareste was probably more sincere: 'I have just read Byron on the lakes. Decidedly verses bore me, as being less exact than prose. Rebecca, in *Ivanhoe*, gave me more pleasure than all of the Parisinas of Lord Byron.'[7]

Praising *Parisina* to Byron, he disparaged Scott, but to Scott himself

---

[1] Ibid. 20 Oct. 1816.
[2] POLIDORI. 8 Dec. 1816. Several weeks written up together.
[3] Hobhouse *Journals*, 23 Oct. 1816.
[4] STENDHAL, *Correspondance*. 1 Oct. 1816.   [5] MOORE, *Memoirs*. 31 Mar. 1820.
[6] STENDHAL, *Correspondance*. 23 June 1823.
[7] Ibid. 20 Oct. 1820.

he had sent copies of his books with the usual duplicates given because 'the friends of the author of *Marmion* must be excellent judges'.[1]

It is not to be supposed that, in this phase of opportunism, Beyle would fail to turn to account his meetings with a young peer who was an object of nearly as much interest in France and Italy as in England and whom he found fascinating for his noble blood as well as his looks and personality— for at that time he was not affecting either the obsessive scorn of titles or the contempt for Britons which, in future years, were to colour his portraits of Byron. On the contrary, he had boasted to Crozet: 'The luckiest chance in the world has just brought me the acquaintance *of 4 or 5 Englishmen of the first rank and understanding*',[2] and the following year it was under the pen name of Stendhal preceded by an aristocratic 'de' that he produced the volume called *Rome, Naples, et Florence*. It contained the author's first published exploitation of Byron. He chose to transport the scene of the meeting from a dinner party at the house of Monsignore de Brême in Milan to a theatre in Venice, and to give it the date, June 27th, 1817, whereas it was actually October 17th, 1816.

> I was introduced at the theatre to Lord Byron. What a heavenly face!— it is impossible to have more beautiful eyes! Ah, the fine-looking man of genius![3] He is scarcely twenty-eight years of age, and he is the first poet in England, probably in the world. When he is listening to music, his is a face worthy of the ideal of the Greeks.

Satirizing the English moral indignation, which sought to make Byron out a monster, he exclaimed:

> He is the most amiable monster I ever knew; in talking of poetry in any literary discussion he is as simple as a child. . . . Were I in his place [he was presumably alluding to the persecution of scandalmongers] I would pass myself off as dead, and commence a new life, as Mr Smith, a worthy merchant of Lima.

He refrained from sending this book to Byron: but Byron, who now read more French than English literature,[4] came across it. He could not but be gratified by the eulogies of his own beauty and charm, and particularly by the sympathy accorded him as the victim of a wave of moral fury in England, but he was at the same time exasperated by a contemptuous observation on Scott in Beyle's pamphlet of 1823, *Racine et Shakespeare*,[5] and it was probably this which decided him to take the unusual course of writing an unsolicited letter. His addiction to facts—a

---

[1] STENDHAL, *Correspondance*. 18 Feb. 1821.
[2] Ibid. 28 Sept. 1816. He wrote the phrase in English and underlined it.
[3] The adjective in French is, untranslatably, *joli*.   [4] GUICCIOLI, *La Vie*.
[5] Much of this is word-for-word plagiarism from Dr Johnson's Preface to Shakespeare's Plays.

feature of his character obscured by biographers who themselves preferred fancy—compelled him to begin with a quiet and ironical protest.

Genoa, May 29, 1823

Sir,

At present [? now] that I know to whom I am indebted for a very flattering mention in the *Rome, Naples, and Florence* in 1817, by M. Stendhal, it is fitting that I should return my thanks (however undesired or undesirable) to M. Beyle, with whom I had the honour of being acquainted at Milan, in 1816.—You only did me too much honour in what you were pleased to say in that work; but it has hardly given me less pleasure than the praise itself, to become at length aware (which I have done by mere accident) that I am indebted for it to one of whose good opinion I was really ambitious.—So many changes have taken place since that period in the Milan circle, that I hardly dare recur to it:—some dead, some banished—and some in the Austrian dungeons. . . .

Of your works I have only seen 'Rome etc.' the lives of Haydn and Mozart, and the brochure on 'Racine and Shakespeare.' The 'Histoire de la Peinture' I have not yet had the good fortune to possess.

There is one part of your observations in the pamphlet which I shall venture to remark upon;—it regards Walter Scott. You say that 'his character is little worthy of enthusiasm,' at the same time that you mention his productions in the manner they deserve.—I have known Walter Scott long and well—and in the occasional situations which call forth the *real* character—and I can assure you that his character *is* worthy of admiration—that of all men he is the most *open*, the most *honourable*, the most *amiable*. With his politics I have nothing to do: they differ from mine, which renders it difficult for me to speak of them. But he is *perfectly sincere* in them,—and Sincerity may be *humble*, but she cannot be servile.—I pray you, therefore, to correct or soften that passage.

You may, perhaps, attribute this officiousness of mine to a false affectation of *candour*, as I happen to be a writer also.—Attribute it to what motive you please, but believe the *truth*. I say that Walter Scott is as nearly a thorough good man as man can be, because I *know* it by experience to be the case.

If you do me the honour of an answer, may I request a speedy one—because it is possible (though not yet decided) that circumstances may conduct me once more to Greece. My present address is Genoa, where an answer will reach me in a short time, or be forwarded to me wherever I may be.—

I beg you to believe me, with a lively recollection of our brief acquaintance, and the hope of one day renewing it,

I am ever your obliged

and obedient humble servant,

Noel Byron.

I make no excuse for writing to you in English, as I understand you are well acquainted with that language.[1]

[1] The text here used is from Martineau's *Cent-Soixante Quatorze Lettres à Stendhal*. It was collated with the original, and has the postscript not given in *L. & J.* The style is so remarkably un-Byronic that he must have been trying to adapt himself to his reader by casting his phrases in a Gallic mould.

Stendhal composed a voluminous reply to Byron, saying that he wished he could share his view of Sir Walter Scott but that he disliked his respect for royalty and acceptance of a baronetcy, and that Scott was condemned everywhere in France for not having refused the title—which came rather strangely from a man who had tried to persuade his father to purchase a barony!

> I am concerned, milord [he continued] that my letter is already so long; but having the unhappiness of being of an opposite opinion to yours, my respect prevents me from curtailing my reasons. I regret sincerely not being of your opinion, and there are not ten men in the world to whom I could say so much with sincerity. . . .
> It was extremely agreeable, milord, to have had some personal contact with one of the two or three men who, since the death of the hero whom I adored, broke up a little the dull uniformity into which the affectations of high society have thrown our poor Europe.[1]

In 1818 Stendhal had numbered Byron with the three most outstanding men he had ever met (the others were Napoleon and Canova),[2] but although he was very much flattered to receive the letter,[3] he had undergone a change of mood and taste that now made him at times almost hostile. As long as three years before, he had been sending gossiping reports to Paris that were fundamentally ill-natured in tone, besides being out of date and generally incorrect. To the Baron de Mareste, for example, he had written in March 1820:

> . . . Your *Journal de Paris* has no more sense in literature than anything else when it doubts my details concerning Lord Byron. He is madly in love and beloved by the young countess whose husband has an income of seventy thousand écus—the écu at five francs thirty-seven centimes; but I reduce that to a hundred and fifty thousand francs income. This good husband has left his young wife three or four months keeping house with the lord, who has been running about Dalmatia with her. . . .
> Like Canova he plays the hypocrite. A scholar told me this morning how Lord Byron says the romantics may go hang, and he adores Tasso, says he, because of his regularity. Myself I despise this vile arithmetic.[4]

In another letter to the same correspondent, after depicting Byron's countess as 'une grosse tétoniére blonde, portant dans la rue ses tétons blancs étalés et des souliers de satin rouges', he proceeded bitterly:

---

[1] STENDHAL, *Correspondance*. 23 June 1823. Though it is improbable that Byron ever received this letter, it is quoted to show the actual nature of their relations.
[2] Ibid. Letter to Mareste, 14 April.
[3] GUNNELL. Letter quoted by Crozet to Colomb, 17 Oct. 1845.
[4] STENDHAL, *Correspondance*. 26 Mar. The 'vil calcul' was regular scansion.

The said lord, to gain supporters, makes himself out quite classical when talking to Italian pedants; for instance, Mezzofanti at Bologna; which appears to me very *jean foutre* and very milord.[1]

The Turkish Ambassador's wife of Proust's invention could not have got hold of the wrong end of the stick more adroitly. Byron never did anything with the object of gaining supporters, and his love of classicism was no hypocrisy; he blamed himself for not being of the school of Pope. It was perhaps because, like so many others, Stendhal was disappointed in his expectation of finding in this pale, dramatic young man the arch-Romantic that adulation became tinged with rancour.

Byron did not see any further public reminiscence about himself by Stendhal, the next to appear being an Appendix to the two-volume biography that Mme Swanton Belloc managed to rush out in the year of his death.

Anne Louise Belloc, *née* Swanton, was pretty, attractive, and not yet twenty-five when she determined to be the first in the field with a full-length book on a poet whose name in France was then an incantation. The daughter of an Irish officer, and bilingual, she had begun her career at the age of nineteen with capable translations of literature for children, such as Maria Edgeworth's *Moral Tales* and *Harry and Lucy*. She was diligent by nature, but had little material in hand for writing a factual story of Byron, and was in too great a hurry to do very much research. She herself explained with engaging candour that she speeded up her work because everyone kept telling her 'Hâtez-vous donc! Vous arriverez trop tard.' But though her errors were numerous, she had an immense graciousness that disarmed severe criticism, and if she romanticized her subject, it was with a certain nobility and splendour of conception:

> Genius is an apparition so beautiful and so rare that one could never go too far in consecrating its passage through the world and honouring its memory.

Mme Belloc was acquainted with only one person who could speak of Byron from first-hand knowledge, and she did not fail to consult him. He began his reply with deceptive sobriety:

> I should be happy, madame, to be able to give you some information for the work you are preparing on Lord Byron. It is true that I passed several months in the society of this great poet, but, in truth, to speak of him is not an easy thing; I did not see Lord Byron in any of those decisive moments which fully reveal a character; what I know about this singular man is only the memory of what I felt in his presence.

[1] Ibid. 30 Aug. 1820.

This ostensible restraint was a stucco camouflaging a construction of bricks made with the barest minimum of straw. He had not passed several months or even several weeks or days in Byron's society. He had never been one hour alone with him, and language difficulties must have prevented their conversation in company from being other than superficial. It is obvious from Byron's postscript, quoted above, that they had not spoken English, which, in any case, Beyle did not know nearly as well as he thought: the common language at Monsignore de Brême's was French, and Byron, though he read French easily, spoke it most reluctantly—possibly owing to some self-consciousness about his accent. Hobhouse was at that date the more fluent linguist, and his diary shows that it was he who took an active part in the various discussions.

Stendhal's version of the meeting for Mme Belloc is different from both the others he published. He first saw the poet, he says, at the Scala in Milan:

> I was struck by Lord Byron's eyes at the moment when he listened to a sextet from an opera of Mayer entitled Elena. I had never in my life seen anything more beautiful or more expressive. Even today if I come to think of the expression a great painter ought to give to genius, this sublime head suddenly reappears before me. I had a moment of enthusiasm, and forgetting the just repugnance that every man with a little pride must have against seeking to be presented to a peer of England, I begged M. de Brême to introduce me to Lord Byron.
>
> I found myself next day at dinner at M. de Brême's, with him, and the celebrated Monti. . . . We spoke of poetry and someone asked which were the twelve finest lines of the past century, in French, in Italian, in English. The Italians present agreed to choose the twelve first lines of the Mascheroniana of Monti [a poem glorifying Napoleon Buonaparte]: Monti willingly recited them to us. I looked at Lord Byron, he was ravished. The shade of hauteur, or rather the air of a man who *finds himself* obliged to repulse an importunity, which slightly spoiled his handsome face, disappeared all of a sudden to give place to an expression of happiness. The first canto of the Mascheroniana which Monti recited almost in its entirety . . . caused the most lively sensation to the author of Childe Harold.
>
> I shall never forget the divine expression of his features; they had the serene look of power and of genius, and he had not at that moment any affectation to reproach himself with. . . . I spent almost every evening from that day with Lord Byron.

If ever there was a safe conjecture, it is that Byron's sensations would have been anything but lively on being compelled to listen to the recitation of a canto at a dinner party. Hobhouse's very capacious journal entry on the occasion speaks of Monti's arrival 'in the middle of dinner', of his violent harangue against everybody in the room, of the delight the Italians seemed to take in making him angry, and of his pouring forth

'torrents of dogmas'. 'When at last he had finished, he talked quietly to
Lord Byron and me.' After this they went to the theatre, where Byron
may or may not have looked inspired while he listened to music—it is the
only feature all Stendhal's narratives have in common, so perhaps it is
true—but where nothing else took place as he described it.

'There was a M. de Beyle, one of Napoleon's secretaries,' Hobhouse
noted, 'Intendant de la Mobilière de la Couronne there, a little fat
whiskered man. Unfortunately, I had hardly a word with him.'[1] He was
disappointed on account of his desire to hear about Napoleon

Stendhal's souvenirs must have been contrived to give Mme Belloc
the sort of thing she wanted, and in doing so to shed a congenial light upon
himself, which would not have been so easy to do if he had repeated, at a
time when all the artistic and intellectual world was paying homage, such
views as he had written in his *Racine et Shakespeare*, when he had
referred to: 'Lord Byron, author of some heroïdes, sublime but always the
same, and many mortally boring tragedies', and had stigmatized *Cain* as
'cette plate amplification de collège'—comments which Byron had politely
ignored in his letter. But sustained applause was too much: presently there
was a flicker of animosity.

> Whenever this singular man was fired and spoke of an enthusiasm, his
> sentiments were noble, great, generous, in a word on a level with his genius.
> But in the prosaic moments of life, the poet's sentiments seemed to me most
> ordinary. He had much petty vanity, a continual and puerile fear of appear-
> ing ridiculous, and, sometimes if I dare to say it, some of that hypocrisy
> which the English call *cant*. It seemed to me that Byron was always ready to
> enter into a compromise with a prejudice in order to win praise.
>
> One thing which struck the Italians was that it was easy to see that this
> great poet thought it much more estimable to be a descendant of those
> Byrons of Normandy who followed William in the conquest of England, than
> to be the author of Parisina and Lara.

Beyle usually lays upon 'the Italians' the onus of passing censure on
Byron. They are represented, with more and more gusto as the years go
by, laughing at him, either behind their hands or with 'Milanese blunt-
ness', while he strives in vain to make headway in their good graces.
They sneer at his pretensions to know either ancient or modern Greek
(in his less disillusioned days Stendhal had allowed him these and even
thrown in Arabic); they are amused at his crass ignorance of Italian
dialects; they find him 'haughty, bizarre, and a little mad', and after he
goes home at night, they irreverently dissect his character, while Stendhal
admires them for the fineness of their perceptions, never duped by
appearances.[2]

---

[1] Hobhouse *Journals*, 17 Oct. 1816.   [2] STENDHAL, *Lord Byron en Italie*.

Hobhouse's view was different. 'The enthusiasm which my poetical friend meets is something extraordinary.'[1] And there is confirmation from the host, Monsignore de Brême, himself: '. . . We are endlessly showing him our private admiration, and this results in a mutual and habitual bond of understanding which leaves him perfectly at ease amid this society with which I have surrounded him.'[2]

Do these very lines in themselves elucidate the mystery of the destructiveness underlying all Beyle's semblances of eulogy? His idea that he spent 'three hundred nights a year' in the company of the Monsignore and the Marquess his brother, with such celebrated poets as Monti and Silvio Pellico, was a fantasy. 'It must be remembered,' says one commentator, 'that in Milan Stendhal was relatively poor, and could not see Byron as often as he would have wished. One may picture him in the brilliant society that surrounded Byron. Proud, sensitive, and without any well-defined social position, Stendhal masked by a correct and reserved bearing his ardent desire to know better this soul which had so many affinities with his own.'[3]

The affinities were probably imaginary, but they were almost certainly imagined. And out of them were conjured pleasing approaches from Byron which the day-dreamer had the exquisite satisfaction of rebuffing:

> I had the good fortune to excite his curiosity by giving him personal details about Napoleon and his retreat from Moscow which, in 1816, were not common knowledge. . . . This species of merit brought me several tête-a-tête promenades in the immense and deserted foyer of the Scala. The great man manifested himself for half an hour each evening, and then there was the finest conversation I ever met with in my life; a volcano of new ideas and generous sentiments so mixed together that we seemed to enjoy those sentiments for the first time. The remainder of the evening, the great man was so much an Englishman and a lord, that I could never bring myself to accept the invitation to go and dine with him which he renewed from time to time.

No doubt if Byron had been able to detect in the unappealing Monsieur Beyle the future author of *Le Rouge et Le Noir*, he would have invited him to dinner, not repeatedly, for that was out of character, but once at least: no doubt, much as he shrank from walking in any public place, he would have taken a turn with him about the *foyer* of La Scala. But Beyle, though he struck people as clever, did not convey by his personality, any more than his illustrious successor, Proust, that he had in him deep resources of vitality and original talent; and besides, Byron left Milan just sixteen days after their first encounter and never saw him again.

---

[1] Hobhouse *Journals*.
[2] MAUROIS, *Byron*. Letter from the Archives of Coppet, quoted without date, but obviously late October 1816.   [3] GREEN, *Stendhal et les Anglais*.

Mme Belloc was a devout Buonapartist. Stendhal, who seems not then to have known that Byron had sung Napoleon's praises when it was intensely unpopular in England to do so, invented an attitude for him:

> I noticed that, in his moments of genius, Lord Byron admired Napoleon, as Napoleon himself admired Corneille. In his ordinary moments, when Lord Byron believed himself a grand seigneur, he sought to pour ridicule on the exile of Saint-Helena. There was envy in Lord Byron for the brilliant side of Napoleon's character; his sublime words vexed him; we yielded to his humour, recalling the famous speech addressed to the army in Egypt: "Soldiers, imagine that from the height of these pyramids, forty centuries are watching over you." He would more readily have forgiven in Napoleon the somewhat flat style of Washington.

What Byron had really not forgiven in Napoleon was that he had gone quietly and sullenly off with his captors, instead of committing suicide or making any other gesture of defiance and desperation: but it is utterly improbable that a man who had the art of pleasing in a pre-eminent degree would have poured ridicule on the deposed Emperor in the presence of his host, who had been Almoner and Councillor of State under him, or of Beyle himself, one of his soldiers in the Russian campaign; or that if he had behaved so boorishly, Stendhal would immediately afterwards have praised him for the charm of his manner.

The novelist was building up a character which had scarcely any point of correspondence with reality, and yet, when shaped and polished in the course of years, was to become an accepted part of the Byron legend. At the stage when Mme Belloc printed the contribution to her book, it was still merely a theatrical puppet, the cardboard figure of an arrogant English nobleman.

> He had not, at least in my view, any true experience of men: his pride, his rank, his fame, had prevented him from ever behaving as equal to equal with them. His hauteur and his caution had always kept them at too great a distance for him to be able to observe them.

Stendhal could not conceivably have believed what he was writing. It was incompatible with what he had said before about the childlike simplicity of the young man's personality, and wholly at odds with anything he could have observed. Byron's easy affability and lack of reserve were the subject of comment, approving or disparaging, from almost everyone who enjoyed any kind of social relations with him. That he had 'fine and just' ideas about women is another opinion that can hardly have been offered with sincerity; and though at first we are struck by the phrase that it was a need with him to 'please them and deceive them', reflection will persuade us that we pity the women who loved Byron precisely because he did not trouble to deceive them, not having enough consideration for their feelings.

This meretricious piece went unnoticed at first by Hobhouse. It was impossible in 1824 for one man to keep count of foreign as well as English publications about Byron. Nor did he know of still another variation on the same theme which the persistent author devised five years later in a long letter, private but clearly meant for a literary record, to his cousin and executor, Romain Colomb.[1] This is likewise full of incompatibilities.

Byron's terrible *hauteur*, canker of the British aristocracy, is now represented as freezing all efforts to make conversation in his presence, and Stendhal's readiness to worship is intimidated by so lofty and inhuman a demeanour. The youthful creature whose amiability had been so engaging has been demolished for ever. A fictitious personage has taken his place.

By 1830 this creation was rounded off and given something more of subtlety. *Lord Byron en Italie* was the finished portrait. It was first translated into English in the *Foreign Literary Gazette* and reprinted soon after in the *Mirror*—a journal run with the utmost economy on abbreviated selections from the contents of other magazines, and at times almost subsisting on Byron, so lavish was the space accorded to him.

Hobhouse, besides having an increasingly busy political career, was now a husband and a father. Lady Julia Hay, whom he had courted with a very moderate degree of passion, had soon won his devoted affection and turned him into a contented family man. The resolution he had once made to expose falsehoods about Byron had naturally weakened under a tide of exaggerated, distorted, and downright fraudulent articles, pamphlets, poems, and books, far exceeding his worst anticipations. On the way to becoming a Cabinet Minister, and with his private life more crowded than ever, he had as little time as inclination for the weary toil of controversy.

But when he found that Galt—the odious and despised John Galt—had appended Beyle's fabrication to his *Life of Lord Byron* with an introductory allusion to 'M. Stendhal, a gentleman of literary celebrity in France', his choler rose again as in its first ebullience, and he decided, in one of his typical impulses, to show this Frenchman up. Years of suffering, both personal and vicarious, embittered remarks that became too vehement for publication:[2]

---

[1] STENDHAL, *Correspondance.* 24 Aug. 1829.

[2] 7 Nov. 1830. Murray MSS. It has been necessary here and there to adjust the punctuation very slightly, and to correct one or two mistakes in the spelling of names. Hobhouse wrote Stendhall or Stendhal, De Beyle or de Beyle, but never simply Beyle. Stendhal's article is given in the English translation that Hobhouse read, and for the benefit of readers who have no copy to refer to, some passages are quoted more fully than in his paper.

If the Reviewing of books be, as Mr Southey calls it, 'an ungentle craft,' the making of them is, for the most part, a dishonest one—and that department of literature which ought to be entrusted to those only who are distinguished for their moral qualities is, not infrequently, in the hands of authors totally devoid of good taste, good feeling, and generous sentiment. The writers of Lives have, in our time, assumed a licence not enjoyed by their more scrupulous predecessors—for they interweave the adventures of the living with the memoirs of the dead; and, pretending to pourtray the peculiarities which sometimes mark the man of genius, they invade the privacy and disturb the peace of his surviving associates.

An end should be put to this dishonest practice—otherwise suspicion and caution and reserve will palsy the warmth of friendship—and social intercourse be sacrificed to the fear of that most unprincipled of all adventurers, a booksellers' hack.

The booksellers' hack in question was Galt, of whom he had a few more sharp things to say before he proceeded to his primary object. He seems not to have heard anything about Beyle since 1816 except that he had written the inaccurate and effusive *Rome, Naples, et Florence* and published it in England under the name of the Count de Stendhal, and as usual he wasted energy and hurt his case by skirmishing about an unessential topic.

. . . Mr John Galt seems altogether unaware that there is no such person as 'M. Stendhal'—that a certain M. de Beyle has chosen to call himself '*Le Comte de Stendhal*' and that the two trumpery volumes containing his supposed adventures in Italy and published under that assumed name are just as much known to us in England as in France and have not procured him 'literary celebrity' in either country. We may now dispose of this 'interesting account of Lord Byron at Milan' which opens thus—

'In 1817, a few young people met every evening at the theatre of La Scala, at Milan, in the box of Monsignor Ludovic de Brême, formerly chief almoner of the ex-king of Italy. . . . One evening a stranger made his appearance in Monsignor de Brême's box. He was young, of middling stature, and with remarkably fine eyes. As he advanced, we observed that he limped a little. "Gentlemen," said Monsignor de Brême, "this is Lord Byron."

To begin with the beginning, Lord Byron was not in Milan in the year 1817, a year which this fictitious Count, however, seems to have had some reason for preferring to the real year in which Lord Byron's visit to Milan occurred. . . .[1]

. . . It must next be told that the first meeting between Lord Byron and Mr de Beyle *alias* Count Stendhal did not take place at the Opera. That event so useful to one of these parties occurred at the Casa Roma the house

[1] Stendhal's reason for changing the year was so that he might use the Byron story in a book which originally purported to deal only with events of 1817. In the Colomb version (1829) he gave 1812 as the date. He seemed to have had a veritable compulsion never to give times and places correctly.

of Monsignor de Brême at a dinner given by that gentleman on the 17th of
October. It would be hardly worth while to notice so trifling an error were
not this interview at the Opera box made the first scene as it were of the
romance . . . and were it not that the aforesaid dinner is also alluded to by
Mr. de Beyle and contrived to hang another fiction upon.

The account proceeds thus: 'We were afterwards presented to his Lordship, the whole scene passing with as much ceremonious gravity as if our
introducer had been de Brême's grandfather in days of yore ambassador
from the Duke of Savoy to the Court of Louis XIV,' and the writer goes on to
state how he knowing the character of the English took little or no notice of
Lord Byron—how his Lordship having heard that a gentleman who had
made the Russian campaign was in the box mistook a tall officer-like looking
person for that person—but soon discovered that de Beyle was the person,
and had a discussion with him on Russia so warm that it was thought angry
—and lastly how Lord Byron the next evening took *me* (that is Mr de Beyle)
'by the arm and walked with me for an hour in the saloon of the theatre
de la Scala.'

The truth is that Lord Byron was formally presented to a small party in
M. de Brême's box on the 14th of October—that Mr de Beyle was not one of
that party—that there was no discussion about Russia—that Lord Byron
did not go to the theatre the next evening and never either on that or any
other evening walked arm in arm with de Beyle in the saloon of that or any
other theatre.

Hobhouse would have been even more scathing if he had seen how, in
the narrative sent the previous year to Colomb, it was not the courtly
formality of the introduction which Stendhal had thought memorable,
but its entire simplicity: 'I was listening to the music when M. de Brême
said to me, indicating my neighbour, "Monsieur Beyle, here is Lord
Byron." . . . I saw a young man whose eyes were superb and had something generous in them; he was by no means tall. I was mad about *Lara*
just then. From the second look I no longer saw Lord Byron as he really
was, but such as it seemed to me the author of *Lara* ought to be. . . . I
was filled with shyness and tenderness. If I had dared I would have kissed
Lord Byron's hand, melting into tears.' (This was a coals-of-fire prelude
to the silence that descended in the English peer's chilling presence.)

In the version read by Hobhouse, Stendhal was no longer the sort of
man who would have burst into tears of emotion about a poet, but an
important character whom the guest of honour was looking forward to
meeting:

The latter [Byron] had been informed that in the course of the evening
he would probably be introduced to a stranger who had performed the
celebrated campaign of Moscow. . . . A fine-looking man, with a military
appearance, happening to be of our party, his Lordship naturally concluded
that he was the hero; and accordingly, in addressing him, relaxed consider-

ably from the natural coldness of his manner. The next day, however, Byron was undeceived.

Byron having thus been made to look faintly absurd, as people do when they have warmed to the wrong man, Stendhal depicts himself as giving very frigid and reproachful replies to his questioning about Napoleon. Hobhouse's diary shows that it was he (Hobhouse) who did the questioning, and that he easily elicited anecdotes, ten pages on one occasion and four on another, many of them discreditable to Beyle's supposed hero. Reflecting on the validity of the same raconteur's anecdotes about Byron, Hobhouse must have thought it a pity he had bothered to record them.

It appears that de Beyle had some predilection for this box at the opera as a convenient scene for his adventures with Lord Byron—for he says 'His progress in the good graces of my Italian friends, who met every evening in Monsignor de Brême's box, was not very rapid. I must confess, that his Lordship, one evening, broached rather a whimsical idea—that, in a discussion which had just been started, his title added weight to his opinion.'

Again, 'On another evening Lord Byron afforded an opening to ridicule by the warmth with which he denied all resemblance between his own character and that of Jean Jacques Rousseau, to whom he had been compared. His principal objection to the comparison . . . was that Rousseau had been a servant, and the son of a watchmaker.[1] We could not avoid a hearty laugh. . . .'

Again 'At Milan we often purposely discussed in his presence the question "if Henry IV could justly pretend to the attribute of clemency, after having ordered his old companion the Duke de Biron, to be beheaded?" . . . It was ludicrous to observe his respect wavering undecided between acquired distinction and his own nobility, which he considered far above that of the Duke de Biron.'

And in another place, 'One evening amongst others, the conversation turned upon a handsome Milanese female, who had eagerly desired to venture her person in single combat with a lover by whom she had been abandoned: the discussion afterwards changed to the story of a prince who in cold blood had murdered his mistress for an act of infidelity. Byron was instantly silent, endeavoured to restrain his feelings, but, unequal to the effort, soon afterwards indignantly quitted the box.'

Also in another place, 'At the theatre our discussions were frequently so energetical as to arouse the indignation of the pit.'

And lastly 'After the lapse of a few weeks, Byron seemed to have acquired a taste for the society of Milan. When the performances for the evening were over, we frequently stopped at the door of the theatre to enjoy the sight of the beauties who passed us in review.'

Who would not collect from these and other passages which might be cited that Lord Byron had passed a season at Milan and had habitually

[1] Stendhal had read and given his own slant to Byron's remarks on a comparison between Rousseau and himself which Moore had published in his biography.

attended at Monsieur de Brême's box at the Opera? But what is the fact? Lord Byron . . . was in Milan only from the *thirteenth* of October 1816 to the *third* of the following November and never went to the opera or the celebrated box of Monsignor de Brême but three times—of which three times Mr de Beyle was present only twice.

It is almost needless to add that the conversation and the anecdotes which the said pseudo-Count appends to and interweaves with the tale of the opera box at the Scala are either pure inventions or framed upon some very scanty and confused recollections of what he heard or saw at the three or four interviews which he had with Lord Byron.

For example, the account given of the arrest of Dr Polidori at the theatre is not a fiction, yet it is all but a fiction. The [illegible word] thus, 'One evening in the middle of a philosophical argument on the principle of *utility*, Silvio Pellico, a delightful poet who has since died in an Austrian prison, came in breathless haste to apprise Lord Byron that his friend and physician, Polidori, had been arrested.'

The person who brought the news to Lord Byron was not Silvio Pellico, whose name it was convenient to introduce to render the narrative interesting. It was a Mr Borsieri. Dr Polidori never had been Lord Byron's friend nor was he at that time his physician. He had been discharged some time before for misconduct.

The narrator goes on, 'We instantly ran to the guard-house. . . . The poet Monti had accompanied us, and, to the number of fifteen or twenty, we surrounded the prisoner. Every one spoke at once; Polidori was beside himself with passion, and his face red as a burning coal. Byron, though he too was in a violent rage, was on the contrary, pale as ashes. His patrician blood boiled as he reflected on the slight consideration in which he was held. . . . The Austrian officer . . . ran from the guard-house to call his men, who seized their arms that had been piled on the outside. Monti's idea was excellent "Sortiamo tutti—restino soli i titolari."[1] De Brême remained, with the Marquis de Sartirana, his brother, Count Gonfalonieri, and Lord Byron. These gentlemen, having written their names and titles, the list was handed to the officer on guard, who instantly forgot the insult offered to his fur cap, and allowed Polidori to leave the guard house'. . . .

The real facts are—that the persons who came down from Monsignor de Brême's box to the guard room where Dr Polidori was disputing with the officer were not fifteen or twenty—they were only five, with Lord Byron— and Monti was not one of them nor was Count Gonfaloniere. They were Monsignor de Brême—his brother the Marquess Gattinara de Brême, a gentleman of the name of Guasco, Signor Borsieri, and Mr de Beyle himself. Mr Hobhouse was with Dr Polidori.[2]

Lord Byron was not at all in a rage—he had no reason or pretext for anger. The Austrian officer was angry but he did not 'run from the guardroom to call his men who seized their arms.' The soldiers were in the guardroom at the time. The officer did not pay the slightest attention to the Italian nobles—but treated their interference with contempt.

[1] 'Let us all leave—let only the titled ones remain.'
[2] Hobhouse was writing in the third person.

To Lord Byron he behaved with much civility and finally accepted his card as a guarantee for Dr Polidori's appearance the next morning. There were not more than Monsignor de Brême and Lord Byron in the guard-room when this arrangement took place, the remainder of the party having gone away, not in consequence of Monti's pleasantry for he was not present, but because the officer ordered them out of the room.[1]

Mr de Beyle, alias Count Stendhal, not satisfied with making this adventure of Dr Polidori serve him in order to work up one picture of Lord Byron seen under excitement, appends thereto another tale for he subjoins 'The morning after Polidori's departure, Byron in a tête-a-tête with me complained bitterly of persecution,' and he then goes on to say he advised Lord Byron to give out an account of his death and retire under the name of Mr Smith to some distant island, thence to reappear after some thirty years —a joke which he says Lord Byron received very coldly, saying "My cousin, who is heir to my title, owes you an infinity of thanks." 'I repressed,' adds de Beyle, 'the repartee which hovered on my lips. Byron had a defect in common with all the spoiled children of fortune. He cherished in his bosom two contradictory inclinations. He wished to be received as a man of rank and admired as a brilliant poet.'

The account of which tête-a-tête so ingeniously introduced apropos of Dr Polidori's departure is most certainly a fiction. Lord Byron never met Mr de Beyle either alone or otherwise after Dr Polidori left Milan which was on the 30th October. It may be added that de Beyle had no tête-a-tête with Lord Byron at any time.

If Hobhouse had glanced again at the 'trumpery volumes' in which the author claimed to have met Byron in Venice, he would have seen in its embryonic form the idea that the celebrity should start a new life as Mr Smith. There no pretence is made that the suggestion was addressed to Byron himself, so the narrator receives no cold retort, nor does any repartee hover upon his lips. Dressed up in successive stages, what must have once been a whimsical private speculation of Beyle's emerges as a verbose speech (Hobhouse has abridged it) intended to provide one more illustration of the obsession with rank which Beyle attributed to Byron, but which was, most apparently, an intense preoccupation of his own.

In 1816 he had shown he was alive to the existence of Byron's insepar- able companion by mentioning him in a letter to Crozet as 'the historian, Hobhouse', and repeating a remark of his. But in all that he wrote with a view to publication, he preferred to ignore this superfluous third party, and he even decided it would be more interesting to put into Byron's mouth the quoted dictum. In the private letter Hobhouse says of Byron: '*He knows not how he is a poet.*'[2] In the recollections for Mme Belloc's book, it is Byron who utters these words, and they are applied to Monti.

[1] See Appendix for two contemporary accounts of this incident, the one by Polidori himself, the other (hitherto unpublished) by Hobhouse.
[2] STENDHAL, *Correspondance.* 31 Dec. 1816.

(They are given in English, so it is difficult to discern their meaning.) Not once is Hobhouse's figure allowed to cast its sturdy, sceptical shadow on the page.

By 1829 Stendhal has become the sole person in the group who knew English. It is to him therefore that Byron turns when he needs directions about getting back to his inn. Stendhal sees that 'he was going to wander in the midst of solitary streets faintly lighted, and without knowing a word of the language. Out of kindness, I had the foolishness to advise him to take a fiacre. Instantly a shade of hauteur marked his brow; he let me understand with all possible politeness that he asked for direction as to the streets, and not for advice on the manner of making his way through them. He went out of the box, and I understood then why he had brought silence with him.'

Hobhouse was spared from any opportunity of comparing this as yet unpublished letter with the printed article at the back of Galt's book, in itself infuriating enough.

. . . This gentleman is not always so cautious as to give something like an air of probability to his romance, or to make himself sole witness of what he narrates. Speaking of the aforesaid meetings at the opera box he says—

'The house in which Lord Byron resided was situated at the further extreme of a solitary quarter at the distance of half a league from the theatre of La Scala. The streets of Milan were at that time much infested with robbers during the night. Some of us, forgetting time and space in the charm of the poet's conversation, generally accompanied him to his own door, and on our return, at two o'clock in the morning, were obliged to pass through a multitude of intricate, suspicious-looking streets. This circumstance gave an additional air of romance to the noble bard's retreat.'

What is the fact? Lord Byron and Mr Hobhouse then travelling together lodged at the Hotel of St. Mark in the most frequented part of Milan, not more than a quarter of a mile from the Opera House; and the only three or four times they were ever at the opera they returned in a carriage, without Mr de Beyle, to their romantic retreat.

But the best is yet to come. 'Polidori informed us that Byron often composed a hundred verses in the course of the morning. On his return from the theatre in the evening, still under the charm of the music to which he had listened, he would take up his papers, and reduce his hundred verses to five-and-twenty or thirty. When he had in this manner put together four or five hundred, he sent the whole to Murray, his publisher, in London. He often sat up all night in the ardour of composition, and drank a sort of grog made from hollands and water.'

The reader has been already told that the nightly visit to the opera is a fiction—of course, the charm of the music evaporates with the supposed opera box: it may now be added that the hundred morning verses, the reduction of these verses after hearing evening music—the accumulation of the reduced fragments—and the sending them from Milan to Mr Murray must be neither more nor less than the offspring of what Dr Polidori may have told Mr de Beyle sometimes happened in the course of Lord Byron's composition whilst residing near Geneva—for most assuredly Lord Byron wrote nothing except a translation of a few lines of Francesca da Rimini whilst at Milan, and if he had, Dr Polidori would have known nothing of it, for he did not live with Lord Byron and very seldom saw his Lordship.

Mr de Beyle is a bold man—for he says—'Never shall I forget the sublime poem which he composed one evening on the subject of Castruccio Castracani, the Napoleon of the Middle Age.' It is somewhat strange that no one should have ever heard of this sublime poem except Mr de Beyle. . . .

It seems that his Lordship had other occupations whilst at Milan most certainly known only to the false Count. Amongst these may be reckoned the absurd story of Lord Byron's '*sensation amounting to horror*' at contemplating Crespi's picture of the monk rising from his coffin, and his following de Beyle on horseback to a monastery at a little distance, after indulging in this trance. Lord B. was very little if at all affected by any picture—and whilst at Milan noticed only the Hagar of Guercino. As to the ride to the 'neighbouring monastery,' he was never on horseback once during his stay in the city.

Here was one more instance where Hobhouse did not know the full extent of the liberties Stendhal had taken with the truth. While in the 1830 composition, he sketches a dramatic picture of Byron's emotion on seeing the painting of a monk whose soul had been condemned to hell, in the contribution to Mme Belloc's work he had told an altogether different story about the young traveller's artistic susceptibilities. M. de Brême, he said, had requested him to take Lord Byron to the Brera Museum— which actually Byron and Hobhouse twice visited together without Beyle —and there 'I admired the profundity of the feeling with which the great poet understood the most diverse types of painters: Raphael, Guercino, Luini, Titian, etc. The Hagar put away by Abraham, of Guercino, electrified him, and while admiration made us dumb, he improvised for an hour, and better in my view than Mme de Staël.'

Whatever percipience Beyle may have had about men in general, his observations of Byron must be said to have produced no enlightenment of any kind whatever if he could part from him in the belief that he had a profound understanding of the arts, and was the sort of person who would hold forth for an hour on the beauties of a picture. In what language was he supposed to address his audience? Not English, for only Beyle, according to himself, understood it. Not Italian, for Byron, Beyle tells us, did not speak a word of it. We are left with French, which good witnesses assure us Byron avoided using whenever he could—French more eloquent than Mme de Staël's!

Of exactly the same authenticity [Hobhouse's paper goes on] is a dialogue with Silvio Pellico to which the Count attributes the 'tone of Lord Byron's subsequent poetical career.' The conversation turned, so says the veridique narrator, on the dialects of Italy—and on the satires of Buratti, of which Pellico gave so favourable an account to his Lordship that he enquired eagerly after the bookseller who sold them, 'a question that excited a hearty laugh at his expense.'

'The next day the charming Contessina N. was kind enough to lend her collection to one of the party. Byron, who imagined himself an adept in the language of Dante and Ariosto, was at first rather puzzled by Buratti's manuscripts. We read over with him some of Goldoni's comedies, which enabled him at last to comprehend Buratti's satires. . . . I persist in thinking, that for the composition of Beppo and subsequently Don Juan, Byron was indebted to the reading of Buratti's poetry.'

What are the facts? Lord Byron saw Silvio Pellico at Milan about as often as he saw de Beyle, that is, three or four times at the utmost. Of Buratti's satires he heard just as little as of 'the charming Contessina N.'—that is, nothing at all. The MSS lent to him was Pellico's own tragedy of which he read only the first two scenes—and this exploit he performed with Mr Hobhouse.

As to the reading over of Goldoni's comedies as a key to Buratti's satires by 'our party' and Lord Byron, no such lecture and no such party would have been or were tolerated by Lord Byron—and the real origin of Beppo was Mr Frere's burlesque poem "Whistlecraft" which the late Lord Kinnaird read to Lord Byron in the autumn of 1817 at Venice. After reading it Lord Kinnaird asked Byron if he did not think it was a very clever and a very difficult performance. Lord Byron replied that he thought it very clever but not very difficult—and two days afterwards he produced Beppo.

So much for the sage conjectures of Count Stendhal who having thereby exhausted his inventive powers considerably exclaims, 'Here, however, I ceased to act the part of an eye witness and here, consequently, I close my narrative.'

The incredible effrontery of this de Beyle in hazarding such a tissue of fictions, whilst there was alive an individual the travelling companion and constant associate of Lord Byron's during the time chosen for the date of these adventures, is only equalled by the convenient and unscrupulous credulity of the wretched novel-monger who has eked out his pretended life of Byron by admitting this 'interesting account' (such is his designation of the Count's falsehoods) amongst the 'pièces justificatives' of his catch-penny volume.

If Hobhouse, after polishing up this criticism, had published it, as he intended, he would have had the moral satisfaction of striking a blow for truth but nothing more. The romance-writer's legendary Byron—fatuous with humourless vanity, pronouncing the name of Brummell 'with a shivering of adoration and jealousy', always dreaming either of his personal beauty or his noble birth, idiotically boasting that only he and Napoleon could use the signature N. B.,[1] yet dowered with incomparable

---

[1] STENDHAL, various passages from *Lord Byron en Italie*. The initials N.B. were not used by Byron till nearly six years after his visit to Milan.

The Holmes Miniature of Byron at the age of 27, shown for comparison

Head from *The Family of Darius before Alexander* by Veronese, said by G. P. R. James to resemble Byron closely in his youth

(and certainly incomprehensible) charm in nocturnal conversations—this figure from a theatrical tinsel picture is much easier for the memory to lay hold of than the features of the very complex man in whom we must reconcile gaiety and melancholy, kindliness and hardness, self-will and self-surrender.

And the anecdotes, ill-grounded though they were, had a vividness that has made them perennial. One modern writer, on the very next page after throwing discredit on Beyle's reminiscences of Napoleon, quotes unquestioningly the story of how Byron was horror-struck at the painting of the monk rising from his coffin crying '*I am damned by a just judgment*', and how he wept and could not be torn away from it, and rode off at last alone to join his awed companions—Beyle of course conveniently at hand to observe him.

Of what use was it for Hobhouse to say: 'He was never on horseback once during his stay in the city'? And yet he should have said it. He who had fought for the burning of the Memoirs, who had so long opposed Moore, and made it practically impossible for any intimate of Byron's to utter his testimony, was under an obligation to bear witness himself.

But whether other matters claimed his attention, or whether, after all he had already endured from arguments in the Press, he lost heart, the final spurt of energy needful for the trimming of his hasty draft was never achieved. It was not till many years later, when he came to write his travel book, *Italy*, that he referred publicly for the first time to one of Stendhal's tall stories. Calling him 'the now celebrated de Beyle', he whittled his criticism down to some subdued words in a footnote:

This gentleman in those days was called *De* Beyle, and afterwards called himself, for authorship, Count Stendhall [*sic*]. . . . I confess I was not aware of the great celebrity of Mr Beyle until this year (1856) when, opening a clever article in the 'Edinburgh Review' for January, I awoke and 'found him famous.'

My previous acquaintance with him as an author, I ought to be ashamed to say, was confined to a quotation from the *History of Painting in Italy*, which I found in Moore's Life of Byron, and which contains an account of what passed at a dinner given by De Brême to Lord Byron, Monti, and others, at Milan, in 1816. I was one of the guests on that occasion, and I can only repeat the old remark, 'All these things happened in my time, but I never heard of them.'

He went on to give in French what Moore had quoted, not, as Hobhouse had written with unwonted carelessness, from Stendhal's book about painting, but from the letter to Mme Belloc; and he cast ridicule—but mildly—on the story.

He was a tired man of seventy years old and the much more plausible recollections which had so enraged him in 1830 had passed completely from his mind. Had he remembered them he would either have refrained from mentioning Stendhal altogether, or else cast his reference in much severer terms.

The angry pages he had dashed off then had been laid aside twenty-six years ago, and at some time between then and now he had scribbled on them in pencil a sad comment:

> I wrote all this at a time when I thought the subject of much more importance than I now know it to be.
> I do not know whether any part of it was ever published.

If a year were named, we might discover what grief, what disgust of life, had cast so sombre a shadow on his mind that friendship and truth suddenly seemed unimportant. Had something heard or read, some old letter or piece of verbal mischief, made him wonder for a moment whether it was worth while to have fought posthumous battles for Byron? Or was the defeatist tone of that unlikely endorsement the consequence of one of those afflictions that for a while reduce everything to triviality?

In 1835, his young wife died, 'the pride and treasure of my heart. . . . I am so stupefied by the blow that I seem to have no feeling.'[1] But that was only five years after he had written his anti-Stendhal paper, and he could not have forgotten in so short a time whether or not he had seen it through the press. In 1849, his much-loved eldest daughter succumbed at the age of nineteen to the cholera. Apart from these two great losses, his domestic life was uncommonly happy.

His political career brought him anxiety and annoyance but also distinction and the satisfaction of having striven for the most progressive causes of the century, the various Reform Bills and the early Factory Acts in defence of children; and though it must have been unpleasant to be nicknamed Flogging Jack after long opposition to brutal sentences of corporal punishment in the Army,[2] it could not be called a disillusionment or a sorrow.

But perhaps his pencilled words were no more than an attempt at a cynical shrug—a gesture of resignation in the face of overwhelming odds. Byron was now a character of mythology. In Greece they sold prints of him wearing a fustanella and exhorting fellow-warriors over the tomb of a hero. In Italy and Switzerland, aged servants, boatmen, innkeepers, Alpine guides, did a thriving business in romantic reminiscences. In France, Byron's 'Secret Amours' were a popular subject for the literature of gallantry; and in England, among the advocates of a less normal kind of eroticism, two dirty, dingy poems, full of sniggering puns, were in

---

[1] Hobhouse *Journals*, 3 April.
[2] He had been obliged to yield on this point in order to take ministerial office. It was a sacrifice of principle which probably did more harm than good to his career.

circulation, glaring with anachronisms, yet purporting to be by Byron.[1]

There was no coping with that sort of thing. To have gone on struggling would have meant never having time for anything else, and in any case, all Hobhouse's repudiations, his complaints of 'impostors', had been unavailing. People believed what they wanted to believe about Byron.

The abortive contest with Stendhal was the last affair of its kind. He continued to keep Byron's memory green amongst his friends and descendants, he was diligent in the promotion of the monument project, he preserved with care every fragment of correspondence and the great hoard of papers that had fallen into his hands as executor; but never again did he attempt any controversy with memoir-writers. The Blessingtons, the Trelawnys, the biographers of contemporary men of letters in general, wrote on and on; even the incorrigible Medwin continued to publish Byroniana; but whatever Hobhouse thought or confided to his diary, his voice was mute.

[1] *Don Leon* and *Leon to Annabella*.

APPENDIX

The row in the Opera House

The published extracts from Hobhouse's *Journals* do not contain any allusion at all to the little fracas in the Opera House which had such serious consequences for Polidori; but Hobhouse wrote about it fully and immediately.

Monday   October 28th

. . . Went to the opera—whilst I was in the pit Polidori came in with Borsieri. P. began to be indignant against the appearance of the soldiery and was silly enough to ask a grenadier officer to pull off his cap. The Captn, who was the officer of the guard, turned round and said vorreste [would you wish it?] Lo voglio [I wish it] returned Polidori—the officer desired him to step out with him. Polidori called me to come out with him thinking he was to fight. He was soon undeceived by being ordered into the custody of two grenadiers into the guardhouse—

At first he would not go—when the officer half drew his sword upon him and was scarcely to be repressed by my intercession. P. was marched in to the guard room and there began a lively altercation with the deutscher whom he told that in the theatre he was equal to any body, the officer replying that he was a verfluchter kerl and not equal to the meanest soldier. The officer was very foul mouthed the doctor very foolish and English but not abusive.

Down came Ld B. de Brême de Beyle Guasco Borsieri [who had gone up to the box to tell the others what was happening] but the officer was not afraid. Brême referred to the Casa di Brême, which did nothing. An English nobleman had a little more power, but still the angry grenadier swore he would make out a species facti or procès verbal and filed us out of the room except Byron and B[rême]

We waited some time without when at last came the Doctor bailed by Ld B. who gave his card for the Doctor's appearance. We returned to the box.

Polidori's diary completely supports Hobhouse, and gives a higher opinion of the writer's veracity than we might expect, considering the passing-off of his tale *The Vampyre* as Byron's (but his posthumous nephew William Michael Rossetti, makes out a good, though not a perfect, case for Polidori's having been innocently involved in that imposture):

. . . Mr Hobhouse, Borsieri, and myself went into the pit, standing to look at the ballet. An officer in a great-coat came and placed himself completely before me with his grenadier's hat on . . . I touched him, and said "Vorrebbe farmi la grazia de levarsi il cappello purch'io vegga?" [Would you do me the favour of taking off your hat so that I may see?] He turning said "Lo vorreste?" with a smile of insult. I answered: "Si, lo voglio." He then asked me if I would go out with him. I, thinking he meant for a duel, said, "Yes, with pleasure"; and called Mr Hobhouse to accompany me. He did.

When passing by the guard-house he said, "Go in, go in there"; I said I would not, that it was not there I thought of going with him. Then he swore in German, and drew half his sabre, with a threatening look, but Hobhouse held his hand.

The police on guard came, and he delivered me to their custody. . . . He began declaiming about the insult to one like him. I said I was his equal, and, being in the theatre, to any one there. "Equal to me?" he retorted; "you are not the equal to the last of the Austrian soldiers in the house"; and then began abusing me in all the Billingsgate German he was master of—which I did not know till afterwards.

In the meanwhile the news had spread in the theatre, and reached de Brême and L. Byron, who came running down, and tried to get me away, but could not on any plea . . . De Brême said he would go to Bubna[1] immediately, and get an order for my dismission; on which the officer took Lord Byron's card, as bail that I would appear to answer for my conduct on the morrow. Then I was released.[2]

Thus two narratives, written independently—and incidentally by persons who heartily disliked each other—prove that Stendhal's story of numerous celebrities and noblemen making an impressive entrance together like the chorus in an opera scene is a work of imagination. Despite the efforts next day of Brême, Byron, Hobhouse, and a Colonel Fitzgerald, Polidori was ordered to leave Milan in twenty-four hours, the banishment to be marked on his passport. His treatment was so severe that Hobhouse could not help concluding he must have been talking dangerously in public somewhere. He was only twenty and very rash.

He committed suicide through a gambling debt in August 1821.

[1] Bubna was apparently the military governor of Milan.   [2] Polidori.

CHAPTER XII

THE COST OF A JOURNEY

Byron and Shelley were the centres of two intersecting circles to which so large a literature has been devoted that the survivors are only brought forward here when, like Medwin, Trelawny, or Hunt, they played an important part in shaping the beliefs that future generations were to hold about Byron. The general drift of events that affected his reputation was given its direction, to a greater extent than has generally been recognized, by a group of persons who, at the time of his death or later, had real or imaginary grievances to redress.

It was inevitable that, after the enormous vogue he had enjoyed, Byron's poetry should have gone for a time into eclipse, and that there would be a process of compensation for his having been more renowned in his lifetime than the two great poets nearest him in age, Keats and Shelley. Their relative obscurity had naturally been resented by their friends who felt that Byron had received homage beyond his due, and unfairly overshadowed names that were more deserving. His impetuous and insensitive criticisms did not conduce to give Keats enthusiasts a good opinion of him: and the rivalry between Byron's fame and Shelley's was yet more pronounced because their lives had been intimately and tragically entwined, and they had just enough in common to make a comparison to Byron's disadvantage highly effective.

That some personal element would tinge the view of those who were concerned to see justice done to Shelley was to be expected; but that a bitter posthumous warfare should have been waged by some of his admirers against Byron was due to several factors which are only by slow stages being brought to light.

Any poet of brilliant gifts and outstanding character who meets a sudden and most untimely end is likely to be enshrined in the hearts of those who loved him rather as a saintly image in a niche than in the human guise he once wore. In Shelley's case the idealization, which scarcely fell short of myth-making, was fostered by his widow's earnest and understandable desire to live down all that had been considered disreputable about his past and hers. The desertion of his first wife, Harriet, and her subsequent suicide, her own elopement with him and the birth of a child before marriage, their practical experiment in 'free love', his rashly flaunted atheism—she wanted these things forgotten, and so decided to erase them from the annals. She was under a monetary as well as a social pressure to take this course, Shelley's father, Sir Timothy, not wishing the turpitude of his son's career to attain further notoriety.

Mary was not untruthful by nature, and would have contented herself with simple suppression, but Leigh Hunt, bent on using Shelley as a stick to beat Byron, found it necessary to indulge in both suppression and distortion, and it was he who first represented Shelley as an unblemished Galahad, or, as Benjamin Jowett more forcefully put it, Jesus Christ.[1] Despite a protest from Mary herself, and in the full knowledge that he was lying, Hunt had represented Shelley as parting from Harriet 'by mutual consent' and after the birth of their two children,[2] whereas his flight with Mary had taken place while Harriet was pregnant (though it is true he had invited her to come and live with him and Mary).

Hunt had laid stress on Harriet's 'inferior rank' and her lack of intellectual attainments, and had hinted at previous immoralities on her part that justified Shelley. In short, he had done a thorough whitewashing job at the expense of a most pitiable young creature, and set the stage for the Victorian biographers to bring on their gentle knight-errant, the 'beautiful and ineffectual angel'. Much new documentary evidence has been produced in the past few decades, and nobody now doubts that Shelley had a fanatical kind of goodness and also a fanatical kind of self-will, that he was not guiltless of inflicting pain, and that he was susceptible and unstable to an eccentric degree in his emotions.

In an illuminating and on the whole very appreciative description of him which appears in her unpublished *Vie de Lord Byron en Italie*, Teresa Guiccioli calls him a perfectionist at odds with the realities of humanity. Reversing the Midas story in which everything touched is turned to gold, Shelley's touch, she says, empoisoned things for those about him and brought a fatality with it: he never wanted to do anything but good and never succeeded in doing anything but harm to those he cared for. Teresa was on terms of close intimacy with Mary, whose journal records sixty-five meetings with her between September 1821 and April 1822, when the Shelleys left Pisa:[3] as both Mary's confidante and Byron's she knew a great deal about Shelley's Italian 'Platonics'[4] and many other subjects glossed over in the 'official' portrait or omitted altogether.

He was, like Byron himself, a bringer of discord; and yet, so greatly has our outlook changed, that the legendary Shelley, so dear to family piety and Victorian prudery, now seems a less appealing figure than the Shelley who emerges in the more candid light of modern biographical research, the man whose rare virtue was that he had the courage to act on his

[1] Letter to Lady Shelley, 16 Apr. 1891: Abinger Papers.

[2] Bowring of the *Westminster Review* had refused Hunt's notice of Shelley's posthumous poems on the grounds that these facts and others were not correct, and said he had consulted Peacock, Coulson, and Mrs Shelley. Hunt was much annoyed with her. To Trelawny she wrote that he had slurred over the real truth (15 Dec. 1829).

[3] PRATT, *Italian Note Book*.

[4] Teresa says Shelley had hallucinations and that Byron regarded his behaviour over Emilia Viviani as the result of them.

beliefs; and whose beliefs, though they could never have conformed to prudent and worldly standards, were gradually being sobered by time and experience of life.

Shelley's feelings towards Byron were intensely variable—laughably so if we were not aware of the stresses and strains imposed on them. At one moment, he would be writing Byron a sonnet, the theme of which was that he was a worm and Byron a god, at another he would see him as the villain of a melodrama:

> My great object has been to lull him into security until circumstances might call him to England. But the idea of contending with him in Italy, and defended by his enormous fortune, is vain.[1]

His friend Peacock receives, in December 1818, a letter telling him that the newest cantos of *Childe Harold* are written in a spirit of 'the most wicked and mischievous insanity that was ever given forth', and conveying scandalous revelations about Venetian debaucheries. In January 1822 the same correspondent learns that Byron is established (it was by Shelley's desire) at Pisa, 'and we are constant companions; no small relief this after the dreary solitude of the understanding and imagination in which past [*sic*] the first years of our expatriation'.

To Horace Smith, and only two weeks later, this welcome companionship is presented as a burden:

> Lord Byron unites us at a weekly dinner, when my nerves are generally shaken to pieces by sitting up contemplating the rest making themselves vats of claret, etc., till three o'clock in the morning.[2]

Shelley lived a stone's throw from Byron, and had a wife waiting for him at home. There does not seem to have been any reason for forcing himself to endure the night-long nerve-strain—except, perhaps, that 'sort of intoxication', that binding spell of the host's conversation which had been commemorated in an earlier poem.[3]

Most unluckily for Byron's after-fame, it was while Shelley was going through one of his anti-Byron phases that his life was cut short. Moreover, he had only just had an affectionate reunion with Leigh Hunt. Death, when it comes catastrophically, confers an air of permanence on situations and relationships which normally are not static. Like the figures on Keats's Grecian urn, those who die young are faithful for ever to the attitudes in which they have been captured. Thus Shelley is fixed as the righteously indignant critic of Byron, and the inseparable friend of Hunt—whom, but for the last week of his life, he had not seen for more than four years. Had he lived, there is every probability that Hunt, who sooner or

---

[1] To Claire Clairmont. Undated. Early 1822. As Claire hated Byron, both Trelawny and Shelley felt obliged to offer elaborate excuses to her for seeking his company.
[2] 25 Jan. 1822.   [3] *Julian and Maddalo.*

later exasperated all his friends, would have exasperated Shelley; and that with Byron, there would have been again and again, as in the past, hours of delight to weigh against hours of bitterness.

It was, after all, no easy situation for a man who was fully and justly conscious of his own under-estimated genius to be in daily companionship with a writer of spectacular career, whose failures commanded more attention than the successes of others: and Shelley disclosed his feelings when he sent Horace Smith the lament that is generally given without the passage he so significantly underlined:

> I do not write—I have lived too long near Lord Byron, and the sun has extinguished the glow worm: for I cannot hope with St John that '*the light came into the world, and the world knew it not.*'[1]

Byron's position also was a most difficult one. Although only thirty-four in Shelley's Pisa days, he was, except for his contemporaries, Medwin and Taaffe, the oldest in the group, and also incomparably the richest and most influential, and this in itself generated a certain refractory spirit among them. He hardly ever visited others, but made them come to him if they wished to see him; it was his whim that ruled the times of the daily riding and shooting diversions; and he never invited the women to his dinner parties nor did anything to suggest that they were other than a cog upon his conviviality. As they had a fantastically exaggerated idea of his income, they marvelled at his boggling over any item of expenditure, and constantly called one another's attention to his avarice. Mary Shelley told Claire Clairmont that he had £12,000 to £15,000 a year.[2] Including the sums earned, it was actually at that date between £3500 and £4000 a year, out of which he was still paying off debts contracted while under age, had a slow-dragging lawsuit on his hands with immense charges, and was trying to amass some capital he would be free to use so that he might fulfil one of his projects for becoming a man of action.

Shelley, whose bounty was so profuse that he indulged in large bene-volence while owing money for years to small tradesmen, was shocked to see that a man of such fabulous wealth checked the accounts of his house-hold steward and counted the cost of many things attentively: and Byron, with his zest for outraging feelings he regarded as priggish or romantic, assumed the miser's role with relish. It is no far-fetched conclusion that this strain of priggishness in Shelley, which had made him so keen an opponent of smoking, drinking, play-going, and bawdy jokes, provoked Byron into many mischievous defiances.

---

[1] Dated only May 1822.

[2] JONES, 11 May 1821. The pound sign is omitted, but no other currency than sterling can be intended. It is quite inconceivable that Byron himself planted the idea of this vast fortune. Money was a topic on which he was always down-to-earth and exact.

Even if the depressing sketch of Shelley's habits offered by Leigh Hunt is misleading, and he was no longer wholly devoted to early rising, taking healthful walks before breakfast, perpetual reading of Greek texts and the Bible, and retiring at ten p.m. after a day of abstinence from all luxury and frivolity, he was still, it may be supposed, on a rather rarefied plane compared with Byron, and as such, likely to be the victim of his sallies.

When Leigh Hunt made his public assault on Byron's memory in 1828, he did not fail to tell of Shelley's desire to break with Byron, and little by little many evidences were produced by which 'the club-footed poet', to use Trelawny's typical epithet, was presented as a Satanic figure in combat with an angelic one, while many other evidences, which would have dissolved that imaginary antithesis, were withheld. There was a veritable epidemic of bowdlerising and dishonest editing, and witnesses of the most doubtful bona fides were treated reverentially as long as their testimony redounded to the glories of Shelley.

Those who had been early with their recognition of his merits now reaped the due praise of their percipience, and sometimes more tangible rewards. Leigh Hunt took all the credit he deserved, and perhaps a good deal more, for his appreciation of Shelley's poetry seems to have been coincidental to a remarkable extent with his learning that the poet was a young man of property. J. Cordy Jeaffreson, who rendered himself obnoxious in 1885 by producing the first 'debunking' book about Shelley, is a quibbling and heavy-handed biographer, but time has not invalidated the general truth of his commentary on Hunt's part in Shelley's career:

> . . . On receiving certain sets of verses from the still youthful literary aspirant, he [Hunt] neither printed them in the *Examiner* nor returned them to the author, but after unfortunately mislaying them, forgot all about them. . . . But if Hunt was tardy in responding to Shelley's repeated overtures of friendship, he atoned for previous negligence by his subsequent pains to plant himself in the affection of the young man, whom he had treated with scant courtesy. The editor of the *Examiner* was too sincere a man to admire aught till he had found it admirable. But on seeing Shelley's titles to his homage, he promptly acknowledged them. . . .
>
> Raising money on . . . ruinous terms, towards the end of 1817, and in the opening weeks of the following year, Shelley raised it with the cognizance of Leigh Hunt. The money came to the younger poet's hands whilst he was living in closest intimacy with the gentleman who, whenever money was passing about, never failed to see why he should not have some of it. . . .
>
> . . . Hunt was a man of middle age, who had been trained by poverty to be keenly mindful of his own interest, though affecting to be wholly regardless of it. . . . This mature man of the world took this young man's money,— not in payment for work done, but as a gift. The affair is all the more discreditable to Hunt, because he was the editor of a powerful journal, whilst Shelley was a literary aspirant. . . .

Endeavouring to correct certain impressions which anyone would derive from Hunt's writings, Jeaffreson adds a footnote:

Like Trelawny, Hunt made the most of his personal intercourse with Shelley. Readers should bear in mind that . . . the period during which they saw much of one another, speaking face to face, began at the close of 1816, and ended in April, 1818—a period of less than eighteen months. Till he saw his way to suck money out of the youngster's pocket, Hunt never troubled himself about Shelley.

The story of how the names of Hunt, Shelley, and Byron came to be linked together in the ill-starred venture of launching an English periodical from Italian soil, has been told many times, and only so much of it will be repeated here as may be the means of introducing new information and of correcting certain perennial errors which proved inexpressibly injurious to Byron. The first narrator was Hunt, who had it all his own way for many years. Sympathy, however, has been gradually shifting over to Byron, as more and more documentation has become available revealing the fecklessness of the slovenly and truculent family which, through Shelley's death, became a leaden weight on Byron's hands.

Hunt blamed Byron exclusively for getting him to Italy, and accused him of purely sordid motives in doing so. The plan of founding a liberal periodical was Byron's own, but it was intended to attract Thomas Moore, and the suggestion that Leigh Hunt should be editor emanated from Shelley. Hunt was quite aware months before he arrived that Byron had grown most doubtful about the whole project, and that he would have been still more so had he been told that he (Hunt) was no longer part-proprietor of the successful *Examiner*, but was intending to become, with all his little tribe, totally dependent upon his two friends in Pisa and the profits of a journal not yet launched. Shelley, in one of his periodical fits of resenting Byron, was behaving with something amounting to duplicity towards him to keep the scheme from falling through.[1] This too was known to Hunt. In fact he boasted that Shelley spoke of Byron—'as a man the most disagreeable to have anything to do with, and one whose connexion he would have given up for ever, had he not thought it might turn to my advantage, and perhaps to the noble Lord's in consequence'.[2]

Nevertheless, Hunt held to his determination to plant himself and his family on the unwilling host about whom he had this evil report.

Shelley himself admitted the entire initiative:

You have perhaps also heard [he told Hogg] of my iniquity in seducing Hunt over to Italy; he is coming with all his children to Pisa. What

---

[1] Of Shelley, Hunt himself wrote: 'If ever he deviated into an error unworthy of him, it was in occasionally condescending, though for the kindest purposes, to use a little double-dealing.' [2] HUNT, *Lord Byron*, Preface to 2nd Edition.

pleasure it would give me and him and all of us if you could follow his example.[1]

Unlike Byron, Shelley was not at ease with Italians, and the idea of forming a little colony of English literary men in Pisa was pleasant to him, while at the same time he saw in it a way of helping the ever-impecunious Hunt, who had already had so much from him.[2] Shelley being, so far as he was known at all, in disgrace with the public, had nothing to lose by associating himself with a man whose reputation in those days was exceedingly malodorous. But Byron, though widely regarded as an enemy of society, still retained, like Lucifer himself, to whom he was often compared, an immense prestige. His entering into any sort of partnership with a most notorious sponger who was also a combative and vulgar person seemed to his friends the portent of a shameful decline.

Moore, Murray, Hobhouse, Kinnaird, and Gifford all conveyed well-founded apprehensions to him, and there was plenty of time to withdraw from the rash venture because Hunt's departure from England was delayed several months; but Byron, though with deepening misgivings, persisted under Shelley's influence in going through with it; and even when it turned out as badly as his advisers had prophesied, he was strikingly restrained in his comments—for it must be remembered that he was not normally a mild or a long-suffering man.

It was only to Mary Shelley, whom he regarded as a fellow-sufferer, that he let himself go about Hunt and his intolerably ill brought-up children, and the conclusion seems unavoidable that, then or afterwards, she allowed that burst of irritation to be read. Not otherwise can we account for the frenzy of resentment which took possession of Hunt—so monstrously out of proportion with any grievance he was ever able to produce. The words that were probably rankling much more than those he could admit to having seen were those in which Byron had said he disliked having anything of Shelley's within the same walls as Mrs Hunt's children—

> dirtier and more mischievous than Yahoos. What they can't destroy with their filth they will with their fingers. . . . Poor Hunt with his six little blackguards. . . . Was there ever such a kraal out of the Hottentot country?[3]

Some weeks after receiving this *cri de cœur* Mary herself became greatly aggrieved against Byron and may then have shown the letter to Hunt, in whose house she was living.

In one of those moods of black exasperation which sometimes descended on him when he considered all the numberless ways in which he was being annoyed, Byron had yielded to a moment of churlishness which was destined to have repercussions that are still echoing.

[1] 20 Oct. 1821.   [2] See p. 282.   [3] *L. & J.* 6 Oct. 1822.

The cause of this was that Mary had written to him in a tiresome, lecturing style reproaching him for having sent Murray a letter that made the new periodical look, she said, like 'a work of charity—a kind of subscription for Hunt's family'.[1] The letter, to his distress, had been shown to Hunt's brother and its contents relayed post-haste back to Pisa; and she asked Byron to send a few words to England 'in explanation or excuse, such as could appear', and to lose no time about it. This was virtually a suggestion that Byron should write an immediate public apology to Hunt; and to add to the tactlessness, she counselled him that it would be a prudent thing to do 'since you would stop effectually the impertinence of Murray, by shewing him that he has no power to make you quarrel with your friend, and that you do not fear his [Murray's] treason'. She asked him to pass over Hunt's vanity, and recall that the independence of his character was at stake, and ended with an admonition that 'really another post ought not to be lost'.

An appeal to Byron's good nature on behalf of a man who had already taxed it to the uttermost was likely to meet with as cool a reception as a remonstrance against compromising the independence of one whom he now regarded as hopelessly wanting in that quality; nor was he likely to appreciate a recommendation to prudence coupled with contemptuous remarks about John Murray and—above all—a reference to Leigh Hunt as his friend. He himself might criticize Murray now that their relationship had become strained, but it had been too long and too glorious for him to hear with patience from an outsider that Murray was a treacherous intervener coming between two friends. His hackles rose at that. He wanted to disclaim friendship with Hunt, who was getting on his nerves, and, also it may be, to discountenance the woman who had presumed to lecture him, and he struck out wantonly:

> As to friendship, it is a propensity in which my genius is very limited. I do not know the *male* human being, except Lord Clare, the friend of my infancy, for whom I feel any thing that deserves the name. All my others are men-of-the-world friendships. I did not even feel it for Shelley, however much I admired and esteemed him; so that you see not even vanity could

[1] *Correspondence*. Undated. Late November 1822. Byron's letter to Murray, about which she was protesting, had been dispatched to England on 9 October. The passage the Hunts so bitterly resented concerned the violent attacks in the Press on *The Liberal*: 'I am afraid the Journal *is* a *bad* business, and won't do; but in it I am sacrificing *myself* for others—*I* can have no advantage in it. I believe the *brothers H.* to be honest men; I am sure that they are poor ones. They have not a rap: they pressed me to engage in this work, and in an evil hour I consented: still I shall not repent, if I can do them the least service. I have done all I can for Leigh Hunt since he came here; but it is almost useless: his wife is ill, his six children not very tractable, and in the affairs of this world he himself is a child. The death of Shelley left them totally aground; and I could not see them in such a state without using the common feelings of humanity, and what means were in my power, to set them afloat again.'

bribe me into it, for, of all men, Shelley thought highest of my talents—
and, perhaps, of my disposition.

I will do my duty by my intimates. . . . But as for friends and friendship,
I have (as I already said) named the only remaining male for whom I feel
any thing of the kind, excepting, perhaps, Thomas Moore.[1]

It was not only churlish, but childish, a mere snarl of anger, but to
Mary, a widow absorbed in grief, it sounded brutal. She was, even to lesser
rebuffs, shrinkingly sensitive, and—as may be gathered from her numerous enthusiasms and disappointments in later life—not dowered with the
slightest capacity to interpret motives. Taking Byron's skin-deep cynicism
at face value, she answered in severe reproof that she had read the principal
part of the letter to Hunt, who had said that *his* friendship was in the
other world—meaning, with Shelley.

Certainly if you did not feel any for one of such transcendant merit, &
whose merit you so freely acknowledged and praised, as Shelley, he [Hunt]
cannot complain. . . .

You cannot tell how I have been pained by entering into this subject. . . .[2]

Thus by Byron's foolish utterance, she was thrown into an alliance of
embitterment with Hunt, who had treated her abominably, reproaching
her when she was in the depths of depair with having made Shelley unhappy, and refusing in words of breathtaking arrogance to give her the
charred heart Trelawny had torn out of the incinerated corpse;[3] but who
at least professed eternal devotion to Shelley. Her relations with Byron
became cool, and Hunt exerted himself to keep them so.

Byron nevertheless went out of his way to serve her. Despite her
neurotic touchiness and his not finding her congenial, he visited her twice a
week, contrived copying work for which she could be paid, and when he
learned that his solicitor Hanson had been unsuccessful in pleading her
cause with Shelley's family, took pen in hand himself and wrote direct to
Sir Timothy. It could not have been very agreeable for him, accustomed
to be addressed by all but his closest friends in strains of adulation, to read
the reply vouchsafed by the upstart baronet:

My Lord,
    . . . The mind of my Son was withdrawn from me, & my immediate
family by unworthy & interested individuals when he was about nineteen,

---

[1] *L. & J.* Undated. Late November 1822.

[2] *Correspondence.* Saturday, early December 1822. The order of the letters is there
reversed.

[3] To discredit Mary, who became the object of his special hate, Trelawny long afterwards stated that she had squeamishly refused to take 'the black and charred piece of
flesh' which was her husband's heart and had asked him to give it to Hunt. (*Athenaeum*,
3 Aug. 1878.) But Hunt's contemporary letter to Mary (17 Aug. 1822) proves that he
asked for this relic and got it 'at the funeral pile'. Byron failed to persuade him to give it
up to Mary, but Jane Williams at length succeeded.

& after a while he was led into a new society & forsook his first associates. In this society he forgot every feeling of duty and respect to me and to Lady Shelley.

Mrs Shelley was, I have been told, the intimate friend of my son in the lifetime of his first Wife, & to the time of her death & in no small degree I suspect estrang'd my son's mind from his Family, & all his first duties in Life: with that impression on my mind, I cannot agree with your Lordship that though my son was unfortunate, that Mrs Shelley is innocent; on the contrary I think that her conduct was the very reverse of what it ought to have been; and I must therefore decline all interference on matters in which Mrs Shelley is interested. . . .

I have thus plainly told your Lordship my determination in the hope that I may be spar'd from all further correspondence on the subject so distressing to me and to my Family. . . .

I have the honour, My Lord to be Yr Lordship's
most Obdt & Hble Sert.
T. Shelley[1]

Byron had suggested that Mary Shelley should remain in Italy, the country she loved, until something was arranged in the way of a home and financial provision for her in England; but on the total failure of his approach to Sir Timothy, he advised her to leave, and offered to pay her travelling expenses. She was a woman of letters, the daughter of the celebrated Godwin, and if her father-in-law refused to assist her, would be better able to practise her profession in England than in Italy, where he for his part did not intend to stay much longer.

Mary had been cast into such unutterable wretchedness by Shelley's death that her preoccupation with her own suffering made her incessantly suspect a failure of sympathy in everyone but Trelawny, whom she regarded with awe and gratitude for the part he had played in the obsequies of Shelley.[2] Inconsiderate in her woe, she wrote Shelley's early friend, Hogg, a letter asking his advice as to whether she should stay or go. Postage was then paid not by the sender but the recipient, and her enquiry was so diffuse that it cost him £4 : 15s. to receive it. Her state of indecision lasted for months, during which she repeatedly appealed to Byron for advice and interviews.[3]

Byron was co-executor with Thomas Love Peacock of Shelley's appallingly encumbered estate, and though she constantly expressed her thankfulness for his kindness, yet she felt that both he and Peacock took but a lukewarm interest in her affairs. She was in the state of wanting perpetual reassurance, but Byron had a great deal on his mind. He was trying to clear the way for his departure to Greece, his Rochdale estate

---

[1] 6 Feb. 1823: Abinger Papers.
[2] 'When I shake his hand, I feel to the depths of my soul that those hands collected those ashes!' 22 Nov. 1822.   [3] *Correspondence*, pp. 265-272.

was the subject of complicated negotiations, and both his poetry and the business side of authorship were also engrossing him. Leigh Hunt's brother was being prosecuted for his part in publishing a 'seditious lebel', *The Vision of Judgement*, in the first number of the unlucky *Liberal*, and while Byron had taken on himself the responsibility for his defence,[1] he was anxious to withdraw from a partnership which had brought him nothing but a storm of public abuse and private trouble.

Always of a restive temperament, he grew irritable with Mary's shilly-shallying, and especially when, having told him at last, 'I think it will be England after all',[2] she announced almost immediately that she had resolved to wait for Mrs Hunt's confinement.[3] Nor could it have been in her favour with him that she was now a resident member of the Hunt household. Yet it is absolutely untrue that he abandoned her without the means to travel, as has been repeatedly and indignantly asserted.

There were ostensibly excellent grounds for the statement. Two of Mary Shelley's letters contained damning passages:

> The day after Marianne's confinement, the 9th June, seeing all went on so prosperously, I told Lord Byron that I was ready to go, and he promised to provide means. When I talked of going post, it was because he said that I should go so, at the same time declaring that he would regulate all himself. I waited in vain for these arrangements. But . . . he chose to transact our negotiation through Hunt, and gave such an air of unwillingness and sense of the obligation he conferred, as at last provoked Hunt to say that there was no obligation, since he owed me £1000.
>
> Glad of a quarrel, straight I clap the door! . . . I have written, therefore, to Trelawny for the sum requisite. . . . In the meantime Hunt is all kindness, consideration, and friendship.[4]

This was some days before Byron left harbour on July 13th. On the 23rd she wrote again to the same correspondent, Jane Williams:

> Lord Byron, Trelawny, and Pierino Gamba sailed for Greece on the 17th inst. I did not see the former. His unconquerable avarice prevented his supplying me with money, and a remnant of shame caused him to avoid me.[5]

With an irony that is truly pathetic in view of the malignance of his subsequent campaign against her, she said of Trelawny that she had 'perfect faith in the unalterable goodness of his heart'. 'They sailed together; Lord Byron with £10,000, Trelawny with £50 and Lord Byron cowering before his eye for reasons you shall hear soon.'

Though Trelawny, when he came to write his reminiscences, repre-

---

[1] He had offered to go to England for the trial. The verdict of Guilty was not brought in till after his death. His executors settled the costs and the fine.

[2] *Correspondence*. No date, probably late May 1823.

[3] Ibid. Early June 1823.   [4] JONES, *Letters of Mary Shelley*. Early July 1823.

[5] Ibid. Byron actually sailed on the 13th, but bad weather occasioned two false starts.

Mary Shelley in 1841, by Richard Rothwell

Leigh Hunt, by Benjamin R. Haydon

sented himself as the man who knew everything, directed everything, and prophesied everything, even he did not pretend that the official leader of the expedition was actually cowering before his eye, so we must suppose that the overwrought feelings which Mary touched upon in her letter were affecting her choice of words. Before exposing the part played by Leigh Hunt in working up these feelings, an explanation of the mysterious thousand pounds mentioned in the first of her two letters must be given.

It was the amount that Byron had lost to Shelley on a wager that his rich mother-in-law would outlive Shelley's rich father (a wager, it may be said, somewhat inconsistent with the 'gentle Shelley' legend). Certain biographers have actually assumed from Hunt's reported words that Byron had borrowed a thousand pounds from Shelley and failed to repay it. He has frequently been described as 'taking' Shelley's money, and even as taking Shelley's money 'morosely'.[1] So far from taking any money from Shelley, morosely or otherwise, Byron lent him £50 immediately before the journey that was to be his last.[2]

The first story that was put into circulation about this bet came from Medwin, who wrote that Shelley's friend, Williams, never entered Byron's house again after he failed to pay it. When Williams's diary was published it showed that he had continued his visits as before on the friendliest terms. On the news of Lady Noel's death reaching Italy, Williams noted with the usual extravagance that Byron must have become richer by £10,000 a year, and recalled the wager. Leigh Hunt read the diary when it was retrieved after Williams was drowned, and made the most of what no one seems to have taken very seriously until grievances were wanted.

There is another point which seems to have escaped all commentators. The bet, whether serious or jocular, was essentially not on death but on accession of fortune, and so it is recorded by Williams in his journal entry for December 25th, 1821: 'It was on this day that Lord B and S proposed to give a thousand pounds to the other who first came to the estate.' The question of Byron's interest in his mother-in-law's property was subject

[1] OLWEN CAMPBELL.

[2] *Correspondence.* Letter to W. Webb, partner in Webb and Barry, Byron's bankers in Italy. 'I greatly doubt if Mr Shelley has left any effects. . . . The extreme liberality of his disposition generally left him in arrear, and the day before he was lost he borrowed of me fifty pounds which were on board in cash when the boat went down.' (2 Sept. 1822.) Ninety crowns of this money were salvaged and applied to Mary's needs. Byron never seems to have mentioned it to anyone but the banker. Trelawny was lying with even more than usual rancour when he said: 'In all transactions between Shelley and Byron in which expense had occurred, and they were many, the former, as was his custom, had paid all, the latter promising to repay.' It was he who first published a statement that Byron had left the widow destitute. (*Recollections.*)

Some of these aspersions were omitted from the revised edition (*Records*).

to arbitration, and the process of appointing Lord Dacre and Sir Francis Burdett as arbitrators in England and awaiting their study of the Marriage Settlement was not instantaneous. Byron was hardly likely to begin settling thousand-pound bets before he was sure of his inheritance.

If Sir Timothy had died first, Shelley, who had involved the entailed estate in debts of almost incredible recklessness, would have been unable to make any settlement with Byron for, literally, years. Lady Noel's financial affairs were more straightforward, but still, many months after Shelley's death, and more than a year after hers, Byron was complaining to Hobhouse that her trustees had as yet paid him nothing.[1] When he was at last informed that his income was substantially increased, at a time of gathering together all his resources for Greece,[2] he may well have thought—if he remembered the bet at all—that it was fairly cancelled by his refusal of Shelley's legacy of £2000.

That legacy was refused, contrary to what has been supposed, before Leigh Hunt taunted him with owing Mary Shelley £1000. The letter in which he renounced it, suppressed except for a single paragraph by Leigh Hunt's son, is given here in full, and shows what he endeavoured to do for Mary:

June 28th 1823

Dear H[unt]
  I have received a Note from Mrs S with a fifth or sixth change of plan, viz, not to make her journey at all—at least through my assistance on account of what she is pleased to call 'Estrangement' etc. On this I have little to say —The readiest mode now may be this which can be settled between you & me without her knowing any thing of the matter.
  I will advance the money to *you* (I desired Mr B[arry] to say what would enable her to travel '*handsomely* and *conveniently* in all respects'—these were the words of my note this Afternoon to him) on Monday—you can say then that you have raised it as a Loan on your own account—no matter with whom or how—and that *you* advance it to *her*—which may easily be made the fact if you feel scrupulous by giving me a scrap of paper as your Note of hand—Thus she would be spared any fancied humiliation, and I am not aware of any thing in the transaction which can render it obnoxious to yourself at least I am sure there was no such intention on my part—nor ever was in any thing which has passed between us, although there are circumstances so plausible—and scoundrels so ready in every corner of the Earth to give a colour of their own to every thing—the last observation is dictated by what you told me today to my utter astonishment—it will however teach me to know my Company better or not at all. And now pray—do not apply or misapply directly or indirectly to *yourself* any of these observations—I knew you

[1] *Correspondence*. 19 Mar. 1823.

[2] Ibid. On 16 June 1823 he wrote to Kinnaird: 'As to my affairs, my anxiety is as much on your account as on my own, as I should not like to overdraw, and yet may have occasion for all the means that I can muster, as I should not like to give the Greeks a *half helping* hand, but rather aid them as much as I can.'

long before Mr. S. knew either you or me—and you and two more of his friends are the only ones whom I can at all reflect upon as men whose acquaintance was honorable & agreeable.

I have one more thing to state, which is that from this moment I must decline the offer of acting as his Executor in any respect and also of further connection with his family in any of its branches—now or hereafter.

There was something about a Legacy of two thousand pounds—which he had left me—this of course I decline—and the more so that I hear that his Will is admitted valid; and I state this distinctly—that in case of any thing happening to me—my heirs may be instructed not to claim it.

Yours ever & truly,
N. B.

P.S. I enclose you Mr B[arry']s answer just received to my Note of this Afternoon.[1]

The 'Mr S' here mentioned is seen in the paragraph that follows to be Shelley himself, and the whole passage indicates that Hunt had not stopped short of implicating his lately dead friend in some accusation that caused Byron to recoil in grief and anger, and, moreover, that he had done so in a way that tended to ingratiate himself while inculpating Shelley.

From the opening words of the letter it is to be seen that Byron was in direct touch with Mary Shelley up to this point, and that any reproach to him for neglecting her welfare would have been absurd. Though it is perfectly clear from her own letters that she was in the frame of mind to be 'glad of a quarrel' with him, his willingness to assist her was so emphatic that he proposed doing so by a subterfuge rather than not doing so at all.

Had Hunt been of a better disposition, he would now have told her of Byron's earnest desire to help her and withheld the severer parts of the letter, and all would probably have been well, but he took the report most calculated to give pain and make mischief. As to this, we have the independent testimony of Countess Guiccioli's *Vie de Lord Byron en Italie*, which is completely in unison with evidence that could not have been known to the writer at the time:

> . . . He told Mary that Byron had often spoken of the insufferable tediousness of her visits, and had said that he did not mind supplying her with money, but wished he need never see her again.[2]

We have only Hunt's side of the correspondence to guide us in this labyrinthine affair. He stated that he had kept Byron's letters on matters of dispute between them, but they are so far missing—with the exception of the one quoted, which we might think he had never received if his son had not seen fit to print the last lines from it.

---

[1] Lovelace Copies.   [2] Quoted by Origo.

Hunt's first communication in the sequence is headed 'Saturday June 1823'. The reference to 'a Greek gentleman' enables us to fix the date as June 28th, which was a Saturday, and distinguishable by the following allusion in a letter from Hunt to his sister-in-law:

> I should have written to you on Saturday, but was interrupted by a Greek gentleman, a cousin of Mavrocordato's, whom I had to introduce to Lord B. So I did, and afterwards had to discuss a very unpleasant matter with the Noble Bard, to wit, the expenses of Mrs S's journey to England, which happens to fall on his shoulders, and which he winces under like an intolerable burden.[1]

It will be observed that Hunt says nothing at all of Byron's proposal addressed to him in writing in a most pressing manner on the very day when he had that talk.

To Byron it was a day of mounting troubles, beginning with Hunt's note:

> Dear Lord Byron,
>
> Mary says, that the reason why she thought of posting was your having observed to her one day, that it was the mode which it would be best for her to take, & that the difficulty of a carriage might be got over. With regard to going by vetturino, she says she prefers it to the diligence, because the latter is extremely bad for a child, as Mrs Williams had occasion to experience.
>
> Lord C[harles] M[urray] says, that the bearer of his letter is 'a Greek gentleman, Mr Constantine Skilitzi . . . who is most anxious to be presented to Lord Byron'. . . .
>
> Will you let me know, when it will be possible to settle matters with regard to Mary, as she will still have some little things to do.
>
> Yours &c.
> L. H.[2]

All the letters in this series were carried by hand so that hardly any time was lost in delivery. Byron must have sent back the messenger with his consent to meet the Greek, who was duly brought to his villa, and whose departure was followed by the portentous talk with Hunt. In the course of this, Hunt made his disclosure involving Shelley, a disclosure of so serious and upsetting a character as to cause Byron to decide upon resignation from the executorship and ending all connection with the family. Doubtless as the result of Hunt's further evil offices, the same day brought Mary's announcement of her unwillingness to accept Byron's assistance.

It must have been within an hour or two that he sat down to write the suggestion that Hunt should supply her needs without revealing the source, and enclosed Barry's estimate for the journey. He underlined his

---

[1] BREWER, 30 June 1823.   [2] Murray MSS.

intention that she should travel '*handsomely* and *conveniently* in all respects' because she had obviously jumped to the conclusion in her edgy and fretful state that he was trying to back out of paying for her to go 'post', which was one of the more expensive methods of travel.

From the next note, sent just three days after Hunt had the important letter containing those words, it may be seen that the situation had deteriorated:

Tuesday. July 1 1823
(a melancholy month)

Dear Lord Byron,

I am sorry to trouble you, but will you have the goodness, by the earliest hour that is convenient to you tomorrow morning, to let me know your final sentiments on this matter or whether you have any other than what you have stated; as I know, that Mary, however against her inclination on account of his own demands upon him for money, will think herself obliged, under certain circumstances, to apply to Trelawny, who offered her (I also know) the use of his purse some time back. She is not aware of my saying a word to you on this point.

Yours in all dutifulness
Leigh Hunt.[1]

There must have been a meeting between the two men on June 29th or 30th—probably the one at which Hunt taunted Byron with owing Mary Shelley a thousand pounds. Two things are certain—that he was far from wishing to promote peace, and that he had a most insolent way of asking for cash ('I must trouble you for another "cool hundred" of your crowns' has become a kind of classic in that line).

Something had taken place in the nature of an angry showdown. Hunt, insensate with self-pity, was glad to add Mary's supposed wrongs to his own. The result was that, on receiving the curt challenge to express his 'final sentiments' immediately, Byron's anger blazed up.

Whatever impatience he may have uttered at Mrs Shelley's readiness to feel injured, there had never been the slightest need for her to turn to Trelawny for assistance. That is palpable from several of her letters, including the first after the quarrel, saying she had refused to receive Byron's '*still proffered aid for the journey*'.[2] Her hostility (as it was represented to him) combined with Hunt's assumption that she had comprehensive claims on him, drove him to sharp protestations. Here they were, a singularly helpless man with an even more helpless wife— the parents by now of seven children—holding him responsible, not only for their existence in a foreign country where they disliked everyone and everything, but also for the existence of a widow whom he had helped in

---

[1] Ibid.

[2] To Jane Williams, early July. Author's italics. She adds that all feeling of alienation from Hunt had disappeared, and he perfectly approved what she had done.

all the ways he could think of, and who took umbrage at every trifle.

He had a hundred other things on his mind, from fitting his ship to parting with the heartbroken Teresa, and was in no mood to be made answerable for the Hunts and Mary. He had heard so much of the superior perfections and generosities of Shelley that he was goaded— recalling the disagreeable things Hunt had repeated to his 'utter astonishment' a few days before—to indulge in one or two home truths. His remarks were immediately passed on to Mary.

> . . . He has written notes and letters so full of contempt against me and my lost Shelley that I could stand it no longer. . . .[1]

For 'notes and letters', Mary would probably have said, in a more sober mood, 'a note and a letter'. The whole of that part of the correspondence took place between July 1st and July 5th, and there were two communications on Byron's side alluding to Shelley, both addressed to Hunt. To the first, Hunt replied with a recrimination which he twice described as 'brief', but which was enormous in length and strangely feeble in its bluster, considering that he had spent time meditating upon it:

Albaro [?4th] July 1823

Dear Lord Byron,
    I have now waited some days in order that I might answer your angry & extraordinary letter in the fittest manner my feelings would allow; yet still I cannot persuade myself . . . to answer it in any way but a very brief & general one. It would only be bandying to & fro extreme differences of feeling. That even a man of wit & talents should not be able to escape the influence of certain conventional notions, does not astonish me after all I have seen of the world. Nor ought they to be treated with any thing but tenderness individually, if they do not lead the holders themselves to play at fast & loose with the feelings & prospects of other people. . . .
    But I confess it does astonish me, that even with reference to those notions & much more on a thousand higher accounts, you could suffer yourself to speak in such a manner of Shelley & his connexions, especially after what you yourself have said of the supereminence of his nature. . . .
    . . . There is one passage in your letter, which will, at all events, excuse me for saying, that should my friend, after all his hard struggles in the cause of humanity, be destined to have a new & most unexpected hand, however formidable, laid upon his drowned head, the occasion will gift me with all the anger, & perhaps with all the power, necessary to make the blow repented,—and this, not as you seem to put it, because he was merely my friend, & therefore to be defended at all hazards, but because he was the friend of all the world, and died daily, inch by inch, in their cause. . . .
    Having now done what I thought my duty by my friend (for after the strange things you have said of her & hers, Mrs Shelley finds it impossible to let me discuss that matter any further, & gives up all thoughts connected

[1] Murray MSS.

with it) I am obliged to trouble your Lordship, extremely against my will, with something relating to myself.

Mary being thus manœuvred into continued refusal of Byron's offer, Hunt proceeded to advance his own claims. He mentioned his wife and seven children and his 'aweful' situation in Italy, and regretted that mere abstract ideas of justice obliged him to ignore a thousand delicacies. Byron, he said, had promised to fill Shelley's place, and though he had modified in his own mind 'the only meaning those words could imply', yet he had not been prepared for what was now befalling him. (What he *had* been prepared for is revealed in a letter when the project was first mooted, addressed to Shelley and assuredly not shown to Byron: 'With regard to the proposed publication of Lord B., about which you talk so modestly, he has it in his power, I believe, to set up not only myself and family in our finances again but one of the best hearted men in the world, my brother and his.'[1])

He was dissatisfied with having to put a stop to a work which might have flourished with the help of reasonable patience and exertion, and his literary character, he said, had thereby been placed at a disadvantage with the public. He grudgingly acknowledged the assistance he had already had and also the 'handsome proposition' to waive any receipts from the magazine, but he complained that Byron had given it up at the behest of his friends after compelling Hunt to incur pecuniary obligations.

> I am in the situation of a poor mercantile man who has been induced to go into a foreign country to set up a firm of some sort with a rich one, & after of necessity becoming a dependent of the latter for some time, is left on the sudden, at the pleasure of the latter, with little better than a shifting of obligations on his head, surrounded by strangers, & in the midst of a family which he sometimes hardly dares to contemplate.

It was the mixture of bombast and whimpering plaintiveness by which he irritated so many of his friends. His literary prestige had stood at its lowest when he had ventured out to Italy, encouraged by Shelley, certainly, but not having a single line from Byron in person. And even Shelley had warned him not to bring his family. The magazine, so far from showing any sign of being likely to flourish if given a longer trial, was losing circulation with each number, while the complaint of being surrounded with strangers could evoke little sympathy coming from a man determined not to be repatriated.

> I have therefore, [he went on] in the first place, to say, that I will avail myself of the spirit, though not of the letter, of the offer which you made me a short time back of replacing me where I came from, & accept, if you

[1] HUNT, *Correspondence*. 21 Sept. 1821. A couple of years later he was in litigation with this good-hearted brother, to whom he owed a huge sum.

please, the payment of my expenses, *not* to *England*, but where I can do much better, situated as I am, & with a wife in such an ill state of health, to *Florence*. In Genoa I can do nothing. Say £50 (fifty pounds) or whatever may be reckoned the reasonable sum, if I have mistaken it.

Secondly, I will beg to be exonerated from the debt of two hundred & fifty pounds, which I incurred in order to leave England, & which Shelley (had he lived and I been unable to pay it) would have paid for me. . . .

Thirdly, & lastly, I have to beg, that you will be kind enough to endorse me another bill on my brother for the sum of a hundred & fifty pounds. . . .

An answer in the course of tomorrow or next day would much oblige me, Lord Byron.[1]

In the absence of Byron's reply, which may yet be discovered, we can only guess at the effect upon him of these several remonstrances—here greatly curtailed. He must have responded at once because Hunt was writing again on the 5th.

Byron was about to go to a new life, from which he only had faint and intermittent expectations of returning. Before he embarked on the evening of July 13th, Hunt and Mrs Hunt and the incorrigible children were already beginning to lose their reality—in the nine months remaining to him, he scarcely referred to their existence again—but he had not the smallest intention of leaving them stranded. He answered without acrimony, granting Hunt's various requests, but pointing out, it may be gathered, that the other was persistently idealizing his relations with Shelley, and minimizing everything he (Byron himself) had tried to do for him. Again at immense length, Hunt defended himself, and renewed his accusations, though more temperately:

Albaro
July 5 1823

Dear Lord Byron,

In the first place, I thank you for answering the second part of my letter so promptly & kindly: in the second I would willingly give you some pangs for those you inflict on me through the medium of my friend:—but to what purpose? You wrong me, especially after the way in which I expressed myself to speak of 'a challenge to a controversy.' I had no wish for such a controversy. It would give me no pleasure nor (without meaning to undervalue my antagonist) even excite my vanity.

You will perhaps believe me when I tell you, that though your blow was not lost on me in one sense, when you alluded to the indifferent opinion Shelley had of my poetry, it was a fact which I knew already, as well as his high opinion of yours. I learnt the former from his own handwriting, since I have been here;[2] & though it mortified me both as an author & as a friend . . . I made it at least yield me a recompense in turning it into a new test of the indestructibility of all my feelings towards him.

---

[1] Murray MSS.

[2] Shelley's papers, salvaged from the foundered yacht, were in Hunt's care for a time.

He reminded Byron that Shelley had not only heaped every kindness upon him but had done so with 'every delicacy of it'—a hint at the annoyance it gave him to accept Byron's contributions at the hands of a secretary; and he made some sarcastic flings at Byron's friends and their 'patrician' pretensions (he was later to tell the public in his book how far they were from being out of the top drawer).

> You can fancy Shelley in heaven. Can your Lordship fancy some other of your acquaintances there?—*Can* Messrs Hobhouse & Gifford become cherubim, or Mr Thomas Moore succeed in the part of any angels but his own? However I shall grow as censorious & forgetful as himself in my old age; & so with this piece of revenge I conclude, jokes & sorrow being almost equally sorrowful things to me just now, as they very often are.
>
> I shall only add that I knew more of Shelley's life from first to last, than you seem to be aware.

Before he could dispatch this decoction of gratitude and reproof, there came another letter from Byron, pressing him again to return with his family to England, and renewing his offer to pay their expenses. Hunt retorted with a tremendous postscript:

> . . . It will save a world of discussion to say at once, that I do not believe either my wife or myself could *exist* in England, till our healths become better. She would certainly not live another winter; and my own health is so much worse than you might guess even by my appearance, & so particularly subject to the influence of cold & wet, that if I struggled through two or three winters more, it would be quite as much as I could do.

He continued in a vague and rambling way to blame Byron for indecision about *The Liberal*, and defended himself for having followed him, contrary to all advice, when he had moved from Pisa. Byron had evidently said, among other things that the climate was unsuitable for Hunt's ailing wife.

> With regard to my coming to Genoa, it was a most unwilling journey on my part, but my wife herself urged me to take it, and I concluded, that it would be less frightful to her to go into a worse climate, which was still Italian, than remain in a place where we should have no one to help us. . . .
> I sometimes feared, even as it was, that my health would not stand out much more writing. . . .
> Of all the pecuniary kindnesses you have done me, I have a particular account, except with regard to the expenses of that journey. . . .

These 'pecuniary kindnesses' were represented in his book as niggardly sums doled out to him as if they were disgraces and, while the 'handsome proposition', by which Byron renounced his share of the profits from

The Liberal,[1] was there passed off as a mere petulant gesture made because those profits fell short of expectation.

The Hunts were destined to live—and in the lethal climate of England —till 1859 and 1857 respectively, but the mere thought of return filled them with alarms in 1823. Some of these may have been connected with the risk, not mentioned to Byron, that Hunt would be arrested for debt on English soil.

> I thank you therefore for the renewal of your offer about England, [he went on stubbornly] but I have only a choice of evils, & Italy is at all events a great deal wholesomer and cheaper for me; I shall set up another set of essays like the Indicator, which succeeded before, & with which my friends in England are well pleased; & I shall live a few years longer, or at least have a chance of it, for the benefit of my family. To Florence therefore, if you please, I will go.

He gave notice that he would call to speak about the arrangements the following day. This postscript was written on July 6th, so it seems likely that affairs between Byron and Hunt were regulated on the 7th. Byron had a large sum in hand ready for the Greek campaign, and may have given Hunt there and then the £50 requested. As to this, there is controversial evidence, and it is essential to examine it because of its bearing on the question of whether Mary Shelley was misled about the 'unconquerable avarice' that has so long disgusted Shelley's admirers and embarrassed Byron's.

In *Lord Byron and Some of His Contemporaries*, Hunt insisted on laying before the public what no one had asked for—a version of his financial transactions with Byron. Here he gives £30 as the amount he received for his journey to Florence, but he is not necessarily to be believed, because in the same pages, he states two or three times that a sum advanced to him by Byron was £200, whereas it was £250—an amount then so considerable that it is not likely a very poor and very money-conscious man would have forgotten it. He not only diminished the gift, but by slyly laying emphasis twice over on the fact that Byron had Shelley's bond for it, he tried to convey the impression to his readers that Shelley, not Byron, was the benefactor.

Moore inflicted a well-merited punishment for this by publishing Shelley's worried and apologetic letter on the topic:

> Hunt had urged me more than once to ask you to lend him this money My answer consisted in sending him all I could spare, which I have now literally done. Your kindness in fitting up a part of your own house for his accommodation I sensibly felt, and willingly accepted from you on his part;

[1] Landré gives the figure of profits on the first number as £377 : 16s. It was much less thereafter.

but, believe me, without the slightest intention of imposing, or, if I could help it, allowing to be imposed, any heavier tax on your purse. As it has come to this in spite of my exertions, I will not conceal from you . . . my absolute incapacity of assisting Hunt farther.

I do not think poor Hunt's promise to pay in a given time is worth very much. . . .[1]

It seems improbable that Byron, having offered Hunt the much more substantial sum requisite for sending the whole family back to England, would have induced him to accept £30 instead of £50 for moving from one Italian city to another. His pride after the quarrel would hardly have permitted him to do so, and he was also desirous of not leaving ill feeling behind him. Not knowing how much he was hated, he sent cordial wishes to Hunt the day before sailing. They were conveyed in a letter from Teresa Guiccioli to Mary Shelley,[2] a letter in which he also greeted Mary and said he had no feeling of enmity towards her—which does not sound like the valediction of one who had given her cause of enmity towards *him*.

A surprising entry in Hobhouse's *Journal* now needs to be studied. At the beginning of 1829, soon after Hunt had taken his lingering and lucrative revenge on Byron in print, Hobhouse visited Genoa for the second time since Byron's death, and on January 5th wrote this:

> . . . Called on Mr Barry who talked a good deal about Byron as usual, and about the scoundrel Leigh Hunt. It seems that Leigh Hunt followed B. to Genoa but did not live with him—indeed did not see him often—
>
> It was on some occasion respecting giving money to Mrs Shelley as I before heard Barry tell, that Leigh Hunt wrote to B. accusing him of abandoning the widow of his best friend, on which Byron wrote a note saying 'I suppose you call yourself also my best friend, but it is by such friends that I have lost my money and what is more my character and I shall now &c' Byron put aside 30 £ for Mrs Shelley, telling Barry that if Hunt did not draw it for her he was not to send it, but Hunt did draw for it and I saw his receipt.
>
> Barry gave me a fragment of this precious scoundrel's writing abusing D. Kinnaird. He lent Blackwood's Magazine to me and I read the article on this man's book—it is ill done[3]—but I was horror struck at the book itself—and I think I must take this thankless villain in hand.

Hobhouse's dependability as a witness has never been disputed by anyone familiar with the vast mass of his accumulated records.[4] He might

---

[1] MOORE, 15 Feb. 1822.   [2] Abinger Papers. Quoted by ORIGO.

[3] *Blackwood's Magazine* fell upon Hunt's book with extreme fury and great shrewdness in March 1828. It is curious that Hobhouse had not seen this famous attack before.

[4] One or two recent critics have made too much of his employing Ugo Foscolo to provide the commentary on modern Italian authors for the Notes to the 4th Canto of *Childe Harold*. This was a matter of literary ethics, entirely distinct from the personal ethics that govern a diary. It is also clear that Hobhouse was drawn on by Foscolo's need of the payment he got for the 'ghost' work, to go much further than he had intended.

judge unsoundly, he might sometimes write evasively, but what he chose to report he reported literally. If he says he saw the receipt, then he did see it, and the only question is whether it was a receipt for the travelling expenses of Mary Shelley or for a sum applied to some other purpose.

It must be remembered, however, that Barry, who told him it was £30 put aside for Mrs Shelley, was very well informed about all these affairs, and it was he who had worked out the estimate for her journey to England. His many letters to Byron and Hobhouse reveal an intelligent man who was, in an amiable way, something of a busybody, and who saw a great deal of Byron, and went on seeing him up to his last hours on Italian soil.[1] It may be doubted whether he would have made any mistake about a financial matter which had aroused his curiosity.

There had been a conversation between him and Hobhouse on the same theme more than two years earlier which was noted thus:

> Leigh Hunt was insolent enough to write a letter to Byron reproaching him with 'abandoning Mrs Shelley, the widow of his best friend.' To this Byron returned a short reply, telling Hunt that 'as for Shelley, his name was unnecessarily introduced; that Mrs Shelley had no claims on him; and that as for him [Hunt], he had only to regret that he had ever communicated so much with him, as he thereby lost not only his money but his character.'
> This letter he read Barry and sent it.[2]

On that occasion Barry had either failed to mention or—what is more likely—Hobhouse had failed to note that Byron's disclaimer of any obligation to Mary Shelley had not prevented his supplying money for her. As Hunt's venomous book was yet to come, Hobhouse was not aware when he wrote the earlier entry that his friend would stand in need of vindication.

Byron does not appear to have kept any letter from Hunt taxing him with abandoning 'the widow of his best friend'. Perhaps that was something he heard by word of mouth on the occasion when he was told about owing Mary £1000, and he may have repeated it indignantly to Barry with the contents of Hunt's brusque note of July 1st. The 'short reply' Byron then dispatched must have been the self-same letter that formed the occasion for Hunt's large and closely filled pages of 'brief' protest here ascribed to July 4th. (This date allows for his deferring his answer 'some days'.)

The sneer at 'conventional notions' must have been elicited by Byron's remarks about what he had lost, materially and otherwise, through association with Hunt. Something said to rebut an assertion that

---

[1] Byron wrote to him: '. . . You know nearly as much of my affairs, public or private, as I do myself.' *L. & J.* 29 Oct. 1823.   [2] 31 Oct. 1826: Hobhouse *Journals.*

Shelley was his best friend was interpreted by Hunt, with characteristic rhetoric, as a threat that Byron intended to lay his hand on Shelley's 'drowned head'. The allusion to how Byron had spoken of 'Shelley and his connexions' of course comprises Mary. Hunt had conveniently forgotten that it was he who had touched off all this choler with his mischievous revelations about Shelley.[1]

On July 16th, three days after Byron embarked for Greece, Barry dispatched a note to him at Leghorn where the *Hercules* was calling:

> I have sent Giraud to Hunt to ask him in what money he wishes to receive the 30 £ and it will be paid this evening.[2]

If this was for the requirements of Mrs Shelley, as Barry believed, then Hunt's own demands were already satisfied. If not, it is strange that the banker should have told such a tale, and in terms by no means casual to judge from Hobhouse's reaction.

Mary's letters to Teresa Guiccioli during the few days before the expedition sailed show that, having thrown down the gauntlet to Byron in her first letter of 'estrangement', she continued to raise such barriers as would have kept any man—except perhaps an ardent suitor—at a distance.

> . . . If I am to understand that you wish to be a peacemaker between me and Lord Byron you will not succeed. I felt no repugnance at the idea of receiving obligations and kindnesses from a friend. . . . A man who does not esteem me cannot be my benefactor. Lord Byron having said it would be disagreeable to him to see me, I cannot have the pleasure of calling upon you, but I shall be delighted to see you here.[3]

Again:

> To tell you the truth, my awkward position weighs less heavily upon my heart than Lord Byron's expressions about me, and still more about Shelley. *From a friend* I would accept anything, and if he will show me the least sign of friendship and will again be *glad* to help me, I will feel a renewed obligation and be grateful.[4]

And again:

> . . . If the friendship of Lord Byron has failed me, the rest [money] is not worth much and could not be accepted by me. If Lord Byron will forget anything painful that he may have endured from me and on account of me, if he will recognize what Shelley deserves, it will be with real pleasure that

---

[1] What these revelations may have been is possibly indicated by a remark of Trelawny's in a letter to Claire Clairmont (1 Feb. 1870) telling her that the scandal about Mrs Leigh recently published was true, and that though he had 'never believed a word' of it, 'Shelley solved the mystery'.   [2] Murray MSS.

[3] ORIGO. About 7 July. The letter may be dated by its being a reply to one in which Teresa had said Trelawny would arrive in a few days.   [4] Ibid. No date.

I shall wish him by word of mouth what I now wish him by letter—a good voyage and all the success that I feel sure his plans will have in Greece.[1]

No doubt if Byron had been less preoccupied, more imaginative and more sympathetic to Mary Shelley as a personality, he would have driven over to see her—but then, there were also at the Casa Negroto the querulous Hunt, the thoroughly inimical Marianne Hunt, and their tribe of 'little Yahoos' encouraged to be impertinent: while to write a letter in the effusive and sentimental strain which alone could appease her would be a surrender to the kind of feminine clamorousness he always detested. Teresa was too unhappy herself, on the verge of losing her lover and her favourite brother, to play a very helpful part; but she transmitted, almost on the last day, a note from Byron, which he handed to her with a sombre look, and a message for Hunt about detailed orders that had been left—she could not remember with whom, but she thought it was Barry.[2]

Teresa's recollections of the affair in old age are not perfectly accurate, but taken in conjunction with Mary's letters they afford some clues. She was not given to invention, though she permitted herself the latitude of a romantic. She might take a year or two off her age, she might speak of her love affair with Byron as if it had been platonic while letting it be seen on every page that it was not; but even the most fantastic statements in her published book turn out to have some solid foundation, while her unpublished book is full of material which can be checked by other testimonies she had no chance of reading.

She recalled forty-odd years later that Mary had seen Byron again, and that he had persuaded her to accept what, out of delicacy, he then called a loan.

> Thus the web woven by the hatred of Mr Hunt was torn asunder. However, his manœuvres were not effective in revealing the depths of his soul to this noble woman.[3]

Unconsciously, it would seem, she was fusing two memories—the letter she had had from Mary before Byron sailed, offering, subject to his making some conciliatory gesture, to see him again, and her knowledge that in his last note to Mary, the one she had forwarded, he had proposed a loan, an advance against what was due to her from *The Liberal*. This was one of the expedients by which he hoped to avert her 'fancied humiliation'. If the tale of 'unconquerable avarice' could have been sustained, we should have expected that those Shelley biographers who have taken pains to represent Byron as darkly as possible would have been glad to produce his final words to Mary. They have never appeared, but her

[1] ORIGO. Undated, but obviously just before Byron's departure.
[2] Teresa's covering letter is in the Abinger Papers, 12 July 1823.
[3] GUICCIOLI, *La Vie*.

answer to them, published in 1944, indicates that he was still making an offer. It appears to be a draft for a letter not sent:

[*? 12th July, 1823*]

Dear Lord Byron,
    I did not wish to spare myself the pain of taking leave. We understood from Conte Pietro today that you did not embark till tomorrow evening or mid-day at the earliest. I intended therefore to settle this pecuniary matter first by letter, there being better subjects for discourse in the world; & then to come down & bid you farewell, which I will do accordingly if you please, tomorrow morning.
    In the meantime as the message which Mad. Guiccioli has been kind enough to transmit to me, still leaves me an uneasy sense of vagueness in my mind, will you do me the favour to state in whose hands you have left this matter & what is its precise nature.
                            Yours sincerely,
                            [No signature][1]

It now seems we are in a position to answer Mary's question. The matter was left in Hunt's hands. Barry was authorized to pay £30 to Hunt for Mrs Shelley, an amount equal to about £180 of present currency. Byron sailed before seeing Mary again, avoiding her, not out of shame, the reason she assigned, but because he was intensely busy and it would have gone against the grain with him to make the parade of feelings she demanded. His request that she would stay a few hours with Teresa after their parting to try to comfort her[2] is quite out of keeping with any knowledge on his part that she was quivering with disapproval of his avarice.

Hunt said nothing about the arrangement with Barry, and so she was aided by Trelawny—an act of generosity which the latter did not fail to publish, together with a plausible expression of regret by Byron for his meanness. We have seen that Trelawny could invent a conversation to denigrate a man he had never had any opportunity of meeting,[3] and that he described the mythical beauties and deformities of a corpse he had never had any opportunity of seeing.[4] It was nothing to him to put into Byron's mouth a confession that could not have been uttered. If what Barry told Hobhouse was true, then Byron went to Greece in the belief that he had provided for Mary's needs, and he must have died under that delusion. If it was false, she had still repelled his persistent offers, and so he could have no occasion for avowing remorseful feelings.

Teresa, who might have unravelled the whole imbroglio if she had known all its coils, was in a state bordering on collapse after Byron sailed, and she left Genoa next day with her father. But Mary, though she may never have heard of the provision that had been made for her, came

---

[1] JONES, *Letters of Mary Shelley*.   [2] GUICCIOLI, *La Vie*.
[3] William Parry, see Chapter .V   [4] See Appendix to Chapter II.

within a year or two to recall of her own accord the kindnesses to her which had far outweighed the imaginary affronts, while Byron soon forgot whatever had momentarily darkened the memory of Shelley for him, and spoke of him in Greece with affection and esteem. It was Hunt who behaved like a guilty person.

His book, wherever it concerns Byron, has the vehemence of a frantic attempt to justify himself not only with the world, but with his own conscience. He works himself up to a greater and greater sense of ill usage and loathing, as if by proving to himself that Byron was absolutely vile, he could excuse any wrongs he had done him. Guilt must have been consuming him for years, for there was nothing impulsive about an attack produced so long after the victim's death. Nor was his mind eased by having given vent to its bitterness. In the Preface to his second edition, he hinted at horrors so awful that 'common humanity' would not let him mention them, magnified Byron's restrained and private comments to John Murray into a shocking injury,[1] and threatened those who criticized him with exposure of what 'their pretended hero' really thought of them, a very artful form of web-weaving in which he excelled.

Moore having taken a sharp but not intemperate revenge in his Life of Byron for the unprovoked aggressions of Hunt's book, Hunt made an onslaught on him in *The Tatler* passing all bounds of decency and forming the subject of the leading article five days running.[2] He actually anticipated Dickens in his ferocious power of conveying sheer repulsiveness; and the novelist might have derived one or two touches for the demeanour of Daniel Quilp from the sketch of Byron encouraging Hunt to write a parody of Moore:

> 'Well, are we never to have the Rhymes?' . . . And then he would retreat a little, doubling himself up in his peculiar manner, and uttering a kind of goblin laugh, breathing and grinning, as if, instead of his handsome mouth, he had one like an ogre, from ear to ear. Then came the inevitable addition—'But mind, you must not publish. You know I'm his *friend*.'

Once again, Hunt had overreached himself. Few could believe that a man given to behaviour so grotesque could have left, wherever he went, an impression of captivating charm.

Disparagement of Moore was set off by the customary running accompaniment in praise of self:

> I am bold as a lion in defending a friend or a principle; timid (I am afraid) as a deer where myself only am concerned. Perhaps I ought to say,

---

[1] After Byron had expressed his dismay that Murray had shown anyone this letter, Hunt wrote to him graciously agreeing to forget the offence (BREWER, 11 Nov. 1822), but even Byron, who was not very perceptive in such matters, could see that he would never be genuinely forgiven and told Murray so.   [2] Jan. 1831.

that I am bold as anyone where I feel that I am in the right: but that I have a great deal less self-love than most people imagine, and am as much inclined to argue in favour of my enemy as myself. . . .

His obsessive self-pity fostered throughout his whole professional life a delusion that he was the sole man of letters who had to support his family by his pen; so that he introduced such irrelevancies, in dealing with the charge that he had struck at a man who could not defend himself, as:

> Mr Moore got hold of a fine commonplace, but a dead man to me was at no such disadvantage. Death with power to leave money to those he loves—how different from life with fear of the reverse!

It must have been most unpalatable to Moore to see 'TOMMY LOVES A LORD' printed in full capitals as one of Byron's dicta, but it was perhaps rather because, than in spite of, this coarse insult that he put his name down as a subscriber to a book of Hunt's poems published that year, and the following year wrote thus to Mary Shelley:

> I have just heard from a friend who has been to Bath that there is some subscription going on there for Leigh Hunt, who (he added, to my very sincere regret) was represented to him as in a state of great distress. Now, if this be true (which is one of the things I want you to tell me) it would be a very great satisfaction to me to contribute my mite, if you think my doing so would not be offensive to *him* or appear ostentation to *others*. I have not time to go further into the subject, but do *you* think & feel *for* me, as my proxy, and say whether, by giving my name & five guineas or so to the subscription, you think I should serve him, *without* at the same time *wounding* him.[1]

No one will doubt that it was a pleasure to Moore to exercise his magnanimous spirit by giving a helping hand to an enemy, but it scarcely seems credible that Hunt could sink to accepting the charity: yet he did so.

The shallow and showy good nature that enabled Moore make light of the injuries not only of himself but of his friend may be contrasted with the staunchness of Hobhouse. Twenty-seven years after Moore's biography came out, with that damaging letter from Shelley to Byron already quoted, Hobhouse had a communication from Hunt asking how Moore, now dead, had obtained the document.

> I suppose L. Hunt thought I might have furnished Moore with the letter—but I did not, and I never saw the Life until it was published.
> L. H. is a good for nothing malignant fellow—but I thought it advisable to answer him by telling him the above fact. . . .[2]

Hunt by this time had changed his tack, and having done all the harm in his power, had become a penitent, and had the effrontery to make

---

[1] 3 Mar. 1832: Abinger Papers.
[2] British Museum: 43761. Journal entry, 29 Apr. 1858.

public excuse for himself on the grounds that he was 'young' when he wrote his virulent book. He had been forty-three and the father of eight children, but with almost everyone except Hobhouse, the bluff worked. Indeed he has been praised by recent biographers for having made 'handsome amends' to Byron, though he never retracted a single syllable.

How Moore came by Shelley's letter remains a mystery, and also whether Mary Shelley was aware beforehand that he was going to use it. Between Hunt and Moore she was in a rather difficult position. She had come to know Moore very well in the course of assisting him with his Byron researches, and had grown to like him warmly. Hunt, on the other hand, though she felt it incumbent on her to speak well of him, had lost a good deal of ground in her favour; his wife's slatternly and intemperate habits were actively disagreeable, and as for his children, she began to see almost eye to eye with Byron.

'The Hunts!' she exclaimed to Jane Williams in a moment of release from idealizing the past. She had found some unpleasant procedure 'completely à la Marianne'.

> I can hardly pity her for she has her *consolation*—but Hunt—what a fate—what a bitter and dread fate is his—& if we say it is partly his own fault, must one not accuse the Gods who formed him to his own ruin—It is the only comfort one has (& that a sorry one) in one's total inability to serve them, that it is impossible to render them service—[1]

It was exactly the point of view expressed by Byron when he described the 'despairing sensation' of trying to do something for Hunt as 'like pulling a man out of a river who directly throws himself in again'. But then, there was Hunt's solemn cult of the memory of Shelley and all he was doing to interpret Shelley to the public in such a way as entirely to lift the stigma of atheism, subversiveness, and immorality. Though Mary would have preferred that Shelley should be known only by his works, still, since it seemed some kind of portraiture was unavoidable, Hunt's was the least objectionable. It revealed Shelley as a Christian gentleman of aristocratic birth, living according to the Sermon on the Mount and contending only with childish superstition and hidebound orthodoxy; and so pure in his morals that he had been obliged to overcome considerable reluctance to 'endure' the comic parts of Byron's poetry (as gross a libel as Shelley ever sustained, his admiration of *Don Juan* being immediate and vociferous).

Shelley's last days on earth had been spent partly in trying to get Byron to lend a further £250 to Hunt,[2] whose brother was in trouble, and

---

[1] JONES, *Letters of Mary Shelley*. 28 June 1828. Mrs Hunt's 'consolation' was drink.
[2] British Museum: 38523. Draft of a letter from Hunt to Byron recapitulating complaints. 7 Apr. 1823.

partly in telling his newly recovered friend all about his unhappiness with Mary, confidences he might have regretted if he had known what misery would result to her from them. Her novels and her conduct often suggest that she had a strain of masochism; and she rewarded the suffering Hunt had inflicted on her when she was ill and distraught with grief, by promising to give him, as soon as Shelley's father died, £2000, the sum Byron had renounced. Both she and Hunt anticipated this event in the near future, and he was not likely to lose touch with her while the promise awaited fulfilment.

Sir Timothy did not die till 1844, and the estate, greatly diminished by Shelley's desperate borrowings on reversion, turned out much less than was expected. Mary had to compromise by giving Hunt £120 a year. He tried hard to get the capital, but she could not manage it. After her death in 1851 he continued to draw this pension from Shelley's son, and to earn it by his lavish contribution to the Shelley legend.

Mary for her part lived in a tormenting state of spiritual dichotomy. To prove her worthiness to Sir Timothy after all his contumely, to establish her son Percy in his rightful position as a baronet's heir, to obliterate the humiliations borne during her most impressionable years, she became externally as circumspect and controlled as a figure walking on a tight-rope. Yet she could not bear to abandon the past or relinquish the strands which bound her to the great man with whom her life had been so richly and so agonizingly linked. She kept in touch with most of the associates of Shelley and practised a kind of idolatry which must have required strenuous double thinking.

Leigh Hunt and Trelawny were much more congenial in sharing this esoteric religion than Shelley's older friends, Hogg and Peacock, who had no anti-Byron axes to grind.

Mary herself was able to combine her devotion to Shelley and the cause of his genius with a high if unstable regard for the memory of Byron. 'Can I forget his attention and consolations to me during my deepest misery? Never.' Such was part of the journal entry in which she recorded the news of his death—'the dear, capricious, fascinating Albé'.[1] The morbid tendency of her nature, which made her able to write one of the world's most successful horror stories while still in her teens, to relish the gruesome narratives of Trelawny, and to consent to the quite unnecessary exhumation of Shelley's mutilated body,[2] gave her a longing to see the dead Byron. She wrote to Hanson, asking his permission to visit 'the remains of our lost and lamented friend'. Excepting the appalled

[1] JONES, *Journal.* 15 May 1824.
[2] Joachim Miller correctly says: 'Shelley was burned because Trelawny willed it to be so . . . not because the Italian Government compelled it. This was not required at all.' Charles Vivian, the boy who was drowned with Shelley, was not exhumed.

Augusta, she was the only woman to whom that far from enviable privilege was granted.[1]

By one of those little revenges of time that abound in the history of this group of personages, it became Mary's eager ambition to have her work published by that same John Murray of whom, under the influence of Leigh Hunt, she had often spoken most scathingly. She wrote him suggestion after suggestion, but he was deterred by her extreme lack of humour—and no doubt also by the faults of construction which weigh down her longer works. He begged her, however, to allow him to turn £100 he had lent her into a gift, as a recognition of her valuable assistance to Moore with his biography. Her refusal with a remark that she was sure Byron's ghost would come and haunt her if ever she were to make any money out of having known him, often quoted as evidence of the ungallant treatment she could not forget, is surely the sadly smiling admission of having behaved foolishly herself. A few weeks later she wrote again to the same correspondent, reiterating her commendation of Moore's book on Byron (about Hunt's she remained discreetly silent) and adding with obvious satisfaction that her father, Godwin, thought it set Byron in the light he best deserved—'generous, openhanded and kind'.[2]

Many Shelley scholars have had access to that letter: none has found those words deserving of a mention.

* * * * * *

In 1826 Mary brought out one of the numberless novels in which Byron figures as a leading character. This was *The Last Man*, a fantasy on a theme totally beyond her powers, the only enduring value of which is that it contains, besides its delineations of both Byron and Shelley, an enormous number of unconscious clues to the nature of their relations with each other and with the several women whose destinies they shadowed or illuminated. The neglect of this *roman à clef* by the biographers of Shelley and Mary is perhaps to be accounted for by the impossibility of analysing it without coming to the conclusion that her feelings for Byron were strongly emotional and tinged with eroticism.[3]

The 'overtopping and towering' Lord Raymond (Byron) is contrasted to his disadvantage with the 'sensitive and excellent' Adrian (Shelley), whose 'slender frame seemed overcharged with the weight of life', and whose 'soul appeared rather to inhabit his body than unite with it'.

[1] 7/9 July 1824. Murray MSS. There is a tradition about the body having been laid out by a woman, but that would have been prior to the ruthless autopsy. Parry, however, speaks of the conspicuous absence of any woman's care at Missolonghi.

[2] Ibid. 26 Jan. 1830.

[3] A conclusion also drawn by Professor Lovell and Professor Marchand in their writings on Byron.

Raymond was emphatically a man of the world. His passions were violent . . . self-gratification at least was the paramount object with him. . . . The earth was spread out as an highway for him. . . . Adrian despised the narrow views of the politician, and Raymond held in contempt the benevolent visions of the philanthropist.

Nevertheless the man of the world, however ignoble his ambitions and amusements, has some striking attributes.

Among his other advantages, Lord Raymond was supremely handsome; everyone admired him; of women he was the idol. He was courteous, honey-tongued—an adept in fascinating arts.

Though Mary takes the rôle of a first-person narrator named Lionel, it is easy to deduce that she is also projecting herself into the woman beloved by Adrian, Evadne. Unfortunately for the virtuous philanthropist, Raymond with all his fascinations 'usurps the empire' of Evadne's heart.

. . . The attentions of Adrian became distasteful to her. She grew capricious; her gentle conduct to him was exchanged for asperity and repulsive coldness. When she perceived the wild, or pathetic appeal of his expressive countenance, she would relent and for a while resume her ancient kindness. But the fluctuations shook to its depths the soul of the sensitive youth. . . .

Here surely is a recapitulation of the emotions which caused her to write verses of bitter remorse for coldness towards Shelley. The necessity of idealizing him did not permit her to remember any provocations on his side.

The portrayal of Byron as Raymond is nearly without an attempt at disguise. He is represented as singing the Tyrolese song of liberty which we know from Mary's journal Byron sang. He is the hero of Greece—where he ultimately dies; the father of a lovely child resembling Allegra (and named Clara): very rich, as the Shelleys imagined Byron to be, but marred by 'worldly principles' which prevent the narrator from applying to him in financial distress, inferior in learning and eloquence to Adrian, but possessed of 'a quick penetration and a practical knowledge of life'; inclined to yield himself up to dissipation and to give rowdy dinner parties, but ennobled by a natural dignity which never forsakes him.

He was gay, playful, fascinating—but never did he overstep the modesty of nature or the respect due to himself, in his wildest sallies. . . . Yet I own I was exceedingly provoked to observe the worthless fellows on whom his time was wasted, and the jovial if not drunken spirit which seemed to be robbing him of his better self. . . .

Adrian flitted like a shadow among them, and, by a word and look of sobriety endeavoured to restore order in the assembly. . . . I was indignant that he should sit at the same table with the companions of Raymond.

How touching is this glimpse of the Pisa dinner parties and Shelley's part in them seen through Mary's eyes! On being remonstrated with—

'My good fellow,' said Raymond, 'this is neither the time nor the place for the delivery of a moral lecture: take my word for it that my amusements and society are not so bad as you imagine. We are neither hypocrites nor fools—for the rest, "Dost thou think because thou art virtuous, there shall be no more cakes and ale?" '

The words had been set by Byron on the title page of the later cantos of *Don Juan*. Though the novel is visionary in the most abstract, and therefore unreadable, style, the almost involuntary realism in the drawing of the two men lends an unmistakable significance to a paragraph about Lord Raymond's dazzling renown:

Relations of what he had done, conjectures concerning his future actions, were the never failing topics of the hour. I was not angry on my own account, but I felt as if the praises which this idol received were leaves torn from the laurels destined for Adrian.

Mary lived just long enough to see the laurel wreath wrested from Byron's head and its leaves divided between Shelley and Keats, the larger share going to Shelley. By the 1850's a swift and total oblivion for Byron was confidently and angrily prophesied, for jealousy of the fame he had enjoyed at what was felt to be Shelley's expense had, from the beginning, been more than a little irate. Though they were of wholly different orders of genius, and it might have been plain to anyone capable of appreciating literature at all that Shelley could no more have written a humorous epic like *Don Juan* than Byron could have written an iridescent lyric like the *Ode to a Skylark*, it was the fashion for more than a hundred years to compare them as if Shelley's claims must necessarily diminish those of Byron.

In 1858, preparing his reminiscences of Italy in Byron's day for the press, Hobhouse, who had never cared much for Shelley,[1] wrote in pained astonishment:

The admiration of Byron has given place to the worship of Shelley and to a fondness for Keats, and it seems to me somewhat unjust that the genius and literary merits of the first of these poets cannot be acknowledged without an attempt to deprecate the author of Childe Harold.

The judgment of the Victorian Age was, of course, largely a moral one. Hobhouse, who had known Shelley when he used to write 'Atheist' after his name in hotel registers, and was living in valiant defiance of conven-

---

[1] When Moore, in his biography of Byron, spoke of Shelley as 'an aristocrat by birth, and, I understand, also in appearance and manners', Hobhouse wrote on the margin of his copy, 'Not in the least unless to be lean and feeble be aristocratical.'

tion as one of the 'Otaheite philosophers', could not realize that he would soon be all but canonized.

Shelley's son had been brought up to become—almost literally—a minister at a shrine where a lamp was kept burning to shed dim light over the relics, spurious and otherwise, of Shelley. Byron's daughter was bred in the knowledge that her father was a man whose portrait was kept veiled under a green curtain, and she had been enabled to 'guess' that he had committed diabolical crimes; so that nothing came as a surprise to her when she received her mother's full confidence.[1] The world knew little of these contrasting family attitudes, yet in a strangely personal way, it partook of them.

One cannot but picture the two poets confronting each other with rather wry smiles in the Elysian fields.

[1] Correspondence in the Lovelace Papers, early 1841. Medwin, publishing the fact that Byron's picture was kept covered up, stated that it was a condition of his mother-in-law's will. This elicited an interesting note from Lady Byron in the margin of a copy of Medwin's book: 'This Portrait in the Albanian Costume was bought of Philips, the Painter by Lady Noel (Ly B's Mother) in 1815—when Ld & Ly B were in London, *he* being unable to afford the money; Sir Ralph being also under pecuniary embarrassments, Lady Noel parted with some of her diamonds to obtain the £300 (or Guineas) for the purchase.—It was hung over a chimney-piece at Kirkby, & *was* covered with a green curtain—*not* for the reason above supposed.' The painting, here reproduced, is now in the British Embassy at Athens.

On another occasion Lady Byron stated its original price was a hundred and fifty guineas. (Letter to her daughter, 22 Dec. 1835).

CHAPTER XIII

'LORD BYRON'S JACKAL'

There is a mad chap come here whose name is Trelawny. . . . He comes as the friend of Shelley, great, glowing and rich in romance. . . . I ought to have seen that this Lord Byron's jackal was rather weak in all the points that I could judge, though strong enough in stilettos. . . . They talk of him as a camelion [*sic*] who went mad on reading Lord Byron's Corsair.

    Joseph Severn in a letter to Charles Armitage Brown, April 1823.

Though he waited till Mary Shelley and most of those who could contradict him were dead before launching full-scale reminiscences, as early as 1831 Trelawny was urging Claire Clairmont to help him to realize 'a double object . . . to wit—the doing justice to Shelley's memory—[and] assisting me to dissipate the cant and humbug about Byron'.[1]

There was another reason, apart from the heightened public interest in Shelley, for this anxiety to deflate the fame of 'the world's greatest man . . . my best friend'. In two recently published books, Trelawny had read with rage that Byron had cast doubts on his truthfulness. There was Dr Kennedy's work, in which he recognized himself under the initial T. as one whose statements were generally deemed to be tall stories. Much more damaging was the account in Dr Julius Millingen's *Memoir of the Affairs of Greece*, where, after a smiling mention of Trelawny's exploits which 'though not new, were marvellous', the author went on scathingly:

> Arrived at Cephalonia, Trelawney [*sic*] discovered that Lord Byron was not romantic enough to be his companion; and he started in consequence for the Peleponnesus; where having roamed in vain in quest of a hero, he passed over to Athens. There he met with Odysseus; and so powerful is the invisible force of sympathy, that, although they could not understand each other's language, they became in an instant, intimate friends.
>
> According to Trelawney, Odysseus was the personification of the *beau ideal* of every manly perfection, mental and bodily. He swore by him, and imitated him in the minutest actions. His dress, gait, air and address were not only perfectly similar, but he piqued himself even in being as dirty; having as much vermin, and letting them loose from his fingers in the same dignified manner as if sparing a conquered enemy.
>
> . . . Owing, no doubt, to his prolonged stay in oriental countries, his imagination got the better of his veracity, or, as Lord Byron observed of him, 'he could not, even to save his life, tell the truth.'

It is a most curious fact that Millingen's apparently far-fetched mockery of Trelawny's style of boasting falls short of the reality, which

---

[1] TRELAWNY, *Letters*. 13 July 1831.

may be gauged by a letter to Leigh Hunt from the Isle of Hydra, October 25th, 1823:

> You see my Dear Hunt I have held firm to my plans. [His plans were to use Byron's name and means for getting to Greece under the best auspices, and then leave him.]¹ I have joined the most enterprising of the Albanian Klefts [Odysseus]—left the most infirm of purpose [Byron]—from an Indolent Italian life become an active soldier—sleeping on mountains— feeding on meal & water—always armed never undressed—allied with barbarous & uncivilised brutes harasing [*sic*] marches—day & night—exposed to wind & rain—cloathed from top to toe—in sheep skin—tortured with multitudes of Lice fleas, & bugs—no linen—no washing—foul ragged & filthy—& this for the whole winter—& this is not exaggerated.²

Trelawny's imagination had got the better of his veracity to the extent of making him forget that his first winter season in Greece was only just beginning, and that, far from spending the whole winter, or any part of it, as an active soldier in the mountains, he had been living, since his arrival in Hydra, in the comfortable house of Orlando, a wealthy shipping merchant, who was preparing to go to London as one of the Government Deputies. (Trelawny repaid his hospitality by writing to the *Examiner* denouncing him as a blockhead whose incompetence had helped to ruin his country.)³ He had parted from Byron only in the previous month, being sent with Hamilton Browne as an emissary to Mavrocordato and the rest of the Provisional Government at Hydra, and there had been no opportunity at all for his participation in mountain warfare.

To be unwashed seems to have been one of the boyish daydreams he was able to realize. His want of fastidiousness was extreme.⁴ In regretting that he did not 'wash his hands', Byron was using the accepted euphemism of the day for general personal negligence. This was a characteristic Trelawny shared with Leigh Hunt, who had found Byron's habit of frequent bathing thoroughly effeminate, and remarked acidly that he was as fond of fine linen as a Quaker—and had 'baby work' on his shirts!⁵ Trelawny knew he would have in Hunt a sympathetic reader when he compared himself to Hotspur and alluded to Byron as 'the certain Lord—who looked so like a waiting gentlewoman so neat & trimly drest &c.'

Hunt would also be delighted to learn that Byron was evading all appeals to assist the Greeks financially. ('They begin to know their man

---

¹ TRELAWNY, *Letters*. To Claire Clairmont, 27 June and 22 July 1823.
² British Museum: MSS. 38523.
³ Letter dated 18 Mar. 1826, published 8 May. On 20 Aug. an anonymous contributor defended Orlando against this attack.
⁴ E.g. 'Mrs Paul tells me she sees Trelawney now & then looking so very dirty & old.' Mary Shelley to Claire Clairmont, 20 Sept. 1843. He was not quite fifty-one at this date.
⁵ HUNT, *Lord Byron*.

now—and expect little from him.') Trelawny, while conspiring with Odysseus to get rid of Mavrocordato, was also conspiring with Mavrocordato, so he said, to force Byron's miserly hand. 'How he will get off this bout heaven knows, for I see no outlet to escape by. I have enmeshed him.'[1] Hunt literally took his idea of Byron's conduct in the Greek war from such letters as this, similar nonsense was written to Mary Shelley.

Byron never had the faintest suspicion of Trelawny's disloyalty, which was masked from him by deferential protestations. '. . . You know that from the first moment I had the honour of knowing you till this day—in every thing in which I have been an actor I have only considered your honour & advantage.'[2]

Trelawny's ebullient lies he took for the yarns of a seafaring man, and although there were occasions when they annoyed him, he failed completely to recognize them as a serious aberration of personality. After their first meetings, he had joked with Teresa about the mock-Corsair's pretence that he left a Gulnare in every port; and when she had spoken of feeling something like fear in his presence, he had replied that the young man was only eccentric and his crimes imaginary. He thought—as Mary Shelley did—that Trelawny's smile was full of good nature and incapable of deceiving him.[3]

Millingen's book, which was the chief publication relating to Byron in 1831, is itself not notable for accuracy, and in certain instances he was paying off old scores. His contact with Trelawny had been very slight—only two meetings in Missolonghi after Byron's death if Trelawny is to be believed. But probably he is not. He represents himself as being impelled by his 'feelings of humanity' to visit Millingen who was ill with malaria fever. 'The ensuing morning I saw him, and he was better; which he mainly attributed to having followed my advice. . . . I never saw anything more of him.'[4] There is a contemporary letter of Trelawny's suggesting a far closer acquaintance than that. 'Millingen has been at Death's door,' he writes to George Finlay, 'but—Death would not let him come in. He is out of great danger and sends his love—cannot write.'[5]

---

[1] Letter of 25 Oct. 1823. None of Trelawny's biographers—Massingham, Armstrong, Grylls—has seen fit to publish these portions of the revealing letter.

[2] 8 Mar. 1824: Murray MSS.

[3] GUICCIOLI, *La Vie*. Mary Shelley wrote in her Journal, 19 Jan. 1822, 'There is an air of good nature which pervades his whole countenance, especially when he smiles, which assures me that his heart is good.' Fanny Kemble was also charmed by the sweetness of his expression.

[4] *Literary Gazette*, 12 Feb. 1831. The communication is dated from Florence, Jan. 20, so Millingen's volume must have been circulating very early in the year. Trelawny's article was 'copied'—which certainly means corrected—for the press by Charles Armitage Brown, and Mary Shelley handled it in England.

[5] TRELAWNY, *Letters*. Addenda, 27 May 1824.

The address is given as 'The Cavern of Ulysses, M't Parnassus', where he had arrived the day before, not having been in Missolonghi for the past three weeks and more, and it is obvious that Millingen, sending his love, could not have been far off. The inference is that Trelawny had brought him with the 'splendid suit' of men, horses, and guns that he had been rounding up for the purpose of making the rebel General's cavern 'the strongest fortress in the world', and certain it is that, in some obscure manner, Millingen ended on the side of the Turks. Each denounced the other as a traitor, and each displayed a contempt for the other that must have been based on something more than two kindly visits by Trelawny to a sick-bed.

Millingen, when he wrote his book, had become physician to the Turkish sultan, and was in a position to learn the history of Trelawny's idol, Odysseus, who in his youth had been the Ganymede of Ali Pasha, one of the rulers nominally under Ottoman dominion. There may have been a deliberate innuendo in the allusion to the immediate intimacy of two men who could not understand each other's speech.

The upshot was an onslaught by Trelawny upon Millingen in the *Literary Gazette* of such violence that the editor was obliged to print a disclaimer of the opinions uttered and to strike out 'epithets which we would not ourselves sanction or apply to the worst of human beings'. The nature of those epithets may be guessed from the portrayal of Millingen as 'a tall delicately-complexioned, rosy-cheeked, dandy-boy, of simpering and affected manners', who whined and cried 'like a sick girl' and was called 'mio caro ragazzino' by Mavrocordato—'which let me into the secret of how he had cajoled him'.[1]

It was now for the first time that Trelawny signed his name to public complaints of the 'apathy and indolence' of Byron, and contrived the specious dialogue in which the latter rejoiced in getting a doctor for the expedition at £20 a year.[2] Once again the carelessness or conscious mischief-making of one of the most distant members of Byron's *entourage* had given impetus to a rankling animosity which powerfully affected the poet's after-fame.

It has been said that Trelawny's long-sustained and highly successful attempts to belittle Byron physically and mentally were due to his having been 'snubbed' by the poet; and his biographers have contrived a painful picture of his sufferings under this cruelty. Thus Massingham, whose book is largely built upon the theory of snubbing, says: 'That Byron trampled remorselessly upon Trelawny's susceptibilities and beliefs is not to be questioned.' It will be questioned now, and with words out of Trelawny's

---

[1] *Literary Gazette*, op. cit.
[2] See Chapter V. The salary was not named in the later version Trelawny published.

own mouth, composed with the most palpable pride ten days after embark-
ing with Byron for Greece:

> . . . Lord B. found me full employment day & night. You could hardly know
> me now transformed into the most active bustling useful fellow you ever
> saw. . . .
>
> Lord B. & myself are extraordinary thick we are inseparable—but mind
> this does not flatter me—he has known me long enough to see the sacrifieses
> [*sic*] I make in devoting myself to serve him—this is new to him, who is sur-
> rounded by mercenaries. . . . Lord B. . . does everything so far I wish him.[1]

This is, of course, typical Trelawny swaggering, but it is in a very
different key from the patronizing air of the *Recollections* of 1858, in
which he is perpetually rebuking Byron and demonstrating his own
infinite superiority. It is not the tone of a man whose feelings have been
remorselessly trampled on. The only authority for that is William
Graham's report of talks with Claire Clairmont in her old age. There is
much that has the ring of truth in it, and the more strikingly so because
he tells things which were altogether at variance with what was popularly
believed. (For example, there is an indication of her love affair with
Shelley, of which no evidence was published till the present century); but
though the record is not to be deprecated, it is not to be implicitly relied
on either. Whether the fault was in her memory or Graham's, he states
that she told him—with his love letters in her possession—that Trelawny
had never been her friend.

> ". . . It seems to me he gives himself airs, and always has done, of
> knowing a great deal more of Shelley, and Byron too (but particularly of
> Shelley), than he has any right. Why, he only knew him six months."
>
> "How he hates Byron, madame!" I said.
>
> "Well, Byron snubbed him, you know. He said, 'Tre was an excellent
> fellow until he took to imitating my *Childe Harold* and *Don Juan*.' This got
> to Trelawney's ears, and he never forgave Byron for it. Trelawney [*sic*] made
> himself quite ridiculous when I lived in London, I remember. He absolutely
> lived, or in any case, dined out, on the strength of his acquaintance with
> Byron. It was always 'Byron said this,' 'Byron did that.' I remember
> Thackeray takes him off rather well somewhere."[2]

This is not fiction, but it is hardly a firm basis for a belief that Byron
was in the habit of lacerating the tender sensibilities of 'the Pirate'.
There is no single occasion on which Claire Clairmont could have seen
Byron and Trelawny together.

A letter from the Marquise de Boissy—better known as Countess
Guiccioli—written very shortly after the appearance of the *Recollections*

---

[1] Letter to Commander Roberts, 23 July 1823. From the original MSS. in the
Keats-Shelley Memorial, Rome.

[2] Graham. The character created by Thackeray was Captain Sumph, a minor figure
in *Pendennis*.

and hitherto unpublished, gives an eye-witness's account of his relations
with Byron. Madame Louise Colet, a French author, had enquired what
credence should be given to the book; a friend of hers, who greatly
admired Byron, had been much disturbed to read how both his feet were
clubbed and his legs withered to the knees. Teresa, apologizing for her
bad French, replied:

> What words to use, when one reads things like this, to explain what one
> knows from experience—and above all when one sees good faith and high
> mind accept (though with regrets)—such lies!
> Never, believe me, did God so lavish and unite in one of his creatures
> such an assemblage of gifts as in Lord Byron, but alas! always at hand are
> men eager to deny them, and, not being able to ascend to his level, to try
> and make him descend to theirs. . . .
> They have found in this fine exercise of their inventive wit food for their
> vanity—and often for their cupidity. Happily, witnesses to this turpitude are
> still living, and will not fail to reestablish the truth of the facts.
> I knew the absurd invention of Mr Trelawny, who fearing perhaps to be
> forgotten, thought to make himself known once more to the world by an
> odious lie about Lord Byron which would be ridiculous if it were not revolting.
> I was in England when this fine work appeared, and I can say that it
> repelled the decent public to the highest degree, and that Lord Br[oughton]
> one of the most intimate friends of Lord Byron, went so far as to say that if he
> met him [Trelawny] he would thrash him as a coward and impudent liar.[1]
> Such was the reception of Mr Trelawny's work in England.
> If then, as you say, M. Paul de [?] Vieton is so great an admirer of Ld.
> Byron and has repeated with regret what this article contains, you can
> relieve him from his error and distress. . . .
> Not knowing the reputation of Mr Trelawny his error was quite natural.
> This reputation, which is completely deserved, is that throughout his whole
> life (which to speak with charity, has been nothing but a tissue of extravag-
> ances), he has never *been able to speak the truth*. Lord Byron, of whom
> Mr Trelawny was never a friend but a simple acquaintance during his last
> days in Italy,—invited to join him in Greece because, in the circumstances
> Greece was in, he might have been of some use—often laughed at him,
> knowing that he aimed at realizing in person the imaginary type of the
> Corsair; however (said Lord Byron) Conrad did one thing more and one less
> than Trelawny—*he washed his hands and he told no lies*.
> On board the ship that took him to Greece, he often jested about Trel-
> awny's lying, and after his death, these jokes were published—thence the
> hostility of Trelawny. . . .

She denied with vigour that Byron had been crippled in the manner
Trelawny described, pointing out that it would have been utterly impossible

---

[1] Lord Broughton was John Cam Hobhouse. He visited Teresa on 18 July 1858, but
does not mention Trelawny's book in his diary. What precisely he had proposed, at the
age of seventy-two, to do to Trelawny, aged sixty-six, is difficult to envisage. Teresa's
verb is '*souffleter*'.

to have concealed such a deformity in infancy or schooldays, and that he had always 'mounted a horse with remarkable elegance, swam better than any other swimmer of his time, and played games with dexterity and grace'. She had up her sleeve a still more telling card:

> One must further add—did he always make love then platonically? . . .
> But I shall never finish if I enumerate to you all the proofs of the lies of Mr Trelawny.[1]

Teresa little knew the vitality of an apocryphal story when she spoke so optimistically of the better witnesses who would establish the facts. The truth is complex, full of nuances, hard to convey and to comprehend: a skilful lie is sure to be much more sharply focused and easily retained in the mind. And Trelawny lived to be nearly ninety, so that veneration for the man who had seen Shelley plain and put Byron boldly in his place, made it seem sacrilege to investigate his statements or to find out the original sources of the genuine material he so freely plagiarized when he was not inventing. Richard Edgcumbe wrote of meeting him in 1875: 'I felt as though drawn by some mysterious agency backwards through the mists of Time, towards those immortal poets who were once proud to call this man their friend.'[2]

Neither Byron nor Shelley left any evidence that they were elated by Trelawny's friendship: that was a legend he himself contrived. And contrivance is an apt word, for nothing could be more ingenious than the way he used the names of the two poets to glorify his own, always indulging the particular *penchant* of the individual he was dealing with; calling Byron 'the Master spirit of the age'—a phrase he had culled from a back number of *Blackwood's*[3]—when he wanted to please John Murray, and single-hearted in his love and reverence for Shelley with the young Victorians. He even claimed that with a prescience exceeding that of any man of his time, he had gone to Pisa, on the strength of *Queen Mab* and some talk with Medwin, for the especial purpose of meeting Shelley. But a letter to him from Edward Williams shows that it was really his chance of meeting Byron that he had been trying to reconnoitre:

> Lord Byron is the very spirit of this place,—that is, to those few to whom, like Mokannah, he has lifted his veil. When you asked me, in your last letter if it was probable to become at all intimate with him, I replied in a manner which I considered it most prudent to do, from motives which are best explained when I see you. Now, however, I know him a great deal better, and think I may safely say that the point will rest entirely with yourself.[4]

[1] 15 Jan. 1859. Gamba Papers, Ravenna. There has been some adjustment of punctuation.　　　　　　　　　　　　　[2] *Temple Bar*, May 1890.
[3] In reviewing Medwin's *Conversations*, Nov. 1824.
[4] JONES, *Shelley's Friends*. 27 Dec. 1821.

There is no reference to Shelley here except as one of the guests at a 'splendid feast' given by Byron and as a member of his 'Pistol Club'. It was as 'the friend of Lord Byron'[1] that Trelawny brought out, in 1831, his *Adventures of a Younger Son*. This book was placed for him by Mary Shelley, who took great trouble over it, gave him excellent advice, and made what were first-rate terms for a beginner who had the disadvantage of writing anonymously. He afterwards denied all credit to her, saying she was 'commissioned to get it published, nothing more; if she read it, it was to satisfy her natural curiosity'. At the same time he asserted with his omniscient air that *Frankenstein* was 'the creation of her husband's brain'.[2] In one of the letters originally bestowing the thankless 'commission' on her, he had written:

> When you have read the work and heard the opinion of the booksellers, write to me before you settle anything. . . . There is no person I have such confidence in as you, and . . . are we not bound and united together by ties stronger than those which earth has to impose?[3]

And in another communication, though protesting against certain alterations she suggested, he told her that every day she became dearer to him.[4] A year or so later, inflated with the success she had procured him, he wrote to Claire Clairmont:

> I am told Colburn the publisher is making a mint of money of it—of which I shall reap no advantages owing to the intrusting others with the disposal of the M.S. . . . Authors think lightly of every work they have no hand in.[5]

The book, overrated as in any case it has been, must have owed much of its merit to the attentions it received from Walter Savage Landor, Charles Armitage Brown, and Horace Smith. Trelawny's style is vigorous —very self-consciously so—but slipshod, disorganized, and repetitive to an extent that seldom permits quotation of anything he wrote without abridgment. 'The first sight of an original letter or page of manuscript of Trelawny's,' says one commentator, 'with its childish spelling, bad grammar, and ignorance of punctuation, usually comes as a shock even though one thinks he is prepared for it.'[6]

Landor and Brown had corrected the copy page by page in Florence, and Shelley's gifted friend, Horace Smith, undertook further revisions in England, as an act of friendship, he said, to Mary and to the memory of Shelley. Mary had given him a glowing report of Trelawny's kindness to her.

---

[1] It was thus advertised.   [2] Letter in *The Athenaeum*, Aug. 1878.
[3] TRELAWNY, *Letters*. 28 Oct. 1830.   [4] Ibid. 19 Jan. 1831.
[5] Ibid. 28 Apr. 1832.   [6] CLINE.

Much as he longed for eminence, he was obliged to publish anonymously, because he had maintained that the work was his life story true and unvarnished—which placed him in an awkward predicament with his formidable mother, his sisters, and other relations and early associates. It seems almost impossible that this romance of his, with its cardboard characters and theatrical tableaux lifted from Smollett, Hope's *Anastasius*, and Byron's youthful Oriental 'tales', could ever have been taken seriously as autobiography, but such was the desire to give the fullest credence to the man who, in his own phrase, had 'elevated Shelley' that honest biographers have for generations been suppressing all misgivings to accept the brutal and bloodthirsty imaginings as a factual record.

Recent research into the history of Trelawny's naval career has disclosed that 'the proportion of truth to fiction in *The Adventures* turns out to be but small, not more than one tenth'.[1] The proportion of truth to fiction in the book he later wrote about Byron and Shelley would probably be slightly higher than that because he had all the work of his predecessors in the same field to draw upon, which he did freely and without acknowledgment. Good but obscure witnesses such as Hamilton Browne, whose recollections were buried in the pages of old magazines, provided much of the material which has any value about Byron. Experts have discredited many of his anecdotes about Shelley.

Trelawny's peculiarities had already begun to irritate members of the Pisa circle months before it was broken up by the deaths of Shelley and Williams. Even Mary who, with her customary susceptibility, was attracted to him, had had to overcome some tendency to doubt his stories: . . . All these adventures took place between the age of thirteen and twenty. I believe them now I see the man. . . .'[2]

Edward Williams, whatever he may have felt at first, seems to have grown sceptical, referring ironically, after the affray in which a dragoon had been injured by one of Byron's servants, to the 'singular circumstance by which an affair of a similar nature occurred to one of this man's brothers—and having been cured of a wound which he had received in a scuffle he awaited concealed for the person whom he suspected—stabbed him to the heart and flung him into the river'.[3]

(Trelawny had only one brother, a resident of Cornwall, described by Richard Edgcumbe as 'tractable, mild, uncomplaining, submissive, in every respect a contrast. . . .')

In the aftermath of the Pisa adventure, Trelawny's part was that of a troublesome tale-bearer.[4] Later he made mischief between Byron, Roberts,

---

[1] HILL, *Keats-Shelley Journal*. Winter 1956.
[2] JONES, *Mary Shelley's Journal*. 19 Jan. 1822.
[3] JONES, *Shelley's Friends Journal*. 26 Mar. 1822.
[4] CLINE gives documentary evidence previously unpublished.

Byron at Missolonghi with his Newfoundland,
Lion, drawn by R. Seymour from a sketch
provided by William Parry

and the crew of the *Bolivar*. He touched on the affair in his *Recollections*, where he says that Byron wrote 'one of his long-winded, offensive epistles' to Captain Roberts, which he (Trelawny) would not forward. Byron's epistolary style was always the reverse of long-winded, and to avoid offensiveness in this instance he stated that 'the most painful part to me is that, after the trouble you have had in building the schooner, etc., anything should have occurred to annoy yourself or your friends.[1] Moreover, Trelawny did not withhold the letter, but sent it the following day, writing to Byron that it was 'perfectly satisfactory as a reply' to Captain Roberts.[2] The matter at issue was Byron's refusal to let two of the four sailors keep their kit, and another letter of his to Roberts is explicit on the subject of Trelawny's responsibility:

> . . . It was in consequence of Mr Trelawney's [*sic*] *former* representations of the *very bad conduct* of Frost towards himself—that I did not allow him to retain the dress—as well as Gaetano and the boy. Bees [*sic*] was impertinent and I treated him accordingly, but Frost was not so to *me* at least— but I heard such an account of him from Mr T. as did not in my opinion entitle him to any indulgence on my part.[3]

Hobhouse, in a passage which has been quoted, called Byron the most munificent man he ever knew but one who had 'a very proper dislike of being cheated'. In one of his letters to Byron about the sailors, Roberts had said that when he was engaging them, he had 'told them they were about serving a Nobleman' and would therefore receive something over and above their pay.[4] Byron replied that as this condition had never been named to him, he could not be supposed to act on it.[5] It was doubtless as a nobleman that he had been grossly overcharged for the building of the schooner by the man who naturally called him afterwards 'a damned close calculating fellow'.[6] According to Barry, Lord Blessington, who had failed as yet to pay for his purchase, was 'heartily sorry' to have made it.

> A Lieutenant of the Navy has come out from England to take charge of her. . . . When Lord Blessington sees this gentleman he will be still more out of humour with his bargain as the Lieutenant says he could build as good a Vessel in England for 200 £ including every thing.[7]

Byron in his ignorance had paid five times this amount to Roberts, although Italy was normally much cheaper than England. Teresa pointed out in her second book that Trelawny had more or less lived on the vessel, with great economy to himself, while it had turned out to be nothing but an expensive nuisance to Byron. Trelawny presented Barry with the final

---

[1] 29 Nov. 1822: Murray MSS.   [2] Ibid. 30 Nov. 1822.
[3] MS. in the Yale University Library, 3 Dec. 1822. The sailor's name was Beeze.
[4] 26 Nov. 1822: Murray MSS.   [5] 29 Nov. 1822: Murray MSS.
[6] TRELAWNY, *Recollections*, quoting Roberts.   [7] 12 Dec. 1823: Murray MSS.

account for running it on departing for Greece, and it was settled three days after the last payment was made to Leigh Hunt.[1] It is necessary to indicate these prosaic and usually neglected facts, because it has never been sufficiently appreciated that those who were loudest in their cry of 'avarice' were precisely the individuals who reaped some advantage from Byron's liberality.

Trelawny is the supreme example in this book of a man taken at his own valuation. He appeared open, hearty, and, if boastful, good-natured. He was actually rancorous, vindictive, and given to vulgar abuse; and as Mary Shelley wrote when she came to know him, 'destroyed by envy'. The shivering need of make-believe he evinced, not merely in youth but to the end of his life, would excite compassion if his posturing and perfidy had not been so triumphantly successful. The adroitness with which he paid homage to Shelley just when the literary world grew ready to hail with gratitude the poet's early supporters and champions caused an eager suspension of disbelief.

In his old age, when the cult of Shelley had become almost an idolatry, he set his face against it, became insulting to the poet's son and daughter-in-law, and began espousing, privately at least, the cause of Harriet, the deserted first wife whom he had never known. This seems to have been due not so much to chivalry as to a desire to score off Mary, now dead; and also to his natural contrariety—the same spirit which made him rebuke the aged Claire Clairmont for her continued hatred of Byron while he allowed his own to remain voluble. As in his youth, he was able to combine this love of contradiction with great dexterity in exploiting the sentiments of whomever he sought to impress.

Richard Edgcumbe, the Byron enthusiast, was persuaded, in the joy of meeting the wonderful old hero, that though 'he might perhaps have been prejudiced against Byron when he compared him with the gentle, unsophisticated Shelley, he never for one moment swerved in his loyalty. . . .'[2] To Edgcumbe he was no uncritical Shelley worshipper. 'The less one has to do with the character of a man like Shelley the better. . . . If Lady Shelley publishes anything against Harriet, I will speak. . . . She seeks to glorify Shelley at the expense of Harriet, but, by God, while *I* live, I will defend her.' (He brandished some documents he had taken out of a box. They remain inscrutable. His only method of defending Harriet was to attack Mary.)

There is something touching about the endeavours of both Edgcumbe

[1] Barry to Byron, 19 July 1823: Murray MSS.
[2] *Temple Bar*, May 1890. The author of the present work was acquainted with Mr Edgcumbe in her youth, and several times heard him speak reverently of Trelawny's friendship for Byron. She did not know Trelawny's *Letters* at the time, and so never enquired how they could be reconciled with unswerving loyalty.

and William Michael Rossetti, the devotee of Shelley, to gloss over or explain away the discrepancies of Trelawny's carefully noted reminiscences. It was Edgcumbe who induced him to alter in his last book, *Records of Shelley, Byron, and the Author* (1878), the description of Byron's lameness given twenty years earlier, confronting him with authentic information he had gathered at Nottingham. But his belief in the hallucinated witness remained unshaken.[1]

'A capital anecdotic touch, this', William Rossetti writes of something Trelawny had told him which was not quite compatible with the printed version. On another occasion: 'Spite of Trelawny's positiveness, I should almost *suspect* some treachery in his recollection. . . .' Hearing how Trelawny remembered seeing Rogers, Hobhouse, and Moore hypocritically ignoring Shelley 'when dining in his company along with Byron', he is obliged to postulate another lapse of memory, since the raconteur could never have seen Moore in company with either Shelley or Byron. (Nor Hobhouse either, whose arrival in Italy in 1822 was after Shelley's death, but Rossetti had no information about that.) He admitted in his journal that Trelawny's narrations were 'possibly (I fancy) a little dressed up in some details':[2] but he could not bear to impose any very severe tests on the spellbinding tales of Shelley's glorious friend.

By this time 'the noble brave Trelawny' was not content to refer to 'lengthy scrawls' he had had from Byron but never produced (because 'they would require tedious notes to explain them'), but had become suddenly rich in relics. There was a dagger which a blind beggar had thrust into his hand in the Pisa scuffle, telling him 'You may have need of this!'[3] (Blind beggars and daggers are absent from all contemporary records.) There was a sword that Byron had given him at Cephalonia 'with great pomp and circumstance, saying in a melodramatic manner; "Here take this, Tre, and use it either like Childe Harold or Don Juan,"'[4] a new version of a speech of Byron's improved on from another narrator and already used—without the sword. There were bits of Shelley's skull which are now deemed to have been bits of Williams's jawbone,[5] and the *Sophocles* alias *Aeschylus* found on Shelley's drowned body but nowhere mentioned in the official report of the Governor of Viareggio.[6] There was a cap of Byron's he had had for forty-eight years without mentioning it,

---

[1] Massingham, the most impassioned of all Trelawny's admirers, says of his widely differing versions of Byron's disability: 'The only explanation seems to be that he did not know that he was lying; in other words that he wrote about Byron's feet not as they were but as he expected to find them. . . . There is nothing true or false but thinking makes it so.' He blames Byron for having, by taking 'pitiless advantage' of Trelawny's intellectual inferiority, got him into the mood for telling this particular (unconscious) lie.

[2] *Athenaeum*, 15 July 1882.   [3] EDGCUMBE, *Temple Bar*.
[4] Ibid.   [5] MARCHAND, *Keats-Shelley Bulletin*, 1952.
[6] Ibid. The only book found on Shelley's body was Keats's *Lamia*.

and, above all, there was Shelley's sofa, so generously given to William Rossetti; a sofa of which he first said that it was bought for Leigh Hunt, then that it had been habitually slept upon by Shelley himself, and ultimately that it was the last couch on which the poet laid his head before his death. Its authenticity was vouched for by a copy of a letter from 'Barone' Kirkup[1] (who also had among his possessions a portrait of Dante completed and signed by that distinguished sitter in the spirit world), but there are reasons for doubting the provenance of the gift to Rossetti either as a Kirkup or a Shelley relic.[2]

Trelawny also told a celebrated story of how he had 'added considerably' to the dignity of Byron's landing in Greece by letting him have a cast-off green jacket of his own. Byron, on the evidence of better witnesses, landed in a scarlet suit, doubtless similar to that of an aide-de-camp, this being an admissible dress for peers on foreign territory; and his five trunks of clothing contained a number of new uniforms,[3] for nobody knew better than he that the Greeks expected their leaders to be clad impressively. Trelawny's jacket is mentioned in his *Recollections*, but there is a less familiar version of the incident written by him to William Rossetti, apparently in answer to an enquiry, on January 14th, 1878.

> Dear Rossetti,
>   On our voyage to Greece, I asked my Black man to bring me a parcel on deck which I had not opened; It contained a military Cavalry jacket that I had had from Vienna. They are the best military Tailors in Europe. I had not seen the tailor, nor had the tailor seen me, and I had neglected to try if it would fit. It was a dark green jacket, with a considerable quantity of braiding of the same colour, or black, I forget which; I could not get it on, and if I could, it would have been more like a straight waist-coat, that I could not have used my arms.
>   I threw it on deck, Byron, who was sitting near me, picked it up, and observed: 'That is just the sort of thing that I want, what have I got, Fletcher, to land with in Greece?'
>   'Nothing but your ordinary clothes.'
>   'Haven't I got a jacket?'
>   Fletcher: 'Only your old plaid one.'
>   Byron then tried on my jacket. 'It's a little too long in the arms,' he said,

---

[1] He had actually received the title of Cavaliere. Kirkup's and Trelawny's accounts of the sofa are in *Rossetti Papers* and Rossetti's *Athenaeum* article already quoted.

[2] If bought for Leigh Hunt, Shelley could not have been in the habit of constantly using it, as the legend claimed, since it would have been delivered to Byron's house and Shelley died at the time of the Hunt's installation there. Byron kept a sofa of Shelley's (see p. 214) but it would not answer to the description of one which Hunt had as a present from Mrs Shelley and disposed of on leaving Italy. Barry occupied Byron's villa with its furniture till after Hunt left Italy. Nobody seems to have considered the inherent improbability of writing to a man of ninety asking him to take the enormous trouble of dispatching a large piece of his furniture to England on the grounds that, after his approaching death, it might not be valued.   [3] Murray MSS. and Marchand.

'otherwise it exactly fits me, when we land at one of the Islands, get me one made exactly like it.'

'There is no Military Tailor,' I said, 'in the Ionian Islands, you are very welcome to that, I have plenty; Fletcher, put this with your Master's things.'

Fletcher said, 'It fits you exactly, and you never had anything so well made.' Byron thought so too; He landed with it in Greece, and never wore anything else. . . .

This is all I know about the Jacket.

Yours

E. J. Trelawny.[1]

The craving of Trelawny to be important, if not in the loftiest then in the paltriest affairs, which could produce so ludicrous a story is only equalled by the credulity of readers who could believe that Byron equipped himself for his Greek expedition with nothing but the helmet Trelawny had elsewhere ridiculed.

The provenance of this interesting jacket, which appears to be the one now on view at Newstead Abbey, is as follows. It was acquired by a Mr C. H. Fairbridge about 1854, and probably in South Africa, from a man named George Gordon Fletcher, a carpenter, who claimed to be, and doubtless was, Fletcher's son and Byron's godson. (Fletcher had two sons, and nothing is more likely than that his employer would have stood sponsor to one of them.) As the valet was given the whole wardrobe on his master's death, the survival of a few items from it in the possession of his son is not improbable.

At some time before he wrote his *Recollections*, Trelawny was asked if he could identify the garment, and it would seem he not only did so, but could not resist claiming to have bestowed it magnanimously on the needy peer—who 'had never had anything so well made'.[2] That Byron, admitted by Trelawny to be 'proud as Lucifer', would have thought it added to his dignity to wear clothing thrown on the deck by a member of his suite is a strain on probability.[3]

There would be little point in exposing the childish impostures of a

---

[1] TRELAWNY, *Letters*.

[2] Fairbridge, a friend of William Frederick Webb, who bought Newstead Abbey from Colonel Wildman in 1860, must have thought it appropriate to give him the relic of the earlier owner. The jacket is certainly of the style and workmanship of the early eighteen-twenties, and would have fitted a well-built man of five feet eight, but could not conceivably have been made by 'the best military Tailors in Europe' for a customer of six feet, who presumably would send measurements with the order.

[3] Byron accepted a pelisse from Colonel Duffie, an officer of the British garrison at Cephalonia, and several writers, not knowing of the extensive wardrobe he had brought with him, have conjectured that he must have worn it for landing at Missolonghi. A pelisse, however, at that date was a full-length overcoat, and Gamba says he had on 'a red uniform'. The colour of Colonel Duffie's gift is not mentioned in Byron's letter of thanks: it may well have been the long blue surtout in which he was depicted with his dog, Lion. See p. 185 and the reproduction facing page 438.

braggart if it were not for the favoured place which, until the last ten years, he occupied, and the mysterious credence that has been given to his statements even by those who have themselves taken their part in the researches that have shown him to be wholly untrustworthy. One might suppose that vividness was a justification for tampering with truth. Indeed, several of his apologists have said so.

'It would seem', writes Mary Shelley's biographer, Mrs Marshall, 'as if, for the conversations at least, Trelawny must sometimes have drawn upon his imagination as well as his memory; if so, it can only be replied that, by his success, he has triumphantly vindicated his artistic right to do so. . . .' What can this mean except that, as long as conversations sound credible, a biographer has the right to invent them?

The same author makes a still stranger excuse for other misrepresentations: '. . . If the history of Trelawny's exploits in Greece somewhat recalls the "Tarasconnade" of his early adventures, it at least puts a thrilling finish to a book it was hard to conclude without falling into bathos.'

The editor of his letters, H. Buxton Forman, averred:

> I for one have always believed in Trelawny as somewhat of the saga-man type, gifted by nature with the faculty of telling boldly and fluently the essential truth in all its important lines, without being scrupulously literal in the minute details of each minor fact.

As an example of departure from the 'minute details of minor fact', we may consider how meanly he shifted the onus of having designed the boat in which Williams and Shelley lost their lives on to the shoulders of his friend.

> Williams had brought with him, on leaving England, the section of a boat as a model to build from . . . believing it to be a marvel of nautical architecture. . . . Roberts, and the builder at Genoa, not approving, protested against it. You might as well have attempted to persuade a young man after a season of boating, or hunting, that he was not a thorough seaman and sportsman; or a youngster flushed with honours, from a university, that he was not the wisest of men. . . . He thought there was no vanity in his believing that he was as good a judge of a boat or horse as any man . . . so the boat was built according to his cherished model.[1]

The boat was built, in reality, according to Trelawny's cherished model.

> Trelawney [sic] called, and brought with him the model of an American schooner, on which it is settled with S[helley] & myself to build a boat 30 feet long, and T. writes to Roberts at Genoa to commence on it directly.[2]

[1] TRELAWNY, *Recollections*.
[2] JONES, *Shelley's Friends*. Williams's Journal, 15 Jan. 1822.

Trelawny's correspondence with Commander Roberts in Genoa confirms that he had the whole matter of the boat-building in hand from first to last, and so he admitted in a letter to Claire Clairmont soon after the tragedy: 'I induced Shelley to reside here,—and I designed the treacherous bark which proved his Coffin.'[1]

Such is the quality of the testimony which has been respectfully used by a large majority of Shelley and Byron biographers!

Other bold and fluent departures by Trelawny from scrupulously literal exactitude are that he read Byron's Memoirs, that it was a letter from him that made the Greek Committee enlist the poet in the Hellenic cause, that Byron clapped him on the shoulder congratulating him on his pagan incantations over Shelley's remains during the cremation, that he was determined to save Shelley's skull from being used by Byron as a drinking cup, that Byron in attempting to force a duel on the Captain of the Pope's guard, produced a Spanish rapier and tried to strike him in the dark, and that when asked by Trelawny to write a word or two that might call attention to Shelley's work, he replied that he would not do it lest comparison prove 'odorous'.[2]

No one who had studied Byron's generous conduct towards fellow writers could believe this last to be anything but a malicious fiction.[3] Selfish as he could be when his comfort was threatened, he had not a trace of professional jealousy. Nor was he either seer enough to anticipate that Shelley's fame would threaten his own, or naïve enough to say so. He might talk of having grown unpopular, but he still knew himself to be renowned on a scale no English poet had hitherto achieved in his lifetime. Even those who are still disposed to show a peculiar tenderness for the weaknesses of Trelawny have become loth to quote that particular dialogue; but there was no limit to the gullibility of partisans in the period when it was assumed that lovers of Shelley ought to be haters of Byron.

Trelawny was skilful enough to throw in amongst all his disparagements just enough little sops of praise to convey to simple-minded readers an air of objectivity (a strategy beyond Leigh Hunt's powers). And nobody thought of asking why a man who said he could hardly refrain from shouting with joy whenever he quitted Byron's 'gloomy hall' should have

---

[1] TRELAWNY, *Letters.* 26 Sept. 1822.

[2] Various passages from Trelawny's *Recollections* and *Records* and his talk noted by Mathilde Blind. There are independent statements by Byron and Leigh Hunt that Byron did not remain to witness Shelley's cremation. The incantations which are supposed to have evoked his praise are never mentioned in any of Trelawny's early narratives of that obsessing experience.

[3] In the Appendix to *The Two Foscari*, published several months before he first met Trelawny, Byron wrote calling *Queen Mab* 'a poem of great power and imagination', and adding that 'in common with all who are not blinded by baseness and bigotry', he highly admired that and Shelley's other publications.

gone back, day after day, to endure further voluntary misery, or why, on his own showing, he and Shelley should have been anxious to make so vain, cynical, pitiful, and played-out a character a member of their Spezia colony.

Of all who came in contact with Byron and Shelley, no one was ever so completely overwhelmed by the experience as Trelawny. His whole long life was devoted to reliving it, reshaping it as he would have liked it to be, and establishing himself as a being fitted for the high romance it had shed round him. Having private means which enabled him to spend a large part of his existence in a series of daydreams, he was spared from ever having to come to terms with reality. Yet by a strange paradox of character, there was a core of pungent realism in him which, if he could have turned it to account for self-knowledge instead of for deflating others, might have made him an honest man.

Thus when Claire Clairmont disclosed a crazy theory that her child was still alive and that Byron, having shut her up in a convent, had fabricated a tale of death out of spite, his rejoinder was couched in ruthlessly forthright terms.

> If I was in Italy I would cure you of your wild fancy regarding Allegra: I would go to the Convent—and select some plausible cranky old dried-up hanger-on of the convent about the age your child would now be, fifty-two, with a story and documents properly drawn up, and bring her to you—she should follow you about like a feminine Frankenstein—I cannot conceive a greater horror than an old man or woman that I had never seen for forty-three years claiming me as Father—do you see any of that age or indeed any age that you should like to have as son or daughter?[1]

The gift of producing searching flashes of truth—though almost never to illuminate himself—gave him the air of a rugged and candid creature, and was an inestimable advantage to him as a liar. He had a vein of grim humour, and seems to have been by no means unconscious of what he was about. 'The few that knew Shelley and have written have deified him —Byron's friends (if he *had any*) have bedevilled him.'[2] Such was his comment to Claire forty-five years after Byron's death. He was perfectly aware of his own great contribution both to the deification and the bedevilment.

The friendless *poseur* who bluffed his way into Byron's society in 1822, and traded on his name and prestige until Shelley's stock stood higher; who began his spurious autobiography with a gloating tale of how, in boyhood, he had mauled and slashed and hanged a pet raven; who traduced Claire Clairmont to curry favour with Byron,[3] and denigrated Byron to

---

[1] TRELAWNY, *Letters*. 27 Nov. 1869.   [2] Ibid. 17 Sept. 1869.
[3] Letter to Byron of 1 May 1822: Murray MSS.

gratify Claire Clairmont; who had rewarded with public abuse the kindnesses of Shelley's widow; lived on till 1881, still posing, still quarrelling,
still bragging, but hallowed by the aura of the legends he had helped to
create. He was painted by Millais as the dear old buccaneer of *The North
West Passage*, and, on dying at last, had his ashes deposited in Shelley's
grave. He was commemorated as 'Worldwide liberty's lifelong lover' in a
poem worthy of its subject by Swinburne.

In the last stanza Shelley is apostrophized:

> Heart of hearts, art thou moved not, hearing
>   Surely, if hearts of the dead may hear,
> Whose true heart it is now draws near?
>   Surely the sense of it thrills thee, cheering
>   Darkness and death with the news now nearing—
> Shelley, Trelawny rejoins thee here.

CHAPTER XIV

TWO COUNTESSES

Among the diverse figures in several countries who were affected by Byron's death, none is more sympathetic than Teresa Guiccioli, who had felt herself to be dying of grief at their parting after more than four years as lovers. She was then not quite twenty-four,[1] the same age as his wife had been on leaving him: but that was the sole point of resemblance between them. Warm, indulgent, sentimental, voluptuous, and brought up to a code of morals which, provided the graces were not abandoned, permitted a certain licence, she did not consign herself to lifelong celibacy. Yet, though she sought consolation in other love affairs and sometimes found it for a while, her memory of Byron remained vernal, and the two books she wrote about him in advanced years have a kind of enthusiasm that is sometimes endearingly, sometimes rather comically, girlish.

It is a remarkable feat for a woman of seventy to recapture the tremulous excitement of an enchanted phase of early youth, as Teresa does in *La Vie de Lord Byron en Italie*; and it seems to have been rendered possible by that inward sunshine of temperament that had dispelled, after the first phase of insecurity, all Byron's defensive cruelty, and attached—when she was forty-seven—the richest marquess in France as a devoted husband.

She had, of course, the advantage of having been the youngest (except her brother Pietro) of the circle in which she had attained notability—younger even than Mary Shelley, who was still a girl by today's reckoning, when Shelley was drowned. Moreover, she was very good-looking, and in the most engaging style, with hair of the true Titian red-gold, long eyelashes, beautiful teeth, and a delightful smile; and if her shortish too-rounded figure gave something for the captious to criticize, it seems to have detracted in no way from her feminine appeal.

Trelawny, when he was in the Pisa circle, thought she was 'certainly a lovely girl',[2] but later, when he had discovered that belittlement of Byron and everything that had been his was a shrewder line than hero worship, he changed his view, and pronounced a total condemnation—'sallow skinned her face without expression small harsh eyes—lardge mouth long bodyed and short limbed—wire haired in short a dumpy woman'.[3] He added, with that omniscience which has before been mentioned, that she 'spoke a provincial language like her brother'. Since

---

[1] Her birth date is slightly uncertain. Iris Origo gives it as either the end of 1799 or the beginning of 1800. She parted from Byron on July 13th, 1823.

[2] CLINE, Letter of 7 Feb. 1822.

[3] Marginal comment in his copy of Medwin's *Conversations*. Houston Library, Harvard University.

Trelawny could scarcely use the simplest phrase of Italian without error and had to have an interpreter in conversation (a fact Shelley biographers have always overlooked when quoting his fluent talk with a Genoese sailor watching Shelley set out on his last voyage) the value of the first disparagement may be gauged by the second.

Teresa's history has been written with rich documentation and in a most scholarly manner by Iris Origo, and the same ground will only be lightly skirted here. About two years after Byron's departure, she had a love affair with Lord Holland's son, Henry Edward Fox, handsome and slightly lame like Byron, but, although younger, a much more hard-bitten character. Though his first journal entries about her were in a carping and even caddish strain ('it is my art always to see the worst first', he acknowledged), he came to appreciate some of her qualities, her sincerity, good nature, 'and talents very superior to what I first supposed them to be'.[1] She was at a great disadvantage with him, because, through all the first stages of their *amour*, he was in love, though she did not know it, with another woman, Theresa Villiers, daughter of that Mrs Villiers who had so dexterously enjoyed the simultaneous friendship of Augusta Leigh and Lady Byron.

As she had resolutely refused to let Byron add a codicil in her favour to his will, her means were very much straitened, and her position made harder by the imprisonment of her liberal father, Count Ruggero Gamba. She surrendered to the pressing demands of the rich husband forty years her senior to return to his house, but the attempt to live a domestic life with him, avaricious and unpleasant as he was, led to a renewal of proceedings for separation by Papal Decree.

Tempered by her many reverses, but still lively, responsive, romantic, she came to England in 1832 with her elder brother Vicenzo. She was now able to speak English, and did so with absurd and captivating errors. Though a woman turned thirty was then considered to have launched upon middle age, she had lost none of her exuberance, and her feathered bonnet, like her impression of almost everyone she met, was rose-coloured. There was the greatest curiosity to see her, and among those who could afford not to be deferential to the moral conventions, she was the undoubted *lionne* of the season, 'caressed and honoured wherever she appeared' as one observer wrote who fell a little in love with her himself.[2] Her papers, now in the Biblioteca Classense at Ravenna, include all sorts of notes, invitations, verses, and flatteries.

She renewed her acquaintance with some of the English people she had met through Byron in Italy; but not with Moore, who was only in London a few days during her sojourn there, nor Hobhouse, who may

[1] Fox. 8 Mar. 1828.   [2] BERKELEY, Vol. III.

have remained annoyed with her for having made a contribution to Moore's book though he had requested her, through Barry, not to assist him. There were many attentions, however, from friends of Byron's earlier years, encountered on her pilgrimage to Newstead Abbey.

One who delighted in her was the brother of Byron's first woman confidante, the very intelligent and observant Miss Elizabeth Pigot of Southwell, who had encouraged his verse-writing and enjoyed his amateur theatricals in his Harrow and Cambridge days—a girl who was full of fun but perfectly decorous, and agreeably sympathetic but free from high-flown sentiment, the nearest approach to a character from Jane Austen's world whom it was his lot to know.

At eighteen years old, Byron had gone with John Pigot on a trip to Harrogate, where he had had the pleasure of cutting a dash in his own carriage, and sending the conveyance to bring one of his Cambridge professors to the theatre. The gay young medical student was now a respected doctor, but still, apparently, susceptible; for after basking in Teresa's radiance, he had written her a long and glowing letter, in which he assured her:

> I should indeed be insensible to everything lovely in person, and every-thing perfect in mind, manners, tact, and conversation, did I not feel and acknowledge the charms of the Countess Guiccioli. I should have felt mystified and disappointed had I found you otherwise, it would have been an impeachment of the taste and judgment of my lamented friend which I should have been most reluctant to be *forced* to admit.

He would not, he said, have trusted himself to utter in her presence all he had written lest she might have suspected 'the animal feelings' had influenced his language, but as they had met probably for the first and last time, he allowed himself to speak freely: and he signed himself her devoted friend.[1] She never replied—she was a dreadfully negligent correspondent—but she endorsed upon the letter a few modest words to the effect that it proved the qualities of Lord Byron. Though she mentioned Dr Pigot to John Murray as 'a very excellent and amiable person', he had been eclipsed for her by Byron's old school-fellow, Colonel Wildman of Newstead Abbey.

> I cannot express you how much gratified I have been with Colonel Wildman[s] reception, and with all the kind attentions he has bestowed upon me. He is a very amiable—and gallant man. And I cannot express how extremely glad I have been to see this interesting spot in the hands of a person who is so very sincerely attached to the memory of Ld Byron. In all the improvements he has done and is doing to the building (which are considerable and of a very refined taste) he seems rather to consult the intentions and wishes of the last possessor of the Abbey than his own.

[1] 6 Dec. 1832: Gamba Papers.

The *arms* of Ld Byron, his *likeness*, his *very name* engraved in a beech-
tree, together with that of his sister are shown by the Colonel to the visitors
of the Abbey with a kind of religious feeling which you may imagine what
sincere though melancholy pleasure has given to me![1]

It must have been a moving experience for her, who had known Byron
only as an exile, to see the ancestral home, losing nothing of its glory from
being in part a ruin, which had remained so deeply engraved on his
memory. His bedroom and several other apartments had been kept exactly
as he had left them, and she could gaze out of the windows upon the same
enchanting view of lake and lawn that had been part of the romantic
landscape of his life.

Of her visit to his grave at Hucknall Torkard she wrote nothing; but
it was not left unnoticed by the newspapers:

> The lady went into the church alone. From the door, and before even
> there was time to close it, the attendant saw the visitor prostrate herself on
> the flags which cover the remains of Byron. . . .
> She remained thus alone in the church, while the servant and the
> attendant waited outside for no very brief space of time—for an hour or
> more, I believe.[2]

Perhaps this was an exaggeration—the young women who, at nineteen, had kept Byron in a fever was a sufficiently strong personality to
inspire a good many high-coloured stories—but surely there must have
been a poignance in the sense of proximity to the lover whose caresses had
turned Venice 'without flowers, without trees, without perfumes, without
birds', into 'the abode of light—of life—paradise upon earth',[3] the sharer
of her utmost rapture and despair.

Among the high-lights of her English journey was a meeting with the
subject of his 'perpetual refrain'—his sister. It was arranged by John
Murray. Augusta, accustomed though she was to the adulteries of English
society, would hardly have been able to perform the daring act of receiving
Byron's foreign mistress—almost a *maîtresse en titre*, so famous had been
the connection—if it had not been for her break with Lady Byron which
had freed her, at any rate, from the necessity of deference to a sterner code
than her own.

Teresa could not and did not admit to disappointment but she may
have felt it. Few except Scrope Davies and Francis Hodgson had ever been
able to understand Byron's unwearied attachment to the shy, hesitant,
untidy, and confused Mrs Leigh; and now there was less to explain his

---

[1] 20 Dec. 1832: Murray MSS.
[2] *The Dial.* Undated contemporary cutting.
[3] GUICCIOLI, *La Vie.*

enthusiasm than ever. She had not worn well, she was dowdy,[1] and the weight of her cares had become crushing.

Georgiana's marriage, the only thing in a dozen years that had seemed to go right, had gone hideously and irrevocably wrong. A few months before the Countess Guiccioli came to England, Hobhouse, now made a rich baronet by his father's death, had briefly noted the dismal facts.

> I have been listening to a sad story from Colonel Leigh and his wife. Trevanion who married their eldest girl has seduced their second daughter 17 years old and had two children by her. The girl told her father that she and the young man read the bible every morning.
>
> Strange to say the poor wife still clings to her husband and says she will follow him to prison—and stranger still Mrs Leigh seemed to me to be afraid of using harsh measures with this pious profligate—The poor girl is very fond of the man—she is hid in London—her father carried her off with a constable and an attorney from Colerne in Wilts. The man is wandering about London trying to find her, with a pistol in his pocket.
>
> The young girl was Lord Byron's favourite niece. I recollect her a little blue eyed chubby cheeked creature whom he used to fondle. What a fate. There is retribution in this as ———— knows.[2]

It was not surprising that Augusta discountenanced harsh measures towards her son-in-law if they were likely to result in such public disgrace as would follow a prosecution for abduction or whatever other charge the enraged Colonel had in mind when he contemplated sending Trevanion to prison. Harsh measures were, in any case, against her timorous nature at all times.

Hobhouse's cryptic mention of 'retribution' might relate to some whisper that Trevanion had been her own lover,[3] or it might conceivably

---

[1] A miniature ascribed to Holmes of a dark young woman with an elaborate coiffure, and a profile by T. G. Wageman of a girl wearing a mantilla, both frequently reproduced as portraits of Augusta Leigh, cannot be deemed to represent her. The costume and hair style in each picture are the height of fashion for about 1830, and by that time she was forty-seven and neither elegant nor showy. Nor is there the slightest resemblance in either work to the authentic drawing of Augusta by Hayter, reproduced facing page 150. If the Wageman picture is of genuine Leigh provenance, which seems by no means established, it is possible that the sitter might be Medora, who was a precocious girl of sixteen in 1830, and said to be Spanish looking. Lady Wentworth told the present author that the attribution of the so-called Holmes miniature (shown in *Astarte*) was made by Lord and Lady Lovelace and herself in about 1905 without consideration of costume evidence. From the late 1820's onwards Augusta Leigh was estranged from Lady Byron and would not have given her a portrait.   [2] Hobhouse *Journals*, 1 July 1831.

[3] Byron's grandson heard this from his father, the 1st Earl of Lovelace, together with an assertion that she had 'promised him the possession of her other daughters as they grew up'. (*Lady Noel Byron*.) 'It is impossible', the 2nd Earl commented, 'to be absolutely certain of the falsehood of these charges.' The difficulty of proving a negative is notorious, but as there is no *contemporary* evidence even of gossip on the subject, let alone foundation for gossip, and as the accuser was the unbalanced and hysterical Medora Leigh, whose source of information was Henry Trevanion himself, it hardly merits serious consideration. Why should a woman who has a seductive young man for her lover raise heaven and earth, and get into debt for years, to send him away married to her daughter?

be an allusion to a suspicion that she had set an ill example by having some other lover; for example, the Colonel D'Aguilar who had caused the rift between her and Douglas Kinnaird and who, when discussing her financial situation with Hobhouse, had actually, to his astonishment, shed tears.[1] It might, on the other hand, take its meaning from some misconduct of Colonel Leigh's that was known to him: and this is much more likely, for, although in his diary entries about Mrs Leigh, he spoke of her great imprudence in monetary affairs, he never let fall the faintest shadow of a criticism of her morals. Nor in those pages, which contain so many revelations, did he even recognize the existence of a rumour that Medora Leigh was Byron's child.

By the early summer of 1832, when Augusta and Teresa had their meeting, the situation had gone from bad to worse. The knavish Trevanion had eloped with Medora to France, leaving his wife and three legitimate children wholly dependent on the already bankrupt Leighs—dependent, in fact, on Augusta, since Colonel Leigh, who had vigorously opposed this marriage, neither could nor would do anything: and though there had been no open publicity, the scandal was pretty widely known. Whether in their talk of three hours it was mentioned, or whether Teresa heard of the disaster elsewhere, it was doubtless that she had in mind when she wrote to John Murray:

> If you happen to see Mrs Leigh do me the favour to tell her how much I regret not to have seen her from a so long time—and present her my best compliments. To say you the truth I fear that in the present state of her domestic annoyances to *receive visits* would be to her rather a troublesome than an agreable thing, and for this reason only I differed [*sic*] day after day to call again upon her. . . . I hope to see her once more when I come back to London. . . .[2]

But it does not appear that she ever saw the unhappy Augusta again.

Teresa's charm of manner drew endearments from almost all her female, and gallantries from her male, correspondents. Among these none took greater pains to be of service to her than John Murray, who even waived the strict rules of propriety so that his wife and daughters might meet her. They dined, they went to the theatre, they exchanged gifts. She thanked him for volumes 'elegantly bounded', and sent him a play by her stepson, apologizing that it was 'non binded'. He gave her a present, unnamed, of which she said: 'His elegance and richness would be worth to be offered to a king!'[3]

When that 'excellent creature' and '*hearty Byronian*', Miss Pigot,

[1] Hobhouse *Journals*, 22 Nov. 1829.   [2] Nov. 1832: Murray MSS.
[3] John Murray's letters are preserved with the Gamba Papers, the Countess Guiccioli's with the Murray MSS.

asked him for a lock of the Countess's hair, which was given, Mr Murray wrote to say he would not forward it till he had one for himself.[1] He begged her to sit for her picture so that he might have it engraved; and on the failure of a remittance she expected to arrive from Italy, dispatched to her, in a characteristic gesture, a bank draft—'conceiving that there cannot be the slightest impropriety in making the publisher of Lord Byron the Guiccioli's Banker, as well as, dear Madame, Her faithful servant'.[2] She would not accept the offering—but it was, of course, an enhancement of cordiality. She promised, when she went back to Italy, to assist him with securing views associated with Byron for a set of illustrations he was planning: and the promise was kept.

Either as a courtesy or because she had several original manuscripts to compare with his fair copies, he gave her a number of proofs to read for a new edition of Byron's works he then had in hand, and as it was combined with the biography, he offered her the chance of altering anything distasteful in what Moore had written. For all her amiability, she could be outspoken and she replied that she thought it highly indelicate—indeed '*remarkable* and *disgusting*'—for Moore to have used such terms as 'enamoured', 'lover', and 'despair' in describing the initial difficulties of her situation with Byron. 'So if you may dear Mr Murray I shall be very obliged to you to see these words suprimed.'[3] She had forgotten that she herself had supplied Moore with an astonishingly candid narrative of her love affair—though it is true she could not have expected to see her name and the names of her family naked on the printed page. Her principal requirements were that the word 'lover', used on a number of occasions, might be changed to 'friend', and 'love' to 'devotion'. (She also took two years off her age, an understandable vanity in a period of almost spiteful cruelty to declining youth.)

The immense, unparalleled wave of prudery we call Victorian cast many premonitory shadows before, and was not solely a British manifestation. Teresa had written her record for Moore in 1827: in 1832 that had already begun to seem an indiscretion. By the 1840's such reminiscences were deemed to be in very bad taste, and by the 1860's a shameful insult to morality. Mrs Beecher Stowe was enabled to pretend that it was the disgraceful effrontery of the poet's mistress in publishing a book that caused her to write her sensational disclosures on his married life.[4]

Teresa had not read Moore's work before coming to England, and its freedom in every way surprised and dismayed her. 'I cannot express you how sorry I am for the want of delicacy and I fear of real friendship on the

---

[1] It is in the Murray archives.   [2] 9 Nov. 1832: Gamba Papers.
[3] Oct. 1832: Murray MSS. Suprimed—*supprimé*.
[4] Her article was in the editor's hands before she had seen the book or the reviews.

Teresa, Marquise de Boissy, aged about 59

part of the Biographer. . . . But the faults are spread all over the entire
work—and how to correct them? It would be as to try to correct the faults
of a building whose greatest fault lies in the foundament—it would be
much better to throw it down.'[1]

Later she concluded:

> This work of Moore is a great Magazine—where a quantity of *useless*,
> *harmful* and *good* things are lying together in a confused manner. Certainly
> it cannot be denied that there are parts in this work which does honour both
> to the author and the *caracter* of Ld Byron—but how many more injurious
> to the memory of our noble friend. I like to believe the most perfect good
> intention presided [over] the composition of this work: but then there has
> been a want of prudence and skill which is scarcely to be believed in such a
> great talent as Mr Moore is.[2]

All this was very much what Hobhouse thought—except that he did
not credit Moore with perfect good intentions.

The biography, said the Countess, would always remain 'a painful
enygma' to her—'but I can now only limit myself to *wish* and *to do* all
who is in my power in order to raise the opinion of the many excellencies
and virtues of my noble friend and that will be the object of my life
henceforth.'[3]

Teresa was much too happily balanced a woman to make any such
endeavour the object of her life, but she did preserve her loyalty in its
pristine lustre through successive experiences of reading all that ill nature
could suggest about Byron's feelings towards her. She sturdily maintained
—and justly—that he wrote and said things 'to relieve his mind' which
he was sorry for afterwards, and which it was foolish to take seriously. She
found excuse for the letters in which he had joked about his rôle of
cavaliere servente to her: 'One might have said that he felt a sort of
shame, that in revealing himself as good-natured he was making a
confession of weakness—of wanting that virility of spirit he so much
admired.'[4] It was a great defect in him, she admitted mildly.

Her diagnosis was not far wide of the mark. We cannot doubt, now his
conduct is laid bare, that in the first years of their *liaison* he was passionately in love with her, and it was precisely during the period when her
hold on him was strongest that he tried to turn his captivity to a jest, or
fretted because 'a man should not consume his life at the side and on the
bosom of a woman, and a stranger', a lament significant chiefly for the
important reservation that soon follows: 'To leave, or to be left would
at present drive me quite out of my senses.'[5]

She had so much instinctive knowledge of Byron's reactions that she

---

[1] Oct. 1832: Murray MSS.   [2] Ibid. 4 Nov. 1832.   [3] Ibid.
[4] GUICCIOLI, *La Vie*.   [5] *Correspondence*. Letter to Hobhouse, 23 Aug. 1819.
L.L.B.—2 G

might even have brought herself to forgive the grosser observations in letters she was spared from seeing, recognizing them as a kind of revenge for the hold she exercised over him. She never allowed her feelings for him to be influenced by the hints, reiterated in more than one publication, that he had gone to Greece simply to make a break with her—a theory which in its belittlement of both parties was most satisfying to malice.

That he had grown bored with his situation in Italy, that he longed for a less irregular domestic life, with children about him and without the complication of the resentful old Count Guiccioli in the background, cannot reasonably be denied; nor that in certain moods he gave expression to his restiveness. But the terms in which he addressed Teresa from Greece have, in their very casualness, the quality of a settled and secure affection and he took their reunion for granted:

> Pray be as cheerful and tranquil as you can—and be assured that there is nothing here that can excite anything but a wish to be with you again. . . .
>
> When we meet again (if it please God) I hope to tell you several things that will make you smile. I kiss your Eyes (occhi) and am most affectly a.a. in e. + + + +[1]
>
> I was a fool to come here but being here I must see what is to be done.
>
> If we were not at such a distance, I could tell you many things that would make you smile—but I hope to do so at no very long period. Pray keep well and love me as you are beloved by yours ever a.a. + + + in e.[2]
>
> You may be sure that the moment I can join you again will be as welcome to me as at any period of our recollection. There is nothing very attractive here to divide my attention—but I must attend to the Greek Cause both from honour and inclination. . . .
>
> I wish . . . that I might return quietly to Italy—and talk over with you *our*, or rather Pietro's adventures—some of which are very amusing—as also some of the incidents of our voyages and travels.—But I reserve them in the hope that we may laugh over them together at no very remote period. . . .
>
> Ever my dearest T. il tuo A.A. in E. + + +[3]
>
> I do not write to you letters about politics—which would only be tiresome, and yet we have little else to write about—except some private anecdotes which I reserve for 'viva voce' when we meet—to divert you at the expense of Pietro and some others. . . .
>
> Salute Costa and his lady—and Papa and Olimpia and Giulia and Laurina—and believe me—dearest T. t[uo] A.A.—in E. + + +[4]

These are the letters of a husband rather than a lover, a husband whom it would not do to trust under temptation, but who is neither in-

---

[1] ORIGO. 11 Sept. 1823. Plus signs were Byron's amorous symbols, 'a.a. in e.' the abbreviation used between them for 'friend and lover for ever' (*Amico ed amante in eterno*).
[2] Ibid. 7 Oct. 1823.   [3] Ibid. 29 Oct. 1823.   [4] Ibid. 17 Mar. 1824.

sensible to his obligations nor unwilling to return them with fondness; the letters of a man whose passion has been sobered by time and usage but not extinguished by disillusionment. He had written a long while before to Augusta:

> It is nearly three years that this 'liaison' has lasted. I was dreadfully in love—and she blindly so—for she has sacrificed everything to this headlong passion. . . . I can say that, without being so *furiously* in love as at first, I am more attached to her than I thought it possible to be to any woman after three years . . . and have not the least wish nor prospect of separation from her.[1]

If since then some of the ties had frayed and weakened, others must have acquired the strength of a habit which, if he had lived, he might have been glad enough to resume.

The conjectures of various biographers that Byron had hankered after a reconciliation with his wife hurt Teresa profoundly—perhaps that was the bitterest thing she ever had to read about him; but whether through pride, vanity, or generosity, she managed to sustain her faith and, sentimental as she was, there were, in her ultimate reminiscences, some judgments of great acuteness. At least, she knew Byron for a man whose natural element was gaiety,[2] not gloom, and his many references to their laughing together suggest that, in the words of her biographer, 'if he came back to anyone, he would come back to her'.[3]

'Byron was certainly tired of her,' wrote Hobhouse, who had never approved of the relationship, 'yet in a letter to Barry from Cefalonia he said he had left his heart in Italy.'[4]

Byron was impressed by the truth of La Rochefoucauld's maxim that in the misfortunes of a friend there is something that does not displease us. There seems also to be an unconscious satisfaction in the breaking-up of a friend's love affair, an unconscious dissatisfaction in its continuance: and if this can be felt even by fundamentally benevolent persons, how much does it rejoice the illiberal to assume that all has ended humiliatingly for one or both parties! Learning English was a doubtful asset to Teresa, who had to grow accustomed to reading descriptions of herself written as bluntly as if she had been dead fifty years.

There was, for example, the hardy John Galt. At the date of her first English visit, she had only managed to familiarize herself with four or five of the books on Byron issued since his death—her brother's of course, and Dallas's and Medwin's, both well-known in Continental editions, Stanhope's, and one by an author she named Bridgerton,[5] presumably Sir Egerton Brydges. She had no idea that John Galt, begging the privilege of being introduced to her, had published a book derogatory on the whole to

[1] LOVELACE, *Astarte* (1921 edition). 5 Oct. 1821.
[2] Letter of 15 Jan. 1859: Gamba Papers.   [3] ORIGO.
[4] Hobhouse *Journals*, 3 Oct. 1826.   [5] 4 Nov. 1832: Murray MSS.

Byron and thoroughly objectionable in its references to herself; any more than that Thomas Campbell, assiduously paying court, offering to be her cicerone in London, had produced a fulsome article about Byron's vices and Lady Byron's trials and virtues two years before in the *New Monthly Magazine*.

Galt had written soliciting from his patroness, Lady Blessington, 'the great favour' of allowing him to call when the Countess Guiccioli might next be at her house. He considered his Life of Byron gave him 'a legitimate cause to seek to know' the Countess, a typically egregious claim, since in that book he had spoken of her as one whom Byron had left destitute, 'his attachment to her having perished', and had added to the fourth edition, just appearing, a note that she had recently been jilted by another English nobleman! He also reprinted Leigh Hunt's unflattering picture of her, as one 'compressing herself artificially into dignity and elegance, and fancying she walked, in the eyes of the whole world, a heroine by the side of a poet'—a heroine prematurely aged by ill usage. Lady Blessington, who wrote much about her own delicate sensibilities, but never displayed any in her conduct, had no hesitation in giving Galt what he called 'an opportunity of personally estimating those attractions which were commonly supposed to be so extraordinary'.

I found her appearance exactly what a friend described who had seen her in Italy. . . . She was better, however, than Mr Leigh Hunt would lead one to suppose when he speaks of her as 'a buxom parlour boarder', although not that 'creature of the element' which enamoured report had delighted to adorn. Perhaps I saw her at first to some disadvantage, for she was exposed to a trying contrast by being seated beside the 'most gorgeous Lady Blessington,'

Her bust reminded me of the description of Dudu in Don Juan; but her general figure was 'of stature low,' and except when sitting she was not particularly graceful. But, though uncommonly fair, I did not think her beauty very brilliant: she possessed, however, one peculiar charm which must have had great influence on a man of Byron's temperament, much naïveté; I think in this respect, more than any other young woman I ever met with, scattering remarks of which she did not herself appear sensible of their force and engaging simplicity.

In manners, she partook of that ease and temperate gaiety which distinguishes the Italian ladies from those of every other country: but in this she was not in any degree superior to many women here. . . . She was, certainly, unaffected without vulgarity, and though always natural, there was occasionally in her naïveté, what the admirers of artificial proprieties might have thought not sufficiently sustained, inflexions liable to be misrepresented by the invidious as allied to silliness: she had, however, none of that quality, yet she may have allowed sayings to escape, sometimes, more pleasing than admirable.

Her regard for the memory of Lord Byron was openly professed, and by

those who knew her best was deemed sincere; but I have heard it said that
she reverenced his Lordship rather too much to love him well: it may be so,
but we know that the fondest female affection may exist along with great
mental admiration. There was a little seasoning of enthusiasm about the
Guicciolli [*sic*] and the indiscriminate might have imagined the expressions
of it as too intellectual to indicate passion.[1]

Who would think the unsuspecting sitter for this sketch would be able
to read it in print within a year?

In 1832, unknown to Teresa, Lady Blessington was on the verge of
serializing, in the *New Monthly* (now edited by Edward Lytton Bulwer),
the so-called Journal of her conversations with Byron, later to be published
in book form, and to become by far the most successful and profitable
work of its author and the only one—apart from *The Idler in Italy* in
which Byron also figures—to enjoy a more than ephemeral existence. It
must have been somewhat disconcerting to her to learn that Mme
Guiccioli was to be in London when the first chapters were about to
appear, for the Italian countess might well be disposed to say that the
English one had had no great success with the poet, and had not been in
his company nearly so much as her book would lead readers to suppose.

But in the course of a career of social climbing, Lady Blessington had
become extremely *rusée*—it was through a little ruse that she had
managed to meet Byron—and, by showering attentions on the visitor,
gushing over her, making her a pet and a confidante (and behind her back
a jest), she manœuvred her firmly into a position from which, when the
offending instalments came out, it was hardly possible to enter into any
hostilities.

Lady Blessington, like Trelawny, with whom she got on exceedingly
well, took whatever attitude to Byron seemed to suit the taste of the
company she was in, while retaining always so much of basic animosity as
to convey the most damaging impression possible. If we except Mme
Swanton Belloc, who never saw him, hers was the first publication about
Byron by a woman, as well as the first by anyone who was taken—outside
the ranks of the aristocracy—to be an aristocrat, a leader of fashion. It was
therefore welcomed with a new access of curiosity and read with amaze-
ment. It appeared that 'the Noble Poet' was vulgar, lacking in taste,
unrefined, flippant, easily put out of countenance, and shockingly ill-
dressed—not on a par at all with anyone so grand as Lord and Lady
Blessington. The book was the first of the patronizing biographies, and set
a tone which lingered until well into our own century.

Leigh Hunt had said Byron had no address, no conversation, but the
same remark might have been made about any lumpish peer; and the

1 GALT, *Autobiography*, 1833.

tireless animus in evidence throughout his pages revealed his sense of having pitted himself against a formidable adversary: Dallas and many others had uttered their censures on the score of religion and morality: Galt had told how he 'relished' seeing the young lord's pride, as he supposed, mortified, but that was sheerly because that pride was high. It remained for Lady Blessington to disclose how, judged by the standards of the exalted circles in which she herself held sway, 'poor Byron', as she called him, was really rather a pitiable figure.

Nothing could be less in keeping with her attitude during her pursuit of him. There have been preserved upwards of seventeen notes and letters from her and her husband to Byron,[1] and two from their companion Count D'Orsay. Their tone from beginning to end is wooing, adulatory. The initiative in all approaches was taken by them, and if Byron's letters are set beside theirs, it will be seen that his are without exception answers to requests, acknowledgments of some attention, or excuses for not accepting invitations; and that there is a combination of politeness and elusiveness in them which must have been most baffling.

But even if she had not been aware, dimly or vividly, of having somehow been frustrated by him, her book would still have had its pitying and patronizing slant, because that was her style—her way of keeping up her pretensions to status. The *Conversations* are, in the modern meaning of the term, a dexterous piece of journalism, the product of a born gossip columnist's skill in providing exactly those touches which convey to the would-be sophisticated a belief that they are being given 'the lowdown'. The hypothesis many critics have offered—including one or two who knew her—is that she wrote with the piqued vanity of one who had hoped to make a conquest of Byron: but, more than sexual vanity, her social vanity needed its outlet. Her state of mind must be gauged, not merely from the two books in which she exploited Byron, but from the whole body of her writings, which are one long sustained and often embarrassingly transparent attempt to persuade the reader of her aristocratic dignity and splendour, the purity of her moral views, her fitness to judge conduct.

She had, as might be guessed from such a preoccupation, much to live down. Given her determination to be deemed a leader of the *beau monde*, the *ton*, the *élite* (she rarely used an English word where a French one would be more *mondaine*), she had to create an illusion that her lineage was ineffably noble, her background that of a rich and pampered society woman.

Her father, who was a country gentleman, occupied with field sports and agricultural pursuits . . . descended from an ancient family in the County of Waterford. Her mother also belonged to a very old Roman Catholic family

[1] Murray MSS.

. . . her genealogical tree was preserved with a religious veneration. . . . 'My ancestors, the Desmonds,' were her household gods and their deeds and prowess were her favourite theme.[1]

So began one of the contemporary sketches of Lady Blessington, whose father, seen with a less visionary eye, was a small-scale Tipperary land-owner practising the trade of a corn-chandler. He had abandoned the Catholic faith to persecute Irish rebels and thereby acquired a magistrate's post from which he was afterwards removed as unfit for office. The religious veneration in which the Desmonds were held never led to any recognition from other ancient families, though it fostered a snobbery which was to have a marked influence on English fashion journalism.

Having lived down her father, Lady Blessington had to cope with the fact of her first marriage. Of this catastrophe she spoke, so far as is known, only to her friend and biographer, Dr Madden. She had been, she told him, sold into matrimony in earliest youth against her will and without her consent. The man, a Captain Farmer, with whom her father had concluded the bargain, was violently insane, beat her, and sometimes starved her, and made it necessary for her to leave him in three months. There was some romanticizing in this account—Farmer's relatives pro-nounced it entirely untrue—but it was needful to evoke a favourable atmosphere for considering the next nine years of her life, nearly the most lived-down episode of all. Madden simply but meaningfully remarks that it is a period about which record is silent. The contemporary sketch-writer already quoted puts it thus:

> Mrs Farmer resided principally in England in the most complete seclusion, indulging to the utmost her natural love of study, to which she devoted the greater portion of her time. Circumstances having at last induced her to fix upon London as a residence, she established herself in a house in Manchester Square where, with her brother Robert . . . she remained for a considerable period, enjoying in his society and her favourite pursuits a degree of tran-quillity which, after the stormy scenes of her early years, was positive happiness. . . .
>
> Hosts of would-be admirers sought to win her favour, but her dignity and reserve forbade any but the most respectful attentions, and drove away idle flatterers, whose ill-advised gallantries met with the coldest rebuffs.
>
> She received at her house those only whose age and character rendered them safe friends. . . .

No explanation is ventured by this reverential writer as to how the runaway wife, daughter of a now ruined corn-chandler, managed to acquire, after her years of studious seclusion, a residence in one of London's most fashionable squares, nor how she came to be surrounded by the hosts

---

[1] Unidentified periodical.

of admirers whose ill-advised gallantries she rebuked. From more prosaic sources comes the report that, after a succession of transient affairs, she lived, until his money ran out, with a Captain Jenkins, and that, like Lady Hamilton, a still more celebrated exponent of the same kind of career, she changed hands ultimately for a very large financial consideration. She had become a notably handsome and accomplished woman, and the newly created Earl of Blessington was said to have given Captain Jenkins ten thousand pounds cash down for her.

The earl, a widower in his thirties, had a very bad squint and drank immoderately, but he was lavish and amiable, and his income was £30,000 a year. He was also sufficiently unconventional, when Captain Farmer died through a fall from a window in King's Bench Prison, to make the widow his second wife. Such an elevation must have seemed like a dream to one for whom rank and money were an obsession; but the portals of society turned out to be closed to her. Attractive and adroit as she was, the rules were remorselessly applied. She could be called upon by men of any rank, she could receive and visit such ladies of lower rank as, for the sake of knowing so resplendent a person, were not too finicky about reputation, she could go to any place to which the entry was achieved by payment: but never could she cut a figure at the balls, the dinners, of the great hostesses whose invitations were an accolade; never could she set foot across the sacred threshold of Almack's, or join, at the end of the London season, the round of house parties at stately country seats. It was not only the matter of her former morals, which, as long as she had not figured in a divorce suit, might have been benignly forgotten: it was the combination of these with showiness and bad breeding.

In later days, when she had come to terms with her lot, and was lion-hunting instead of tuft-hunting, her skill as a hostess won praise (though even the partial Madden admitted her turn for throwing ridicule on absent guests); but as late as 1839, Greville described her as 'ignorant, vulgar, and commonplace;'[1] and in the first years of her grandeur, her propensity to show off gave rise to many criticisms which were not invariably the outcome of envy.

No fortune could have long remained equal to the spendthrift mania of the Blessingtons. Lord Blessington's extravagance, which had been extreme before the marriage, grew feverish after it, for his wife's greed for luxury, as may be seen in her pseudo-journals, *The Idler in Italy* and *The Idler in France*, was insatiable. 'No expense spared' was the recurring theme of those books, stated sometimes in so many crude words, and most patently devised as a counterpoint to the voices of disapprobation. As early as 1820, only two years after the marriage, the absentee landlord was

[1] Greville. 17 Feb.

raising large amounts of money on his Irish estates, and a question arose of his getting a loan from an old acquaintance—Lord Byron. He approached Douglas Kinnaird.

The £60,000 settled on Lady Byron was in Government funds, yielding a very low rate. Byron, who had the income for life, considered that suitable mortgages would be a much better investment, and Kinnaird was of the same opinion. The proposition was that £30,000 should be lent to Lord Portsmouth and the other £30,000 to Blessington, whose security, Kinnaird told him, was 'a good & unencumber'd title to the estate in question' (in Dublin) and a rental 'ample to doubly cover the interest of the Mortgage'.[1] Since the approval of Lady Byron's trustees would have to be obtained, the project formed the subject of four of Byron's rare letters to his wife.

> The Mortgage as represented to me is most eligible—and has my full consent and concurrence—but yours is as necessary as mine—so do let us concur for once—if we never agreed before—for the singularity of the thing as well as the importance of the object. . . .
>
> Your consent will save me the horrors of a journey to England which I assure you I contemplate with the most repugnant feelings. Since I was twenty-one I have passed six years out of the eleven in other countries so that I am as much expatriated in habits or in climate, and should feel hardly less strange in London than in Pekin.———
>
> I perceive that the King is dead—but I shall not trouble you with my company at the Coronation—unless compelled by business to return. . . .
>
> I recommend this affair to your earnest consideration—. . . .
>
> P.S. . . . Recollect one thing only—that in all acts of Settlement I gave you *every advantage*—that you will be a great gainer by my decease—and that by yours I stand where I am—only in that I acted fairly and liberally in such transactions previous to our marriage—recollect all this—when the time comes—and then do not forget my *Sister Augusta—and her children*—were I but sure of this—I should be relieved from a weight that was upon my heart like lead when I was ill three months ago—it was my last request on leaving England—and it would be my last on leaving this world.[2]

These were scarcely sentiments to render Lady Byron amenable to the plan, even though the postscript included an assurance that he could never contemplate the idea of her death without a heavy heart, and hoped he would rather precede than follow her. She was, moreover, much annoyed at his representing his marriage settlement as liberal. In April he approached her again, somewhat more doubtfully, for Hanson was heartily against the business:

> In February last, at the suggestion of Mr Douglas Kinnaird, I wrote to you on the proposition of the Dublin investment. . . . I now enclose you a

---

[1] 1 Feb. 1820: Murray copies.   [2] 20 Feb. 1820: Lovelace Papers.

statement of Mr Hanson's & to say the truth—I am at a loss what to think or to decide upon between such very opposite views of the question.

Perhaps you will lay it before your trustees. . . . Excuse all this trouble—but as it is your affair as well as mine—you will pardon it. . . .[1]

Blessington and Portsmouth, however fundamentally sound their property might be, were not names to appeal to Lady Byron and her advisers. In October Kinnaird had to announce that they refused to transfer money to a mortgage investment. Byron wrote to her again assuring her that she could not count on Government funds because 'the Exasperation of men's minds is extreme and general. . . . The Spanish and Neapolitan Revolutions have changed every thing'; and trying to give her some notion of the unsettled and rebellious state of Italy under Austrian domination.

The suspicion of the government here is extreme—even of strangers—(most of whom have retired) they sent an order the other day to *disarm my servants*—(who by the way did not carry arms)—imagine what must be the state of things when a solitary stranger puts upon them such precautions!—I answered them that they might make what regulations they chose for such servants as were Papal—but that they should not disarm *me*—unless by actual force—in a country where they 'shoot a man a week'—like Bob Acres 'in the country.' They said no more—but there is a general espionage. . . .[2]

Almost everyone thought of Byron's belief that he was spied on as an egocentric delusion, but it is now known, from Austrian and Italian archives, that he was indeed the object of constant police vigilance. It all seemed very far-fetched to the English recipients of his letters, and his stories of Austrian tyranny, of being watched, and of upheavals that would make gilt-edged securities insecure, exasperated Augusta Leigh particularly and made her write one of her most treacherous letters to Lady Byron:

. . . I *cannot* at some moments resist laughing—it does appear so *very* odd sitting quietly by one's own fire side—not dreaming of such things to read all this vehemence—& think of a person *clawing & scratching* for what he can get! . . . Surely *if not insanity*, it is *akin* to it! I begin to think South America wd be the best thing for I see no peace in *this* quarter of the Globe—perhaps ye extreme change might be of use—God knows! it is *very* melancholy![3]

Ironically enough, while Augusta was ridiculing him thus bitterly, his own letters to the same recipient continued to plead and to exhort on her behalf.

And if in these '*kittle* times' any accident should occur which may throw the settlement into your own hands—be kind to my sister and her children—as I have all along entreated you—though apparently to no great purpose.[4]

[1] *L. & J.* 6 Apr.   [2] 25 Oct. 1820: Lovelace Papers.
[3] Ibid. 24 Jan. 1821. Byron had toyed with a plan for going to South America.
[4] Ibid. 25 Oct. 1820.

This at any rate drew an answer, a few cool and distant but apparently, sincere words from Lady Byron herself, the first he had had for years promising kindness to Augusta and her children[1]—a promise which in after years Augusta's conduct deprived her of the 'opportunity of *acting* up to'. By a coincidence, it is dated December 10th, the day on which Byron directed another communication to her.

> About six weeks ago—more or less—I wrote to you requesting your assent & that of the trustees to the transfer of property in a Loan to Lord Blessington. Since that letter was written—I have had an intimation from Mr Kinnaird that the deed had been examined by Counsel and approved. . . .[2]

He begged her to sell out of the 'funds', and to give her some idea of the menacing aspect of European affairs, he told her of the assassination of an Austrian Military Commandant which had taken place with a sawn-off gun so near his own door that the victim, whom no one else would risk aiding, had died on Fletcher's bed. It was an affair which had impressed him tremendously and which he mentioned, without making any effect, to a number of his English correspondents who were living snugly and smugly by their own firesides. His alarmism was not unjustified, but it was a generation too early.

Byron's attempts to humanize his letters on business matters to his wife by giving utterance to feelings and opinions and telling her pieces of news, were painfully ill-judged and occasioned many sarcastic comments on the other side; but even without these ineptitudes, her trustees would never have recommended the Blessington loan, which fell through after protracted negotiations.

Lady Blessington was a shrewd, materialistic woman who could not have failed to understand that the scale on which she and her husband were living was making heavy inroads on his fortune; and the abortive transaction with Byron had probably not been concealed from her. The knowledge that there had been a question of £30,000 between them, and that to him their parade of inexhaustible opulence was entertaining rather than convincing, may have added to the uneasiness occasioned by his cool reception at their first visit; and later, there was the further uneasiness of remembering Lord Blessington's dishonoured cheque for the *Bolivar*,[3] and that bill for four hundred guineas being presented time after time by Barry. To be uncomfortable on any score was not to be borne without compensation by a woman so precariously poised as Lady Blessington.

That her reception had been cool her biographer easily guessed: and his observation that she was mortified by finding Byron not 'so highly

---

[1] Lovelace, *Astarte*.   [2] Lovelace Papers.   [3] See p. 216.

gratified' to meet her as she had expected is shown to have been sound by the diary of one who was present on that occasion,—Lord Holland's son, Henry Edward Fox.

> I went to Ld Byron's at two o'clock. . . . To my great dismay the family of Blessington were forcing their way, and his Lordship had already gained admittance. I found Ld Byron very much annoyed at their impertinence and rather nervous.
>
> He received me most kindly, and indeed his good nature to me has always been most marked and flattering. . . . D'Orsay was with them, and to my surprise I found that Ld Byron could not, or would not, talk French. While the B[lessington]s staid, the conversation rather flagged.
>
> As soon as they were gone he talked most agreeably and most openly on every subject. . . . He was sorry not to converse with D'Orsay. Having lived so long out of the world it was rather an amusement to him to see what sort of an animal a dandy of the present day is.[1]

This account, not published until a hundred years after the event, dovetails perfectly with Teresa's, and not at all with Lady Blessington's. Teresa declared that when Lord Blessington paid his unheralded call at the villa near Genoa, the weather was very threatening. While he lingered, the expected downpour came on, and Byron was surprised and by no means pleased to be told that Lady Blessington and her sister, Miss Power, were sitting outside in a carriage. He could do nothing else than ask them into the house.[2] Henry Fox arrived, it is apparent, before they came in and must therefore have been an eye-witness to their entrance. 'The lady's plot' to be caught in the rain was perhaps an exaggeration of Teresa's. The weather may have served her accidentally, but she was so pushing that, if it had not, some other device would have been brought into play. 'She forces herself into the correspondence or acquaintance of all who have (unhappily for them) acquired any sort of fame', Fox wrote in his ruthless, perpetually exasperated way.[3] He was to have many opportunities of watching her at it, including an occasion when she turned up uninvited at a ball given by the ex-Queen of Holland.[4]

Lady Blessington always represents Byron as making the advances.

> Lord Byron requested to be presented to me; which led to Lord Blessington's avowing that I was in the carriage at the gate, with my sister. Byron immediately hurried out into the court, and I, who heard the sound of steps, looked through the gate, and beheld him approaching quickly towards the carriage without his hat, and considerably in advance of the other two gentlemen. . .
>
> In the vestibule stood his chasseur, in full uniform, with two or three other domestics: and the expression of surprise visible in their countenances

---

[1] Fox. 31 Mar. 1823. The entry is misdated by one day, his visit and the Blessington's having taken place on 1 Apr.
[2] GUICCIOLI, *La Vie*.   [3] Fox. Early 1825.   [4] Fox. 16 Feb. 1828.

evinced that they were not habituated to see their lord display so much cordiality to visitors.

Our visit was a long one; for when we proposed abridging it, he so warmly urged our stay. . . . He expressed warmly, at our departure, the pleasure which our visit had afforded him—. . . . We are to see him to-morrow at our hotel; for he has asked at what hour we would admit him.[1]

This was written, or written up, in 1839, sixteen years later, and it is not in key with Fox's more immediate impressions, nor her own of 1832, which, as Madden commented, had 'a tincture of asperity . . . very evident appearances of annoyance of some kind or another', which he put down to 'the reception given her by Byron'.

Despite his irritation at being taken unawares at this first encounter, on paying the return call which courtesy demanded the following day, he was in a pleasanter humour and after it he wrote charmingly to Moore, both about Henry Fox, who had not over-estimated Byron's liking for him and 'some friends of yours', the Blessington party—'very agreeable personages, with a very handsome companion in the shape of a French Count'—whom he summed up with the luminous phrase '*a Cupidon dechainé*'.[2]

It was the phenomenon, D'Orsay, and the Blessingtons' *ménage à trois*, which engaged the attention of Byron. D'Orsay, the gay, superb, conceited, attractive, and unscrupulous society adventurer, was of all Lady Blessington's luxuries the most expensive, the most difficult to live up to, and the most difficult to live down. How to be accepted as respectable, and how at the same time to flaunt this splendid acquisition, and how to be sure of keeping him at her side—a lover twelve years her junior—formed, at the time Byron knew her, the science of her life. The scheme by which the feat was to be achieved was already worked out before the three presented themselves at the Villa Saluzzo.

The watchful and disapproving Fox noted in his journal on March 23rd, '. . . Dined with the Blessingtons. D'Orsay is established with them and, she says, is to marry Ld. B[lessington]'s daughter, whom he has never seen and who is only 13. This, I suppose, is only a blind.' The object of the marriage, planned thus early and eventually accomplished, was to secure the bride's large fortune for D'Orsay and at the same time, by making him a member of the family, to give a pretext for his being on a permanent footing in the household. Lady Blessington's feelings would be spared from the disquiet of jealousy because he had vowed not to consummate the union. Such was the all but incredible story that was whispered everywhere, and for once the gossip hardly kept pace with the reality.

[1] BLESSINGTON, *The Idler in Italy.*   [2] *L. & J.* 2 Apr. 1823.

In the 1930's there was a composite biography of the Blessingtons and Alfred D'Orsay, which was built on the theory that Lady Blessington was asexual, D'Orsay impotent, and Blessington homosexual, and their relations with one another therefore free from physical impropriety—an aspersion against which the author defends his heroine as earnestly as if he had been writing in her own century rather than ours. Her first matrimonial experience was presumed to have annulled her capability of normal feeling for men: Lord Blessington had paid Captain Jenkins £10,000 for her because she was a cultivated and graceful hostess, 'an ideal ornament to his house', and Captain Jenkins was in the position of one who was 'anxious to do his best for an agreeable ward, and glad to have found her a satisfactory establishment'.[1] Henry Fox's diary, though it contained intimate first-hand information about the characters concerned, received no mention in this book.

Fox, besides meeting the Blessingtons with waning and waxing distaste for years, and having been an inmate of their house in Rome for seven weeks, had D'Orsay's confidence and was for a time most warmly attached to him. He knew him to be Lady Blessington's lover and remonstrated with him over the mercenary marriage, which he regarded as 'sacrificing the happiness of a poor child to his own convenience, or rather to the indulgence of his passion for Ly B.'[2] This verdict of a contemporary, friendly to one at least of the parties when it was written, is surely incontestable. On the other hand, Lord Blessington does not seem to have been quite the ordinary *mari complaisant* he was often taken for. His alacrity in providing magnificently for D'Orsay was perhaps not induced solely by the persuasions of his wife. Fox thought him a mere drunkard ('When not drunk he is below contempt'),[3] but the letter in which he announced to Byron the death of his only legitimate son, Lord Mountjoy, is remarkable enough to lend support to the idea of his being somewhat abnormal.

Albergo della Villa
April 6th 1823

My dear Lord Byron,
    The contents of your agreeable and to Alfred D'Orsay very flattering letter shall be communicated to him as soon as I have the pleasure of seeing him, but I understand he is not yet up.[4] I write from my Bed to which I am

---

[1] SADLEIR.

[2] FOX. 17 Nov. 1827. D'Orsay replied to a letter of protest from Fox with attempts at reasoning on the subject which Fox considered childish. 'He only makes bad worse by professing his connection with Lady B., his indifference to his hapless bride, and the many advantages of fortune, &c, &c, he hopes to acquire.' (Same date.)

[3] FOX. 23 Oct. 1827.

[4] D'Orsay, aged twenty-two, was writing his memoirs of London society, which Byron had just praised. In his postscript he mentioned a rumour of an uprising in the Pyrenaean section of the French army.

not confined by the slight attack of Gout, but in which I am endeavouring to recover from languor—

I will not trespass on your patience with any account of our mental sufferings, suffice it to say I yesterday received by an express from Calais a letter from my Sister announcing that she had just closed the Eyes of my angelic son Mountjoy. From letters received at Nice I had no right to hope, but yet hope lingers. Lady B., who loved him as fondly as if he had been her own firstborn, has suffered much, and Alfred, who has received his father's assent to a marriage with one of my daughters, felt as if he had lost a brother. My sister says that my daughters have been attacked by the Influenza but are recovered still I fear that the grief they must feel in losing their beloved playfellow & companion may bring on a relapse. You must have heard your Sister speak of mine. Mrs Fowler is with Miss Gardiner [his sister] & their attentions to my poor child were beyond description.

I read your letter to Lady B. & she hopes that you will not avoid us in our misfortune.

With respect to the Pyrennean News I hope it is not true. Strongly as I am opposed to the unjust, oppressive aggression of France, yet for Alfred's sake whom I love as if he was my own Son, or Brother, I should be sorry that such Prophecies of Evil as Revolt and Insurrection should be realized. . . .

Alfred . . . selected our house for his home, altho' the only person in it that spoke French was Miss P[ower]. Lady B. begs me to give her compliments & remembrances, & you are Miss P.'s Son—so of course you have a mother's regards.

Alfred will be overjoyed at hearing what you say of him—He is a clever creature with a heart more valuable & *more pure* than gold. When he travelled with us we called him Le Jeune Lion. When you know him you will be charmed with him. I am sure he will also be very happy to hear the approbation of the fair Countess [Guiccioli].

Believe me Very truly & sincerely
Yours
Blessington.[1]

When every allowance has been made for the comparatively resigned spirit in which the loss of children was accepted at a time when half that were born were not expected to survive, this letter is a strange production for a father deprived of a boy who had attained the age of nine years, the sole heir to his purchased earldom and its privileges. There is an air of irresponsibility and even callousness in the continued pleasure tour of the trio who had heard weeks before that the child was dying, and who, if they had turned back, could easily have arrived before his end. The coupling of this unhappy news with raptures about the delightful Alfred, the unparalleled extravagance with which husband as well as wife pandered to every whim of 'the young lion', lend colour to the theory of some aberration—an aberration which becomes more puzzling when we find

[1] Murray MSS.

that the handwriting as well as the language, not only of this but of a whole succession of letters addressed by Blessington to Byron, are peculiarly difficult to distinguish from Lady Blessington's own.

Byron must have been hard put to it to frame his condolences, which, until seen with the letter he was answering, have always had a somewhat perfunctory air.[1] But they were adequate for the Blessingtons, who put aside their grief for the dead infant to inveigle the living celebrity.

> It is bad taste at all times to intrude private misfortune on Society [wrote the Earl, still apparently using his wife's pen] but in the present case it would be cruelty to ourselves to permit any selfish indulgence in sorrow to keep us from the pleasure which we feel in the society of Men of Genius, when their Genius is accompanied by kindness of heart. . . .
>
> Our Alfred is grateful for what you say, but I can see he wishes you had addressed it to himself direct in English. Every man ought to write in his own tongue let him speak what Language he will, and as you have conferred distinction on yours Alfred would be more proud of your letter than the decoration of the Legion d'Honneur unless it was gained on the Champs de Bataille.[2]

With compliments of this kind Byron was absolutely sated, and he could not have been otherwise than bored by a flourish of gossip about Royal dukes which was quite out of his line; his own zest for gossip being confined to friends and enemies. In any case, what with his Leigh Hunt troubles, his Greek plans, and his hard work on the English cantos of *Don Juan*, he had little time to devote to passing travellers.

Lady Blessington's statement that they enjoyed 'a nearly *daily* intercourse of ten weeks' deserves more sifting than it has had, for a person capable of one gross exaggeration is capable of another. The number of her meetings with Byron may easily be worked out from their letters and the sequence of dates given in her second account, *The Idler in Italy*, more nearly based on a diary than the *Conversations*—though there are discrepancies even here, and in several instances her phrasing is calculated to give an impression that they met when the correspondence shows that they did not.

Their introduction was effected on April 1st, their parting on June 1st. Between those dates there were about a dozen meetings, some of which were achieved fortuitously when riding. Lady Blessington tries to make it appear as if almost all the riding excursions were planned, but Byron's amiable observation, made not years later but at the time, is supported by letters: 'As they were friends of Moore's and have been civil to me I could not easily (in my usual way) escape being occasionally with them,

---

[1] *L. & J.* 6 Apr. 1823.   [2] 7 Apr. Murray MSS.

especially as they are equestrians and I met them frequently in my rides about Genoa.'[1]

It was not for want of persuasions on their side that meetings by appointment were only occasional. Byron's first courtesy call at their hotel was followed up at once by a letter from Lord Blessington asking for English papers—a request which seems to have been a pretext for mentioning that his intended son-in-law, Count D'Orsay, whose reception in London had been 'equal to Grammont's', was willing to lend Byron his account of that visit.[2] A second letter brought thanks for the papers with a reminder from Lady Blessington that he had promised to dine with them.[3]

The dinner took place on the 3rd.[4] The Blessingtons—or their servants—had spread the news that he was coming, so that the stairs and corridors were filled with English people from that and other hotels who were eager to get a glimpse of him. Lady Blessington says he was not annoyed, but his lameness had always made him shrink from this kind of curiosity. On the 5th he returned D'Orsay's memoir, with high commendation in a letter to Blessington. D'Orsay then wrote him 'a very handsome and flattering note', offering to make him a present of the manuscript, and Byron responded with a polite message, in his letter about Lord Blessington's bereavement, saying that he 'would not on any account deprive him of the production'.[5]

A week passed without a meeting, then on April 10th they went for a ride to Nervi. (Lady Blessington was shocked at Byron's recollection of seeing someone looking 'devilish well' in pale lemon-coloured gloves. 'Strange', she wrote, 'that such a mind should retain such puerilities.') On the 12th there was a ride in another direction, and Byron asked if he could introduce Count Pietro Gamba. Lady Blessington thought this was a high compliment, but the truth—and it receives confirmation from an independent source—was that Teresa was jealous of Byron's least contacts with other women, and had secured a promise from him that in future on these little excursions he would always be accompanied by her brother.[6]

On the 13th the introduction briefly took place, and Pietro with Byron was invited to dine next day, but neither of them came. Byron excused himself in what was, unconsciously, a most unflattering manner, for he explained in a letter that he had applied caustic to a wart that was forming

---

[1] *Cornhill*, Jan. 1928. Letter of 17 May 1823, to Lady Hardy, a cousin of Byron's half sister and wife of Vice-Admiral Sir Thomas Hardy, Bt., Nelson's friend.

[2] 2 Apr. 1823: Murray MSS.   [3] Ibid. Same date.

[4] Lady Blessington says the 4th, but a letter from Byron to Kinnaird written at the time is probably more dependable.

[5] *L. & J.* 6 Apr. D'Orsay's note seems to have been lost or not preserved.

[6] ORIGO. See also Colonel Montgomery's letter infra.

on his face, and that it had gone black and the skin had come off 'an inch square' on his upper lip.[1] This was not the sort of avowal he would have made if he had been anxious to maintain the slightest glamour. Lady Blessington professed in her second book to have noticed the disfigurement and smiled, whereas Lord Blessington (in his wife's hand) wrote to him almost archly: 'With your short upper lip I cannot comprehend how the burning venom could find an *inch square*.'[2]

The Irish peer took the opportunity of begging support for his Committee for improving the condition of his native peasantry. Byron replied with an exceedingly brief note sending more newspapers and promising a subscription. (Lord Blessington's own peasants were among the most miserable in Ireland, and even the reactionary John Galt had warned Lady Blessington about the consequences of his continued absenteeism.[3])

With Pietro, Byron joined their ride on the 16th and 17th, but failed to accept an invitation to dinner. (Lady Blessington noted that he was ignorant of the fine arts, and that it was torture to him to be reminded of malevolent paragraphs against him in the newspapers.) They only met twice in the next fortnight: on the 22nd, when he introduced Mr Barry to them while out riding, and the 29th, another riding occasion.

The Blessingtons had meanwhile sent several more invitations. On the 22nd, Byron acknowledged a 'billet' from Lord Blessington, and apologized for not having been able to go to tea; he had been calling on the French Ambassadress.[4] Next day the good-natured earl—or his very feminine amanuensis—wrote again, beginning, 'Milor, Hail King that may be or what think you of *Emperor of the Greeks*'.[5] They had bought a set of his works and were hoping the author would dine with them on the morrow. Byron replied pleasantly but using the semi-formal address, 'My dear Lord', which, with a single exception, he never dropped. He taxed Lord Blessington with quizzing him about Greece, since all he hoped for was 'a grey Greek stone' to cover him; and he said he dared not venture to dine with them tomorrow or any day that week, as dinners made him 'head-achy and sulky'.[6]

The next Blessington letter enquired, after various pleasantries, when he *could* be got for dinner.[7] There seems to have been no reply—or none the Countess cared to publish. Her state of mind may be divined by an entry, genuine or concocted, in her 'journal' for the 28th, saying that she respected Byron's wife: he was obviously a man whom a high-minded

---

[1] *L. & J.* 14 Apr. 1823.   [2] 14 Apr. Murray MSS.
[3] Letter of 27 July 1822 telling her she ought to conquer her repugnance and persuade Lord Blessington to go to Ireland. 'He must not listen to any complaints on the spot or he would become a mere administrator of petty relief.' *Blessington Papers.*
[4] *L. & J.*   [5] 23 Apr. Murray MSS.   [6] *L. & J.* 23 Apr.
[7] 25 Apr. Murray MSS.

woman would have found it difficult to live with, being quite without perception or considerateness of the feelings of others, and capable of giving grievous wounds, not through ill nature but sheer obtuseness.

At this point there is tampering with the dates and facts of an incident that can be checked. In the second chapter of her *Conversations*, she mentions the arrival of 'a friend of ours, Colonel Montgomery', whose sister was a confidante of Lady Byron's, and the embarrassment Byron showed when he discovered that the Blessingtons had been seeing him. Regarding the Colonel as an enemy, 'he expected that he would endeavour to influence us against him, and finally succeed in depriving him of our friendship'. Lady Blessington strove to calm his apprehensions, and he then begged for her good offices in using Colonel Montgomery as a means of approach to Lady Byron. By fixing this talk almost at the beginning of her book, she conveys the idea of a very swiftly ripening intimacy between herself and the affectionate poet.

Her later account of the same incident, in *The Idler in Italy*, is yet more circumstantial, but is dated April 29th, when more than half the meetings she was destined to have with Byron were already accomplished. In this second version 'his pale face flushed crimson when one of our party inadvertantly mentioned that Colonel M. was in Genoa'. He had not known of it before, and again the story is told of his fear that the Colonel would drive a wedge between them. It happened that Colonel Montgomery wrote a letter to Lady Byron on this subject which discredits Lady Blessington. Referring to the loathed Byron as 'Cain', he told her:

> I saw him frequently at Genoa, & met him at dinner at Mr Hill's our Minister. I very much feared a presentation, but this I fortunately escaped by his late arrival. I sat at the opposite side of a wide table whence I had a very good opportunity of observing him without having occasion to communicate—I thought at first he did not know me, but afterwards I found that he spoke about me to Lord Blessington, saying that I was a great friend of his Wife, & that he would have procured an introduction, but did not know whether it would be agreeable. In this he conjectured right, & I took very good care to avoid anything of the kind afterwards.[1]

The dinner party at the British Minister's at which Byron saw Montgomery—the most priggish and mischief-making of all Lady Byron's male friends—took place on April 20th, so Lady Blessington could not have surprised him on the 29th with the news of the Colonel's arrival, and part at least of that conversation is made up. Nor is it likely that he spontaneously asked her to 'use her influence' to transmit a request to his wife through this channel, because there had been memorable

[1] 15 May 1823: Lovelace Papers.

unpleasantness between him and the Montgomerys in Venice in 1818. More probably, prompted by a longing to be cast for some rôle in his drama, she initiated the offer of mediation.[1]

Byron joined her riding party with Pietro on May 1st, and on the 3rd he sent her in writing the message she had undertaken to transmit. It was delivered by hand in response to a note he received from her,[2] and so the sentimental interview with him she sketches under that date is fictitious.

Early in May there were two meetings with the Blessingtons for riding and a dinner.[3] D'Orsay then made the most famous of all his drawings, and they went to see the dilapidated Villa Paradiso, where Byron gave Lady Blessington a few lines which owe such point as they have to her expressing a wish to buy and restore the house.

> Beneath Blessington's eyes
> The reclaimed Paradise
> Should be free as the former from evil:
> But if the new Eve
> For the apple should grieve
> What mortal would not play the devil?

It is extremely difficult to believe that, when presenting this most trifling of bagatelles, he said: 'In future time, people will come to see Il Paradiso, where Byron wrote an impromptu on his—countrywoman; thus our names will be associated when we have long ceased to exist.' No instance of boastfulness so fatuous is known of him.

Her eager effort to please and serve him by acting as intermediary with Colonel Montgomery he took at face value, and for those two days there was a flaring-up of warmth and confidence which a receptive atmosphere too easily evoked in him. He rashly told her, probably to explain his elusiveness, that Teresa was jealous of his being in her company, and he promised to send her Constant's *Adolphe*, a work he greatly admired, and also a letter he had written but never posted to his wife containing a sort of diagnosis of the deadlock between them.[4]

She received these on May 7th and replied the same day:

Dear Lord Byron,

   I have read the letter to Lady B. and I cannot help wishing (much as I prize its possession) that it had been sent—It speaks a language that would I do believe have found an echo in her bosom.

---

[1] See Appendix to this Chapter for an account of how Colonel and Miss Montgomery carried out their commission, and a description sent to Lady Byron of Byron's life in Genoa.   [2] Murray MSS.

[3] Lady Blessington places them at the 4th and 5th. Letters indicate the second of the two dates should be the 6th.

[4] *L. & J.* His unsent letter to his wife is the one dated 17 Nov. 1821. The covering letter to Lady Blessington is dated 6 May 1823, but it was written just before he went to bed in the small hours, and was not delivered till next day.

Did you get scolded yesterday? and how are you today?

I have smiled more than once at the grave face of fear you put on before we parted, and I could have told you all that was at that moment passing in your mind.

Lord B. desires kind remembrances, and Believe me, Dear Lord Byron, What I truly am

Your sincere well wisher

Marguerite Blessington

P.S. I dare not send you my answer to your lines on Paradise—you may guess why.[1]

The coyness with which she alludes to Teresa's dislike of their meetings is that of a woman who would be glad to be giving cause for such jealousy. Later that day she sent him some flattering verses, immensely different from those scornful ones she published with a tale of having read them to him, making him 'red and pale by turns with anger', as D'Orsay drew him.[2] If there is one thing certain in the story, it is that Lady Blessington took no risk during the two months of their acquaintance of rousing Byron's indignation against her, but did everything she could to impress him with her sympathy and graciousness. These are the lines he actually received:

> When I ask'd for a verse pray believe,
>   'Twas not vanity caus'd the desire
> For no more can my mirror deceive
> And no more, can I Poets inspire.
>
> Time has press'd with rude fingers my brow,
>   And the roses have fled from my cheek
> Then it surely were folly if now
>   I the strains due to beauty should seek.
>
> But as Pilgrims who visit the Shrine
>   Of some Saint bear a relic away
> So I sought a Memorial of thine
>   As a treasure when distant I stay.
>
> Then while thus inspired thou canst sing
>   Never say that thy Hippocrene's dry
> In thy breast is its ne'er failing Spring
>   And its powers in each line we espy.

[1] Murray MSS.

[2] In *Conversations*:

> And canst thou bare thy breast to vulgar eyes?
>   And canst thou show the wounds that rankle there?
> Methought in noble hearts that sorrow lies
> Too deep to suffer coarser minds to share
>   etc. etc.

> Tho' sorrow ere yet youth has fled
> May have altered thy locks jetty hue
> The bays which encircle thy head
> Hide the Ravager's marks from our view.[1]

At this point Byron reverted to brevity and distance. A comparison of pressing invitations with polite but evasive replies gives rise to scepticism when we read in Lady Blessington's books of his struggles to persuade her not to leave Genoa and his 'pouting sulkiness' when she resisted him. The rides almost cease, there is only one dinner in three weeks, and on May 23rd he writes to Lord Blessington begging to be forgiven for not dining with them again. '. . . The truth is, that your banquets are too luxurious for my habits. . . . I am sure you will not be angry, since I have already more than sufficiently abused your hospitality.'[2]

There had been a note from the earl saying he had a great mind to try bargaining with Byron for his boat, and asking what was the lowest he would take for her with her furniture.[3] Byron with little enthusiasm turned the matter over to Barry. The transactions by which he bought the horse, Mameluke, and unwillingly sold to Blessington the yacht, *Bolivar*, receive a very different light in the letters from that shed by Lady Blessington's published recollections.[4] After acceptance of the offer for Mameluke, the purchase of another horse as well was almost urged. ('He will follow you like a dog when he knows you & likes bread.')

Blessington, who was under the affliction of a hangover, ventured to hope that Byron was finished with *Don Juan*—'which I will fairly say is no favourite of mine'.[5] It was no favourite of Lady Blessington's either, and she represents herself as remonstrating with him on 'ever writing a page which could bring the blush of offended modesty to the cheek of his daughter',[6] a sentiment Dickens seems to have pigeonholed in readiness for the use of Mr Podsnap.

An accidental meeting out riding on the 20th and a final dinner on the 29th rounded off all the intercourse Byron had with the Blessingtons during the last fortnight in May. On the evening of June 1st he paid his farewell visit, their parting causing him, according to the Countess, to

---

[1] Murray MSS. It is rather mysterious that in her letter which preceded this poem, dated May 7th, and received on that date by Byron (she says May 6th in her 'journal'), Lady Blessington refers only to Byron's 'lines on Paradise'—the single stanza quoted—and not in this or any other communication to the five stanzas she gave to Moore as having been addressed by Byron to her, to which those above appear to be an answer. It is not beyond the bounds of possibility that Byron made verbally the excuses to which she thus replied, and that the exceedingly bad poem Moore published as his composition was actually her own. She states explicitly that Byron sent her the 'copy of verses'—i.e. the five stanzas—on the 6th, but in neither side of the correspondence are they anywhere mentioned.

[2] *L. & J.*

[3] No date. About 20 May: Murray MSS.

[4] See pp. 215-216.

[5] 24 May: Murray MSS.

[6] BLESSINGTON, *Conversations*.

weep copiously, his lips quivering, his voice inarticulate. As is well known, Hobhouse wrote: *'Very unlike him'* beside the passage in Moore's book which treats of this outburst. Teresa insists that, on the contrary, as she heard from Pietro, who was present, as well as from Byron himself, it was Lady Blessington who was overcome,[1] and it is certain that in a postscript to his letter to her next morning he says: 'I hope your *nerves* are well today . . .'[2] to which she replied: 'My Nerves are not better today, but I will not bore you about them.' She said she would always sincerely prize the souvenir of a chain from him, and she begged him to sign his gift of a book—the Armenian Grammar to which he had contributed. 'If you add underneath your name that you give it to me you will oblige me. God bless you.'[3]

There is no reason why a woman who meets an interesting man some fifteen times—or even half a dozen times, or only once—should not put down her recollections of him; but should she persist in trebling or quadrupling the number of their opportunities for conversing, there are grounds for mistrust, and especially when, having eagerly courted him, she devotes herself to showing up his weaknesses and showing off her own wisdom, taste, and social superiority. Teresa's comment that the account betrays 'a secret feeling of spite and uneasiness' in the author is justified. And by an all unconscious irony, there is scarcely a failing of which Lady Blessington accused Byron which was not contemned in herself— triviality, self-love, vanity of rank, sententiousness, insincerity, affectation, coarseness, talking too much[4]—and making an excessive use of coronets!

When the work came out, the prodigal earl had died leaving his estate encumbered with every kind of debt; and his widow was fast declining from the heyday of affluence, beauty, and such position as she had managed to attain. Her continued *ménage* with D'Orsay and their treatment of his wife, her young step-daughter, whose fortune he had already squandered, had for ever defeated the ambitions she had made so manifest: but the thousands of middle-class readers for whom the magazines now catered knew little or nothing of this and had no means of differentiating between the hauteur of the aristocrat and the snobbery of the parvenue. All that society had denied her, she gathered to herself in those lofty pages where she told how she had studied Lord Byron *de haut en bas*. At the same time, she was able to use his dressed-up speeches for castigating anyone against whom she had a grudge.

'The conversations of a dead man cannot be contradicted,' wrote her

---

[1] GUICCIOLI, *La Vie.*   [2] *L. & J.*   [3] 2 June: Murray MSS.
[4] Fox says her abusiveness was 'almost Billingsgate', and that she never stopped when she once started talking, repeating the same thing 'thirty times'. (30 Dec. 1825.) On another occasion he mentions her ribaldry, but she was always very genteel in print.

aged friend, Joseph Jekyll, 'so if Miladi is not scrupulous on the score of veracity she may report Byron as she pleases.'[1] That Jekyll, although he had an octagenarian's gallantry towards one whom he regarded as still most attractive, could harbour suspicions of her veracity is in itself significant. Teresa Guiccioli is not a disinterested critic, but her remark that Lady Blessington 'had much imagination and almost a necessity of making a romance out of the simplest story'[2] receives full support from the reminiscences of the Hon. Grantley Berkeley who, through his friendship for D'Orsay, knew her well.

Whenever Byron is represented as deriding or disparaging anybody, it is invariably someone who had aroused her resentment, and when he is in a complimentary vein, it is towards someone with whom she wished to ingratiate herself. The first long conversation in the series must be the nearest to exact reporting, both because she would lead off with the best cards in her hand, and because, like Medwin, when the excitement of finding herself in Byron's company was fresh, she probably did jot down what she could recall of their talk, growing more lax, as all but the most assiduous chroniclers will, when the novelty wore off. Always foolishly unguarded, he may have called Lady Holland imperious and dictatorial, selfish and unfeeling. These were the views expressed by many, including Lady Holland's son; and Lady Blessington, who had never been received by that great hostess, must have encouraged and rejoiced in such strictures. Whether he spoke of Lord Holland's wife as contriving, by impudence or courage, 'to get herself into society' is more questionable, for the envious rancour has a Blessington rather than a Byron savour, and the woman who would publish that deratction, allowing the victim to be recognizable, would not be unequal to embroidering it.

But it is when she comes to Lady Holland's son that she gives herself away. Henry Fox's most enthusiastic sentiment for Lady Blessington was that he regretted not being able to like her: his considered opinion after some years was that she was a woman whose trade had been immorality, thrusting herself forward; one who, 'having persuaded a drivelling drunkard to marry her, dishonours him and makes the future misery of his young daughter by sacrificing her at 15 years old to a worthless adventurer whom, as the husband of this poor child, she may contrive to keep in the house on the score of the relationship. It is one of the basest and most barbarous transactions I ever knew.'[3] Fox's friendship with D'Orsay had fallen to pieces soon after the unconsummated marriage,[4] which he had refused to attend, protesting against it in a letter; and later

---

[1] JEKYLL, Aug. 1832.   [2] GUICCIOLI, *La Vie*.   [3] 16 Feb. 1829. Fox.
[4] Fox reported a conversation of Lord Blessington's in which he said that D'Orsay would not consummate the marriage (23 Mar. 1828).

they had nearly fought a duel through certain insults the Count had written to Lady Blessington's implacable enemy, Lady Westmorland. Lady Blessington thus had a score to settle with Fox, and she put into Byron's mouth some artfully contrived criticism:

> He said that he had formerly felt very partial to Mr [Fox]; his face was so handsome, and his countenance so ingenuous, that it was impossible not to be prepossessed in his favour. . . . 'He has, however, degenerated sadly,' said Byron, 'but as he is yet young he may improve; though to see a person of his age and *sex* so devoted to gossip and scandal, is rather discouraging to those who are interested in his welfare.'

Byron mentioned Fox in at least three letters at the time he was supposed to be lamenting his degeneration:

> I think that he [Henry Fox] has the softest and most amiable expression of countenance I ever saw, and manners correspondent. . . . I have ever found that those I liked longest and best, I took to at first sight; and I always liked that boy.[1]

> On Monday I saw Henry Fox (Lord Holland's son) and was delighted with him; he seems to me, on so slight a glimpse, the *ne plus ultra* of the amiable, even to the very features of his face.[2]

> . . . saw Henry Fox, Lady Holland's firstborn in *second* wedlock, and I was delighted to see him again for he was always an especial favourite of mine.[3]

It is not credible that, writing unqualified eulogies to friends, Byron would speak of Fox's disappointing character to strangers; and we may wonder whether he would have been allowed, in Lady Blessington's book, to say anything in the young man's favour at all if Moore had not already published the letter of praise.

Doubtless because of extensive embellishments they received, whatever notes were taken at the time were never produced. (Medwin's and most of Trelawny's also vanished.) *The Idler in Italy*, purporting to be the actual diary, does not contain more than fractional indications of Byron's talk, and these, like other entries, bear numerous evidences of being filled out with later knowledge. The homage to Shelley, 'the passionate, visionary poet, dreaming away life in a world of his own creation', was assuredly not written on September 16th, 1822, a few weeks after his death. It is the verdict of the 1830's. Lady Blessington's poetical tastes, as revealed in a long career of editorship, were neither advanced nor sensitive.

Byron's panegyric of Trelawny, attributed to the date May 20th, 1823,

---

[1] To Thomas Moore, 2 Apr. 1823.
[2] To Douglas Kinnaird, 2 Apr. 1823.　　　[3] To Lady Hardy, 17 May 1823.

contains Trelawny's error of 1824—that Byron sent to Rome inviting him
to come on the Greek expedition. Byron had the best of reasons to know
that Trelawny was in Florence, because Lady Hardy had just addressed a
letter to him from that city telling him Trelawny had, by his own request,
been presented to her as a great friend of Byron's.[1] Nor, wherever
Trelawny was, could Byron have told Lady Blessington he had invited
him to go to Greece, because the invitation was not sent till a fortnight
after she left Genoa! The speech full of tributes is therefore a fiction, the
reward of Trelawny's frequent patronage of Lady Blessington's *salon*.

The passage on Leigh Hunt (in the *Conversations*) is palpably retrospective. She and Hunt professed mutual admiration, and she told Henry
Crabb Robinson that his account of Byron was just.[2] Her close association
with John Galt, one of her literary advisers, probably accounts for an
ingenious posthumous apology from Byron for faults that biographer had
complained of in his book:

> When I knew Galt, years ago, I was not in a frame of mind to form an
> impartial opinion of him. . . . To say the truth, his manner had not deference
> enough for my then aristocratical taste, and finding I could not awe him into
> a respect sufficiently profound for my sublime self, either as a peer or an
> author, I felt a little grudge towards him that has now completely worn off.

Lady Blessington had an advantage over Medwin inasmuch as she was
able to draw upon a number of books for helpful facts. Her *Conversations*,
being much more diffuse than his, may be judged to contain more invention. Discourses running into pages on end are often so far out of character in opinions and expression that they cannot be supposed even
accurately reconstructed, far less accurately remembered. They are inter-
larded everywhere with genteelisms, French words, and clumsy pedantries
typical of Lady Blessington's style and highly untypical of Byron's. In a
condemnation of the attempts of Englishwomen to be women of fashion—
a condemnation which anticipates sneers uttered frequently by Lady
Blessington in *propria persona*—Byron is made to talk of *les dames à la
mode*, *les usages du monde*, the *bienséances*, the *légèrete* of the French,
their *espièglerie* and their *politesse*. Trelawny told William Michael Rossetti that this was not in the least his manner, and for once his statement
is irrefutable.

[1] 15 May: Murray MSS. 'In quality of your friend I was very glad to know him',
Lady Hardy wrote, 'though I should have rather he had his *Hair* like other people as
everybody was staring at my acquaintance with the raven ringlets which however as I
am a valiant woman when my friends are in question I did not mind but got all I could
from him about you.'

[2] ROBINSON. 28 Sept. 1832. 'Nearly the whole of her conversation was about Lord
Byron, to whose name, perhaps, Lady Blessington's will be attached when her beauty
survives only in Sir Thomas Lawrence's paintings. . . . She, however, is by no means an
extravagant admirer of Lord Byron.'

The book abounds in vast monologues which cannot be quoted at all without extensive cutting:

> I was thought a devil, because Lady Byron was allowed to be an angel; and that it formed a pretty antithesis, *mais hélas*! there are neither angels nor devils on earth, though some of one's acquaintance might tempt one into the belief of the existence of the latter. After twenty, it is difficult to believe in that of the former, though the *first* and *last* objects of one's affection have some of its attributes. Imagination resembles hope—when unclouded, it gilds all that it touches with its own bright hue: mine makes me see beauty wherever youth and health have impressed their stamp. . . . Sentimentalists may despise 'buxom health, with rosy hue,' which has something dairy-maid like, I confess, in the sound (continued he)—for buxom, however one may like the reality, is not euphonious, but I have the association of plumpness, rosy hue, good spirits, and good humour, all brought before me in the homely phrase; and all these united give me a better idea of beauty than lanky languor, sicklied o'er with the pale cast of thought, and bad health, and bad humour, which are synonymous, making tomorrow cheerless as today. [Lady Blessington herself was becoming very buxom, and had always been rosy.]
>
> Then see some of our fine ladies, whose nerves are more active than their brains, who talk sentiment, and ask you to 'administer to a mind diseased, and pluck from memory a rooted sorrow,' . . . . The best dower a woman can bring is health and good humour; the latter, whatever we may say of the triumphs of the mind, depends on the former. . . .

If Byron really held forth like this—and it is but a fraction of the printed speech—in long unbroken stretches of triteness, platitude, and quotation, then somebody else must have written his letters for him. If he did not, then we must be careful of according credit even to what sounds more Byronic, especially where the author is making him a mouthpiece to insult her enemies or rectify the grievances of her friends.

> With the strongest regard for Lady Blessington [wrote Madden in his biography] . . . it cannot be denied that, whether discoursing in her salons, or talking with pen in hand on paper in her journals, she occasionally aimed at something like stage effects . . . or passed off appearances for realities. This was done with a view to acquiring esteem, strengthening her position in the opinion of persons of exalted intellect or station, and directing attention to the side of it that was brilliant and apparently enviable. . . .

The book that social uncertainty produced was ultimately to give a great deal of pain to Teresa Guiccioli, but when she first saw it coming out, in small sections month by month, its impact was naturally less than when she read it with rage as one volume. At the time of her leaving England, in January 1833, only half—the more authentic half—had as yet appeared, and she was consoled by knowing it was widely derided as 'Imaginary Conversations', a title Landor had recently made popular.

She protested as well as she could, but she was placed in an awkward dilemma—on the one hand, there was the hospitality she had accepted and the overwhelming show of affection she had received and was still receiving when the first article appeared (July 1832); on the other, the nature of her relations with Byron. She did not know that Lady Blessington's flowery compliments disguised a malice towards herself of which some unpleasant examples survive.

> Lady Blessington told us yesterday that the Guiccioli used to watch Byron with a Telescope when he went out.
> She (Lady B) asked Lord Byron why he did not take her out, & he drawled out in his usual way, "Consider what a fright she would be in a habit."
> She asked him if he thought her handsome. He replied, "She is a horror —she has *red* hair"—which is not true. She said, "Why do you not walk with her?" He replied, "She shuffles like a Duck & I am lame—a pretty couple!" She said, "Do you ever tell her this?" "Yes." "What does she say?" "She scra-a-a-tches me," replied Byron.[1]

We might think this was reckless misreporting on Haydon's part if there were not so many other testimonies of Lady Blessington's ill will. In Rome, where she had first met Teresa, she had tried to divide her from Henry Fox by telling her that Fox said Byron went to Greece to get rid of her.[2]

If Byron really spoke so crudely and cruelly about Teresa to Lady Blessington, then the laudatory remarks on the same theme that she ascribes to him in her two books are obviously fabricated, since it would be impossible even for the most capricious lover to say one day that his mistress was a fright and a horror, and another that she was most worthy of attachment, attractive, and well-bred! The appreciation of Teresa, being in accord with what he said of her in a number of letters which Lady Blessington had no chance of seeing, has indeed a striking note of authenticity, though he may have laughed in his usual indiscreet way about her 'fits of Italian jealousy'.

Byron's attitude to both women was summed up in a letter written, six days after the Blessington cortège moved on, to one of his liveliest and most charming correspondents, Lady Hardy. It was to her that he had first mentioned the rides with the Blessingtons and the disquiet they were giving to 'la mia dama'.[3] She replied on June 7th:

> Your last letter amused me very much, My dear Cousin, as I can imagine (& even pity) the jealousy of a Person that feels you may grow tired of the perpetual presence she has entailed on you, & seek variety

---

[1] POPE, Haydon's Diary, 11 May 1835. In an entry of some weeks earlier he writes, 'Mrs [Leicester] Stanhope told me she had seen a letter from Byron saying 'Can any one relieve me of Lady Blessington or rather Count D'Orsay?' (16 Feb. 1835.)
[2] Fox. 9 May 1828.   [3] *Cornhill*, Jan. 1928. 17 May 1823.

in other Society. I have seen Lady Blessington in the Park & I thought her very handsome but am surprised to hear she is a literary Lady as I believe her first rudiments of learning were learned at Cahir in Tipperary where she was the post Master's Daughter, but when women take to writing there is no saying where they will stop.

I am afraid had that been her only quality you might not have given poor Mde. G. any excuse for uneasiness & I am very sorry to say that if a man does take a fancy to a woman past five and twenty it is more dangerous than before, as she knows her powers of mind as well as of appearance, & makes the most of both. Am I not right? I had rather hear of your falling into the sea than in Love as you would find no difficulty in swimming ashore, whereas in the other quagmire there is no saying how deep one flounders.[1]

Lady Hardy was on Teresa's side against the interloper. She had been to see the young Countess's portrait by West and 'admired her very much. What lovely hair and sweet countenance.'

To the suggestion that he had been in peril from Lady Blessington, Byron answered explicitly:

'Very right,' my dear Cousin (or Cozen), but you see there was no danger, for I have an awful dread both of new love and learning and besides, to say truth, thought that I was as well off at home. I suspect that it is only for a young man these enchantments [i.e. the enchantments of mature women] are paramount and indeed I know in one instance at least of my own experience that at entering into life those full blown beauties have the power you describe. But at present besides my long foreign liaison of five years and my being exceedingly governed and kept tight in hand, I do not know how it is, but it would be difficult for me to fall in love again with an Englishwoman of any description.

Besides I have laid down a rule never to have a feeling of that kind (that is a new one) after thirty. My present attachment began before I had turned that awkward corner of my existence, so that it was but just in time. Having begun, it will probably continue to the end of the chapter unless something out of the way stops it, as it does many things of that kind.

To return to our Irish Aspasia, I did not know that she had been Post-mistress of Cahir, but I had heard that she had been a mistress of some kind or other before she espoused the Earl of Bln. Her slight acquaintance with me was of the most decorous description; the poor woman seemed deranged with ennui, entirely bored with her Lord and a little sick of her Parisian Paladin also, though why I could not perceive, for he is not only remarkably hand-some but certainly clever and apparently amiable—but it was hinted that his

[1] Murray MSS. Of Lady Blessington she told Byron in a later letter (17 June 1823): 'I believe she began life as the lady fair in a most humble occasional way of the late Lord Glengall, at Cahir & supplied the absence of the lawful lady, she then succeeded in the usual routine of that life till she found the present Lord in deep despair at his first wife's Death who though what is called in England a *naughty* woman, was I believe as near an angel as possible. I know a person that knew her well & from his account she was an example to other women of every high & noble feeling. . . .'

temper was not good, in fact that he was exigeant, though I saw few signs of either. I saw very little of them especially latterly, and now they are gone.[1]

After some news of other English visitors to Genoa, he returned to the question of Teresa and what was to happen to her when he went to Greece. It was her fancy to retire to a convent since she could not go with him— 'till we can find our way back again or till Greece is quiet enough for me to send for her. I am glad you like her picture.' It was the letter of a much-married man (and Teresa would not have minded that) who is quite unconscious that a *femme fatale* has been making a play for him. Lady Blessington had thought him obtuse with women, and she was right.

[1] *Cornhill*, Jan. 1928. 'Paramount' has been substituted for 'permanent' as a more likely reading in the first paragraph.

The Montgomerys' mission to Lady Byron

We learn from their letters that neither Colonel Hugh Montgomery nor his sister had ever met Byron until he addressed a few words to Miss Montgomery in Venice in 1818, yet both of them wrote about him in so damaging and destructive a manner to his wife and others that one might suppose they had some personal cause for animosity. All the most unpleasant reports about him were conveyed to Lady Byron by one or other of them, and Colonel Montgomery in Venice, as years later in Genoa, spent his time 'trembling' (the word is his own) lest Byron should somehow succeed in scraping an acquaintance with him. Miss Montgomery did not disguise her opinion, when visiting the salons of his Venetian hostesses, that he was 'a very bad man'.[1]

She was one of several ladies, either celibate or unhappily married, who were attached to Annabella with an almost maternal devotion, and determined that she never should be recaptured by her infamous husband. Once again Byron, who seemed quite incapable of grasping what hatred and fear he inspired, was pitifully misguided in his choice—or acceptance —of a mediator. Miss Montgomery transmitted Lady Blessington's letter with this comment: '. . . He appears to think himself a very innocent and injured personage—but I am disposed to believe all this tenderness is directed to the £3,500 per an: which in case of a reconciliation would return to his possession.'[2]

Colonel Montgomery followed this up a week later with a letter of his own telling Lady Byron that he had seen a rough copy of 'some very severe lines' Byron had written about her, in which she was compared to Nemesis. These were the *Lines on Hearing that Lady Byron was Ill*, written in 1816, which Lady Blessington, never able to resist the temptation to make mischief, first showed to Montgomery and later published. (They are among the best of their kind that Byron ever produced. Perhaps it was because he had some idea that they would eventually find their way to Lady Byron through that medium that he left them in Lady Blessington's hands.)

The rest of Montgomery's account is chiefly what Lady Blessington told him, and it will be seen that some of it was what she had picked up through gossiping with Byron's doctor:

> He was always talking about you and Ada, with tears *running down* his cheeks—He has been told that you are ever abusing him and Vilifying his character & to the reports of your calumnies are to be attributed the Various attacks upon you that have appeared in his Works—

[1] 7 May 1818: Lovelace Papers.   [2] Ibid. c. 7 May 1823.

. . . He is quite thin compared with what he was at Venice in 1818. He lives upon Vegetables at home, but when he dines out eats and drinks as copiously as any of the Company. His time is disposed of as follows—he rises at 9, reads writes & c till 2; rides (always with pistols) till 6, dines & lies down immediately, is called at 12. Writes and studies till 5, then gets into bed & sleeps till 9.—

There is no apparent intercourse between him & the lady—they live quite separate he on one side of the house, & she her father & brother on the other—having their respective establishments. The Brother Count Gamba, accompanies him in all his excursions & to dinner or wherever he may be invited—

She is a small, fair, delicate bashful person much more resembling a British Subject than one of any Southern nation. She is very agreeable and very Ladylike.—All these details I had from Lady B[lessington] who obtained them from a Doctor Alexander settled at Genoa who attends the parties.

In case you comply with his request about the picture he intends to ask for Ada's, at first he thought of both, but on reflection preferred getting one favor at a time. When he first mentioned this matter he asked if I had children, for were it otherwise he would not have appealed to me.

He observed that if I knew him he was sure I should think otherwise of him than most of those who had judged him wrongfully. He lamented the unfortunate temper which had been his ruin, & the cause of all his misfortunes, took every opportunity of praising and extolling you, & declaring over & over again that he had no wish upon earth greater than that 'our daughter, (for she is our daughter) may resemble her mother in every thing' —Those were his exact words.

Among the many things of which he accuses you one in particular was that of going to Newstead, & cross questioning a housekeeper there relative to his conduct previous to his Marriage, and as it regarded Mrs Leigh.

He accuses himself of having allowed you to form an acquaintance with some person to whom he was previously attached. He added that you are the only unmarried woman he ever loved, and declared most solemnly that during the time you lived together he never was guilty of any infidelity. He is totally at a loss to know why you wont live with him, but has been told that your objection is grounded upon the most violent personal *hate*. He accused Mrs Clermont of having done the principal mischief in fabricating stories to his disadvantage in particular while you were confined.

Lady B. told me that it was evident there was some person that was continually poisoning his mind. He wears Mrs L[eigh']s hair in a large brooch, and a bracelet on his left arm, and mentioned the locket sent with his hair to Ada. . . . He seemed desirous of knowing if she would be allowed to wear it.

I believe I have now related all that I heard, at least the principal part.[1]

[1] 15 May 1823: Lovelace Papers.

Lady Blessington in 1841, by Count Alfred D'Orsay

CHAPTER XV

'IMPLORA PACE'

Byron told his wife that it might be the destiny of authors to have to linger about the earth after their death till the effects of their work should have ceased, and that for his release (he said it mournfully) he might have to wait five centuries.[1] She was recalling the conversation after thirty-five years, and it may not have been for authors only that he fancied such a bondage—indeed she recorded at an earlier time that he had a low opinion of the durable qualities of his work.[2] Whether as author or as man, if his notion were realized, the 19th century must have provided his unquiet shade with an intricate pattern of ironies.

In 1828 Cawthorne published *The Beauties of Don Juan* 'including only those passages which are calculated to extend the real fame of Lord Byron'. It was described by the *Literary Gazette* as 'a captivating volume with all the impurities of *Don Juan* expurgated. . . . It may with perfect propriety be put into female hands, from which the levities and pruriencies of the entire poem too justly excluded it.' *Don Juan* without its levity was not grasped as eagerly by female hands as the publishers hoped; and presently John Murray—the same John Murray who had conferred with Hobhouse as to how in the world to get Byron to suppress the poem—took the risk of purchasing the entire copyright, although Lord Chancellor Eldon had decided it was too immoral and too flippant to deserve the protection of the law. (It was perhaps because of this verdict that, though it had made excellent profits, it was withdrawn from the auction sale at three hundred and ten guineas, no publisher being willing to venture more.)

Hobhouse himself had come to the conclusion, requiring a profound rearrangement of his ideas, that it was a 'very extraordinary performance', and there were critics who found it even more than that. Yet for a generation, the view of Lady Blessington and Harriette Wilson was the accepted one.[3] The Rev. William Bowles, with whom Byron had argued in print somewhat in the style of a jovial cat with a daring mouse, wrote to the *Devizes and Wilts Gazette* to ask whether, if his Lordship had gone to Westminster instead of Harrow and been flogged as Southey was, he could have created such a poem, and answered himself, 'I trow not'.[4] Thackeray thought the epic was the result of dieting and physic. 'If that

[1] Letter to the Rev. F. W. Robertson, 9 Aug. 1850: Lovelace Papers.
[2] Ibid. Statement headed *Lord Byron and Literature*.
[3] Harriette Wilson, the most notorious courtesan of the epoch, wrote to Byron protesting against the indecency of the work. (Quennell and Paston.)
[4] Bowles seems not to have known that Southey was expelled from Westminster School—and for a protest against corporal punishment!

man had respected his dinner, he would never have written *Don Juan*.'[1]

Various people put forward various theories, serious or jocular, as to what might have averted Byron's poetical downfall; nevertheless the reading of his works continued, and even through the pruderies of an age with a new kind of puritanism, there were voices—a few—which cried that his strength had lain in the very style which had been deemed the symptom of his ruin and depravity. And though other and louder voices proclaimed, decade after decade, that no one read Byron any more or ever would read him again, Murray continued to bring out large new editions, which, illustrated or unillustrated, in small print or big, in few volumes or many, somehow found their way to bookshops, libraries, and—strange portent—school-rooms.

No matter how often Byron was consigned to oblivion, the vitality of his Muse—negligent, insolent, moping, glowering, ribald, witty, and flashy—continued to defy the prophets. Not less irrepressibly, despite frequent assurances to the public that interest in the personal life of the misguided poet was at last decently exhausted and could not be revived, there he was furnishing the subject of another book, another article, another forgery; or inspiring another fiction writer. Never in novels has one model so often served for either hero or villain. Self-willed, self-doomed Satanic noblemen with a quality of magnanimity, fascinating rakes haunted by nameless sins, gifted remorseful seducers, ran their romantic course through a thousand circulating libraries.

The most realistic, in so far as the introduction of recognizable features constitutes realism, was perhaps Disraeli's *Venetia* (1837), a story about Byron and Shelley, 'two of the most renowned and refined spirits that have adorned these latter days'. Disraeli knew many friends of Byron's, his father had some first-hand reminiscences, and Tita the gondolier, now his own servant, was an intimate link. Yet often the dialogue can hardly be called convincing.

> 'Plantagenet, I have a father.'
> Lord Cadurcis started, and for an instant his arm quitted Venetia's. At length he said in a gloomy voice, 'I know it.'
> 'Know it!' exclaimed Venetia with astonishment. 'Who could have told you the secret?'

Plantagenet Cadurcis and Marmion Herbert are not the most persuasive names for Byron and Shelley, but many of their actual utterances are incorporated in the book. (Shelley has, however, discreetly given up atheism.) Lady Byron is boldly introduced under the thin disguise of 'Lady Annabel'—a woman given to making a sombre mystery of the past and

---

[1] *Memorials of Gormandizing*, 1841.

keeping her husband's portrait under a curtain. There is a sketch of the hero's childhood, showing his mother as socially ludicrous and also intemperate. Invited to a collation, Mrs Cadurcis says:

> Thank you, I never eat, my dear lady, except at my meals. But one glass of Mountain, if you please, I would just take the liberty of tasting, for the weather is so dreadfully hot; and Plantagenet has so aggravated me, I really do not feel myself.

Such hints of extravagant silliness may have been based on the information of good witnesses, but possibly they were only the crystallizing of a tradition that was unjust to the ill-starred Mrs Byron. Under the title *Sketches from the Portfolio of a Sexagenarian*,[1] Pryse Lockhart Gordon published recollections of Byron and his mother which suggested that, though Mrs Byron may unrepentantly have spoken with a Scottish accent, the poet's boyhood was no such sordid affair as biographers fond of dramatic contrasts have enjoyed depicting. The house at Banff, where he spent much time in his most impressionable years, is described by one who often stayed there as handsome and spacious, facing on to 'a large well-stocked garden', and having a balcony giving on to a noble view of the bay of Macduff and Banff and the river Deveron.[2] Whatever thrift his mother may have had to exercise, his playmates there were children of the best families in the district. Scottish writers appear to be well justified in complaining that the 'poverty' and 'squalor' of his upbringing have been overplayed.

The English side of Byron's ancestry was made the theme of a very dull novel by Miss Cursham, *Norman Abbey*. She corresponded about it with Augusta Leigh, who wrote to her in her own pathetic, ineffectual way:

> You tell me you are anxious to promote the sale of your Book. Do you think it wd have the effect . . . to dedicate it to *me*!! . . . not my name—but 'To the Sister of ——!' Now <u>pray</u> do not set this down to vanity or conceit—on my *own* individual acct.—I know I am *worse* than Nobody—'I by myself —I—' but—the Sister of —— you know alters the case—& it has occurred to me whether it might not *attract*! I beseech you *never to breathe* this—but burn it instantly & be honest & candid in your use of it.[3]

Did the request emanate from a hope that the little *cachet* of a dedication from a highly respectable author would help her in some measure to

---

[1] *New Monthly Magazine*, 1829. Gordon, who makes a few mistakes such as an honest man can make, but is generally dependable, describes Miss Gordon of Gight, as 'a romping, comely, good humoured girl . . . inclined to corpulency. She was fond of running races and swinging between two trees on the lawn.' When Byron came to London for his holidays, after his accession to the title, Gordon lent him a pony.

[2] WELLS.   [3] 10 Jan. 1832: Roe-Byron Collection, Newstead Abbey.

rise above the scandal of the previous year, when one of her daughters had been forcibly—but vainly—separated from the husband of another? However that may have been, her wish was not gratified nor her plea for secrecy respected.

In November 1834 Byron figured under his own name as the hero of a play by Jacques Ancelot at the *Comédie Française, Lord Byron à Venise*. Several living characters were represented, including Lady Byron and that great friend, Trelawny, who could not have much liked his portrayal as 'a little fellow with a pug nose, a long pipe in his mouth, and a sailor's jacket'.[1]

Besides the candidly fictitious works, there were the spurious and semi-spurious works. These had existed in substantial numbers in Byron's lifetime and were multiplied enormously after his death—continuations of *Don Juan*, bogus translations, pornographic verses fathered, irrespective of anachronisms, on the defenceless victim, and biographies which are either wholly invented or an amalgam of fact and fiction. There were also some items which remain puzzling.

What of T. Sheldrake, who wrote in the *New Monthly Magazine* about the treatments and appliances he had provided for Byron's lame foot, and was violently denounced in the following number by the editor, Campbell, as a self-advertising quack?[2] Was he altogether an impostor, taking on himself the credit due to another practitioner of the same name (said to be his brother), or was there some groundwork for at least part of his fanciful structure? The story of a play which Byron undertook to put before the Drury Lane Committee, and which was subsequently seen by Douglas Kinnaird, has a ring of truth, though there are obvious falsehoods in the rest. What of an anonymous Frenchwoman who claimed to have approached Leigh Hunt for an introduction to Byron in 1823 and, being refused, to have forced her way into his presence without that formality? Many details are more correct than is usual in faked memoirs, and there is a certain convincing naïveté in the writer's manner of admitting her tiresome persistence; but her reconstruction of Byron's conversation is far-fetched,[3] and we wonder whether she is expressing his opinion or her own in such a passage as:

> Do you know another amateur writer, Baron de Stendhal who once amused himself by denouncing me to the liberals of France as an aristocrat? The reproach amused me a good deal. There is, however, this difference between us—that I was born an aristocrat and am become a liberal, whereas the Baron de Stendhal, of his own private authority, makes himself a baron on the title pages of his books in favour of a liberal press.

[1] Unidentified English Journal.
[2] Sept. 1830. Under the title *Lord Byron—Theatricals.*
[3] *Court Magazine*, 10 Apr. 1830.

He is, however, a man of genius, of original talent even, a very rare thing among authors who are men of the world. . . .

Then there is the rambling and disjointed *Angler in Wales,* published in 1834 by Thomas Medwin, who, now lost to scruple, was printing anything that would avenge the scorn cast on his *Conversations* by Byron's friends. All the amiability of his first book had been curdled by the diatribes of Hobhouse and others, and two years before, he had sought to prove serious plagiarisms against Byron in an article in the *Literary Gazette,* a case much weakened by the outrageous inaccuracies so typical of him. Introduced into his new book, only by his initial but perfectly recognizable, was the self-styled Captain Roberts, R.N., Trelawny's friend, the boat-builder.[1]

If Roberts really made all the statements Medwin attributed to him, he was a liar of no common turpitude: if he did not, then Medwin himself was as great a cheat as Hobhouse thought him. Roberts, as reported here, knew Hobhouse well and viewed him with unadulterated and very libellous disgust. His anecdotes of Byron and Shelley outdid those of Trelawny himself. He claimed to have passed many years of his life with Byron, knowing him 'better than any other individual—*au fond*', and traced his association with both poets to Geneva in 1815, when neither of them was there.

He always took, says Medwin, 'a very dark estimate of Byron's character. It is the only point on which I have ever had reason to suspect the freedom from bias and prejudice in his opinions.' He also took a very dark estimate of Byron's figure—'short and devoid of symmetry', 'grossly corpulent', 'vulgarly fat'—and his face, which was 'pallid and fleshy, and betrayed no sign of a single hair, being closely shaved up to the ears, giving his visage an unmanly and unbecoming appearance'. (Copious whiskers were *de rigueur* in the 1830's, and a naked male face was henceforward for many years to be regarded as an unseemly sight.)

Byron was given at all times, Roberts told Medwin, to wearing shabby and shrunken apparel, and even in Switzerland, in the prime of his youth, had been anything but presentable. His voice was effeminate, his tones were affected, he had 'the misanthropy of the snarling Apemantus', and was 'steeped in vices that fitted him for the Bolgi of the Inferno'. Yet this repulsive being—who even rode a repulsive horse!—would 'charm away the night', and Roberts boasted of having spent many 'glorious hours' with him. Whether any of these extensive recollections were uttered to Medwin, or whether Medwin vindictively contrived them so as to put into another person's mouth an attack on Byron he could not make in his own person, having formerly given so different a picture, is a question that may

[1] Correctly called Commander by Medwin.

yet be solved, for much material about the remoter planets revolving round Byron and Shelley is being brought to light.[1]

The only certainly genuine thing in the two vituperative volumes is a first-rate account of Byron at Missolonghi ascribed simply to 'Forrester', and ignored till recently because of the falsity of its setting.[2] Surgeon James Forrester, R.N., was a real person, however, with a traceable career, one of the three officers of the sloop *Alacrity* who came on shore to demand compensation from the Greeks for the detention of a neutral Ionian vessel —an affair Byron handled with great dexterity and courtesy, satisfying everyone except the jaundiced Stanhope.[3] Since this is one of the last sketches of Byron before illness and hopelessness cast their shadows over him, and has never been reprinted, it is given with slight abridgements at the back of this volume.[4]

The reputation he had left behind him as licentious in literature and a debauchee in life made him a popular subject for the mythology of gallantry, especially in France, where a book called *La Vie Privée et Amours Secrètes de Lord Byron* went through many editions from as early as 1837 onwards. It was supposed to be a translation of an English work by one John Mitford; but on the strength of the description of Harrow School alone, it may be asserted without a qualm that no Englishman could have written it. There would seem to have been more than one version of this *Vie Privée*—justly described in booksellers' catalogues as 'curious'.

In the first, Harrow is what Southey might have called 'a preparatory school for the brothel and the gallows'. One of the masters, by name Gazelee, is in the habit of acting as procurer for the young Byron; and even the headmaster only gives him 'a severe reprimand' when he finds him in the most compromising of situations on his favourite tomb in the churchyard accompanied by a young married lady. 'The reverend director'—whether Dr Drury or Dr Butler is not stated—refuses to accept a denial of the offence. 'He knew too well that the Harrow scholars were not over scrupulous for truth when there was a woman in the case.'

No wonder the editor of the second version begins:

. . . On a dit, raconté, écrit, imprimé tant de sottises, d'absurdités à ce sujet, que l'incredulité des lecteurs est bien pardonnables.

[1] It may also be asked whether Medwin had got the story of Byron frightening Rogers with his dog from Trelawny, or Trelawny lifted it from this book—which he showed many signs of having read when he came to write his own; and whether, whoever told it first, there is the slightest truth in it.

[2] Marchand makes some use of it in his *Byron*.

[3] Byron saved face for both sides by handing over a sum, nominally from the Greeks but actually out of his own pocket. Stanhope wrote an embittered report to the Secretary of the Greek Committee. (28 Jan. 1824.)

[4] Appendix to this chapter.

His own more restrained narrative, however (and he warns readers to be on guard against the temptation of believing it a fable), does not omit the most astounding features of the first. The corrupt tutor Gazelee still plays his rôle, and we are treated to such nearly untranslatable dialogues as the following:

"Mon cher Gazelee" [it is Byron who speaks] . . . "j'aime une femme charmante, divine; je l'adore, et je sens que je deviendrai la possèder."

". . . Quelle est donc cette charmante personne qui vous tourne ainsi la tête. . . .?"

"Mon cher precepteur, c'est une jeune personne que vous connaissez particulièrement . . . à laquelle vous voulez beaucoup de bien, j'en suis sûr; en un mot, c'est votre sœur."

"Comment! Milord!"

Milord Byron, the son of a rich woman with castles in Scotland, puts a purse into the preceptor's hand and overcomes his brotherly reluctance. Each day at Harrow School there are hunting or fishing parties in which fascinating women are usually included. Byron makes friends too with those farmers of Harrow-on-the-Hill who have good-looking wives and daughters, the menfolk not realizing, says the author, that they were letting a wolf into the fold. There is an occasion when the tutor acts as sentinel all night while his lordship indulges in one of his least creditable amours.

At a later stage in his depraved career, Milord takes round with him, disguised as a lacquey, a girl called Miss Page, the daughter of a Neapolitan nobleman. Thus accompanied, he goes to stay at the house of an uncle, who is horrified to hear from his valet that the lacquey and master are in another of those compromising situations which are the *raison d'être* of the book. He rushes into the bedroom to put an end to so monstrous an abuse of his hospitality and sees enough of the page, Miss Page, to withdraw laughing: 'Doucement! Doucement! Le mal n'est pas aussi grave que je le croyais.'

The oddities of this wild but much-reprinted romance must have been rendered somewhat confusing to French readers by the occasional mention of places and people that really had some Byron association—a death-bed scene (attended by the Countess Guiccioli) in Greece, a translation of Fletcher's actual letter describing his master's death, and a poem eulogizing as a hero one who has been delineated throughout two volumes as a scoundrel.

Such shams were too crude to take in anyone, but serious forgers were not wanting. The most effective of all, a very expert collector of data and imitator of handwritings, went to the length of passing himself off as Byron's son by a Spanish Countess he had loved and deserted on his 1809 travels. It was useless for Hobhouse, from whom the charlatan had tried to raise £1500,[1] to insist that he had been with Byron every day of that journey in Spain and kept a detailed journal, and that no such amour could have taken place without his knowledge: it was equally useless for Augusta Leigh to deny, through her solicitors, that she had given her sanction, as advertised, to a book this 'Major Byron' was proposing to bring out about his 'father', or for the Society of Guardians for the Protection of Trade against Swindlers to issue warnings against him. He was a criminal of considerable cleverness and panache, and, brazenly calling his illusory mother the Countess de Luna, he was able to impose on a number of British and American supporters.[2] The desire for a re-incarnated Byron was very strong, and the adventurer was said—though not by anyone who knew the poet—to bear a resemblance. Perhaps it was the look that started the make-believe.

For a man whose life and work were in disrepute, Byron's name continued to be marvellously lucrative. Even the tragedies which the critics of his own day had so roundly condemned turned out adaptable for the theatre. All were played, and the weakest of them, *Werner*, was one of Macready's most triumphant 'vehicles'. More fraudulence was perpetrated in April 1834 when the playbills of the Theatre Royal, Drury Lane, announced *Sardanapalus* with Mrs Mardyn in the rôle of Myrrha, adding the surprising information that the Noble Author had intended it for her.

Mrs Mardyn was the actress whose name had been luridly and quite erroneously linked with Byron's in the matrimonial crisis of 1816. The gossip, which might have been of value to her in a later age, was then most injurious. There had been indignant denials, assurances of virtuous conduct. Yet here she was positively boasting that a part written nearly five years afterwards had been designed for her.[3]

> My late regretted friend ever paid me the flattering compliment, that in his portraiture of the 'Ionian Myrrha,' I had been associated by his Muse in every image of her trance, and that if ever the poem strayed in publicity, beyond the closet, it was his wish that the Greek girl's sandals should be worn upon the stage by *me*.[4]

Mrs Mardyn, as the enraged Macready noted in his diary, had become 'a quadragenarian' and had never been an important actress. (She had

---

[1] 30 June 1844. British Museum: Broughton Papers. Hobhouse was very much annoyed with Mrs Leigh for being so silly as to write a somewhat credulous letter to the forger before making enquiry. It was immediately turned to account.

[2] Much of the story is told in *Major Byron, The Incredible Career of a Literary Forger*, by Theodore G. Ehrsam.

[3] The part was written into the play at the instance of Mme Guiccioli, and was perhaps no bad likeness of her voluptuous yet loyal and courageous character.

[4] Letter received on 25 Mar. 1834. Quoted by Trewin, whose book *The Night Has Been Unruly* treats this incident more fully.

retired from the stage at the age of twenty-four.) Macready had prepared
to do the play with the accomplished Ellen Tree, whom the manager,
Bunn, now thrust aside without compunction so that old scandals might
be exploited. To add injury to insult, the retired actress was only coming
from Paris at the last moment and there would not even be time for
effective rehearsal with the company.

An enquiry was set going by John Murray, and Augusta Leigh got in
touch with Fletcher to ask whether there had been any meetings between
Mrs Mardyn and Byron in his latter years.

> His statement quite confirms me in my belief that the whole is a fabri-
> cation of the *Enemy*—or *Enemies* or a Fraud on the public. *Both* ought to be
> convicted or undeceived.
>
> I send Fletcher with this who is quite as *feverish* on the point as I am—
> and will have the greatest pleasure in doing anything in the way of contra-
> diction.[1]

After infuriating delays and confusions, the Greek girl's sandals were
worn by Ellen Tree after all, and with only two rehearsals, one of them
being on the day of the performance. Bunn had been the victim of an
elaborate hoax. Mrs Mardyn's complicity seems unlikely; yet, very
strangely, she never repudiated any of the claims that had been made on
her behalf. After the first night, Macready received an envelope sealed
with an impression of Byron's head, and containing a lock of grey hair
fastened by gold thread and wrapped in a sheet of paper bearing only the
words 'Werner, November 1830; Byron, Ravenna, 1821: and Sardanapalus, April 10th, 1834'.[2] He was much pleased to conclude that it was
Byron's hair, and that it had been sent to him by Mrs Leigh, an assumption afterwards confirmed by a friend of hers, the wife of Colonel
D'Aguilar.

Sardanapalus had what was then a good run, during which Captain
Medwin, who seemed to Macready 'a complete shuffler', sent a messenger
to ask for a free seat.[3]

The dramatic version of another work of Byron's, *Mazeppa*, provided
the Victorian stage with one of its greatest spectacles, the perilous ride of a
Tartar prince tied to a wild horse—a feat which became yet more
sensational when undertaken by a woman. This was the redoubtable
American, Ada Menken, young Swinburne's friend, who had the courage
not merely to perform the ride, but to do so in a breathtakingly daring
costume, pink fleshings.

Byron's effect on musicians was even greater than on dramatists.
Rossini composed a choral elegy on his death, and took part in it himself.

---

[1] 28 Mar. 1834: Murray MSS.
[2] MACREADY. 11 Apr. 1834.   [3] Ibid. 10 May 1834.

Byron would have been pleased at that, for he had constantly attended Rossini's operas and had sung his tunes, much to Leigh Hunt's contempt, 'in a swaggering style, though in a voice both small and veiled'. (Hunt, who prided himself on being musical, had a low opinion of the popular Rossini.) The new composers, the romantics, from Berlioz to Tchaikowsky, found Byronism an inspiration for many works.

Nor was he neglected by the choreographers. There were at least two versions of *Le Corsaire*, somewhat fantastic but containing Conrad, Medora, and Gulnare, and danced many times in Paris, London, and St Petersburg.[1] The great Italian master at the Scala in Milan, Carlo Blasis, listed among his works *Lord Byron à Venise*, a ballet of a 'Mixed Character'. If any record of its production could be found, it might turn out that the opponent of the waltz was first portrayed on the stage by a *premier danseur*.

Of the innumerable painters who chose Byronic subjects for their canvases, Delacroix was the most fitted by temperament to catch the vigour and vividness of the prototype. Byron's comic vein, however, was almost never of interest to the artists, and their Juans and Haidees, Mazeppas, Manfreds, and picturesque modern Greeks paid tribute to him under only two aspects—the lover and the sublime rebel.

'The genius of Byron, which appeared at the beginning of this century, is like a funeral torch sculptured on our cradles', wrote the Spaniard Emilio Castelar. In the 20th century, which has placed a much higher value on Byron's astringent realism than on his rhetoric, his humour rather than his melancholy, a funeral torch would seem the least appropriate of symbols. The reader of our time would be more inclined to compare him to an inexhaustible Roman candle, or one of those rockets that goes on breaking out in varied coruscations and leaves in the air a luminous smoky trail, an acrid tang of gunpowder.

It is difficult to imagine so dæmonic a spirit attaining peace, but that was what he longed for when he saw the tombs in the Bologna cemetery and was moved by their simple and humble inscriptions:

Martini Luigi
Implora Pace

Lucrezia Picini
Implora eterna quiete

'Pray, if I should be shovelled into the Lido churchyard in your time,' he instructed Hoppner, the British Consul at Venice, 'let me have *implora*

---

[1] Medora was danced in the present century by Pavlova and Karsavina.

pace, and nothing else, for my epitaph.'[1] For at least twenty-four hours he meant it, writing next day to John Murray:

> Those few words say all that can be said or sought. . . . There is all the helplessness, and humble hope, and deathlike prayer, that can rise from the grave—'implora pace'. . . . I am sure my bones would not rest in an English grave, or my clay mix with the earth of that country.[2]

Compelled to watch the aftermath of his life and labour, he would have found little to calm him though much to revive sardonic amusement in the shifting relationships of his friends and enemies. There was Caroline Lamb's lethargic husband Prime Minister, and frequently in company with Hobhouse who regarded him highly. There was the odious, detested Henry Brougham wearing the Robes of the Lord Chancellor, and likewise in amity with Hobhouse, who had once thought him intolerable—and was sometimes to think so again. What was more wonderful still, the day was to come when Brougham of all people stood up in the House of Lords and protested against the exclusion of Byron's monument from Westminster Abbey! And the intimidating Lady Holland, whom Hobhouse, using the word in its strictest sense, had called 'awful'—in widowhood she came to depend greatly on him for news and companionship, writing him little notes asking him to *tête-à-tête* dinners; and, for all the mischief-making of Lady Blessington and others, speaking very fondly of Byron.

Hobhouse, as may happen with fundamentally good-natured men who are somewhat pugnacious in youth, grew mellow with time, a fond and slightly strait-laced father with three daughters who were the pride of his heart. The resentments which had darkened so many days and driven him to 'walk about', fuming, gradually wore themselves out. He had written in 1831 of 'the thousand and one squabbles' that Byron's affairs had entailed on him,[3] and one cannot keep quarrelling about a dead man for ever. He had no great regard for Thomas Campbell, but he came to realize that poverty is a hard taskmaster to a journalist, and when he found himself in Hastings where Campbell was living, he banished from his mind the offensive *New Monthly* article that had followed Lady Byron's 'Remarks', and their intercourse was amicable.

In May 1844, he was induced to call on Count D'Orsay to see his picture of Byron (which he immediately persuaded him to alter), and he met Lady Blessington, whose connection with his friend he had once deemed 'not much more respectable than that of the Hunts'[4]. He found the *ménage* 'singular'—particularly the large boar-hounds in the court-yard, which were unleashed at night to keep creditors at bay: but he

[1] *L. & J.* 6 June 1819.   [2] Ibid. 7 June.   [3] Hobhouse *Journals*, 25 Nov.
[4] Marginal comment in his copy of Moore's biography, 1831.

thought D'Orsay a talented person, and he talked pleasantly of Byron with Lady Blessington. She had on the whole used Hobhouse well in her book, and he was very much inclined—though he would have been the last to recognize this—to judge books on Byron by whether or not they had accorded him his due place.

He did not know it was this charming hostess who had secretly caused Byron's unmerciful lampoon on Samuel Rogers to be published—the expression of a black mood and a furious sense of injury which the head-strong poet would have done well to tear up before he went to Greece. It had been left among other papers in Genoa, and Lady Blessington on a second visit there had managed, through Barry's carelessness, to take a copy. No one with a vestige of good feeling would have allowed it to be circulated, but—either as an act of spite against Rogers or to injure Byron's memory when her articles about him were under criticism, she had first regaled her friends with it,[1] and then given it to *Fraser's Magazine*—a brutal blow to Rogers who had written generously of Byron in his poem *Italy*.

Twenty years after Byron's death, Hobhouse was tending to enjoy the common ground he could share with the friends of his friend and to forget that it had once been a battlefield. The day came when even Moore was a welcome guest at his fine country house, Erle Stoke. Moore was by that time sixty-five years old and 'much shattered'. His memory was slowly failing, his social gaiety dimming. Everything in his once brilliant life was going wrong, and he was destined to outlive in sorrow all his children and much of his fame.

Perhaps it was because 'merry Tom Moore, clever Tom Moore', whose merriment and cleverness had so often seemed a provocation to a less dexterous man, had so little now to arouse envy that at last he awoke a sort of protective affection.

> T. Moore told me he should go away this morning but he forgot it, and staid without a word of explanation. I was glad of it for he is very agreeable. . . .
> Moore sang four or five of his songs to the great delight of my girls.[2]

Sir John Hobhouse knew everyone and went everywhere. His diary is full of balls and concerts at Buckingham Palace, ducal dinner parties, talks

---

[1] E.g. JEKYLL. 1 Aug. 1832. 'She recited to me the most dreadful verses by Byron against his friend Rogers, but will not publish them, or the poet must inevitably plunge into the Serpentine.' Correspondence in the Gamba Papers and the Murray MSS., however, shows that it was she who got them published the following year. Trelawny, who pretends in his book to have been shocked by Byron's readiness to believe ill of Rogers, actually wrote (in error of course) to John Murray congratulating him on printing the savage verses. Augusta also wrote to Murray. Deeply distressed for Rogers, she exclaimed: 'Thank God! none of my children have an atom of poetry in their composition!' (1 Jan. 1833: Murray MSS.)   [2] 24 Sept. 1844. British Museum: Broughton Papers.

with great statesmen, attendance as an interested and alert spectator at historic ceremonies: but he always made time to keep up certain quiet and reposeful friendships. The best of these in his latter years was with one of the companions of Shelley's youth, Thomas Love Peacock.

They had originally sensed an affinity in their mutual dislike of Moore and Hunt. When Hobhouse had been asked to do an article on Moore's Life of Byron in the *Westminster Review*, he was obliged, knowing Moore and feeling as he did about the book, to refuse; but he had proposed to Bowring that the assignment should be offered to Peacock.[1] The resulting criticism seems to reveal traces of Hobhouse's influence, but it is doubtful if Peacock needed much urging to castigate Hunt in passing. He despised all who were engaged in falsifying Shelley for posterity, and was one of those who had advised Bowring against publishing the justification by Hunt of Shelley's conduct towards his first wife. Reviewing Moore, he had therefore taken the opportunity of condemning Hunt's assault on Byron for—

> the querulous egotisms, the scaturient vanity bubbling up in every page like the hundred fountains of the river Hoangho, the readiness to violate all the confidences of private life, the intrinsic nothingness of what the writer had it in his power to tell, the shallow mockeries of philosophical thinking, the quaint and silly figures of speech, the out-of-the-way notions of morals and manners, the eternal reference of everything to self, the manifest labour and effort to inflate a mass of insignificancies . . . the constantly recurring 'Io triumphe' over the excellent hits and clinches of the author and his family, and the obvious *malus animus* of the whole work. . . .[2]

There was even less love lost among Shelley's various friends than Byron's. Trelawny too attacked Hunt, but waited till he was dead.

> Leigh Hunt often said he was the dearest friend Shelley had. I believe he was the most costly. His theory was that between friends everything should be in common: he said you could not do your friend a greater favour than constitute him your banker, and that he could receive no greater pleasure than answering your drafts.[3]

This was almost literally true. In his second edition to *Lord Byron and Some of His Contemporaries* Hunt had remarked 'that the world would have been losers in a very large way . . . if certain men of lively and improvident genius, humanists of the most persuasive order, had not sometimes left themselves under the necessity of being assisted'. Yet it was an ironical thing that Trelawny should have exposed his weakness because he happened to be in the almost unique position of a man from whom Hunt had refused the positive offer of a loan![4]

[1] NESBITT.   [2] April 1830.   [3] TRELAWNY, *Records*.
[4] BREWER. Letter of 14 July 1823.

Hunt, who had been visited by Byron in prison when he was serving
a two-year sentence for a libel judged subversive in tendency, lived to be
the recipient of a civil pension—and to inspire the portrait of a calculating
sponger who presents to the world a façade of airy and whimsical indifference to money. Charles Dickens was obliged to make a general disclaimer
of having depicted Hunt as Harold Skimpole in *Bleak House*, but privately
he not only admitted it was a likeness but affirmed that, as to character, it
could not have been a more faithful one.

> Skimpole. I must not forget Skimpole—of whom I will proceed to speak
> as if I had only read him and not written him. I suppose he is the most exact
> portrait that ever was painted in words! I have very seldom, if ever, done
> such a thing, but the likeness is astonishing. I don't think it could possibly
> be more like himself. It is so awfully true that I made a bargain with myself
> 'never to do so any more.' There is not an atom of exaggeration or sup-
> pression. It is an absolute reproduction of the real man. Of course I have been
> careful to keep the outward figure away from the fact; but in all else it is life
> itself.[1]

Teresa Guiccioli, transformed into a rich marquise of the Second
Empire frequenting the court of Napoleon III, could not bring herself to
read what Hunt had written about Byron until 1857, when the book was
given to her by John Murray's successor, the son who had been brought
into the drawing-room expressly to see Byron's Memoirs burnt in 1824.
He was now a great traveller and the author of guide books which formed
the model for Baedeker. Teresa had no need to struggle with English for
him. Torrents of French, not impeccable but remarkably eloquent (for
some reason she had come to prefer French to Italian), flooded page after
page with a disgust, a horror, that could not have been more vehement if
she had read the work on the day of publication.

> *All—all* is lying and perfidy! There is only one true thing in this book
> crammed with malice—and that is involuntary—the portrait of the author. . . .
> . . . Calumny never passes without leaving some trace. . . . Abroad and above
> all in France, most biographies and estimates of Lord Byron's character,
> through a union of superficiality and want of research, are based on hostile
> English books. . . . For this reason the too absolute silence of Lord Byron's
> friends and of Lord Broughton in particular has always distressed me—since
> for many people, while the words of enemies and of ill nature accuse, the
> silence of friends condemns. . . . It is true that most of the facts about Lord
> Byron are to be found in Moore but . . . mixed like gold in a mine—so that
> the reader, who is nowadays always short of time . . . having to work to get
> at the truth, does not reach it.
> What Moore lacked was a social position in harmony with his tastes—
> more independence—perhaps even a little more generosity in his character to

[1] *Harper's Magazine*, 1906. To the Hon. Mrs Richard Watson, 25 Sept. 1853.

say frankly, courageously, what he thought—to explain himself so that he would carry conviction to his readers. I presume also that the part he had played (active or passive) in the destruction of Lord Byron's Memoirs always weighed on his conscience, because he had to answer to the world for that trust—but it is a subject too painful for me to dwell on.

As the last word on Lord Byron (not as a poet but as a man—moral and social) is far from being said I have always hoped and I always do hope that it will be said one day by Lord Broughton.

No one lived so long and so intimately with Lord Byron. . . . Who better than Lord Broughton, for whom he had so great a friendship, to show the world the true Lord Byron with his so few faults and his so great virtues? I am persuaded that Lord Broughton will not fail in this sacred duty—that he will not forget posterity demands it of him as a debt of honour that he must pay. . . .

You, Monsieur, who see him, you must press this on him—and in doing it you will have the satisfaction of thinking that justice and honour rendered to the memory of Lord Byron must be an accomplishment of the wishes of your excellent father.

As to what it is in my power to do . . . I hope that after my death it will be done. . . . Whatever may be the consequence to my memory matters little so long as the documents and letters that can put the great and good heart of Lord Byron in their true light are not lost.[1]

The book that could provoke that cry for redress in an ageing woman with a well-filled life was an extraordinary book; the love that could surge up in such a rush of loyalty and resolve was an extraordinary love; and the man who could inspire hatred and love of so intense a quality needed a greater interpreter than he ever had—a Goethe, not a Lady Blessington, a Medwin, a Dallas, or even a Moore.

Goethe had taken the measure of Byron, though they never met. 'And when', he wrote to a friend who might see him, 'you . . . have an opportunity to give news of yourself to that remarkable man, tell him also about me and mine, and the inexhaustible reverence, admiration, and love which we feel for him. Speak out and tell him that we should look upon any of us as most fortunate who might happen to meet him, wherever it might be, on this globe.'[2] He had addressed a little poem to Byron which had arrived too late to be translated before the voyage to Greece, and which, knowing no German, the other could not read.

It was Goethe who first exclaimed against the folly of those who judged such a poet by standards of purity and morality, instead of 'boldness, audacity, and grandeur'.[3] From him too came the sublime tribute in the second part of *Faust*—the symbolic portrayal of Byron as Euphorion, the offspring of Faust and Helen of Troy.

[1] 2 Jan. 1858: Murray MSS.
[2] BUTLER. Letter to Charles Sterling, 13 Mar. 1824.
[3] Ibid. Talk with Eckermann, 16 Dec. 1828.

Goethe was on Hobhouse's distinguished Committee for the presentation of a monument to Westminster Abbey, and helped to pay for Thorwaldsen's statue. 'For even though the departed has already erected a glorious spiritual monument to himself, it is very right and proper that an actual, permanent memorial should bring him visibly to the memory of posterity.'[1]

The Dean and Chapter of the Abbey, however, continued not to see eye to eye with the illustrious German. Ten years after they had rejected Byron's body, a new application was made in the hope that at least the statue might be acceptable. A refusal rapidly followed. In June 1840 the *Philadelphia Public Ledger* reported more or less accurately:

> The statue of Lord Byron, made by Thorwaldsen, the first of living sculptors, is, and has been for five years, in the vaults of one of the English Custom Houses. The ecclesiastical authorities objected to its erection in Westminster Abbey and the exertions of those for whom it was made have died away—until this exquisite work of art lies almost forgotten in its packing case of rough boards, amidst rum puncheons and bonded sacks of corn in the Custom House cellars.

The error here was that the exertions of Hobhouse, chief promoter and permanent chairman of the memorial project, had 'died away'. His desire to win for Byron the official status conferred by a monument in the nearest approach to a national Pantheon, remained stubborn, and as soon as Dean Ireland, the principal objector, was removed by death in 1842, he set about preparations for a new assault on Poets' Corner. It was an unpleasant surprise to learn there were as many obstacles as ever.

In 1844 Thomas Campbell died, and was given Abbey burial. 'Something should be done about Byron', was Hobhouse's first thought;[2] and after attending the funeral, full of pomp and ceremony and almost empty of grief, he wrote: 'I cannot help feeling more indignant than ever at the exclusion of my friend's monument from those precincts which received the remains of his not superior rival.'[3]

The eight pall-bearers, chosen solely for their rank and eminence, had included the Prime Minister, Sir Robert Peel; and it was embittering for Hobhouse to remember that a few months before, this old school-fellow of Byron's had broken to him the news that there was no hope of getting the statue into the Abbey, and had suggested trying the Library of Trinity College, Cambridge, instead.[4] A feeler had already been thrown out by

---

[1] BUTLER. Letter to F. Benecke, 3 Apr. 1826.
[2] 30 June. British Museum: Broughton Papers.   [3] Ibid. 3 July.
[4] Ibid. 12 Feb. Byron had links, by a curious coincidence, with four famous Prime Ministers—Melbourne, Peel, Lord John Russell, a close friend of Moore's and acquaintance of his own, and Disraeli who—apart from other connections—was a prime mover in the erection of the monument near Hyde Park Corner.

The Countess of Lovelace, Byron's daughter Ada,
aged about 32, from a daguerreotype

Dr Whewell, the Master, but Hobhouse had set his heart on the Abbey and was disposed to make an agitation about it.

A meeting of the subscribers was called—such few of them as were still alive and available: and the very aged Sam Rogers, who with great magnanimity had remained on the Committee despite the lampoon, said he didn't wish to lie in the Abbey because the company wasn't good.[1] The meeting was in favour of Trinity, but Hobhouse was so much annoyed at the slight upon Byron by bishops and deans that he actually toyed with the idea of letting the statue go to the Louvre. (The French Government had tendered promising enquiries.)

In a last bid for Poets' Corner, he set himself to write a pamphlet in his old, extreme style, telling the whole history of the rejected monument and explaining why he was not in accord with those who were willing to see it in Trinity College, the British Museum, or any other honourable situation which had been proposed.

. . . Persons who are not fit to be held up to public regard in a church are not fit to be so distinguished anywhere. If the example is that which is likely to become pernicious, that effect will be just as likely to be produced by a monument placed in a public gallery as in a church; and it is difficult to conceive what other apprehensions, except that of bad example, can be supposed to influence the church authorities in desiring this exclusion. They can hardly be so vindictive as to aim at punishment—the punishment of the living for the offences of the dead; nor so sanguine as to think that anyone will become more careful in his writings merely to procure a niche in Westminster Abbey.[2]

It could not be hoped that such arguments would convince the Dean and Chapter or that very strong objector, the Bishop of London; but the value of the pamphlet was that it incorporated Hobhouse's considered opinion of Byron's character and of the treatment he had had from society:

Lord Byron had hard measure dealt to him in his lifetime, but he did not die without leaving behind him friends, deeply and affectionately attached friends. . . . Those friends, however, do not prefer their late much loved associate to truth—they would not sacrifice the best interests of society at the shrine even of his surpassing fame. They were not blind to the defects of his character, nor of his writings, but they knew that some of the gravest accusations levelled against him had no foundation in fact; and perhaps the time may come, when justice may be done to the dead without injury to the feelings of the living.

[1] 29 July 1844. British Museum: Broughton Papers.
[2] HOBHOUSE, *Remarks*.

Even now it may be permitted to say something of him, and it will be said by one who, perhaps, knew him as well as he was known by any human being.

Lord Byron had failings—many failings, certainly, but he was untainted with any of the baser vices; and his virtues—his good qualities—were all of the higher order. He was honourable and open in all his dealings, and he was kind. He was affected by the distress—and, rarer still, he was pleased with the prosperity of others. Tender-hearted he was to a degree not usual with our sex—and he shrunk, with a feminine sensibility, from the sight of cruelty.

He was true-spoken—he was affectionate—he was very brave, if that be any praise—but his courage was not the result of physical coolness or indifference to danger; on the contrary, he entertained apprehensions and adopted precautions, of which he made no secret, and was by no means ashamed. His calmness and presence of mind, in the hour of peril, were the offspring of reflection and of a fixed resolution to act becomingly and well.

He was alive to every indication of good feeling in others—a generous or noble sentiment, a trait of tenderness or devotion, not only real, but in imaginary characters, affected him deeply, even to tears.

He was, both by his habits and his nature, incapable of any mean compliance, any undue submission towards those who command reverence and exact flattery from men of the highest genius: and it will be the eternal praise of his writings, as it was one of the merits of his conversation, that he threw no lustre on any exploit, however brilliant, nor character, however exalted, which had not contributed to the happiness or welfare of mankind.

Lord Byron was totally free from envy and from jealousy. . . . He was well aware of his own great reputation; but he was neither vain-glorious, nor overbearing. Of his lesser qualities very little need be said, because his most inveterate detractors have done justice to his power of pleasing and to the irresistible charms of his general deportment. There was indeed something about him not to be definitely described—but almost universally felt, which captivated those around him, and impressed them, in spite of occasional distrusts.

Part of this fascination may, doubtless, be ascribed to the entire self-abandonment, the incautious, it may be said, the dangerous sincerity of his private conversation, but his very weaknesses were amiable; and, as has been said of a portion of his virtues, were of a feminine character—so that the affection felt for him was as that for a favourite and sometimes froward sister.

In mixed society Lord Byron was not talkative, neither did he attempt to surprise by pointed or by humourous remarks; but in all companies he held his own, and that, too, without unbecoming rivalry with his seniors in age and reputation, and without any offensive condescension towards his inferior associates. In more familiar intercourse, he was a gay companion and a free, but he never transgressed the bounds of good breeding, even for a moment. Indeed he was, in the best sense of the word, a gentleman.

Hobhouse sent advance copies of this warm, straightforward, and spirited appreciation to a number of persons who were fitted to judge its accuracy. Thomas Moore called it 'perfect', Lady Holland said 'admirable', John Murray III was eager to publish it, and Macaulay urged him to expand it to a full account of his friend; but Hobhouse explained that while Lady Byron lived, he could not do so, because there would be the difficulty of dealing with the Separation.[1] He sent the pamphlet, however, to the Countess of Lovelace.

The Countess of Lovelace was Ada, Byron's longed-for daughter, the symbol of every deprivation he had suffered through becoming a wanderer. She had married Lord King, holder of an ancient barony, raised to an earldom under Lord Melbourne's Ministry. She was a handsome, delicate, eccentric young woman who had inherited her mother's talent for mathematics but developed it much further—far enough to make her a protegée of the great Mrs Somerville and an intimate friend of Charles Babbage; far enough, unhappily, to tempt her into contriving systems for betting which would have been infallible had it not been for the interference of horses and jockeys.

Life had been full of special pitfalls for her. The knowledge that she was an object of intense curiosity wherever she went had given her a somewhat self-conscious and high-handed manner. Her education had been supervised with all the minute and analytical watchfulness of which her mother was capable, her conscience continually probed. Her husband too, though affectionate and devoted, aspired to discipline her character. At that time the 1st Lord Lovelace's friendship with his mother-in-law was as extreme as his subsequent hostility, and they took counsel together about all Ada's pursuits and habits, as well as the system of education for her three children. Ada was supposed to be so absorbed in scientific study that she must feel glad to shift some of the burden of responsibility.

She had inherited her mother's precise and considered style of speaking, which Hobhouse did not care for, but he found her 'amiable and interesting', and her speculative and independent mode of thinking was very much to his taste. That independence was the reason why she could meet and talk to him, disregarding the maternal warnings which, some years before, had caused her to tell him rudely at a party that she disliked him. Lady Byron had never ceased to hold the opinion that he was an 'infamous' man whom none of her descendants ought to know:[2] but Hobhouse had no notion of that, and no notion either of the astounding confidences Ada and her husband had received, nor the dramas in which

---

[1] 12 Nov. 1844. British Museum: Broughton Papers.
[2] Written after the dedication of *Childe Harold* in a copy given to her grandson, 6 Sept. 1854.

they had shared. A mysterious begging letter in 1843 had simply been endorsed by Hobhouse: 'Elizabeth Medora Leigh—stating herself to be *child* of Lord Byron and starving—some impostor I *hope*.'[1] That Lord and Lady Lovelace had been first encouraged to receive Mrs Leigh's ruined daughter as a half-sister of Ada's, and then required to close their door implacably upon her—all that would have seemed to him almost too fantastic to be believed; but Ada, unlike her father, could keep secrets.

Byron's character as drawn by Hobhouse was in every possible way a contradiction of what she had heard about him from her mother, who remained perfectly unable to apprehend, till the day of her death, that he might have matured into a better, more restrained, less neurotic being than the spoiled and guilt-ridden young man she had so briefly known. Lady Byron was under the impression that she had never attempted to bias Ada's feelings, but her need of esteem for the heroic position she believed she had taken made it an impossibility for her to act up to her resolutions, and Ada's adherence to what her mother called 'the Mythic idea generally entertained of your father'[2], contributed to an estrangement which lasted till nearly the end of her short life. What view, if any, she expressed to her father's friend about his pamphlet, and whether she showed it to her mother, does not appear in his journal.

A decision was taken against publication because, if the protest failed to achieve its object, it would have damaged the chance of arranging matters gracefully with Trinity College, and Hobhouse was at last induced to see that Wren's library was no such poor *pis aller* as he had imagined. He went to Cambridge in person in November 1844, travelling very enjoyably by railway train: the wonders of the modern age always had an immense fascination for him. The Master of Trinity turned out most sympathetic and enlightened, and the library a far nobler building than he had remembered. In his day, undergraduates had not been allowed to enter, and he had supposed that none but tutors, fellows, and dignitaries would be able to see the memorial. So at last, if only in effigy, there was to be a home for Byron.

Before leaving London after its imprisonment of many years, the statue was placed in the studio of Sir Richard Westmacott and shown to visitors. Among these was the poet's widow and the author, Anna Jameson—for a time her inseparable friend. According to Mrs Jameson's report, Lady Byron looked at Thorwaldsen's work in silence for some minutes, and then, her eyes filling with tears, murmured: 'It is very

---

[1] 12 Aug. Murray MSS.

[2] MAYNE. A long letter on this topic quoted without date, p. 388. Ada died in 1852, aged thirty-six, and by her own request was buried in her father's grave.

beautiful, but not half beautiful enough for my dear Byron!'[1] Was this a novelist's embroidery? It is not easy to reconcile such a sentiment with the unrelenting, and if anything intensifying, condemnation of the narratives written later, and explicitly intended for publication.

Tom Campbell got a full-length monument in the Abbey which made him look very much larger than he was in life. It was trying for Hobhouse, but even he came to see that Byron was really better off musing alone among the splendours of the library than in that curious mason's yard of sculptural litter called Poets' Corner.

Hobhouse could take a pride in what was the fruit not only of his obstinacy, toil, and influence, but also his enterprise in getting Byron to sit to Thorwaldsen, and his extravagance too in commissioning a bust that was then rather beyond his means. Without it, there would have been no one but the immensely inferior Bartolini to turn to for a sculpture done from life, and little support would have been forthcoming for that. He had wanted the head to be crowned with laurels, but this Byron had effectually resisted; and now, except for the hair being brought forward in the classical manner instead of brushed back from the forehead, it was a capital likeness of the poet at the age of thirty.[2]

The bust had a place of honour in Hobhouse's London house, and he was able to show it to Lady Lovelace at one of his dinner parties. 'She certainly reminded me much of her father's expression—especially the upper part of his face. She looked a great deal at her father's bust, and appeared affected by it. When going away she thanked me for giving her an opportunity of seeing it.'[3]

In February 1847 he took another railway trip to Cambridge—'a merry journey'—and by now he was quite reconciled.

I walked to Trinity College Library and saw the Byron statue. It is a beautiful work of art and is in an admirable position. Little did he or I think, when we used to idle about the college—that he would have a statue, and the only statue, in that splendid building.

The white marble figure looked so serene, gazing beyond the leather bindings and the gleaming busts of noble men. If only it had not been for Mrs Leigh's money troubles, dismal, nagging, irretrievable, and her ne'er-do-well sons and disgraced daughters, and the shocking rumours

[1] Trelawny either read this story when it came out in *The Literary Life of the Rev. William Harness* (1872) or heard it from Mrs Jameson, whom he knew; and in his own version of it for Richard Edgcumbe, he made himself Lady Byron's companion on this occasion. He never, in fact, met her.

[2] There is a copy of it in the Borghese Gardens, Rome, and another in the Town Hall of Missolonghi.

[3] 15 June 1845. British Museum: Broughton Papers.

revived from time to time and countenanced by Lady Byron's friends; and that plausible scoundrel still passing himself off as Byron's son, and poor stupid old Fletcher, despite all efforts at rescue, practically destitute; and the Lovelaces' very peculiar new ideas about bringing up Byron's grandsons—actually wanting one of them to be an engineer!—if only it were not for these and all the other worries and mysteries and absurdities, one might almost have believed that turbulent spirit was at rest.

Forrester's account of Byron at Missolonghi

Medwin does not say where he procured Forrester's two letters about Byron, but their style is perfectly distinguished from his own, and the verifiable particulars are authentic. Forrester went down with a convict ship in which he was serving. The date of his meeting with Byron was January 26th, 1824.

Missolonghi is just as wretched a collection of houses and huts as can well be imagined. . . . The season was very rainy and the houses were insulated among mire and water, the communication being kept up by stepping-stones. . . . A visit to Lord Byron was our first step in landing. . . .

The principal and only tolerable room was approached by an outward stair. Three sides were furnished with sofas in the Turkish taste. A deal shelf, apparently stuck against the wall, was loaded with books. . . . Round the walls were appended to numerous nails and pegs, fowling-pieces and pistols of various descriptions and nations; sabres and yataghans. The corridor or antichamber, or whatever else it might be termed, swarmed with Mainotes and others, armed to the teeth.

We were ushered in by Tita, his Lordship's chasseur, who reminded me of the French sapeurs, as he wore a bushy beard, with his livery which was set off by two silver epaulettes. He was an immense fellow, upwards of six feet in height, and although well-proportioned for such a herculean figure, his frame was too large and heavy for his stature to come within the description of elegant. His page was a young Greek, dressed as an Albanian or Mainote, with very handsomely chased arms in his girdle, and his maitre d'hotel, or fac-totum, an honest-looking, though not remarkably elastic Northumbrian, named Fletcher, who seemed, and doubtless with reason, a great favourite with his master.

. . . Of course, I entered his house as in a certain degree familiarised to the appearance of its master, but great was my astonishment, although prepared to make a fair allowance to artists, to see before me a being bearing as little resemblance to the pretended fac-simile, as I to Apollo. True . . . I had certainly been taught to expect one thing I found—a long oval face with a handsome nose, and a kind of rapt expression of thoughtfulness, blended with a cynical hint amounting to 'don't think me thoughtful for want of thought'; but instead of . . . the absent, unsociable, and supercilious deportment I had been prepared to meet, we were presented with the personification of frankness itself; his countenance enlivened with smiles, and his whole manner the very reverse of anything like abstraction, not to say misanthropy.

. . . Our intercourse was under some ludicrous restrictions. Any communication with Turkey would have classed us as unclean at any of the Ionian Islands, or other parts where certain precautions against the plague are attended to . . . we made it a sort of quarantine case of conscience to sit on a wooden stool and packing cases, and to deny ourselves the luxury of his Lordship's Turkish cushions and sofa.

. . . In communicating with Mavrocordato, Lord Byron spoke French, but oftener Italian, the latter beautifully. As there arose some demur at the idea of restitution [for the Ionian caïque] he became warm, and even went so far as to declare that rather than not have it made, he would advance the money out of his own pocket. . . . The interview ended in a promise from the prince, to send the sum required at a specified time to the house of Lord Byron.

On returning, his lordship went into a very animated and desultory conversation, which savoured much of Beppo and Don Juan, more than his other productions. Far from showing any of the gloomy misanthropy or wayward shyness he affected in most of his writings, he rattled away in such a harum-scarum manner, that it required an effort to recollect that he had ever written on a grave or affecting subject, and with such a profusion of smiles upon his countenance as seemed to leave no space where care might throw in a single sable touch. Now and then, indeed . . . four or five very expressive furrows would streak his forehead, but they disappeared with the fleeting rapidity of the Aurora Borealis.

. . . He laughingly apologized for his table, which, from the circumstances wherein he was then placed, was not, as he said, *trop bien montée*; but he felt the less annoyed when he reflected that persons of our profession understood those things, and were of course prepared for all sorts of privations. He then bustled about, actively assisted by Fletcher, who was but poorly aided by the Greek menials in placing dishes to the best advantage, drawing corks and all the *et cætera* of the table. . . . On opening a bottle of wine, and inspecting the complexion of its contents, his lordship questioned Fletcher as to its name and lineage.

'I really don't know, my lord,' was the reply.

'Then away with it,' he rejoined; 'I hate anonymous wine.'

We were five at table, and Count Gamba . . . was one. . . . His Lordship was extremely amusing on the subject of an impression on the minds of some, that Greek liberty was to be achieved by the establishment of a printing-press. . . .

On looking over the arms about the room, his Lordship asked the principal of the party if he would like to try a shot with pistols? On his answering affirmatively, they walked up to the landing-place of the outside stairs, from which they fired at Maraschino bottles, placed on a pilaster in the court. . . . They had an equal number of shots. Byron struck each time. His antagonist missed once, although a very good shot. But one of Lord Byron's was excellent:—the upper rim of a bottle which his competitor broke fell on the top of the pilaster, and remained there, reduced to a size not much larger than a finger ring. Instead of having another bottle placed, he took aim at this fragment, and reduced it to dust. His precision was the more surprising because his hand shook as if under the influence of an ague fit, and the time he took to take aim would have made any other man's hand unsteady.

. . . As each fired, a large Labrador dog, named Lion, ran and picked up the bottle, which he laid at the bottom of the stair. I remarked to Lord Byron, as we were laughing at his officiousness.

'That is an honest tyke of yours.'

'Oh! Oh!' he replied, 'I find you are half a countryman of mine.'
I answered I was a whole Scotsman.

'Then, we are half countrymen,' said he; 'my mother was Scotch.'

Lord B is, as near as I can judge, about five feet nine inches in height, and of an athletic make, which is most apparent from the loins downward, the breast having suffered from the attitude acquired through his lameness. [This is contrary to the description of Byron's body by Millingen, who states that the *upper* portion was fine and well developed; and the same thing was stated by Hobhouse in a letter to Thorwaldsen, to guide him in modelling the figure.] . . . His face is pale, and from the angle of one jaw to the other unusually broad. The forehead is remarkably striking and fine . . . the hair receding at the temples; its surface as smooth as alabaster, except when a moment of abstraction leaves it with lines of thought.

His eyes are strikingly expressive . . . somewhat between a light blue and grey. His eyelashes are long and thick; eyebrows distinct and finely arched, both nearly the colour of his hair. His nose, so far from aquiline and thin, as represented in plates I have seen, rather inclines to turn up at the point; it is of moderate length, somewhat broad between the alæ . . much of that style which is found among athletic, full-faced highlanders of a fair complexion. The upper lip rather short than otherwise; the mouth well-proportioned, the lips round and plump without being thick, with a pleasing curl or curve outwards, which, on their being separated in speaking or smiling, display to great advantage a beautifully white, regular set of teeth. His chin is dimpled. . . .

His hair is parted all over his head into innumerable small spiral curls, about three inches long, which is somewhat surprising, as it is as fine as silk. The effect is very becoming. Its colour light auburn, or perhaps it may be more properly described as light brown, inclining to auburn. [The grey mixed with what was naturally *dark* auburn hair must have lightened its appearance.] It is very glossy. . . . His beard is shaved all over the face, except the upper lip, but his *moustache* is certainly no ornament, as it is of a flaxen whiteness. . . . Complexion fair and florid.

. . . His hands are exquisitely formed, very white and the nails beautiful. Of the feet I cannot judge as he wore boots; that on the sound foot was clumsily made, with the view, I suppose, of rendering the shapelessness of the other less apparent. . . . Though not so deformed as many I have known, yet it is sufficiently so to occasion a considerable limp in his walk.

He wore a deep green hussar jacket, with black woollen shag collar and cuffs, with a profusion of cording, braid, and frogs, a plain black waistcoat, blue trowsers with a broad scarlet stripe on the sides, and a blue foraging cap with a scarlet border and leathern shade. He told me he had for field duty two fancy uniforms, besides that of Lord Sligo's militia. . . .

He had a slight burr in uttering words in which the letter *r* occurred, such as Corinth, for instance, and it was far from disagreeable. His voice was sweet and sonorous, his most prevailing mode of expression deliberate, though not slow, and I thought I detected a slight touch of a Scottish accent, which, however, I could not satisfy myself existed.

. . . A young man, whom his Lordship laughingly styled Secretary of

State made his appearance, with a canvas bag in his hand, containing the dollars in question [the compensation money].

Byron laughed at the grave carriage the man put on while counting them, and said—'Well, I am wronging the poor devils if each dollar is not like a drop of their heart's blood.' My firm opinion is, that the sum ultimately will be made up from his coffers. . . .

'I do not know how it will end,' said his Lordship gaily, 'but one thing is certain, there is no fear of my running,' at the same time glancing at his lame foot.

MINIATURE BIOGRAPHY

1788. Jan. 22. George Gordon Byron born at 16 Holles Street, London.

c. 1790. Mrs Byron, her fortune spent by her husband, takes her son to Scotland where they live, chiefly in Aberdeen, for some years.

1791. Captain John Byron, father of George Gordon, dies in France, aged thirty-six.

1794. By the death of the 5th Lord Byron's grandson, George Gordon becomes heir to the barony.

1798. May. George Gordon succeeds to the title, and soon afterwards is brought to England, a peer aged ten.

1798–1799. Byron is taught by an American, 'Dummer' Rogers, in Nottingham, and undergoes painful treatments for his lameness from a quack surgeon. The family solicitor, Hanson, learns of base conduct by Byron's Calvinist nurse and recommends her dismissal.

1799–1801. Byron is a boarder at Dr Glennie's school, Dulwich. His mother's interferences exasperate the headmaster.

1801. He is placed in Dr Drury's house at Harrow School.

1803–1808. Newstead Abbey being let, Mrs Byron lives at Burgage Manor, Southwell, a few miles away. There Byron spends his holidays, makes friends with local families, and is encouraged to write by Miss Elizabeth Pigot.

1803. He becomes violently infatuated with Mary Chaworth, a distant cousin, heiress of Annesley Park, and refuses to return to school.

1804. Induced after months to go back to Harrow, he grows popular and makes ardent friendships. He corresponds with his half-sister, the Hon. Augusta Leigh, chiefly about difficulties with his mother.

1805. Byron leaves school in summer after playing in the annual cricket match against Eton. He enters Trinity College, Cambridge.

1806. Augusta consenting to stand security for him with a money-lender, at eighteen he is entrapped in serious debt. At Southwell he enjoys amateur theatricals and circulates his poems. His first volume, *Fugitive Pieces*, is destroyed at the request of a friendly clergyman.

1807. He prepares a new volume, *Poems on Various Occasions*, and later publishes *Hours of Idleness*. His indiscretions with girls in Southwell cause some scandal, but shortage of money keeps him from college. Drastic fasting and exercise reduce his weight, strikingly changing his appearance. In Cambridge, from summer onwards, he enters a new life. He is drawn into the circle of college intellectuals, including J. C. Hobhouse, Scrope Davies, and C. S. Matthews. It is also the period of his 'violent though pure' attachment to a middle-class youth, Edleston. He works on a satire called *British Bards*.

1808. Hours of Idleness is severely mauled by the *Edinburgh Review*. Byron polishes *British Bards* and throws in North British reviewers. He fits up part of Newstead Abbey, now regained, and entertains friends there.

1809. March. He publishes the revised satire with considerable effect, and a few days later takes his seat in the House of Lords. Though prospects are opening for him in England, he raises a large loan from Scrope Davies and goes abroad with Hobhouse. They journey adventurously through Portugal, Spain, Gibraltar, Malta, Albania, and Greece.

1810. March. At Smyrna he finishes the first draft of *Childe Harold*, Cantos I and II. With Hobhouse he travels about Asia Minor and in May swims the Hellespont. At Constantinople he has audience with the Sultan. In July Hobhouse sails for England. Byron settles in a 'far from ecclesiastical' monastery in Athens. He becomes acquainted with numerous Philhellenes and travellers. At Patras he nearly succumbs to a fever (probably malaria, which remains with him all his life). His companion is Nicolo Giraud, a youth of mixed nationality who teaches him Italian.

1811. Regretfully he returns to England, bringing *Childe Harold* and a second satire, *Hints from Horace*. He gives both to a kinsman, Robert Dallas, with *carte blanche* as to publication. Dallas introduces John Murray. In swift succession, Byron learns of the death of his mother, his great friend Matthews, two old school-fellows, Wingfield and Long, and the beloved Edleston. Some months are passed in deep gloom at Newstead, but later he comes to London and, in November, meets literary celebrities for the first time, and forms a friendship with Thomas Moore.

1812. Feb. 27. He makes a humane and adroit maiden speech in the House of Lords, but is depressed by the infidelity of a pretty housemaid, Susan Vaughan, who had solaced him at Newstead; financial difficulties press upon him, and he longs to return to the East. But when in March John Murray publishes *Childe Harold* with brilliant success, Byron suddenly becomes a social lion. He joins the ultra-fashionable Melbourne House circle, charms the great Whig hostess, Lady Melbourne, and captivates her daughter-in-law, Lady Caroline Lamb. A brief affair with Caroline involves him in melodramatic scenes.

In April he meets Lady Melbourne's niece, Miss Milbanke. A large offer for Newstead Abbey gives promise of freedom from debt, and he contemplates marriage. Miss Milbanke's refusal of his rather haphazard proposal is something of a relief. He becomes the lover of Lady Oxford, a beautiful woman of forty.

1813. The would-be purchaser of Newstead defaults. Byron is harassed by financial and emotional entanglements. In June Lady Oxford goes abroad. He has renewed his acquaintance with his half-sister, now married to a wastrel and mother of an increasing family. In July Caroline reanimates gossip by staging an hysterical scene at a ball. Byron makes energetic preparations to leave the country, but is soon telling Moore that he is engaged in a new and serious 'scrape' with a woman, and postpones his travel plan. He sees Augusta frequently.

Miss Milbanke opens correspondence with him, assuring him that her love is bestowed elsewhere. In autumn he recounts in letters to Lady Melbourne his amatory manœuvrings with Lady Frances Webster. Her effect is seen in *The Bride of Abydos*, a new narrative poem following the successful *Giaour* (June). Lady Frances's husband takes occasion to borrow £1000. Byron cannot go abroad for, of the funds amassed, he has given another £1000 to enable his friend, Francis Hodgson, to marry.

1814. Involved with several women, Byron thinks of marriage as a re-birth. An avowal from Miss Milbanke that her affections are really free encourages him to renew his addresses. He is accepted. Torn between his hope of being reformed by a virtuous bride and his more realistic misgivings, he delays visiting her. Misgiving is uppermost on both sides when at last they do meet, after very slight acquaintance; but he cannot withdraw, and she believes she can reform him.

During this year his fame is increased by *The Corsair* and *Lara*, and he receives a memorable ovation from the students in the Cambridge Senate House. In December he reluctantly travels North again for his wedding, pausing to spend Christmas with Augusta.

1815. Jan. 2. Byron and Anna Isabella Milbanke are married in the Milbanke's drawing-room, with Hobhouse as best man. A bitterly cold carriage journey to Halnaby starts the honeymoon off inauspiciously. Byron exhibits a vein of cruelty, yet throughout the short-lived marriage, he seems unaware of the lacerating effects of his changeful moods and provocative utterances on his rigidly self-controlled partner. They spend some wintry weeks with the bride's parents, and then occupy a much too expensive mansion in Piccadilly, where he is soon beset by duns. On a visit to Augusta, Byron's evident preference for her company distresses Lady Byron. Nevertheless she cultivates Augusta's friendship.

In April Murray auspiciously brings Byron and Walter Scott together. In May Byron joins the Management Committee of the Drury Lane Theatre, and, during his wife's pregnancy, is much occupied with scripts and productions and endeavours to assist literary men, amongst whom is Coleridge. He becomes recklessly intemperate, and lets loose at home his guilt and irritation. Augusta is Lady Byron's comforter and defender.

On Dec. 10 a daughter is born, Augusta Ada.

The only 1815 publication is *Hebrew Melodies*, written for musical settings.

1816. Jan. *15.* After secretly arranging an investigation of her husband's mental state, Lady Byron goes to her parents. Learning that his conduct has not the excuse of insanity, she has him notified of her intention never to return. Byron, who has had affectionate letters from her, is astounded, incredulous, and for some weeks resistant. The Deed of Separation is signed on Apr. 21, and, amidst unprecedented scandal, he leaves England for ever on Apr. 25.

During the struggle he has consented to meet a head-strong persistent girl who has repeatedly written to him—'Claire' Clairmont, stepdaughter of William Godwin. She brings Godwin's daughter, who is living with Shelley, to see him. Byron meets both again at Sécheron in Switzerland, and a mutually influential friendship with Shelley ensues. He takes a villa on Lake Geneva, and the Shelley party occupies one near by: but Byron recoils from Claire's importunities. He is joined by Hobhouse and Scrope Davies, and frequently sees Mme de Staël and her circle at Coppet. Caroline Lamb dramatizes herself as the injured heroine of a novel, *Glenarvon*, with Byron as the wicked seducer.

An overture of reconciliation to his wife, made through Mme de Staël, is a humiliating failure. Hobhouse accompanies him on an Alpine tour, and afterwards they travel to Italy, staying nearly three weeks in Milan, where they meet Henri Beyle, not yet known as Stendhal. They make for Venice, where Byron falls in love with Marianna Segati, wife of his landlord.

This year sees the publication of *The Siege of Corinth* and *Parisina*, written in 1815, and also a third Canto of *Childe Harold*, as well as *The Prisoner of Chillon*, produced after sailing round Lake Geneva with Shelley.

1817. Byron finishes *Manfred*. In April, after a severe fever, he goes to Rome to meet Hobhouse, and while there learns that Claire has given birth to a daughter (Allegra) on Jan. 12 in Bath. He has promised Shelley and Mary, now married, to take care of the child, but is adamant in keeping the mother at arms' length.

Returning to Venice, he takes a summer villa on the Brenta. A handsome illiterate young woman, Margharita Cogni, becomes Marianna's rival and gradually supersedes her. In this period the last Canto of *Childe Harold* is written. October sees his first full-scale experiment in comic poetry, *Beppo*.

1818. Tiring of Margharita, Byron abandons himself to a generally dissolute life, yet retains unbounded literary energy. The sale of Newstead Abbey to an old school friend, Colonel Wildman, is at last completed. Byron takes the Palazzo Mocenigo on the Grand Canal. The Shelleys bring his illegitimate daughter to Italy. His house proving an unfit home for her, he consigns her for a time to the care of the British Consul's wife.

In summer he begins *Don Juan*. *Mazeppa* is another 1818 production. He also writes substantial memoirs.

1819. Byron's friends in England beg him to suppress *Don Juan*. After a temporary yielding, he overrules them. In April he is drawn to the young, naïvely romantic Teresa Guiccioli, married to a rich elderly Count. He follows her to Ravenna and later to Bologna, and sends for Allegra. Dismaying her family and risking exclusion from society, Teresa stays with him in his summer villa on the Brenta. There he is visited in October by Moore, to whom he makes a gift of his memoirs.

Teresa's husband grows restive. Byron resolves to leave Italy with Allegra. An illness of Allegra's delays his departure, and at the last moment, he impulsively decides to go back to Ravenna, where Teresa joyfully welcomes him, having won over her family.

Don Juan (Cantos I and II) is greeted with torrents of abuse.

1820. Count Guiccioli, outwardly complaisant again, lets off part of his Ravenna Palazzo to Byron; but the situation leads to fresh resentments. Teresa's father, Count Ruggero Gamba, supports her in applying to the Pope for a separation. In July it is granted—on condition that she lives under the parental roof. Byron is now fully accepted by her relatives, and friendly with her brother Pietro.

Constantly watched by secret police, he has become a member of the Carbonari, pledged to overthrow Austrian domination. On Dec. 9, however, he goes to the aid of a dying commandant of the government troops. Though discouraged, he continues *Don Juan* and writes a tragedy in verse, *Marino Faliero*.

1821. Byron is still living with Allegra in the Palazzo Guiccioli, though on the worst terms with his landlord. His difficult environment and the prospect of an insurrection induce him to place the little girl in a convent. Claire, whose former infatuation has turned to obsessive hatred, protests.

Despite a legal injunction to prevent it, *Marino Faliero*—not written for the stage—is played at Drury Lane. In May Byron is depressed by exaggerated reports of its failure, but goes on writing deliberately non-theatrical pieces in drama form—*Sardanapalus*, *The Two Foscari*, *Cain* and others. Teresa has prevailed on him to give up *Don Juan* after three more cantos have been completed.

In July the men of the Gamba family are suddenly sent into exile, the authorities hoping that the dangerous poet will soon follow. While he lingers in Ravenna, he has a visit from Shelley and decides to settle near his English friends in Pisa. Shelley finds houses both for him and Teresa's family. In November Byron takes up residence at the Palazzo Lanfranchi.

1822. He now sees Shelley almost daily, and meets English-speaking people again. Among these is Thomas Medwin, Shelley's cousin, and Edward John Trelawny, a young man who models himself on Byron's Corsair and pretends to a similar lawless career. Trelawny fires Shelley with enthusiasm for building a boat.

From England comes news of a fresh outcry against Byron through the publication of *Cain* in Dec. 1821. There has been further offence to British decencies from Cantos III, IV, and V of *Don Juan*. Relations with Murray become strained because the publisher flinches from the poet's more challenging works though they are still profitable.

On Feb. 16 Byron hears of his mother-in-law's death. By matrimonial settlements he will share in her estate, and the Hon. Douglas Kinnaird as his Power of Attorney informs him that he must legally add Noel to his name.

Shelley is indignant at Byron's lack of sympathy for Claire's anxieties about Allegra; but he cannot quarrel with him, having engaged him in a project to bring Leigh Hunt to Italy to collaborate in running a periodical—an idea originated by Byron but with Thomas Moore in view. Hunt, in perpetual difficulties, sees in Byron his future means of support.

On Mar. 24 a cavalry sergeant is severely wounded by one of Byron's servants after a scuffle involving Byron himself. This affray causes a considerable stir and jeopardizes Byron's already precarious position with the Tuscan government.

On April 25 Allegra dies. Claire's animosity is intensified. Byron reveals his grief only to Augusta, writing of 'my poor little natural baby'.

He takes the Villa Dupuy near Leghorn for the summer. On May 21 he is warmly received on board two American ships. He too has had a boat built by Trelawny's friend, Commander Daniel Roberts, the luxurious *Bolivar*; but the authorities, suspecting some subversive purpose, place obstacles in the way of his using it. Trelawny alone has the benefit of this costly toy.

Leigh Hunt arrives just when, by a decree once more aimed at Byron, the Gambas are ordered out of Tuscany. 'This is virtually my own exile', writes Byron. Shelley settles Hunt with his pregnant wife and six children in Byron's Pisa house, where rooms have been furnished for them. On July 7 Shelley leaves Pisa intending to sail from Leghorn to Lerici, where his wife awaits him. Several days later Byron and Hunt learn he has never arrived. His body and those of two companions are washed ashore. Trelawny arranges cremation ceremonies.

The Gambas take a house at Albaro near Genoa for themselves and Byron. On Sept. 15, while he is preparing to move, Hobhouse arrives on a five-day visit. Like Moore and others, he warns his friend against association with Hunt, but Byron sees no retreat. He decides to sever his business relationship with Murray, transferring his work to Hunt's brother, John Hunt. Teresa consenting, he has resumed *Don Juan* and produced three more cantos.

The first number of the magazine, *The Liberal*, out on Oct. 15, raises a storm. Even his friends feel his partnership with Hunt is a shameful come-down, and John Hunt is arraigned for printing *The Vision of Judgement*, a sparkling satire, written the year before in revenge for an insulting attack by Southey, the Poet Laureate. Hunt has become a dead weight, but Byron continues to supply copy for the doomed *Liberal*.

1823. More cantos are added to *Don Juan*. At the Casa Saluzzo, Albaro, Byron now lives a retired life. His affair with Teresa has calmed down, on his side, to a rather bored conjugality. The Hunt family and Mary Shelley, in another villa, are on uneasy terms with him.

Hobhouse is active on a Committee formed in London to help the Greeks throw off the Turkish yoke. He enlists Byron's interest.

The Earl and Countess of Blessington, in a *ménage à trois* with Count Alfred D'Orsay, spend April and May in Genoa, seeing Byron fairly frequently.

By May it is arranged that Byron will leave for Greece, and Teresa's brother determines to accompany him. Teresa is in despair. Trelawny, regarded as a man of action and experience, is invited to join the expedition. He eagerly assents, but lingers five weeks in Florence, where he is courting a Mrs Wright: and while Byron, with the help of his banker, Charles Barry, is doing the practical work of preparation, Trelawny turns up only a day or two before the chartered vessel sails.

Byron pressingly urges Hunt to return with his family to England, and offers to pay the expenses. Hunt refuses and gets instead a sum to go to Florence. He fosters discord between Byron and Mary Shelley.

On July 13 Byron embarks. He has raised a large sum from his own resources for the succour of the Greeks, and takes with him medical supplies. On the *Hercules* (Captain Scott) besides Byron, Trelawny, and Count Pietro Gamba, are Count Schilizzi, a Greek, Dr Bruno, a young Italian physician, several servants including the reluctant but faithful valet Fletcher and the ex-gondolier Tita, and James Hamilton Browne, a Scottish Philhellene, who joins the ship at Leghorn.

They arrive at Argostoli in Cephalonia, an island under British rule, on Aug. 3, and Byron is made welcome by the Resident, Colonel Charles Napier, and the officers of the garrison. He learns that Greece is full of internal strife and determines to remain on neutral ground until he is sure he will not become a tool of political intrigue. The party makes a strenuous excursion to Ithaca by mule and rowing-boat (Aug. 11 to 17). On the way back, Byron has an outburst of apparently frantic, uncontrollable rage, which is probably his first seizure. He contributes generously to the relief of refugees.

He is beset with confusing appeals from faction leaders. In September Browne and Trelawny are dispatched on a mission to get authentic information; but Trelawny, jealous and disaffected, after some comfortable weeks in Hydra, decides to throw in his lot with the brigand chieftain, Odysseus, and they go off on a hunting expedition. In October Browne returns to Byron with two Greek Deputies representing Mavrocordato, the leader most likely to prove reliable. Byron resolves to give full support to Mavrocordato's Provisional Government, and in November advances a substantial loan to maintain the Greek fleet.

On Nov. 22, Col. the Hon. Leicester Stanhope arrives from the Committee, with highly unrealistic views of the Greeks. Byron's down-to-earth tone disturbs him. He soon leaves for the mainland, entrusted with letters from Byron stressing the folly of Greek disunity.

Mavrocordato establishes himself at Missolonghi and begs for Byron's presence. His course now clear, the poet sets sail on Dec. 28, calling at Zante for a further large sum to aid the insurgents.

1824. Jan. 5. After an adventurous passage, Byron is rapturously greeted at Missolonghi. He is immediately besieged with claims on his purse. A corps of Suliotes is placed under his command, of which he is obliged to support 500. His large suite includes, besides Gamba and his personal staff from Italy, two English aides-de-camp, Hesketh and Fowke, and a Greek page, Lukas, whose family, ruined by the war, Byron has rescued from destitution. Byron starts to form an artillery corps from the many foreign volunteers Germans, Swiss, Americans, and others—who have hitherto been given no direction; but Stanhope devotes himself to setting up a printing-press though few of the Greek population can read.

In February the congenial William Parry arrives, an engineer sent out by the Committee to assist in works of fortification; but they have shown great ineptitude in equipping him. From now on there are daily disappointments and mishaps. Incessant rains turn the town into a swamp. The dissensions of the soldiers are violent and unpredictable. On Feb. 15 Byron has a dangerous seizure, and next day is bled till he faints. His health henceforward deteriorates.

Though almost hopeless, he refuses to leave, and displays courage, humanity, and commonsense that arouse even Stanhope's admiration.

On Feb. 21 Stanhope leaves to set up printing-presses in Athens. In March he meets Trelawny and Odysseus. They win his artless support for the romantic brigand chieftain's party, and detach him from Mavrocordato. It is important to prevail over Byron who, apart from his own wealth, is expected to control £800,000 raised in England, largely on the strength of his name—more than the entire national revenue of Greece. They write urging him to come to a congress. Byron is mistrustful of Odysseus but

L.L.B.—2 L

consents to go, accompanied by Mavrocordato himself. Torrential rains make roads impassable and delay their journey.

There are perpetual demands for money. Byron asks Kinnaird for 'all possible credits to the extent of my resources'.

The Turkish fleet comes to blockade Missolonghi. There is suspected treachery by a chieftain, Karaiskakis, while the report of a plot by Odysseus to kill Mavrocordato and coerce Byron increases the latter's perplexity. He fears the money from England will merely promote civil war.

On April 9 he is caught in heavy rain when riding, and in the evening complains of fever and severe rheumatic pain. The following day he rides again. Pain and fever increase. The inexperienced Dr Bruno knows no remedies except bleeding, drastic purging, and thirst-provoking medicines. Byron resists bleeding, but on April 16, a second youthful doctor—Millingen —persuades him by saying that, unless bled, he may lose his reason. After this, his blood is repeatedly drained in very large amounts. He strives for lucidity and, despite phases of delirium, often talks coherently of Greek affairs and faces impending death.

On Easter Sunday, the 18th, he tries to give Fletcher messages of importance for his wife, his sister, and Hobhouse, but cannot make himself understood. After vain struggles to speak audibly, he goes into a coma. His last words are 'I want to sleep now'. He lies motionless for twenty-four hours, opens his eyes for a moment at six on the evening of April 19, and dies.

SOME LEADING CHARACTERS

BEYLE, Marie-Henri (1783–1842), famous as author under the name of Stendhal.

BROUGHAM, Henry Peter (1778–1860), Scottish lawyer, one of the founders of the *Edinburgh Review*. Defended Queen Caroline during her trial, a proceeding largely of his own making. He was Lord Chancellor 1830–1835. Created Baron Brougham and Vaux 1830.

BYRON, Anne Isabella (1792–1860), born Milbanke, married 6th Lord Byron in 1815, separated 1816. Added Noel to her name on her mother's death in 1822. Became Baroness Wentworth in her own right in 1856, a title she never used. Supported philanthropic projects, chiefly educational.

BYRON, Captain (later Admiral) George Anson, R.N., 7th Lord Byron (1789–1868), Byron's cousin and successor. He and his wife were close friends of Lady Byron, and took charge of Ada on her entrance into society.

CAMPBELL, Thomas (1777–1844), Scottish poet with great contemporary reputation. Edited *New Monthly Magazine*, 1820–1830. Helped to found London University.

DALLAS, Robert Charles (1754–1824), kinsman by marriage of Byron whose literary affairs he managed for a time. Wrote novels and moral works. Died in France.

DOYLE, Colonel Francis Hastings (1783–1839), created baronet in 1828. He and his two sisters, Selina and Adelaide, were among Lady Byron's most intimate confidants and advisers.

GALT, John (1779–1839), Scottish traveller, novelist, and journalist.

GIUCCIOLI, Teresa, Countess (late 1799 or early 1800–1873), born Ghiselli Gamba. Married at eighteen to an elderly husband. Her *liaison* with Byron began in spring 1819 and was still in being when he left Italy for Greece in 1823. She was separated by Papal decree from Count Guiccioli, and, after his death, married the Marquis de Boissy in 1847. She wrote two books about Byron, one unknown until the 1940's and not yet published in full. Her brother, Count Pietro Gamba, accompanied Byron to Greece, and died there in 1827.

HOBHOUSE, John Cam (1786–1869), M.P. for Westminster 1820–1833; for Nottingham 1836–1847; for Harwich 1849–1851; Secretary for War 1832–1833; Chief Secretary for Ireland 1835; First Commissioner of Woods and Forests 1835; President of the Board of Control 1846–1852. Succeeded to his father's baronetcy in 1831. Created Baron Broughton de Gyfford 1851. In the course of a distinguished career, he presented or supported many progressive and humane Bills. Married Lady Julia Hay in 1828, by whom he had three daughters. He knew Byron intimately from their college days, accompanied him on his Grand Tour, was best man at his wedding, acted as his official 'friend' in the separation proceedings, travelled with him on the Continent afterwards, and was the executor of his will. He kept diaries which are an invaluable source of information.

HOLLAND, Henry Richard Fox, 3rd Lord (1773–1840), influential Whig host and politician. Held various offices and was a considerable scholar and reformer. In 1797 he married Elizabeth Lady Webster (born Vassall) after her divorce from Sir Godfrey Webster. Their coveted hospitality was sometimes marred by her outspokenness.

HORTON, Sir Robert John Wilmot (1784–1841). He was born Wilmot, a kinsman of Byron and Augusta Leigh, but added Horton to his name in 1823 after an inheritance from his wife's father. His political career included the Colonial Office and the Governorship of Ceylon. He succeeded to his father's baronetcy in 1834 shortly after being knighted. He and his wife were members of Lady Byron's confidential circle.

HUNT, James Henry Leigh (1784–1859), critic, essayist and minor poet. Went to prison for libelling the Prince Regent but ended with a civil pension.

KINNAIRD, the Hon. Douglas (1788–1830), a younger son of the 7th Lord Kinnaird. He was one of Byron's most loyal friends as well as his banker and Power of Attorney.

LAMB, Lady Caroline (1785–1828), born Ponsonby, daughter of Viscount Duncannon, afterwards Earl of Bessborough. Married in 1805 to the Hon. William Lamb, younger son of Viscountess Melbourne who later became Byron's friend. The actual period of her love affair with Byron was only a few months early in 1812, but she made the most of it by publicity-attracting devices, including a novel *Glenarvon*, 1816. She separated from her husband in 1825.

LEIGH, the Hon. Augusta Mary (1783–1851), daughter of Captain John Byron and the Marchioness of Carmarthen, Baroness Conyers in her own right, with whom he eloped. Married her cousin, Lt.-Col. George Leigh of the 10th Dragoons in 1807. He was a racing enthusiast in the *entourage* of the Prince of Wales. Mrs Leigh was later appointed to attend the Prince's mother, Queen Charlotte. She had seven children, most of whom followed Col. Leigh's irresponsible footsteps. Despite her inheritance from her half-brother, Byron, and a royal pension, financial difficulties beset her life. Her eldest daughter, Georgiana, married Henry Trevanion, who deserted her and eloped with her sister, Elizabeth Medora.

LUSHINGTON, the Rt. Hon. Stephen (1782–1873), an eminent civil lawyer. He held high offices and became a Privy Councillor in 1838. He acted as Lady Byron's legal adviser, and both he and his wife (born Carr) were her confidential friends.

MEDWIN, Thomas (1788–1869), a second cousin of Shelley's. Became a Lieutenant in the 24th Dragoons, but soon retired on half-pay. Afterwards acquired a commission in the Life Guards, from which he likewise briskly retired. In 1825 he married a Swedish heiress, but her fortune did not last. He wrote much, but only Byron and Shelley proved lucrative subjects.

MOORE, Thomas (1779–1852), celebrated Irish poet, musician, and wit. Wrote a *Life* of Byron.

MURRAY, John II (1778–1843), Byron's principal publisher, to whom many of his most amusing and revealing letters are addressed. His house at Albemarle Street was the resort of famous men of letters.

SHELLEY, Mary (1792–1851), daughter of Mary Wollstonecraft and William Godwin. She married Percy Bysshe Shelley in December 1816, having lived with him since 1814. She wrote *Frankenstein* and several other novels. Her stepsister was Mary Jane Clairmont, mother of Byron's Allegra.

STANHOPE, Col. the Hon. Leicester (1784–1862), strongly doctrinaire Philhellenist, who came to Greece to practise the teachings of Jeremy Bentham. He became an adherent of the Odysseus faction, and printed republican propaganda. He was recalled by the Foreign Office, and accompanied Byron's body to England in the *Florida*. In 1851 he became 5th Earl of Harrington.

TRELAWNY, Edward John (1792–1881), a member of the minor landed gentry of Cornwall. He was bred for the Navy, from which he represented himself (untruly) as having deserted. He wrote *The Adventures of a Younger Son*.

VILLIERS, the Hon. Mrs George (1775–1856), born Hon. Therese Parker, daughter of Lord Boringdon. She married a son of the Earl of Clarendon. A very intimate friend of Augusta Leigh, she also had the entire confidence of Lady Byron.

PRINTED SOURCES CONSULTED

Periodicals

A list of contributions on Byron in British and foreign journals would extend to scores of pages. It has therefore been deemed sufficient to give the names and dates of newspapers and magazines only when they are explicitly quoted. References will be found in the footnotes.

Books and Pamphlets

This bibliography comprises material, significant or trivial, reliable or controversial, that has formed the background of the present volume. To keep it within manageable compass, all publications prior to Byron's death have been excluded, as well as a great many later writings which, however valuable, have shed no direct light on the topics in these pages.

The source references in the footnotes consist of the author's or editor's name with an easily recognizable abridgement of the title of the book quoted. Where an author's name is given without a book title, it is because there is little likelihood of confusion as to which work is alluded to. The editor's name is given instead of the author's in certain cases where more than one edition or selection is in existence.

All publications are English except where otherwise stated.

The following abbreviations are used for principal published sources:

> *Moore*—Letters and Journals of Lord Byron, 1830/1831.
> *Correspondence*—The two volumes of *Lord Byron's Correspondence* edited by John Murray IV, 1922.
> *L. & J.*—The six volumes of Byron's *Letters and Journals* forming the monumental edition of R. E. Prothero, 1898/1900.
> *Poetry*—The seven volumes of Byron's works edited by E. H. Coleridge in the same series.
> *Lady Noel Byron*—The book printed privately and anonymously by Lord Wentworth, *Lady Noel Byron and the Leighs*, 1887.

ABERDEIN, JENNIE W. *John Galt*. 1936.
AIRLIE, MABEL COUNTESS OF. *In Whig Society*. 1921.
ARMSTRONG, MARGARET A. *Trelawny, A Man's life*. New York, 1940.
ARNOLD, REV. FREDERICK. *Robertson of Brighton with some Notices of His Times and Contemporaries*. 1886.
AUSTIN, ALFRED. *A Vindication of Lord Byron*. 1869.
BARBER, REV. T. G. *Byron and Where he is Buried*. 1939.
BEATTIE, *see* Thomas Campbell.
BELLOC, MADAME LOUISE SW- - - - -. *Lord Byron*, 2 vols. Paris, 1824.
BERKELEY, THE HON. GRANTLEY F. *My Life and Recollections*, 4 vols. 1865/1866.
BESSBOROUGH, EARL OF (with A. ASPINALL). *Lady Bessborough and Her Family Circle*. 1940.

BEYLE, MARIE-HENRI, *see* STENDHAL.

BIAGI, DR GUIDO. *The Last Days of Percy Bysshe Shelley, New Details from Unpublished Documents.* 1898.

BLAQUIERE, EDWARD. *Narrative of a Second Visit to Greece, including facts concerning the Last Days of Lord Byron.* 1825.

BLESSINGTON, COUNTESS OF. *The Idler in Italy*, 2 vols. 1839.
Journal of the Conversations of Lord Byron. 1834.

Blessington Papers. *The Collection of Autograph Letters and Historical Documents formed by Alfred Morrison*, catalogued by R. C. Jeaffreson. 1895.

BLUNDEN, EDMUND. *Leigh Hunt, A Biography.* 1930.

BORST, WILLIAM A. *Lord Byron's First Pilgrimage.* Yale University Press, 1948.

BREWER, LUTHER A. *My Leigh Hunt Library, The Holograph Letters.* Iowa, 1938.

BROUGHTON, THE RT HON. LORD, *see* Hobhouse, J. C.

BROWNE, DENIS, F.R.C.S. *The Problem of Byron's Lameness.* Proceedings of the Royal Society of Medicine. 1960.

BRUCE, IAN. *Lavalette Bruce, His Adventures and Intrigues before and after Waterloo.* 1953.

BRYDGES, SIR EGERTON, Bt. *An Impartial Portrait of Lord Byron.* 1825.
Letters on the Character and Poetical Genius of Lord Byron. 1824.

BULLOCK, J. B. *The House of Gordon-Gight.* Privately Printed, 1903.

BUTLER, E. M. *Byron and Goethe.* 1956.

BYRON, CAPTAIN THE RIGHT HONBLE. Lord Byron [7th Lord]. *Voyage of the H.M.S. Blonde to the Sandwich Isles in the Years 1824–1825.* 1826.
Lord Byron, The Poetical Works, Life and Letters, edited by E. H. Coleridge and R. E. Prothero, 13 vols. (referred to herein as *Poetry* and *L. & J.*). 1898/1904.
Lord Byron, The Ravenna Journal, now for the first time issued in book form, with an introduction by the Rt Hon. Lord Ernle, P.C., M.V.O. First Edition Club, 1928.

CAMPBELL, OLWEN WARD. *Shelley and the Unromantics.* 1924.

CAMPBELL, THOMAS. *Life and Letters of*, edited by William Beattie, M.D., 3 vols. 1849.

CANTONI, FULVIO. *Lord Byron e la Guiccioli a Bologna.* Bologna, 1927.
La Prima Dimora di Lord Byron a Bologna. Bologna, 1926.

CASTELAR, EMILIO. *Life of Lord Byron.* 1875.

CECIL, DAVID. *Lord M, or the Later Life of Lord Melbourne.* 1954.
The Young Melbourne. 1939.

CHEW, SAMUEL C. *Byron in England, His Fame and After-Fame.* 1924.

CLARKE, ISABEL C. *Shelley and Byron, A Tragic Friendship.* 1934.

CLINE, C. L. *Byron, Shelley and Their Pisan Circle.* 1952.

CLINTON, GEORGE. *Memoirs of the Life and Writings of Lord Byron.* 1825.

COLERIDGE, E. H. editor of Byron's *Poetical Works* (herein referred to as 'Poetry'). 1898/1904.

DALLAS, R. C. *Correspondence of Lord Byron with a Friend, also Recollections of the Poet*, 3 vols. Paris, 1825.

Recollections of the Life of Lord Byron from the Year 1808 to the end of 1814. 1824.

DALLAS, REV. ALEX. R. C. *Incidents in the Life and Ministry of*, by his Widow. 1871.

DE MORGAN, SOPHIA ELIZABETH. *Threescore Years and Ten*, edited by her Daughter. 1895.

[DEVONSHIRE] *The Two Duchesses, Georgiana Duchess of Devonshire, Elizabeth Duchess of Devonshire—Family Correspondence*, edited by Vere Foster. 1898.

DISRAELI, BENJAMIN. *Venetia, or The Poet's Daughter*. 1837.

DRINKWATER, JOHN. *The Pilgrim of Eternity*. 1924.

DU BOS, CHARLES. *Byron and the Need of Fatality*. 1932.

DUDLEY, 1st Earl of, *see* Romilly.

DUFF, SIR M. E. GRANT. *Notes from a Diary*, 2 vols. 1897.

DYCE, REV. A., *see* Rogers.

EDGCUMBE, RICHARD. *Byron: The Last Phase*. 1909.
   The Diary of Lady Frances Shelley, 1787–1817, edited by her grandson. 1912.
   Edward Trelawny, A Biographical Sketch. 1882.

EHRSAM, THEODORE G. *Major Byron, The Incredible Career of a Literary Forger*. 1951.

ELZE, KARL. *Lord Byron, A Biography with a Critical Essay on his Place in Literature*. 1872.

ERNLE, THE RT HON. LORD, *see* Prothero.

ESCARPIT, ROBERT. *Lord Byron, Un Tempérament Littéraire*, 2 vols. Paris, 1957.

FIELD, MAUNSELL B. *Memories of Many Men and of Some Women*. 1874.

Finden's Illustrations to the Life and Works of Lord Byron, Text by William Brockedon, 3 vols. 1833/1834.

FINLAY, GEORGE L. L. D. *History of the Greek Revolution*, 2 vols. 1861.

FORMAN, H. BUXTON, *see* Trelawny.

FOX, SIR JOHN S. *The Byron Mystery*. 1924.

[FOX, JOHN]. *Vindication of Lady Byron*. Published anonymously. 1871.

Fox, The Journal of the Hon. Henry Edward, edited by the Earl of Ilchester. 1923.

GALLENGA, A. *Episodes of My Second Life*, 2 vols. 1884.

GALT, JOHN. *Autobiography*, 2 vols. 1833.

GAMBA, COUNT PETER. *A Narrative of Lord Byron's Last Journey to Greece*. 1825.

GORDON, SIR COSMO. *The Life and Genius of Lord Byron*. 1824.

GORDON, THOMAS. *History of the Greek Revolution*, 2 vols. 1832.

GRAHAM, WILLIAM. *Last Links with Byron, Shelley and Keats*. 1898.

GRANT, JAMES. *Memoirs of Sir George Sinclair, Bt. of Ulbster*, 3 vols. 1870.

GREEN, F. C. *Stendhal*. 1939.

GREVILLE. *The Greville Diary*, edited by Philip Whitwell Wilson, 2 vols. 1927.

GRONOW, CAPTAIN R. H. *Reminiscences and Recollections*, 1810–1860, 2 vols. 1892.

GRYLLS, R. GLYNN. *Claire Clairmont, Mother of Byron's Allegra*. 1939.
   Trelawny. 1950.
   Mary Shelley, A Biography. 1938.

[GUICCIOLI, COUNTESS] *Lord Byron Jugé par les Témoins de Sa Vie*, 2 vols. Paris, 1868.

  My Recollections of Lord Byron (the English version of the above, translated by Hubert E. H. Jerningham), 2 vols. 1869.

GUNNELL, DORIS. *Stendhal et l'Angleterre*. Paris, 1909.

HARNESS, REV. WILLIAM, *see* L'Estrange.

HAYDON, BENJAMIN ROBERT. *Autobiography and Memoirs, 1786–1846*, edited by Tom Taylor, 2 vols. 1926.

  The Diary of, edited by Willard B. Pope, Harvard University Press, 2 vols. 1960.

  Table Talk, with a Memoir by his son F. W. Haydon, 2 vols. 1876.

HILL, ANNE. *Trelawny's Strange Relations*. 1956. (The same author provided the Keats-Shelley Journal with an important paper 'Trelawny's Family Background and Naval Career'.]

[HOBHOUSE, JOHN CAM, THE RT HON. LORD BROUGHTON] *Contemporary Account of the Separation of Lord and Lady Byron, also of the Destruction of Lord Byron's Memoirs*. Privately Printed, 1870.

  Italy. Remarks made in Several Visits from the Year 1816 to 1856. Revised Edition, 1861.

  Recollections of a Long Life, edited by his daughter Lady Dorchester, 6 vols. 1909/1911.

  Some Account of a Long Life, 5 vols. Privately printed, 1865.

  Remarks on the Exclusion of Lord Byron's Monument from Westminster Abbey. 1844.

HODGSON, REV. FRANCIS, B.D. *Memoir*, by his son the Rev. James T. Hodgson, M.A., 2 vols. 1878.

HOUSSAYE, ARSÈNE. *Voyage à Venise*. Paris, 1850.

HOWE, SAMUEL G., M.D. *An Historical Sketch of the Greek Revolution*, New York, 1828.

HUNT, LEIGH. *Autobiography*. Edition of 1860.

  Lord Byron and Some of his Contemporaries, 2 vols. 2nd edition, 1828.

  The Correspondence of, edited by his eldest son, 2 vols. 1862.

ILCHESTER, EARL OF, *see* the Hon. H. E. Fox.

  Elizabeth Lady Holland to her Son, 1821–1845. 1946.

IRVING, WASHINGTON. *Life and Letters*, edited by his nephew, Pierre M. Irving. 1865.

  Abbotsford and Newstead Abbey. 1835.

JEAFFRESON, JOHN CORDY. *The Real Lord Byron*, 2 vols. 1883.

  The Real Shelley, 2 vols. 1885.

JERNINGHAM, HUBERT E. H. *Reminiscences of an Attaché*. 1886.

JONES, FREDERICK L. *Mary Shelley's Journal*. Oklahoma, 1947.

  Maria Gisborne and Edward E. Williams, Shelley's Friends, Their Letters and Journals (referred to herein as *Shelley's Friends*). Oklahoma, 1951.

  The Letters of Mary Shelley, 2 vols. Oklahoma, 1944.

JOYCE, MICHAEL. *My Friend H, John Cam Hobhouse Baron Broughton de Gyfford*. 1948.

KENNEDY, JAMES, M.D. *Conversations on Religion with Lord Byron and others held in Cephalonia a Short Time Previous to His Lordship's Death*. 1830.

KNIGHT, G. WILSON. *Lord Byron's Marriage, The Evidence of Asterisks.* 1957.

LAMARTINE, ALPHONSE DE. *Le Dernier Chant du Pélérinage d'Harold.* Paris, 1825.

LANDRÉ, LOUIS. *Leigh Hunt, Contribution à l'histoire du Romantisme anglais* Paris, 1935.

LAYARD, G. S. [editor]. *Sir Thomas Lawrence's Letter Bag.* 1906.

L'ESTRANGE, REV. A. G. *The Literary Life of the Rev. William Harness.* 1871.

LEONARD, WILLIAM ELLERY. *Byron and Byronism in America.* Boston, 1905.

LEVER, TRESHAM. *The Letters of Lady Palmerston.* 1957.

LOVELACE, MARY COUNTESS OF. *Ralph Earl of Lovelace, A Memoir.* 1920.

LOVELACE, 2ND EARL OF. *Astarte, A Fragment of the Truth concerning George Gordon, Sixth Lord Byron.* Privately printed, 1905.

Astarte. Another edition edited by Mary Countess of Lovelace (with additional letters). 1921.

[LOVELACE, 2ND EARL OF, when he was Lord Wentworth] *Lady Noel Byron and the Leighs, Some Authentic Records of Certain Circumstances in the Lives of Augusta Leigh and others of her Family, that concerned Anna Isabella Lady Byron in the Course of Forty Years after Her Separation* (referred to herein as *Lady Noel Byron*). Privately printed, 1887.

LOVELL, ERNEST J., Jr. *His Very Self and Voice: Collected Conversations of Lord Byron.* New York, 1954.

MACAULAY, THOMAS BABINGTON. *Lord Byron.* Reprint of Essay of 1831. 1853.

MACKAY, CHARLES. *Medora Leigh, A History and an Autobiography.* 1869.

MACKAY, WILLIAM. *The True Story of Lady Byron's Life—Christmas Comic Version, MS recently discovered in the 'Milbanke' Penitentiary.* 1869.

MACREADY, WILLIAM CHARLES. *The Diaries of,* edited by William Toynbee, 2 vols. 1912.

MADDEN, R. R. *The Literary Life and Correspondence of the Countess of Blessington,* 3 vols. 1855.

MARCHAND, LESLIE A. *Byron, A Biography,* 3 vols. 1957.

MARSHALL, MRS JULIAN. *The Life and Letters of Mary Shelley,* 2 vols. 1889.

MARSHALL, WILLIAM H. *Byron, Shelley, Hunt and the Liberal.* Philadelphia, 1960.

MARTINEAU, HARRIET. *Biographical Sketches.* 1869.

MASSINGHAM, H. J. *The Friend of Shelley, A Memoir of Edward John Trelawny.* 1930.

MAUROIS, ANDRÉ. *Byron.* 1930.

MAYNE, ETHEL COLBURN. *Byron,* 2 vols. 1912.

The Life and Letters of Anna Isabella Lady Byron. 1929.

MEDWIN, THOMAS. *Journal of the Conversations of Lord Byron Noted during a Residence with his Lordship at Pisa in the Years 1821 and 1822.* 1824. Revised, 2 vols. in one, 1832.

The Angler in Wales, or Days and Nights of a Sportsman, 2 vols. 1834.

The Life of Percy Bysshe Shelley, 2 vols. 1847.

[? MEDWIN, THOMAS] *Captain Medwin Vindicated from the Calumnies of the Reviewers,* by 'Vindex' (purports to be by a writer unknown to Medwin, but is generally attributed to his own hand). 1825.

MILLER, BARNETTE, Ph.D. *Leigh Hunt's Relations with Byron, Shelley and Keats*. New York, 1910.

MILLER, JOAQUIM. *Trelawny with Shelley and Byron* (written in 1893). New Jersey, 1922.

MILLINGEN, JULIUS. *Memoirs of the Affairs of Greece*. 1831.

MOLLOY, F. J. *The Most Gorgeous Lady Blessington*, 2 vols. 1896.

MOORE, THOMAS. *Letters and Journals of Lord Byron with Notices of his Life* (referred to herein as MOORE), 2 vols. 1830/1831.

Memoirs, Journal, and Correspondence of, edited by the Rt Hon. Lord John Russell, 8 vols. 1853/1854.

Prose and Verse, Humorous, Satirical and Sentimental. 1878.

Lady Morgan's Memoirs, Autobiography, Diaries and Correspondence, 2 vols. 1863.

[MURRAY, JOHN, II]. *Notes on Captain Medwin's Conversations of Lord Byron.* 1825.

MURRAY, JOHN, IV. *Lord Byron's Correspondence chiefly with Lady Melbourne, Mr Hobhouse, the Hon. Douglas Kinnaird, and P. B. Shelley*, 2 vols. 1922. (Referred to herein as *Correspondence*.)

John Murray III, 1808–1892. 1920.

Contribution to *Lord Byron and his Detractors* (q.v. under Various Authors). 1906.

NATHAN, ISAAC. *Fugitive Pieces and Reminiscences of Lord Byron and also some original Poetry, Letters and Recollections by Lady Caroline Lamb.* 1829.

NESBITT, GEORGE L. *Benthamite Reviewing, The First Twelve Years of the Westminster Review.* 1934.

NICOLSON, HAROLD. *Byron, The Last Journey.* 1924.

Small Talk. 1937.

NOEL, THE HON. RODEN. *Life of Lord Byron.* 1890.

NORMAN, SYLVA. *After Shelley.* 1934.

The Flight of the Skylark. 1954.

ORIGO, IRIS. *The Last Attachment.* 1949.

PARRY, WILLIAM. *The Last Days of Lord Byron with his Lordship's Opinions on Various Subjects*, etc. 1825.

PASTON, GEORGE, *see* Quennell, '*To Lord Byron*'.

PHILLIPS, W. ALISON, M.A. *The War of Greek Independence.* 1897.

PICKERING, LESLIE P. *Lord Byron, Leigh Hunt and the 'Liberal'.* N.D.

POPE, WILLARD B., *see* HAYDON, B. R.

POPE-HENNESSY, UNA. *Durham Company.* 1941.

POLIDORI, DR JOHN WILLIAM. *The Diary of*, edited and elucidated by Willam Michael Rossetti. 1911.

PRATT, WILLIS W. *Byron at Southwell, The Making of a Poet.* Texas, 1948.

An Italian Pocket Notebook of Lord Byron. Texas, 1949.

Lord Byron and his Circle, A Calendar of Manuscripts in the University of Texas Library. Texas, 1947.

PRAZ, MARIO. *La Fortuna di Byron in Inghilterra.* Florence, 1925.

PROTHERO, R. E. Contribution to *Lord Byron and His Detractors* (q.v. under 'Various Authors'). 1906.

Editor of Lord Byron's *Letters and Journals* (referred to herein as *L. & J.*).

QUENNELL, PETER. *Byron in Italy.* 1941.
   Byron, a Self-Portrait, 2 vols. 1950.
   Byron, The Years of Fame. 1935.
   With George Paston. '*To Lord Byron*'. *Feminine Profiles based upon un-published letters* (referred to herein as 'QUENNELL AND PASTON'). 1939.
RAYMOND, DORA NEILL, Ph.D. *The Political Career of Lord Byron.* N.D.
ROBERTS, R. ELLIS. *Samuel Rogers and His Circle.* 1910.
ROBINSON, HENRY CRABB. *Diary, Reminiscences, and Correspondence of*, edited by Thomas Sadler, Ph.D., 3 vols. 1869.
Roe-Byron Collection, Newstead Abbey. The *Catalogue.* 1937.
ROGERS, SAMUEL. *Recollections and Table Talk*, edited by the Rev. Alexander Dyce. 1887.
ROMILLY, S. H. *Letters to 'Ivy' from the First Earl of Dudley.* 1905.
ROSSETTI, WILLIAM MICHAEL. *Rossetti Papers, 1862–1870*, 1903.
   Some Reminiscences, 2 vols. 1906.
RUSKIN, JOHN. *Essays on Literature.* 1836.
SADLEIR, MICHAEL. *Blessington D'Orsay, A Masquerade.* 1933.
SALVO, MARQUIS DE. *Lord Byron en Italie et en Grèce.* Paris, 1825.
SHELLEY, MARY, *Lodore*, 3 vols. 1835.
   The Last Man, 3 vols. 1826.
   Letters, see Jones.
   Journal, see Jones.
Shelley Memorials from Authentic Sources, edited by Lady Shelley. 1859.
Shelley and Mary. [Documents edited by Lady Shelley.] Privately printed, 1882.
SHELLEY, PERCY BYSSHE. *Complete Works.* Julian Edition, edited by Roger Ingpen and Walter E. Peck, 10 vols. 1929.
Shelley's Lost Letters to Harriet, edited by Leslie Hotson. 1930.
New Shelley Letters, edited by W. S. Scott. 1948.
SHELLEY, LADY FRANCES, *see* Edgcumbe.
SIMMONS, JACK. *Southey.* 1945.
SIMMONS, J. W. *An Inquiry into the Moral Character of Lord Byron.* 1826.
SMILES, SAMUEL, LL.D. *A Publisher and his Friends. Memoirs and Correspondence of the late John Murray*, 2 vols. 1891.
SMITH, MARY R. DARBY. *Recollections of Two Distinguished Persons.* Philadelphia, 1878.
SMITH, ROBERT METCALF. *The Shelley Legend, see* 'Various Authors'.
STANHOPE, THE HON. COL. LEICESTER. *Greece in 1823 and 1824, being a Series of Letters and other Documents on the Greek Revolution.* 1825.
STENDHAL (MARIE-HENRI BEYLE). *Correspondance Inédite Précédée d'une Introduction par Prosper Merimée.* Paris, 1855.
   Correspondance, 1800–1842. Publiée par Ad. Paupe et P.-A. Cheramy, Preface de Maurice Barrès, 3 vols. Paris, 1908.
   Journal, annoté par H. Debraye et L. Royer. Paris, 1923/1924.
   Œuvres Complètes. Paris, 1854.
   The Private Diaries of, edited and translated by Robert Sage. 1955.
   Cent Soixante Quatorze Lettres à, edited by H. Martineau. Paris, 1947.

STOWE, HARRIET BEECHER. *Lady Byron Vindicated, A History of the Byron Controversy*. 1870.

SYMON, J. D. *Byron in Perspective*. 1924.

TICKNOR, GEORGE. *Life, Letters, and Journals*, 2 vols. Boston, 1876.

THOMAS, JOHN WESLEY. *Byron and the times, or an Apology for Don Juan.* 1855.

TRELAWNY, EDWARD J. *Recollections of the Last Days of Shelley and Byron.* 1858.

Records of Shelley, Byron and the Author. 1878.

Letters, edited by H. Buxton Forman. 1910.

VINCENT, E. R. *Byron, Hobhouse and Foscolo, New Documents in the History of a Collaboration*. 1949.

VULLIAMY, C. E. *Byron, with a View of the Kingdom of Cant, etc.* 1948.

WELLS, NANNIE KATHARIN. *George Gordon, Lord Byron, A Scottish Genius.* 1960.

WENTWORTH, LORD, *see* Lovelace, 2nd Earl of.

WHITE, NEWMAN IVEY. *Shelley*, 2 vols. 1947.

WILSON, FORREST. *Crusader in Crinoline, The Life of Harriet Beecher Stowe.* 1902.

WISE, THOMAS J. *A Byron Library, Catalogue of Printed Books, Manuscripts and Autograph Letters*. 1928

Anonymous, Pseudonymous and Spurious Publications (a brief selection)

Les Amours de Lord Byron, Traduit de l'anglais, 2 vols. Paris, 1838.

Les Amours Secrètes de Lord Byron and variants of the above, from 1839 onwards.

Byroniana—Bozzies and Piozzies. 1825.

Captain Medwin Vindicated, *see* Medwin.

Don Leon. A poem by the Late Lord Byron . . . to which is added Leon to Annabella, etc. (apparently written in the 1830's, printed much later). N.D.

MITFORD, JOHN. *La Vie Privée et Amours Secrètes de Lord Byron, Traduites de l'Anglais par F. Paris*, 2 vols. Paris, 1842.

Newstead Abbey. Lord Byron. Colonel Wildman. A Reminiscence. 1856.

PINTO, FERDINAND MENDEZ. *Narrative of Lord Byron's Voyage to Corsica and Sardinia during the Summer of 1821 . . . in his Lordship's Yacht 'Mazeppa'.* 1824.

Seventeen Letters of George Noel Gordon, Lord Byron, to an Unknown Lady, 1811–1817. Edited by Walter E. Peck, D.Phil (Oxon) (reprint of forgeries by De Gibler which appeared in the Schultess-Young volume, see *infra*). New York, 1930.

The Unpublished Letters of Lord Byron, edited by H. S. Schultess-Young. (These consist of letters which had, in fact, been published by Dallas and others now recognized as De Gibler forgeries. The book was suppressed by injunction.) 1872.

WILSON, HARRIETTE. *The Memoirs of, written by Herself*, 2 vols. (Contains spurious recollections of Byron whom she wrote to but never met.) Privately printed, 1924.

Various Authors—Compiled Works

Anecdotes of Lord Byron (Collection attributed to Dr A. Kilgour). 1825.

Byron the Poet. Essays edited by Walter Briscoe. 1924.

Byron Painted by His Compeers, or All About Lord Byron from his Marriage to his Death as given in the Various Newspapers of his Day. 1869.

Byroniana—The Opinions of Lord Byron . . . with the Parish Clerk's Album kept at his Burial Place, Hucknall Torkard. 1834.

Life of Lady Byron . . . to which is appended a Vindication of the Late Lord Byron. Police News Pamphlet. N.D.

Lord Byron and his Detractors, by John Murray IV, E. H. Pember, and R. E. Prothero. Roxburghe Club, 1906.

Nos Anciens et Leurs Œuvres. Recueil Genevois D'Art, 2me Série. Geneva, 1912.

The Shelley Legend. Robert Metcalf Smith in collaboration with Martha Mary Schlegel, Theodore Ehrsam and Louis Waters. New York, 1945.

An Examination of the Shelley Legend. Newman I. White, Frederick L. Jones, Kenneth N. Cameron. Philadelphia, 1951.

The Stowe-Byron Controversy, A Complete Resumé . . . together with an Impartial View of the Merits of the Case. By the Editor of *Once a Week*. 1870.

The True Story of Lord and Lady Byron in answer to Mrs Beecher Stowe. N.D.

INDEX